THE PAPERS OF
BENJAMIN FRANKLIN

SPONSORED BY

The American Philosophical Society
and Yale University

Peter Collinson

THE PAPERS OF
Benjamin Franklin

VOLUME 3   *January 1, 1745, through June 30, 1750*

LEONARD W. LABAREE, *Editor*

WHITFIELD J. BELL, JR., *Associate Editor*

Helen C. Boatfield and Helene H. Fineman, Assistant Editors

New Haven YALE UNIVERSITY PRESS, 1961

©1961 by the American Philosophical Society
Held at Philadelphia for Promoting Useful Knowledge; by
Yale University; and by Yale University Press, Inc.

All rights reserved. No part of the editorial contents
of this volume in excess of 300 words may be reprinted
in any form without permission in writing from the
Yale University Press. Much of the textual material
in this book is included by special permission of the owners
of the original manuscripts or holders of existing copyrights
and should not be reprinted without their authorization.

Designed by Alvin Eisenman and Walter Howe,
and printed in the United States of America
at The Lakeside Press,
R. R. Donnelley & Sons Company, Chicago, Illinois,
and Crawfordsville, Indiana.

Library of Congress catalogue number: 59-12697

Administrative Board

Roy F. Nichols, University of Pennsylvania, *Chairman*
Frederick B. Adams, Jr., The Pierpont Morgan Library
James T. Babb, Yale University Library
Chester Kerr, Yale University Press, *Secretary*
William E. Lingelbach, American Philosophical Society
Richard H. Shryock, American Philosophical Society Library
Walter M. Whitehill, Boston Athenaeum

Editorial Advisory Committee

Samuel F. Bemis, Yale University
Lyman H. Butterfield, *The Adams Papers*
I. Bernard Cohen, Harvard University
Robert E. Spiller, University of Pennsylvania
Lawrence C. Wroth, The John Carter Brown Library

Cooperating Committee

Thomas Boylston Adams
Bromwell Ault
Charles Braibant
Prince Louis de Broglie
Julien Cain
Gilbert Chinard
William Bell Clark
Norman V. Donaldson
Gaylord Donnelley
Luther P. Eisenhart
F. C. Francis
Lawrence H. Gipson
Wayne C. Grover
Philip M. Hamer
Andrew Heiskell
Bernhard Knollenberg

Waldo G. Leland
Wilmarth S. Lewis
Henry R. Luce
William S. Mason
David C. Mearns
Sir Owen Morshead
Sir Lewis B. Namier*
Howard H. Peckham
John E. Pomfret
Sir Sydney Roberts
Clifford K. Shipton
St. George L. Sioussat
S. K. Stevens
R. W. G. Vail
R. Norris Williams, 2nd
   *Deceased

Contents

1746

1747

CONTENTS

List of Illustrations

Peter Collinson   *Frontispiece, opposite title page*

Gainsborough painted Collinson's portrait at Bath in 1767; that painting
has disappeared, but this may be a copy of it by an artist unknown. It
hangs in the Mill Hill School, which occupies Collinson's house.
Peter Collinson had an incalculable influence on American culture in the
middle of the eighteenth century, as Franklin generously acknowledged: he was the patron and London agent of the Library Company
of Philadelphia, which was the model for more than a score of subscription libraries in the colonies; and his gift of pamphlets and electrical equipment set the Philadelphians, and Franklin in particular, to
experimenting and studying the new science. It was through Collinson,
as the contents of this volume show, that Franklin's discoveries were
communicated to the Royal Society and the learned world. "Their
minds," wrote Dr. Fothergill, who knew them both, "were congenial,
ever intent upon promoting public good." John Fothergill, "Some
Account of the late Peter Collinson," *Works* (London, 1781), p. 615;
Norman G. Brett-James, *The Life of Peter Collinson, F.R.S., F.S.A.*
(London, 1926), pp. 284–6. Reproduced by permission of the Governors of the Mill Hill School, London.

Illustrations of Electrical Experiments

In the reports of electrical experiments which he sent Peter Collinson
from time to time and which he had Lewis Evans copy for James
Bowdoin in 1750, Franklin inserted illustrative sketches in the text and
the margins. Evans' neatly executed drawings of Leyden jars and other
apparatus add to both the charm and the meaning of Franklin's letters,
as the Bowdoin manuscript shows. To Collinson on July 28, 1747,
Franklin reported the results of eleven experiments, of which he
illustrated five. These illustrations, reproduced in the text of this
volume, are listed here, with the number of the experiment to which
each refers and its number on the plate (made from the sketches Collinson received) in the first printed edition of *Experiments and Observations on Electricity* (London, 1751). Reproduced from the Bowdoin
manuscript by permission of the American Academy of Arts and
Sciences.

This sketch map locates the principal places on the approaches to Philadelphia associated with war and defense in 1747–48. Drawn by Crimilda Pontes.

Plain Truth was Franklin's answer to the Pennsylvania Assembly's continued refusal to provide for defense against the French and Spanish attacks. He "determined to try," he wrote, "what might be done by a voluntary Association of the People." Although the Association formed in response to his appeal never saw the enemy and quietly disbanded in the fall of 1748, Franklin had indeed shown what might be done by voluntary action, and his fame was spread wide through the province. Reproduced by permission of The Historical Society of Pennsylvania.

A woodcut, graphically reinforcing Franklin's argument that the Pennsylvanians could defend themselves only by their own efforts, appeared on the back of the title page of *Plain Truth*. Franklin had used this illustration (adapted to the American environment—note the Conestoga wagon—from Croxall's popular translation of Aesop) in his edition of Dilworth's *A New Guide to the English Tongue,* published earlier in 1747. It shows a farm wagon mired in a muddy lane, and a farmer on his knees "bawling and praying" to Hercules to help him. The god's answer is an order to get up, whip up the horses, put a shoulder to the wheel, and push. The woodcut in *Plain Truth* bears the caption *Non Votis, &c.,* which was taken from the Latin quotation on the title page— "Not by prayers and womanish supplications is help from the gods obtained." Although the cut was originally prepared for a schoolbook, William Murrell (*A History of American Graphic Humor,* N.Y., 1933, I, 11) says it is "the first attempt printed in America to symbolize a political situation." Sinclair Hamilton, *Early American Book Illustrators and Wood Engravers, 1670–1870* (Princeton, 1958), p. 8. Reproduced by permission of The Historical Society of Pennsylvania.

Top: A ticket (but not a winning one) in the First Philadelphia Lottery signed by one of the managers. Reproduced by permission of the owner, Philip G. Nordell, Ambler, Pa.

Bottom: The Association Battery, erected with proceeds of the Philadelphia Lotteries, where Franklin stood guard as a common soldier in the spring and summer of 1748. From an inset in George Heap and Nicholas Scull's *An East Prospect of the City of Philadelphia.* Undertaken at the urging of the proprietor, this perspective view of the city was drawn by Heap, who died in 1752 while en route to England to have it engraved. The drawing was acquired by Scull, a relative by marriage, who had it published in London, 1754. A second printing was made in 1755 and, because of the enormous size of the original— 80 by 20 inches—a smaller, "contracted view" was made and issued in 1756. Nicholas B. Wainwright, "Scull and Heap's East Prospect of Philadelphia," *PMHB*, LXXXIII (1949), 16–25. Reproduced from a copy of the second state by permission of The Historical Society of Pennsylvania.

After fifteen years of success with it, Franklin enlarged *Poor Richard's Almanack,* increasing both the number and the size of the pages. The new almanacs contained the familiar elements of calendars, astronomical data, aphorisms, and verses, and in addition printed so many poems, short essays, historical notes, and statistical tables that each issue became almost a small magazine. A comparison of the title pages of the first *Poor Richard* (above, I, 287) and the first *Poor Richard improved* makes clear that only the contents of the latter were "improved," not its typographical design. Reproduced by permission of the Yale University Library.

Tickets in the third and fourth drawings, signed by Abraham Taylor, one of the managers. Ticket No. 2106 drew a blank, but No. 2114 won £30. Reproduced by permission of the Yale University Library.

By Gustavus Hesselius. The artist came to Philadelphia from Sweden in 1711. He lived in Wilmington, Del., and in Prince George's County, Md., but returned to Philadelphia about 1735 (see below, p. 299 n). He is thought to have painted this portrait between 1735 and 1745. William Sawitzky, *Catalogue Descriptive and Critical of the Paintings and Miniatures in the Historical Society of Pennsylvania* (Phila., 1942), pp. 96–7. In the years when Franklin knew him, Logan lived at his country place, Stenton, "where," in the words of his obituary in the *Pennsylvania Gazette*, "he enjoy'd among his Books that Leisure which Men of Letters so earnestly desire." Unlike in most ways, he and Franklin were united by their common devotion to science and the public welfare. Reproduced by permission of The Historical Society of Pennsylvania.

Title page of *Proposals for the Education of Youth*, 1749   395

Written and printed by Franklin, but distributed gratis and anonymously as though from unnamed public-spirited citizens, this pamphlet prepared the minds of "the principal Inhabitants" of Philadelphia for Franklin's scheme to establish an academy. Pledges of money were forthcoming and the subscribers carried the plan into immediate execution, with Franklin as their president. The modern result is the University of Pennsylvania. Reproduced by permission of the Yale University Library.

Contributors to Volume 3

The ownership of each manuscript, or the location of the particular copy used by the editors of each contemporary pamphlet or similar printed work, is indicated where the document appears in the text. The sponsors and editors are deeply grateful to the following institutions and individuals for permission to print in the present volume manuscripts or other materials which they own:

INSTITUTIONS

American Academy of Arts and Sciences
American Antiquarian Society
American Philosophical Society
Boston Athenaeum
Boston Public Library
Bostonian Society
Buffalo Historical Society
Columbia University Library
Free Library of Philadelphia
Harvard College Library
Haverford College Library
Historical Society of Pennsylvania
Henry E. Huntington Library and Art Gallery
Library Company of Philadelphia
Library of Congress
Massachusetts Historical Society
Munson-Williams-Proctor Institute, Utica, New York
New-York Historical Society
New York Public Library
Pennsylvania Hospital
Pierpont Morgan Library
Princeton University Library
Prothonotary of the Supreme Court of Pennsylvania
Recorder of Deeds, Philadelphia
Riverdale Country School, New York City
The Philip H. and A. S. W. Rosenbach Foundation
The Royal Society
Edgar Fahs Smith Library of the History of Chemistry, University of Pennsylvania
Trustees of the University of Pennsylvania
University of Pennsylvania Archives
University of Pennsylvania Library
Western Reserve Historical Society
Yale University Library

INDIVIDUALS

Miss S. Berenice Baldwin, Woodbridge, Connecticut
Noël J. Cortés, Philadelphia
Joseph W. P. Frost, Kittery Point, Maine
Mrs. Thomas S. Gates, Philadelphia
Drayton M. Smith, Philadelphia
Mrs. Richard D. Wood, Jr., Wawa, Pennsylvania

Method of Textual Reproduction

An extended statement of the principles of selection, arrangement, form of presentation, and method of textual reproduction observed in this edition appears in the Introduction to the first volume, pp. xxxiv-xlvii. A condensation and revision of the portion relating to the method of reproducing the texts follows here.

Printed Material:

In general Franklin's writings printed under his direction should be regarded as his ultimate intention and should therefore be reproduced without change, except as modern typography requires. In fact, however, newspapers and pamphlets were often set by two or more journeymen with different notions of spelling, capitalization, and punctuation. Although the resulting inconsistencies and errors did not represent Franklin's intentions, they are not eliminated by the editors. Again, in cases where Franklin's writings were printed by another, they were sometimes carelessly or willfully revised without his consent. He once complained, for example, that an English printer had so corrected and excised one of his papers "that it can neither scratch nor bite. It seems only to paw and mumble."[1] What was thus printed was obviously not what Franklin wrote, but, in the absence of his manuscript, the editors have no alternative but to reprint it as it stands. Still other Franklin letters are known only in nineteenth-century printings, vigorously edited by William Temple Franklin, Duane, or Sparks. Here, too, the editors follow the texts as printed, only noting obvious misreadings.

In reproducing printed materials, the following general rules are observed:

1. The place and date of composition of letters are set at the top, regardless of their location in the original printing.

2. Proper nouns, including personal names, which were often printed in italics, are set in roman, except when the original was italicized for emphasis.

1. BF to William Franklin, Jan. 9, 1768.

3. Prefaces and other long passages, though italicized in the original, are set in roman. Long italicized quotations are set in roman within quotation marks.

4. Words in full capitals are set in small capitals, with initial letters in full capitals if required by Franklin's normal usage.

5. All signatures are set in capitals and small capitals.

6. Obvious typographical errors are silently corrected. An omitted parenthesis or quotation mark, for example, is inserted when the other of the pair was printed.

7. Every sentence is closed with a period or other appropriate mark of punctuation (usually a question mark).

8. Longhand insertions in the blanks of printed forms are set in italics, with space before and after.

Manuscript Material:

a. *Letters* are presented in the following form:

1. The place and date of composition are set at the top, regardless of their location in the original.

2. The complimentary close is set continuously with the text.

3. Addresses, endorsements, and docketing are so labeled and printed at the end of the letter.

b. *Spelling* of the original is retained. When, however, it is so abnormal as to obscure meaning, the correct form is supplied in brackets or footnote, as: "yf [wife]."

c. *Capitalization* has been retained as written, except that every sentence is made to begin with a capital. When there is doubt whether a letter is a capital, it is printed as like letters are in the same manuscript, or, that guide failing, as modern usage directs.

d. Words underlined once in the manuscript are printed in *italics;* words underlined twice or written in large letters or full capitals are printed in SMALL CAPITALS.

e. *Punctuation* has been retained as in the original, except:

1. Every sentence ends with a period or other appropriate mark (usually a question mark), unless it is not clear where the sentence ends, when the original punctuation (or lack of it) is preserved.

2. Dashes used in place of commas, semicolons, colons, or periods are replaced by the appropriate marks; and when a sentence ends with both a dash and a period, the dash is omitted.

3. Commas scattered meaninglessly through a manuscript are eliminated.

4. When a mark of punctuation is not clear or can be read as one of two marks, modern usage is followed.[2]

5. Some documents, especially those of a legal character, lack all punctuation. This is supplied with restraint, and the fact indicated in a footnote. In some other, inadequately punctuated documents, it is silently added when needed for clarity, as in a long series of names.

f. *Contractions and abbreviations* in general are expanded except in proper names. The ampersand is rendered as "and," except in the names of business firms, in the form "&c.," and in a few other cases. Letters represented by the thorn or tilde are printed. The tailed "p" is spelled out as per, pre, or pro. Symbols of weights, measures, and monetary values follow modern usage, as: £34. Superscript letters are lowered. Abbreviations in current use are retained, as: Col., Dr., N.Y., i.e.

g. *Omitted or illegible words or letters* are treated as follows:

1. If not more than four letters are missing, they are silently supplied when there is no doubt what they should be.

2. The omission of more than four letters or one or more words is supplied conjecturally within brackets. The addition of a question mark within the brackets indicates uncertainty as to the conjecture.

3. Other omissions are shown as follows: [*illegible*], [*torn*], [*remainder missing*], or the like.

4. Missing or illegible digits are indicated by suspension points in brackets, the number of points corresponding to the estimated number of missing figures.

5. Blank spaces are left as blanks.

---

2. The typescripts from which these papers are printed have been made from photocopies of the manuscripts, and marks of punctuation are sometimes blurred or lost in photography. It has often been impossible to consult the originals in these cases.

h. *Author's additions and corrections.*

1. Interlineations and brief marginal notes are brought into the text without comment. Longer notes are brought into the text with the notation: [*in the margin*].

2. Author's footnotes are printed at the bottom of the appropriate pages between the text and any editorial footnotes.

3. Canceled words and phrases are in general omitted without notice; if significant, they are printed in footnotes. The canceled passages of important documents, such as drafts of treaties, are brought into the text enclosed in angle brackets *before* the words substituted.

4. When alternative words and phrases have been inserted in a manuscript but the original remains uncanceled, the alternatives are given in brackets, preceded by explanatory words in italics, as: "it is [*written above:* may be] true."

5. Variant readings of several versions are noted if important.

Abbreviations and Short Titles

ADS	Autograph document signed.[1]
ALS	Autograph letter signed.
APS	American Philosophical Society.
BF	Benjamin Franklin.
Bigelow, *Works*	John Bigelow, ed., *The Complete Works of Benjamin Franklin* . . . (10 vols., N.Y., 1887–88).
Cohen, *BF's Experiments*	I. Bernard Cohen, ed., *Benjamin Franklin's Experiments. A New Edition of Franklin's Experiments and Observations on Electricity* (Cambridge, Mass., 1941).
Colden Paps.	*The Letters and Papers of Cadwallader Colden.* New-York Historical Society *Collections* for 1917–23, 1934, 1935.
DAB	*Dictionary of American Biography.*
DNB	*Dictionary of National Biography.*
DS	Document signed.
Darlington, *Memorials*	William Darlington, *Memorials of John Bartram and Humphry Marshall* (Phila., 1849).
Dexter, *Biog. Sketches*	Franklin B. Dexter, *Biographical Sketches of the Graduates of Yale College* . . . (6 vols., N.Y. and New Haven, 1885–1912).
Duane, *Works*	William Duane, ed., *The Works of Dr. Benjamin Franklin* . . . (6 vols., Phila., 1808–18). Title varies in the several volumes.
Eddy, *Ledger "D"*	George Simpson Eddy, *Account Books Kept by Benjamin Franklin* [Volume II]. *Ledger "D," 1739–1747* (N.Y., 1929).
Evans	Charles Evans, *American Bibliography* (14 vols., Chicago and Worcester, Mass., 1903–59). Surviving imprints

1. For definitions of this and other kinds of manuscripts, see above, I, xliv–xlvii.

are reproduced in full in microprint in Clifford K. Shipton, ed., *Early American Imprints, 1639–1800* (microprint, Worcester, Mass.).

Exper. and Obser.   *Experiments and Observations on Electricity, made at Philadelphia in America, by Mr. Benjamin Franklin,* ... (London, 1751). Revised and enlarged editions were published in 1754, 1760, 1769, and 1774 with slightly varying titles. In each case the edition cited will be indicated, e.g., *Exper. and Obser.,* 1751 edit.

P. L. Ford, *Franklin Bibliog.*   Paul L. Ford, *Franklin Bibliography. A List of Books written by, or relating to Benjamin Franklin* (Brooklyn, 1889).

Kalm, *Travels*   Adolph B. Benson, ed., *Peter Kalm's Travels in North America. The English Version of 1770* (2 vols., N.Y., 1937).

Lib. Co. Phila.   Library Company of Philadelphia.

LS   Letter signed.

MS, MSS   Manuscript, manuscripts.

Montgomery, *Hist. Univ. Pa.*   Thomas H. Montgomery, *A History of the University of Pennsylvania from its Foundation to A.D. 1770* (Phila., 1900).

OED   *Oxford English Dictionary.*

PMHB   *Pennsylvania Magazine of History and Biography.*

Pa. Arch.   Samuel Hazard and others, eds., *Pennsylvania Archives* (9 series, Phila. and Harrisburg, 1852–1935).

Pa. Col. Recs.   *Minutes of the Provincial Council of Pennsylvania* ... (16 vols., Phila., 1838–53). Title changes with volume 11 to Supreme Executive Council.

Pa. Gaz.   *The Pennsylvania Gazette.*

Par. Text edit.   Max Farrand, ed., *Benjamin Franklin's Memoirs. Parallel Text Edition* ... (Berkeley and Los Angeles, 1949).

Parton, *Franklin*   James Parton, *Life and Times of Benjamin Franklin* (2 vols., N.Y., 1864).

Phil. Trans.	The Royal Society, *Philosophical Transactions.*
Sibley's Harvard Graduates	John L. Sibley, *Biographical Sketches of Graduates of Harvard University* (Cambridge, Mass., 1873–). Continued from volume 4 by Clifford K. Shipton.
Smyth, *Writings*	Albert H. Smyth, ed., *The Writings of Benjamin Franklin* ... (10 vols., N.Y., 1905–07).
Sparks, *Works*	Jared Sparks, ed., *The Works of Benjamin Franklin* ... (10 vols., Boston, 1836–40).
Thomas, *Printing*	Isaiah Thomas, *The History of Printing in America, with a Biography of Printers* ... (2 vols., American Antiquarian Society *Transactions and Collections*, V–VI, 1874).
Tyerman, *Whitefield*	Luke Tyerman, *The Life of the Rev. George Whitefield* ... (2 vols., London, 1876–77).
Van Doren, *Franklin*	Carl Van Doren, *Benjamin Franklin* (N.Y., 1938).
Van Doren, *Franklin-Mecom*	Carl Van Doren, ed., *The Letters of Benjamin Franklin & Jane Mecom* (*Memoirs* of the American Philosophical Society, XXVII, Princeton, 1950).
WTF, *Memoirs*	William Temple Franklin, ed., *Memoirs of the Life and Writings of Benjamin Franklin, LL.D., F.R.S. &c.* ... (3 vols., 4to, London, 1817–18).
Watson, *Annals*	John F. Watson, *Annals of Philadelphia, and Pennsylvania, in the Olden Time* ... (3 vols., Phila., 1891).

Genealogical references. An editorial reference to one of Franklin's relatives may be accompanied by a citation of the symbol assigned to that person in the genealogical tables and charts in volume 1 of this work, pp. xlix–lxxvii, as, for example: Thomas Franklin (A.5.2.1), Benjamin Mecom (C.17.3), or Benjamin Franklin Bache (D.3.1).

Chronology

January 1, 1745, through June 30, 1750

1745

January 16: BF's father Josiah dies in Boston.

June 17: Louisbourg surrendered to British and colonial force.

1746

April 16: Duke of Cumberland defeats the army of Charles Stuart at Culloden Moor.

November–December: BF visits Boston.

Pieter Van Musschenbroek investigates properties of the Leyden jar.

1747

March 28: BF's first mention of his electrical experiments in a letter to Collinson.

November 24: The Association signed.

1748

January 1: BF and David Hall form a partnership for printing; BF retires from active business thereafter and moves his residence to corner of Race and Second Streets.

February 8: First Philadelphia Lottery drawn.

September 10: Second Philadelphia Lottery drawn.

October 4: BF elected a member of the Philadelphia Common Council.

October 18: Treaty of Aix-la-Chapelle signed, ending the War of the Austrian Succession (in America, King George's War).

1749

June 3: BF appointed justice of the peace of the City of Philadelphia.

July 10: BF appointed Provincial Grand Master of Masons of Pennsylvania by Thomas Oxnard of Boston, Provincial Grand Master of all North America.

November 13: BF elected president of the trustees of the Academy of Philadelphia.

1750

March 13: BF deposed as Provincial Grand Master of Pennsylvania by William Allen, newly appointed from England as Provincial Grand Master, who immediately appoints him Deputy Grand Master.

THE PAPERS OF
BENJAMIN FRANKLIN

VOLUME 3

January 1, 1745, through June 30, 1750

Poor Richard, 1745

Poor Richard, 1745. An Almanack For the Year of Christ 1745, ... By Richard Saunders, Philom. Philadelphia: Printed and sold by B. Franklin. (American Antiquarian Society)

Courteous Reader,

For the Benefit of the Publick, and my own Profit, I have performed this my thirteenth annual Labour, which I hope will be as acceptable as the former.

The rising and setting of the Planets, and their Conjunctions with the Moon, I have continued; whereby those who are unacquainted with those heavenly Bodies, may soon learn to distinguish them from the fixed Stars, by observing the following Directions.

All those glittering Stars (except five) which we see in the Firmament of Heaven, are called fixed Stars, because they keep the same Distance from one another, and from the Ecliptic; they rise and set on the same Points of the Horizon, and appear like so many lucid Points fixed to the celestial Firmament. The other five have a particular and different Motion, for which Reason they have not always the same Distance from one another; and therefore they have been called wandering Stars or Planets, viz. Saturn ♄, Jupiter ♃, Mars ♂, Venus ♀, and Mercury ☿, and these may be distinguished from the fixed Stars by their not twinkling. The brightest of the five is Venus, which appears the biggest; and when this glorious Star appears, and goes before the Sun, it is called Phosphorus, or the Morning Star, and Hesperus, or the Evening Star, when it follows the Sun. Jupiter appears almost as big as Venus, but not so bright. Mars may be easily known from the rest of the Planets, because it appears red like a hot Iron or burning Coal, and twinkles a little. Saturn, in Appearance, is less than Mars, and of a pale Colour. Mercury is so near the Sun, that it is seldom seen.

Against the 6th Day of January you may see ♂ rise 10 35, which signifies the Planet Mars rises 35 Minutes after 10 o'Clock at Night, when that Planet may be seen to appear in the East. Also against the 10th Day of January you will find ♀ sets 7 13, which shows Venus sets 13 Minutes after 7 o'Clock at Night. If you look towards the West that Evening, you may see that beautiful

3

Star till the Time of its setting. Again, on the 18th Day of the same Month, you will find ♄ rise 9 18, which shews that Saturn rises 18 Minutes after 9 at Night.

Or the Planets may be known by observing them at the Time of their Conjunctions with the Moon, viz. against the 14 Day of January are inserted these Characters ♂ ☽ ♄ , which shews there will be a Conjunction of the Moon and Saturn on that Day. If you look out about 5 o'Clock in the Morning, you will see Saturn very near the Moon. The like is to be observed at any other time by the rising and setting of the Planets, and their Conjunctions with the Moon; by which Method they may be distinctly known from the fixed Stars.

I have nothing further to add at present, but my hearty Wishes for your Welfare, both temporal and spiritual, and Thanks for all your past Favours, being, Dear Reader, Thy obliged Friend,

R. SAUNDERS

> Go, wond'rous Creature! mount where Science guides,
> Go measure Earth, weigh Air, and state the Tides;
> Shew by what Laws the wand'ring Planets stray,
> Correct old Time, and teach the Sun his Way.
> Go soar with Plato to th'empyreal Sphere,
> To the *first* Good, *first* Perfect, and *first* Fair;
> Or tread the mazy Round his Follow'rs trod,
> And, quitting Sense, call *imitating* God,
> As Eastern Priests in giddy Circles run,
> And turn their Heads to imitate the Sun.
> Go teach Eternal Wisdom how to rule,
> Then drop into thyself, and be a Fool.

XI Mon. January hath xxxi days.

> "I give and I devise (old Euclio said,
> And sigh'd) my Lands and Tenements to Ned."
> Your Money, Sir? "My Money, Sir! what all?
> Why—if I must—(then wept) I give it Paul."
> The Mannor, Sir? "The Mannor! hold," he cry'd,
> "Not that—I cannot part with that"—and dy'd.

4

Beware of little Expences, a small Leak will sink a great Ship.

Wars bring scars.

A light purse is a heavy Curse.

As often as we do good, we sacrifice.

> Help, Hands;
> For I have no Lands.

XII Mon. February hath xxviii days.

> *Self Love* but serves the virtuous Mind to wake,
> As the small Pebble stirs the peaceful Lake;
> The Centre mov'd, a Circle strait succeeds,
> Another still, and still another spreads,
> Friend, Parent, Neighbour, first it will embrace,
> His Country next, and next all human Race;
> Wide and more wide, th' o'erflowings of the Mind
> Take every Creature in of every Kind.

It's common for Men to give 6 pretended Reasons instead of one real one.

I Mon. March hath xxxi days.

> *Fame* but from Death a Villain's Name can save,
> As Justice tears his Body from the Grave;
> When what t'oblivion better were resign'd
> Is hung on high to poison half Mankind.
> All Fame is foreign but of *true Desert,*
> Plays round the Head, but comes not to the Heart.
> One *Self-approving Hour* whole Years outweighs
> Of stupid Starers, and of loud Huzza's.

Vanity backbites more than *Malice.*

He's a Fool that cannot conceal his Wisdom.

Great spenders are bad lenders.

All blood is alike ancient.

II Mon. April hath xxx days.

> 'Tis not for Mortals always to be blest:
> But him the least the dull and painful Hours
> Of Life oppress, whom sober SENSE conducts,
> And VIRTUE, thro' this Labyrinth we tread.
> Virtue and Sense are one; and, trust me, he
> Who has not Virtue, is not truly wise.

You may talk too much on the best of subjects.

A Man without ceremony has need of great merit in its place.

No gains without pains.

III Mon. May hath xxxi days.

> VIRTUE, (for meer GOOD-NATURE, is a Fool)
> Is Sense and Spirit, with HUMANITY:
> 'Tis sometimes angry, and its Frown confounds;
> 'Tis ev'n vindictive, but in Vengeance just.
> Knaves fain would laugh at it; some great Ones dare;
> But at his Heart, the most undaunted Son
> Of Fortune, dreads its Name and awful Charms.

Had I revenged wrong, I had not worn my skirts so long.

Graft good Fruit all, or graft not at all.

IV Mon. June hath xxx days.

> Unhappy Italy! whose alter'd State
> Has felt the worst Severity of Fate;
> Not that *Barbarian* Bands her *Fasces* broke,
> And bow'd her haughty Neck beneath her Yoke;
> Nor that her Palaces to Earth are thrown,
> Her Cities desart, and her Fields unsown;
> But that her ancient Spirit is decay'd,
> That sacred Wisdom from her Bounds is fled.
> That there the Source of Science flows no more,
> Whence its rich Streams supply'd the World before.

6

Idleness is the greatest Prodigality.

Old young and old long.

> Punch-coal, cut candle, and set brand on end,
> Is neither good house-wife, nor good house-wife's friend.

V Mon. July hath xxxi days.

> Hot from the Field, indulge not yet your Limbs
> In wish'd Repose, nor court the fanning Gale,
> Nor taste the Spring. O! by the sacred Tears
> Of Widows, Orphans, Mothers, Sisters, Sires,
> Forbear!—No other Pestilence has driven
> Such Myriads o'er th' irremeable Deep.

>> He who buys had need have 100 Eyes,
>> But one's enough for him that sells the Stuff.

There are no fools so troublesome as those that have wit.

VI Mon. August hath xxxi days.

> Has God, thou Fool! work'd solely for thy Good,
> Thy Joy, thy Pastime, thy Attire, thy Food?
> Who for thy Table feeds the wanton Fawn,
> For him as kindly spread the flow'ry Lawn.
> Is it for thee the Lark descends and sings?
> Joy tunes his Voice, Joy elevates his Wings.
> Is it for thee the Mock-bird pours his Throat?
> Loves of his own, and Raptures, swell the Note.

Many complain of their Memory, few of their Judgment.

One Man may be more cunning than another, but not more cunning than every body else.

VII Mon. September hath xxx days.

> The bounding Steed you pompously bestride,
> Shares with his Lord the Pleasure and the Pride.
> Is thine alone the Seed that strows the Plain?

7

The Birds of Heav'n shall vindicate their Grain.
Thine the full Harvest of the golden Year?
Part pays, and justly, the deserving Steer.
The Hog that plows not, nor obeys thy Call,
Lives on the Labours of this Lord of all.

To God we owe fear and love; to our neighbours justice and charity; to our selves prudence and sobriety.

Fools make feasts and wise men eat them.

Light-heel'd mothers make leaden-heel'd daughters.

VIII Mon. October hath xxxi days.

For Forms of Government let Fools contest,
Whate'er is best administer'd is best:
For Modes of Faith let graceless Zealots fight,
His can't be wrong, whose Life is in the right:
All must be false, that thwart this one great End,
And all of God, that bless Mankind, or mend.

The good or ill hap of a good or ill life,
Is the good or ill choice of a good or ill wife.

'Tis easier to prevent bad habits than to break them.

IX Mon. November hath xxx days.

Fair Summer's gone, and Nature's Charms decay.
See gloomy Clouds obscure the chearful Day!
Now hung with Pearls the dropping Trees appear,
Their faded Honours scatter'd here and there.
Behold the Groves that shine with silver Frost,
Their Beauty wither'd, and their Verdure lost.
Sharp Boreas blows, and Nature feels Decay,
Time conquers all and we must Time obey.

Every Man has Assurance enough to boast of his honesty, few of their Understanding.

Interest which blinds some People, enlightens others.

X Mon. December hath xxxi days.

These Blessings, Reader, may Heav'n grant to thee;
A faithful Friend, equal in Love's degree;
Land fruitful, never conscious of the Curse,
A liberal Heart and never-failing Purse;
A smiling Conscience, a contented mind;
A temp'rate Knowledge with true Wisdom join'd;
A Life as long as fair, and when expir'd,
A kindly Death, unfear'd as undesir'd.

An ounce of wit that is bought,
Is worth a pound that is taught.

He that resolves to mend hereafter, resolves not to mend now.

COURTS.

The Christian Doctrine teaches to believe
It's every Christian's Duty, to forgive.
Could we forgive as fast as Men offend
The LAWS slow Progresses would quickly end.
Revenge of past Offences is the Cause
Why peaceful Minds consented to have Laws.
Yet Plaintiffs and Defendants much mistake
Their Cure, and their Diseases lasting make;
For to be reconcil'd, and to comply,
Would prove their cheap and shortest Remedy.

Presentment of the Philadelphia Grand Jury[1]

AD: Historical Society of Pennsylvania

Jan. 3. 1744, [5]
To the Worshipful the Mayor, the Recorder[2] and the rest of the Justices of the City of Philadelphia.

The Grand Jury of the said City, met at the present Sessions,

1. Except for the foreman's signature at the end, the MS is in the handwriting of BF, who was a member of the Jury.
2. The mayor was Edward Shippen (1703–1781), later "of Lancaster"; the recorder was William Allen (1704–1780).

9

do, in Compliance with the Direction of the Court, [make] the following *particular* Presentments of unlawful Bakehouses, Coopers Shops, Disorderly Houses, &c. but believing from the Reprimand they yesterday received from the Court, that the *general* Presentment they then made was misapprehended, and that, thro' the Clerk's hasty Reading, the Court did not sufficiently advert to the Tenor and Import of that Presentment, they beg Leave here to repeat it.[3]

"The Grand Jury observe with great Concern the vast Number of Tipling Houses within this City, many of which they think are little better than Nurseries of Vice and Debauchery, and tend very much to encrease the Number of our Poor. They are likewise of Opinion, that the profane Language, horrid Oaths and Imprecations, grown of late so common in our Streets, so shocking to the Ears of the sober Inhabitants, and tending to destroy in the Minds of our Youth, all Sense of the Fear of God and the Religion of an Oath, owes its Increase in a great Measure to those disorderly Houses. The Jury therefore beg Leave to recommend it to the Court, to fall on some Method of limiting or diminishing the Number of Publick Houses, and preserving Good Order in such as shall be licenced for the future."

The Jury would only observe, that they had no Intention in the least to break in upon the Authority of the Magistrates; that they only complain'd of the great Number of Tipling Houses as a Grievance which they feel, and, far from prescribing to the Justices, they only requested them to fall upon some Methods among themselves of preventing it for the future: Which is no more than is practiced in like Cases by the Grand Juries of the City of London, as the Presentment they made of the great Increase of Gin Shops, to the Lord Mayor and Justices of that City, fully shows.[4] [*In the margin:* Here read the Middlesex Presentment.][5] For this Presentment the Jury were, as we are inform'd,

3. The original MS of the presentment of Jan. 2 is also in Hist. Soc. Pa. It is not, however, in BF's hand, as stated in *PMHB*, XXII (1898), 497–8, where both presentments are printed.

4. The findings of the London and Middlesex grand juries and justices on excessive gin drinking from 1725 onwards are briefly summarized in M. Dorothy George, *London Life in the XVIIIth Century* (N.Y., 1925), pp. 32–4.

5. The Middlesex presentments of 1729 and 1735 were especially well

thank'd by that honourable Court, and a Committee of the Bench appointed to enquire into the Grievance complain'd of, upon whose Report Measures were afterwards taken to remove it. The Grand Jury do therefore still think it their Duty to complain of the enormous Increase of Publick Houses in Philadelphia, especially since it now appears by the Constables Returns that there are upwards of One Hundred that have Licences, which, with the Retailers, make the Houses that sell strong Drink, by our Computation, near a tenth Part of the City; a Proportion that appears to us much too great, since by their Number they impoverish one another as well as the Neighbourhoods they live in, and, for want of better Customers, may, thro' Necessity, be under greater Temptations to entertain Apprentices, Servants, and even Negroes. The Jury therefore are glad to hear from the Bench, that the Magistrates are become sensible of this Evil, and purpose to apply a Remedy; for which they will deserve the Thanks of all good Citizens.

We do further hereby particularly present the following Persons for keeping Disorderly Houses in this City, to wit, Katharine Mason, John Browne, Joseph Webb,[6] Margaret Cook, Widow Finley, Ralph Highrick, William Jones, Jane Bond[7], Katharine Carr, Sarah Levine.

The Jury observ'd with Concern in the Course of the Evidence, that a Neighbourhood in which some of these disorderly Houses are, is so generally thought to be vitiated, as to obtain among the common People the shocking Name of *Hell-Town*.[8]

We do farther present the following Persons for having Coopers Shops not regulated according to Law, and dangerous to the City on Account of Fire, to wit. Hugh McMachen, Samuel Powel,

---

known. The presentment of 1729 is reprinted in William Maitland, *The History and Survey of London* (London, 1756), I, 544, and that of 1735 in [Thomas Wilson], *Distilled Spirituous Liquors the Bane of the Nation* (2d edit., London, 1736), appendix, pp. iv–vii.

6. This name is struck out as though it was not to be presented.

7. Jane Bond was convicted of the charge, fined £5, but, on petition that she was unable to pay, the Common Council remitted the fine, May 20, 1745. *Minutes of the Common Council of . . . Philadelphia, 1704 to 1776* (Phila., 1847), p. 445.

8. Hell-Town was on the west side of Third Street, extending south from Race. Watson, *Annals*, I, 446.

Andrew Farrel, Benjamin Betterton, Thomas James, Jonathan Evans, Aaron Jenkins, Jacob Kollock, Thos. Glentworth, Thomas Fisher, Richard Brockden,   Cateer, Jacob Shute, William Nixon, Hugh McCullough, Edmund Beech.[9]

We do farther present the following Persons for keeping Bakehouses not regulated according to Law, and dangerous to the City on Account of Fire, to wit. William Darvell, Marcus Kuhl, John Fitzharris, John Fer[nal], Daniel Button [or Britton], Francis Johnson, Samuel Reed, Joseph Clark, Stephen Jenkins. And we do present Norton Prior, Wight Massey, and Marcus Kuhl for having Piles of Faggots dangerously situated and contrary to Law.[1]

We do farther present Lynford Lardner for abusing and assaulting the Constable of the Watch then upon Duty.[2]

And lastly, we do present Samuel Hasell Esqr. as a Magistrate who not only refused to take Notice of a Complaint made to him against a Person guilty of profane Swearing, but (at another Time) set an Evil Example by swearing himself.[3]

We beg Leave only to add, that as a good Grand Jury (which the Recorder was pleased to say we had the Appearance of being) may, if there is no Misunderstanding between the Magistrates and them, greatly assist and strengthen the Court in the Suppression of Vice and Immorality, we hope no Cause will be given hereafter of the least Disagreement; and that well meaning Persons may not be made unwilling to serve in that Office by unkind Reprimands from the Bench, tho' they should sometimes happen to mistake their Duty, but be treated—at least with some Indulgence.

By Direction and in Behalf of the Grand Jury

WILLM. BELL foreman

9. This paragraph has been struck out, apparently by another hand than BF's.

1. This paragraph has also been struck out.

2. Lynford (or Lyn Ford) Lardner (1715–1774), receiver general of quitrents; keeper of the Great Seal of the Province, 1746; provincial councilor, 1755. Charles P. Keith, *The Provincial Councillors of Pennsylvania* (Phila., 1883), p. 317. Between "for" and "abusing" in this paragraph the words "prophane Cursing, and for" were first written, then struck out.

3. Samuel Hassell, alderman of Philadelphia, had been mayor, 1731–33, 1740–41. This paragraph has been struck through by another hand than BF's.

To William Strahan

MS not found; reprinted from *The Atlantic Monthly*, LXI (1888), 22–3.

Sir, Philad. Feb. 12, 1744, 5
I received your Favour per Mr. Chew[4] dated Sept. 10, and a
Copy via Boston. I received also Mr. Middleton's pieces.[5] I am
pleased to hear that my old Acquaintance Mr. Wygate[6] is promoted, and hope the Discovery will be compleated. I would not
have you be too nice in the Choice of Pamphlets you send me. Let
me have everything, good or bad, that makes a Noise and has a
Run: for I have Friends here of Different Tastes to oblige with the
Sight of them. If Mr. Warburton publishes a new Edition of Pope's
works,[7] please to send me as soon as 'tis out, 6 Setts. That Poet has
many Admirers here, and the Reflection he somewhere casts on
the Plantations as if they had a Relish for such Writers as Ward
only, is injurious.[8] Your authors know but little of the Fame they
have on this Side the Ocean. We are a kind of Posterity in
respect to them. We read their Works with perfect Impartiality,
being at too great a Distance to be byassed by the Fashions,
Parties and Prejudices that prevail among you. We know nothing
of their personal Failings; the Blemishes in their character never
reach us, and therefore the bright and amiable part strikes us with
its full Force. They have never offended us or any of our Friends,
and we have no Competitions with them, and therefore we praise
and admire them without Restraint. Whatever Thomson writes,
send me a Dozen Copies of. I had read no Poetry for several
years, and almost lost the Relish of it, till I met with his *Seasons*.

4. Benjamin Chew, who, admitted to the Middle Temple, Oct. 27, 1743,
returned to Philadelphia a year later because of the death of his father, Dr.
Samuel Chew. Burton A. Konkle, *Benjamin Chew, 1722–1810* (Phila., 1932),
pp. 41, 48.
5. Christopher Middleton. See above, II, 410 n.
6. John Wygate. See above, II, 412 n.
7. At his death in 1744 Pope had left the rights to his published works to
his friend Bishop William Warburton, so his edition was to be expected. It
was published in 1751.
8. Pope's aspersion on the colonies and on Edward Ward, author of *The
London Spy*, appeared in the first edition of *The Dunciad Variorum* (London, 1729), I, 200: "Or shipp'd with W--- to ape and monkey lands," and
was elaborated in the 1743 edition.

That charming Poet has brought more Tears of Pleasure into my Eyes than all I ever read before. I wish it were in my Power to return him any Part of the Joy he has given me. I purpose to send you by a Ship that is to sail shortly from this Port a Bill, and an Invoice of Books that I shall want for Sale in my Shop, which I doubt not you will procure as cheap as possible; otherwise I shall not be able to sell them, as here is one who is furnished by Oswald[9] that sells excessively low; I cannot conceive upon what terms they deal. The Pamphlets and Newspapers I shall be glad to receive by way of N York and Boston, when there is no Ship directly hither; If you direct them for B.F. Boston and Philada. they will come directly to hand from those Places. Mr. Hall is perfectly well and gains ground daily in the Esteem of all that know him. I hope Caslon[1] will not delay casting the English Fount I wrote to you for, so long as he has some that have been sent me. I have no doubt but Mr. Hall will succeed well in what he undertakes. He is obliging, discreet, industrious but honest; and when these Qualities meet, things seldom go amiss. Nothing in my Power shall be wanting to serve him. I cannot return your Compliments in kind; this Quaker plain Country producing none. All I can do is, to demonstrate, by a hearty Readiness in serving you when I have an Opportunity, or any Friend you recommend, that I do truly esteem and love you, being, Sir, Your obliged humble Servant B FRANKLIN

P.S. Please continue the Political Cabinet.[2]

Notes on Assembly Debates MS: American Philosophical Society

These fragments are part of an account Franklin wrote of Assembly debates, February 26–28, 1745, on aid to Massachusetts' expedition against Louisbourg. Governor William Shirley had written Governor Thomas on February 4 about preparations and requested him to excite "an Emulation" in the Pennsylvanians and encourage them to do their

9. John Oswald, London bookseller and publisher. H. R. Plomer and others, *A Dictionary of the Printers and Booksellers . . . in England . . . 1726 to 1775* (Oxford, 1932), pp. 186–7.
1. William Caslon (1692–1766), English typefounder.
2. *The Political Cabinet*, a periodical published from July 1744 through June 1745.

part to promote "His Majesty's Service and the common Interest of these Provinces."[3] Thomas laid Shirley's request before the Assembly in a special session on February 25. "Dispatch, you will see, is the Life of the Undertaking," he pointed out. The Assembly showed dispatch only in rejecting the governor's request. A committee was appointed on February 27 to draft an answer, which was read, considered, approved, and sent to the governor on the 28th.

The Assembly put their rejection of Shirley's call on the grounds of dignity and policy. "If they expected the Assistance of the neighbouring Colonies, it is reasonable they should have consulted them." Furthermore, the Assembly pointed out, the Crown might call for action with which New England's plans might interfere. "Had we not other Reasons to determine us," they concluded, with a veiled reference to the Quakers' religious scruples, "we should think it not prudent to unite in an Enterprize, where the Expence must be great, perhaps much Blood shed, and the Event very uncertain."[4] The expedition remained an undertaking of the New England colonies alone, chiefly Massachusetts, aided by a squadron of the Royal Navy under Commodore Peter Warren.[5]

[February 26–28, 1745]

[*Pages missing*] Crown, he did not see how we could come into it, our Principles considered. After some Minutes Silence, Mr. Trotter[6] said, We have often been importun'd to do something in our own Defence, and have always refus'd: Therefore it will not become us to raise Men and Money to go and disturb those that neither meddle nor make with us; People with whom we have nothing to do. [This Gentleman forgot, that a Privateer from Cape Breton, took 4 of our Vessels near the Mouth of our Bay last Summer; and sent Word to the Governor that he should cruise there a fortnight.][7] Mr. Norris said, That if the Crown had recommended the Affair we might possibly do something; for as we are protected by the Crown we think we ought to give Money when

3. Shirley to Thomas, Feb. 4, 1744/5. Charles H. Lincoln, ed., *Correspondence of William Shirley* (N.Y., 1912), I, 179–80.

4. *Pa. Col. Recs.*, IV, 753–5; 8 *Pa. Arch.*, IV, 3025–28.

5. For BF's further comments on this expedition see below, p. 26.

6. Joseph Trotter. Other members of the Assembly mentioned in this manuscript are Isaac Norris, Thomas Leech, Joseph Pennock, John Hall, and Joseph Harvey.

7. Brackets in the MS, but not BF's. See Thomas' message to the Assembly on this contemptuous invasion of Pennsylvania waters. *Pa. Col. Recs.*, IV, 749.

demanded: But it would be inconsistent for those who would not defend themselves to attack their *Neighbours,* (as we might in some sense call them, tho' Enemies. There is no particular Commission for this Expedition, and if Commands should come from the Crown hereafter it may be of as much Use to give Money then as now; for now it is too late, and therefore he thought it might well enough be postpon'd at present. Mr. Leech said, That tho' a few of the Members might be dispos'd to encourage and assist in this Expedition, it would be to no purpose to lay their Reasons before the House, or to speak in the Affair, considering *the religious Principles* of the Majority; and therefore he should hereafter be silent in it. Mr. Norris, added, that it was well known an Application had been made to the Crown by the Agent of New England last Spring to take Cape Breton which if the Crown had approv'd, there had been time enough to send Orders for the purpose; but as no Orders had been sent, it would appear forward in us to join in the Enterprize. Some Pause intervening, Mr. Pennock said, He wish'd the Members would speak their Minds freely: let them consider their Principles and they must soon come to a Result. Mr. Hall, then said that since it was inconsistent with our Principles, and not required by the Crown, he thought we should do nothing in it: And Mr. Harvey said the same. So some proposed a Committee might be appointed to prepare an Answer to the Governors Message agreeable to the Sentiments of the House: But others observing that it was an Affair of Importance, and it would look too hasty and Precipitate if it appear'd on our Minutes that the House came to so sudden a Resolution; the farther Consideration of it was adjourned to the Morning: and then the House adjourned. [*Pages missing*] opposite to Defense, and more so to an offensive War. Together with the Absurdity they would be involv'd in, who have always refus'd the one, if they should agree to the other. When I compare the Governor's Message to the House, with his private Conversation, I cannot but admire at his Insincerity, to commend the Undertaking publickly, that he might gain the Applause of the Governor and People of New-England; and the Ministry at home. At the same time that he privately does all in his Power to disappoint it. He is not therefore the Man of Honour his former Friends cry'd him up to be; I say his former Friends for those Gentlemen [*obliterated*] differently of him of late. Nor can

I justify the Assembly from Disingenuity in their Answer. For tho' if it be against their Consciences, they ought not by any Means to encourage Military Proceedings in others more than themselves; yet I think they ought to be open and honest and give the true Reason; and not trifle in the Manner they do; by pretending among other Things, that they are offended at not being consulted in such an Affair, &c. In short the Governor and Assembly have been only acting a Farce and playing Tricks to amuse the World.

Several of the Members told me to day that they heartily wished the N E People Success. I told them those People were as much oblig'd to them for their Good Wishes as the Poor in the Scripture to those that [say] Be ye warmed be ye filled &c.[8] I ask'd them what should hinder the House from sending a little Provision to their fellow Subjects, who were going [to be at?] so useful an Undertaking and probably might suffer for want of it. One Answered, That would be encouraging War, and they [*remainder missing*].

From John Mitchell

MS not found; reprinted from *The American Medical and Philosophicaι Register; or Annals of Medicine, Natural History, Agriculture, and the Arts*, IV (1814), 383–7.

[March? 1745][9]

In the short account of the yellow fever, which I left with you at

8. "If a brother or sister be naked, and destitute of daily food, And one of you say unto them, Depart in peace, be ye warmed and filled: notwithstanding ye give them not those things which are needful to the body: what doth it profit?" James 2:15–16.

9. On Oct. 25, 1744, BF sent to Cadwallader Colden a copy of Mitchell's essay on yellow fever at the author's request (see above, II, 418). Lacking time for more than a cursory reading at the moment, Colden returned it to BF with some remarks (not found) in order that Mitchell, whom he did not know, "might have every hint that I could suggest to make your performance more perfect." Colden to Mitchell, June 8, 1745, *Amer. Med. and Philos. Reg.*, IV (1814), 378. The MS and comments may have reached BF in December, and the comments, forwarded to Virginia, may have reached Mitchell in January or February. Mitchell replied to Colden's comments in the letter to BF here printed. This was probably written between February and April, for Colden acknowledged it, June 8, in his first letter directly to Mitchell. The March date is an approximation.

Philadelphia, I have not endeavoured to establish any theory, or even to make any deductions from any established theory of that, or like diseases; but have only delivered a few matters of fact, as they occurred to me in practice, (which are chiefly or only such as I thought were either new or not well confirmed and known before,) as a foundation to build a theory upon, and on which to deduce a rational cure of this disease; and it is such which I humbly conceive may be most pertinent to the laudable designs of your society, of promoting rather that repeating the knowledge of the arts and sciences; nor have I either health or leisure at present, to deduce any theory or particular applications of it, from these *data;* however, I am glad to see myself so well prevented in this by your worthy colleague, Dr. Colden, as far as relates to malignant fevers in general, in this paper which you favoured me with. But as all diseases are generally attended with some peculiar and distinguishing symptoms, whereby they differ very materially from those of the same general denomination, especially in their cure, so I shall mention the concomitants of this disease, which seem to distinguish it as much from other malignant and pestilential fevers, and are to be had as much regard to in the cure, as the eruption of pustles in the measles or small pox, or of carbuncle and buboes in the plague; for beside the general affections of the solids and fluids, we must likewise have particular regard to the symptoms which they produce in the cure of diseases.

The first of these concomitants of our yellow fever, which is so material to be regarded, is an inflammation of the stomach, or liver, or both, with the adjacent parts. This appears not only from dissections, but from all outward symptoms or appearances of the disease, to be a most constant and aggravating circumstance of it; inasmuch that I never knew any one to die in this disease, without manifest tokens of this inflammation of the stomach or adjacent parts: this, as well as the inflammation of other *viscera,* generally of the brain, it is true, sometimes happens in other fevers of this class, but not so constantly, and almost surely, as in this. The next appearance of our malignant, or rather pestilential fever, as it may be called, which ought to be regarded, is an icterus, or yellow effusion. This, it is true, has imposed upon some so far as to make them take this symptom for a cause; to take this nominal, for the real essence of the disease; whereby they reckon this fever to be entirely of the bilious kind; but it would be equally wrong, and of as bad consequence almost, in practice, to have no regard to this most fatal appearance in the disease, as to deduce its nature solely from thence. These two constant concomitants of the disease, wherever it is severe and mortal, joined to the general state of the fluids, which is very well explained by Dr. Colden, may give us a good idea of this disease, and point out the several indications of cure. The principal of these indications, which has been so well explained by many, is sweating, or at least promoting a constant *diaphoresis,* well known to be necessary in all malignant fevers. But, alas! it is much easier to propose a general method, than to perform a cure, when we come to practice; for that accurate observer, Sydenham, tells us, that the method which will prove successful in one year, (not to mention particular cases) will be prejudicial in another. Thus, in the years 1737 and 1741, when this disease was epidemic in Virginia, the sick could not be made to sweat in the winter and spring seasons; at least, not so plentifully as was necessary to check the violence of the fever, and avert the impending inflammation; which, indeed, is very often the case, when this distemper is very severe; for you must observe, that it differs as much in degree, at different times, as the measles or small-pox does. All heating sudorifics, in these cases, bring on the inflammation, and hasten on the gangrenous state of the *viscera;* and plentiful bleeding (which I have known to be urged by some in these urging occasions) causes a no less fatal dissolution of the fluids, or mortal debility, both which are but too well known in practice, and are easily deduced from the theory of these diseases. It is upon such occasions, as you may perceive, that I recommend purging in this disease, agreeably to the practice of all physicians who have had any considerable experience in it; for there are no parts, through which the lymphatic humours (which, as Dr. Colden justly observes, are the principal seat of this distemper,) go off with more ease and more freely, than through the glands of the *primae viae.* Helvet. *Anim. Econ.*[1]

Another advantage, and even necessity of purging, is obvious to be perceived from the necessity of cleansing the *primae viae* of their

1. Jean Claude Adrien Helvétius, *An Essay on the Animal Oeconomy. Together with Observations upon the Small Pox ... Translated from the French* (London, 1723).

feculent and corruptible contents, which is of great service, when they come to be so severely affected. When this alone is indicated, by purging it may be done without any danger of driving the humours to the bowels; for the action of lenitives is no more to be referred to purgation, than the washing of the skin is to be referred to the action of sudorifics. Pitcairn. *Dissertat. de Febr. curat.*[2] But it is very certain, what Dr. Colden rightly inculcates, that purging in this disease, requires much medical skill and prudence, (as well as most other applications in it,) and ought not to be rashly attempted; for which reason I have been more particular in explaining the reasons of it, and wish I had leisure to be as particular in delivering the practical observations which confirm and illustrate this part of practice, and the cautions requisite in it; but in general it might be observed, that it is rather out of necessity than choice, that we have recourse to purging before, or rather, at the decline of this disease. But on the decline it is so necessary that I never knew the yellow effusion to be carried off, except in one single instance, without a purge; the reason of which appears to be the viscidity of the bile, which occasions this icterus, which cannot pass off by other outlets. Dr. Colden desires to know, if any recover after purging without sweats? I can inform him, that sometimes they do, although sweats are the most general critical evacuations of all fevers. But the miasmata of contagious fevers, seem to be so subtile, that when they are disengaged from the more viscid humours, they make their escape insensibly through the pores of the skin and other parts; by which you may see some recover suddenly and surprisingly, without the least perceptible evacuation. As to the relapse, which Dr. Colden thinks may proceed from the sick being exposed to the cold air after the fever, you must observe, that this was not an accidental, but a constant circumstance of the disease, at least at four times, when it has been epidemic in Virginia, and as much to be expected, as the return of an intermittent fever at its stated periods, whenever care was not properly taken to prevent it. What seemed to aggravate it most, was a too plentiful or gross diet. I imagined it might proceed from some lentor of the fluids, not removed nor evacuated, on account of the extreme debility of the body, which might afford, as it were, a *nidus*, for the subtile

2. Archibald Pitcairne, *Dissertatio de curatione febrium quae per evacuationes instituitur* ([Edinburgh?], 1695).

contagious vapours; in the same manner as some people, who have a great fluidity of their humours, and free execretions, never contract any contagious disease; whilst others, whose fluids are more viscid, can hardly avoid it, and suffer most severely from them.

p.s. What I understand by the lymphatic humours being affected in this disease, is chiefly a morbid acrimony of all the serous parts of the blood, which dissolves or assimilates the globular part of the blood, whenever the circulation is languid. *Qu.* Whether the contagious vapour, which affects the blood in this manner, is not derived from the internal, rather than the external, surface of the body? and whether the affections of the bile and liver, do not proceed originally from the same cause or minera of disease: since most of the blood which is carried to the liver, and from which the bile is secerned, proceeds from the stomach, intestines, pancreas, &c. by the venae portarum, very different from the other veins of the body? and whether this may not make discharges from the internal surface of the body more necessary than in like diseases of the malignant kind: since, in this fever, the morbid humours not only proceed from thence in all probability, but likewise fix there; whilst in others of the eruptive kind, as they generally are, they are thrown on the external surface?

To William Strahan Duplicate:[3] Rosenbach Foundation

Sir Philada. April 14. 1745
I wrote to you lately via New York, and sent a Copy via Maryland, one or other of which I hope may come to hand. I have only Time now to desire you to send me the following Books,[4] viz.

1 Doz Cole's Eng. Dictionaries
3 Doz. Mather's Young Man's Companion
2 Doz Fisher's Ditto
2 Quarter Waggoners for America

3. Written at the top of the sheet which carried the second letter of the same date, printed here directly following.
4. The identifiable works in this list were probably the following: Elisha Coles, *An English Dictionary* ... *Now Corrected and Much Improved* (London, 1732); William Mather, *The Young Man's Companion* (15th edit., London, 1737); George Fisher, *The Instructor: or, Young Man's Best Com-*

6 Echard's Gazetteer
4 Doz Grammars with const[ruin]g Book
1 Doz Clark's Corderius
1 Doz London Vocabulary
1 Doz Bailey's English Exercises
6 Clark's Introduction
6 Esop's Fables, Latin
1 Doz Accidences.
6 Brightland's English Grammar

I am, Sir, Your most humble Servant   B FRANKLIN
Copy

To William Strahan   ALS: Rosenbach Foundation

Sir,   Philada. April 14. 1745
The above is a Copy of mine per Capt. Martyn. I have only to
desire you to add the following Books. 6 French Testaments. 12
Boyer's Grammars, 12 Cord[ier]. Colloqu[es]. French. 3 Cambray's Fables. 3 Telemaque, 2 Travels of Cyrus, French. 2 Boyer's
Dictionaries 8vo. 1 New German and Eng. Dictionary and Grammar by Professor A. of Leipsig.[5] Yours &c.   B FRANKLIN

Addressed: To   Mr   William   Strahan   Printer   In   Wine   Office
Court   Fleetstreet   London   per Capt. Mesnard

---

panion; "Quarter Waggoners for America": *The English Pilot. The Fourth
Book. Describing the West India Navigation, from Hudson's-Bay to the River
Amazones* (London, 1737 or 1745. "Wagoner" was a term used for an atlas
of charts, derived from a work of this nature published in Leyden in 1588
by Lucas Wagenaer); Laurence Echard (or Eachard), *The Gazetteer's: or,
Newsman's Interpreter* (15th edit., London, 1741); John Clarke, *Corderii
Colloquiorum centuria selecta* (10th edit., London, 1740); *The London Vocabulary, English and Latin* (London, [1700?]); Nathan Bailey, *English and
Latin Exercises* (5th edit., London, 1720); John Clarke, *An Introduction to
the Making of Latin* (13th edit., London, 1742); John Brightland, *A Grammar of the English Tongue* (4th edit., London, 1721).

 5. The identifiable works in this list were probably the following: Abel
Boyer, *The Compleat French-Master, for Ladies and Gentlemen* (14th edit.,
London, 1744); Mathurin Cordier, *Nouvelle Traduction des Colloques* (Paris,
1672); Archbishop of Cambrai [Fénélon], *Dialogues des morts anciens et
modernes avec quelques fables* (2d edit., Paris, 1725); Fénélon, *Les Aventures*

Report of Viewers of a Road in the Northern Liberties[6]

MS Appearance Docket, 1740–1751, Prothonotary of the Supreme Court of Pennsylvania, Philadelphia

[April 1745][7]

Joseph Fox & al.
      vs
Mary Ball
} The Persons appointed to View and lay out a Road &ca. Report as followeth.

To the Honourable the Judges of the Supream Court of the Province of Pennsylvania now Sitting

WHEREAS by an Order of the Supream Court held at Philadelphia the Twenty fourth day of September last, We the Subscribers were appointed "To View a certain Road leading from a Dam across the Creek called Gunners Creek to the plantation lately in Possession of Joseph Lynn and Jeremiah Elfreth near the Mouth of Frankfort Creek and to lay out a Road there if we should See Occasion and to judge whether for Publick or Private use and to Examine thro' whose Improved Lands the same should pass and the Value of such Improved Lands as shall be taken up for the Use of such Road and to Certify all our Proceedings therein to this Court."[8]

AND we having pursuant to the said Order Carefully viewed the premises Do Report to this Court that We are of Opinion

---

de Télémaque, fils d'Ulysse (London, 1734 and other edits.); Andrew Michael Ramsay (Chevalier Ramsay), Les Voyages de Cyrus (Paris, 1727; London, 1730); Abel Boyer, The Royal Dictionary Abridged (6th edit., London, 1738); Theodor Arnold, Neues teutsch-englisches Worterbuch (Leipzig, 1739).

6. The Court of Quarter Sessions had approved the survey of a road from Philadelphia to the Northern Liberties that would take up land belonging to the Widow Ball. She appealed to the Supreme Court and won a reversal in April 1744. The Court, with the consent of the parties, appointed a board of six, "or any four of them," to view and, if they saw occasion, to lay out a road, and make return at the next term. In September the case was continued and the viewers were again ordered to report at the following term. MS Appearance Docket, 1740–1751, pp. 44, 52. In addition to Fox, the petitioners were Edward Warner, Michael Hillegas, Robert Hopkins, Edward Cathrall, Samuel Parr, White Massey, William Callender, Joseph Oldman, Hugh Roberts, and William Logan. The original report has not been located.

7. The April term of court opened April 10. Individual hearings are not dated in the Appearance Docket.

8. Not found.

there is Occasion for a publick Road between the places aforesaid Begining at the Dam abovementioned and extending thence on the Land late of William Ball deceased North East One hundred and ten Perches thence on the same Land North Sixty one Degrees East Three hundred and Seventy one perches, thence continuing the last mentioned Course on the unimproved Lands of divers Persons Six hundred and Eighty four Perches to a Line dividing the Land of William Logan and Samuel Parr at Forty Perches distance on the said Line from the River Delaware. And we have accordingly laid out a Publick Road as the same is above Described (a Draught whereof is hereunto annexed). But as the said Road as far as it passes over the Land late of William Ball (tho' hereafter it may be of great Advantage to that Land) will in the Present Circumstances of the Plantation and Possessors be a much greater Damage thereto than benefit to the publick; And as there is a private Road now Subsisting by Agreement thro' the said Plantation, which if Established a Private Road by this Court may Accommodate Sufficiently well all Persons concerned for the Present: We therefore think the publick Road abovementioned need not be opened thro' the same 'till the Youngest Children of the said William Ball become of Age; At which time also Judgment may be better made what Allowance should be given to that Estate for the Ground which such Road will take up.

The Private Road thro' the said Plantation begins at the Dam afd [aforesaid], thence South Seventy two Degrees and a half, East Forty Six perches towards the River Delaware Thence North fifty Six Degrees East Forty six perches to a Small Walnut Tree, Thence North Fifty nine Degrees East Eighty Eight Perches to a place a little beyond the Widow Balls House Thence North fifty nine Degrees and a half East Seventy perches to a place called the Red Gate, And thence North fifty four Degrees and three Quarters East Two hundred and Fifty five Perches to the above Described Publick Road at Edward Warners Corners: which private Road we are of Opinion should Subsist no longer than until the Publick Road through the said Plantation is opened as abovesaid, but be then given up and abolished in favour of that Estate. Read and Confirmed by the Court.

THOS. HOWARD   JOHN STAMPER
PHILIP SYNG   SAMLL. BURGE
JAMES MORRIS   B. FRANKLIN

Agreement about the Road DS: Historical Society of Pennsylvania

[April 1745]
Whereas we the Subscribers have by a Written Agreement dated the day of 17 made with the late William Ball deceased a Right to a certain private Road thro the said William Ball's plantation beginning at a Dam over Gunner's Run and extending to the Land belonging to Edward Warner. And whereas by an Order of the Supreme Court held at Philadelphia the 10 day of September last Benjamin Franklin James Morris Philip Syng Thomas Howard John Stamper and Samuel Burge or any four of them were Appointed to view and lay out a Road thro' the said Plantation if they Saw Occasion and they have accordingly laid out a publick Road thro' the same which is to be opened when the Children of the said Willm. Ball become of Age, provided the private Road now used to the said Edward Warner's Land be then given up. We therefore who have by the above mentioned agreement a Right to the use of the said private Road, do hereby Agree and promise for our Selves our Heirs Executors Administrators and Assigns, that if the said publick Road is Confirmed by the Court and laid open as aforesaid we will whenever the same shall be done, and we do hereby for our Selves our heirs Executors and Administrators relinquish and quit Claim from that time forever to the said private Road as far, as to the Land of the said Edward Warner. Wittness our Hands and Seals the day of April 1745.

WIGHT MASSEY [Seal]	WM CALLENDER [Seal]
MICHL HILLEGAS [Seal]	JOS FOX [Seal]
EDWD: WARNER [Seal]	JAMES PARROCH [Seal]
	JOHN TILL [Seal]
	JOHN COATS [Seal]

Signed sealed and delivered (the above Interlineation first made) by James Parroch, John Till, and John Coats, in the Presence of us. JAS: MORRIS
B FRANKLIN

Sealed and deliver'd by Wight Massey, Michael Hilligas, Joseph Fox, William Callender and Edward Warner, in the presence of us HUGH ROBERTS
JOS. OLDMAN

To John Franklin

MS not found; reprinted from extract in Sparks, *Works*, VII, 16–17.

Philadelphia, [May ?], 1745[9]

Our people are extremely impatient to hear of your success at Cape Breton.[1] My shop is filled with thirty inquiries at the coming in of every post. Some wonder the place is not yet taken. I tell them I shall be glad to hear that news three months hence. Fortified towns are hard nuts to crack; and your teeth have not been accustomed to it. Taking strong places is a particular trade, which you have taken up without serving an apprenticeship to it. Armies and veterans need skilful engineers to direct them in their attack. Have you any? But some seem to think forts are as easy taken as snuff. Father Moody's prayers look tolerably modest.[2] You have a fast and prayer day for that purpose; in which I compute five hundred thousand petitions were offered up to the same effect in New England, which added to the petitions of every family morning and evening, multiplied by the number of days since January 25th,[3] make forty-five millions of prayers; which, set against the prayers of a few priests in the garrison, to the Virgin Mary, give a vast balance in your favor.

9. Sparks printed this letter incomplete and dated it only "Philadelphia, 1745." Smyth (*Writings*, II, 283) assigned the date March 10 on the basis of his interpretation of BF's "ecclesiastical mathematics," but this is clearly too early. BF printed the first news of the expedition's departure from Boston, March 24, in the *Gazette*, April 12, and that of the arrival of most of the troops at Canso, the rendezvous, April 10, in the *Gazette*, May 2. Inquirers at BF's shop could hardly have begun to "wonder the place is not yet taken" much before the middle of May at the earliest. Actually Louisbourg's capitulation took place on June 17 and was announced to the Pennsylvania Council on July 11. *Pa. Col. Recs.*, IV, 764.

1. See above, p. 14.

2. Rev. Samuel Moody (1676–1747) of York, Maine, although "much impair'd by old Age," accompanied the expedition which his neighbor from Kittery Point, William Pepperrell (1696–1759), commanded. After the capitulation he preached the first Protestant sermon ever delivered at Louisbourg ("the citadel of Popish darkness"). *Sibley's Harvard Graduates*, IV, 356–65.

3. This was the date on which the Massachusetts General Court approved Shirley's proposal for the expedition. Charles H. Lincoln, ed., *Correspondence of William Shirley* (N. Y., 1912), I, 169–70.

If you do not succeed, I fear I shall have but an indifferent opinion of Presbyterian prayers in such cases, as long as I live. Indeed, in attacking strong towns I should have more dependence on *works,* than on *faith;*[4] for, like the kingdom of heaven, they are to be taken by force and violence; and in a French garrison I suppose there are devils of that kind, that they are not to be cast out by prayers and fasting, unless it be by their own fasting for want of provisions. I believe there is Scripture in what I have wrote, but I cannot adorn the margin with quotations, having a bad memory, and no Concordance at hand; besides no more time than to subscribe myself, &c. B. FRANKLIN

Old Mistresses Apologue[5]

AL: The Rosenbach Foundation; also copy and transcript: Library of Congress

In both manuscript and print, this composition has had an unusual history. Three versions of it were among the papers which William Temple Franklin inherited from his grandfather. One was entirely in Benjamin Franklin's autograph; this is the text reproduced here. The second was a contemporary copy, to which Benjamin Franklin himself made two additions. The third manuscript, made early in the nineteenth century, seems to have been intended for Temple Franklin's edition of his grandfather's writings. He decided, however, not to include it and the piece remained unknown to the public.

In 1850, nearly 30 years after Temple Franklin's death, what remained of the Franklin papers he had owned were purchased by the London bookseller Henry Stevens of Vermont. Stevens' catalogue offering the collection for sale in 1881 listed "Essays in form of Letters, on 'Perfumes' and 'Choice of a Mistress,' witty and explosive, but perhaps too Dean Swiftian for the press;" but Stevens did not enumerate the manuscript versions.[6] The United States Government purchased

4. Moody and Pepperrell were both enthusiastic supporters of the Great Awakening. George Whitefield preached at Portsmouth to the "Gentlemen bound on the Expedition" while it was being organized. *Pa. Gaz.,* April 12, 1745.

5. Known better as "Advice to a Young Man on the Choice of a Mistress," and sometimes as "A Letter on Marriage," the title here used is that which BF himself gave the copy in Lib. Cong. An undated French translation, in BF's hand, of the first two and a half sentences is in APS.

6. Henry Stevens, *Benjamin Franklin's Life and Writings: A Bibliographical Essay* (London, 1881), p. 18.

the collection in 1882. It contained, as the librarians of the Department of State were startled to discover, two copies of the Old Mistresses—the copy with Franklin's two additions, and the transcript that had been made for the printer.

Presumably Henry Stevens had withdrawn the Franklin autograph draft from the collection. In any event, it was subsequently acquired by the Chicago collector Charles Frederick Gunther, who later offered his library to the city of Chicago on condition that the city construct a fireproof building to house it. Mr. Gunther died in 1920 before any action had been taken on his offer; the collection became part of his estate; and his widow sold it—some 50,000 items—to the Chicago Historical Society.[7] The Society disposed of those items which did not fall within its fields of interest. Thus Franklin's autograph Old Mistresses' Apologue was discarded. The manuscript passed through the hands of Forrest G. Sweet into the collection of Dr. A. S. W. Rosenbach of Philadelphia in 1926.[8] Dr. Rosenbach prized it as "the most famous and the wittiest essay" Franklin ever wrote and gave it the place of honor in the exhibition of his Frankliniana at the Free Library of Philadelphia in 1938.[9]

Meanwhile the letter had been frequently, if furtively, printed. In the catalogue of his collection Stevens listed two copies (one "on the purest vellum") of "Dr. Franklin's Two New Bagatelles [on Perfumes, and on Marriage]," edited and printed in London in 1881 from the original manuscripts in his possession; but it seems that this never got past the stage of printer's proof.[1] Possibly from Stevens' unfinished printing, but more than likely from the two manuscript versions which gentlemen might see at the Department of State despite the special restrictions placed on them, other limited editions were privately issued. The first was made in 1885; Paul L. Ford did another in 1887, entitled "A Philosopher in Undress;" and two other printings were run off before 1889, one of them designed by form and type to be inserted between appropriate pages of Bigelow's edition of Franklin's writings.[2]

Ford has recounted the story of his printing. In the Department

7. *DAB.*

8. This sober recital is less colorful than the account Dr. Rosenbach liked to give of the manuscript's history. See his *A Book Hunter's Holiday* (Boston, 1936), p. 26.

9. *The All-Embracing Doctor Franklin . . . Illustrated by Books and Manuscripts from the Collection of Dr. A. S. W. Rosenbach* (Phila., 1938).

1. Stevens, *Benjamin Franklin's Life and Writings*, pp. 39, 40. No completed copy of this printing is known. A proof copy was found and presented to Lib. Cong. in 1935 by Henry Stevens, Son & Stiles, of London.

2. Ford, *Franklin Bibliography*, nos. 52–5.

of State, he explained to a friend, the Franklin letter "was kept very private, and when Bigelow wanted to add it to his edition, permission was refused by Bayard.[3] To a distinguished politician and intimate friend, however, he gave an MSS. copy, which was read aloud at a dinner party in New York (after the ladies had left, it is needless to remark). Several gentlemen at once requested copies, which were declined on account of the troubled [*sic*] to the dis. Pol. involved, so the suggestion was made that he should have it printed. Very well— find me a safe printer—this was a poser to all but himself. He was a friend of mine and knew that for many years I had owned a press and was in the habit of printing little tracts, varying in editions from 1 to 50 copies; and so he came to me and asked me to do it as a favor, as it could not be done by an ordinary printer. Agreed. I added a title page, in keeping, as I thought with the matter, and put it into type, receiving [?] two copies, and sundry shekels in return. One copy went into my Franklin collection, and one into my press file. . . . You are at liberty to use as much or as little of this story as you please, only kindly omit my name, as I do not care to harness it, even with that of B.F. to such a cart."[4]

By such means Franklin's essay acquired a clandestine fame. No nineteenth century editor or biographer, however, dared to print it. John Bach McMaster, who warmly praised The Speech of Polly Baker, thought the Old Mistresses' Apologue "unhappily too indecent to print."[5] Ford was certain it would "shock modern taste."[6] Without being specific, Smyth spoke of Franklin manuscripts "the printing of which would not be tolerated by the public sentiment of the present age."[7] Not even that cheerful iconoclast Sydney George Fisher would quote it without deep excisions.[8] Slowly, however, the national taste changed. In 1926 Phillips Russell printed the complete essay in his widely read biography of the man he called "the first civilized American."[9] Fifteen years later Franklin's little essay achieved acceptance, if not complete respectability: Simon and Schuster included it in their *Treasury of the World's Great Letters,* and that volume was delivered as a dividend to 225,000 members of the Book-of-the-Month Club.

3. Thomas F. Bayard, Secretary of State, 1885–89.
4. Goodspeed's Book Shop, Inc., *Catalogue* 268 (1936), item 74.
5. *Benjamin Franklin as a Man of Letters* (Boston, 1887), p. 266.
6. *The Many-Sided Franklin* (N.Y., 1899), p. 410.
7. *Writings,* I, 171.
8. *The True Benjamin Franklin* (Phila., 1899), pp. 126–8.
9. *Benjamin Franklin, The First Civilized American* (N. Y., 1926), pp.171–3.

My dear Friend,[1]   June 25. 1745

I know of no Medicine fit to diminish the violent natural Inclinations you mention; and if I did, I think I should not communicate it to you. Marriage is the proper Remedy. It is the most
natural State of Man, and therefore the State in which you are
most likely to find solid Happiness. Your Reasons against entring
into it at present, appear to me not well-founded. The circum-
stantial Advantages you have in View by postponing it, are not
only uncertain, but they are small in comparison with that of the
Thing itself, the being *married and settled*. It is the Man and Woman
united that make the compleat human Being. Separate, she wants
his Force of Body and Strength of Reason; he, her Softness, Sensi-
bility and acute Discernment. Together they are more likely to
succeed in the World. A single Man has not nearly the Value he
would have in that State of Union. He is an incomplete Animal.
He resembles the odd Half of a Pair of Scissars. If you get a prudent healthy Wife, your Industry in your Profession, with her
good Œconomy, will be a Fortune sufficient.

But if you will not take this Counsel, and persist in thinking
a Commerce with the Sex inevitable, then I repeat my former
Advice, that in all your Amours you should *prefer old Women to
young ones*. You call this a Paradox, and demand my Reasons.
They are these:

1. Because as they have more Knowledge of the World and
their Minds are better stor'd with Observations, their Conversation
is more improving and more lastingly agreable.

2. Because when Women cease to be handsome, they study to
be good. To maintain their Influence over Men, they supply the
Diminution of Beauty by an Augmentation of Utility. They learn
to do a 1000 Services small and great, and are the most tender

---

1. The addressee is unknown; and the letter may in fact be an essay in
the form of a letter. Paul L. Ford believed it was addressed to William Franklin; but William was only a lad of 14 or 15 in 1745. Smyth noted a tradition
in the Colden family that it was written to one of their young men, and Va.
Hist. Soc. owns a facsimile of a late 19th century transcript of the letter on
which the name of Cadwallader Colden has been inserted—as unlikely a
recipient as can be imagined. These statements of Ford and Smyth are made
in letters laid in a copy of Ford's *A Philosopher in Undress* (1887) that was
offered for sale in Goodspeed's *Catalogue* 268, item 74.

and useful of all Friends when you are sick. Thus they continue amiable. And hence there is hardly such a thing to be found as an old Woman who is not a good Woman.

3. Because there is no hazard of Children, which irregularly produc'd may be attended with much Inconvenience.

4. Because thro' more Experience, they are more prudent and discreet in conducting an Intrigue to prevent Suspicion. The Commerce with them is therefore safer with regard to your Reputation. And with regard to theirs, if the Affair should happen to be known, considerate People might be rather inclin'd to excuse an old Woman who would kindly take care of a young Man, form his Manners by her good Counsels, and prevent his ruining his Health and Fortune among mercenary Prostitutes.

5. Because in every Animal that walks upright, the Deficiency of the Fluids that fill the Muscles appears first in the highest Part: The Face first grows lank and wrinkled; then the Neck; then the Breast and Arms; the lower Parts continuing to the last as plump as ever: So that covering all above with a Basket, and regarding[2] only what is below the Girdle, it is impossible of two Women to know an old from a young one. And as in the dark all Cats are grey, the Pleasure of corporal Enjoyment with an old Woman is at least equal, and frequently superior, every Knack being by Practice capable of Improvement.

6. Because the Sin is less. The debauching a Virgin may be her Ruin, and make her for Life unhappy.

7. Because the Compunction is less. The having made a young Girl *miserable* may give you frequent bitter Reflections; none of which can attend the making an old Woman *happy*.

8[thly and Lastly][3] They are *so grateful!!*

Thus much for my Paradox. But still I advise you to marry directly; being sincerely Your affectionate Friend.

2. BF first wrote "viewing."

3. "thly and Lastly" is added from BF's own correction of the copy in Lib. Cong.

To James Alexander[4]

ALS: American Philosophical Society

Sir   Philada. Augt. 15. 1745

I return you herewith your Draughts,[5] with a Copy of one of them per Mr. Evans[6] and a few Lines relating to it from him. I wrote to Mr. Parker last Post that they might be got done in Boston by one Turner who is said to be a good Engraver.[7] Our only tolerable Engraver here will not undertake the Jobb.[8] And for my own Part I would rather chuse you should get them done there, or by Mr. Evans, than abide by the Proposal I made you: Tho' I will do them for you with what Dispatch I can, if you conclude on that Method.[9] I have mislaid yours of June 17. and forget what further Explanation you desir'd. I am, Sir, Your most humble Servant   B FRANKLIN

Addressed: To   James Alexander Esqr   at   Perth Amboy

4. James Alexander (1691–1756), lawyer, politician, and mathematician. Fleeing Scotland, where he had supported the Jacobite cause, he settled in America, 1715, living alternately in New Jersey and New York and holding office in both colonies, usually simultaneously. In 1718 he was appointed both recorder of Perth Amboy, N. J., and deputy secretary of New York. He served on the New York Council, 1721–32, and on the New Jersey Council, 1723–35; and later was again a member of both. He was attorney general of New Jersey, 1723–37, and appeared as counsel for John Peter Zenger until he was disqualified for contempt. He was one of the first members of APS. *DAB;* see above, II, 407.

5. The drafts were the maps of New Jersey which Alexander used as counsel for the East Jersey Proprietors in a land suit in chancery, 1745. They were engraved by James Turner in Boston, and are printed in *A Bill in the Chancery of New-Jersey, at the Suit of John Earl of Stair, and others, Proprietors of the Eastern-Division of New-Jersey* . . . printed for the subscribers by James Parker in New York, 1747 "and a few Copies are to be Sold by him, and Benjamin Franklin, in Philadelphia."

6. Lewis Evans.

7. For James Turner, silversmith and engraver of Boston, see below, p. 144 n.

8. Possibly Samuel Leach, who advertised as an engraver in 1741–42. David M. Stauffer, *American Engravers upon Copper and Steel* (N.Y., 1907), I, 158–9.

9. What this method was is not known.

To Cadwallader Colden ALS: New-York Historical Society

Sir   Philada. Augt. 15. 1745

I receiv'd your Favour of the 20th past, with your medical Piece enclos'd,[1] the Reading of which gave me a great deal of Pleasure. I show'd it to our Friend Mr. Bertram, who carried it home, and, as he since tells me, is taking a Copy of it; His Keeping of it for that End has prevented my Showing it to any other Gentlemen as you desired; and hitherto prevented my Writing to you upon it as I intended. But lest you should conclude me the very worst Correspondent in the World, I shall delay no longer giving you some Thoughts that occur'd to me in Reading of it; chusing rather to be blam'd for not writing to the Purpose, than for not Writing at all.

I am extreamly pleas'd with your Doctrine of the *absorbent Vessels* intermix'd with the perspiratory Ducts both on the external and internal Superficies of the Body. After I had read *Sanctorius,*[2] I imagin'd a constant Stream of the perspirable Matter issuing at *every* Pore in the Skin: But then I was puzzled to account for the Effects of mercurial Unctions, for the Strangury sometimes occasion'd by an outward Application of the Flies, and the like, since whatever Virtue or Quality might be in a Medicine laid upon the Skin, if it would enter the Body it must go against Wind and Tide, (as one may say). Dr. Hales help'd me a little, when he inform'd me, (in his Vegetable Statics)[3] that the Body is not always in a perspirable but sometimes in an *imbibing State,* as he expresses it; and will at Times actually grow heavier by being expos'd to a moist Air. But this did not quite remove my Difficulty, since, as these Fits of Imbibing did not appear to be regular or frequent, a Blistering Plaister might lie on the Skin a Week, or a mercurial

1. Probably a version or abstract of a part of Colden's treatise on "The Animal Œconomy," composed in 1733 or 1734. The MS is in the Colden Papers in N.-Y. Hist. Soc.

2. Santorio Santorio (1561–1636), called Sanctorius, professor of medicine at Padua; founder of the physiology of metabolism by his discovery that the loss by "insensible perspiration" exceeds that by all other bodily excretions together. His best known work was translated and edited by John Quincy in London, 1712, as *De Medicina Statica: being Aphorisms of Sanctorius.*

3. Rev. Stephen Hales, *Vegetable Staticks: Or, An Account of some Statical Experiments on the Sap in Vegetables* (London, 1727).

Unguent be us'd a Month, to no purpose, if the Body should so long continue in a perspirable State. Your Doctrine, which was quite new to me, makes all easy, since the Body may perspire and absorb at the same Time, thro' the different Ducts destin'd to those different Ends.

I must own, however, that I have one Objection to the Explanation you give of the Operation of these Absorbents. That *They* should communicate with the Veins, and the Perspirants with the Arteries only, seems natural enough; but as all Fluids by the hydrostatical Law press equally in all Directions, I question whether the *mere Direction* of one of those minute Vessels (where it joins with a Vein or Artery) *with* or *against* the Stream of Blood in the larger Vessel, would be sufficient to produce such contrary Effects as *perspiring* and *absorbing*. If it would, both Perspirants and Absorbents might proceed from the Arteries only, or from the Veins only, or from both indifferently; as by the Figure in the Margin, whether the Vessel *a b* is a Vein or an

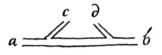

Artery, if the Stream moves from *a* to *b,* the minute communicating Vessel *c* shall be a Perspirant, and *d* an Absorbent, and contrary if it moves from *b* to *a.* Yet I cannot say, I am certain the mere Direction of the Vessels will have no Effect; I only suspect it, and am making a little Machine to try an Experiment with for Satisfaction. 'Tis a Syphon made of two large Joints of Carolina Cane united at *e,* into which two small glass Tubes *f* and *g* are to be inserted one on the descending and the other on the ascending Side. I propose to fill the Syphon and the two glass Tubes with Water, and, when 'tis playing, unstop at the same Instant the Tops of both glass

Tubes, observing in which the Water sinks fastest. You shall know the Success. I conceive the Pressure of the Atmosphere on the Apertures of the two glass Tubes to be no way different from the Pressure of the same on the Mouths of the Perspirants and Absorbents; and if the Water sinks equally in the two Tubes, notwithstanding the Direction of one *against* and the other with the Stream, I shall be ready to think we must look out for another

Solution. You will say, perhaps, that 'twill then be time enough, when the Experiment is try'd and succeeds as I suspect; yet I cannot forbear attempting at one beforehand, while some Thoughts are present in my Mind. If a new Solution should be found necessary, this may be ready for Consideration.

I do not remember that any Anatomist that has fallen in my Way, has assign'd any other Cause of the Motion of the Blood, thro' its whole Circle, than the contractile Force of the Heart, by which that Fluid is driven with Violence into the Arteries, and so continually propell'd by Repetitions of the same Force, till it arrives at the Heart again. May we, for our present Purpose, suppose another Cause, producing half the Effect; and say, that the Ventricles of the Heart, like Syringes, *draw* when they dilate, as well as *force* when they contract? That this is not unlikely, may be judg'd from the Valves Nature has plac'd in the Arteries to prevent the Drawing back of the Blood in those Vessels when the Heart dilates, while no such Obstacles prevent its Sucking (to use the vulgar Expression) from the Veins. If this be allow'd, and the Insertion of the Absorbents into the Veins, and of the Perspirants into the Arteries, be agreed to, it will be of no Importance in what Direction they are inserted: For, as the Branches of the Arteries are continually lessening in their Diameters, and the Motion of the Blood decreasing, by means of the encreas'd Resistance, there must, as more is continually press'd on behind, arise a kind of *Crouding* in the Extremities of those Vessels, which will naturally *force out* what is contain'd in the Perspirants that communicate with them. This lessens the Quantity of Blood, so that the Heart cannot receive again by the Veins all it had discharg'd into the Arteries, which occasions it to draw strongly upon the Absorbents that communicate with them. And thus the Body is continually perspiring and imbibing. Hence, after long Fasting, the Body is more liable to receive Infection from bad Air; and Food, before 'tis sufficiently chylified, is drawn crude into the Blood, by the Absorbents that open into the Bowels. To confirm this Position, that the Heart *draws* as well as *drives* the Blood, let me add this Particular. If you sit or lean long in such a Manner as to compress the principal Artery that supplys a Limb with Blood, so that it does not furnish a due Quantity, you will be sensible of a pricking Pain in the Extremities like that of a thousand Needles; and the Veins, that us'd to raise your Skin in Ridges, will be (with the Skin) sunk into Channels; the Blood being drawn out of them, and their Sides press'd so closely together, that 'tis with Difficulty and slowly that the Blood afterwards enters them when the compress'd Artery is reliev'd. If the Blood was not drawn by the Heart, the Compression of an Artery could not empty a Vein; and I conjecture that the pricking Pain is occasion'd by the Sides of the small Vessels being press'd together.

I am not without Apprehensions, that this Hypothesis is either not new, or, if it is new, not good for any Thing. It may however, in this Letter, (with the enclos'd Paper on a kindred Subject)[4] serve to show the great Confidence I place in your Candour, since to you I so freely hazard myself (*ultra crepidam*) in Medling with Matters directly pertaining to your Profession, and entirely out of the way of my own. If you give yourself the Trouble of Reading them, 'tis all I can modestly expect. Your Silence about them afterwards will be sufficient to convince me, that I am in the wrong; and that I ought to study the Sciences I dabble in, before I presume to set Pen to Paper. I will endeavour however to make you some Amends, by procuring you from better Judges some better Remarks on the Rest of your Piece; and shall observe your Caution not to let them know from whom I had it.

The Piece on Fluxions I purpose shortly to read again, and that on the several Species of Matter, when you shall have what little I shall be able to say about them.

The Members of our Society here are very idle Gentlemen; they will take no Pains. I must, I believe, alter the Scheme, and proceed with the Papers I have and may receive, in the Manner you advise in one of your former Letters. The mention of your former Letters puts me in mind how much I am in Arrear with you: Like some honest insolvent Debtors, I must resolve to pay ready Money for what I have hereafter, and discharge the old Debt by little and little as I am able.

The Impertinence of these Moskito's to me, (now I am in the Humour of Writing) prevents a great deal of mine to you, so that for once they are of some Use in the World. I am Sir Your most humble Servant   B FRANKLIN

Endorsed: Benj Franklin

4. Printed immediately following.

[Enclosure]

A GUESS at the Cause of the Heat of the Blood in Health and of the hot and cold[5] Fits of some Fevers.

The Parts of Fluids are so smooth, and roll among one another with so little Friction, that they will not by any (mechanical) Agitation grow warmer. A Phial half full of Water shook with Violence and long continued, the Water neither heats itself nor warms the Phial. Therefore the Blood does not acquire its Heat either from the Motion and Friction of its own Parts, or its Friction against the Sides of its Vessels.

But the Parts of Solids, by Reason of their closer Adhesion, cannot move among themselves without Friction, and that produces Heat. Thus, bend a Plumbet to and fro, and in the Place of Bending it shall soon grow hot. Friction on any Part of our Flesh heats it. Clapping of the Hands warms them. Exercise warms the whole Body.

The Heart is a thick Muscle, continually contracting and dilating near 80 Times in a Minute; By this Motion there must be a constant Interfrication of its constituent solid Parts; That Friction must produce a Heat, and that Heat must consequently be continually communicated to the perfluent Blood.

To this may be added, That every Propulsion of the Blood by the Contraction of the Heart, distends the Arteries, which contract again in the Intermission; and this Distention and Contraction of the Arteries may occasion Heat in them, which they must likewise communicate to the Blood that flows thro' them.

That these Causes of the Heat of the Blood are sufficient to produce the Effect, may appear probable, if we consider that a Fluid once warm requires no more Heat to be apply'd to it in any Part of Time to keep it warm, than what it shall lose in an equal Part of Time. A smaller Force will keep a Pendulum going than what first set it in Motion.

The Blood thus warm'd in the Heart, carries Warmth with it to the very Extremities of the Body, and communicates it to them; but as by this Means its Heat is gradually diminished, it is return'd again to the Heart by the Veins for a fresh Calefaction.

5. In the MS an arabic 2 has been placed under "hot" and an arabic 1 under "cold," as if the author intended the words should be reversed.

The Blood communicates its Heat not only to the Solids of our Body, but to our Clothes, and to a Portion of the circumambient Air. Every Breath, tho' drawn in Cold, is expir'd Warm; and every Particle of the *Materia Perspirabilis* carries off with it a Portion of Heat.

While the Blood retains a due Fluidity, it passes freely thro' the minutest Vessels, and communicates a proper Warmth to the Extremities of the Body. But when by any Means it becomes so viscid as not to be capable of passing those minute Vessels, the Extremities, as the Blood can bring no more Heat to them, must grow Cold.

The same Viscidity in the Blood and Juices checks or stops the Perspiration, by clogging the perspiratory Ducts; or, perhaps, by not admitting the perspirable Parts to separate. Paper wet with Size and Water will not dry so soon as if wet with Water only.

A Vessel of hot Water, if the Vapour can freely pass from it, soon cools. If there be just Fire enough under it to add continually the Heat it loses, it retains the same Degree. If the Vessel be clos'd so that the Vapour may be retain'd, there will from the same Fire be a continual Accession of Heat in the Water, till it rises to a great Degree: Or, if no Fire be under it, it will retain the Heat it first had for a long time. I have experienc'd that a Bottle of hot Water stopp'd, and put in my Bed at Night, has retain'd so much Heat 7 or 8 Hours, that I could not in the Morning bear my Foot against it, without some of the Bedclothes intervening.

During the cold Fit then, Perspiration being stop'd, great Part of the Heat of the Blood that us'd to be dissipated, is confin'd and retain'd in the Body; The Heart continues its Motion, and creates a constant Accession to that Heat, the Inward Parts grow very hot, and, by Contact with the Extremities, communicate that Heat to them: The Glue of the Blood is by this Heat dissolved, and the Blood afterwards flows freely as before the Disorder.

To James Read[6]

MS not found; reprinted from *The Port Folio*, I (1801), 165–6.[7]

Dear J[emmy],   Saturday morning, Aug. 17, '45

I have been reading your letter over again, and since you desire an answer, I sit me down to write you one; yet, as I write in the market, [it] will, I believe, be but a short one, tho' I may be long about it. I approve of your method of writing one's mind, when one is too warm to speak it with temper: but being myself quite cool in this affair, I might as well speak as write, if I had an opportunity. Your copy of Kempis, must be a corrupt one, if it has that passage as you quote it, *in omnibus requiem quaesivi, sed non inveni, nisi in angulo cum libello.*[8] The good father understood

6. James Read (1718–1793), son of Charles Read who was a cousin of Deborah Read Franklin; went into business with his widowed mother Sarah Harwood Read, 1737, in a shop next to BF's. He visited London, 1739–40, meeting Peter Collinson, Charles Wesley, and William Strahan. Admitted to the bar, 1742, he was clerk of the Crown and prothonotary of the Supreme Court of Pennsylvania, 1746, and tried unsuccessfully to replace BF as clerk of the Assembly, 1747; removed to Reading, Pa., where he was appointed prothonotary, 1752, and subsequently and simultaneously held the offices of register of wills, clerk of Quarter Sessions, and justice of the peace; held minor appointments from the Board of War and Supreme Executive Council, 1776–77; elected to the Assembly, 1777, to the Supreme Executive Council, 1778–81, 1787–90, and to the Council of Censors, 1783; appointed register of the Court of Admiralty, 1781. His career, related in terms of a long-standing and unpaid debt to Strahan, is recounted at length in J. Bennett Nolan, *Printer Strahan's Book Account: A Colonial Controversy* (Reading, Pa., 1939).

7. This letter has been reprinted at least seven times since 1801, and there is an 1859 transcript of an earlier transcript in APS. These versions vary significantly. Sparks (*Works*, VII, 17–18) was the first to indicate that the addressee was James Read and to print out "Jemmy" in the salutation and the final paragraph, where previous editors had given only "J———." But Sparks (and Bigelow and Smyth, apparently copying from him) silently omitted all that part of the first paragraph that follows the word "opportunity." Two versions incorrectly dated the letter August 27. The ALS was listed in Parke-Bernet Galleries Sale No. 79 (Jan. 11–12, 1939), but has not been found.

8. These words are inscribed on a picture of Thomas à Kempis at Zwolle, Holland. According to Heribert Rosweyde (preface to *Imitatio Christi*, 1617), the author wrote them in a copy of the *Imitatio*. Burton Stevenson, *The Home Book of Quotations* (8th edit., N.Y., 1956), p. 189.

pleasure (requiem) better, and wrote, *in angulo cum puella.* Correct it thus, without hesitation. I know there is another reading, *in angulo puellae;* but this reject, tho' more *to the point,* as an expression too indelicate.

Are you an attorney by profession, and do you know no better, how to chuse a proper court in which to bring your action? Would you submit to the decision of a husband, a cause between you and his wife?[9] Don't you know, that all wives are in the right? It may be you don't, for you are yet but a young husband. But see, on this head, the learned Coke, that oracle of the law, in his chapter *De Jus Marit.Angl.*[1] I advise you not to bring it to trial; for if you do, you'll certainly be cast.

Frequent interruptions make it impossible for me to go thro' all your letter. I have only time to remind you of the saying of that excellent old philosopher, Socrates, *that in differences among friends, they that make the first concessions are the* WISEST; and to hint to you, that you are in danger of losing that honour in the present case, if you are not very speedy in your acknowledgments; which I persuade myself you will be, when you consider the sex of your adversary.

Your visits never had but one thing disagreeable in them, that is, they were always too short. I shall exceedingly regret the loss of them, unless you continue, as you have begun, to make it up to me by long letters. I am dear J[emmy], with sincerest love to our dearest Suky, Your very affectionate friend and cousin,

B. FRANKLIN

9. Nolan surmises that the misunderstanding or quarrel was between Read and Deborah Franklin, and that it may have arisen from there being too many women in the house in Market Street. Read had married, April 20, 1745, Susanna (the "Suky" of BF's letter) Leacock, and brought her to live at his mother's house next door to the Franklins on Market Street. *Printer Strahan's Book Account*, p. 27.

1. Neither Coke *On Littleton* nor the *Institutes* employed such chapter-headings; and this may very well be one of BF's small jokes, and (a parody of pomposity) *de Jus Marit. Angl.* his translation of *The Lady's Law: or, a Treatise of Feme Coverts, containing all the Laws and Statutes relating to Women* . . . (London, 1727), largely drawn from Coke, of which a copy of 2d edit., 1732, is in Lib. Co. Phila.

From John Mitchell

ALS: New-York Historical Society

Sir   Urbanna, Septr. 12th. 1745

I was surprised to see yours of Jun. 15th.[2] come to my hands only by last Post. What I then received by it from Dr. Colden,[3] I suppose I owe to you; for which I am sorry I can make no other acknowledgement but thanks. I perceive likewise, that you are desirous (if I am not mistaken), that the small Paper I left with you on the yellow fever should come forth.[4] I was highly delighted to see so good an opportunity any one might

2. Not found.

3. Colden's letter to Mitchell, June 8, 1745, *Amer. Med. and Philos. Reg.*, IV (1814), 378–83. This was Colden's first direct communication with Mitchell, although in the autumn of 1744 he had sent to BF for Mitchell some "remarks" he had written out after "cursorily" reading the copy of Mitchell's essay on yellow fever which BF had sent him. To these "remarks" Mitchell had replied via BF some months later (see above, p. 17 and note). On Sept. 10, 1745, two days before writing the present letter to BF, Mitchell addressed a long communication to Colden in answer to Colden's of June 8 and, as the last sentence and the postscript of this letter to BF show, enclosed it to BF for the latter to read and forward to Colden. It is printed in *Colden Paps.*, VIII, 314–28. The correspondence between the New Yorker and the Virginian continued thereafter without an intermediary.

4. Mitchell's essay had an unusual history and an important influence, although it was not printed until after both its author and BF had died. In November 1745 BF promised to have Lewis Evans make a copy for Colden (see below, p. 48) and shortly before his death he gave his own copy (or still another made from it) to Benjamin Rush, who read it "with pleasure" and secured permission to make extracts to be read before the College of Physicians. Rush to Samuel P. Griffitts, March 24, 1790, College of Physicians of Phila. In his *Account of the Bilious remitting Yellow Fever . . . in the Year 1793* (2d edit., Phila., 1794), pp. 196–9, Rush told how, "baffled" by the epidemic then raging in Philadelphia, he "ransacked" his library for anything that might tell him how to treat it and found "among some old papers" this MS account of the fever in Virginia in 1741. He was "much struck" by Mitchell's recommendation of strong purges and his warning against "an ill-timed scrupulousness about the weakness of the body." At this "a new train of ideas suddenly broke in upon my mind," Rush wrote. "Dr. Mitchell in a moment dissipated my ignorance and fears" on the subject of purges. The result was Rush's controversial heroic treatment by bleeding and purging. Nathan G. Goodman, *Benjamin Rush, Physician and Citizen* (Phila., 1934), p. 176; John H. Powell, *Bring out Your Dead* (Phila., 1949), pp. 76–8.

Rush sent extracts of Mitchell's essay to be printed in the *Philadelphia Medical Museum*, I (1805), 1–20, but the MS copy "perished in the printing

have to oblige the publick, and promote the arts and Sciences, as your Press affords; better than I expected to have found in our new world. I look upon myself obliged, thro' gratitude to you, as well as the justice due to your laudable industry and improvements in that way, to encourage your press as much as I can. The Debt likewise which we all owe to the publick, would make me do what I could to discharge it. But for many very good reasons, I can do neither at present. My health is so impaired by this summer and fall, that I am not able to follow my own necessary calling. Since the last of June I have been afflicted with a Diarrhoea several times, a slow hectic, with spitting of Blood, and troublesome Piles: I had no sooner got over these, (when our weather began to break in the fall, with Rains and Easterly winds) than I was seized with an Intermittent fever, the origin and source of all my disorders. With this I was afflicted, when I received yours, and as I kept the house, I have been more prolix in what I have wrote, having nothing else to amuse me; which is the reason, why I have said so little in so many words; which I hope Dr. Colden and you will excuse. I am so farr from being able to come to Philadelphia this fall again, as you kindly invite me, that I was not able to go to the upper parts of our own Countrey, as I had appointed and firmly resolved, to avoid what I expected in the fall, and have accordingly met with. But my bad state of health puts me under a necessity of going to England very soon, or of loosing my life. I shall let you hear from me before I go; which I am afraid will not be before next Spring, but it must be before Summer, or never. What I shall do there or afterwards, I am not determined, nor can I be, 'till I see what my bad State of health is likely to come to.

As for the small piece on the yellow fever in your hands, you know I left it to be transmitted to Dr. Colden, since we were disappointed of seeing him. But lest I might seem to refuse others

office." After the death of Dr. John Redman, Rush's "old master," in 1808, his daughter found among his papers a copy of the Mitchell essay, together with two of the communications Mitchell and Colden had exchanged on the subject, and gave them to Rush. He in turn sent them to Dr. David Hosack of New York, who published them in his journal, *The American Medical and Philosophical Register*, IV (1814), 181–215, 378–87. Lyman H. Butterfield, ed., *Letters of Benjamin Rush* (Princeton, 1951), II, 1057–8. See also Saul Jarcho, "John Mitchell, Benjamin Rush, and Yellow Fever," *Bull. Hist. Med.*, XXXI (1957), 132–6.

any benefit that might be reaped from it (if there is any) I consented, that your Physicians might see it. But it is by no means
fit to be printed by itself, nor never was intended to be. It contains only a brief account of some things that I thought might be
improvements on this Disease, or at least more clearly shown
than is common to be met with, Especially the Dissection of the
bodies that dyed of it, for which alone it was wrote, as that is not
any where to be met with, as far as I know. It was wrote to a
Master of the Art (like compendious Institutes, extracted from a
much longer account) to whom I thought Explications might be
as impertinent, as they are necessary for others, Especially among
us. Had I wrote it for (the generality at least of) your Readers,
what I have herein left out, would be most necessary to have insisted upon, and what is herein contained ought to be more fully
explained. You know very well, this would be necessary all over
America, as far as I can perceive at least. My friends in Scotland
(to whom I first sent it) desired me to let them print it by itself;
but Mr. Monro[5] and Dr. Clarke[6] at Edinburgh were of Opinion,
that in that manner it could not miss to perish (which they were
pleased to say it was a pity it should) among the many other
little pieces of that sort, which daily come out. They desired me
to preserve it by a fuller Account of the other things relating to the
Disease. But I laid down all thoughts of that, when I first extracted these observations from the others I had made, not out
of any discommendable design I hope. My views then were to
inform myself, as well as to qualify myself to inform others (if any
desired such information, which very few, too few among us,
so much as do) of the nature and Cure of our other popular
Maladies, as well as this; as well as of the nature and effects
of our Climate, minerals, vegetables and animals, &c. With these
pursuits I was busied at some times, when this yellow fever came
in my way; and I thought it much better to go on with them, than
suffer myself to be interrupted with this: hoping I might preserve
my account of it in a Natural and Medical History of my Countrey;
for which I have kept Journals of Observations for many years,

5. John Monro (1670–1740), surgeon-apothecary in Edinburgh. He had
studied medicine at Leyden and been an army surgeon. The idea of establishing the medical school and hospital in Edinburgh was his.
6. Dr. John Clark, a graduate of St. Andrews, Fellow of the Royal College
of Physicians of Edinburgh, 1714.

but left them all off, the beginning of this Monthe, and when, or if ever, I shall be able to begin them again, He only knows who disposes of all things. But still I should be glad of your information about any of these things, for which reason I mention them to you and Dr. Colden; and in return you may command any thing from me, hoping you will use it as a friend, as you see I take you to be, by being so very plain with you. I am fond and ambitious of corresponding with all candid and ingenious Persons about these things I here mention, as I find their Information to be necessary, and am as willing and ready to give them the best accounts of things I can, in return. But you must excuse my not publishing any thing yet a while. I think the world is pestered with this Itch of many to appear in print, which makes many so little regarded that do. Authors ought to be Masters not only of the particular subject, but of the whole art, they undertake to instruct the world in; and when they are—*Nonum prematur in annum*, saies Horace.[7]

What is enclosed suppose wrote equally to yourself as to Dr. Colden, for whom it is directed, and persist to oblige Sir Your very humble Servant   JOHN MITCHELL

P.S. I wrote for my baggs by Mr. Miron,[8] the first opportunity I had to send for them. If you have any pray send them. They are not of great value. I enclosed one to Mr. Bartram.

The enclosed &c. are only for your perusal and Dr. Colden's, as well as any thing else I write to you   J:M:

Addressed: For Mr. B. Franklin

From John and Elizabeth Croker:[9] Deed

Copy: Department of Records, Recorder of Deeds, City of Philadelphia

October 12, 1745

ABSTRACT: John Croker of Staten Island, N.Y., yeoman, and Elizabeth his wife grant to Benjamin Franklin forever, for £60 proclamation

7. Horace, *Ars Poetica*, 388.
8. Not identified.
9. Deborah Franklin's sister Frances Read had married John Croker, who described himself in 1734 as a tailor of Philadelphia. Following her death in 1740 he had apparently married again and was now farming on Staten Island.

money, their undivided half of a messuage and lot on the south side of High Street, Philadelphia, 16½ ft. in breadth and 306 ft. in length, bounded north by High Street, east by a lot late of William Boulding deceased, south by the ends of Chestnut Street lots, and west by a messuage and lot now or late of John Read,[1] together with all buildings, outhouses, improvements, and appurtenances thereto belonging, and all estate, title, interest, and possession therein claimed by the Crokers. They covenant their right to make this conveyance and he warrants a clear title. Signed by John Croker and Elizabeth Croker; witnessed by George Spencer and Lanc[aste]r Green, who appeared November 12, 1745, before Samuel Hasell, justice of the peace, and swore to having seen the grantors sign, seal, and deliver the indenture and to having subscribed as witnesses. Recorded, February 21, 1757.

To William Strahan   ALS: New York Public Library (Berg)

Sir   New York, Nov. 7. 1745
   Finding a Vessel here about to sail to London, I take the Opportunity to enclose you a second Bill, the first of which I sent via Maryland. I left Mr. Hall and all Friends well at Philada last Week, and hope to see them again in a few Days. I have not Time to add but that I am Sir Your very humble Servant
                                                          B FRANKLIN
The English and Books are safe arriv'd.

Addressed: To   Mr Wm Strahan   Printer in   Wine Office Court Fleetstreet   London   Per Capt Bryant

To William Strahan   ALS: University of Pennsylvania Library

Sir   Philada. Nov. 16. 1745
   I wrote a Line to you via Maryland, and another via New York, lately, enclosing with each a Bill for £15 Sterl. The Third I now

1. The property here transferred was the eastern half of the Read lot on High (Market) St. with the dwelling house that stood on it. Mrs. Sarah Read deeded this portion in undivided half-interest to her two daughters and their husbands April 9 and 10, 1734, and they had leased it back to her for life April 11. At the same time she deeded the western half of the lot with its dwelling house to her son John. See above, 1, 362–70.

send you. I receiv'd the Books and Letter you sent in good Order, and purpose to write for another Parcel of Books by Mesnard who is to sail in 2 or 3 Weeks. I have now every Thing ready for Mr. Hall to go to the W. Indies, but feel some Reluctance to part with him these hazardous Times. He continues to enjoy his Health, as I hope you and yours do, being, Sir with sincere Respect, Your obliged humble Servant   B FRANKLIN

To Cadwallader Colden   ALS: New-York Historical Society

Sir   Philada. Nov. 28. 1745
I shall be very willing and ready, when you think proper to publish your Piece on Gravitation, &c., to print it at my own Expence and Risque.[2] If I can be a Means of Communicating anything valuable to the World, I do not always think of Gaining, nor even of Saving by my Business; But a Piece of that kind, as it must excite the Curiosity of all the Learned, can hardly fail of bearing its own Expence.

I must not pretend to dispute with you on any Part of the animal Œconomy:[3] You are quite too strong for me. I shall just mention two or three little Things that I am not quite clear in. If there is no Contrivance in the Frame of the Auricles or Ventricles of the Heart, by which they dilate themselves, I cannot conceive how they are dilated. It is said; By the Force of the Venal Blood rushing into them. But if that Blood has no Force which was not first given it by the Contraction of the Heart, how can it (diminish'd as it must be by the Resisting Friction of the Vessels it has pass'd thro') be strong enough to overcome that Contraction? Your Doctrine of Fermentation in the Capillaries helps me a little; for if the returning Blood be rarified by the Fermentation, its Motion must be encreas'd: but as it seems to me, that it must by

2. Colden did not accept BF's offer. The essay was printed the next year (though dated 1745 on the title page) by James Parker in New York, under the title *An Explication of the First Causes of Action in Matter, and, of the Cause of Gravitation*.

3. The ideas to which BF responds here are expressed in Colden's "Inquiry into the Principles of Vital Motion," especially secs. 15–18, and his treatise on "The Animal Oeconomy," surviving in several MS versions in N.-Y. Hist. Soc. Colden may have sent BF a revised or abridged version of either of these.

46

its Expansion resist the Arterial Blood behind it, as much as it accelerates the Venal Blood before it, I am still somewhat unsatisfied. I have heard or read somewhere too, that the Hearts of some Animals continue to contract and dilate, or to beat, as 'tis commonly express'd, after they are separated from the other Vessels and taken out of the Body. If this be true, their Dilatation is not caus'd by the Force of the returning Blood.

I should be glad to satisfy myself too, whether the Blood is always quicker in Motion when the Pulse beats quicker. Perhaps more Blood is driven forward by one strong deep Stroke, than by two that are weak and light: As a Man may breathe more Air by one long common Respiration when in Health, than by two quick short ones in a Fever.

I apply'd the Syphon I mention'd to you in a former Letter, to the Pipe of a Water Engine. E is the Engine; a its Pipe bbb the Sy-

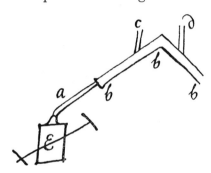

phon; c and d the two glass Pipes communicating with the Syphon. Upon working the Engine, the Water flow'd thro' the Syphon, and the Glass Tube c; but none was discharg'd thro' d. When I stop'd with my Finger the End of the Syphon, the Water issu'd at both Glass Tubes with equal Force; and on only half Stopping the End of the Syphon it did the same. I imagine the sudden Bending of the Syphon gives such a Resistance to the Stream, as to occasion its Issuing out of the Glass Tube c: But I intend to try a farther Experiment, of which I shall give you an Account.

I am now determin'd to publish an American Philosophical Miscellany, Monthly or Quarterly. I shall begin with next January, and proceed as I find Encouragement and Assistance. As I purpose to take the Compiling wholly upon my self, the Reputation of no Gentleman or Society will be affected by what I insert of anothers; and that perhaps will make them more free to communicate. Their Names shall be publish'd or conceal'd as they think proper; and Care taken to do exact Justice in Matters

47

of Invention, &c. I shall be glad of your Advice in any Particulars that occur'd to you in Thinking of this Scheme; for as you first propos'd it to me, I doubt not but you have well consider'd it.

I have not the Original of Dr. Mitchel's Tract on the Yellow Fever. Mine is a Copy I had taken with his Leave when here. Mr. Evans[4] will make a Copy of it for you.

I hope it will be confirmed by future Experiments that the Yaws are to be cured by Tar Water. The Case you relate to Dr. Mitchel gives great Hopes of it, and should be publish'd to induce People to make Trials: for tho' it should not always succeed, I suppose there is no Danger of its doing any Harm.[5]

As to your Pieces on Fluxions and the different Species of Matter, it is not owing to Reservedness that I have not yet sent you my Thoughts; but because I cannot please my self with them, having had no Leisure yet to digest them. If I was clear that you are anywhere mistaken, I would tell you so, and give my Reasons, with all Freedom, as believing nothing I could do would be more obliging to you. I am persuaded you think as I do, that he who removes a Prejudice or an Error from our Minds, contributes to their Beauty; as he would do to that of our Faces, who should clear them of a Wart or a Wen.

I have a Friend gone to New York with a View of Settling there if he can meet with Encouragement. It is Dr. Jno. Bard,

4. Lewis Evans (c.1700–1756), surveyor, draftsman, geographer; born in Wales, he was settled in Pennsylvania before 1736, and seems to have been employed by BF as a clerk. He accompanied John Bartram and Conrad Weiser to Onondaga, 1743; lectured on natural philosophy in Newark, N. J., New York (at the house of Rev. Ebenezer Pemberton), and Philadelphia, 1751. As a draftsman he prepared the diagrams for BF's *Account of the New Invented Pennsylvanian Fireplaces*, 1744 (see above, II, 432, 445), and compiled *A General Map of the Middle British Colonies in America*, 1755. Deborah Franklin was godmother of his daughter Amelia. *DAB;* Lawrence H. Gipson, *Lewis Evans* (Phila., 1939), pp. 1–14.

5. Mitchell had asked Colden on Sept. 10, 1745, what he knew about yaws; Colden, replying on Nov. 7, enclosed an account of a cure by tar water, which he had received from Rev. Samuel Johnson of Stratford, Conn. *Colden Paps.*, VIII, 322, 334–5. Bishop George Berkeley's *Siris: A Chain of Philosophical Reflexions and Inquiries Concerning the Virtue of Tar water* (Dublin and London, 1744) was then making a great impression. Johnson borrowed BF's copy and Colden published an abstract with his own "reflexions" on the value of tar water in the treatment of diseases frequent in America. *Colden Paps.*, III, 98, 102, 108, 121, 149, 206.

whom I esteem an ingenious Physician and Surgeon, and a discreet, worthy and honest Man.[6] If upon Conversation with him, you find this Character just, I doubt not but you will afford him your Advice and Countenance, which will be of great Service to him in a Place where he is entirely a Stranger, and very much oblige, Sir Your most humble Servant   B FRANKLIN

I shall forward your Letter to Dr. Mitchel.[7] Thank you for Leaving it open for my Perusal.

To William Strahan

ALS: Pennsylvania Hospital; also duplicate: New York Public Library (Berg)

[Sir]   Philada. Dec. 11. 1745
    While the War continues I find it will not answer to send for any considerable Quantities of Books; for that Business, as well as others grows duller daily, and People are unwilling to give the advanc'd Prices we are now obliged to put on Books, by the excessive Charges of Insurance &c. So at present I only send for a few School Books and Books of Navigation which they cannot do without.
    I sent you sometime since a Bill for £15 Sterl. and part of Mr. Hall's Bill £10 which I hope will come to hand and be readily paid. I purpose to send you another soon, and am Sir with much Repect Your very humble Servant   B FRANKLIN

P.S. Our Library Company send yearly for about £20 worth of Books. Mr. P. Collinson does us the Favour to buy them for us.[8] Perhaps on your speaking to that Gentleman he would take them of you.

6. John Bard (1716–1799), physician; educated under Alexander Annand in Philadelphia; apprenticed to Dr. John Kearsley; practiced in Philadelphia. BF encouraged him to move to New York, as to a place of greater opportunity, two physicians having recently died there. He became health officer of New York, wrote several scientific papers, and was first president of the Medical Society of the State of New York, 1788. *DAB*. BF's Ledger D, p. 5, contains an account with Bard, 1739–45, for advertisements, paper, and books.
    7. Probably Colden's letter of Nov. 7, cited in note 5 above.
    8. Peter Collinson, London Quaker mercer and merchant, was the Library Company's agent and benefactor. See above, I, 248, and below, p. 115 n.

To William Strahan ALS: New York Public Library (Berg)

Sir   Dec. 22. 1745
The above is a Copy of what I wrote you per Mesnard[9] who
sailed about 10 Days ago from this Port. This goes per Capt.
Hargrave, who is soon to sail from Maryland. Enclos'd I send
you a Bill for £15.7.1, which I hope will be readily paid. Enclos'd
is also a Letter to Mr. Collinson, containing an Order for Books
for the Library, which when you deliver you will have an Opportunity of proposing to furnish them. Please to add to the enclos'd List the following Books for me,[1] viz. Starkey's Pyrotechny
asserted, an old Book. 6 Echard's Gazetteer. 6 Watts's Lyrick
Poems. 6 Watts's Logic with Supplement. 1 Watts's Essays. also
5 or 6 lbs. of Long primer Fractions, i.e. to use with Long Primer
in Arithmetic Work. Mr. Hall and all your Friends here are well,
as I hope [*obliterated*].

From Robert Grace: Lease DS: Haverford College Library

Robert Grace (see above, I, 209 n), whose parents died when he was
young, was brought up by his grandmother and her second husband,
Hugh Lowden, in their home on the north side of Market Street, between Front and Second, facing the Jersey Market. Under Lowden's
will, Grace inherited the life use of the property when his grandmother
died in 1725. He was living there as a young bachelor when he and
Franklin began their lifelong friendship, and it was there that the Junto
held its meetings. Franklin's first establishment was apparently a little
west of Grace's house on the same side of the street. Grace went abroad
in 1733, remaining away for several years, and seems never to have

---

9. BF's letter of Dec. 11, the duplicate of which was written on the same
sheet as this of Dec. 22.
   1. The books wanted were probably the following: George Starkey, *Pyro-
techny Asserted and Illustrated, to be the Surest and Safest Means for Arts
Triumph over Natures Infirmities* (London, 1696); Laurence Echard (or
Eachard), *The Gazetteer's: or Newsman's Interpreter* (15th edit., London,
1741); Isaac Watts, *Horae Lyricae. Poems chiefly of the Lyric Kind* (8th edit.,
London, 1743); Watts, *Logick: or the Right Use of Reason in the Enquiry after
Truth* (7th edit., London, 1740), with *The Improvement of the Mind: or, a
Supplement to the Art of Logick* (2d edit., London, 1743); and Watts, *Philo-
sophical Essays on Various Subjects* (3d edit., London, 1742).

lived in the former Lowden house again.[2] On January 11, 1739, Franklin announced in the *Gazette* that he had moved "four doors nearer the River," and it was probably at this time that he first rented the property from Grace, although no lease for the years 1739–45 has been found.[3] Here he lived with his family, and here he maintained his printing office and shop and the post office. After Franklin formed his partnership with David Hall in January 1748 and withdrew from the active conduct of his printing business he "remov'd to a more quiet Part of Town," occupying a house on the northwest corner of Sassafras (Race) and Second streets.[4] The printing office and post office remained at the Grace property until 1752.[5] Hall, who had married a week after the formation of the partnership, probably moved into the vacated living quarters at once and continued to make his home there until at least 1764.[6]

December 30, 1745

ABSTRACT: Robert Grace, merchant, leases to Benjamin Franklin, "Typographer," for 14 years beginning Jan. 1, 1746, the lot, with all buildings and other improvements thereon, beginning at John Jones's lot on the north side of Market St., running eastward 17 ft. to the Widow Read's[7] lot, then northward 164 ft. to Jones Alley (or Pewter Platter Alley, now Church St.), westward 34 ft. to Thomas Shute's lot, southward 62 ft., then eastward by John Jones's lot 17 ft., and then southward 102 ft. to Market St. Franklin is to pay £55 lawful money of Pennsylvania annually, in equal installments on July 1 and January 1, with a right to Grace to enter and distrain in case of default. Franklin is to keep the property in repair. No one is to exercise the trade of baker or brewer on the premises.[8] By a memorandum at the end, dated March 28, 1757, the lease is extended for seven years beyond its original term at an annual rental of £60.

2. Mrs. Thomas Potts James, *Memorial of Thomas Potts, Junior* (Cambridge, Mass., 1874), pp. 378–85.

3. As early as Sept. 22, 1740, BF began the practise of paying on Grace's behalf ground rent due on this property, a practise he and David Hall continued throughout their occupancy, debiting the amounts paid against Grace's running account. Ledger D and Receipt Book, APS; MS account of Robert Grace with Franklin and Hall, March 17, 1764, Haverford Coll. Lib.

4. See below, p. 318. *Pa. Gaz.*, May 31, 1750.

5. *Pa. Gaz.*, Jan. 14, 1752.

6. BF Receipt Book, Dec. 27, 1763, APS.

7. Not BF's mother-in-law, but another Sarah, widow of Charles Read, a cousin of Deborah Franklin's father.

8. Since Grace was neither a baker nor a brewer, this restriction was probably inserted as a precaution against fire. See above, p. 12.

The Antediluvians Were All Very Sober

Draft: American Philosophical Society

[*c.* 1745][9]

The Antediluvians were all very sober
For they had no Wine, and they brew'd no October;[1]
All wicked, bad Livers, on Mischief still thinking,
For there can't be good Living where there is not good Drinking.

Derry down

'Twas honest old Noah first planted the Vine,
And mended his Morals by drinking its Wine;
He justly the drinking of Water decry'd;[2]
For he knew that all Mankind, by drinking it, dy'd.

Derry down.

From this Piece of History plainly we find
That Water's good neither for Body or Mind;
That Virtue and Safety in Wine-bibbing's found
While all that drink Water deserve to be drown'd.

Derry down

So For Safety and Honesty put the Glass round.

Extracts from the Gazette, 1745

Printed in *The Pennsylvania Gazette*, January 1 to December 31, 1745.

[ADVERTISEMENT] Lost on Friday, the 21st of December, 1744, betwixt Frankfort and Philadelphia, a Fowling-Piece, mounted with Brass, Dutch Make, a black Barrel, with a pretty wide Bore. Whoever has found it, and will return it to the Printer hereof, shall be sufficiently rewarded. [January 1]

9. This MS in BF's autograph was dated "*circa* 1745" in I. Minis Hays, *Calendar of the Papers of Benjamin Franklin* (Phila., 1908), III, 435. Van Doren accepted this in *Benjamin Franklin's Autobiographical Writings* (N.Y., 1945), p. 48. There is no reason for changing it except, perhaps, that BF has suggested alternative words in pencil, which he used more frequently in his later years. The watermark provides no clue to a date.

1. October: ale or cider brewed in October; any good ale.

2. Penciled alternatives for the last two lines of the second stanza read:

Thenceforth as unwholesome he Water decry'd;
For he saw that by drinking it Millions had dy'd.

After a long Dearth of News, we have, by the late Ships, received English Papers to the 12th of November. The War, tho' it
creates a more general Appetite for News, does, we find, in this
distant Part of the World, very much disconcert us News Writers.
During the Peace, Ships were constantly dropping in at some Port
or other of this Continent, and we had fresh Advices almost every
Week from Europe; but now, by their waiting for Convoy, and
other Hindrances and Delays, we are sometimes Months without
having a Syllable. The Consequence is, that a Series of News
Papers come to hand in a Lump together; and being each of us
ambitious to give our Readers the freshest Intelligence, we croud
all the latest Events into our *First* Paper, and are obliged to fill up
the *Succeeding* Ones with Articles of prior Date, or else omit them
intirely, as being anticipated and stale, and entertain you with
Matters of another Nature. Hence the Chain of Occurrences is
broken or inverted, and much of the News rendered thereby unintelligible. Hence you have tedious Accounts of the raising of
Armies, the Motion of Fleets, or the Sieges of Cities, after you
have been some Weeks acquainted with the taking of those Cities,
and the beating of those Fleets and Armies; or perhaps you are
never told at all by what Steps those great Events were brought
about. Such a confused Method must make any Writings of a historical Nature less entertaining and instructive to the intelligent
Reader. We purpose therefore to avoid it for the future in this
Paper, as much as may be, and doubt not, but that for the sake of
a clear and regular Account of the Affairs of Europe, our Readers
will excuse us if we happen now and then to be a Week or two
later than others with some particular Articles.   [January 22]

[ADVERTISEMENT] Lost or left at some House, a good Kersey
Great Coat of a dark Dove Colour; having a large Cape, with a
Cap in its Lining, a Pocket on the right-side of the Coat. Whoever
leaves it at the Post-Office, shall be Thank'd or Rewarded.
N.B. The said Coat has Hair Buttons.[3]   [February 5]

[ADVERTISEMENT] Any Gentleman, or Gentlemen, inclined to
employ a Schoolmaster, by enquiring at the Printer's hereof, may

3. This advertisement first appeared Jan. 22, but without the note about
buttons.

53

be informed of one well qualified, and whose Conduct and Method is well recommended. [February 19]

Mr. Franklin,

As Privateering is now so much in Fashion, the printing the following Question may be an Amusement, if not to the Privateers, yet to some of your Correspondents or Readers.

Suppose a Privateer, in the Latitude of 10 Degrees North, should, at 6 in the Morning, spy a Ship due South of her, distant 20 Miles; upon which she steers directly for her, and runs at the Rate of 8 Miles an Hour. The Ship at the same time sees the Privateer, but not being much afraid of her, keeps on her Course due West, and sails at the Rate of 6 Miles an Hour; how many Hours will it be before the Privateer overtakes the Ship?

N.B. The Sailing is supposed on a Plane as plain Sailing, and the Privateer keeps her Course constantly directed toward the Ship.

T.G.[4]

[March 5]

[ADVERTISEMENT] Left at the Post Office, some Time ago, a Cane, with a wrought Head. The Owner, describing it, may have it again without any Charge. [March 12]

Saturday Night last died after a long Indisposition, CLEMENT PLUMSTED,[5] Esq; many Years an eminent Merchant and Magistrate of this City, and one of the Governor's Council. His Funeral was respectfully attended by a great Number of People, who (instead of Wine and Biscuit heretofore customary) were serv'd each with one of Bishop Tillotson's Sermons, suitable to the Occasion.

[May 30]

Philadelphia, June 6. 1745

As the CAPE-BRETON Expedition[6] is at present the Subject of most Conversations, we hope the following Draught (rough as it is, for want of good Engravers here) will be acceptable to our Readers; as it may serve to give them an Idea of the Strength and Situation

4. Thomas Godfrey. See above, I, 190 n. No solution of the problem was published.
5. Clement Plumsted (1680–1745) had been mayor of Philadelphia in 1723, 1736, and 1741.
6. See above, pp. 14, 26.

of the Town now besieged by our Forces, and render the News we receive from thence more intelligible.[7]

CAPE-BRETON Island, on which Louisburgh is built, lies on the South of the Gulph of St. Lawrence, and commands the Entrance into that River, and the Country of Canada. It is reckon'd 140 Leagues in Circuit, full of fine Bays and Harbours, extreamly convenient for Fishing Stages. It was always reckon'd a Part of Nova-Scotia. For the Importance of this Place see our *Gazette*, No. 858.[8] As soon as the French King had begun the present unjust War against the English, the People of Louisburgh attack'd the New-England Town of Canso, consisting of about 150 Houses and a Fort, took it, burnt it to the Ground, and carried away the People, Men, Women and Children, Prisoners.[9] They then laid Siege to Annapolis Royal, and would have taken it, if seasonable Assistance had not been sent from Boston.[1] Mr. Duvivier[2] went home to France last Fall for more Soldiers, &c. to renew that

7. Here follows a "Plan of the Town and Harbour of Louisbourgh" with an explanatory key. This is the first news illustration to appear in the *Gazette*. Four days later, June 10, James Parker printed the same map and key in his *New-York Weekly Post-Boy*, apparently using the identical block. The source for the map and the maker of the cut are unknown.

8. The *Gazette* of May 23 devoted nearly a column to an essay by an unknown author on Cape Breton and the strategic and economic advantages to be gained by the capture of Louisbourg. The same article had appeared in Parker's *New-York Weekly Post-Boy*, May 20. Internal evidence suggests that the piece may have been based on a much longer paper written in London, April 9, 1744, by Robert Auchmuty, vice-admiralty judge of Boston, entitled "The Importance of Cape-Breton to the British Nation." 1 Mass. Hist. Soc. *Colls.*, v, 202–5.

9. Canso, or Canseau, at the extreme northeastern tip of the Nova Scotia mainland, was an important fishing station of the British colonists. The French commander at Louisbourg, who learned of the declaration of war by France four weeks before the news reached Boston, dispatched a small expedition against Canso, about 70 miles away, which captured the place on May 24, 1744, destroyed the blockhouse, and carried the garrison and inhabitants as prisoners to Louisbourg.

1. Within a month after learning of the declaration of war Governor Shirley of Massachusetts dispatched reinforcements to Annapolis Royal on the Bay of Fundy, the principal British post in Nova Scotia. The New Englanders arrived in time to help the commander, Paul Mascarene, and his small garrison to withstand an Indian attack in July 1744, and a more formidable siege conducted by forces from Louisbourg in the late summer and early fall.

2. Captain Duvivier, aide-major of Louisbourg, led the expeditions against both Canso and Annapolis Royal.

Attempt, and for Stores for Privateers, of which they proposed to fit out a great Number this Summer, being the last Year unprovided: Yet one of their Cruisers only, took 4 Sail in a few Days, off our Capes, to a very considerable Value. What might we have expected from a dozen Sail, making each 3 or 4 Cruises a Year? They boasted that during the War they should have no Occasion to cut Fire Wood, for that the Jackstaves of English Vessels would be a Supply sufficient. It is therefore in their own NECESSARY DEFENCE, as well as that of all the other British Colonies, that the People of New-England have undertaken the present Expedition against that Place, to which may the GOD OF HOSTS grant Success. *Amen.* [June 6]

By some of our People, who have lately been Prisoners at the Havanna, we learn, that while they were there, an English Ship, from Jamaica, commanded by Captain William Lyford, which had met with the Hurricane at Sea, and lost her Masts, put in there in Distress; the Capt. waited upon the Governor, and surrendered himself a Prisoner, with his Vessel. But the Governor generously told him, no Advantage should be taken of his Misfortune: And Leave was given him to sell Part of his Cargo, in order to refit his Vessel, and pursue his Voyage. *Thus have we at length taught our Enemies Humanity.* [July 4]

From Trenton we hear, that on Friday the 21st past, two Lads, Benjamin and Severns Albertis, Brothers, going in a Canoe to fish near the Falls, the Canoe overset by running against a Log, and the latter was drowned, the other hardly escaping. Great Search was made for the Body on that and the three following Days, by a great Number of People in Boats and Canoes; but to no Effect, it being driven down, to the Surprize of many, as low as Burlington, and there taken up and interr'd on Monday.

From Abington we hear, that on Saturday, the 22d of June last, a Woman, who had been subject to the Falling-sickness, was found drowned in a Spring, into which it was thought she fell when in a Fit, having gone out to fetch Water.

Saturday last a Boy about 7 Years of Age, playing with some other Children in a Boat, accidentally fell into the River, and was drowned.

The same Day the Body of one John Holmes, who belonged to one of our Privateers, and was accidentally drowned, by falling into the River between the Boat and the Vessel a few Days before, was taken up and buried.

And on Sunday last a Woman of this City, who had been subject to Fits, was found dead in her Bed. [July 4]

Wednesday last, a great Number of Guns were distinctly heard in several Places round this City, the Occasion of which, as well as the Place where they were fired, was unknown till the Evening of the Day following, when an Express arriv'd with Advice of the Surrender of Louisbourg, which had caus'd great Rejoycings at New-York.[3] 'Twas near 9 o'Clock when the Express came in, yet the News flying instantly round the Town, upwards of 20 Bonfires were immediately lighted in the Streets. The next Day was spent in Feasting, and drinking the Healths of Governor Shirley, Gen. Pepperel, Com. Warren, &c. &c. under the Discharge of Cannon from the Wharffs and Vessels in the River; and the Evening concluded with Bonfires, Illuminations, and other Demonstrations of Joy. A Mob gathered, and began to break the Windows of those Houses that were not illuminated, but it was soon dispersed, and suppress'd. [July 18]

[ADVERTISEMENT] Choice Bohea Tea to be sold by the Dozen or half Dozen Pound, at the Post-Office, Philadelphia. [August 8]

Thursday Night last the Rev. Mr. Whitefield arrived here from New-York. He was met and conducted into Town by about 50 Horse. The Evening following he preach'd at the New-Building, and twice or thrice every Day since to large Audiences. He purposes to set out speedily for Georgia, by Land, thro' Maryland, Virginia, and the Carolina's.[4] [September 12]

[ADVERTISEMENT] Lost, about four Months ago, a dark coloured Cloth Surtout Coat. Whoever brings the said Coat to the Post-Office, in Philadelphia, shall have Ten Shillings Reward. [September 12]

3. The French surrendered Louisbourg June 17.
4. Whitefield's movements after this date are not precisely known. Tyerman, *Whitefield*, II, 153.

[ADVERTISEMENT] Notice is hereby given to all Persons, who have old Pewter to dispose of, that by applying to the Printer hereof, they will be informed where they may have 12*d.* half Penny per Pound, for any Quantity, from One Pound, to a Thousand Weight, in Cash. [September 26]

[ADVERTISEMENT] On Monday next will be published, POOR RICHARD'S ALMANACK, for the Year of our Lord 1746, containing, besides what is usual; His Account of himself and his Way of Life with his Dame Bridget. A Table for the more easy and ready casting up of Pieces of Eight, Pistoles, Moidores, &c. Verses on several Subjects; viz. The Fool out of Fashion. Man's insatiable Appetite. The best Wealth. Sacred Solitude. Zara. On Pleasure. Man's Reward. Gold insolvent. Lavinia at threescore. The Opiate. Definition of Female Beauty. Together with many wise Sayings, Jokes, &c. &c. Sold by B. Franklin, at the customary Price. [October 31]

[ADVERTISEMENT] THE PENNSILVANIA FIRE-PLACES, made by Robert Grace, are sold by Lewis Evans, in Strawberry Alley; who takes care, if required, that they are fitted up, and set to the best Advantage, in Philadelphia, or the Parts adjacent.[5] [November 14]

Several counterfeit Pistoles made of fine Brass, have lately appeared among us. They may be known by their being harder to the Teeth than Gold, and by their extream Lightness; a Piece of Brass equal in Bulk to a Piece of Gold, being not quite half the Weight. [November 21]

Just Published, The Pocket Almanack for the Year 1746. Printed and sold by B. Franklin. [November 28]

Philadelphia, December 24. 1745.
Taken away from the Post-Office, the 11th Instant, a Silver Spoon, marked T C, Philip Syng Maker: The Person supposed to have taken it, is desired to return the same, before exposed. [December 24]

5. See above, II, 419–46.

Williamsburg, December 13. 1745.

Ran away from Hanover Court-house, on Thursday Night the 6th of this Instant, a Servant Man, belonging to the Subscriber, named Daniel Whealon, aged about Thirty, 5 Feet 9 Inches high, smooth-tongu'd, his Legs much swell'd. He had a dark grey Beaver Coating Jacket, with Metal Buttons, a Coat near the same Colour, with Metal Buttons, and other good Cloathing. He is an Irishman, a Convict, and a Smith by Trade; shoes Horses very well, makes Locks, and is dexterous at picking of any Locks. He has committed some Felonies lately, and is suspected of others; Has Money, a Silver Watch with only the Hour Hand, Silver Shoe and Knee Buckles, and other Things of Value: He stole when he went off, a middle-siz'd dark bay Horse, branded on the near Shoulder with a Heart; and a Virginia-made Saddle, with a Cut on the Seat, sew'd up with Silk: The Horse belongs to Abraham Bedel, living near the Place where the Upper Southanna Bridge stood, in Hanover County. It is thought he has a forg'd Pass. He ran away before, went to Carolina; and returned to his former Master, Mr. John Fitzgerald of King William County; but now will endeavour to get off, for fear of Prosecution for Felony.

Whoever will apprehend the said Servant, and secure him, so that he be brought to Justice, shall have Three Pistoles Reward, if taken in Virginia, or Six Pistoles if taken in any other Government. And for the Horse, Saddle and Bridle, One Pistole, if deliver'd to the above-mention'd Owner, or to me in Williamsburg.

WILLIAM PARKS[6]

N.B. It's supposed he'll go to the Northward.

P.S. If the said Servant and Horse should be taken up and secur'd in Pennsylvania, or any of the Northern Governments, the Rewards will be paid at Philadelphia, by   B. FRANKLIN

[December 31]

PHILADELPHIA: Printed by B. FRANKLIN, Post-Master, at the New-Printing-Office, near the Market.

6. William Parks, printer of the *Virginia Gazette*. See above, II, 363 n.

Poor Richard, 1746

Poor Richard, 1746. An Almanack For the Year of Christ 1746, . . . By Richard Saunders, Philom. Philadelphia: Printed and sold by B. Franklin. (Yale University Library)

PREFACE.

Who is Poor Richard? People oft enquire,
Where lives? What is he?—never yet the nigher.
Somewhat to ease your Curiositie,
Take these slight Sketches of my Dame and me.
 Thanks to kind Readers and a careful Wife,
With Plenty bless'd, I lead an easy Life;
My Business Writing; hers to drain the Mead,
Or crown the barren Hill with useful Shade;
In the smooth Glebe to see the Plowshare worn,
And fill the Granary with needful Corn.
Press nectarous Cyder from my loaded Trees,
Print the sweet Butter, turn the drying Cheese.
Some Books we read, tho' few there are that hit
The happy Point where Wisdom joins with Wit;
That set fair Virtue naked to our View,
And teach us what is *decent,* what is *true.*
The Friend sincere, and honest Man, with Joy
Treating or treated oft our Time employ.
Our Table neat, Meals temperate; and our Door
Op'ning spontaneous to the bashful Poor.
Free from the bitter Rage of Party Zeal,
All those we love who seek the publick Weal.
Nor blindly follow Superstition's Lore,
Which cheats deluded Mankind o'er and o'er.
Not over righteous, quite beyond the Rule,
Conscience perplext by every canting Tool.
Nor yet when Folly hides the dubious Line,
Where Good and Bad their blended Colours join;
Rush indiscreetly down the dangerous Steep,
And plunge uncertain in the darksome Deep.
Cautious, if right; if wrong resolv'd to part
The Inmate Snake that folds about the Heart.
Observe the *Mean,* the *Motive* and the *End;*

Mending our selves, or striving still to mend.
Our Souls sincere, our Purpose fair and free,
Without Vain Glory or Hypocrisy:
Thankful if well; if ill, we kiss the Rod;
Resign with Hope, and put our Trust in GOD.

A TABLE for the more ready casting up of COINS, in Pennsylvania.

No.	Ps. Eight.			Spanish Pistoles.			English Guineas.			Moidores.		
	£	s.	d.	£	s.	d.	£	s.	d.	£	s.	d.
1	0	7	6	1	7	0	1	14	0	2	3	6
2	0	15	0	2	14	0	3	8	0	4	7	0
3	1	2	6	4	1	0	5	2	0	6	10	6
4	1	10	0	5	8	0	6	16	0	8	14	0
5	1	17	6	6	15	0	8	10	0	10	17	6
6	2	5	0	8	2	0	10	4	0	13	1	0
7	2	12	6	9	9	0	11	18	0	15	4	6
8	3	0	0	10	16	0	13	12	0	17	8	0
9	3	7	6	12	3	0	15	6	0	19	11	6
10	3	15	0	13	10	0	17	0	0	21	15	0
11	4	2	6	14	17	0	18	14	0	23	18	6
12	4	10	0	16	4	0	20	8	0	26	2	0
13	4	17	6	17	11	0	22	2	0	28	5	6
14	5	5	0	18	18	0	23	16	0	30	9	0
15	5	12	6	20	5	0	25	10	0	32	12	6
16	6	0	0	21	12	0	27	4	0	34	16	0
17	6	7	6	22	19	0	28	18	0	36	19	6
18	6	15	0	24	6	0	30	12	0	39	3	0
19	7	2	6	25	13	0	32	6	0	41	6	6
20	7	10	0	27	0	0	34	0	0	43	10	0
30	11	5	0	40	10	0	51	0	0	65	5	0
40	15	0	0	54	0	0	68	0	0	87	0	0
50	18	15	0	67	10	0	85	0	0	108	15	0
60	22	10	0	81	0	0	102	0	0	130	10	0
70	26	5	0	94	10	0	119	0	0	152	5	0
80	30	0	0	108	0	0	136	0	0	174	0	0
90	33	15	0	121	10	0	153	0	0	195	15	0
100	37	10	0	135	0	0	170	0	0	217	10	0

EXPLANATION.

Find your Number in the 1st Col. under No. and right against the same you have the Sum of that Number of Pieces of Eight, Spanish Pistoles, English Guineas, Moidores. But if your Sum cannot be found at one View, it must be taken at two or more Operations.

XI Mon. January hath xxxi days.

> Nothing exceeds in Ridicule, no doubt,
> A Fool *in* Fashion, but a Fool that's *out;*
> His Passion for Absurdity's so strong
> He cannot bear a Rival in the Wrong.
> Tho' wrong the Mode, comply; more Sense is shewn
> In wearing others Follies than your own.
> If what is out of Fashion most you prize,
> Methinks you should endeavour to be wise.

When the Well's dry, we know the Worth of Water.

> He that whines for Glass without G
> Take away L and that's he.

XII Mon. February hath xxviii days.

> Man's rich with little, were his Judgment true,
> Nature is frugal, and her Wants are few;
> Those few Wants answer'd, bring sincere Delights,
> But Fools create themselves new Appetites.
> Fancy and Pride seek Things at vast Expence,
> Which relish not to *Reason* nor to *Sense.*
> Like Cats in Airpumps, to subsist we strive
> On Joys too thin to keep the Soul alive.

> A good Wife and Health,
> Is a Man's best Wealth.

A quarrelsome Man has no good Neighbours.

I Mon. March hath xxxi days.

> O sacred *Solitude!* divine Retreat!
> Choice of the Prudent! Envy of the Great!
> By thy pure Stream, or in thy waving Shade,
> We court fair Wisdom, that celestial Maid:
> The genuine Offspring of her lov'd Embrace,
> (Strangers on Earth) are Innocence and Peace.

There blest with Health, with Business unperplext,
This Life we relish and ensure the next.

Wide will wear,
But Narrow will tear.

Silks and Sattins put out the Kitchen Fire.

Vice knows she's ugly, so puts on her Mask.

II Mon. April hath xxx days.

Zara resembles Ætna crown'd with Snows,
Without she freezes, and within she glows;
Twice e'er the Sun descends, with Zeal inspir'd,
From the vain Converse of the World retir'd,
She reads the Psalms and Chapters of the Day,
In—some leud Novel, new Romance, or Play.
Thus gloomy Zara, with a solemn Grace,
Deceives Mankind, and *hides* behind her *Face*.

It's the easiest Thing in the World for a Man to deceive himself.

Women and Wine,
Game and Deceit,
Make the Wealth small
And the Wants great.

All Mankind are beholden to him that is kind to the Good.

III Mon. May hath xxxi days.

Pleasures are few, and fewer we enjoy;
Pleasure like *Quicksilver,* is bright and *coy;*
We strive to grasp it with our utmost Skill,
Still it eludes us, and it glitters still.
If seiz'd at last, compute your mighty Gains,
What is it but rank Poison in your Veins.

A Plowman on his Legs is higher than a Gentleman on his Knees.

Virtue and Happiness are Mother and Daughter.

The generous Mind least regards money, and yet most feels the Want of it.

For one poor Man there are an hundred indigent.

IV Mon. June hath xxx days.

> What's Man's Reward for all his Care and Toil?
> But *One;* a female Friend's endearing Smile:
> A tender Smile, our Sorrow's only Balm,
> And in Life's Tempest the sad Sailor's Calm.
> How have I seen a gentle Nymph draw nigh,
> Peace in her Air, Persuasion in her Eye;
> Victorious Tenderness, it all o'ercame,
> Husbands look'd mild, and Savages grew tame.

Dost thou love Life? then do not squander Time; for that's the Stuff Life is made of.

Good Sense is a Thing all need, few have, and none think they want.

V Mon. July hath xxxi days.

> Who taught the rapid Winds to fly so fast,
> Or shakes the Centre with his Western Blast?
> Who from the Skies can a whole Deluge pour?
> Who strikes thro' Nature, with the solemn Roar
> Of dreadful *Thunder,* points it where to fall,
> And in fierce Light'ning wraps the flying Ball?
> Not he who trembles at the darted Fires,
> Falls at the Sound, and in the Flash expires.

What's proper, is becoming: See the Blacksmith with his white Silk Apron!

The Tongue is ever turning to the aching Tooth.

Want of Care does us more Damage than Want of Knowledge.

VI Mon. August hath xxxi days.

> Can Gold calm *Passion,* or make *Reason* shine;
> Can we dig *Peace* or *Wisdom* from the Mine?
> Wisdom to Gold prefer, for 'tis much less
> To make our *Fortune,* than our *Happiness.*
> That Happiness which Great Ones often see,
> With Rage and Wonder, in a low Degree,
> Themselves unblest. The Poor are *only* poor;
> But what are they who *droop* amid their Store?

Take Courage, Mortal; Death can't banish thee out of the Universe.

The Sting of a Reproach, is the Truth of it.

Do me the Favour to deny me at once.

VII Mon. September hath xxx days.

> Can Wealth give Happiness? look round and see,
> What gay Distress! What splendid Misery!
> Whatever Fortune lavishly can pour,
> The Mind annihilates, and calls for more.
> Wealth is a Cheat, believe not what it says;
> Greatly it promises, but never pays.
> Misers may startle, but they shall be told,
> That Wealth is Bankrupt, and *insolvent* Gold.

The most exquisite Folly is made of Wisdom spun too fine.

A life of leisure, and a life of laziness, are two things.

VIII Mon. October hath xxxi days.

> Some Ladies are too beauteous to be wed,
> For where's the Man that's worthy of their Bed?
> If no Disease reduce her Pride before,
> Lavinia will be ravisht at threescore.
> Then she submits to venture in the Dark,
> And nothing, now, is wanting—but her Spark.

Mad Kings and mad Bulls, are not to be held by treaties and packthread.

Changing Countries or Beds, cures neither a bad Manager, nor a Fever.

IX Mon. November hath xxx days.

> There are, who, tossing on the Bed of *Vice,*
> For *Flattery's* Opiate give the highest Price;
> Yet from the saving Hand of *Friendship* turn,
> Her Med'cines dread, her generous Offers spurn.
> Deserted *Greatness!* who but pities thee?
> By Crowds encompass'd, thou no *Friend* canst see.
> Or should kind *Truth* invade thy tender Ear,
> We pity still, for thou no Truth canst bear.

A true great Man will neither trample on a Worm, nor sneak to an Emperor.

Ni ffyddra llaw dyn, er gwneithr da idd ei hûn.[7]

X Mon. December hath xxxi days.

> What's Female Beauty, but an Air divine,
> Thro' which the Mind's all gentle Graces shine?
> They, like the Sun, irradiate all between;
> The Body *charms,* because the Soul is *seen.*
> Hence, Men are often Captives of a Face,
> They know not why, of no peculiar Grace.
> Some Forms tho' bright, no mortal Man can *bear;*
> Some, none *resist,* tho' not exceeding fair.

> Tim and his Handsaw are good in their Place,
> Tho' not fit for preaching or shaving a face.

Half-Hospitality opens his Doors and shuts up his Countenance.

7. Man's hand alone, without God's help, cannot do himself good.

66

COURTS.

From Earth to Heav'n when *Justice* fled,
The Laws decided in her Stead;
For Heav'n to Earth should she return,
Lawyers might beg, and Lawbooks burn.[8]

To Cadwallader Colden

ALS: New-York Historical Society

Sir   [February 1746][9]

I receiv'd yours with others enclos'd for Mr. Bertram and Mr. Armit,[1] to which I suppose the enclos'd are Answers. The Person who brought yours said he would call for Answers, but did not; or, if he did, I did not see him.

I understand Parker has begun upon your Piece.[2] A long Sitting of our Assembly has hitherto hinder'd me from beginning the Miscellany. I shall write to Dr. Gronovius as you desire.[3]

I wish I had Mathematics enough to satisfy my self, Whether the much shorter Voyages made by Ships bound hence to England, than by those from England hither, are not in some Degree owing to the Diurnal Motion of the Earth; and if so, in what Degree?[4] 'Tis a Notion that has lately entred my Mind; I know not if ever any other's. Ships in a Calm at the Equator move with the Sea

---

8. The verses were repeated in the 1747 almanac, where "for," in the third line, is corrected to "from."

9. This conjectural dating depends on two facts: that BF was preparing his Philosophical Miscellany in the spring and summer of 1746 (see below, p. 92); and that the long session of the Assembly, which hindered him from working on it, lasted Jan. 6 to Feb. 24, 1746.

1. John Armitt, probably a lawyer, was Colden's business agent in Philadelphia. *Colden Paps.*, III, 177–8.

2. James Parker printed Colden's *Explication of the First Causes of Action in Matter*.

3. Johann Friedrich Gronovius (1690–1762?), physician and botanist of Leyden, was a correspondent of Colden and Bartram. Darlington, *Memorials*, p. 349. No letter from BF to Gronovius has been found.

4. BF recurred to this problem several times in the ensuing 30 years and finally solved it with the help of his Nantucket kinsman, Captain Timothy Folger, who charted the Gulf Stream for him. BF to Anthony Todd, Oct. 29, 1768.

15 Miles per minute; at our Capes suppose 12 Miles per Minute; in the British Channel suppose 10 Miles per Minute: Here is a Difference of 2 Miles Velocity per Minute between Cape Hinlopen and the Lizard! no small Matter in so Weighty a Body as a laden Ship swimming in a Fluid! How is this Velocity lost in the Voyage thither, if not by the Resistance of the Water? and if so, then the Water, which resisted in part, must have given Way in part to the Ship, from time to time as she proceeded continually out of Parallels of Latitude where the Earths Motion or Rotation was quicker into others where it was slower. And thus as her Velocity tends eastward with the Earth's Motion, she perhaps makes her Easting sooner. Suppose a Vessel lying still in a Calm at our Cape, could be taken up and the same Instant set down in an equal Calm in the English Channel, would not the Difference of Velocity between her and the Sea she was plac'd in, appear plainly by a violent Motion of the Ship thro' the Water eastward? I have not Time to explain my self farther, the Post waiting, but believe have said enough for you to comprehend my Meaning. If the Reasons hinted at should encline you to think there is any Thing in this Notion, I should be glad of an Answer to this Question, (if it be capable of a precise Answer) viz.

Suppose a Ship sails on a N. East Line from Lat. 39 to Lat. 52 in 30 Days, how long will she be returning on the same Line, Winds, Currents, &c. being equal?

Just so much as the East Motion of the Earth helps her Easting, I suppose it will hinder her Westing.

Perhaps the Weight and Dimensions or Shape of the Vessel should be taken into the Consideration, as the Water resists Bodies of different Shapes differently.

I must beg you to excuse the incorrectness of this Scrawl as I have not time to transcribe. I am Sir Your most humble Servant
B FRANKLIN

Addressed: To Cadwalader Colden Esqr Coldengham Free
B FRANKLIN

From Cadwallader Colden

Draft: New-York Historical Society

[February 1746][5]

There is no Question but in the case you mention of a ships being taken up in a Southern latitude and let down in one some degrees more northerly the same moment she would have a degree of Motion Eastward but that it would shorten a Voyage from America to Europe I cannot think because as the alteration is made by insensibly small steps it can only be so much as an alteration of the Velocity in the least conceivable part of a degree of Latitude is greater than the resistance of the Water which in all cases remains the same and equally resists the smallest alteration of Velocity as the greatest. Suppose for example in the alteration of one second of latitude how much greater will the Velocity be in the Southward than northward? If it be 60 miles at the Œquator what will it be at 1 second on either side of the Œquator? The Difference is the force which the ship can acquire from the diurnal rotation of the earth in this second. Now it may be asked whether this Difference will be sufficient to overcome the resistance of the Water in any degree whatsoever, that is, whether it be not infinitely small in respect to the resistance of the body of Water which resists the motion of a ship and if so it can neither add to nor diminish the ships way in the time she alters her latitude one second, and if this be the case it cannot either forward or stop her way in a greater change of latitude because it is done by a continual addition of these seconds or rather of less than thirds or of any imaginable quantity so that according to my way of computation in answer to your question the difference of time in the going and return will be = 0.

The shorter Voyages to Europe without doubt are chiefly owing to the more frequent westerly winds but this does not account for the reason why in going to Europe a ship is generally a head of the reckoning or you meet with the land sooner than by the computation of the ships way if it be well kept, whereas in coming to America the reckoning is generally a head of the ship. The true reason I think is from the Tides. The High Water every day is nearly three quarters of an hour more easterly on the globe

5. Colden wrote this draft reply on the back of BF's letter to him (see above, p. 67). Punctuation, omitted in the draft, has been supplied.

than the day before or following the course of the moon advances daily about twelve degrees eastward and therefor they every day in sailing Westerly meet with the contrary current of the Water sooner than they do in sailing easterly, as in a river in going down the river you meet the flood sooner than you do the ebb in going up the river where the flood and ebb are nearly equal; for the difference of the force and length of the ebb more than the flood in rivers from the force of the accumulated fresh water cannot take place at sea. If you think proper to give this in your Miscellany as the reason of the shorter voyages from America to Europe than from Europe to America other things being alike, I'l u[nder]take to support it against any objection. There are some mistakes that I would be so far from being ashamed of them after I knew them to be such that I would be vain of them because none but those of a lively and quick and pierceing Imagination can fall into them. A Blockhead is uncapable of making such mistakes. There is even a pleasure in telling it after the mistake is discover'd and the person to whom it is told values the ingenuity which occasion'd the mistake and on reflection is conscious to himself that he would have valued himself for that very thought. There is a use likewise in mentioning these mistakes to others to guard them against those conceptions which please and flatter the Imagination most.

Suppose the difference between the lands end and the coast of America to be 72 degr. of longitude (I choose this number to avoid fractions), then the same high Water on the coast of America will happen six hours later at the lands end and therefor a ship will meet with one whole tide of flood against her there which would be an ebb in her favour on the coast of America and supposing her voyage perform'd in 30 days, every day equally approaching to America, she would every day have that tide lessen'd 1/30 of the time as she approaches. I once had thoughts to calculate an Equation to rectify a ships easting and westing but upon reflecting that a general equation cannot serve for every ship but must be different for every ship according to the several molds by which the ship is built and her being loaded or in ballast, I believe it will be of little use for according to the different molds of a ship and her being deep or light the tides have greater or less force on her way. The heavy dull ships must make much larger allowences than the best saylors and accordingly we generally find these heavy saylers most out in their reckoning.

To ————   Draft (fragment): American Philosophical Society

[February 1746?][6]
has been blown off that Coast. Our Governor thinks they contain the Commissions for the Officers, and Orders to draw for the Pay of the Troops &c. and therefore directs me to forward them per Express to N. York, that they may overtake the Post. In haste I am &c.

[On back]   One Month at £45 per Ann. is   3. 15. 0
            Hire of Horse 2 Trips at 25 s.   2. 10.
                                              ——————————
                                              £6:   5: 0
                              Paid   1.   17. 6
                                              ——————————
                                              4:   7: 6[7]

From George Whitefield

Printed in *The Pennsylvania Gazette*, May 22, 1746.

Mr. Franklin,   [April 16], 1746
As it is a Minister's Duty to provide Things honest in the Sight of all Men, I thought it my Duty, when lately at Georgia, to have the whole Orphan House Accounts audited, from the Beginning of that Institution to January last; the same I intend to do yearly for the future: An Abstract of the whole, with the particular Affidavits, and common Seal of Savannah affixed to it, I have sent you with this;[8] be pleased to publish it in your weekly

6. This scrap is too short and the reference too general for precise dating. It could have been written in any of the years from 1745 through 1747. It is inserted here because of its possible connection with an episode of which Governor Gooch informed the Virginia House of Burgesses, Feb. 20, 1746: "Several Transports with Two Regiments bound to Cape Breton, to preserve the valuable Conquest of Louisbourg, . . . by bad Weather and contrary Winds, have been forced with their Convoys into this Colony." *Jour. House of Burgesses, 1742–1747, 1748–1749* (Richmond, 1909), p. 155.

7. These notes may refer to wages of a post rider.

8. The following account and affadavit appeared in Whitefield's *A Further Account of God's Dealings . . . To which is annex'd A brief Account of the . . .*

Paper. My Friends thought this was the most satisfactory Way of proceeding. To print every particular Article, with the proper Voucher, would make a Folio, and put me to a greater Expence than my present Arrears will permit me to be at; however, if any want further Satisfaction, they may consult the original Vouchers, &c. at Savannah, in the Hands of Mr. Habersham;[9] or, if they desire it, and will defray the Expence of Printing, every single Article of Debtor and Creditor shall be published by, Sir, Your very humble Servant,   GEORGE WHITEFIELD

Orphan-House, in Georgia,	Dr.	Orphan-House, in Georgia,	Cr.
	Sterling.		*Sterling.*
	£ s. d.		£ s. d.
To Cash received from the 15th December, 1738, to the 1st January, 1745–6, by publick Collections, private Benefactions, and annual Subscriptions, per Account,	4982 12 8	By Cash paid Sundries by particular Accounts examined, from the 15th Decem. 1738, to the 1st January, 1745–6, for Buildings, Cultivation of Lands, Infirmary, Provisions, Wearing Apparel, and other incident Expences,	5511 17 9¼
To Ballance superexpended, January 1. 1745–6,	529 05 1¼		
	£5511 17 9¼		

SAVANNAH, in GEORGIA.

L.S. This Day personally appeared before us Henry Parker and William Spencer, Bailiffs of Savannah aforesaid, the Reverend Mr. George Whitefield, and James Habersham, Merchant of Savannah aforesaid; who, being duly sworn, say, That the Accounts relating to the Orphan House, now exhibited before us, of which the above is an Abstract, amounting on the Debit Side (namely, for Collections and Subscriptions received) to the Sum of Four Thousand, Nine Hundred, Eighty Two Pounds, Twelve

Orphan-House in Georgia, printed by Bradford, 1746. They were reprinted in Whitefield's *Works* (London, 1771), III, 487–8. Their purpose was to silence rumors and asseverations, especially in New England, that the Orphan-House did not exist and that Whitefield had misappropriated the funds. Tyerman, *Whitefield*, II, 153–4.

9. James Habersham (1712–1775) came to Georgia with Whitefield, 1738, opened a school for poor children, and helped with the establishment of the Bethesda Orphanage, of which he was superintendent until 1744, when he entered business. He became a wealthy planter, merchant, and active public servant: a member of the Council, secretary of the province, president of the upper house of the Assembly, and acting governor of Georgia. *DAB*.

Shillings and Eightpence, Sterling, and on the Credit Side (namely, for Disbursements paid) to the Sum of Five Thousand, Five Hundred, Eleven Pounds, Seventeen Shillings, and Ninepence Farthing, Sterling, do, to the best of their Knowledge, contain a just and true Account of all the Monies collected by, or given to them, or any other, for the Use and Benefit of the said House; and that the Disbursements, amounting to the Sum aforesaid, have been faithfully applied to and for the Use of the same. And the Reverend Mr. Whitefield further declareth, that he hath not converted or applied any Part thereof to his own private Use and Property, neither hath charged the said House with any of his travelling, or any other private Expences whatsoever.

GEORGE WHITEFIELD,
JAMES HABERSHAM

SAVANNAH, in GEORGIA.

This Day personally appeared before us, Henry Parker and William Spencer, Bailiffs of Savannah aforesaid, William Woodrooffe, William Ewen, and William Russell, of Savannah aforesaid; who being duly sworn, say, That they have carefully and strictly examined all and singular the Accounts relating to the Orphan House, in Georgia, contained in Forty One Pages, in a Book intituled, *Receipts and Disbursements for the Orphan House in Georgia,* with the original Bills, Receipts, and other Vouchers, from the Fifteenth Day of December, in the Year of our Lord One Thousand Seven Hundred and Thirty Eight, to the First Day of January, in the Year of our Lord One Thousand Seven Hundred and Forty Five; and that the Monies received on Account of the said Orphan House, amounted to the Sum of Four Thousand, Nine Hundred, Eighty Two Pounds, Twelve Shillings, and Eightpence, Sterling, as above; and that it doth not appear that the Reverend Mr. Whitefield hath converted any Part thereof to his own private Use and Property, or charged the said House with any of his travelling, or other private Expences; but, on the contrary, hath contributed to the said House many valuable Benefactions; and that the Monies disbursed on Account of the said House, amounted to the Sum of Five Thousand, Five Hundred, Eleven Pounds, Seventeen Shillings, and Ninepence Farthing, Sterling, as above; which we, in Justice to the Reverend Mr.

73

Whitefield, and the Managers of the said House, do hereby declare, appear to us to be faithfully and justly applied to and for the Use and Benefit of the said House only.

WILLIAM WOODROOFFE,
WILLIAM EWEN,
WILLIAM RUSSEL

Sworn this 16th Day of April, 1746, before us Bailiffs of Savannah; in Justification whereof, we have hereunto fixed our Hands, and the common Seal.

HENRY PARKER,
WILLIAM SPENCER

[Reflections on Courtship and Marriage]

Reflections on Courtship and Marriage: in Two Letters to a Friend. Wherein a Practicable Plan is laid down for Obtaining and Securing Conjugal Felicity. Philadelphia: Printed and Sold by B. Franklin, M,DCC,XLVI.

The *Gazette* of April 17, 1746, announced this pamphlet as "Just Published." Charles R. Hildeburn assigned it to Franklin on the authority of a note, which he quoted as "By Benjamin Franklin. B.R. [Benjamin Rush]," in the copy belonging to the Library Company of Philadelphia.[1] Paul L. Ford and Carl Van Doren accepted this attribution.[2] However, the Library Company's copy belonged in fact to James Read of Reading, who acquired it in 1774; and the inscription, in Read's hand, actually reads "By Mr. Franklin (the printer of it) I believe. J R." Another note on the title page, made by Lloyd P. Smith, librarian of the Library Company, on May 26, 1880, reads, "Jos. Sabin wrote me he had ascertained that Franklin was the author." The editors do not know what evidence Sabin had, but their judgment is that the pamphlet's style is too unlike Franklin's to ascribe it to him.

Memorandum

MS: American Philosophical Society

Memorandum 1746   [April 18, 1746]

Sally[3] was inoculated April 18, being Fryday at 10 a Clock in the Morning.

1. *A Century of Printing: The Issues of the Press of Pennsylvania* (Phila., 1885), no. 976.
2. Ford, *Franklin Bibliog.*, no. 57; Van Doren, *Franklin*, pp. 152–3.
3. Sarah Franklin (Genealogy, D.3) was about two and a half years old. Her

74

To William Strahan

ALS: University of Pennsylvania Library; also duplicate: Boston Public Library

Sir   Philada. April 26. 1746

I have had no Line from [you] since that dated June 1745, which, with your equal Silence to our Friends Hall and Read, made me apprehend that Death had depriv'd me of the Pleasure I promis'd myself in our growing Friendship: But Lieut. Grung[4] writing in February last that you and your Family were well, convinces me that some unlucky Accident has happen'd to your Letters. I sent you in mine of December 11. and December 20.[5] a List of some Books, &c. which I wanted, with a Bill for £15.7.1 Sterling and as Mr. Collinson had his Letter which I then enclos'd to you, there can be no need of Copying what I sent you. I shall expect those Books in the next Vessel that arrives from London, and send you now enclos'd another Bill for £15 Sterling.

I have not time to add but that I am with sincere Respect Your obliged humble Servant   B FRANKLIN[6]

Please to forward the enclos'd to Mr. Watkins.[7]

---

brother Francis had died of smallpox before he was inoculated. See above, II, 154. The memorandum is in BF's hand.

4. Peter Grung, lieutenant of one of the Pennsylvania companies raised for the Cartagena expedition, 1740. Charles P. Keith, *Chronicles of Pennsylvania* (Phila., 1917), II, 809.

5. December 22; see above, p. 50.

6. On the duplicate BF indicated that a "Copy" (i.e. the original) had been sent "per Martyn who sail'd Ap. 26." This duplicate is addressed "To Mr. Wm. Strahan   Printer   in Wine Office Court, Fleet street   London   via Maryland."

7. Possibly Adrian Watkins, Edinburgh printer and bookseller, who printed an edition of the Bible in 1748. H.R. Plomer and others, *A Dictionary of the Printers and Booksellers . . . in England, . . . 1726 to 1775* (Oxford, 1932), p. 363.

From George Scholtze[8]   ALS: American Philosophical Society

upper Hanover May 5. 1746

Mr. Benj: Franklin to Geo: Scholtze . . . . Dr.

	£		
1733. october 30. To 22 yards of Dowlas[9] at 2s. 6d. per	£2	15	0
1734. october 31. To 1 lb. of Green Tea at 11s. per lb.	0	11	0
December 21. To 1 lb. bohea tea at 11s.	0	11	0
	3	17	0
1733. December 18. To Seven yards of Dowlas at 2s. 6d. per Yrd.			
amounts £0 17s. 6d. But this is Credit it [sic] in my Book by			
Settling once You will find it in your Receipt book.[1]			
Do. by a note of hand Remains Ballance Due	1	11	2
	£5	8	2

If there be any Errors in this, you Can Search your books; and if you Cannot [settle?] with my Brothers, then it must be Referred untill I Come to Town me Self. I Donot think that you will Wrong me nor I you. You may Continue the Gazette in my name or in my Brothers name, you shall get paid for it. Further Remain With my Humble Respects to you and Famile, and Remain your affectioned old Friend and Servant   GEO: SCHOLTZE

N.B. Mr. Franklin have you heard any thing of Thomas Butwell.[2] If he is in Philada. Let me know of it. He Owes me near £19.0.0. He Did live in your House about 13 years ago. A Staymaker.

Addressed: To Mr. Benjamin Franklin. Printer and Post master in Philadelphia These

8. George Scholtze (1711–1779), first Schwenkfelder to come to America, 1731; merchant in Philadelphia. With his brother David he acquired 260 acres of land in Upper Hanover Township, Pa., 1736; he moved to Frederick Co., Md., before 1757. David Scholtze (1717–1797) was a surveyor, scrivener, "bush lawyer," and farmer in Upper Hanover Township. Samuel K. Brecht, ed., *The Genealogical Record of the Schwenkfelder Families* (Pennsburg, Pa., 1923), pp. 68, 88–9, 92–6.

George Scholtze is charged in BF's Ledger D with 3s. for a pocket compass, and BF has closed the account with the notation, "Settled with Mr. Scholtz and received of his Brother £2 6s. 1d. Ballance being in full to the 14th September 1745."

9. Strong, coarse linen cloth.

1. Opposite this entry, but probably applying to the entire account, is written in another hand: "This Account settled and paid. David Scholtze."

2. Thomas Butwell, "from England," rented a shop under BF's printing-office. He advertised his wares in *Pa. Gaz.*, July 17, 1732.

76

To William Strahan

ALS: American Philosophical Society; also duplicates: New York Public Library and Pierpont Morgan Library

Sir   Philada. May 22. 1746

This is only to enclose a third Bill, for £15.0.0 Sterling the first and second of which went from this Port directly and from Annapolis: And to desire you to send me two setts of Popple's Mapps of N. America one bound the other in Sheets,[3] they are for our Assembly; they also want the Statutes at large, but as I hear they are risen to an extravagant Price, I would have you send me word what they will cost before you send them.[4] Mr. Hall is well but has not time to write. We have heard nothing from you since yours of June 1745. I am Sir Your most humble Servant

                                                        B FRANKLIN

P.S.[5] I forgot to mention, that there must be some other large Map of the whole World, or of Asia, or Africa, or Europe, of equal Size with Popple's to match it; they being to be hung, one on each side the Door in the Assembly Room; if none can be had of equal Size, send some Prospects of principal Cities, or the like, to be pasted on the Sides, to make up the Bigness.

To William Vassall[6]   ALS: Harvard College Library

Sir   Philada. May 29. 1746

I have your Favour of the 19th Instant,[7] with some Queries relating to the Small Pox; in Answer to which I am to acquaint

---

3. Henry Popple, *A Map of the British Empire in America with the French and Spanish Settlements adjacent thereto*, London, 1733. The publication prices were: £1 11s. 6d. in sheets, £1 16s. 6d. bound, and £2 12s. 6d. on rollers, colored. Writing to Strahan, Oct. 19, 1748, BF acknowledged receipt of the maps the previous April.

4. Probably William Hawkins' edition of the *Statutes at Large*, which began publication in 1734.

5. The postscript is omitted in both duplicates of this letter.

6. William Vassall (1715–1800), son of a rich Jamaica planter who moved to Philadelphia about 1717 and then to Boston two years later; A.B., Harvard College, 1733. Living on income from his plantations and Maine lands, Vassall had no business or profession, held no significant public offices (he considered small, beginning posts unworthy), but engaged in spectacular lawsuits

you, That by the best Informations I have been able to procure, and which I believe are pretty near the Truth, between 150 and 160 Persons (mostly Children, the Small Pox having gone thro' this Place twice within these 15 Years) have been inoculated since the 10th of April last, when the Distemper began to spread here; of which Number one only died, a Child of two Years old, who expired the third Day after the Operation, no Signs of the Small Pox appearing, and therefore its Death is not ascribed to that Distemper, but to another Disorder it laboured under when inoculated; the Operation being perform'd at the earnest Request of the Father, contrary to the Judgment of the Physician. Of the Rest who recovered or are on the Recovery, none have had so much as one dangerous Symptom. And yet perhaps all this Success will not serve to establish an Opinion of Great Advantage in the Practice of Inoculation, when it is known that at this Season the Small Pox have been of so benign a kind, in the common Way of Infection, that only five Persons of all Ages have died out of 160 or 170 who have had the Distemper without Inoculation; of which 5, one was a weak rickety Child; another a young Maid labouring under a violent Disorder incident to the Sex; and of the other three, tho' I know not the Circumstances, yet since no Choice was made of Subjects, nor Preparation of Bodies generally used, we may suppose that sundry Accidents might possibly concur with the Distemper to carry them off. Especially if it be true as I have heard, that 171 Persons have this Spring had the Small Pox at Brunswick in the Jersies in the Common Way and all recovered, not one dying in the whole Town. Our Physicians however agree, that those who have taken the Infection in the Common Way here, have not generally had the Distemper so light as those that were inoculated. I could give you their Reasonings on the Subject, but as you principally require Facts, and Hypotheses however ingenious have a deal of Uncertainty in them, I forbear. The principal Advantages I see

which "helped to support all of the abler members of the Boston bar." He visited Jamaica, 1747–50. He presented a set of twelve framed anatomical drawings to Harvard, 1750. Generous, sybaritic, sometimes pungent in speech but often garrulous, he was never popular in Boston, where he consorted with Anglican newcomers. A Tory in the American Revolution, he spent the last 25 years of his life in England vainly trying to recover his lost property. *Sibley's Harvard Graduates*, IX, 349–59.

7. Not found.

in Inoculation, are, that it gives an Opportunity of laying hold of a favourable Season (as the present seems to be) to go thro' the Distemper; when otherwise a Person might not be taken down till it becomes generally more malignant, And that, the Time being fix'd for the Operation, you can prepare the Body by Temperance and a little Physic, where such Precautions may be of use. As to your going to New York to be inoculated, perhaps such a Journey is not quite necessary; since, as has been try'd here with Success, a dry Scab or two will communicate the Distemper by Inoculation, as well as fresh Matter taken from a Pustule and kept warm till apply'd to the Incision. And such might be sent you per Post from hence, cork'd up tight in a small Phial. You can hardly doubt of their taking Effect, since you seem to apprehend there might be Danger from my Letter, if it should have been near an infected Room. And I have somewhere read, that the Chinese actually preserve Scabs taken from a healthy Person for the Purpose, tho' their Manner of Inoculation is different from ours. The Esteem I contracted for you in the short Acquaintance we had in Boston,[8] will always render every Service in my Power to do you, a Pleasure, to, Sir, Your most humble Servant   B FRANKLIN

Please to favour me with a Character of Treatise of Morality propos'd to be publish'd in Boston by Aristocles.[9]

Addressed: To Wm. Vassal Esqr Boston Free B FRANKLIN

Endorsed: From Benj. Franklin Phila. May 29th. 1746

To William Vassall   ALS: Harvard College Library

Sir   Philada. June 19. 1746
I received your Favour of the 9th Inst. with the New System of Morality.[1] We have nothing lately publish'd here fit to send you in Return. A few Copies of the Enclos'd have been just

8. Probably on the occasion of BF's visit in the summer of 1743.

9. *Ethices Elementa. Or the First Principles of Moral Philosophy* (Boston, 1746), by Samuel Johnson of Stratford, Conn. Johnson had used this pseudonym the year before in *A Letter from Aristocles to Authades, concerning the Sovereignty and the Promises of God.*

1. Samuel Johnson's *Ethices Elementa* (Boston, 1746). Vassall's letter not found.

printed at New York, at the Expence of the Author, who is a Friend of mine.[2] His Intention in this small Impression, is, by distributing the Pieces among the few Learned and Ingenious in these Colonies, to obtain their Opinions, Censures, Corrections or Improvements, before he hazards a more general Publication. Five or Six Copies have been put into my Hands for this Purpose and I send one of them to you enclos'd. If you have Leisure and Inclination for these kind of Studies, please to read it with Attention, and favour the Author with your Remarks, through my Hands. I can assure you, he is a most candid and ingenuous Man, and will think himself more oblig'd to you for pointing out to him one Mistake, than to any one for 20 Encomiums. You may also communicate it to any of your Friends that you think likely in any Degree to answer the Author's Intention.

Since the Account I gave you of the Small Pox here, I have been well informed, that about 3 Weeks since, 260 Persons had had that Distemper at New Brunswick in the Common Way, and that one only of the Number had died, who was an ancient Woman, and a Drinker of Rum. It spreads more and more among us, and continues favourable. We have never known so dry a Season. The upland Grass is almost all lost; the Country parch'd up. This *dry Season* may be remembred with the *favourable Small Pox;* perhaps one may be in some Degree a Cause of the other. I am, Sir, Your obliged humble Servant   B Franklin

Addressed: To   Wm. Vassall Esqr   Boston   Free B Franklin

Endorsed: From Mr. Benjamin Franklin June 19th. 1746 June 19. 1746. From Mr. Benj Fra[nklin]

To Cadwallader Colden   ALS: New-York Historical Society

Sir   Philada. July 10. 1746
     I have your Favours of June 2d. and the 7th Instant. I thank you for your little Treatise.[3] I have interleav'd it, and am Reading

---

2. Cadwallader Colden's *Explication of the First Causes of Matter* (N.Y., 1745, but actually 1746). See above, II, 446.
     3. Colden's *Explication of the First Causes of Action in Matter.* His letters of July 2 and 7 have not been found.

it and Making Remarks as Time permits. I deliver'd one, as you directed, to Mr. Evans; another to Mr. Bertram. The former declares he cannot understand it; the latter told me the other Day, that he could not read it with the necessary Attention, till after Harvest, but he apprehended he should find it out of his Reach. I have not seen Mr. Logan since I sent him one. Two other Gentlemen to whom I gave each one, have not yet given me their Opinions; and in Truth I think you are somewhat too hasty in your Expectations from your Readers in this Affair. There are so many Things quite new in your Piece, and so different from our former Conceptions and Apprehensions, that I believe the closest and strongest Thinker we have amongst us, will require much longer Time than you seem willing to allow before he is so much a Master of your Scheme, as to be able to speak pertinently of it. Indeed those whose Judgment is of Value, are apt to be cautious of hazarding it: But for my Part, I shall, without Reserve, give you my Thoughts as they rose, knowing by Experience that you make large candid Allowances to your Friends. In a Post or two more I shall send them, with Mr. Logan's Sentiments, if he will give them me, as I intend to see him in a few Days. Dr. Mitchel (as you will see by the enclos'd, which please to return me) is gone to England. I have sent one of your Pieces to Mr. Rose.[4]

I wish our Governor would go to Albany, for I imagine the Indians have some Esteem for him. But he is very infirm of late; and perhaps your Governor has not invited him in such a Manner as to make him think his Company would be really acceptable.[5]

4. Robert Rose (1705–1751), rector of St. Anne's parish, Essex County, Va., 1727–48, and of St. Anne's parish, Albemarle (later Amherst) County, 1748–51; successful planter; friend of Governor Spotswood and executor of his estate. By descending the James River in a canoe with one or two friends in 1749, he determined its navigability from the present Amherst to Richmond; then, joining two canoes together, he showed his fellow planters how to float tobacco hogsheads from the back country down to market. His epitaph describes him as "a friend of the whole human race." William Meade, *Old Churches, Ministers and Families of Virginia* (Phila., 1857), I, 396–402; Thomas J. Wertenbaker, *The Old South: The Founding of American Civilization* (N.Y., 1942), pp. 121–3, 128–9; James Fontaine, *Memoirs of a Huguenot Family*, tr. Ann Maury (N.Y., 1853), pp. 388–9.

5. Governor George Clinton of New York and the governors of the New England colonies had urged Governor Thomas to appoint commissioners to meet with the Indians, but the Pennsylvania Assembly refused on the ground

Of this, however, I know nothing. If you go, I heartily wish you a safe and pleasant Journey, with Success in your Negociations. I am, with much Respect, Sir Your most humble Servant

B FRANKLIN

Addressed: To The Honble. Cadwallader Colden Esqr New York Free B FRANKLIN

To William Strahan

ALS (2): Western Reserve Historical Society and Pierpont Morgan Library; also duplicate: Yale University Library

Sir   Philada. Sept. 25. 1746
    Your Favours of Feb. 11. and May 1. are come to hand. Mesnard arrived safe this Morning, and I suppose I shall have the Trunks out in a Day or two. Our other Ships Lisle and Houston not yet come, but daily expected. I am much oblig'd to you for your ready Compliance with my Requests. I sent you in the Spring a Bill on Messrs. Hoare and Arnold for £15 which I hope came to hand, and will be as readily paid as that on George Rigge for £15.7.1. I now send you the following Bills, viz.

	Sterling
John Dening's for	3. 5.7
George Copper for	2. 8.0
J. Bordely's for	4. 3.3
Ra. Page's for	4.15.0
Sarah Gresham's for	4.10.0
Jno. Bond's for	13.17.9
	£32:19:7

I wish the Sum had been all in one Bill, as the Trouble to you would be less; but Bills have been scarce lately, and we were glad to get any. I think however to send you no more such small ones.

---

that the purpose of the conference was to get the Six Nations to engage in war. They did offer to pay the governor's expenses, under certain circumstances, if he should go to Albany himself, but bad health, which Richard Peters attributed to his drinking no wine, prevented his taking the trip. *Pa. Col. Recs.*, v, 43, 48–9; Paul A.W. Wallace, *Conrad Weiser* (Phila., 1945), p. 238.

I shall as you desire deliver one of Ainsworth's Dictionaries[6] to Mr. Read. You will please to take the Charge of it, off my Account in your Book, and add it to his.

Please to send me per next Vessel 6 Dozen of Dyche's Spelling Books, and as many of Owen's,[7] with a Dozen of Post-Horns of different Sizes. I shall speedily send you another Bill.

My Wife joins with me in Thanks to you and good Mrs. Strahan and young Master, for your great Kindness to our Daughter.[8] She shall make her Acknowlegements herself as soon as she is able.

I congratulate you on the Defeat of Jacobitism by your glorious Duke, and the Restoration of Peace and Good Order within the Kingdom.[9] We have just now an Account that a French Fleet of about 30 Sail were lately seen off Cape Sables; They are sup-pos'd to be from Brest.[1] I hope they are follow'd by a superior Force from England, otherwise a great Deal of Mischief may be done in North America.

I am sorry it so happen'd that Mr. Collinson had bespoke the Books. The next Catalogue sent to him will be accompanied with a Request that he should purchase them of you only.[2]

6. Robert Ainsworth, *Thesaurus linguae Latinae compendiarius; or, a compendious dictionary of the Latin tongue*, 2d edit., London, 1746.

7. The books ordered were probably Thomas Dyche, *A Spelling Dictionary* (3d edit., London, 1731), and John Owen, *The Youth's Instructor in the English Tongue; or a Spelling Book* (London, 1732).

8. Strahan's eldest son, William, then a boy of six. BF's daughter Sarah was three.

9. Charles Stuart's forces were decisively defeated at Culloden Moor, April 16. BF printed the first news of the "glorious Duke" of Cumberland's victory in a supplement to *Pa. Gaz.*, July 5. Fuller accounts appeared in the issue of July 10 and the supplement of July 12.

1. The Duke d'Anville, commanding a squadron of 11 ships of the line, 30 smaller vessels, and transports carrying land forces of 3130 men, sailed from Brest on June 22, to recapture Louisbourg and Cape Breton Island. Storm and sickness reduced the force; d'Anville died four days after the fleet reached Chebucto; an attack on Annapolis was frustrated when the ships were scattered in a storm; and the remnant of the fleet limped back to France. Thomas Hutchinson, *The History of Massachusetts Bay* (3d edit., Boston, 1795), II, 383–5.

2. BF had earlier suggested that Strahan might solicit the Library Company's business from Collinson. The Library's new catalogue was printed by BF in 1746.

83

Our Friends Messrs. Hall and Read continue well.[3] I am Sir
Your most obliged humble Servant   B FRANKLIN

To [Thomas Hopkinson?]

Copy: Library of Congress; also transcripts: Library of Congress and
American Philosophical Society

Vaughan (*Political, Miscellaneous, and Philosophical Pieces*, London,
1779, pp. 478–86) thought the addressee was Andrew Baxter; Duane
(*Memoirs, . . . with a Postliminious Preface*, Phila., 1834, II, 383–5)
thought it was Francis Hopkinson; Sparks (*Works*, VI, 87–93) and
Bigelow (*Works*, II, 211–18) believed it was Thomas Hopkinson;
Smyth (*Writings*, II, 317–22) named Cadwallader Colden. The present
editors believe that Thomas Hopkinson was the most likely original
addressee, although this copy, in Franklin's own hand, was sent to
Colden as an enclosure in his letter of October 16.[4]

Further confusion has arisen because none of the surviving manuscripts is dated. Duane dated the essay 1748; Sparks, Bigelow, and
Smyth, 1747; while Vaughan's footnote that the market referred to in
the final paragraph was Hungerford, near Craven Street, where Franklin
lived in London, in effect dated the paper after 1757 (when Baxter, to
whom he said it was addressed, was seven years dead). Franklin's
letter to Colden makes it clear that his "Remarks" on Baxter's book
were already written by October 16, 1746. Subsequently Franklin lost
his own draft and asked Colden, on July 30, 1747, to return the copy
sent him. In time Colden seems to have done so, since it survives
among Franklin's papers instead of his.[5]

[October 16, 1746]

According to my Promise I send you *in Writing* my Observations
on your Book.[6] You will be the better able to consider them;
which I desire you to do at your Leisure, and to set me right
where I am wrong.

3. Thus in the ALS in the Western Reserve Hist. Soc. and the duplicate in
Yale Univ. Lib.; the ALS in Pierpont Morgan Lib. reads: "Our Friends Hall
and Read are well, and desire to be remember'd to you. Mr. Hall will write
via New York."

4. See below, p. 89.

5. See below, pp. 166, 273.

6. Andrew Baxter, *Enquiry into the Nature of the Human Soul* (3d edit.,
London, 1745).

I stumble at [the] Threshold of the Building, and [therefore have not read farther.]⁷ The Author's *Vis Inertiae essential to Matter,* upon which the whole Work is founded, I have not been able to comprehend. And I do not think he demonstrates at all clearly (at least to me he does not) that there is really any such Property in Matter.

He says, No. 2. "Let a given Body or Mass of Matter be called A, and let any given Celerity be called C: That Celerity doubled, tripled, &c. or halved, thirded, &c. will be 2C, 3C &c. or ½C, ⅓C &c. respectively. Also the Body doubled, tripled or halved, thirded; will be 2A, 3A, or ½A, ⅓A, respectively." Thus far is clear. But he adds, "Now to move the Body A with the Celerity C, requires a certain Force to be impressed upon it; and to move it with a Celerity as 2C, requires twice that Force to be impressed upon it, &c." Here I suspect some Mistake creeps in occasioned by the Author's not distinguishing between a *great* Force apply'd *at once,* and a *small* one *continually* apply'd, to a Mass of Matter, in order to move it. I think 'tis generally allow'd by the Philosophers, and for aught we know is certainly true, That there is no Mass of Matter how great soever, but may be moved by any Force how small soever (taking Friction out of the Question) and this small Force continued will in Time bring the Mass to move with any Velocity whatsoever. Our Author himself seems to allow this towards the End of the same [No. 2] when he is subdividing his Celerities and Forces: For [as] in continuing the Division to Eternity by his Method of ½C, ⅓C, ¼C, ⅕C, &c. you can never come to a Fraction of Celerity that is equal to oC, or no Celerity at all; so dividing the Force in the same Manner, you can never come to a Fraction of [Force] that will not produce an equal Fraction of Celerity. [Where] then is the mighty *Vis Inertiae,* and what is its Strength when the greatest assignable Mass of Matter will give way to [or be moved by] the least assignable Force? Suppose two Globes each equal to the Sun and to one another, exactly equipoised in Jove's Ballance: Suppose no Friction in the Center of Motion in the Beam or elsewhere: If a Musketo then were to light on one of them, would he not give Motion to them both, causing one to descend and the other to

7. The MS is mutilated. Except where otherwise indicated, missing or illegible words have been supplied, in brackets, from Vaughan's edition of 1779.

rise? If 'tis objected, that the Force of Gravity helps one Globe to descend: I answer, The same Force opposes the other's Rising: Here is an Equality, that leaves the whole Motion to be produc'd by the Musketo, without whom those Globes would not be moved at all. What then does Vis Inertiae do in [this] Case? And what other Effect could we expect if there were no such Thing? Surely if it was any Thing more than a Phantom, there might be enough of it in such vast Bodies to annihilate, by its Opposition to Motion, so trifling a Force?

Our Author would have reason'd more clearly, I think, if, as he has us'd the Letter A for a certain Quantity of Matter, and C for a certain Degree[8] of Celerity, he had employ'd one Letter more, and put F (perhaps) for a certain Quantity of Force. This let us suppose to be done; and then, as it is a Maxim that the Force of Bodies in Motion is equal to the Quantity of Matter multiply'd by the Celerity, or $F = C \times A$; and as the Force received by and subsisting in Matter when it is put in Motion, can never exceed the Force given; so if F move A with C, there must needs be required (See No. 3) 2F to move A with 2C; for A moving with 2C would have a Force equal to 2F, which it could not receive from 1F; and this, not because there is such a Thing as Vis Inertiae, for the Case would be the same if that had no Existence; but, *because nothing can give more than it hath*. And now again, if a Thing can give what it hath; if 1F can to 1A give 1C, which is the same thing as giving it 1F; i.e. if Force apply'd to Matter at Rest, can put it in Motion, and give it *equal* Force; Where then is Vis Inertiae? If it existed at all in Matter, should we not find the Quantity of its Resistance subtracted from the Force given?

In No. 4. our Author goes on and says, "The Body A requires a certain Force to be impressed on it, to be moved with a Celerity as C, or such a Force is necessary; and therefore it makes a certain Resistance, &c. A Body as 2A, requires *twice* that Force to be moved with the same Celerity, or it makes *twice* that Resistance, and so on." This I think is not true, but that the Body 2A moved by the Force 1F, (tho' the Eye may judge otherwise of it) does really move with the same Celerity as 1A did when impell'd by

8. Vaughan edition reads: "quantity" for "degree."

the same Force: For 2A is compounded of 1A+1A; And if each of the 1A's or each Part of the Compound were made to move with 1C, (as they might be by 2F) then the whole would move with 2C, and not with 1C as our Author Supposes. But 1F apply'd to 2A makes each A move with ½C, and so the Whole moves with 1C, exactly the same as 1A was made to do by 1F before. What is *equal Celerity* but a Measuring of the same Space by moving Bodies in the same Time? Now if 1A impell'd by 1F measures 100 Yards in a Minute; and in 2A impell'd by 1F, each A measures 50 Yards in a Minute, which added make 100, are not the Celerities as well as the Forces equal? And since Force and Celerity in the same Quantity of Matter are always in *Proportion* to each other, why should we, when the Quantity of Matter is doubled, allow the Force to continue unimpair'd, and yet suppose one Half of the Celerity to be lost? I wonder the more at our Author's Mistake in this Point, since in the same No. I find him observing, "We may easily conceive that a Body as 3A, 4A, &c. would make 3 or 4 Bodies equal to once A, each of which would require once the first Force to be moved with the Celerity C." If then in 3A, each A require once the first Force F to be moved with the Celerity C, would not each move with the Force F, and Celerity C; [and consequently] the whole be 3A moving with 3F, and 3C? After so distinct an Observation, how could he miss of the Consequence, and imagine that 1C and 3C were the same? Thus as our Author's Abatement of Celerity in the Case of 2A moved by 1F, is imaginary, so must be his additional Resistance. And here again I am at a Loss to discover any Effect of the Vis Inertiae.

In No. 6 he tells us, "That all this is likewise certain when taken the contrary way, viz. from Motion to Rest; For the Body A moving with a certain Velocity as C requires a certain Degree of Force or Resistance to stop that Motion, &c. &c." That is, in other Words, equal Force is necessary to destroy Force. It may be so; but how does that discover a Vis Inertiae? Would not the Effect be the same if there were no such Thing? A Force 1F strikes a Body 1A, and moves it with the Celerity 1C, i.e. with the Force 1F. It requires, even according to our Author, only an opposing 1F to stop it. But ought it not, (if there were a Vis Inertiae) to have [not only the] Force 1F, but an additional Force equal to the Force of Vis Iner-

87

tiae, that *obstinate Power, by which a Body endeavours with all its Might to continue in its present State, whether of Motion or Rest?* I say, ought there not to be an opposing Force equal to the Sum of these? The Truth however is, that there is no Body how large soever, moving with any Velocity how great soever, but may be stopped by any opposing Force how small soever, continually apply'd. At least all our modern [Philosophers] agree to tell us so.

[Let] me turn the Thing in what Light I please, I cannot [discover] the Vis Inertiae nor any Effect of it. Tis allowed [by all] that a Body 1A, moving with a Velocity 1C, and [a Force 1]F, striking another Body 1A at Rest, they [will after]wards move on together, each with $\frac{1}{2}$C, and $\frac{1}{2}$F; which, as I said before, is equal in the Whole to 1C and 1F. If Vis Inertiae as in this Case neither abates the Force nor the Velocity of Bodies, What does it, or how does it discover itself?

I imagine I may venture to conclude my Observations on this Piece, almost in the Words of the Author, "That if the Doctrines of the Immateriality of the Soul, and the Existence of God, and of Divine Providence are demonstrable from *no plainer* Principles, the *Deist*[9] hath a desperate Cause in Hand." I oppose my *Theist* to his *Atheist*, because I think they are diametrically opposite and not near of kin, as Mr. Whitefield seems to suppose where (in his Journal) he tells us, *Mr. B. was a Deist, I had almost said an Atheist.* That is, *Chalk,* I had almost said *Charcoal.*

Shall I hazard a Thought to you [that?] for aught I know is new, viz. If God was before all Things, and fill'd all Space; then, when he form'd what we call Matter, he must have done it out of his own Thinking immaterial Substance. The same, tho' he had not fill'd all Space; if it be true that *Ex nihilo nihil fit.* From hence may we not draw this Conclusion, That if any Part of Matter does not at present act and think, 'tis not from an Incapacity in its Nature [but from] a positive Restraint. I know not yet [what other] Consequences may follow the admitting of [this position] and therefore I will not be oblig'd to defend [it. *Torn*] 'tis with some Reluctance that I either [*torn*] in the metaphysical Way. The great Uncertainty I have found in that Science; the wide Contradictions and endless Disputes it affords; and the horrible Errors I led my self into when

9. Vaughan edition adds: "[i.e. theist]."

a young Man, by drawing a Chain of plain Consequences as I thought them, from true Principles,[1] have given me a Disgust to what I was once extreamly fond of.[2]

The Din of the Market encreases upon me, and that, with frequent Interruptions, has, I find, made me say some things twice over, and I suppose forget some others I intended to say. It has, however, one good Effect, as it obliges me to come to the Relief of your Patience, with Your humble Servant   [B FRANKLIN]

Endorsed: Vis Inertia deny'd

To Cadwallader Colden   ALS: New-York Historical Society

Sir   Philada. Oct. 16. 1746

I have receiv'd your Favour of the 13th. Instant,[3] and am glad to hear you are return'd well from Albany, which I understand has been a very sickly Place this Fall. I did not imagine you would have been detain'd there so long, or I should have done my self the Pleasure of writing to you by my Son.[4] Our Interpreter Mr. Weiser is return'd.[5] He tells me that as soon as he came to Albany

---

1. Keyed to this word BF wrote in the margin of the MS, possibly when going over his papers in old age: "In my Pamphlet call'd a Dissertation on Liberty and Necessity, Pleasure and Pain, printed in London in 1725 when I [*remainder missing*]." The pamphlet is printed above, I, 57.

2. This paragraph is omitted in all printed versions of the letter, and in the transcripts as well, though William Temple Franklin's copyist (Lib. Cong. version) began the paragraph, stopped, and canceled what he had transcribed. The bracketed words without question marks have been supplied from James Bowdoin's letter to BF, Jan. 27, 1755, a critique of BF's remarks, which quotes most of the paragraph.

3. Not found.

4. William Franklin was commissioned an ensign in Capt. John Diemer's company, one of four companies of 100 men each, raised under authority of Governor Thomas' proclamation of June 9, 1746 (*Pa. Col. Recs.*, V, 39–41) for an expedition against Canada. The troops passed the winter of 1746–47 at Albany, where they suffered from lack of supplies (1 *Pa. Arch.*, I, 724). The expedition was called off, and the men were discharged Oct. 31, 1747.

5. Conrad Weiser (1696–1760), as "Province Interpreter," was a principal architect and agent of Pennsylvania's Indian policy after 1730. He went to the Albany meeting in September on his own responsibility. *DAB;* Paul A. W. Wallace, *Conrad Weiser* (Phila., 1945), p. 238.

he went to the Fort and waited on the Secretary,[6] that his being there might be made known to the Governor, in Case he should have any Commands for him; and that 2 Days after being told by Major Rutherfurd[7] that the Governor wonder'd he had not seen him, he immediately waited on his Excellency.

I am sorry I have so little to tell you relating to your Treatise, that may afford you any Satisfaction. Seven or eight of our Gentlemen, have, within my Knowledge, read more or less of it, viz. Mr. Hopkinson our Judge of the Admiralty; Mr. Taylor, Collector of the King's Customs; Mr. Francis our Attorney General, (who is a pretty close attentive Thinker) Mr. Coleman and Mr. Graydon, and Mr. Sober, Merchants and ingenious Men;[8] with some others. And all I can learn of their Sentiments concerning it is, that they say they cannot understand it, it is above their Comprehension. Mr. Logan, from whom I expected most, when I desired his Opinion, said just the same; only added, that the Doctrine of Gravity's being the Effect of Elasticity was originally Bernouilli's,[9] but he believ'd you had not seen Bernoulli. Mr. Norris,[1] his Son in law, lately one of our Commissioners at the Treaty of Albany, was present. He had been reading of it too, and said he was not able to make anything of it. Thus, tho' you should get no Praise among us, you are like to escape Censure, since our People do not seem to suppose that you write unintelligibly, but charge all to the Abstruseness of the Subject, and their own Want of Capacity.

6. John Catherwood was secretary to the province. He returned to England, 1748, appearing before the Board of Trade as agent of Governor George Clinton.

7. John Rutherfurd (1712–1758), commandant of the fort at Albany; M.P. for Roxburghshire, 1734–41; commissioned captain of an Independent Company of Foot in the British Army, 1741; killed in the unsuccessful attack on Fort Ticonderoga. His family and Colden's in Scotland were friends, and he maintained a correspondence and association with Colden in America, 1743–58, delighting that his duties at Albany allowed him to spend his time on "Mathematicks, Philosophy, Politicks, &c." *Colden Paps.*, III, 3; Livingston Rutherfurd, *Family Records and Events* (N.Y., 1894).

8. Thomas Hopkinson, Abraham Taylor, Tench Francis, William Coleman, Alexander Graydon, and John Sober.

9. Probably Jacques (James) Bernouilli (1654–1705), whose *Dissertatio de Gravitate Aetheris* (Amsterdam, 1683) was in Logan's library. Max Savelle, *Seeds of Liberty* (N.Y., 1948), pp. 97–8.

1. Isaac Norris (1701–1766), merchant, Speaker of the Assembly, leader of the Quaker party, one of Pennsylvania's commissioners at the Albany Conference of 1745.

For my own Part I have read no more than I send you enclos'd. What little Leisure I have is so broken and interrupted, and it requiring methinks a steady continued Consideration for some Time to become a Master of your Doctrine in all its Parts, I am almost ready to join with the rest, and give it up as beyond my reach. Yet I imagine, that if I had an Opportunity of reading it with you, and proposing to you my Difficulties for Explanation as they rise, I might possibly soon succeed. The Notes I have made were only for my own Consideration; they are Queries which I put down that I might remember to look out for Answers to them, which I suppos'd I might find as I read further. From the whole I intended to draw the Observations I should communicate to you, after due Consideration, and rejecting what was not to the purpose. But since I am not like to compleat the Reading soon, being embarras'd in much Business, and obliged to take a Journey to Boston in a Week or two, I send them as they are.[2] I have shown them to no one. If you would have me continue them, you will please after Perusal to return them. They will at least show you that I have been endeavouring to read and understand your Piece; and perhaps either your Approbation or Opposition of something I have said, may spirit me up to return to it with fresh Vigour.

Some of our Gentlemen to render themselves more capable of comprehending your Doctrine, have been mustering up and reading whatever else they could find on Subjects anyway akin to yours. Among other Pieces, they got a Book not long since publish'd, said to be wrote by an ingenious Man in Scotland, one Baxter, on the human Soul:[3] This was handed about and extoll'd as the plainest and clearest Thing that ever was wrote on such a dark Subject. At length it came to my Hands, and I was desir'd to read it. The Author lays down the Vis Inertiae of Matter as a Foundation on which all Philosophy and even Religion are to be built. In Company one Night, I express'd my Dissatisfaction with his Demonstrations, to the Surprize of some, who desir'd me to give my Reasons in Writing, that they might examine them at better Leisure. I did so the next Morning. And as I imagine they may give you some Amusement, I will send you the Book and my Remarks, if I can get them home time enough for the Post.

2. Not found.
3. Andrew Baxter, *Enquiry into the Nature of the Human Soul* (3d edit., London, 1745). See above, p. 84.

Mr. Bertram acquaints you with the Contents of a Letter he has just receiv'd from Gronovius. I congratulate you on the Immortality conferr'd on you by the learned Naturalists of Europe. No Species or Genus of Plants was ever lost, or ever will be while the World continues; and therefore your Name, now annext to one of them, will last forever.[4]

I see my Account of the Fireplaces translated into Dutch is printed at Leiden. Mr. Bertram has two of them come over.[5]

Dr. Mitchel was taken in his Passage home, and plunder'd of all his learned Observations. He got to London from France sometime in May last, bravely recover'd in his Health.

It will not be long after my Return from Boston before you will see the first Number of the Miscellany. I have now Materials by me for 5 or 6. The want of a good Engraver is a great Difficulty with me. The Mention of Engraving puts me in mind, that Mr. Evans told me you would permit me to take off some Copies from a Plate you have of the N American Coast. I shall be oblig'd to you for that favour.

When Capt. Honeyman[6] was here, I gave him at his Request, a Paper containing some Account of Experiments relating to wooden Cannon. Enclos'd is a Copy of it, which please to return with your Sentiments, when you have read it. I sent a Copy (without a Name) to Gov. Shirley.[7]

4. In honor of Colden Linnaeus had given the name *Coldenia procumbens* to an herb of the borage family growing in tropical India. For Gronovius' letter to Bartram, June 2, 1746, see Darlington, *Memorials*, pp. 354–7. Bartram informed Colden of this, Oct. 6, 1746, *Colden Paps.*, III, 270–1.

5. Colden sent a copy of BF's pamphlet on the Pennsylvania fireplace to Gronovius, probably in December 1744. It was, he explained, the invention of BF, a printer of Philadelphia, "a very Ingenious man," and had been shown to be efficient. *Colden Paps.*, III, 91. Gronovius had the pamphlet translated and printed at Leyden. He sent Bartram two copies, one to be forwarded to Colden, "who hath been so kind to communicate that book, in English, to me. That invention hath found a great applause in this part of the world. . . ." In the Dutch edition a slight alteration was made in the plates. Gronovius to Bartram, June 2, 1746, Darlington, *Memorials*, p. 355.

6. Capt. John Honeyman raised a company of volunteers to go on an expedition to Canada, 1746.

7. No paper on wooden cannon has been found among the papers of BF, Colden, or Shirley.

Having sufficiently tired your Patience, I will not add to the Trespass by an Apology, but conclude Your most humble Servant

B FRANKLIN

Addressed: To Cadwalader Colden Esqr

Receipt to Sarah Read

MS Receipt Book: American Philosophical Society

Among Franklin's papers in the American Philosophical Society is a receipt book of his mother-in-law, containing 27 receipts between 1715 and 1760, most of them between 1733 and 1747. Payments are recorded to William Rakestraw for carpentry, to Samuel Alford for making a silver spoon, to Anthony Nicholas "for Iron work Done too pump & Seller Dores of house," to Bridget Sullivan for beef and veal, to Simon Edgell, Samuel Coates and others for various kinds of goods. Richard Warder signed two receipts for rent paid by Mrs. Read, Christopher Thompson signed one. There are receipts from three different Receivers General for quitrents paid the Proprietaries "on half a lot in high Street."[8] The only one given by Franklin is printed below. Mrs. Read's signed receipt to her son-in-law on this settling of accounts is in his Ledger D.

Oct. 21. 1746

Settled all old Accounts with Mother Mrs. Sarah Read, and I am Dr. to Ballance, One Pound Seventeen Shillings and seven pence half penny; the Bond of Portues's[9] which I took up not reckon'd. Witness my hand   B FRANKLIN

£1. 17s. 7½d.

Settled as above written, and the Ballance with £20 Cash making in all the Sum of Twenty-one Pounds Seventeen Shillings and seven pence half penny receiv'd towards that Bond per me

B FRANKLIN

Mem[orandu]m. The Cash was paid to my Wife some time ago.

8. This is the property Mrs. Read's husband John purchased from Henry Hayes. See above, I, 362.

9. Probably the wealthy James Portues (d. 1737), member of the Carpenters' Company. *PMHB*, XXXII (1908), 178.

From James Smith[1] ALS: Drayton M. Smith, Philadelphia (1958)

Sir   Chester Town, Ocbr. 25th 1746
  Yours of the 17th mentioning my chance in the New York Lottery[2] for which I return you thanks And when you Shall get the money Please to Acquaint me. I may have Occation of Somthing in your way So that if you please to let the money lye with you tell then. I am with respects Sir Your Most humble Servant
                                                            JAM. SMITH
Addressed: To   Mr. Benjamin Franklin   Philadelphia

From Mary Lucas[3] ALS: Haverford College Library

Mr. Franklin   December the 2d 1746
  As my husbeand Robt. Lucas in his Life time Did take the Newes Papers, and now is Decesed I now think it no Longer Proper to have them, these are to Requst the faver of you to Stoop them, and Send Down what his Estate is indebted to you for them and I Shall Pay for them at the time oppointed by Law. From Sir your humble Servant   MARY LUCAS Executrix
Addressed: To   Mr. Benjamin Franklin, Post-   master in Philadelphia   this

Extracts from the Gazette, 1746

  Printed in *The Pennsylvania Gazette*, January 7 to December 30, 1746.

  [ADVERTISEMENT] All Persons indebted to the Printer hereof for a Year's Gazette, or more, are desired to make Payment.
                                                            [February 11]

1. James Smith, clerk of Kent Co., Md., for many years. He was one of the commissioners for building the Kent County court house, 1750; and his name heads a list of petitioners for authority to hold a market twice weekly at Chestertown, 1761. *Arch. of Md.,* VI, 30; XLVI, 458; LVIII, 579.
2. BF sold tickets for the New York Lottery. See below, p. 96.
3. Unidentified. BF's Ledger D records that Mary Lucas paid 20s., March 25, 1742, presumably for two years of the *Gazette*. Her husband may have been son of Robert Lucas, who came from England to Bucks County in 1679. *PMHB*, IX (1885), 228.

From Lancaster County, and the upper Parts of Philadelphia County, we have received several Accounts of the Mischiefs done by mad Dogs, among the black Cattle, Horses, Sheep, &c. many of which run mad, and die a few Days after they are bitten, as do also the wild Creatures, Wolves, Foxes, &c. some sorts of which that us'd to be very shy of Man, have run madly into the People's Houses and been kill'd there. To prevent the Spreading of this Evil, some whole Townships have kill'd all their Dogs. In our next we shall insert a Receipt, which is said to be an infallible Cure for the Bite of a mad Dog.[4]   [March 11]

Mr. John Bartram, Botanist, informs us, that he has had two fair Specimens of the English ash-colour'd Ground-Liverwort, sent him by Dr. Dillenius,[5] Chief Professor of Botany at Oxford; which appears to be exactly the same Species with ours in Pennsylvania, and the Places and Manner of their Growth near alike. It grows, he says, flat and spreading on the Ground, as broad as the Palm of one's Hand, in divided Lobes, in shady, poor, cold, clayey, or gravelly Ground; the upper Side is of an Ash Colour, the other is whitish, thick set with fibrous Roots by which it adheres close to the Ground. It is sufficiently plenty in many Parts of the Country.   [March 27]

The Northern Post begins his Weekly Stage this Day at Three o' Clock in the Afternoon, till next Winter, during which Time this Paper will be published on Thursdays.   [March 27]

[ADVERTISEMENT] Found this Morning, a Pair of Silver Knee-Buckles; the Owner by applying to the Printer, describing their Marks, and paying the Charge of this Advertisement, may have them again.   [March 27]

Notice is hereby given to the Constables of the several Wards in the City of Philadelphia, and to the Constables of all the Townships and Burroughs in the several Counties of the Province of Pennsylvania, That by a late Act of Assembly of the said Province, entitled, *An Act for the more effectual Suppressing profane Cursing*

4. Dr. Richard Mead's cure was printed March 27.
5. John James Dillenius (1687–1747), F.R.S., professor of botany at Oxford from 1728 until his death; author of *Historia Muscorum*, 1741. *DNB*.

and Swearing, they are enjoined and required, to affix a Copy of the said Act in the most publick Place in their respective Wards and Districts, under the Penalty of *Five Pounds*, to each Constable who shall neglect his Duty therein; which Copies are now printed on single Sheets as the Act directs, and ready to be delivered by the Printer of this Paper, to the several Constables, for the Purpose aforesaid, on their calling or sending for the same.[6]   [April 3]

[ADVERTISEMENT] To be LET, A Large Dwelling House on Society Hill, with a Kitchen, Wash House, Chaise House, Stable, and a Garden improved. Enquire of Robert Grace, Merchant, in Philadelphia, or the Printer hereof.   [April 24]

‡New-York Lottery Tickets, sold by B. Franklin. Price 30*s*. each.   [May 15]

The Revd. Mr. Whitefield arrived in Town on Saturday, and has preached every Day since in the New Building, to crouded Auditories.   [May 22]

Philadelphia, May 29. 1746.
To ALL Concerned. Whereas I, the Subscriber, employed B. Franklin to print £27.10.0 of Notes of Hand, viz. Twopenny, Threepenny, and Sixpenny Ones, out of meer Necessity for want of Pence for running Change, but made no more by him, nor any other Printer; whoever takes any of said Notes by me signed, shall have the same exchanged upon Demand with the best Money I have. Witness my Hand,   JOSEPH GRAY[7]
[May 29]

[ADVERTISEMENT] Lent from the Post-Office, Philadelphia, the second Volume of *Pamela;* the Person that has it, is desired to return it.   [June 26]

There are great Rejoicings in Town on account of the Defeat of the Rebels by the Duke of Cumberland.[8]   [July 10]

6. The bill became law March 7, 1746.
7. Unidentified.
8. The Pretender's army of Highlanders was defeated and routed in battle at Culloden Moor, April 16.

[ADVERTISEMENT] Those who have any Muskets or Guns of a good sizeable Bore, or Cutlasses, to dispose of, may hear of a Purchaser, by applying to the Printer hereof.   [July 24]

In Pursuance of the Governor's late Proclamation for that Purpose, Thursday last was observed here with a becoming Solemnity, as a Day of Publick Thanksgiving to Almighty God, for the Suppression of the Rebellion in Scotland, &c.⁹ Great Numbers of People attended at all the Places of Worship in the fore Part of the Day; and his Honour the Governor entertained near a hundred of the principal Gentlemen and Inhabitants of the City at Dinner; where our Happiness under the present Constitution, both in Church and State, and the great Obligations we have to the Family on the Throne, were properly and decently remember'd.   [July 31]

[ADVERTISEMENT] Lost, a Fortnight ago, in the Market Place, a Stone Sleeve Button, set in Gold. The Person that has found it, and will bring it to the Post-Office, Philadelphia, shall be sufficiently rewarded.   [July 31]

[ADVERTISEMENT] Henry Pratt¹ is removed from the Sign of the *Ship a-Ground* in Front-street, to the Royal Standard in Market Street, opposite the Butcher's Shambles; where he keeps TAVERN as formerly.   [August 14]

Saturday last the Rev. Mr. Whitefield arrived here from New-York: He preached twice on Sunday, and once every Day since, in the New-Building, to crowded Auditories.   [August 21]

Last Sunday Evening the Rev. Mr. Whitefield preach'd to a very large Auditory (among whom were many of the principal Persons of this City) a most excellent Sermon on Occasion of the late Victory over the Rebels; in which he set the Mischiefs of Popery and arbitrary Power, and the Happiness the Nation has enjoy'd under the present Royal Family, in the strongest Lights; and pathetically exhorted to Repentance and Amendment

9. The proclamation, dated July 14, is printed in *Pa. Col. Recs.*, V, 50.
1. On Henry Pratt, see I, 233.

of Life in Gratitude for that signal Deliverance.[2] No Discourse of his among us has given more general Satisfaction; nor has the Preacher ever met with a more universal Applause; having demonstrated himself to be as sound and zealous a Protestant, and as truly a loyal Subject, as he is a grand and masterly Orator.

[August 28]

On Thursday last the Reverend Mr. Whitefield left this City, after having preached here the greatest Part of the Summer to large Congregations, which the longer he staid increased the more. He never was so generally well esteemed by Persons of all Ranks among us; nor did he ever leave us attended with so many ardent Wishes for his happy Journey thro' Maryland and Virginia, and to Georgia, and a safe Return to this Place. We shall probably see him next Summer in his Way to Boston, unless he should embark in the Spring for Barbados, and the other West India Islands.

[September 25]

[ADVERTISEMENT] Just imported, and to be sold by B. Franklin, Bibles of various Sizes, from large Folio, down to the smallest Pocket Bibles; Testaments, Common Prayers, Confessions of Faith, large and small, Gray's Works, compleat, Vincent on Judgment, Dyer's Golden Chain, Life of Monsieur De Renty; Journals of the Siege of Cape-Breton, with a large Map of Louisburgh, &c. Salmon's Gazetteer, better than Echard's; Watts's Lyric Poems; Watts's Logic, with Supplement; Watts's Essays; Medical Essays of Edinburgh; Cocker's Arithmetick, &c. &c.

NAVIGATION Books. Quarto Waggoners for America; Mariner's Compass Rectified; Mariner's Calendar; Atkinson's Epitome, with Scales and Dividers.

LATIN SCHOOL BOOKS. Accidences; Lilly's Grammars; Ruddiman's Rudiments; Bayley's Exercises; Vocabularies; Parsing Books; Roberts's Cato; Wayett's Phedrus; Selectae è Profanis Historiae; Selectae è Veteri Testamenti Historiae; Clark's Grammars, Esop, Eutropius, Erasmus, Ovid, Nepos, Salust, Justin and Florus.

FRENCH SCHOOL BOOKS. Boyer's Grammar; Blair's Ditto;

---

2. Whitefield's sermon was *Britain's Mercies, and Britain's Duty*, and was printed by William Bradford. Evans 5883.

Boyer's Dictionary; Sterling's Cordery; French Testaments; Palaitet's Arts and Sciences, French and English; Cambray's Tales and Fables, Ditto; History of England, Ditto.

DUTCH SCHOOL BOOKS. Beiler's German Grammars; Ludwig's Dictionary, High Dutch and English.

With Psalters, Primmers, Paper, Sealing Wax, Ink-powder, and all Sorts of Stationary Ware.   [October 2]

Monday next will be published, and sold by B. FRANKLIN, The VOTES of the last Sessions of the ASSEMBLY of the Province of Pennsylvania. To which is added, The TREATY held with the INDIANS at Albany, in October, 1745. Price 3s. 6d.

N.B. Those who incline to take the Treaty without the Votes, may have it separate.   [October 2]

JUST PUBLISHED, AND SOLD BY B. Franklin, POOR RICHARD'S ALMANACK, For the Year 1747. Likewise The POCKET AL-MANACK, For the Year 1747.   [November 6]

Philadelphia, November 6. 1746.

Lent, but forgot to whom, Locke's essay on human understanding, and the two volumes of the Guardians. The persons that borrowed them, are desired to return them, to William Logan.

N.B. Locke's essay has my father J. Logan's name in the tital page.   [November 6]

Philadelphia, November 13. 1746.

Dropt about two weeks since, in Market-street, between the Market-house and Third-street, a dirty white linnen shirt, and a pair of thread stockings: The person that pick'd them up, is desir'd to send them to the Post-Office.   [November 13]

Philadelphia, November 20. 1746.

[ADVERTISEMENT] All Sorts of Deeds and Conveyances, carefully drawn, by Thomas Hopkinson, in Front-street. [November 27]

*⁎*The Northern Post begins his Fortnight's Stage at Two o'Clock this Afternoon; during which Time this Paper will be publish'd on Tuesdays.   [December 2]

Tuesday last died here THOMAS GRIFFITTS, Esq; Keeper of the Great Seal of this Province; he was for some Years one of the Judges of the Supream Court, and has been twice Mayor of this City.

He is succeeded in his Office as Keeper of the Great Seal by LYN-FORD LARDNER, Esq; the Proprietaries Receiver General.

[December 16]

PHILADELPHIA: Printed by B. FRANKLIN, Post-Master, at the New-Printing-Office, near the Market.

Poor Richard, 1747

Poor Richard, 1747. An Almanack For the Year of Christ 1747, ... By Richard Saunders, Philom. Philadelphia: Printed and sold by B. Franklin. (Yale University Library)

Courteous Reader,

This is the 15th Time I have entertain'd thee with my annual Productions; I hope to thy Profit as well as mine. For besides the astronomical Calculations, and other Things usually contain'd in Almanacks, which have their daily Use indeed while the Year continues, but then become of no Value, I have constantly interspers'd *moral* Sentences, *prudent* Maxims, and *wise* Sayings, many of them containing *much good Sense* in *very few* Words, and therefore apt to leave *strong* and *lasting* Impressions on the Memory of young Persons, whereby they may receive Benefit as long as they live, when both Almanack and Almanack-maker have been long thrown by and forgotten. If I now and then insert a Joke or two, that seem to have little in them, my Apology is, that such may have their Use, since perhaps for their Sake light airy Minds peruse the rest, and so are struck by somewhat of more Weight and Moment. The Verses on the Heads of the Months are also generally design'd to have the same Tendency. I need not tell thee that not many of them are of my own Making. If thou hast any Judgment in Poetry, thou wilt easily discern the Workman from the Bungler. I know as well as thee, that I am no *Poet born;* and it is a Trade I never learnt, nor indeed could learn. *If I make Verses, 'tis in Spight—Of Nature and my Stars, I write.* Why then should I give my Readers *bad Lines* of my own, when *good Ones*

of other People's are so plenty? 'Tis methinks a poor Excuse for
the bad Entertainment of Guests, that the Food we set before
them, tho' coarse and ordinary, is *of one's own Raising, off one's
own Plantation,* &c. when there is Plenty of what is ten times
better, to be had in the Market. On the contrary, I assure ye, my
Friends, that I have procur'd the best I could for ye, and *much
Good may't do ye.*

I cannot omit this Opportunity of making honourable Mention
of the late deceased Ornament and Head of our Profession, Mr.
JACOB TAYLOR,[3] who for upwards of 40 Years (with some few
Intermissions only) supply'd the good People of this and the
neighbouring Colonies, with the most compleat Ephemeris and
most accurate Calculations that have hitherto appear'd in America.
He was an ingenious Mathematician, as well as an expert and
skilful Astronomer; and moreover, no mean Philosopher, but
what is more than all, He was a PIOUS and an HONEST Man.
Requiescat in pace.

I am thy poor Friend, to serve thee,   R. SAUNDERS

XI Mon. January hath xxxi days.

To show the Strength, and Infamy of Pride,
By all 'tis follow'd, and by all deny'd.
What Numbers are there, which at once pursue
Praise, and the Glory to contemn it too?
To praise himself Vincenna knows a Shame,

3. Jacob Taylor (d. 1746), Quaker schoolmaster and poet, who compiled
an almanac each year from 1702 through 1746, and was a printer in Philadelphia about 1706–12. The author of "The Wits and Poets of Pennsylvania"
(*Amer. Weekly Mercury*, May 6, 1731) thus characterized his verses:

His fancy's bold, Harmonious are his Lays,
And were He more correct, He'd reach the Bays:

* * *

Yet such a Sweetness trills thro' all his Strains,
To have Our Ears so pleas'd, We could away with Brains.

The notice of his death in *Pa. Gaz.*, March 11, 1746, calls him "formerly
Surveyor-General of this Province, a very ingenious Astronomer and Mathematician." J. William Wallace, "Early Printing in Philadelphia," *PMHB*, IV
(1880), 441–2; Thomas, *Printing*, I, 224–7; see above, II, 135 n. Letters to
Taylor are printed in *PMHB*, III (1879), 114–5; XXI (1897), 130–1.

And therefore lays a Stratagem for Fame;
Makes his Approach in Modesty's Disguise,
To win Applause, and takes it by Surprize.

Strive to be the *greatest* Man in your Country, and you may be disappointed; Strive to be the *best,* and you may succeed: He may well win the race that runs by himself.

XII Mon. February hath xviii days.

See *Wealth* and *Pow'r!* Say, what can be more great?
Nothing—but *Merit* in a low Estate.
To Virtue's humblest Son let none prefer
Vice, tho' a Croesus or a Conqueror.
Shall Men, like Figures, pass for high, or base,
Slight, or important, only by their *Place?*
Titles are Marks of honest Men, and Wise;
The Fool, or Knave that wears a Title, lies.

'Tis a strange Forest that has no rotten Wood in't
And a strange Kindred that all are good in't.

None know the unfortunate, and the fortunate do not know themselves.

I Mon. March hath xxxi days.

Celestial PATIENCE! How dost thou defeat
The Foe's proud Menace, and elude his Hate?
While Passion takes his Part, betrays our Peace;
To Death and Torture swells each slight Disgrace;
By not opposing, Thou dost Ill destroy,
And wear thy conquer'd Sorrows into Joy.

There's a time to wink as well as to see.

Honest Tom! you may trust him with a house-full of untold Milstones.

There is no Man so bad, but he secretly respects the Good.

II Mon. April hath xxx days.

RELIGION's Force divine is best display'd,
In a Desertion of all human Aid:
To succour in Extreams is her Delight,
And cheer the Heart when Terror strikes the Sight.
We, disbelieving our own Senses, gaze,
And wonder what a Mortal's Heart can raise,
To smile in Anguish, triumph in his Grief,
And comfort those who come to bring Relief.

　　When there's more Malice shown than Matter:
　　On the Writer falls the satyr.

III Mon. May hath xxxi days.

Girls, mark my Words; and know, for Men of Sense
Your strongest Charms are native Innocence.
Shun all deceiving Arts; the Heart that's gain'd
By Craft alone, can ne'er be long retain'd.
Arts on the Mind, like Paint upon the Face,
Fright him, that's worth your Love, from your Embrace.
In simple Manners all the Secret lies.
Be kind and virtuous, you'll be blest and wise.

Courage would fight, but Discretion won't let him.

Delicate Dick! whisper'd the Proclamation.

Cornelius ought to be Tacitus.

IV Mon. June hath xxx days.

O, form'd Heav'n's Dictates nobly to rehearse,
PREACHER DIVINE! accept the grateful Verse.
Thou hast the Power, the harden'd Heart to warm,
To grieve, to raise, to terrify, to charm;
To fix the Soul on God, to teach the Mind
To know the Dignity of Human Kind;
By stricter Rules well-govern'd Life to scan,
And practise o'er the Angel in the Man.

Pride and the *Gout,*
Are seldom cur'd throughout.

We are not so sensible of the greatest Health as of the least Sickness.

A good Example is the best sermon.

V Mon. July hath xxxi days.

Men drop so fast, ere Life's mid Stage we tread,
Few know so many Friends *alive* as *dead;*
Yet, as *immortal,* in our uphill Chace,
We press coy Fortune with unslacken'd Pace;
Our ardent Labours for the Toy we seek,
Join Night to Day, and Sunday to the Week,
Our very Joys are anxious, and expire
Between *Satiety* and fierce *Desire.*

A Father's a Treasure; a Brother's a Comfort; a Friend is both.

Despair ruins some, Presumption many.

A quiet Conscience sleeps in Thunder,
But Rest and Guilt live far asunder.

VI Mon. August hath xxxi days.

A *decent Competence* we fully taste;
It strikes our *Sense,* and gives a constant Feast:
More, we perceive by Dint of *Thought* alone;
The Rich must *labour* to possess *their own,*
To feel their great Abundance; and request
Their humble Friends to *help* them to be blest;
To *see* their Treasures, *hear* their Glory told,
And *aid* the wretched Impotence of Gold.

He that won't be counsell'd, can't be help'd.

Craft must be at charge for clothes, but *Truth* can go naked.

Write Injuries in Dust, Benefits in Marble.

VII Mon. September hath xxx days.

> But some, great Souls, and touch'd with Warmth divine,
> Give *Gold* a *Price,* and teach its *Beams* to *shine;*
> All *hoarded* Treasures they repute a Load,
> Nor think their Wealth *their own* till well bestow'd.
> Grand *Reservoirs* of public Happiness,
> Thro' *secret* Streams diffusively they bless;
> And while their Bounties glide conceal'd from View,
> *Relieve* our *Wants,* and *spare* our *Blushes* too.

What is Serving God? 'Tis doing Good to Man.

What maintains one Vice would bring up two Children.

Many have been ruin'd by buying good pennyworths.

VIII Mon. October hath xxxi days.

> One to destroy, is Murder by the Law,
> And Gibbets keep the lifted Hand in Awe.
> To murder Thousands, takes a specious Name,
> *War's glorious Art,* and gives immortal Fame.
> O great Alliance! O divine Renown!
> With Death and Pestilence to share the Crown!
> When Men extol a wild Destroyer's Name,
> Earth's Builder and Preserver they blaspheme.

Better is a little with content than much with contention.

> A Slip of the Foot you may soon recover:
> But a Slip of the Tongue you may never get over.

What signifies your Patience, if you can't find it when you want it.

d. wise, *£* foolish.

IX Mon. November hath xxx days.

> I envy none their Pageantry and Show;
> I envy none the Gilding of their Woe.

Give me, indulgent Heav'n, with Mind serene,
And guiltless Heart, to range the Sylvan Scene.
No splendid Poverty, no smiling Care,
No well bred Hate, or servile Grandeur there.
There pleasing Objects useful Thoughts suggest,
The Sense is ravish'd, and the Soul is blest,
On every Thorn delightful Wisdom grows,
In every Rill a sweet Instruction flows.

Time enough, always proves *little enough*.

It is wise not to seek a Secret, and Honest not to reveal it.

A Mob's a Monster: Heads enough, but no Brains.

The Devil sweetens Poison with Honey.

X Mon. December hath xxxi days.

Old Age *will* come, Disease may come before,
Fifteen is full as mortal as *Threescore*.
Thy Fortune and thy Charms may soon decay;
But grant these *Fugitives* prolong their Stay;
Their Basis totters, their Foundation shakes,
Life that supports them, in a Moment breaks.
Then, *wrought* into the Soul, let Virtue shine,
The *Ground* eternal, as the *Work* divine.

He that cannot bear with other People's Passions, cannot govern
his own.

He that by the Plow would thrive,
Himself must either hold or drive.

COURTS.

From Earth to Heav'n when *Justice* fled,
The Laws decided in her Stead;
From Heav'n to Earth should she return,
Lawyers might beg, and Lawbooks burn.

To William Strahan

Duplicate: Yale University Library

Philada, Jan. 1. 1746, 7.

This is only to enclose a Bill of Exchange for £25 Sterling, and to wish you and good Mrs. Strahan, with your Children &c. many happy new Years. Mr. Hall continues well. We shall both write largely per Seymour. This via New York. I am, &c. B FRANKLIN

To William Strahan

ALS: Mrs. Thomas S. Gates, Philadelphia (1957); also duplicate: Yale University Library

Sir,   Philada. Jany. 4. 1746[,7]

I wrote a Line to you some days since, via New York, enclosing a Bill of £25 Sterling; the second in a Copy by some other Vessel from that Port; the third you have herein, together with a Bill of £60 Sterling, which I hope will be duly honour'd. My Wife wrote to you per Mesnard for 6 Nelson's Justice, 6 Dyche's Dictionary, 12 Cole's English ditto, 6 Female Fables, 6 Croxall's Ditto, and Mrs. Rowes Works compleat.[4] If not sent before, please to add them to the within Invoice, and send the whole per first Ship; add also Lemery on Foods, and Dr. Moffet on Health.[5] Please to deliver the enclos'd Procuration to Mr. Acworth[6] with the Bill. The Books you sent per Mesnard turn'd out all right and in good Order, except that the Prayer Books had all wrong Psalms the old Version: I do not know if they will ever sell. The

4. Deborah Franklin's letter has not been found. The books she ordered were probably: William Nelson, *The Office and Authority of a Justice of the Peace* (London, 1718); Thomas Dyche, *A New General English Dictionary* (3d edit., London, 1740); Elisha Coles, *An English Dictionary ... Now Corrected and Much Improved* (London, 1732); Edward Moore and Henry Brooke, *Fables for the Female Sex* (London, 1744; 2d edit., 1746); Samuel Croxall, *Fables of Aesop and Others* (London, 1722 and later edits.); Mrs. Elizabeth Rowe, *Miscellaneous Works in Prose and Verse* (London, 1739).

5. Louis Lémery, *A Treatise of All Sorts of Foods, Both Animal and Vegetable* (London, 1745); and Thomas Moffett (or Moufet), *Health's Improvement* (London, 1745).

6. Possibly a son or other heir of John Acworth, "formerly an eminent Wine Merchant in the City of London," who died in Philadelphia, Dec. 13, 1744. *Pa. Gaz.*, Dec. 18, 1744.

Paper should not have been cut at the Edges, being to be bound in Accompt Books. Our Friends Hall and Read continue well. My Wife joins me in best Respects to Mrs. Strahan and your self: She will write per Seymour, as will Mr. Hall. The Life of Du Renty,[7] charg'd at 6s. per Doz. has *Price stitch'd Four pence* under the Title Page. Is there not some Mistake in the Charge? I am, Sir, Your obliged humble Servant   B FRANKLIN

Your Government sent no Fleet to protect us from the French under D'Anville. But they have been defeated by the Hand of God.[8]

Addressed: To   Mr Wm Strahan   Printer in Wine Office   Court. Fleetstreet   London   per Capt. White

To Thomas Darling[9]   ALS: Yale University Library

Sir   Philada. Jan. 27. 1746/7

I receiv'd yours of the 26th past,[1] which I shall endeavour to answer fully per next Post. In the mean time please to tender my best Respects and Service to good Mr. and Madam Noyes,[2] and the most agreable Ladies their Daughters, with Thanks for

7. *An Extract of the Life of Monsieur de Renty, a Late Nobleman of France* [Abridged and translated from the French of J. B. de Saint Jure] (London, W. Strahan, 1741).

8. See above, p. 83 n.

9. Thomas Darling (1720–1789), A.B., Yale, 1740; licensed to preach, 1743; tutor in Yale College, 1743–45, where Ezra Stiles was one of his students. After his marriage, 1745, to Abigail, daughter of Rev. Joseph Noyes, he entered business and was for a time a partner of Nathan Whiting. He was subsequently a justice of the peace, county court judge, and delegate to the General Assembly. He was quietly Loyalist during the Revolution. Dexter, *Biog. Sketches*, I, 642–3.

1. Not found.

2. Rev. Joseph Noyes (1688–1761), A.B., Yale, 1709; tutor in the College, 1710–15; ordained minister of Center Church, New Haven, 1716; was instrumental in bringing Yale to New Haven. During the Great Awakening a part of his congregation grew dissatisfied with his theology and dull preaching and formed a separate church; the Yale students were withdrawn for their own services, 1753; and this student congregation became a church in the College, 1757. Dexter, *Biog. Sketches*, I, 85–9. BF visited Noyes on his return from Boston, December 1746. Darlington, *Memorials*, p. 333.

the Civility they were pleased to shew me when at Newhaven. We have printed nothing new here lately, except the Enclos'd Pamphlet,[3] which I send, in hope it may afford the Ladies and yourself some Amusement these long cold Winter Evenings. I am, Sir, Your most humble Servant   B FRANKLIN

Endorsed: I Received this Letter Feb 12 1746/7[4]

To Thomas Darling

ALS: Miss S. Berenice Baldwin, Woodbridge, Conn. (1959)

Sir   Philada. Feby. 10. 1746/7
    I wrote a Line to you per last Post, which I hope came to hand. The Ingredients of Common Window and Bottle Glass are only Sand and Ashes.[5] The Proportions of each I do not exactly know. The Heat must be very great. Our Glasshouse consumes Twenty-four Hundred Cords of Wood per Annum tho' it works but Seven Months in the Year. (But the Wood is only of 3 Foot Length, which lessens the Quantity One Fourth.) It is split small and dried well in a Kiln before 'tis thrown into the Furnace. The Cutting, Hauling, Splitting and Drying of this Wood, employs a great many Hands, and is the principal Charge; for this Consumption of Wood in Making the necessary Heat furnishes at the same Time great Part of the Ashes that are wanted: An Advantage

3. Perhaps *Reflections on Courtship and Marriage*, which BF printed in April 1746. See above, p. 74.
4. On the back of this letter Darling made notes for questions he submitted to BF in February. They are printed below, pp. 112–13.
5. Darling was interested in starting a glass factory in Connecticut, and secured from the next Assembly, May 1747, the exclusive right to make glass in the colony for twenty years, the privilege to be revoked if, after an initial period of four years for establishing the works, he failed to make 500 feet of good window pane in any of the remaining sixteen years of the monopoly. He did not exercise his privilege. Charles H. Hoadly, ed., *The Public Records of the Colony of Connecticut*, IX (Hartford, 1876), 281–2; George S. and Helen McKearin, *American Glass* (N.Y., 1941), p. 584. Probably Darling had discussed his plan with BF during the latter's visit to New Haven in December 1746, and BF had promised to send back information about Caspar Wistar's glasshouse in Salem Co., N. J., after he should reach home. For further correspondence on this subject, see below, pp. 112–13, 114–15.

they have not in England, where they burn Sea Coal, the Ashes of which will make no Glass, nor even Soap.

The House and Furnace may cost about a Thousand Pounds of your Money. The Tools a Trifle, being only a few Iron Rods made hollow, with wooden Handles, Sheers &c. The Pots which contain the melted Glass Metal, are made of a particular Clay, which will stand a violent Fire. At first 'twas brought from England; 'tis now found here. They may be large enough to contain about 100 lb. of Metal.

There are no Workmen to be had here. But as several Glasshouses about London have blown out, since the discouraging Act which lays so heavy a Duty on Glass, possibly Hands may be easily procured from thence.

It will be adviseable, if you go on with this Affair, to procure a Tract of Land well wooded. 1500 or 1000 Acres may do, seated on or near some navigable Water. By dividing your Land, and cutting suppose a Thirtieth Part of your Wood yearly, suffering it to grow again, you may always be supply'd. And by Means of the navigable Water, carry your Glass to Market cheaper and with less Risque of Breakage.

It will not suit me to be concern'd at such a Distance. I heartily wish you Success, and if you need any further Information that I can procure for you, please to command me. My Wife joins with me in presenting our Service to good Mr. and Madam Noyes, to your good Spouse and amiable Sister. I hope little Miss continues well, and am, Sir, Your very humble Servant   B FRANKLIN

Addressed: To   Mr Thomas Darling   in   Newhaven   Free   B FRANKLIN

Endorsed: B Franklens Letter 10 feby 46/7

From James Logan   Transcript: Harvard College Library (Sparks)

My friend B. Franklin,   Stenton February 23. 1747

Yesterday was the first time that I ever heard one syllable of thy Electrical Experiments, when John Bartram surpriz'd me with the account of a Ball turning many hours about an Electrified Body, with some other particulars that were sufficiently amazing. I have now by me Fr: Hawkesbee's Experiments printed in 1709[6] and saw his whole Apparatus in 1710 amongst which he had a Globe with thrums in it, which being whirled round with a wheel excited fire &c. I have also seen St: Grey's[7] account of his discovering what he did by his fixing on a ball of Wax, which is the last I think he ever gave that Society in or about the year 1738, when he died. Therefore only to the English that most remarkable Discovery as well as that equally surprizing one of the Magnetism by Dr. Gowen Knight[8] is due, and the further Improvements whether by the Germans, Low Dutch or French (of whose Experiments by one called Buffon[9] Peter Collinson sent me this last Summer a printed piece). But your own Experiments in my judgment exceed them all. I could therefore wish as soon as it can suit thee that thou wouldst step up hither bringing an Account with thee, (as well as of?)[1] of your last addition to your Library[2] both which especially the first will very much oblige thy assured friend   J. LOGAN

6. Francis Hauksbee (d. 1713?), an early experimenter in electricity, who described an electrical discharge as appearing *"like Flashes of Lightning,"* but without appreciating the identity. He invented an electrical machine consisting of "a pretty large glass cylinder, turned by a winch and rubbed by hand"; and wrote *Physico-Mechanical Experiments* (London, 1709; 2d edit., 1719). *DNB;* Cohen, *BF's Experiments,* pp. 32–6. Not to be confused with the chemist and mechanician of the same name (1687–1763).

7. Stephen Gray (d. 1736), F. R. S., whose papers in *Phil. Trans.* attracted wide attention and stimulated theoretical speculation. He provided the concept of static electricity. *DNB;* Cohen, *BF's Experiments,* pp. 37–41. The experiment with the cake of rosin was dictated by Gray the day before he died, and was published in *Phil. Trans.,* XXXIX (1738), 400–3.

8. Gowin Knight (1713–1772), F. R. S., studied the effects of lightning on the ship's compass; received the Royal Society's Copley Medal, 1747. He made a special study of magnetism, manufactured artificial magnets, and made improvements in the compass which the Admiralty adopted. He was appointed first Principal Librarian of the British Museum, 1756. *DNB.* Knight's account of this experiment is in *Phil. Trans.,* XLIII (1745), 161–6.

9. Georges-Louis Le Clerc, Comte de Buffon (1707–1788), naturalist. He informed Turbervill Needham of French experiments in electricity, especially Monnier's, 1746; Needham reported them to the Royal Society, Oct. 23, 1746. *Phil. Trans.,* XLIV (1748), 247–63. Buffon suggested to Dalibard, 1751, that BF's electrical experiments be translated into French.

1. Apparently inserted by Sparks's copyist.

2. The Library Company's *Catalogue.* See below, p. 113 n.

It would be no small addition to the favour if thou couldst conveniently bring with thee some of the Apparatus as the Glass Tube.

From Thomas Darling MS notes for a letter:[3] Yale University Library

[February? 1747]

1. How many men imployed in the whole?
2. How many men imediately about the Glass blowing?
3. How maney feet of Glass Do they make a Day?
4. How Do they Sell it per foot in their Philedalphia?
5. What are the Stone they make their furnace of and
6. Where Do they Git them?
7. Where are the pots made that Contain the metal?
8. Who makes them?
9. Can they be bought amonst you and what a peace?
10. How Large the furnace and where Does it Stand?
11. How Do you think workmen are to be hired i.e. glass mongers: are they to be had by the Day and how much their money per Day: if they be or are they to be hiered in as partners?
12. [How] Maney pots Shall I need per Annum [and] how Long will they Last?
13. How maney men Shall I Have Need to Send for to England?
14. How Soon may the furnice be got a going?
15. What Do you think their furnice Clears per annum?
16. Where Does their furnice Stand? in what town? how far from Philedalphia?
17. Whether there be any thing Special to Seperate the Glass from the Sedements?
18. Why Dont the Iron Grates between the first and Second Chambers melt when the fire is So Extream? Cramer upon Metals.[4]

3. These notes for a reply to BF's letter of Jan. 27, 1747, appear on the back of it, above, pp. 108–9. The questions concern glass making in New Jersey, and were answered by BF, March 27, 1747, below, pp. 114–15. The interrogation points have been supplied.
4. John Andrew Cramer, *Elements of the Art of Assaying Metals* (London, 1741).

19. What the Reason workmen may not be had with you?
20. When will their Furnace begin to work this Spring: because &c.
21. What is the Contrivance of their Kiln?
22. Do they in England Use potashes in m[aking] Glass?
23. What part of Sand and ashes is Converted into Glass?

From James Logan   Transcript: Harvard College Library (Sparks)

My friend B. Franklin,   Stenton March 6. 1747
I utterly forgot to send thee the N York Paper by my Son who was here this Morning but I now do it with my hearty thanks. I ordered him further to see thee to day and to beg thy Excuse for my desiring thee to send me a List of your Addition of Books to your Library which I did not the least apprehend would be sufficient to fill so much as one Quarter of a sheet of common paper, and indeed I am surpriz'd to hear the number is so considerable since the year 1742 as to require the Press.[5] But for my justification thou may'st remember I had from thee about two years since (I think it was) a written List from thy own hand of the last Addition before. But I own I am grown very forgetful notwithstanding Cicero's expression (de Senectute) Omnia quae curant senes meminerint.[6] Tho I shall scarce forget that I am thy obliged friend   J. LOGAN

From William Dames[7]

ALS (fragment): American Philosophical Society

[Missing] 16th: March 1746/7
[Missing] letters frequently are sent down by the westren [missing] post to Annapolis, which occasions a [missing] delay, Ex-

5. Books added to the Library since the Year 1741, a 28-page supplement to The Charter of the Library Company, which BF printed, 1746.
6. Cicero, De Senectute, vii. Logan inserted "senes" and changed the tense of the verb. His own translation (in Cato Major, p. 43) reads: "The Oldest will remember what engages their Thoughts and Care."
7. William Dames lived at Chestertown, Kent Co., across the Chesapeake Bay from Annapolis. In 1749 he is listed as owning also a lot in Kingston, a

pence, and trouble, Shall be obliged [*missing*] if you give your Young Man directions [*missing*] all my Letters for our New town, or [Chester?]town post, to be by him forwarded me. [*Missing*] Can in any shape serve you here [*missing*] freely Command Sir Your Obedient Servant   WM. DAMES

[My ser]vice to your good spouse.

Addressed: To   Mr: Ben: Franklin   at the post Office   Philadelphia

To Thomas Darling   ALS: Noël J. Cortés, Philadelphia (1954)

Sir   *Philada. March 27. 1747*
    There are, I am informed, Six Hands employed in blowing Glass;[8] at first there were but two, who instructed the Rest. The two first Workmen were taken in as Partners by the Person who found Stock, and set up the Business, the others are Servants, therefore there are no Workmen to be engag'd here for you. They work seven Months in the Year, and 'tis said make 20 Pounds worth of Glass per Diem. The Furnace is made of Bricks of white Clay, and renew'd every Blast. The old Bricks are Pounded fine and mix'd with fresh Clay to make the new. The Pots are made of Clay found here; they are made by the Workmen, and often fail. Cotton Stone[9] might possibly be of Service. The Furnace is about 12 foot long, 8 wide, 6 high, has no Grate, the Fire being made on its Floor. Cramer's is a Furnace for Ex-

---

new town laid out on the Queen Anne's side of the Chester River, where he was warden and vestryman of St. Paul's parish, and for whose new church he furnished the brick, 1767–71. He owned several ships, one of which, he said, in advertising it for charter to England, could carry 200 hogsheads of tobacco. Frederic Emory, *Queen Anne's County, Maryland* (Baltimore, 1950), pp. 120, 167, 169, 321; *Md. Hist. Mag.*, XXVI (1931), 254, 256–7, 261; *Md. Gaẓ.*, Jan. 13, 1748.
    8. This letter is a reply to Darling's questions about glass making, above, p. 112. It describes Caspar Wistar's glasshouse in Salem Co., N. J. Wistar (1696–1752) came from Germany, 1717; an enterprising businessman, he built the first successful cooperative factory in America at Wistarburg. *DNB;* George S. and Helen McKearin, *American Glass* (N. Y., 1941), pp. 37–41.
    9. Cotton stone: asbestos.

periments only, therefore small.[1] Its Grate melts not because of the fierce Draught of cold Air continually passing between the Bars. On each Side in the Furnace is a Bench or Bank of the same Materials with the Furnace, on which the Pots of Metal stand, 3 or 4 of a Side. I think the likeliest Way to get good Workmen from England, would be to invite them into Partnership. I suppose the Works might be compleated ready to go on, in a few Months. In England they get Salt by burning Kelp and Fern; they also buy foreign Potash. Our Works are now going, and as you propose to visit them this Spring, you will then have such an Opportunity of Satisfying your self in every Thing you want to know, as makes a more particular Answer to your Queries at this Time unnecessary. The Glasshouse is about 35 Miles beyond this City. I shall be glad to see you here, and am, with Respects to good Mr. Noyes[2] and Family, Sir, Your humble Servant

B FRANKLIN

Please to give the enclos'd with my humble Service, to Mr. President Clap.[3]

Addressed: To Mr Thomas Darling at the Revd Mr Noyes's in Newhaven Free B FRANKLIN

Endorsed: This Letter Received Apr 4[?] per Thos Darling
B: Franklen Letter
From Benj B Franklin To Thomas Darling

To Peter Collinson[4]

MS not found; reprinted from extract in Benjamin Franklin, *Experiments and Observations on Electricity* (London, 1769), pp. 1–2.[5]

This is the earliest surviving letter in which Franklin alludes to his electrical investigations. It introduced the fourth edition of his *Ex-*

1. Plate VI in Cramer's book (above, p. 112 n.) on assaying metals answers BF's description of this furnace.
2. On Noyes, see above, p. 108 n.
3. Rev. Thomas Clap, president of Yale College.
4. Peter Collinson (1694–1768) was one of the most important persons in BF's life. His name has appeared before in this work, and will appear many more times. The success of the Library Company, BF testified, was "greatly owing to his kind Countenance and good Advice," and BF's inquiry into

periments and Observations in 1769. That edition, its predecessors and its successor, will be discussed below, under their respective dates of publication. This note is concerned rather with the several manuscript and printed versions of Franklin's reports of his electrical experiments.[6]

Franklin's practice was to keep drafts of his letters to Collinson, from which he made other copies for friends in America. Cadwallader Colden, for example, received several such copies.[7] In the late summer of 1750 Franklin had Lewis Evans copy all his reports on electricity for young James Bowdoin of Massachusetts, who had shown keen

---

electricity was "encouraged by the friendly Reception he gave to the Letters I wrote to him upon it." BF to Michael Collinson, Feb. 8, 1770. In 1757 BF spent his first night in London at Collinson's house.

Born in London of Quaker parents, he entered his father's mercery business, which he and his brother expanded, especially by developing trade with America. He had early been interested in natural history; he helped increase the collections of Sir Hans Sloane (see above, I, 54 n), was encouraged in his studies by the Earl of Bute, and corresponded with Linnaeus. In his garden and greenhouses at Mill Hill, near London, he introduced more than 50 new American plants, and demonstrated the principles and pleasures of horticulture to his countrymen. He warmly encouraged John Bartram, bringing him as customers for American seeds, plants, and shrubs many owners of estates, including Lord Petre, and the Dukes of Norfolk, Bedford, Richmond, and Argyll. In turn, he urged his American correspondents to cultivate flax, hemp, silk, and grapes. Some 45 articles of Collinson's on natural history appear in *Gent. Mag.*, and eleven in *Phil. Trans.*, one (LI, 459–64) disproving the widely-held notion that swallows hibernate in the mud of streams and ponds. He was elected to the Royal Society, 1728.

His letters to Bartram are printed in Darlington, *Memorials*, and another group has been edited by Earl G. Swem as "Brothers of the Spade: Correspondence of Peter Collinson of London and John Custis of Williamsburg, 1734–1746," Amer. Antiq. Soc. *Proc.*, LVIII (1948), 17–190. See also Norman G. Brett-James, *The Life of Peter Collinson, F.R.S., F.S.A.* (London, 1926); *DNB.* His penmanship was loose and careless, and his capitalization and punctuation are the despair of the transcriber who must divine what he produced and meant.

5. Letter I in the 1769 and 1774 editions of *Exper. and Obser.*

6. The principal study of BF's electrical work is I. Bernard Cohen, *Benjamin Franklin's Experiments* (Cambridge, Mass., 1941). In this work the experiments, which are reprinted from the 1774 edition, are preceded by a long historical introduction, describing the scientific background of BF's contribution. His *Franklin and Newton* (Phila., 1956) covers some of the same material in a full, definitive evaluation of BF's place in eighteenth-century experimental science.

7. See below, pp. 169, 482.

interest during his summer visit to Philadelphia. Franklin corrected the 155–page manuscript and forwarded it to Bowdoin, October 25, 1750.[8] Along with Franklin's notes and corrections, there are marginal headings and notes in another hand, perhaps added from the printed editions. This manuscript belongs to the American Academy of Arts and Sciences, Boston.[9]

Collinson showed Franklin's letters to friends, read some of them to the Royal Society, and allowed copies to be made. He decided, late in 1750, to publish them, and they appeared in April 1751 with the title *Experiments and Observations on Electricity, Made at Philadelphia in America, by Mr. Benjamin Franklin, and Communicated in several Letters to Mr. P. Collinson, of London, F.R.S.*, a thin pamphlet of 86 numbered pages, which included corrections and additions supplied by Franklin. Twenty more pages of letters, numbered 89–109 and called *Supplemental Experiments and Observations . . . Part II . . .* , were published in 1753; and another 44 (pp. 111–54), entitled *New Experiments and Observations . . . Part III*, appeared in 1754. Parts I and II were reprinted as a second edition in 1754; and all three parts, continuously paged, as a third edition in 1760, 1762, and 1764 respectively. Franklin was in London in 1769, and could supervise personally the publication of the fourth edition. He annotated the original parts of the first three editions with many corrections and additions, and added a number of scientific letters on other subjects. A fifth edition followed in 1774.

Thus five English editions of the *Experiments and Observations* appeared during Franklin's lifetime: the first, 1751, with two additional parts, 1753 and 1754; the second, 1754, of Parts I and II only; the third, 1760, with the two additional parts, 1762 and 1764; the fourth, 1769; and the fifth, 1774.

The first three editions are similar, but not identical; and the differences, some of which go to the substance of the matter, cannot be explained by the vagaries of eighteenth-century printing offices. The fourth edition shows, naturally, significant differences; and there are only a few variations between the fourth and fifth editions. Since all five printed editions differ from the Bowdoin manuscript, the question arises which version of these six should be printed here.

In general, a printed work is the effective and authoritative one, and in Franklin's case it was the printed editions which established his principles of electricity among the largest number of people. After

8. BF to Bowdoin, Oct. 25, 1750.
9. The Bowdoin MS, first used by Cohen, is described in *BF's Experiments*, pp. 152–5.

1754, however, the question arises, which printed edition? On the other hand, the manuscript reports Franklin sent Collinson, beginning with this letter in the spring of 1747, introduced him to the philosophers of the Royal Society and provided William Watson and other experimenters with hypotheses to test, discuss, and refine. If these manuscripts had survived they would take precedence here over any printed version.

The Bowdoin manuscript, though a copy, was supervised and corrected by Franklin. Made in 1750, it antedates the first printed edition of *Experiments and Observations*. It is also in several instances fuller than any printed version. It is therefore followed here.

Appreciating, however, the historical and scientific importance of the several printed versions, with their significant changes and corrections, the editors have collated them and indicated the changes between manuscript and printed editions. Footnotes appear as they did in the printed editions, corrections and other emendations have been incorporated in the texts, and though it seemed unnecessary to note changes in spelling, capitalization, punctuation and paragraphing and verbal differences not affecting sense (the editions improved, generally, on the Bowdoin MS), all changes of substance are indicated, such as differences in singular and plural nouns and verbs.

Two additional sources provide important material for annotating these letters. One is a copy of the 1751 edition which Franklin presented to Yale College before 1755. The other is Franklin's own volume of pamphlets, including the 1751 and 1754 editions. In both of these he made marginal notes and corrections. Both are in the Yale University Library. Citation will be precise as to which copy is meant—the Yale presentation copy, Franklin's own copy, or any copy of the 1751 or 1754 editions.

Sir,   Philadelphia, March 28, 1747
Your kind present of an electric tube, with directions for using it, has put several of us[1] on making electrical experiments, in which we have observed some particular phaenomena that we look upon to be new. I shall, therefore communicate them to you in my next, though possibly they may not be new to you, as among the numbers daily employed in those experiments on your side the water, 'tis probable some one or other has hit on the same observations. For my own part, I never was before engaged in

1. Footnote in 1774 edition: "i.e. of the Library-Company, an institution of the Author's, founded 1730. To which company the present was made."

any study that so totally engrossed my attention and my time as this has lately done; for what with making experiments when I can be alone, and repeating them to my Friends and Acquaintance, who, from the novelty of the thing, come continually in crouds to see them, I have, during some months past, had little leisure for any thing else. I am, &c.   B. FRANKLIN

To [John Franklin]² Transcript: American Philosophical Society

Brother   Philada. April 2th. 1747
I should be glad you'd send me the first informations you receive, of what Admiral Warren is doing or like to do in England.³ And whether the wasted[?]⁴ is returning in Orders. We want much to hear that the Fleet is preparing to come from England, in Order to carry on the Expedition.
Billy is so fond of a military Life, that he will by no means hear of leaving the Army. We have good Accounts of him from his Captain and Brother Officers.
I must desire you to send me per first Vessel as much single Refin'd Loaf Sugar as Sixty Pounds Old Tenor will purchase neither less nor more. Love to dear Sister &c. &c. &c. from Your affectionate Brother   B FRANKLIN

2. Believed to be addressed to John Franklin (C.8), tallow chandler and soapmaker of Boston, rather than to Peter (C.9), merchant and shipmaster of Newport, because transcripts of two other letters by BF, Sept. 27, 1750, and Jan. 2, 1753, both almost certainly addressed to John, appear to have been made by the same copyist.
3. Admiral Peter Warren (1703–1752), commander of the British naval forces at the capture of Louisbourg, 1745, and governor of Louisbourg and Cape Breton Island, sailed for England, Nov. 30, 1746, to oppose as impracticable the expedition against Canada proposed for the next year. Before he could return to America, he was sent on an expedition against the French, which culminated in a decisive British naval victory off Cape Finisterre, May 3, 1747. In rapid succession he was knighted, elected to Parliament, and promoted to be vice-admiral of the White. DAB.
4. Obviously a misreading by the transcriber. Not identified.

The Speech of Miss Polly Baker

Printed in *The General Advertiser*, April 15, 1747.

When Franklin wrote The Speech of Miss Polly Baker is not now known, though 1746 is a likely date.[5] How a copy found its way to London is also a matter for speculation. All that is certain is that the earliest printing of the piece yet discovered was in a London newspaper, the *General Advertiser*, of April 15, 1747. Within a week five London papers reprinted it, and by the end of the month it had appeared in a number of provincial papers. Five monthly magazines picked it up—three in London, including the *Gentleman's*,[6] one in Edinburgh, and one in Dublin. The English magazines and papers reached America in midsummer. From one of them the *Boston Weekly Post-Boy* reprinted the Speech on July 20; both the *New-York Gazette* and the *New-York Weekly Journal*, each taking it from the *Post-Boy*, published it on August 3. Finally, on August 11, Franklin's former journeyman Jonas Green of Annapolis published a somewhat different version in the *Maryland Gazette*. In an introduction that may have been designed to puff the printer, Green asserted that the Speech had been "published in the *London* and *Gentleman's Magazines* for April past, as well as in some other British Papers; but was there printed incorrectly, which I suppose was occasioned by the Mutilation it suffer'd, in passing through the Hands of Transcribers before it reach'd the Press in London: And happening to have a correct Copy of it by

5. Most of the information in this headnote was taken from Max Hall, *Benjamin Franklin and Polly Baker: The History of a Literary Deception* (Chapel Hill, N.C., 1960); Mr. Hall also generously provided additional data to the editors and revised this note in the light of his special knowledge.

6. To the title of the Speech in its April 1747 issue, this magazine added that Polly bore 15 more children by the judge she married the day after her trial. This set off a curious correspondence. In the May issue one William Smith claimed to have seen the celebrated Polly Baker, who, he said, was now a woman of 60 and the wife of Paul Dudley of Massachusetts. He was constrained to make this statement, he added, as some persons had charged the speech was a fabrication. The following month "L. Americanus" vindicated the eminent and respected Dudley from the imputation in Smith's letter: Paul Dudley was chief justice of Massachusetts, had never served in any judicial capacity in Connecticut, where the trial had reportedly taken place, had been long married to a woman of good family and reputation, and had no children who survived infancy. The speech, he asserted firmly, was a fiction. The editor closed the matter in July 1748 with an apology to Chief Justice Dudley and his wife. *Gent. Mag.*, XVII (1747), 211, 295; XVIII (1748), 332. Abridgements of the "William Smith" and "L. Americanus" letters are printed in Smyth, *Writings*, II, 463–4.

me, I cannot think it amiss to give it my Readers, not doubting it's favourable Reception."[7]

In London the crusading deist Peter Annet included Polly's defense of her conduct in his *Social Bliss Considered*, 1749, a work on marriage, fornication, and divorce, which was later reprinted in his *Collection of the Tracts of a Certain Free Enquirer*. From time to time American newspapers revived the Speech. Probably from Annet or one of the London magazines the Abbé Raynal took it for his popular *Histoire Philosophique et Politique*, 1770. Citing Polly's case as an example of the severity of New England's laws, Raynal made changes and additions to suit his purpose. He reduced the humor and amplified the indignation in Polly's outburst. Delivered "il n'y a pas long-tems," Raynal asserted, the Speech had had such an effect on every mind that the court absolved Polly from punishment and, "pour comble de triomphe," one of her judges married her: "tant la voix de la raison est audessus des prestiges de l'éloquence étudiée."[8] The piece was by this time so well known that one of the English translators of Raynal felt justified in omitting it, "as this speech is in the hands of every English reader."[9] Still other versions appeared in French, one of them in the *Courier de l'Europe*, printed in London, 1777.[1]

Thus far, however, the authorship of the Speech was unknown, or at least unpublished. Raynal apparently had no suspicion that Polly Baker was not a real person or her case not authentic. How Franklin confessed his authorship Mazzei revealed in 1788.[2]

7. The "correctness" of Green's copy is open to question: its paragraph on abortions is quite unlike the style of the rest of the Speech. On the other hand, as Green knew and corresponded with BF, it cannot be asserted without reservation that Green concocted this new paragraph in the text he printed. In any event, the *Maryland Gazette* (like all the other journals) presented the Speech as an actual occurrence.

8. [Guillaume-Thomas François Raynal], *Histoire Philosophique et Politique, Des Établissments & du Commerce des Européens dans les Deux Indes* (Amsterdam, 1770), VI, 257–62. Polly's Speech was dropped from the new edition of Raynal's *Histoire* (Avignon, 1786), VII, 239; but was included in the Paris edition of 1820–21, IX, 53–58.

9. J. Justamond, trans., *A Philosophical and Political History of the . . . Indies* (2d edit., London, 1776), V, 200.

1. The *Courier's* version (June 17, 1777) was prefaced with a statement that the Speech had been recently received from America, communicated by one who had the highest title to recognition and whose rank gave him a claim to profound veneration. Such terms suggest BF, but they may be meaningless.

2. Translated from [Philip Mazzei], *Recherches Historiques et Politiques sur les États-Unis de l'Amérique Septentrionale* (Paris, 1788), III, 23–4; also

"At the end of 1777 or the beginning of 1778, the Abbé Raynal, having gone one evening to visit Dr. Franklin, found Silas Deane at Franklin's house. 'We were just speaking of your work,' Deane remarked, 'and were saying that you had been poorly served by those who gave you information about America and particularly my country.'

"As the Abbé would not admit this, Deane cited several passages in which there was not a word of truth. Finally they came to speak of the tale of Polly Baker. This subject brought on a most serious dispute since the Abbé maintained that he had taken it from an authentic account. Dr. Franklin after having enjoyed listening to the debate for some time, broke his silence and, addressing the Abbé Raynal, said, 'M. l'Abbé, I am going to set you straight. When I was young and printed a newspaper, it sometimes happened, when I was short of material to fill my sheet, that I amused myself by making up stories, and that of Polly Baker is one of the number.'

" 'My word,' replied the Abbé Raynal, giving up the argument, 'I would rather have included your tales in my book than many other men's truths.' "

Mazzei may have heard this anecdote from his friend Thomas Jefferson who was fond of telling the same story and who put it on paper in 1818, saying that he had heard it from Franklin himself in Paris—that is, in 1784 or 1785.[3]

Four other authorities may also be cited on the question of authorship. John Adams, writing to James Warren on April 13, 1783, listed Polly Baker's Speech as one of Franklin's many "Outrages to Morality and Decorum."[4] The Abbé Morellet recorded the episode of Franklin and Raynal in his *Ana*, a systematized commonplace book now in the British Museum. In the posthumous Kehl edition of Voltaire's works, in a volume published in 1784, appears the statement that Franklin wrote the Speech—the first time this statement is known to have been made in print.[5] And William Franklin told Jonathan Williams, Jr., in 1807 that his father "wrote and printed a Piece called the Speech of

---

translated by Alfred Owen Aldridge, *Franklin and his French Contemporaries* (N.Y., 1957), pp. 95–6.

3. Thomas Jefferson, *Writings*, Andrew A. Lipscomb and Albert E. Bergh, eds. (Washington, 1904–05), XVIII, 171–2. How Jefferson provided facts and opinions for Mazzei's book is related in Richard C. Garlick, Jr., *Philip Mazzei, Friend of Jefferson* (Baltimore, 1933), pp. 100–14.

4. *Warren-Adams Letters*, II (Mass. Hist. Soc. *Colls.*, LXXIII), 209. Adams also mentioned Polly Baker as one of BF's productions in his autobiographical notes under date of May 27, 1778, Adams Microfilm, Reel 180.

5. Voltaire, *Oeuvres Complètes* (Kehl, 1784–89), XXXVII, 277–8.

Polly Baker, a young Woman supposed to have had several natural Children."[6]

Though Miss Baker's awkward predicament had its humorous side and Franklin presented only that, the plea he wrote for her moved many Europeans to sympathy. Raynal and other French *philosophes* used her, as they used the Good Quaker and the Noble Savage, as yet another weapon in the arsenal of revolution and reform.[7]

The SPEECH of Miss POLLY BAKER, before a Court of Judicature, at Connecticut near Boston in New-England; where she was prosecuted the Fifth Time, for having a Bastard Child: Which influenced the Court to dispense with her Punishment, and induced one of her Judges to marry her the next Day.

MAY it please the Honourable Bench to indulge me in a few Words: I am a poor unhappy Woman, who have no Money to fee Lawyers to plead for me, being hard put to it to get a tolerable Living. I shall not trouble your Honours with long Speeches; for I have not the Presumption to expect, that you may, by any Means, be prevailed on to deviate in your Sentence from the Law, in my Favour. All I humbly hope is, That your Honours would charitably move the Governor's Goodness on my Behalf, that my Fine may be remitted. This is the Fifth Time, Gentlemen, that I have been dragg'd before your Court on the same Account; twice I have paid heavy Fines, and twice have been brought to Publick Punishment, for want of Money to pay those Fines. This may have been agreeable to the Laws, and I don't dispute it; but since Laws are sometimes unreasonable in themselves, and therefore repealed, and others bear too hard on the Subject in particular Circumstances; and therefore there is left a Power somewhat to dispense with the Execution of them; I take the Liberty to say, That I

6. William Franklin to Jonathan Williams, Jr., July 30, 1807, MS, Indiana Univ. Lib.

7. Johan V. Johansson, *Études sur Denis Diderot* (Göteborg, 1927), pp. 161–92; Aldridge, *Franklin and his French Contemporaries*, pp. 95–104. Of the several American printings after the Revolution, that in *Amer. Museum*, I (1787), 243–5, is especially interesting. It ends with a note that reads: "This judicious address influenced the court to dispense with her punishment, and induced one of her judges to marry her the next day. She supported an irreproachable character, and had fifteen children by her husband.

"N.B. Another account says her name was Sarah Olitor."

think this Law, by which I am punished, is both unreasonable in itself, and particularly severe with regard to me, who have always lived an inoffensive Life in the Neighbourhood where I was born, and defy my Enemies (if I have any) to say I ever wrong'd Man, Woman, or Child. Abstracted from the Law, I cannot conceive (may it please your Honours) what the Nature of my Offence is. I have brought Five fine Children into the World, at the Risque of my Life; I have maintain'd them well by my own Industry, without burthening the Township, and would have done it better, if it had not been for the heavy Charges and Fines I have paid. Can it be a Crime (in the Nature of Things I mean) to add to the Number of the King's Subjects, in a new Country that really wants People? I own it, I should think it a Praise-worthy, rather than a punishable Action. I have debauched no other Woman's Husband, nor enticed any Youth; these Things I never was charg'd with, nor has any one the least Cause of Complaint against me, unless, perhaps, the Minister, or Justice, because I have had Children without being married, by which they have missed a Wedding Fee. But, can ever this be a Fault of mine? I appeal to your Honours. You are pleased to allow I don't want Sense; but I must be stupified to the last Degree, not to prefer the Honourable State of Wedlock, to the Condition I have lived in. I always was, and still am willing to enter into it; and doubt not my behaving well in it, having all the Industry, Frugality, Fertility, and Skill in Oeconomy, appertaining to a good Wife's Character. I defy any Person to say, I ever refused an Offer of that Sort: On the contrary, I readily consented to the only Proposal of Marriage that ever was made me, which was when I was a Virgin; but too easily confiding in the Person's Sincerity that made it, I unhappily lost my own Honour, by trusting to his; for he got me with Child, and then forsook me: That very Person you all know; he is now become a Magistrate of this Country; and I had Hopes he would have appeared this Day on the Bench, and have endeavoured to moderate the Court in my Favour; then I should have scorn'd to have mention'd it; but I must now complain of it, as unjust and unequal, That my Betrayer and Undoer, the first Cause of all my Faults and Miscarriages (if they must be deemed such) should be advanc'd to Honour and Power in the Government, that punishes my Misfortunes with Stripes

124

and Infamy. I should be told, 'tis like, That were there no Act of Assembly in the Case, the Precepts of Religion are violated by my Transgressions. If mine, then, is a religious Offence, leave it to religious Punishments. You have already excluded me from the Comforts of your Church-Communion. Is not that sufficient? You believe I have offended Heaven, and must suffer eternal Fire: Will not that be sufficient? What Need is there, then, of your additional Fines and Whipping? I own, I do not think as you do; for, if I thought what you call a Sin, was really such, I could not presumptuously commit it. But, how can it be believed, that Heaven is angry at my having Children, when to the little done by me towards it, God has been pleased to add his Divine Skill and admirable Workmanship in the Formation of their Bodies, and crown'd it, by furnishing them with rational and immortal Souls. Forgive me, Gentlemen, if I talk a little extravagantly on these Matters; I am no Divine, but if you, Gentlemen, must be making Laws, do not turn natural and useful Actions into Crimes, by your Prohibitions. But take into your wise Consideration, the great and growing Number of Batchelors in the Country, many of whom from the mean Fear of the Expences of a Family, have never sincerely and honourably courted a Woman in their Lives; and by their Manner of Living, leave unproduced (which is little better than Murder) Hundreds of their Posterity to the Thousandth Generation. Is not this a greater Offence against the Publick Good, than mine? Compel them, then, by Law, either to Marriage, or to pay double the Fine of Fornication every Year. What must poor young Women do, whom Custom have forbid to solicit the Men, and who cannot force themselves upon Husbands, when the Laws take no Care to provide them any; and yet severely punish them if they do their Duty without them; the Duty of the first and great Command of Nature, and of Nature's God, *Encrease and Multiply*. A Duty, from the steady Performance of which, nothing has been able to deter me; but for its Sake, I have hazarded the Loss of the Publick Esteem, and have frequently endured Publick Disgrace and Punishment; and therefore ought, in my humble Opinion, instead of a Whipping, to have a Statue erected to my Memory.

To [William Strahan?]

ALS: Munson-Williams-Proctor Institute, Utica, N.Y. (1955)

Dear Sir   Philada. May 1. 1747

This is only to cover a Bill of Exchange for Eleven Pounds
2*s*. 2½*d*. Sterl. drawn on Richd. Atkinson[8] of Colthouse by Wm.
Satterthwaite,[9] and to inform you that we are all well, as I hope
this will find you and yours. I am Your most humble Servant

B FRANKLIN

This via New York. Copy with first Bill and Letter of Advice via
Boston by the Mermaid Man of War

To Peter Collinson Copy: American Academy of Arts and Sciences[1]

Sir   Philada. May 25. 1747[2]

In my last[3] I informed you that In pursuing our Electrical Enquiries, we had observ'd some particular Phaenomena, which we

8. Not identified.

9. A native of England, Satterthwaite was employed by Lawrence Growdon
and Jeremiah Langhorne to keep a school at Durham in Bucks Co., Pa. He
wrote several poems, including an elegy on Langhorne and one called "Mys-
terious Nothings," 1734, whose title, one critic has written, "precisely describes the contents." *PMHB*, VII (1883), 83–4; XVII (1893), 29. Purchases
from BF are recorded in Ledger D.

1. In Bowdoin MS: Letter I; in all printed editions of *Exper. and Obser.*:
Letter II. See above, pp. 115–18, for a discussion of MS and printed versions.

2. This letter has been given almost as many dates as it has had printings.
It is dated Sept. 1, 1747, in the editions of 1751, 1754, and 1760; but July 11
in those of 1769 and 1774 and by the principal editors—Dubourg, Duane,
Sparks, Bigelow, Smyth—of Franklin's collected works. William Watson,
who quoted part of it in "Some further Inquiries into the Nature and Properties of Electricity," *Phil. Trans.*, XLV (1748), 98–100, gave its date as June 1.
An autograph note by BF in both his own copy of the 1751 edition and the
Yale presentation copy of the same edition (both in Yale Univ. Lib.) reads:
"The two first Letters transpos'd, except the Dates"—which would date
this letter July 28. Franklin's note, however, should not be taken as assigning
the letter to that date; BF only recognized that the first two letters were mis-
placed. The date of the Bowdoin MS is the correct one. BF confirms this in a
letter to Collinson, Aug. 14, where he says he had sent a long letter on electricity by the "Governor's Ship." This was the *Greyhound*, Captain Budden,
which sailed from Philadelphia on June 1. I. Bernard Cohen discusses the

lookt upon to be new, and of which I promised to give you some Account; tho' I apprehended they might possibly not be new to you, as so many Hands are daily employed in Electrical Experiments on your Side the Water, some or other of which would probably hit on the same Observations.

The first is the wonderful Effect of Points[4] both in *drawing* off and *throwing* off the Electrical Fire. For Example,

Place an Iron Shot of three or four Inches Diameter on the Mouth of a clean dry Glass Bottle. By a fine silken Thread from the Ceiling, right over the Mouth of the Bottle, suspend a small Cork Ball, about the Bigness of a Marble: the Thread of such a Length, as that the Cork Ball may rest against the Side of the Shot. Electrify the Shot, and the Ball will be repelled to the Distance of 4 or 5 Inches, more or less according to the Quantity of Electricity. When in this State, if you present to the Shot the Point of a long, slender, sharp Bodkin at 6 or 8 Inches Distance, the Repellency is instantly destroy'd, and the Cork flies to it.[5] A blunt Body must be brought within an Inch, and draw a Spark to produce the same Effect. To prove that the Electrical Fire is drawn off by the Point: if you take the Blade of the Bodkin out of the wooden Handle, and fix it in a Stick of Sealing Wax, and then present it at the Distance aforesaid[6] no such Effect follows; but slide[7] one Finger along the Wax till you touch the Blade, and the Ball flies to the Shot immediately. If you present the Point in the Dark, you will see, sometimes at a Foot Distance and more, a Light gather upon it like that of a Fire-Fly or Glow-Worm; the less sharp the Point, the nearer you must bring it to observe this Light: and at whatever Distance you see the Light, you may draw off the Electrical Fire, and destroy the Repellency. If a Cork Ball, so suspended, be repelled by the Tube, and a Point be presented quick to it, tho' at a considerable Distance, tis surpriz-

---

problem fully in *BF's Experiments*, p. 166, and in "Some Problems in Relation to the Dates of Benjamin Franklin's First Letters on Electricity," APS *Proc.*, C (1956), 537–9.

3. See above, p. 118.
4. In all printed editions: "Points" is replaced by "pointed bodies."
5. In all printed editions: "it" is replaced by "the shot."
6. All printed editions add: "or if you bring it very near."
7. In all printed editions: "slide" is replaced by "sliding."

ing to see how suddenly it flies back to the Tube. Points of Wood do as well[8] as those of Metal,[9] provided the Wood is not dry.[1]

To shew that Points will *throw* off,[2] as well as *draw* off the Electrical Fire: Lay a long sharp Needle upon the Shot, and you can not electrise the Shot, so as to make it repel the Cork Ball.[3] Fix[4] a Needle to the End of a suspended Gun Barrel,[5] so as to point beyond it like a little Bayonet, and while it remains there, the Gun Barrel can not be electrised (by the Tube applied to the other End) so as to give a Spark;[6] the Fire is[7] continually running out silently at the Point. In the Dark you may see it make the same Appearance as it does in the Case before mentioned.

The Repellency between the Cork Ball and Shot is likewise destroy'd; 1. By sifting fine Sand on it; this does it gradually: 2. By breathing on it: 3. By making a Smoke about it from burning Wood:* 4. By Candle Light,[8] even tho' the Candle is at a Foot

*We suppose every Particle of Sand, moist Breath[9] or Smoke, being first attracted and then repelled, carries off with it its Portion of the Electrical Fire, but that it[1] still subsists in those Particles, till they communicate it to something else, and that it is never really destroyed. So when Water is thrown on common Fire, we do not imagine the Element is thereby destroy'd or annihilated, but only dispersed; each Particle of Water carrying off in Vapour its Portion of the Fire which it had attracted and attacht to itself.

8. In 1751, 1754, and 1760 editions: "will do as well"; in 1769 and 1774 editions: "will do near as well."

9. In all printed editions: "iron" replaces "Metal."

1. All printed editions add: "for perfectly dry wood will no more conduct electricity than sealing-wax."

2. Footnote in 1769 and 1774 editions: "This power of points to *throw off* the electrical fire, was first communicated to me by my ingenious friend Mr. Thomas Hopkinson, since deceased, whose virtue and integrity, in every station of life, public and private, will ever make his Memory dear to those who knew him, and knew how to value him." In the margin of his own copy of the 1751 edition BF had written Hopkinson's name.

3. Footnote in the 1769 and 1774 editions: "This was Mr. Hopkinson's Experiment, made with an expectation of drawing a more sharp and powerful spark from the point, as from a kind of focus, and he was surprized to find little or none." In the 1774 edition, the footnote is keyed to "bayonet."

4. In all printed editions this sentence begins with "Or."

5. All printed editions add: "or iron rod."

6. In all printed editions altered to: "the gun-barrel, or rod, cannot by applying the tube to the other end be electrised so as to give a spark."

Distance: These do it suddenly. The Light of a bright Coal from a Wood Fire, and the Light of a red-hot Iron do it likewise; but not at so great a Distance. Smoke from dry Rosin dropt into a little hot Letter Founders Ladle[2] under the Shot does not destroy the Repellency; but is attracted by both the Shot and the Cork-Ball, forming proportionable Atmospheres round them, making them look beautifully; somewhat like some of the Figures in Burnets or Whiston's Theory of the Earth.[3]

N.B. This Experiment should be made [in a closet] where the Air is very still.[4]

The Light of the Sun thrown strongly on both Shot and Cork by a Looking Glass for a long Time together does not impair the Repellency in the least. This Difference between Fire Light and Sun Light is another Thing that seems new and extraordinary to us.[5]

We had for some Time been of Opinion, that the Electrical Fire was not created by Friction, but collected, being an Element[6]

---

7. All printed editions omit "is."

8. BF's emendation in MS: "This is since found to be by the *Smoke* and not the *Light* of the Candle. All burning Candles give more or less Smoke; this Smoke attracted, electrified and repell'd, carries off the Electricity." Printed emendation in 1751, 1754, and 1760 editions: "From some observations since made, I am inclined to think, that it is not the light, but the smoke or non-electric effluvia from the candle, coal, and red-hot iron, that carry off the electrical fire, being first attracted and then repelled."

9. In all printed editions: "moist Breath" is replaced by "moisture."

1. In all printed editions: "it" is replaced by "the same."

2. In all printed versions: "dropt on hot iron." The words "under the Shot" are omitted from all printed editions.

3. Thomas Burnet, *The Sacred Theory of the Earth: containing an Account of the Original of the Earth* (6th edit., 2v. London, 1726), and William Whiston, *A New Theory of the Earth . . . Wherein the Creation . . . Deluge and . . . Conflagration as laid down in the Holy Scriptures are shown to be perfectly agreeable to reason and philosophy* (5th edit., London, 1737).

4. This is a marginal note in MS in another hand; it is incorporated in the 1751 and all later editions with the bracketed words, as here. The 1769 and 1774 editions also add: "or it will be apt to fail."

5. Footnote in 1769 and 1774 editions: "This different Effect probably did not arise from any difference in the light, but rather from the particles separated from the candle, being first attracted and then repelled, carrying off the electric matter with them; and from the rarefying the air, between the glowing coal or red-hot iron, and the electrised shot, through which rarified air the electric fluid could more readily pass."

6. In all printed editions: "being really an Element."

diffused among, and attracted by other Matter, particularly by Water and Metals. We[7] had even discovered and demonstrated its Afflux to the Electrical Sphere, as well as its Efflux, by Means of little light Wind-Mill Wheels[8] made of stiff Paper Vanes, fixt obliquely, and turning freely on fine Wire Axes. Also by little Wheels of the same Matter, but formed like Water Wheels. Of the Disposition and Application of which Wheels, and the various Phaenomena resulting, I could, if I had Time, and it were necessary,[9] fill you a Sheet.

The Impossibility of Electrising one's self (tho' standing on Wax) by Rubbing the Tube and drawing the Fire from it: and the Manner of doing it by passing the Tube near a Person, or Thing standing on the Floor &c. had also occurred to us some Months before Mr. Watsons ingenious *Sequel*[1] came to hand; and these were some of the new Things I intended to have communicated to you: But now I need only mention some Particulars not hinted in that Piece, with our Reasonings thereon; tho' perhaps the latter might well enough be spared.

1. A Person standing on Wax and rubbing the Tube; and another Person on Wax drawing the Fire, they will both of them (provided they do not stand so as to touch one another) appear to be electrised to a Person standing on the Floor; that is, he will perceive a Spark on approaching each of them.[2]

7. In his own copy of the 1751 edition BF wrote in the margin: "Philip Syng."

8. BF's emendation in MS: "These Wheels are since found to move from no other Causes than Attraction, Electrification and Repulsion of their circumferent Parts." Printed emendation in 1751, 1754, and 1760 editions: "We afterwards discovered, that the afflux or efflux of the electrical fire, was not the cause of the motions of those wheels, but various circumstances of attraction and repulsion." The same information appears in a footnote in 1769 and 1774 editions, keyed to the end of the paragraph: "These experiments with the wheels were made and communicated to me by my worthy and ingenious friend Mr. Philip Syng; but we afterwards discovered that the motion of those wheels was not owing to any afflux or efflux of the electric fluid, but to various circumstances of attraction and repulsion. 1750."

9. All printed editions omit "and it were necessary."

1. William Watson, *A Sequel to the Experiments and Observations Tending to illustrate the Nature and Properties of Electricity* (London, 1746), pp. 31–2.

2. Added in all printed editions: "with his knuckle."

2. But if the Persons standing[3] on Wax touch one another during the exciting of the Tube, neither of them will appear to be electrised.

3. If they touch one another after exciting the Tube, and drawing the Fire as aforesaid, there will be a stronger Spark between them than was between either of them and the Person on the Floor.

4. After such strong Spark, neither of them discovers any Electricity.

These Appearances we attempt to account for thus. We suppose as aforesaid, That Electrical Fire is a common Element, of which every one of the three Persons[4] abovementioned has his equal Share before any Operation is begun with the Tube. *A* who stands on Wax, and rubs the Tube, collects the Electrical Fire from himself into the Glass; and his Communication with the common Stock being cut off by the Wax, his Body is not again immediately supply'd. *B*, who stands upon Wax likewise, passing his Knuckle along near the Tube, receives the Fire which was collected by the Glass from *A;* and his Communication with the common Stock being likewise cutt off, he retains the additional Quantity received. To *C,* standing on the Floor, both appear to be electrised; for he having only the middle Quantity of Electrical Fire receives a Spark on approaching *B,* who has an over-quantity, but gives one to *A,* who has an under-quantity. If *A* and *B* touch[5] each other, the Spark between them[6] is stronger, because the Difference between them is greater. After such Touch, there is no Spark between either of them and *C;* because the Electrical Fire in all is reduced to the original Equality. If they touch while Electrising, the Equality is never destroyed, the Fire only circulating. Hence have arisen some new Terms among us. We say *B* (and other Bodies alike circumstanced) are[7] electrised *positively;* *A* negatively: Or rather *B* is electrised *plus* and *A minus*. And we daily in our Experiments electrise Bodies *plus* or *minus* as we

3. All printed editions omit "standing."
4. In all printed editions: "the three persons."
5. In all printed editions: "approach to touch."
6. All printed editions omit "between them."
7. In all printed editions: "We say *B* (and bodies like circumstanced) is."

think proper. *These Terms* we may use till your Philosophers give us better.[8] To electrise *plus* or *minus,* no more needs to be known than this; that the Parts of the Tube or Sphere, that are rub'd, do, in the Instant of the Friction, attract the Electrical Fire, and therefore take it from the Thing rubbing: the same Parts immediately, as the Friction upon them ceases, are disposed to give the Fire they have received, to any Body that has less. Thus you may circulate it, as Mr. Watson has shewn; You may also accumulate or subtract it upon, or from any Body, as you connect it[9] with the Rubber or with the Receiver; the Communication with the common Stock being cut off. We think that ingenious Gentleman was deceived, when he imagined (Page [64] of the Sequel)[1] that the Electrical Fire came down the Wire from the Cieling to the Gun Barrel, thence to the Sphere and so electrised the Machine,[2] the Man turning the Wheel &c. We suppose it was *driven off* and not *brought on* thro' that Wire; and that the Machine and Man &c. were electrized *minus,* i.e. had less electrical Fire in them than Things in common.

As the Vessel is just sailing,[3] I can not give you so large an Account of American Electricity as I intended. I shall only mention a few Particulars more.[4] We find granulated Lead better to fill the Vial with than Water, being easily warmed, and keeping the Vial[5] warm and dry in damp Air. We fire Spirits with the Wire of the Phial. We light Candles just blown out, by drawing a Spark among the Smoke between the Wire and Snuffers. We represent Lightning, by passing the Wire, in the Dark, over a China Plate, that has gilt Flowers; or applying it to gilt Frames of Looking Glasses &c. We electrise a Person 20 or more Times running, with the Touch of the Finger on the Wire, thus;* He stands on

*The person standing on wax, holding the electrised bottle, when you touch the Hook of the bottle and receive a Spark from it, is electrified minus; a Quantity of electrical fire going out of him into the Coating of the bottle, equal to the Quantity taken from the Hook: in this state a person on the Floor touching him, will give him the quantity he has lost.[6]

8. All printed editions omit this sentence.
9. In all printed editions "it" is replaced by "that body."
1. In all printed editions: "(in his *Sequel*)." The page reference, left blank in MS, has been inserted by the editors.

Wax; give him the electrised Bottle in his Hand; touch the Wire with your Finger, and then touch his Hand or Face, there are Sparks every Time.[7] We encrease the Force of the electrical Kiss vastly, thus; Let *A* and *B* stand on Wax;[8] give one of them the electrised Vial in Hand; let the other take hold of the Wire; there will be a small Spark; but when their Lips approach, they will be struck and shockt. The same, if *C* and *D*[9] (standing also on Wax) and joyning Hands with *A* and *B,* salute or shake Hands. We suspend by a fine Silk Thread a Counterfeit Spider, made of a small Piece of burnt Cork, with Legs of Linen Thread, and a Grain or two of Lead stuck in[1] to give him more Weight. Upon the Table, over which he hangs, we stick a Wire upright, as high as the Vial and Wire, 2 or 3 Inches[2] from the Spider: then we animate him, by setting the electrified Vial, at the same Distance on the other Side of him: he will immediately fly to the Wire of the Vial, bend his Legs in touching it, then spring off and fly to the Wire in the Table; thence again to the Wire of the Vial; playing with his Legs against both in a very extraordinary[3] Manner, appearing perfectly alive to Persons unacquainted. He will continue this Motion an Hour or more in dry Weather.

We electrify upon Wax, in the Dark, a Book that has a double Line of Gold round upon the Covers, and then apply a Knuckle to

2. All printed editions insert "and."

3. In all printed editions: "just upon sailing."

4. In his own copy of the 1751 edition BF wrote Philip Syng's name in the margin at this point.

5. All printed editions omit "the Vial."

6. All printed editions omit this footnote, which appears in MS, probably in Bowdoin's hand.

7. Footnote in 1769 and 1774 editions: "By taking a spark from the wire, the electricity within the bottle is diminished; the outside of the bottle then draws some from the person holding it, and leaves him in the negative state. Then when his hand or face is touch'd, an equal quantity is restored to him from the person touching."

8. Emendation in 1751, 1754, and 1760 editions: "We soon found that it was only necessary for one of them to stand on wax." Added in 1769 and 1774 editions: "or *A* on wax, and *B* on the floor."

9. In all printed editions: "if another gentleman and lady, *C* and *D*."

1. In all printed editions: "stuck in him."

2. In 1774 edition: 4 or 5 inches.

3. In all printed editions "extraordinary" is replaced by "entertaining."

the Gilding; the Fire appears every where upon the Gold like a Flash of Lightning; not upon the Leather; nor if you touch the Leather instead of the Gold. We rub our Tubes with Buck Skin, and observe always to keep the same Side to the Tube, and never to sully the Tube by Handling. Thus they work readily and easily without the least Fatigue, especially if kept in tight Pastboard Cases, lined with Flannel and fitting close to the Tube.[4] This I mention, because the European Papers on Electricity frequently speak of rubbing the Tube as a fatiguing Exercise. Our Spheres are fixt on Iron Axels,[5] which pass thro' them.[6] At one End of the Axis there is a small Handle with which we[7] turn the Sphere like a common Grind-Stone. This we find very commode;[8] as the Machine takes up but little Room, is portable, and may be enclosed in a tight Box, when not in Use. 'Tis true the Sphere does not turn so swift as when the great Wheel is used; but Swiftness we think of little Importance, since a few Turns will charge the Vial &c. sufficiently.[9]

I must say no more of Electricity at present, or I shall not leave myself Time to answer your Favour of March last, which came to Hand by Dowers,[1] with the Magazines and LeBlank's Letters, Martin's Electricity and Watson's first Part and Sequel.[2]

We are, as we always have been, extreamly obliged to you for

4. Footnote in 1751, 1754, and 1760 editions: "Our tubes are made here of green glass, 27 or 30 inches long, as big as can be grasped. Electricity is so much in vogue, that above one hundred of them have been sold within these four months past." The 1769 and 1774 editions include only the first sentence of the footnote.

5. In all printed editions: "axes."

6. At this point BF wrote Philip Syng's name in the margin of his copy of the 1751 edition.

7. In 1760, 1769, and 1774 editions: "we" is replaced by "you."

8. In all printed editions: "commodious."

9. Footnote in 1769 and 1774 editions: "This simple easily-made machine was a contrivance of Mr. Syng's." In all printed editions BF's letter ends at this point.

1. Not found. But see Collinson's letter of June 1 (below, p. 141) for confirmatory evidence of date and contents.

2. Jean Bernard LeBlanc, *Letters on the English and French Nations* (2v., London, 1747); Benjamin Martin, *An Essay on Electricity* (Bath, 1740); William Watson, *Experiments and Observations Tending to illustrate the Nature and Properties of Electricity* (London, 1746), and *A Sequel to Experiments and Observations . . .* (London, 1746).

your kind Care in sending us, from Time to Time, what is new and curious, tho' not wrote for.

The rest of the Letter on private Affairs and Matters relating to the Philadelphia Library.[3]

To Peter Collinson Esqr. F.R.S. London

Verses on the Virginia Capitol Fire

Printed in *The New-York Gazette, revived in the Weekly Post-Boy,* June 1, 1747, Supplement.

The capitol at Williamsburg, Virginia, was destroyed by fire on January 30, 1747. Addressing a special session of the General Assembly on April 1, Governor Sir William Gooch plunged directly into the matter: "The astonishing Fate of the Capitol occasions this meeting, and proves a Loss the more to be deplored, as being apparently the Effect of Malice and Design. I must indeed own it is difficult to comprehend how so flagitious a Crime could be committed, or even imagined, by any rational Creature. But when you have considered that the first Emission of the Smoke through the Shingles, was from an upper retir'd Room, without Chimney or Wainscot; that the Persons who on its first Appearance hasten'd thither to discover the Causes, found all the Inside of the Room in one Blaze, impossible to be extinguished; and that a Fire kindled by Accident could not have made so rapid a Progress; you will be forced to ascribe it to the horrid Machinations of desperate Villains, instigated by infernal Madness." And he called upon the Assembly, as "the Fathers of your Country," to take steps to repair the "Royal Fabrick."

The Council replied in terms yet more fulsome. Saluting their governor as "a great Instrument under divine Providence, of conveying many Benefits to the Community, over which you so deservedly pre-

3. This sentence and the address are in BF's hand.
Collinson showed BF's report to the president and some members of the Royal Society, including William Watson. Quick to appreciate its merit, Watson quoted nearly three pages of the most important part of it—BF's statement of the single-fluid theory (pp. 130–2 above)—in the paper he read the Society, Jan. 21, 1748. BF's electrical experiments, made before the American could have learned about similar experiments in England, Watson declared, showed that he was "very conversant in this part of Natural Philosophy." *Phil. Trans.,* XLV (1748), 98–100. See also Cohen, *BF's Experiments,* pp. 78–9.

side," they asserted that "the raging Fire, which consumed the Capitol," was "an awful Incitement to a general Reformation of Manners, the best Expedient for averting the wrathful Indignation of an incensed God. . . ," and expressed concern lest the religious enthusiasm introduced into Virginia by itinerant preachers should implant "a Spirit more dangerous to the common Welfare, than the furious Element, which laid the Royal Edifice in Ashes." Finally they congratulated Gooch on his having been recently created baronet.

Gooch expressed his appreciation and thanks for the Council's concern and congratulations, assuring them that he would "oppose the Progress of Heterodoxy and Immorality; and . . . promote true Religion and Virtue, the sure Foundation of our present Happiness, and the only Hope of our future Reward." Neither Council nor Governor said anything more at this time about plans for rebuilding.[4]

Franklin printed the addresses in the *Gazette*, May 14. At the same time, amused by the extravagant compliments and irrelevancies, he composed a humorous paraphrase in blank verse, which he sent to James Parker with copies of the original speech, address and answer, and a covering letter. Parker printed them at once in a supplement to his *New-York Gazette* for June 1. The *Maryland Gazette* reprinted the verses, which "made a deal of Laughter" in Annapolis.[5] Parker printed them again in a supplement to the *New-York Gazette*, May 20, 1751.

The verses are ascribed to Franklin on authority of a letter from William Franklin to Jonathan Williams, Jr., in 1807, in which he listed some of his father's uncollected writings and recalled that "one of them was written in Doggrel Rhime, travesting the Addresses of the Council and Assembly of Virginia to the Governor, on the Burning of an old Court-House, which they pompously stiled the CAPITOL! . . . It must, I think, be between 50 and 60 Years since that Piece was publish'd."[6]

Mr. Printer,

It may entertain the curious and learned Part of your Subscribers, if you give them the following genuine *Speech* and *Address*, which, for the *Importance* of the *Subject, Grandeur* of *Sentiment,* and *Elegance* of *Expression,* perhaps exceed Any they have hitherto seen. For the Benefit of more common Readers, I have turn'd them, with some Paraphrase, into *plain English Verse.* I am

4. The documents are printed in *Jour. House of Burgesses, 1742–1747, 1748–1749* (Richmond, 1909), p. 239.

5. *Md. Gaz.*, June 16, 1747; see below, p. 154.

6. William Franklin to Jonathan Williams, Jr., July 30, 1807, MS, Indiana Univ. Lib.

told by Friends, that my Performance is excellent: But I claim no other Praise than what regards my *Rhyme,* and my *Perspicuity.* All the other Beauties I acknowledge, are owing to the *Original,* whose true Sense I have every where follow'd with a scrupulous Exactness. If envious Critics should observe, that some of my Lines are *too short* in their Number of Feet, I own it; but then, to make ample Amends, I have given *very good Measure* in most of the others. I am, Sir, your constant Reader,   NED TYPE

[*Here follow The Speech of Sir William Gooch, the Humble Address of the Council, and the Governor's Answer.*]

The SPEECH Versyfied.

L--D have Mercy on us! — the CAPITOL! the CAPITOL! is burnt down!
O astonishing Fate! — which occasions this Meeting in Town.
And this *Fate* proves a *Loss,* to be deplored the more,
The said *Fate* being th' *Effect* of Malice and *Design,* to be sure.
And yet 'tis hard to comprehend how a Crime of so flagitious a Nature
Should be committed, or even *imagined,* by any but an *irrational* Creature.
But when you consider, that the first *Emission of Smoke* was not from below,
And that Fires kindled by Accident *always burn slow,*
And not with half the Fury as when they *burn on Purpose* you know
You'll be forced to ascribe it (with Hearts full of Sadness)
To the horrid Machinations of desperate Villains, instigated by infernal Madness.
God forbid I should accuse or excuse any without just Foundation,
Yet I may venture to assert — for our own Reputation,
That such superlative Wickedness never entred the Hearts of Virginians, who are the CREAM of the British Nation.
The Clerks have been examin'd, and clear'd by the May'r,
Yet are willing to be examin'd again by you, and that's fair.
And will prove in the Face of the Country, if requir'd,
That it was not by their *Conduct* our Capitol was fir'd.

137

I must add, to do 'em Justice, that the Comfort we have,
In enjoying our authentic Registers, which those Clerks did save,
Is owing to their Activity, Resolution and Diligence,
Together with Divine Providence
All which would have been in vain, I protest,
If the Wind, at the bursting out of the Flames, had not changed
    from *East* to *Northwest*.
    Our Treasury being low, and my Infirmities great,
I would have kept you prorogu'd till the Revisal of the Laws
    was compleat;
But this Misfortune befalling the *Capitol* of the Capital of our
    Nation
Require your immediate Care and Assistance for its *Instauration*.
    To press you in a Point of such Usefulness manifest,
Would shew a Diffidence of your sincere Zeal for the public
    Interest
For which you and I always make such a laudable Pother,
And for which we've so often *applauded one Another*.
    The same public Spirit which within these Walls us'd to direct
    you all,
Will determine you (as Fathers of your Country) to apply Means
    effectual
For restoring the ROYAL FABRIC to its former Beauty
And Magnificence, according to your Duty;
With the like Apartments, elegant and spacious
For all the *weighty* purposes of Government, so capacious.
    Mean time the College and Court of Hustings our *Weight* may
    sustain,
But pray let us speedily have our CAPITOL, our *important* CAPITOL
    again.

            The COUNCIL's Answer.

We the King's *best Subjects*, the Council of this Dominion,
Are deeply affected (as is every true Virginian)
With the unhappy Occasion of our present Meeting:
——In Troth we have but a sorry Greeting.
    We are also not a little touch'd (in the Head) with the same
    Weakness as your Honour's,
And therefore think this raging Fire which consum'd our *Capitol*,
    should incite us to reform our Manners:
The best *Expedient* at present to avert the Indignation divine,

138

And *nobly* to express our *Gratitude* for the *Justiae*, which (temper'd
  with Mercy) doth shine,
In *preserving* our Records, tho' Red hot,
And like Brands pluck'd out of the Flames, in which they were
  going to pot,
Without this *Expedient* we shall be ruin'd quite.
Besides, This FIRE puts us in Mind of NEW-LIGHT;
And we think it Heav'n's Judgment on us for tolerating the Pres-
  byterians,
Whose Forefathers drubb'd ours, about a hundred Year-hence.
We therefore resolve to abate a little of our Drinking, Gaming,
  Cursing and Swearing,
And make up for the rest, by persecuting some itinerant Presby-
  terian.
  An *active Discharge* of our *important* Trusts, according to your
  Honour's Desire,
Is the wisest *Project of Insurance* that can be, of the Public Safety,
  from the Attempts of such as would *set it on fire.*
'Tis *a Project* also for advancing the Honour and Interest of our
  King and Nation,
And *a Project* for engaging Heaven's Protection from Generation
  to Generation.
  We take this Opportunity, that we may not be suspected of
  Malignity,
To congratulate you, Sir, on your Promotion to the Baronet's
  Dignity;
A fresh Instance of just Regard to your long and faithful Services,
  we say,
Because from Carthagena your Honour came safe away.[7]
And you lent and sent such *great Assistance** for reducing CANADA.

*One WHOLE Company.[8]

7. Sir William Gooch, governor of Virginia, 1727–49, had raised and led
400 men to assist British forces in the attack on Cartagena, 1740, where he
was seriously wounded and contracted a fever. He was created a baronet
Nov. 4, 1746. *DAB.*
8. Virginia's claims for reimbursement from the British government for
the expenses of this company are mentioned in *Executive Journals of the
Council of Colonial Virginia,* v (Richmond, 1945), 246; and *Journal of the
Commissioners for Trade and Plantations, 1741/2 to 1749* (London, 1931),
pp. 457, 460, 470.

The BARONET's Reply.

The just Sense you express for the Loss of our CAP-
ITOL, which to be sure was a fatal Mishap,
Your affectionate Concern for the *Infirmities of my Honour,*
And Joy at my new Title, of which our good K—g is the Donor,
Claim sincere Acknowledgments of Thankfulness,
And Gratitude, for this obliging Address.
   And, (lest here and hereafter we're left in the Lurch)
To promote *true Religion,* (I mean our own Church)
I'll heartily concur with you, and lend a few Knocks
To suppress these confounding New Light Heterodox.
Then if from our Sins, we also refrain,
Perhaps we may have our CAPITOL! our dear CAPITOL! our glo-
rious ROYAL CAPITOL again.

To William Strahan   ALS: American Philosophical Society

Dear Sir   Philada. June 1. 1747
   Mr. Hall will acquaint you of the Footing we are about to go
upon &c. &c.[9] I have only time to acquaint you, that I have sent
you several Bills lately, and will speedily remit you whatever
shall be due to you after the Receipt of the Parcel of Books some
time since wrote for. My best Respects to Mrs. Strahan and
Wishes of Happiness to you and all Yours, in which my Wife joins
me heartily, is all at present from Your obliged Friend and Servant
                                                    B FRANKLIN

Add Feuquiere's Memoirs of the late War 2 Vols. 8vo. Also
Parker's military Memoirs printed for Austin price 3s. 6d.[1]

Addressed: To   Mr William Strahan   Printer in Wine-Office
Court Fleetstreet   London   Per Capt. Budden

9. BF and Hall formed a partnership, Jan. 1, 1748. For their Articles of
Agreement, see below, p. 263.
   1. The books ordered were probably Marquis de Feuquières, *Memoirs
historical and military* (London, 1736); and Captain Robert Parker, *Memoirs
of the Most Remarkable Military Transactions, from the year 1683 to 1718*
([London], Stephen Austen, 1747). See *Gent. Mag.*, XVII (1747), 108.

From Peter Collinson
ALS: American Philosophical Society

Respected friend   Londn. June 1: 1747

I shall be pleased to Hear that Mine per Mesnard and Dowers are come safe to your Hands with the books &c. and 4 Transactions[2] all Committed to the Care of Elias Bland[3] to putt up with his Letters. via N York I advised of your Bill on Oliver[4] for £47 5s. 5d. is received and placed to Account.

Inclosed are some proposals.[5] Pray send one to J: Logan.

I am with Respects thine   P COLLINSON

Books &c. by Dowers and Mesnard   £2: 2: 6
Ditto by this Ship   4: −

I doubt not but your proprietors fine present of an Electrical aparatas setts you all to Work.[6]

Addressed: To   Benn. Francklin   These

To Cadwallader Colden
ALS: New-York Historical Society

Sir   Philada. June 5. 1747

Mr. Harrison[7] tells me you are still in New York, as deeply engag'd in Publick Affairs, I suppose, as ever. When I consider your present Disposition to Retirement and Philosophical Meditation, I pity you: But I hope that Success will attend your Cares for the Publick Good; and the Satisfaction arising thence will make you some Amends.

2. *Philosophical Transactions* of the Royal Society.

3. Elias Bland, Quaker merchant of London, served a five-year apprenticeship to the Philadelphia merchant John Reynell before 1743. He failed, 1750, but was permitted to continue trading for a time under the direction of his creditors. BF lent him £300 in 1759; the loan was repaid promptly. *PMHB*, LV (1931), 121; LVI (1932), 170–86; LXXII (1948), 354 n, 362.

4. Not identified.

5. Probably the proposals for publishing the *Universal History* (London, 1747), which BF printed in *Pa. Gaz.*, July 9. Logan acknowledged receiving a copy, July 13. See below, p. 146.

6. For the Library Company's thanks for this gift, see below, p. 164.

7. George Harrison, whose wife was a sister of Mrs. Alexander Colden, daughter-in-law of Cadwallader Colden. *Colden Paps.*, IX, 61 n.

The Deserters who are come hither from the Forces on your Frontiers, are, 'tis said, unanimous in hating and Cursing the People of Albany.[8] I wonder at it: For I should have imagin'd that a People to be defended, would, from mere Views of Self Interest, have treated Strangers that came to defend them, with such Kindness and Hospitality as entirely to gain their Affections. Our Governor is gone, and no Measures are taken to send the Deserters back to their Colours, nor perhaps will be, unless the Expedition goes on; which I am sorry to hear from Boston, is thought to be laid aside, at least for this Summer. If this comes to be known among the Troops, I am afraid the Desertion will become yet more general; unless the Attempt on Crown Point, or something else to employ them, is enter'd upon; Men without Action generally growing uneasy and mutinous.[9]

My Son, who will wait upon you with this, is returning to the Army, his military Inclinations, (which I hoped would have been cool'd with the last Winter) continuing as warm as ever. If the Forces are to remain in your Government, it may sometimes fall in your Way to assist him with your Advice or Countenance, in which you would exceedingly oblige me.

I send you by him, a Glass Tube; and enclose you the first Part of my Electrical Journal,[1] which, rough as it is, may afford you some Amusement when you have a Leisure Hour. You will find in it, my Manner of Rubbing the Tube; to which I need only add, That it should be kept perfectly clean, and never sully'd by

8. "A Party of above 100 of the Pennsylvania Troops" deserted, and most of the other forces were mutinous. The reason was that only the New Jersey troops had been paid in full, and rumors were being spread among the German troops in Albany that their officers were cheating them and that they would never be paid in full. The captains of the Pennsylvania companies made a dignified protest to Governor Clinton against "low, evil minded people" who propagated malicious rumors. E. B. O'Callaghan, ed., *Documents relative to the Colonial History of the State of New-York*, VI (Albany, 1855), 375–6; *Colden Paps.*, III, 385–6.

9. Not only was there no expedition against the French in Canada this summer, but the Duke of Newcastle, May 30, ordered the immediate discharge of most of the American troops. Charles H. Lincoln, ed., *Correspondence of William Shirley* (N.Y., 1912), I, 386–7, 393, 403. Great Britain and France signed a peace at Aix-la-Chapelle the next year.

1. Not found. BF discussed the effects of points and the differences between firelight and sunlight in his letter to Collinson, May 25, above, pp. 128–9.

Handling, &c. By the Time you have read and return'd this, I shall have a second Part ready to send you, containing a greater Number of Experiments, and more curious. It is now discovered and demonstrated, both here and in Europe, that the Electrical Fire is a real Element, or Species of Matter, not *created* by the Friction, but *collected* only. In this Discovery, they were beforehand with us in England; but we had hit on it before we heard it from them. What relates to the wonderful Effect of *Points,* the Difference between *Candle Light* and *Sun Light,* and several other Things in these Papers, the Philosophers at home, are still, as far as we know, ignorant of. I am, Sir, with great Respect Your obliged and most humble Servant   B FRANKLIN

Addressed: To   The honble. Cadwallader Colden Esqr   at   New York

From George Whitefield   ALS: American Philosophical Society

Dear Mr. Franklin   [Philadel]phia June 23. 1747
     I thank You heartily for Your kind preamble to the Subscription.[2] I only object against its being made publick so as to engage persons in America and Great Britain. I think such a procedure would betray somewhat of meaness of Spirit and of a confidence in Him who *hitherto* has never left me in extremity, since I think a private subscription among my Friends here and *elsewhere* would raise as much as I want.[3] The publication of such a subscription would raise I believe more than is sufficient to pay my debts. I seek no such thing. If I can say I owe no man anything but love, I do not desire to save a groat, any more than will serve for a *visible* fund for the Orphan-house after my decease. [That?] institution I cannot give up. I know it would grieve thousands. Besides I am persuaded the New plantation in South Carolina

2. No copy of this subscription form has been found.
3. The expenses of the Bethesda Orphan-House ran ahead of receipts, and by the winter of 1746–47, when there were 26 inmates, Whitefield was over £500 in debt. In January 1747 he raised £300 in Charleston, but used it to buy a plantation of 640 acres—60 of them cleared—complete with house, barn, outbuildings, and slaves; and the original indebtedness remained undischarged. Tyerman, *Whitefield,* II, 155–8, 169–70.

will more than supply Bethesda with what (as it now subsists) it stands in need of. Need I add that there are several fatherless Children, [*torn:* whom I] look upon as my own who must then be turned out into a [*torn*] I cannot bring them to Pensylvania, because I [*torn*] to [*torn*] here; and if the Orphan-house should be given up [before?] my departure to my Native Country, America, in all probability, would see me no more. Whilst that stands, I shall have *a visible call* to visit these parts again. If this reasoning be not sound, let me be indulged in the Orphan-house since it is my *darling,* and a darling in which my own private interest cannot be concerned. Let it suffice to inform You that if I am helped out of my present embarrassments, I intend troubling no one for the Orphan-house any more. Excuse me from adding anything further. You know how generous minds work. I think it more blessed to give than to receive. But I submit to [*torn*] once tho' *Lord of all* condescended to live [*torn*] alms. At the same I would be humbled for all im [*torn*] cies in his service, and committing all my concerns to [His] hands, I subscribe myself Dear Sir Your very affectionate Friend and Servant   G W.

Would it not be for a few Trusty Friends to [have?] Copies of the preamble and to agree to call upon such persons as they have most interest with? I depend on my Friends Readiness and dispatch. Bis dat qui cito dat.[4]

From James Turner[5]   ALS: American Philosophical Society

Mr. Franklyn   Boston July 6th. 1747
Sir
    Herewith I send the Seal which you so long ago Spoke to me for, for Mr. Read.[6] The Occasion of my sending it to you and not

4. He gives twice who gives promptly. BF had printed this in his almanac, March 1742.
5. James Turner (d. 1759), Boston silversmith and engraver; engraved John Franklin's bookplate (see above, II, 230); the maps for James Alexander's *Bill in the Chancery of New-Jersey* (N.Y., 1747), printed on behalf of the East Jersey Proprietors and sold by James Parker and BF; and probably Lewis Evans' drawings for BF's fireplace pamphlet; moved, about 1754, to Philadelphia, where he engraved bookplates and did the plates of the maps

directly to him was because that the Seal being very heavy might cause him a great Charge which I thought he might be eased of by my sending it to you as you are Postmaster. I am very Sorry that I disappointed the Gentleman of it so long but it has been my Ill fortune ever Since I have been for my Self to be Involved in a great deal of large Unprofitable Silver Smiths work which was particularly my Case when your Brother Mr. J Franklyn procured me a large Job of Engraveing so that I cou'd not begin on that work till some time after you was last in Town but I hope as I have now Just got these plates ready for the press that I shall be able to mend this fault of keeping work so long, for the future. I have sent with the Seal 2 Impressions from it one on wax taken off by hand the other on a Wafer taken off in Colonel B Pollards[7] Press. The Letters show best on the latter because of its being such a large body of Metal that it chils the Wax before it can enter the Letters, but I think that either of 'em are legible enough. Soon after I began to work upon it I found that the Price I mentiond to you was much too little, and that I cou'd not afford to take pains to do it well under at least £3 more, but however depending on the Gentleman's Generosity I have taken no less pains about it than if I had actually agreed for £15. One thing I must Confess seems sufficient to stop my mouth on this Account viz. my keeping it so long in hand but I think my Self punish'd enough by the Constant falling of our money. But after all I do not demand any more than £12 the Sum I Mentiond to you

---

of Lewis Evans, 1755, and Nicholas Scull, 1759, and Joshua Fisher's *Chart of the Delaware Bay.* David McN. Stauffer, *American Engravers upon Copper and Steel* (N.Y., 1907), I, 278–9; II, 548–50; Lawrence C. Wroth, "Joshua Fisher's 'Chart of Delaware River and Bay,' " *PMHB*, LXXIV (1950), 90–109. Turner engraved the Penn coat of arms which first appeared in the masthead of *Pa. Gaz.* April 12, 1759. Sinclair Hamilton, *Early American Book Illustrators and Wood Engravers, 1670–1870* (Princeton, N. J., 1958), p. 7. The seal for the Pennsylvania Hospital was probably his work, and in 1758 he offered to do a mezzotint of BF. John Franklin to BF, Nov. 4, 1751; Turner to Deborah Franklin, May 1, 1758, Duane, *Works*, VI, 30–3.

6. James Read (see above, p. 39 n), clerk of the Crown and prothonotary of the Supreme Court of Pennsylvania. Turner's description suggests the seal was an official rather than a personal one.

7. Benjamin Pollard (1696–1756), sheriff of Suffolk Co., Mass., since 1743; commander of a company of cadets raised in Boston at the time of the Louisbourg expedition, 1745. 6 Mass. Hist. Soc. *Colls.*, X, 100.

145

(tho it was but a guess as I had never done one of this Size and but one great or Small in Steel before) for I always make it my rule to stand strictly to any bargain I make tho I lose by it and £12 I shall account to be the bargain that I made with you about this Seal Unless the Gentleman is Convinc'd that it is worth more and he is willing to allow it so hoping it will give him Satisfaction and resting the price Intirely with him I remain his and Your most Obliged humble Servant   JAMES TURNER

P.S. Unless the Gentleman has Money already in Boston he may direct it Either to me or to your Brother Mr. J Franklyn and if you or any Other Gentlemen wants any graveing work done of any Sort I should be glad of an Oppertunity of retrieveing the Credit I may have lost by keeping this and the things I did for you long.   Yours JT

Addressed: To   Mr. Benj: Fraklyn Postmaster   In   Philadelphia

From James Logan   Transcript: Harvard College Library (Sparks)

My friend B. Franklin   July 13. 1747
I received this afternoon a Copy of the Proposals for printing another Edition of Universal History of which I had a sight of the first vol:[8] about two or three years since from my Friend Richd Peters, of which notwithstanding I could not approve

---

8. A folio edition of *An Universal History, from the Earliest Account of Time to the Present* began to appear in London in 1736. Seven volumes, completing the ancient history part of the work, had been published by 1744, when George Faulkner, bookseller of Dublin, pirated them. In January 1747 the London printers Thomas Osborne, John Osborn, and Andrew Millar issued the first volume of a revised edition, octavo. In their Proposals (*Gent. Mag.*, XVII, 1747, 61–2) they announced that others would follow, one a month at 5s. a volume, until the work was completed in twenty volumes. The promised rate of publication was maintained for more than a year, but the twentieth volume was not issued until March 1749. The second part of the *History*, comprising the modern history, sixteen volumes in the folio edition and forty-four in the octavo, began to appear in London in 1759, and was completed in 1765 and 1766 respectively. *Gent. Mag.*, XIV (1744), 624; XVII (1747), 52, 61–2, 108; XVIII (1748), 96; XIX (1749), 144. BF reprinted the Proposals in *Pa. Gaz.*, July 9, 1747, offering the volumes at 13s. 6d. Pennsylvania currency.

of some particulars in the Preface which I was very sensible were wrong, tho' I cannot remember at present what they were, yet I very much approve of the design, and should be much pleased with the sight of these 20 volls, tho' I conceive there must be at least as many more to compleat the work. I should be pleased to know whether R.P. has the whole 9 volls in folio[9] that have been publish'd. But I am of opinion that the Modern History of Europe had as well be omitted, and that they had as good only give what concerns the Asiaticks and Africans. Since these proposals are dated the 30th of May 1746 I admire they should not publish the first till January last.[1] I presume thou hast not yet received any or more than one or two at most. I thank thee for thy new Catalogue[2] but am sorry thy Friend Parker[3] could have no help to range their Library into some tolerable order. Old as I am, now near 73, and much fail'd in all respects, I want to lay out about £200 Sterling more in Books which I shall do if I am so happy as to see a peace without farther disturbance and I have my Catalogue ready drawn. I should take it as a favour if I could see thee oftner here, for I want to ask divers questions; but shall add no more at present but that I am with great Truth and Reality Thy sincere Friend

J. LOGAN

To Jared Eliot[4]   ALS: Yale University Library

Dear Sir   Philada. July 16. 1747

I receiv'd your Favour of the 4th Instant.[5] I ought before this Time to have acknowledg'd the Receipt of the Book, which came

9. Volumes 6 and 7 each appeared in two parts—which probably explains Logan's speaking of nine volumes, instead of seven.

1. See below, p. 164, on the *Universal History*. For its importance in historiography, see Harry E. Barnes, *A History of Historical Writing* (Norman, Okla., 1937), pp. 171–2. The work is a bibliographical challenge, which deserves special study.

2. Probably BF's printed list of *Books Added to the Library Since the Year 1741* (Evans 5853). Logan had inquired earlier about the Library's new accessions (see above, p. 111).

3. Not identified.

4. Jared Eliot (1685–1763), B.A., Yale, 1706; schoolmaster at Guilford, Conn., 1706–07; minister at Killingworth, Conn., 1707–1763. Eliot was one of those examined on their theological views at the Yale commencement of 1722 (see above, I, 43), but he reconsidered his position and was not

very safe and in good Order, to hand. We have many Oil Mills in this Province, it being a great Country for Flax. Linseed Oil may now be bought for 3s. per Gallon; sometimes for 2s. 6d: But at New York I have been told it generally holds up at about 8s. Of this you can easily be satisfy'd, it being your Neighbour Government. In your last, you enquir'd about the kind of Land from which our Hemp is rais'd. I am told it must be very rich Land; sometimes they use drain'd Swamps and bank'd Meadows:[6] But the greatest Part of our Hemp is brought from Canistogo which is a large and very rich Tract [of Land] 70 Miles [west] from this City on the Banks of Sasquehanah a large fresh Water River. It is brought down in Waggons. If you should send any of your Steel Saws here for Sale, I should not be wanting where my Recommendation might be of Service. We have had as wet a Summer as has been known here these Thirty Years, so that it was with Difficulty our People got in their Harvest. In some Parts of the Country a

troubled further. He was a Yale trustee from 1730 until his death, and left the college an endowment of £10 for the purchase of books, which continues to yield an income. He studied medicine, acquired an extensive practice, and was the last of New England's eminent clerical physicians. One of his apprentices was Benjamin Gale. In the 1740s he turned to agriculture, reporting his experiments on his farms in the six parts of *Essays upon Field-Husbandry in New-England*, 1748–59. (The first three were printed at New London, the fourth and fifth at New York, and the last at New Haven. All six were reprinted in a single volume at Boston, 1760.) Eliot encouraged silk culture in Connecticut, and for inventing a process of "making very good, if not the best Iron" from black sea sand, 1762, he received a gold medal from the Society of Arts of London, of which he was a corresponding member. Defending experimentation against scoffers and belittlers, Eliot cited BF, who "very judiciously observed, that such Treatment was neither just nor political; that the Germans acted a wiser Part, for if a Project failed, unless it was ridiculous in itself, the Undertaker was named with Respect, saying though it failed, yet it was well imagined." Eliot's essays on agriculture and iron manufacture, together with a number of letters to and from him, and a biographical sketch by Rodney H. True, were edited by Harry J. Carman and Rexford G. Tugwell (N.Y., 1934). See also *DAB* and Herbert Thoms, *The Doctors Jared of Connecticut* (Hamden, Conn., 1958), pp. 3–31.

5. Not found.

6. Eliot used this information in the first of his *Essays upon Field-Husbandry* as follows: "It is not a meer Conjecture that the dreined Lands will produce Hemp. I am informed by my worthy Friend Benjamin Franklin Esq; of Philadelphia, that they raise Hemp upon their dreined Lands."

great Deal of Hay has been lost, and some Corn mildew'd: but in general the Harvest has been very great. The two preceding Summers (particularly the last,) were excessively dry. I think with you, it might be of Advantage to know what the Seasons are in the Several Parts of the Country. One's Curiosity in some philosophical Points might also be gratified by it. We have frequently along this North American Coast, Storms from the N East, which blow violently sometimes 3 or 4 Days. Of these I have had a very singular Opinion some years, viz. that tho' the Coarse of the Wind is from NE. to S.W. yet the Course of the Storm is from S.W to NE. i.e. the Air is in violent Motion in Virginia before it moves in Connecticut, and in Connecticut before it moves at Cape Sable, &c. My Reasons for this Opinion (if the like have not occur'd to you) I will give in my next.[7] I thank you for the curious Facts you have communicated to me relating to Springs. I think with you, that most Springs arise from Rains, Dews, or Ponds, &c. on higher Grounds: Yet possibly some that break out near the Tops of high Hollow Mountains, may proceed from the Abyss, or from Water in the Caverns of the Earth, rarified by its internal Heat, and raised in Vapour, 'till the cold Region near the Tops of such Mountains condense the Vapour into Water [again?] which comes forth in Springs and runs down on the outside of the Mountain, as it ascended on the [Inside?]. There is said to be a large Spring near the Top of Teneriffe;[8] and that Mountain was formerly a Volcano, consequently hollow within. Such Springs, if such there be, may properly be call'd Springs of *distill'd* Water. Now I mention Mountains it occurs to tell you, that the great Apalachian Mountains, which run from York River back of these Colonies to the Bay of Mexico, show in many Places near the highest Parts of them, Strata of Sea Shells, in some Places the Marks of them are in the solid Rocks. 'Tis certainly the *Wreck* of a World we live on! We have Specimens of those Sea shell Rocks broken off near the Tops of those Mountains, brought and deposited in our Library as Curiosities.[9] If you have not seen the

7. See below, p. 463.
8. Teneriffe: largest of the Canary Islands, with a 12,000-foot peak at its center.
9. On his return from Onondago, 1743, John Bartram wrote Peter Collinson that he had "observed the fossil shells over the country—even on top of

like, I'll send you a Piece. Farther, about Mountains (for Ideas will string themselves like Ropes of Onions) when I was once riding in your Country, Mr. Walker[1] show'd me at a Distance the Bluff Side or End of a Mountain, which appeared striped from top to Bottom, and told me the Stone or Rock of that Mountain was divided by Nature into Pillars; of this I should be glad to have a particular Account from you. I think I was somewhere near New-haven when I saw it.[2] You made some Mistake when you intended to favour me with some of the new valuable Grass Seed (I think you call'd it Hurd Seed) for what you gave me is grown up, and proves meer Timothy; so I suppose you took it out of a wrong Paper or Parcel.[3]

I wish your new Law may have the good Effect expected from it, in extricating your Government from the heavy Debt this War has oblig'd them to contract.[4] I am too little acquainted with your particular Circumstances to Judge of the Prudence of such a

the mountain that separates the waters of Susquehanna and St. Lawrence . . . ." Darlington, *Memorials*, p. 169. The Library Company's catalogue of 1770 listed "Pennsylvania fossils &c. given by Mr. Bartram." Dorothy F. Grimm, "Franklin's Scientific Institution," *Pa. Hist.*, XXIII (1956), 460.

1. Robert Walker, Jr. (1705–1772), lawyer of Stratford, Conn., member of the General Assembly, 1745–64, one of the governor's Assistants, 1766–72, judge of the Superior Court, 1760, and a colonel of militia. He and Eliot were two of the patentees of an ore bed near Salisbury, Conn. Dexter, *Biog. Sketches*, I, 418–9; *Public Records of the Colony of Connecticut*, VII (1873), 499; Walker to Eliot, July 12, 1758, MS, Yale Univ. Lib.

2. Several such formations are visible near New Haven. East Rock is "a Bluff Side or End of a Mountain," while good examples of pillars or columnar formations are found at Rabbit Rock, near Montowese, a few miles to the north. "The cylindrical columns are certainly in New England," Bartram wrote Collinson, July 20, 1747. "Benjamin Franklin saw them at three miles distance; but being very cold, did not care to turn out." Darlington, *Memorials*, p. 180.

3. BF must have misunderstood. Eliot had compared "Herd Grass (known in Pennsylvania by the Name of *Timothy-Grass*)" with fowl meadow grass, which he said was much better, made softer and more pliable hay, and stood unspoiled longer if cutting was delayed. *Essays* (1934 edit.), pp. 61–2.

4. Connecticut's law of May 1747 "for the Regulating and Encouragement of Trade in this Colony," levied a duty of 5 per cent (7½ per cent for importers not residents of Connecticut) on goods, above the value of £15 new tenor currency, imported from any New England colony, New York, New Jersey, or Pennsylvania. Exceptions included cast, bar, and slit iron, steel, salt, beaver, leather, deerskins, dried and pickled fish, whalebones, rice, tar,

Law for your Colony with any Degree of Exactness. But to a
Friend one may hazard one's Notions right or wrong. And as
you are pleas'd to desire my Thoughts, you shall have 'em and
welcome. I wish they were better. First, I imagine that the Five
Per Cent Duty on Goods imported from your Neighbouring
Governments, tho' paid at first Hand by the Importer, will not
upon the whole come out of his Pocket, but be paid in Fact by
the Consumer: For the Importer will be sure to sell his Goods as
much dearer as to reimburse himself: So that it is only another
Mode of Taxing your own People, tho' perhaps meant to raise
Money on your Neighbours. Yet if you can make some of the
Goods, heretofore imported, among yourselves, the advanc'd
Price of 5 percent may encourage your own Manufacture [*torn*]
and in time make the Importation of such Articles unnecessary,
which will be an Advantage. Secondly, I imagine the Law will
be difficult to execute, require many Officers to prevent Smugling,
in so extended a Coast as yours; and the Charge considerable:
And if Smugling is not prevented, the fair Trader will be under-
sold and ruined. If the Officers are many and busy, there will
arise Numbers of vexatious Lawsuits, and Dissensions among
your People. Quere whether the Advantages will overballance.
Thirdly, if there is any Part of your Produce that you can well
spare and would desire to have taken off by your Neighbours in
Exchange for something you more want, perhaps they, taking
Offence at your selfish Law, may in Return lay such heavy Duties
or Discouragements on that Article, as to leave it a Drug on your
Hands. As to the Duty on transporting Lumber,[5] (unless in Con-

---

turpentine, window glass, and ship timbers. Collectors were to be appointed
for each county. The quantity and value of the goods imported had to be declared within three days, under penalty of confiscation, with the burden
of proof, in case of suit, on the importer. The act also offered a 5 per cent
premium to anyone importing goods at his own risk from Great Britain or
Ireland. The law was to run five years. It was not renewed. *Public Records
of the Colony of Connecticut*, IX (1876), 283–6.

5. Connecticut's "Act for laying a Duty on the Exportation of Lumber
to the neighbouring Governments," May 1747, was supposed to conserve the
colony's timber resources and promote shipbuilding and trade with the West
Indies. It applied to all barrel staves and headings, ships timbers, planks,
boards, and bark shipped to the neighboring coastal colonies of New England
and New York. *Ibid.*, pp. 286–7.

necticut Bottoms to the West Indies) I suppose the Design is to raise the Price of such Lumber on your Neighbours, and throw that advanc'd Price into your Treasury: But may not your Neighbours supply themselves elsewhere; or if Numbers of your People have Lumber to dispose of, and want Goods from, or have Debts to, pay to your Neighbours, will they not, (unless you employ Numbers of Officers, to watch all your Creeks, and Landings) run their Lumber, and so defeat the Law; or if the Law is strictly executed, and the Duty discourage the Transportation to your Neighbours, will not all your People that want to dispose of Lumber, be laid at the Mercy of those few Merchants that send it to the W. Indies, who will buy it at their own Price, and make such Pay for it as they think proper. If I had seen the Law, and heard the Reasons that are given for making it, I might have judg'd and talk'd of it more to the purpose. At present I shoot my Bolt pretty much in the Dark: But you can excuse, and make proper Allowances. My best Respects to good Madam Elliot and your Sons; and if it falls in your Way, my Service to the kind hospitable People near the River, whose Name I am sorry I've forgot. I am, Dear Sir, [with] the utmost Regard, Your obliged humble Servant   B FRANKLIN

From James Logan   Transcript: Harvard College Library (Sparks)

My friend B. Franklin,   Stenton July 19   1747
   I can scarce ever forgive thee for not shewing me, in now above two years and a half, Dr. Colden's Answer to my Objections to his Fluxions:[6] For he had good reason to say that either my Memory had fail'd me, or I had read that piece with little attention; the last of which is exactly true, tho' I remember not now what other business diverted me from it; but some there was: And the whole piece prov'd to me intolerably tedious, for so it truly appears to me at this time. But then he was exceedingly himself to blame, for writing in page 10 at the $2d^x+x+1$ which ought according to the usual notation to have been wrote $\dot{x}+.1$ and even then with the point on the line itself which in that case

6. BF had sent Colden Logan's first criticism of his essay, Oct. 25, 1744. See above, II, 417.

is the only common method. I might have overlooked it but as he wrote it, I took no manner of notice of the point. And as himself says, but by a mistake in too much haste I presume I own they more properly might have been mark'd thus $\sqrt{10+0\cdot1}$ instead of $\sqrt{10+01}$, and it is a mistake to say the [*remainder missing*].

From G. Row[se?][7]   ALS: American Philosophical Society

Sir   North East July 21st. 1747
I'm informd of Some Letters from Virginia being directed for your care, if any arrived please send per Enoch Story[8] and if any shoud Soon come to hand please to Order the Post to deliver them at my house which will much oblige Sir Your humble Ser[vant]   G. Row[se?]
To Mr. Franklin
Addressed: To Mr. Benjn. Franklin Postmaster in Philadelphia By favour Captn. West

From Jonas Green[9]   ALS: American Philosophical Society

Dear Sir,   Annapolis, July 25. 1747.
You will receive by this Mail two Packets from Barbadoes,

7. The signature is torn, but only two or three letters can be missing. At least four persons named Rouse were heads of families in 1790 in Cecil County, Md., where North East is located.
8. Probably Enoch Story, son of the proprietor of Pewter Platter Tavern in Philadelphia. Enoch was a co-founder of the *Pennsylvania Mercury*, 1755; served the British during their occupation of Philadelphia, 1777–78; was attainted of treason; and sought refuge in England. Lorenzo Sabine, *Biographical Sketches of Loyalists of the American Revolution* (Boston, 1864), II, 337.
9. Jonas Green (1712–1767), born in Boston; learned his trade from his father Timothy, who settled as a printer in New London, Conn., 1714. Young Green worked for a time for his brother in the firm of Kneeland and Green of Boston, and he issued at least one book over his imprint—Judah Monis' Hebrew grammar, the first published in America, 1735. For three years he was a journeyman in Philadelphia, working with both BF and Bradford. Settling at Annapolis, 1738, he became official printer for Maryland and published, after 1745, the *Maryland Gazette*, of which Thomas (*Printing*, II, 156)

153

which came inclosed to me from Mr. Ja. Bingham.[1] One of them incloses the W. India Monthly Packet, which Mr. Bingham wrote me word he sent open that I might have a sight of it. They came by Capt. Seager. Our Assembly added this Session 5 Pounds in each County to my Salary, but added to the Work likewise, which I am well content with; They give me now 260 Pounds our Currency a Year:[2] And we are very busy in dispatching the Public Work. I wish I could get another Hand. The Assembly has hinder'd me from Time to go to the Courts to collect my Money, otherwise should have got you a Bill by this Time; But as soon as the Public Work is done, or sooner, I will get you a good Bill. I wish I could get another parcel of Paper from Philadelphia; a very favorable opportunity now offers; Mr. Daniel Rawlings[3] is gone up the Bay in a Schooner, and brings down Goods from Philadelphia, and would bring some Paper for me. He went up yesterday. If you could send me such a parcel as before I'll get you a large Bill of £40 or 45 Sterling, and send [it]. I likewise want some Varnish, (a Bottle by the post,) and 4 or 5 Pound of Lampblack per Rawlings. My Paper sinks fast; we now use 3 or 4 Reams a Week. I have about 450 or 460 good Customers for Seal'd Papers, and about 80 unseal'd. The Virginian's Speech made a deal of Laughter here; and was well approved of by some in that Colony; how the Baronet himself lik'd it I have not heard.[4] We have had a Severe Hot Spell of Weather; and I have been a little troubled with Fevers; but they are, I hope, gone from me. We are all well. I hope you are so too. Our hearty Respects to yourself and Mrs. Franklin, not forgetting Miss Sally. I rejoice to see that our brave Countrymen are to be rewarded for their

---

said that typographically it was as good as any printed in America. He was postmaster of Annapolis, held several minor political appointments, was a vestryman of St. Anne's Parish, and had an active social life, being secretary of his Masonic lodge and a member of the Tuesday Club with Dr. Alexander Hamilton. *DAB;* Lawrence C. Wroth, *A History of Printing in Colonial Maryland* (Baltimore, 1922), pp. 75–84.

1. Not identified.
2. The text of the act increasing Green's compensation is in *Arch. of Md.*, XLIV, 663–4.
3. A Daniel Rawlings was sheriff of Calvert Co., 1748.
4. Green reprinted BF's Verses on the Virginia Capitol Fire (see above, pp. 135–40) in *Md. Gaz.*, June 16.

Expence in taking Cape Breton.[5] I am, Dear Sir, Your obliged Friend and humble Servant   JONAS GREEN

Addressed: To   Mr. Benjamin Franklin   Post Master   at   Philadelphia

Endorsed: Jonas Green July 30. 47

From Joseph Dowse[6]   ALS: American Philosophical Society

Sir   Boston July 27 1747

Mrs. Steel[7] who got here last week desires me to write you in her behalf, to acknowledge the many kind Acts of Freindship she hath received from you and at the same time to sollicit you to let me or her know what new Matter you had received after her leaving Philadelphia to be displeased with her or her conduct as you Seem to be in a letter she received after she left you.[8] She assures me she is not consious of any thing either said or done and doth with the utmost Sincerity esteem you her freind, and therefore thinks she can fairly chalange your open Answer to this earnest demand. I tell her Im assured from your Character there must have happned some Mistake between you, or some ill minded persons delivered wrong representations or fashoods. To

5. Soon after the capture of Louisbourg in 1745, Massachusetts, followed by the other New England colonies, petitioned the Crown for repayment of their expenses in the expedition. After extended inquiry the Privy Council issued an order, Jan. 15, 1747, approving the requests. *Acts of the Privy Council, Colonial Series, 1745–1766* (London, 1911), pp. 10–11.

6. Joseph Dowse (1708–1785), was auditor of Boston, 1759, and in 1760 was named surveyor and searcher of customs at Salem, where he was a substantial merchant. Robert F. Seybolt, *The Town Officials of Colonial Boston, 1634–1775* (Cambridge, Mass., 1939), p. 289; Joseph B. Felt, *Annals of Salem* (Salem, Mass., 1827), p. 456. A Loyalist during the Revolution, he received a pension from the British government, as did his son Jonathan, also a customs official. E. Alfred Jones, *The Loyalists of Massachusetts* (London, 1930), pp. 120–1. Dowse was not related to BF's sister Elizabeth Douse.

7. Mrs. Thomas Steel's daughter Jane had married Joseph Dowse in 1734. Record Commissioners of the City of Boston, *Report . . . containing Boston Births from A.D. 1700 to A.D. 1800* (Boston, 1894), p. 65; same, *Report . . . containing the Boston Marriages from 1700 to 1751* (Boston, 1898), p. 222.

8. Not found. BF alluded to his "dissatisfaction" with Mrs. Steel in a letter to his brother John, Aug. 6, 1747 (below, p. 169), but without explanation.

this desire of Mrs. Steel, I would add my own and pray you would be so kind as to comply with her request and let me know, if you please, what hath been the cause of these surmises. Please also let me know whether you have sold her Horse and Chair and what she may be indebted to you which I will with the utmost care see you reimbursd: Your complyance with this request will greatly oblidge Sir Your Most Humble Servant   JOSEPH DOWSE

I beleive it would be best to dispose of the Horse &c. assoon as may be for what it will fetch. I can assure you Mrs. Steel speaks of you, and your kindness with the greatest esteem.

Addressed: To   Mr: Benja Franklin   at   Philadelphia

To Peter Collinson   Copy: American Academy of Arts and Sciences[9]

Sir   Philada. July 28. 1747[1]

The inclosed is a Copy of my last, which went by the Governour's Vessel: since which we have received, by Mesnard and Ouchterlony, Hill's Theophrastus, Pemberton's Dispensatory, Wilson's Electricity and some other Pamphlets.[2] The Proprietor's handsome Present of a complete Electrical Apparatus &c. is also come to Hand in good Order, and is put up in the Library; but little has been done with it yet, the Weather having been excessively hot and moist ever since it arrived. The Directors have ordered his very kind Letter to be answered with the Thanks of the Company.[3] I suppose it will be done by this Ship, if her unexpected sudden Departure does not prevent.[4]

9. In Bowdoin MS: Letter II; in 1751, 1754, and 1760 editions of *Exper. and Obser.*: Letter I; in 1769 and 1774 editions: Letter III. See above, pp. 115–18, for a discussion of manuscript and printed versions.

1. For the dating of this letter, see above, p. 126 n. Confirmatory evidence for the July 28 date is provided by BF's letter to Collinson, August 14, in which he says he has already sent Collinson two long letters on electricity, one on the "Governor's Vessel," the other by Captain Mesnard. Mesnard's ship *Carolina* was reported in *Pa. Gaz.*, July 30, as having cleared Philadelphia for London.

2. John Hill, *Theophrastus's History of Stones* (London, 1746); Henry Pemberton, *The Dispensatory of the Royal College of Physicians* (London, 1746); and Benjamin Wilson, *An Essay towards an Explication of the Phaenomenon of Electricity* (London, 1746).

3. See below, p. 164.

4. The first paragraph is omitted in all printed editions.

The necessary Trouble of copying long Letters which perhaps, when they come to your Hands, may contain Nothing new or worth your Reading, so quick is the Progress made with you in Electricity, half discourages me from writing anymore on that Subject. Yet I can not forbear adding a few Observations on Mr. Muschenbroek's wonderful Bottle. vizt.

1 The Non-electric, contained in the Bottle, differs, when electrised from a Non-electric electrised out of the Bottle in this; That the Electrical Fire of the latter is accumulated *on it's Surface,* and forms an Electrical Atmosphere round it, of considerable Extent; but the Electrical Fire is crouded *into the Substance* of the former; the Glass confining it.[5]

2 At the same Time that the Wire and Top of the Bottle &c. is electrised *positively* or *plus,* the Bottom of the Bottle is electrised *negatively* or *minus* in exact Proportion. i.e. Whatever Quantity of Electrical Fire is thrown in at [the] Top,[6] an equal Quantity goes out of the Bottom.[7] To understand this, Suppose the common Quantity of Electricity in each Part of the Bottle, before the Operation begins, is equal to 20, and at every Stroke of the Tube, suppose a Quantity equal to 1 is thrown in; then after the first Stroke, the Quantity contained in the Wire and upper Part of the Bottle will be 21, in the Bottom 19. After the second, the upper Part will have 22, the lower 18, and so on, till after 20 Strokes, the upper Part will have a Quantity of Electrical Fire equal to 40,

5. Emendation in MS: "The Difference here mention'd between a Non Electric confin'd in Glass and one not so confin'd; and the Supposition of crouding into and condensing the Electric Fire in a Non Electric Body, were afterwards found to be Mistakes; the true Cause of the Bottle's Force being discover'd by subsequent Experiments. What follows is right, if only the Words *Top* and *Bottom* of the Bottle, be changed for the Words *Inside* and *Outside Surfaces.*" Printed emendation in 1751, 1754 and 1760 editions: "We since find, that the fire in the bottle is not contained in the non-electric, but *in the glass.* All that is after said of the *top* and *bottom* of the bottle, is true of the *inside* and *outside* surfaces, and should have been so expressed. See Sect. 16, p. 24." (below, p. 356). Footnote in 1769 and 1774 editions: "See this opinion rectified in Letter IV, §16 and 17 [below, p. 356]. The fire in the bottle was found by subsequent experiments not to be contained in the non-electric, but *in the glass.* 1748."

6. Inserted as a correction in 1769 edition, and in the text of 1774 edition.

7. Footnote in 1769 and 1774 editions: "What is said here, and after, of the *top* and *bottom* of the bottle, is true of the *inside* and *outside* surfaces, and should have been so expressed."

the lower none: and then the Operation ends; for no more can be thrown into the upper Part, when no more can be driven out of the lower Part. If you attempt to throw more in, it is spued back thro' the Wire, or flies out in loud Cracks *thro' the Sides of the Bottle.*[8]

3 The Equilibrium can not be restored in the Bottle by *inward* Communication, or Contact of the Parts; but it must be done by a Communication form'd *without* the Bottle, between the Top and Bottom, by some Non-electric touching[9] both at the same Time. In which Case, if the Contact be large especially,[1] it is restored with a Violence and Quickness inexpressible; or touching each alternately, in which Case the Equilibrium is restored by Degrees.

4 As no more Electrical Fire can be thrown into the Top of the Bottle, when all is driven out of the Bottom. So in a Bottle not yet electrised, none can be thrown into the Top, when none *can* get out of[2] the Bottom; which happens either when the Bottom is too thick, or when the Bottle is placed on an Electric-per-se. Again, when the Bottle is electrised, but little[3] of the Electrical Fire can be *drawn out* from the Top, by touching the Wire, unless an equal Quantity can at the same Time *get in* at the Bottom.[4] Thus place an Electris'd Bottle on clean Glass or dry Wax, and you will not, by touching the Wire, get out the Fire from the Top. Place it on a Non-electric, and touch the Wire, you will get it out in a short Time; but soonest, when you form a direct Communication, as above.

So wonderfully are these two States of Electricity, the *plus* and *minus* combined and ballanced in this miraculous Bottle! situated and related to each other in a Manner that I can by no Means comprehend! If it were possible that a Bottle should in one Part contain a Quantity of Air strongly comprest, and in another Part

8. For the last six words another hand has substituted in the margin of MS: "to the Sides or Coating of the Bottle from the wire Hook." This correction appears in no printed edition.

9. Added in 1769 and 1774 editions: "or approaching."

1. Deleted in another hand in MS: "if the Contact be large especially." These words are also omitted from all printed editions.

2. In all printed editions: "at" replaces "of."

3. In the margin of the MS in another hand: "The little that can be drawn out, is the quantity in, or accumulated on, the non-electric within the Bottle. The power to Shock resides in the Glass as Glass. See Analysis of the Bottle Page 40. §17 [below, p. 356]."

4. Footnote in 1769 and 1774 editions: "See the preceding note [p. 157], relating to *top* and *bottom.*"

158

a perfect Vacuum; We know the Equilibrium would be instantly restored *within*. But here we have a Bottle, containing at the same Time a *Plenum* of Electrical Fire and a *Vacuum* of the same Fire; and yet the Equilibrium can not be restored between them but by a Communication without! Tho' the Plenum presses violently to expand, and the hungry Vacuum seems to attract as violently in Order to be filled.

5 The Shock to the Nerves (or Convulsion rather) is occasioned by the sudden Passing of the Fire thro' the Body in its Way from the Top to the Bottom of the Bottle. The Fire takes the shortest Course,[5] as Mr. Watson justly observes; but he was mistaken in supposing, that for a person to be shock'd[6] a Communication with the Floor is necessary (see *Sequel* p. 67, 68, 69).[7] He that holds the Bottle with one Hand, and touches the Wire with the other, will be shockt as much, tho' his Shoes be dry, or even standing on Wax, as otherwise. And on the Touch of the Wire (or of the Gun Barrel, which is the same Thing) the Fire does not proceed from the touching Finger to the Wire, as he supposes,[8] but from the Wire to the Finger, and passes thro' the Body to the other Hand, and so into the Bottom of the Bottle. We are all obliged to that Gentleman for Publishing his ingenious Observations. It is likely he has seen these little Mistakes himself before this Time; and therefore it is hardly necessary to shew him what I write: If you should, I hope, he will excuse the Freedom I have taken; it being only in a private Letter; There is also some apparent Contradiction between his No. XLVII and LXII in the Sequel which I need not further point out.[9]

Experiments confirming the above

Exper. I. Place an electrised Vial on Wax. A small Cork Ball suspended by a dry Silk Thread held in your Hand, and brought near to the Wire, will first be attracted and then repell'd. When in this State of Repellency, sink your Hand, that the Ball may

5. Footnote in 1774 edition adds: "other circumstances being equal."

6. In all printed editions: "as Mr. Watson justly observes: But it does not appear from experiment that in order for a person to be shocked . . ."

7. The reference to William Watson's *A Sequel to the Experiments and Observations Tending to illustrate the Nature and Properties of Electricity* (London, 1746), is omitted from all printed editions; and the next clause begins with "for."

8. In all printed editions: "as is supposed" replaces "as he supposes."

9. All printed editions omit the sentences from "We are all obliged to that Gentleman . . ." to the end of the paragraph.

be brought towards the Bottom of the Bottle, it will there be instantly and strongly attracted, 'till it has parted with it's Fire. If the Bottle had an Electrical[1] Atmosphere as well as the Wire, an Electrified[2] Cork would be repell'd from one as well as from the other.

Exper. II [fig. 1].[3] From a bent Wire [(a)] sticking in the Table, let a small Linen Thread [(b)] hang down within half

an Inch of the Electrised Vial [(c)]. Touch the Wire of the Vial repeatedly with your Finger; and at every touch you will see the Thread instantly attracted by the Bottle. This is best done with a Vinegar Cruet, or some such belly'd Bottle. As soon as you draw any Fire out from the upper Part, by touching the Wire, the lower Part of the Bottle *draws* an equal Quantity *in* by the Thread.

Exper. III [fig. 2]. Fix a Wire in the Lead, with which the Bottom of the Bottle is armed [(d)], so as that bending upwards, it's Ring End may be level with the Top, or Ring End of the Wire in the

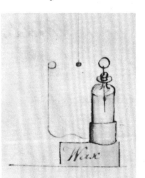

Cork [(e)], and at 3 or 4 Inches Distance. Then electrise the Bottle, and place it on Wax. If a Cork suspended by a Silk Thread [(f)] hang between these two Wires, it will play incessantly from one to the other, 'till the Bottle is no longer electrised. That is, it fetches and carries Fire from the Top to the Bottom[4] of the Bottle till the Equilibrium is restored.

Exper. IV [fig. 3]. Place an electricised[5] Vial upon Wax. Take a Wire

1. In 1769 and 1774 editions: "a positive electrical atmosphere." In 1754 edition: "electrified" for "Electrical."

2. In his own copy of the 1754 edition BF has underlined this word and written "electrical plus" in the margin.

3. The numbers of the figures and the letters of particular apparatus refer to the plate in the printed edition, reproduced in the next volume.

4. Footnote in 1769 and 1774 editions: "i.e. from the inside to the outside."

5. In 1760, 1769, and 1774 editions: "electrised" replaces "electricised."

[(g)] bent in the Form of a C,[6] the Ends at such a Distance when bent, as that the upper may touch the Wire of the Bottle,

when the lower touches the Bottom; stick the outer Part to a Piece[7] of Sealing Wax [(h)] which will serve as a Handle. Then apply the lower End to the Bottom of the Bottle, and gradually bring the upper End near the Wire in the Cork: the Consequence is; Spark follows Spark till the Equilibrium is restored. Touch the Top first, and on approaching the Bottom with the other End, you have a constant Stream of Fire from the Wire entering the Bottle. Touch Top and Bottom together, and the Equilibrium will soon be restored

but silently[8] and imperceptibly, *the Contact being small;*[9] the crooked Wire forming the Communication.[1]

Exper. V [fig. 4]. Let a Ring of thin Lead or Paper surround the Bottle [(i)],[2] even at some Distance from or above the Bottom: From that Ring let a Wire proceed up till it touch the Wire of the Cork [(k)]. A Bottle, so fixt, cannot by any Means be electrised; the Equilibrium is never destroyed. For while the Communication between the upper and lower Parts of the Bottle is continu'd by the outside Wire[3] what is driven out at Bottom is constantly

6. In all printed editions: "Take a wire (g) in form of a C."

7. In all printed editions: "to a Piece" is replaced by "on a stick."

8. Printed emendation in 1751, 1754, and 1760 editions: "This must have been a mistake. When the bottle is full charged, the crooked wire cannot well be brought to touch the top and bottom so quick, but that there will be a loud spark; unless the points be sharp, without loops."

9. All printed editions omit *"the Contact being small."*

1. In 1769 and 1774 editions: "Touch the top and bottom together, and the equilibrium will be instantly restored; the crooked wire forming the communication."

2. In all printed editions: "surround a bottle (i), even at some distance from or above the bottom."

3. Added in the MS in another hand, and in all printed editions: "the fire only circulates:"

supplied from the Top.[4] Hence a Bottle can not be electrised that is foul or moist on the Outside.[5]

Exper. VI. Place a Man on a Cake of Wax and present him the Wire of the Electrified Vial to touch, you standing on the Floor, and holding it in your Hand. As often as he touches [it][6] he will be electrified *plus*, and any one standing on the Floor may draw a Spark from him. The Fire in this Experiment passes out of the Wire into him; and at the same Time out of your Hand into the Bottom of the Bottle.

Exper. VII. Give him the electrified[7] Vial to hold, and do you touch the Wire. As often as you touch it, he will be electrified *minus*, and may draw a Spark from any one standing on the Floor. The Fire now Passes from the Wire to you, and from him into the Bottom of the Bottle.

Exper. VIII. Lay two Books on two Glasses back towards back, 2 or 3 Inches distant, set the electrified Vial on one, and then touch the Wire; that Book will be electrified *minus;* the Electrical Fire being drawn out of it by the Bottom of the Bottle. Take off the Bottle, and holding it in your Hand, touch the other Book with the Wire; that Book will be electrified[8] *plus;* the Fire passing into it from the Wire, and the Bottle at the same Time supplied from your Hand. A suspended small Cork Ball will play between these Books, 'till the Equilibrium is restored.

Exper. IX. When a Body is electrised *plus* it will repel an electrified Feather[9] or small Cork Ball. When *minus* (or when in [the][1] common State) it will attract them; but stronger when *minus* than when in the Common State, the Difference being greater.

4. Footnote in 1769 edition: "See the preceding note. [8];" footnote in 1774 edition: "See the preceding note relating to top and bottom."

5. Printed addition in 1751, 1754, and 1760 editions: "such moisture continuing up to the cork or wire." Added in 1769 and 1774 editions: "if such moisture continue up to the cork or wire."

6. Added in all printed editions.

7. In 1754 and all subsequent editions: "electrical" replaces "electrified."

8. In 1751, 1754, 1760, and 1769 editions: "electrised" replaces "electrified;" but in 1774 edition: "electrified."

9. In 1774 edition: "a positively electrified feather."

1. Added in all printed editions.

Exper. X. Tho' as in Expert. VI. a Man standing on Wax may be electrised a Number of Times by repeatedly touching the Wire of an electrised Bottle held in the Hand of one standing on the Floor, he receiving the Fire from the Wire each Time; yet holding it in his own Hand, and touching the Wire, tho' he draws a Strong Spark, and is violently shockt, no Electricity remains in him; the Fire only passing thro' him from the upper to the lower Part of the Bottle. Observe, before the Shock, to let some one on the Floor touch him, to restore the Equilibrium in his Body; for in taking hold of the Bottom of the Bottle, he sometimes becomes a little electrised *minus*, which will continue after the Shock, as would also any *plus* Electricity he might have given him before the Shock. For, restoring an Equilibrium in the Bottle, does not at all affect the Electricity in the Man thro' whom the Fire passes: that Electricity is neither increased nor diminished.

Exper. XI. The Passing of the Electrical Fire from the upper to the lower Part[2] of the Bottle to restore the Equilibrium, is rendered strongly visible by the following pretty Experiment. Take a Book, whose Cover[3] is filletted with Gold; bend a Wire of 8 or 10 Inches long in this Form,[4] slip it on the End of the Cover of the Book, over the Gold line, so as that the Shoulder of it may press on one End of the Gold Line, the Ring up, but leaning towards the other End of the Book. Lay the Book on [a][5] Glass or Wax;[6] and on the other End of the Gold Line[7] set the Bottle electrised. Then bend the springing Wire, by pressing it with a Stick of Wax, 'till it's Ring approaches the Ring of the Bottle Wire: instantly there is a strong Spark and Stroke, and the whole Line of Gold, which completes the Communication between the Top and Bottom of the Bottle, will appear a vivid Flame, like the

2. Footnote in 1769 and 1774 editions: "i.e. from the *inside* to the *outside.*"
3. In 1769 and 1774 editions: "covering" replaces "cover."
4. In all printed editions: "in the form of (m) fig. 5."
5. Added in all printed editions.
6. Footnote in 1774 edition: "Placing the book on glass or wax is not necessary to produce the appearance; it is only to show that the visible Electricity is not brought up from the common stock in the earth."
7. In all printed editions: "lines" for "line."

sharpest Lightning. The closer the Contact between the Shoulder of the Wire and the Gold at one End of the Line, and between the

Bottom of the Bottle and the Gold at the other End, the better the Experiment succeeds. The Room should be darkned. If you would have the whole Filleting round the Cover appear in Fire at once, let the Bottle and Wire touch the Gold in the diagonally opposite Corners.

The rest of this Letter on private Affairs.[8]

To Peter Collinson Esqr. F. R. S. London

Library Company to Thomas Penn

MS Minutes: Library Company of Philadelphia

Franklin informed the Library Company Directors on July 13, 1747, that he had received a letter from the Proprietor Thomas Penn, "with a compleat Electrical Apparatus" as a gift to the Library. John Sober, William Coleman, and Franklin were appointed to acknowledge it. A copy of their letter was spread on the Library Company's minutes of September 14.

Sir   Philadelphia July 29th, 1747.

We embrace this Opportunity of acknowleging the Honour done us in your Letter by Capt. Mesnard and the Receipt of your kind Present of an Electrical Apparatus, which gave us a Satisfaction so much the greater, as it is a Confirmation, that at this Distance of Time and Place, we are remembered by you with the same Regard which you have from the first testifyed by such repeated Instances of your Bounty. We are under a Difficulty for Terms new or significant enough to convey a proper Acknowlegement, but hope it may be done in the best Manner by putting your Present to the Use intended. And some of our Members who employ themselves in such Researches may, by its Assistance, shew

8. This sentence and the address are in BF's hand.

that this fresh Mark of your Favour has been judiciously, as well as generously bestowed upon Your most obliged &c.

To William Strahan

 MS not found;[9] reprinted from *The Atlantic Monthly*, LXI (1888), 26.

Sir,   Philada. July 29. 1747

Your Favours of March 18 and April 1[1] are come to Hand with all the Books, &c. mentioned in the invoice, in good Order, and am much obliged to you for your ready Compliance with all my Requests.

I believe I could have got Subscriptions for 20 Sets of the Universal History, and perhaps more, but unluckily a Ship from Ireland has, since the Receipt of your Letter, brought in 20 Setts compleat, and they are offer'd at a lower Rate than the English Edition can be afforded at, even if I paid but 4s. per vol.[2] I do what I can to lessen the Credit of that piratical Edition, and talk much of the Improvements made in this; but that being to be had entire immediately, and this not until after many Months, weighs a good deal with Some; and others object, that 'tis to be appre-hended the London Booksellers will either curtail the folio Edi-tion greatly to save Money, or put the Subscribers at last to the Expense of a greater Number of Volumes than 20; seeing the Volumes are much less than those of the Irish Edition, the 3 first of the one containing but little more than the first of the other. If they think fit to venture a Parcel here Hall will do his best to dispose of them, and I will assist him what I can. They may send a Parcel also to Mr. Parker Printer of New York, a very honest punctual Man.[3]

I am glad all the Bills I sent you have been paid or accepted. You may expect more in a short Time, and after the next Parcel of Books are paid for you will chiefly have to deal with Mr. Hall, into whose Hands I have agreed to put the Shop, &c.

9. The ALS is listed in Anderson Galleries Sale No. 1008 (Oct. 30–31, 1913), item 198.
1. Letters not found.
2. See above, p. 146 n.
3. James Parker. See above, II, 341 n.

With all our best Respects to you and yours, heartily wishing you Health and Happiness, I conclude Your obliged humble Servant B. FRANKLIN

Per Mesnard

To Cadwallader Colden

ALS: Yale University Library

Sir   Philada. July 30. 1747

I receiv'd your Favour of the 26th.[4] which I shall answer at large per next Post. In the mean time please to send me, if you have it with you, my Paper of Observations on Baxter's Book, which I want to make some present Use of, and have no other Copy.[5]

Mesnard sail'd this Day for London. But here is a Vessel bound to Bristol, which the next Post will reach. In haste I am, Sir Your oblig'd humble Servant B FRANKLIN

P S. Upon farther Enquiry I find that next Post will not reach the Bristol Vessel, she being to sail on Saturday.[6]

From Daniel Cheston[7]

ALS: American Philosophical Society

Sir   Chester Augt. 2d 1747

I received your Favour of the 23d Ulto With Mr. Thos Fayerweathers order on Mr. Edward Scott in favour of Mr. Jeremiah

4. Not found.
5. See above, p. 84.
6. On the reverse is a memorandum in Colden's hand: "The Expence of One ps[?] of Service in the plan concerted by the Council amounting to £2000 is proposed to be entirely born by this Province. And that the remaining £12000 of the £14000 be at the joint expence of this Govt. Massachusetts Bay and Connecticut." This seems to refer to an attack on Crown Point by New York, Massachusetts, and Connecticut forces, discussed in the New York Council in July–August, 1747.
7. Daniel Cheston, sheriff of Kent Co., Md., merchant and shipowner, appears in BF's Ledger D as "Capt. Danl. Cheston." He may have moved to England, where the firm of Sedgely and Daniel Cheston of Bristol did business with Maryland, and where his widow died, 1766. *Arch. of Md.*, XLIV, 302; *Md. Hist. Mag.*, II (1907), 375; XXV (1930), 55–7; XXVI (1931), 252,

Osborn[8] Inclosed and Immediately Applyed to Mr. Edwd Scott for the Money who promised Me to pay It before the Return of our Mercury. But being Gone Down to Talbott County am afraid Shall not see him time Enough to Send It per this next return. You may Depend I will Doe Every Thing in my power to Get It as soon as possible and Send It up.

I am Sir Your Servant to Command   DANL CHESTON

P S please send me per the post a Corderie and A Latin Clerk's Introduction.[9]

Addressed: To   Mr Benj Franklin   In   Philadelphia

From Cadwallader Colden   ALS: New-York Historical Society

Sir   New York Aug 3d 1747

Baxters [book] was gon so much out of my memory that I could not for some time recollect any thing of it.[1] I cannot now recollect whether I sent back your observations on it. If I have not they are among my papers which I carried to the Country and are now there. I can remember that when I lookt into that book I thought that he did not understand the subject on which he treated as appear'd to me from several passages in the book. Assoon as I return home I shall look carefully for the papers you sent but what they were I donot at present remember. Please therefor to assist my memory.

Some Gentlemen here are desirous to go on Electrical experiments. We hear that you have the whole Apparatus sent over

---

261. Cheston's son James (b. 1747) was educated in England and was in business there and in Maryland, 1767–80. He was a Loyalist, but a quiet one, and decided to remain in America. BF required him to take the oath of allegiance, Nov. 19, 1780, before giving him a passport to proceed to England on business. MS, APS.

8. Scott was a ship owner of Chestertown, Md. *Md. Hist. Mag.*, XXVI (1931), 346. Fayerweather and Osborn have not been identified.

9. John Clarke, *Corderii Colloquiorum centuria selecta* (10th edit., London, 1740), and his *Introduction to the Making of Latin* (13th edit., London, 1742).

1. This answers BF's request, July 30 (see above, p. 166), that Colden return the former's comments on Andrew Baxter's *Enquiry into the Nature of the Human Soul*.

from England. They would purchase the like if they can be made at Philadelphia from what you have sent to you. Please to let me know whether any of your Artists can do it and what may be the price. I am Sir Your most obliged humble servant

CADWALLADER COLDEN[2]

Addressed: Mr Be[njamin Franklin] Pos[tmaster] *The* [*rest cut off*]

Endorsed: C Colden 1747

To Cadwallader Colden

ALS: New-York Historical Society; draft: American Philosophical Society

Sir   Philada. Augt. 6. 1747.

The Observations I sent you on Baxter's Book were wrote on a Sheet or two of Paper in Folio.[3] He builds his whole argument on the Vis Inertiae of Matter: I boldly deny'd the Being of such a Property, and endeavour'd to demonstrate the contrary. If I succeeded, all his Edifice falls of course, unless some other way supported. I desir'd your Sentiments of my Argument. You left the Book for me at N York, with a few Lines containing a short Censure of the Author; and that your Time had been much taken up in Town with Business, but you was now about to retire into the Country, where you should have Leisure to peruse my Papers; since which I have heard nothing from you relating to them. I hope you will easily find them, because I have lost my rough Draft; but don't give yourself much Trouble about them; for if they are lost, 'tis really no great Matter.

I am glad to hear that some Gentlemen with you are enclin'd to go on Electrical Experiments. I am satisfy'd we have Workmen here, who can make the Apparatus as well to the full as that from London; and they will do it reasonably. By the next Post I will send you their Computation of the Expence: If you shall conclude to have it done here, I will oversee the Work, and take Care that every Part be done to perfection, as far as the Nature of the Thing admits.

2. A fragment of a draft of BF's reply, Aug. 6, is visible at the bottom of the MS.

3. See above, p. 84.

Instead of the Remainder of my Rough Minutes on Electricity, (which are indeed too rough for your View) I send you enclos'd Copies of two Letters I lately wrote to Mr. Collinson on that Subject.[4] When you have perus'd them, please to leave them with Mr. Nichols,[5] who I shall desire to forward them per next Post to a Friend in Connecticut.[6]

I am glad your Philosophical Treatise meets with so good Reception in England. Mr. Collinson writes the same Things to Mr. Logan; and Mr. Rose of Virginia writes me, that he had receiv'd Accounts from his Correspondents to the same Purpose. I long to see some of their Observations on it. I perceive by the Papers, that they have also lately reprinted in London, your History of the Five Nations in 8vo. If 'tis come to your Hands, I should be glad to have a Sight of it.

Mr. Logan, on a second Reading of your Piece on Fluxions, lately, is satisfied, that some of the Faults he formerly objected to [in] it, were his own, and owing to his too little Attention at that Time;[7] he desires me to tell you so, and that he asks your Pardon. Upon what Mr. Collinson wrote, he again undertook to read and consider your Philosophical Treatise: I have not seen him since, but shall soon, and will send you his Sentiments. I am, Sir, with great Respect, Your most humble Servant   B FRANKLIN
Dr. Colden

To John Franklin   ALS: American Philosophical Society

Dear Brother   Augt. 6. 1747
I am glad to hear that Mr. Whitefield is safe arriv'd,[8] and recover'd his Health. He is a good Man and I love him.

Mr. Douse has wrote to me per this Post at Mrs. Steele's Request desiring an Explanation from me with regard to my Dissatisfaction with that Lady.[9] I have wrote him in answer, that I

4. See above, pp. 126, 156.
5. Richard Nicholls, postmaster of New York. See above, II, 407 n.
6. Possibly Thomas Darling.
7. For Logan's first impression of Colden's work, see above, II, 417.
8. Whitefield reached Boston July 20. Tyerman, *Whitefield*, II, 174.
9. See above, p. 155.

think a Misunderstanding between Persons at such a Distance, and never like to be further acquainted, can be of no kind of Consequence, and therefore had better be dropt and forgot than committed to Paper; but that however, if Mrs. Steele after Recollection still desires it, I will be very particular with her in a Letter for that purpose to herself. If such a Letter should be written, I will send you a Copy of it, for your and Sister's Satisfaction; but think 'twill be best that you do not show it, or any of the Letters in which I have mention'd her nor speak of them, but keep quite unconcern'd for perhaps there may be a little Squabble.

With Love to Sister, &c. &c. I am, Sir Your affectionate Brother
B FRANKLIN

To Cadwallader Colden
ALS: New-York Historical Society

Sir   Philada. Augt. 13. 1747
I am glad the electrical Observations please you.[1] I leave them in your hands another Week. Our Workmen have undertaken the Electrical Apparatus, and I believe will do it extreamly well: It being a new Job they cannot say exactly what their Work will come to, but they will charge reasonably when done, and they find what Time it has taken. I suppose the whole will not exceed ten or twelve Pounds.

I send you enclos'd the Advertisement of the History of the 5 Nations.[2]

We are told here, that Gov. Belcher has brought Orders to disband the Forces raised for the Expedition against Canada;[3] you know before this Time whether this is true, and whether the

1. See above, p. 169. This letter is apparently in reply to one of about Aug. 9 or 10, now lost.
2. Possibly a handbill or an advertisement from a London paper; it does not appear in *Pa. Gaʒ*. Colden's *History of the Five Nations*, first published in 1727, was republished in the summer of 1747 by Thomas Osborne, London printer, with revisions and extensive additions. Collinson had urged Colden to prepare a new edition; Dr. John Mitchell helped to draw up the title page. Collinson also suggested that Osborne send 50 copies to James Read to sell in Philadelphia. *Colden Paps.*, II, 207, 245–6; III, 369, 402–3; IX, 18–19.
3. These orders were issued. Charles H. Lincoln, ed., *Correspondence of William Shirley* (N.Y., 1912), I, 386–8.

Expedition is postpon'd only, or the Thoughts of it entirely laid aside.

I am, Sir, with great Respect, Your most humble Servant

B FRANKLIN

Addressed: To The honble. Cadr Colden Esqr New York Free B FRANKLIN

To Peter Collinson

ALS: Pierpont Morgan Library

Sir   Philada. Augt. 14. 1747

I have lately written two long Letters to you on the Subject of Electricity, one by the Governor's Vessel, the other per Mesnard.[4] On some further Experiments since, I have observ'd a Phenomenon or two that I cannot at present account for on the Principles laid down in those Letters, and am therefore become a little diffident of my Hypothesis, and asham'd that I have express'd myself in so positive a manner.[5] In going on with these Experiments, how many pretty Systems do we build, which we soon find ourselves oblig'd to destroy! If there is no other Use discover'd of Electricity, this, however, is something considerable, that it may *help to make a vain Man humble.* I must now request that you would not expose those Letters; or if you communicate them to any Friends, you would at least conceal my Name. I have not Time to add, but that I am, Sir, Your obliged and most humble Servant   B FRANKLIN[6]

Addressed: To Mr Peter Collinson Mercht London via Dublin

4. BF's letters of May 25 and July 28 (see above, pp. 126, 156). Governor Thomas embarked for London, June 1, on the *Greyhound*, Capt. Richard Budden. *Pa. Gaz.*, June 4, 1747. On July 30 the *Gazette* reported Capt. Stephen Mesnard's ship *Carolina* as having cleared in the preceding week.

5. The revision of the hypothesis was doubtless made in the "Corrections and Additions" printed in 1751 and subsequent editions. These emendations are printed with the letters.

6. A postscript has been torn away.

To Cadwallader Colden

ALS: Yale University Library

Sir   Philada. Augt. 27. 1747
   This just serves to enclose you a Letter from our Friend Bertram;[7] and to request you would deliver my Papers on Electricity
to the Bearer Mr. Darling.[8] I have not Time to add, but that I
am, with great Respect, Sir, Your most humble Servant
                                                    B FRANKLIN
P.S. I think you wrote me Word you had lent Watson's Book on
Electricity[9] which I sent you last Winter to Dr. Bard.[1] Please to
direct Mr. Darling to Dr. Bard's for it, if he has not return'd it to
you.
Addressed: To   The honble. Cadwalr Colden Esqr   New York
per favr of Mr Darling

From James Parker[2]

ALS: American Philosophical Society

Dear Sir   New York. Sept. 7. 1747.
   Mr. Whiting[3] came and [paid the] whole last Saturday Evening
in Jersey Money, except 5s. in York, of the Pay[ment] for the
Postage. I don't know any Body has any of the Spanish Paper
to sell cheap. I believe 5 or 6s. will be the lowest. I know several
ask 8s. I can yet gladly spare you 4 or 5 Bales of that I have,
having got about 10 Bales yet entire. If you please to order it I
will send it by the first Oppertunity. I will make Enquiry if any be
to be got else where.
   As to what relates to the Copper Plate, tis thus; The Engraver
is a Silver-Smith. During the Proposing of the Thing I gave him
some Silver to make me two Silver Spoons; but he has not done

---

7. John Bartram's letter to Colden, Aug. 16. *Colden Paps.*, III, 419–20.
8. On Thomas Darling of New Haven, see above, p. 108 n.
9. William Watson, *Experiments and Observations Tending to illustrate the
Nature and Properties of Electricity* (London, 1746), or his *Sequel to the Experiments and Observations* (London, 1746).
1. On John Bard, see above, p. 49 n.
2. New York printer; BF's partner. See above, II, 341–5.
3. Possibly Nathan Whiting (1724–1771), New Haven merchant. See
above, p. 108 n.

'em yet.[4] I have been at him several Times: but one time he has been sick, another Time his Wife is sick, &c. I tell him we want him to go about the Plate, but I fear he is an idle lazy Fellow. I will try him again this Week, and I think if he don't go on it, as he is well enough now, we may despair of getting him to do it at all.

As my Long-Primer is almost worn out I have had Thoughts of trying to get some new for which I have not seen an easier Way than to send home some Money by the Man of War now going in about 3 Weeks; but know not well the Price, or whom to apply to, or what Quantity will do. I could make up about £12 or 14 Sterl: and I would run my own Risk—but this I will not do without your Advice and Permission.[5]

I received the Pocket Companion[6] safe, tis well enough. May I ask, if the Young Man's Companion[7] be almost done?

I rejoice to hear you all keep your Health: May it continue! Our Son is recovered pretty well but my Wife is poorly, tho' not with the present Sickness, but one She is pretty much accustomed to.

With all our hearty Respects, I remain, Sir Your most obedient Servant,   JAMES PARKER

P.S. I send 4 Quire Marble Paper, it cost 3s. 6d. a Quire. A Sheet of a different sort is sent, if you are minded for any of that. Payment for a little more than 1½ Dollar is coming to you; which with the 5s. York Money paid by Mr. Whiting will just clear this Paper.

4. If the plates were wanted for the East Jersey Proprietors' *Bill in the Chancery of New-Jersey*, which Parker printed, the New York silversmith's dilatoriness may explain why the job was finally given to James Turner of Boston (see above, p. 144 n).

5. Ledger D shows that on May 5, 1748, BF charged Parker for "a fount of Pica." George S. Eddy has suggested that BF sent this pica type instead of letting Parker order the long primer (two sizes smaller) from London. Eddy, *Ledger "D,"* pp. 95, 97.

6. Probably BF's *Pocket Almanack*, which Parker used as a model for his own series of pocket almanacs, the first of which was for 1748. Evans 6053.

7. See below, p. 304, for *The American Instructor: or, Young Man's Best Companion*, printed by Franklin and Hall, 1748.

From James Parker

ALS: American Philosophical Society

Dear Sir   New York. Sept. 21. 1747.

Last Week I accidently met Mr. DeLancey[8] in the Streets: I ask'd him, if he had heard any Thing about the Affair, and he said No. I ask'd him, if he were willing to take the Money? He said Yes. I ask'd him how much it was? and he said £37 principal: which is more than what you mention. However, I will pay it, let it be what it may; On which I told him, I had Money of Yours in my Hands, and expected your Orders to pay it: and he said, It was well. I shall see him, God willing, Wednesday or Thursday.

I am heartily concerned at your frequent Losses. I will see about sending the Paper the first Boat.

Mr. H.[9] is deprived of his being Councillor, and as he's out of the Governor's Favour, 'tis suppos'd he will be turn'd out of both his other Places before long.

The History of the Rebels[1] will make about 24 Sheets; 8½ are done as you will perceive by what I send you.

As to what you say about the Materials I don't think myself a competent Judge at all of the Prices, &c. I shall therefore rather entirely Submit it to you; tho' unless you can better imagine it already than I, I am of Opinion, We had best wait till the Expiration of the Time; as we are both uncertain of our Lives so long; and if it please God to call me hence, I have none to leave either the Materials to, or a Desire to leave so much in Debt; you will

8. Neither DeLancey nor the subject of this conversation has been identified.

9. Daniel Horsmanden (1694–1778), a lawyer trained in the Middle and Inner Temples, by 1747 was a member of the Governor's Council, Recorder of the City of New York, and third judge of the Supreme Court. For his outspoken opposition Governor Clinton stripped him of all his offices, 1747. He was reappointed to the Supreme Court in 1753, becoming chief justice in 1763, and he was restored to the Council in 1755. *DAB*. He was one of the New Yorkers who applied for membership in APS in 1744. *Colden Paps.*, III, 82.

1. Parker reprinted John Marchant's *The History of the Present Rebellion* (London, 1746) under the title *The History of the Late Rebellion, In Great-Britain*, 1747. The work was done for John Hyndshaw (or Hinshaw), New York bookbinder, and John Thomson of Elizabeth, N. J., by whom it was offered for sale.

174

then be obliged to take 'em again: I can then, if I live, give you a List of every Thing and you can set your Price on them.[2]

The first Half Sheet of the History of the Rebellion, is of the new Letter, it sets up all the Italick, to about Half a Page more. It is not bottle-ars'd; but is unhappily about a Hair-space shorter than the other, i.e. the Old: so won't stand in the same Word, but will do in the same page. This Letter will do very well for what Long-primer is in the Spelling-Books, &c.

I have not got Pay of the Undertakers of the History; but am promis'd some this Week: if tis not done, I must stop yet; for I begin to have less confidence than before: Hynshaw being poor, and t'other I'm afraid not honest.

I will see about the Marble Paper, &c. with all convenient Speed.

I was about purchasing a Saw of Mr. Meredith;[3] if you have not already nail'd up the Box, and it is long enough to put the Plate in, I should be glad if you would put that in with the Books. Those sort of Saws are not to be got here.

I could wish you would send me One Ream of Cartridge Paper Along with the other Things, I not having above 8 Quire of that sort in the House.

The Sickness is greatly abated, thank God, tho' there be a pretty many yet down with it, and some die of it still; By God's Mercy, we are all well. With all our Respects, &c. remain Sir your most obliged Servant   JAMES PARKER

To Cadwallader Colden   ALS: New-York Historical Society

Sir   Philada. Sept. 24. 1747

I have one of your Histories come in among some Books sent me per Mr. Strahan: But Osborne I understand has sent 50 to Mr. Read per Recommendation of Mr. Collinson. I should sell them more readily than he can, I imagine; and he talks of putting them into my hands.[4] Are any of them arriv'd in N York?

Enclos'd are two Letters for you. No others are yet come to

2. See the partnership agreement between BF and Parker, above, II, 341–5.
3. Not identified.
4. *Colden Paps.*, III, 402; above, p. 170. James Read gave up bookselling

175

hand; but perhaps we shall find more when the Ship is unloaded; for Mr. Collinson's Letters are often in Trunks among Goods, &c. I should be glad to know if Mr. Darling,[5] by whom I wrote a Line to you, had my Papers on Electricity. I am, Sir, Your most humble Servant   B Franklin

Addressed: To   The honble Cadwalader Colden Esq   New York Free   B Franklin

Receipt to Hector Gambold[6]   ADS: Princeton University Library

[September 28, 1747]
    Receiv'd Sept. 28. 1747 of Mr. Gambold Twenty three Pounds Ten Shillings, being in full for Fourteen hundred German Spelling Books; also One Pound Ten Shillings and three Pence for 50 lb. Pasteboard.   per me   B Franklin

£23.10.0
  1.10.3
———————
£25: 0:3

Endorsed: 1747 Sepr: 28. Franklin's Rect: £25.—.3.

From Daniel Cheston   ALS: American Philosophical Society

Sir   Chester Septr: 28th 1747
    I am sorry to Acquaint you that with Assiduity Equal to the Want of the Gentleman In whose favour the order was Drawn I

---

this year. BF offered to sell the 50 copies but withdrew the offer when he and Hall decided they were too expensive. At 5s. the work sold poorly in London and the printer remaindered it in 1750, at a loss of more than £30. *Ibid.*, IV, 66, 103, 271; VII, 344.
    5. For Thomas Darling, see above, p. 108 n.
    6. Hector Ernest Gambold (1719–1788), born in Wales, became a Moravian at Oxford, migrated to Pennsylvania, 1742, with a group of German and Welsh Moravians. Ordained in 1755, he preached in Pennsylvania, New Jersey, and New York, and in 1763 settled on Staten Island as the first Moravian minister there. He died at Bethleham. Frederick Lewis Weis, "The Colonial Clergy of the Middle Colonies," Am. Antiq. Soc. *Proc.*, LXVI, pt. 2 (1956), 223.

have not Been able to procure anything But Promises.[7] I would
Advise (if It meet with yours and the Gentlemans Approbation)
a threatning Line or two to Mr. Edward Scott who has made
Such an Assumption in favour of Mr. Osborn As may [torn] on an
Action though the Bringing One would not Answer the Gentle-
mans End As by our most Salutary Constitution he may Be kept
out of It about 18 Months. If A Line of that Kind is thought
necessary if Its Inclos'd To me I will take Care to Deliver It and
at the Same time will Enforce It in the Best Manner I am Able.
My best respects Waits on Mrs. Franklin and am Sir Your Most
Humble Servant   DANL CHESTON
Addressed: To   Mr Benj Franklin   In   Philadelphia

From Cadwallader Colden   ALS: American Philosophical Society

Dear Sir   New York Septr 28th 1747
    I am obliged by your favour of the 24th and the Information
you give. I have not heard that any of the Indian History are in
this place and am very desirous to see one of them assoon at least
as any other in this place may because I really do not know of what
papers it consists. I sent Mr. Collinson accounts or relations on
that subject at several times and now I do not remember particularly what I sent him, perhaps some things which I had no
thoughts of their being published.[8] Please therefor to procure me
one Copy to be sent by next post. One of the letters you inclos'd
was from Mr. Osborn the Publisher of that piece wherein I learn
that he has given Mr. Collinson 12 copies for me but it is probable
these may not arive this year or not till late in November at
soonest.[9] I am at this time hurried with the publick despatches

7. See Cheston to BF, Aug. 2, above, p. 166.
8. Colden had sent Collinson in 1742 revisions of the 1727 edition of his
History of the Five Indian Nations, as well as the Continuation, which appeared
as Part II of Osborne's 1747 edition. He also forwarded other materials on
Indian affairs, from time to time, sent copies of Indian treaties, and suggested
including his memorial on the fur trade (printed at New York in 1724) in a
new edition of the Indian History. Collinson had a free hand in putting the
book together, but he and Colden both disapproved of Osborne's title page
and new dedication. *Colden Paps.,* III, 410; IX, 19.
9. Thomas Osborne to Colden, June 12, 1747, *Colden Paps.,* III, 402–3.

to go by the Man of war which is to sail to morrow morning. If I can have so much time I shall answer his letter. He desires me to recommend some correspondents to him for trade in his way. I shall mention you as one that can be the most useful to him.

I deliver'd your piece on Electricity to Mr. Darling assoon as [I] receiv'd yours by him.

You may see by the inclos'd that Mr. John Hughes Tanner and Tavern keeper in Exeter township[1] has a servant man who run away from me last summer. If you will take the trouble to agree for his time or to send him back to me or in my absence to Mr. Nicholls[2] I shall be obliged to you and [it] will be an addition to many favour. Or desire Mr. Ermit[3] to do it. I was told Mr. Ermit was gon to Boston. I have now for a considerable time expected his return through this place but have never heard of him. Please to let me know whether he be well and return'd. I have no time to write to him by this Post. Your most obliged servant

CADWALLADER COLDEN

Addressed: To   Mr Benjn Franklin   Post Master in   Philadelphia

To Cadwallader Colden

ALS: New-York Historical Society

Sir   Philada. Oct. 1. 1747

I send you herewith the History of the Five Nations. You will perceive that Osborne, to puff up the Book, has inserted the Charters &c. of this Province, all under the Title of *History of the Five Nations,* which I think was not fair, but 'tis a common Trick of Booksellers.[4]

Mr. James Read, to whom Mr. Osborne has sent a Parcel of Books by Recommendation of Mr. Collinson, being engag'd in

1. BF recorded in Ledger D purchases by Hughes, whom he described as "Tanner of Oley." Oley and Exeter are adjoining townships in Berks County, Pa.

2. Richard Nicholls, lawyer, postmaster of New York, whose daughter married Colden's son Alexander. See above, II, 407 n.

3. John Armitt of Philadelphia, who handled Colden's business there.

4. Osborne's edition of Colden's *History* had a second, separately paged, section of 283 pages containing the author's early papers on the Indian trade in New York; reports of Indian treaties at Philadelphia, 1742, at Lancaster, 1744, and at Albany, 1746; and—the particular object of BF's scorn—the charters and other basic laws of Pennsylvania.

Business of another kind, talks of declining to act in Disposing of them, and perhaps may put them into my Hands. If he should, I will endeavour to do Mr. Osborne Justice in disposing of them to the best Advantage, as also of any other Parcel he may send me from your Recommendation.

Mr. Armit is return'd well from N England; As he has your Power of Attorney, and somewhat more Leisure at present than I have, I think to put your Letter to J. Hughes into his Hands, and desire him to manage the Affair of your Servant. I shall write a Line besides to Hughes, that he would assist in obliging the Servant to do you Justice, which may be of some Service, as he owns himself oblig'd to me for recovering a Servant for him that had been gone above a 12 month. I am, Sir Your most humble Servant   B FRANKLIN

To Abiah Franklin

MS not found; reprinted from Duane, *Works*, VI, 8.

Honoured Mother,   Philadelphia, October 16, 1747⁵
This has been a busy day with your daughter and she is gone to bed much fatigued and cannot write.

I send you inclosed, one of our new almanacks; we print them early, because we send them to many places far distant. I send you also, a moidore inclosed, which please to accept towards chaise hire, that you may ride warm to meetings this winter. Pray tell us, what kind of a sickness you have had in Boston this summer: besides the measles and flux, which have carried off many children, we have lost some grown persons, by what we call the *Yellow Fever;* though that is almost if not quite over, thanks to God, who has preserved all our family, in perfect health. Here are cousins Coleman, and two Folgers, all well.⁶ Your grandaughter is the greatest lover of her book and school, of any child I ever

5. Correctly dated by Duane, but changed to 1749 in Sparks (*Familiar Letters*, pp. 16–17; *Works*, VII, 41), Bigelow (*Works*, II, 153–4), and Smyth (*Writings*, II, 379). The reference to yellow fever establishes the correct date. I *Pa. Arch.*, I, 769.
6. The "cousins Coleman" were probably children or grandchildren of BF's aunt Joanna Folger Coleman (B.1.1); the "two Folgers" cannot be identified among his many Nantucket relatives of that name.

knew, and is very dutiful to her mistress as well as to us.[7] I doubt not but brother Mecom[8] will send the collar as soon as he can conveniently. My love to him, sister, and all the children. I am, Your dutiful son, B. FRANKLIN

Plain Truth

Plain Truth: or, Serious Considerations On the Present State of the City of Philadelphia, and Province of Pennsylvania. By a Tradesman of Philadelphia. Printed in the Year MDCCXLVII. (Yale University Library)

During the late spring and early summer of 1747 the activity of French and Spanish privateers had been increasing off the Delaware capes, and each week's newspapers reported some new action. To prevent their learning too much about the river and the defenseless condition of Philadelphia, the Council on July 4 tried to close the Delaware to foreign vessels, even those carrying flags of truce, by forbidding pilots to bring such vessels up the river above Marcus Hook except with special license. This measure was ineffective, however, for New Jersey imposed no similar restriction, and any hostile force might make its own way into the river in small boats. This was clearly demonstrated a few days afterwards when, on July 12, a raiding party of fifteen or twenty armed men from a French privateer actually landed at Edmund Liston's plantation near Bombay Hook in New Castle County. They seized four slaves, carried off bedding, clothes, and furniture, and forced Liston to lead them to the neighboring plantation of James Hart, whose house they attacked and plundered, wounding Mrs. Hart, and taking a slave and goods to the value of £70. A few days later the same privateer seized the ship *Mary* off Cape Henlopen; her captain was wounded resisting the boarding party.[9]

The alarming news was brought to Philadelphia by express. Rumors multiplied and spread. The landing party at Bombay Hook, for example, was first reported to have numbered one hundred armed men. Spanish prisoners, Negroes, and other desperate characters were said to be plotting to seize a ship's boat in the harbor and join the enemy at the mouth of the river; and the city watch was given special instructions to prevent them. The Council debated whether to call the Assembly into special session, but the Speaker successfully discouraged the

7. Sarah Franklin had just turned four.
8. BF's brother-in-law Edward Mecom (C.17), a saddler.
9. *Pa. Col. Recs.*, V, 80–2, 89–93, 111, 117–8, 226.

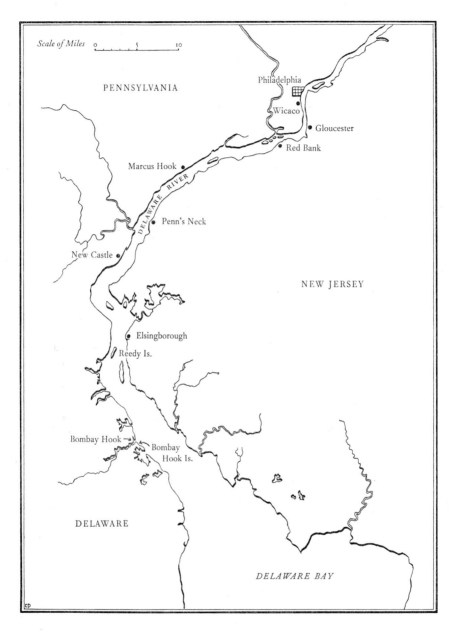

PENNSYLVANIA

Philadelphia

Wicaco

Gloucester

Red Bank

Marcus Hook

DELAWARE RIVER

Penn's Neck

New Castle

NEW JERSEY

Elsingborough

Reedy Is.

Bombay Hook

Bombay Hook Is.

DELAWARE

DELAWARE BAY

The Defenses of the Delaware, 1747–48

proposal. With Governor Thomas on his way to England for his health, the Council could only wish that the Proprietor himself might "come over and undertake the cure."[1] In this atmosphere of frustration and fear the Assembly convened in its regular session in mid-August.

The President of the Council, Anthony Palmer, told the Assembly urgently that he believed the enemy planned to attack Philadelphia in the spring. "The Terror and Confusion, the Ruin of vast numbers of Families, the Destruction of Trade, the Bloodshed, Cruelty, and other fatal Consequences which must unavoidably attend the plundering or burning this City, are too obvious to need a Description." The Assembly were unmoved: they approved the Council's action respecting the Delaware pilots as "a prudent Step," but thought that nothing practicable could be done to prevent raids like that on Liston's and expressed the opinion that the enemy's threats of attack on Philadelphia "rather appear to us as so many Bravados than what they either really intended or had the Power to do." Palmer's insistence that Philadelphia was defenseless would not only do nothing to avert danger, but would even increase popular apprehension.[2]

Privateering continued; interference with shipping increased. William Kelly, passenger on the sloop *Elizabeth*, bound from Providence to Philadelphia, deposed in Philadelphia on September 21 that he had been taken prisoner a month before off the North Carolina coast by a French privateer from Cap François, which had already taken three English prizes and took three more off the Virginia capes, another fifteen leagues from the Delaware capes, and two in Delaware Bay itself. "From the Success which attends our Enemies by Cruizing in our Bay without risque or opposition," Palmer told the Assembly on October 16, "it may reasonably be expected that they will continue their Depredations in the Spring, and in all likelyhood block up the Trade of this flourishing Colony—a Loss which we apprehend will be sensibly felt by all sorts of People." But the Assembly remained impervious to appeals and alarms. If any enemy privateers came up the river, they replied, it was the pilots' fault for bringing them; and as for an attack on Philadelphia, "we hope there is no Danger."[3]

To all but Quaker pacifists it seemed that something must be done, if not by the Assembly, then by the people. To win over moderate Quakers who, like James Logan, appreciated the obligations of power, Franklin printed in his *Gazette* of October 22 verses complimentary to Barclay's *Apology* and the Quakers ("His works at least shall make me moderate prove,/And those who practice what he writes, I'll love."), and two weeks later the paper contained a short piece arguing that the

1. *Ibid.*, 89, 92–4.　　2. *Ibid.*, 99, 101–3.　　3. *Ibid.*, 113, 125–6.

Quakers' doctrine was not "absolutely against *Defensive War.*" Meanwhile he composed and published in pamphlet form on November 17 a strongly worded appeal for voluntary action.[4]

Plain Truth, Franklin remembered in his autobiography, "had a sudden and surprizing Effect."[5] It was defended, approved, recommended, and explained by citizens, printers, and ministers. He printed 2000 copies; it went into a second edition;[6] it was translated into German;[7] and extracts were reprinted in other colonies.[8] Samuel Smith answered it on behalf of the Quakers, Christopher Saur on behalf of the German pacifists.[9]

Franklin promised in his pamphlet to submit a plan for a volunteer association for defense. This he did on November 21. Approved first at a meeting of tradesmen and mechanics, then by "the principal Gentlemen, Merchants and others" of the city, the Association was signed by more than 500 citizens on November 24.[1] Within a few days the number of signatures exceeded 1000. Things were moving at last. The Mayor and Corporation of Philadelphia appealed to the Proprietor in London for "a Number of large Cannon" for a battery,[2] the Council made a similar request, and Secretary Peters told Thomas Penn that small arms were said to be available at the Tower "for a Trifle." The city's merchants petitioned the Admiralty for a man-of-war in Delaware Bay[3] and subscribed £1500 to buy sixteen 28-pounders and some

---

4. Although *Pa. Gaz.*, Nov. 12, 1747, announced that the pamphlet would be published Saturday, i.e., Nov. 14, Richard Peters stated explicitly that it appeared Nov. 17. According to Peters (see below, p. 215) BF received advice on strategy from Tench Francis, William Coleman, and Thomas Hopkinson.

5. Par. Text edit., p. 278.

6. This edition contained at the end a translation of the Latin exordium which BF had placed on the title page. See below, p. 204 n.

7. By the Philadelphia German printer, Joseph Crellius (or Crell), as *Die Lautere Wahrheit;* and printed by Gotthard Armbrüster. BF supplied the Association with 1000 "Dutch Plain Truths" at 3*d.* each. Eddy, *Account Books. Ledger "D,"* p. 80.

8. *N.-Y. Gaz.*, Dec. 14, 1747.

9. Smith, *Necessary Truth* (Evans 6241), and Saur, *Verschiedene Christliche Wahrheiten* (Evans 6233). Of the first printing of 1000 copies of Smith's pamphlet, 500 were distributed free by the printer and the remaining 500 by the author. Albert C. Myers, ed., *Hannah Logan's Courtship* (Phila., 1904), p. 133.

1. See below, p. 205.

2. *Minutes of the Common Council of the City of Philadelphia. 1704 to 1776* (Phila., 1847), pp. 488–90.

3. *Pa. Col. Recs.*, v, 160–2.

smaller guns in Boston.[4] The Assembly was called into special session on November 23; some 260 citizens, including, it was said, 62 Quakers formerly opposed to even defensive war, petitioned it to protect the city. The Assembly still took no action, and on November 28, in the midst of the crisis, adjourned. Carried along by popular feeling and not knowing what else to do, the Council resolved "to give all due Protection and Encouragement to the Members of the Association, it being the only Method thought on likely to preserve the Lives and Properties of their Fellow-Citizens in case of a Descent."[5]

Franklin was intimately involved in all aspects of the Association. The volunteers had to be organized—he suggested how. They had to be trained—the New Printing-Office sold manuals of arms and even "good Muskets, all well fitted with Bayonets," belts and cartouche boxes.[6] To pay for fortifying the approaches to Philadelphia Franklin proposed a lottery, and then had to explain how it worked. He even designed the companies' standards, decorating them with heraldic devices and sentiments of patriotic defiance. Documents recording these activities are printed below; and there are other reflections of Franklin's involvement in the Association in his letters to Colden and Logan. A chronological outline may be helpful:

November 17, 1747: *Plain Truth* published.
    21: Franklin addresses meeting at Walton's schoolhouse.
    23: The principal gentlemen approve the Association.
    24: Citizens begin to sign the Association. See below, p. 205.
December 7: Franklin addresses Associators at the Court house. See below, p. 225.

4. Peters to Penn, Feb. 1, 1748. Penn MSS, Official Corres., IV, 89, Hist. Soc. Pa.

5. *Pa. Col. Recs.*, V, 158, 160–3.

6. *Pa. Gaz.*, March 8, 1748. Writing Penn in warm praise of BF, James Logan summed up the latter's services in the Association: "He it was that by publishing a small piece in the year 1747 with his further private contrivances, occasioned the raising of ten Companies of near one hundred men each in Philadelphia and above one hundred companies in the Province and Counties, of which I have a List. He it was who set on foot two Lotteries for Erecting of Batteries, purchasing great guns and to dispatch which he went himself to New York and borrowed there 14— which were brought thro' New Jersey by land, and here mounted till such Time as there could be others had from England, in which thy assistance is in some Measure expected; and all this without much appearing in any part of it himself, unless in his going to New York himself in Company with others of whose going he was the occasion, for he is the principal Mover and very Soul of the Whole." Nov. 24, 1749, transcript (Sparks), Harvard Coll. Lib.

5: Scheme of the Philadelphia Lottery published. See below, p. 220.

9: Public Fast Day proclaimed. See below, p. 226.

January 1, 1748: Associators reviewed; officers elected.

7: Public Fast Day observed.

February 8: First drawing of the Lottery.

March 21: Meeting of Associator Officers to draft regulations. See below, p. 279.

August 17: Cessation of hostilities proclaimed at Philadelphia.

September 10: First drawing of the Second Philadelphia Lottery. See below, p. 288.

May 17, 1749: Peace proclaimed at Philadelphia.

The Association was not regarded everywhere with approval or even equanimity. Jealous of his proprietary rights and sensitive to his position in the eyes of the British government, Thomas Penn wrote Lynford Lardner that Franklin's pamphlet had "done much mischief," adding dryly, "I am sure the people of America are too often ready to act in defiance of the Government they live in, without associating themselves for that purpose."[7] He considered the popular scheme hasty and ill advised, believed it threatened his interests. "This Association is founded on a Contempt to Government," he wrote Secretary Richard Peters, "and cannot end in anything but Anarchy and Confusion. The People in general are so fond of what they call Liberty as to fall into Licenciousness, and when they know they may Act . . . by Orders of their own Substitutes, in a Body, and a Military manner, and independant of this Government, why should they not Act against it." To establish "a Military Common Wealth"—which he thought the Association was—within the government of the province seemed to Penn "acting a part little less than Treason."[8] Franklin's doctrine, he continued in a subsequent letter, "tho very true in it self, that Obedience to Governers is no more due than Protection to the People [see below, p. 199], yet it is not fit to be always in the heads of the Wild unthinking Multitude. . . . He is a dangerous Man and I should be very Glad he inhabited any other Country, as I believe him of a very uneasy Spirit. However as he is a Sort of Tribune of the People, he must be treated with regard."[9]

7. Penn to Lardner, March 29, 1748, Penn Letter Book, II, 223, Hist. Soc. Pa.

8. Penn to Peters, March 30, 1748, *ibid.*, 225; quoted in Hubertis Cummings, *Richard Peters: Provincial Secretary and Cleric, 1704–1776* (Phila., 1944), pp. 134–6.

9. Penn to Peters, June 9, 1748, Penn Letter Book, II, 232, Hist. Soc. Pa.

Penn objected particularly to the clause of the Association by which the subscribers bound themselves to obey the laws and regulations of the military council, though the officers received commissions from the Governor's Council. This, he warned, "is giving the power of the Militia, or calling the People together for their defence, from the King to themselves, and . . . I fear will be esteemed greatly Criminal."[1] The military council was in fact "the most dangerous part" of the Association, for it usurped "the King's power of ordering the Militia, which you know our Kings are very jealous of, and if it should be known to the Ministers, would incline them to look with an Evil Eye over us on all Applications."[2] It was strange, Penn wrote with irritation, that "people cannot walk in a plain path, but when Men set up for refined polititians everything common plain sence dictates, is beneath their notice."[3]

Like the members of the Council Secretary Richard Peters[4] had approved the Association; he put it in a good light before the Proprietor, assuring Penn that the Associators' "Conduct hitherto has been remarkably regular and moderate, without any angry Expressions or blustering behaviour."[5] Their election of their own officers, he explained, "was look'd upon by the Council only in the nature of a recommendation, the tenor of their Commissions being to receive their Orders from the Governor for the time being according to the rules of

1. Penn to President and Council, March 30, 1748, *ibid.*, 228.
2. Penn to Peters, June 9, 1748, *ibid.*, 234.
3. Same to same, March 30, 1748, *ibid.*, 225.
4. Richard Peters (*c.* 1704–1776), secretary of the Province and clerk of the Council, 1743–62, was born in England, studied at Leyden, the Inner Temple, London, and at Wadham College, Oxford, and was ordained an Anglican clergyman, 1731. When his second marriage was discovered to be bigamous, he came to America, 1734; served briefly as assistant rector of Christ Church, Philadelphia, 1736; and in 1737 was appointed secretary of the Provincial Land Office, a post he held until 1760. He was named to the Governor's Council, 1749. In his public roles he attended the Albany Congress, 1754, and the Treaty of Fort Stanwix, 1768. Always loyal to the proprietary interest, he resigned his office in 1762 and returned to the ministry as rector of Christ Church and St. Peter's. A High Churchman, who once suspected the Quakers and opposed George Whitefield, he grew tolerant as he grew older, and even allowed the latter to preach in his churches, 1763. He was one of the first trustees of the Academy and College of Philadelphia, preached the sermon on the opening of the Academy, 1751, and served as president of its trustees, 1756–64. Hubertis Cummings, *Richard Peters* (Phila., 1944); *DAB*.
5. Peters to Proprietaries, Feb. 1, 1748, Penn MSS, Official Corres., IV, 89, Hist. Soc. Pa.

war." Peters even expressed a belief that the Association would promote the proprietary interest by reconciling the Quakers to defense and so save the British Government "the Trouble, and the Quakers the Shame, of an Act of Parliament to incapacitate them from sitting in Assembly."[6] But Penn's disapproval, repeated in letter after letter reaching Philadelphia in the spring of 1748, soon changed Peters' opinions. Writing to Penn on June 16, he viewed it as his master did, as an illegal combination, expressed a strong abhorrence of it, was apprehensive of its leaders' intentions, and hinted that it would be used to advance the political interests of those hostile to the proprietary party.[7]

But peace was already in prospect; the Association soon dwindled away; and though its leaders, notably Franklin, had won a province-wide fame and influence, they made no use of it in the October elections. "We are well pleased to find that the Association has had so good an Effect," Penn informed Peters on August 31, "that the persons associated have Commissions in the Common Form, and do not act but by Authority from the president and Council, as well as that they have been so ready to attend their Duty when in Times of danger; their readyness to defend their Country is very commendable, and it was with reluctance that we objected to any thing done by persons that in general might intend nothing more than to defend themselves under their legal Commanders, . . . We shall ever be wel pleased to encourage preparations for defence, as is our Duty and hope before another War something more regular may be done, and as Peace will very soon be declared that they will become good Friends with those who think differently from them, or at least live quietly with them."[8]

PLAIN TRUTH, &C.

It is said the wise Italians make this proverbial Remark on our Nation, viz. *The English* FEEL, *but they do not* SEE. That is, they are sensible of Inconveniencies when they are present, but do not take sufficient Care to prevent them: Their natural Courage makes them too little apprehensive of Danger, so that they are

6. Peters to Penn. March 25, June 13, 1748, *ibid.*, 93, 94.

7. Same to same, June 16, 1748, *ibid.*, 97. Theodore Thayer, *Pennsylvania Politics and the Growth of Democracy, 1740–1776* (Harrisburg, Pa., 1953), pp. 21–3. The Council defended the Association and their support of it in a letter to the Proprietors, July 30, 1748. *Pa. Col. Recs.*, V, 319–23.

8. Penn to Peters, Aug. 31, 1748, Penn Letter Book, II, 242, Hist. Soc. Pa. There is a summary account of the Association and the construction of the batteries, with quotations from the Council minutes and *Pa. Gaz.*, in 1 *Pa. Arch.*, XII, 437–42.

PLAIN TRUTH:

O R,

SERIOUS CONSIDERATIONS

On the PRESENT STATE of the

CITY of PHILADELPHIA,

A N D

PROVINCE of PENNSYLVANIA.

By a TRADESMAN of *Philadelphia.*

Capta urbe, nihil fit reliqui victis. Sed, per Deos immortales, vos ego appello, qui semper domos, villas, figna, tabulas vestras, tantæ æstimationis fecistis ; si ista, cujuscumque modi sint, quæ amplexamini, retinere, si voluptatibus vestris otium præbere vultis ; expergiscimini aliquando, & capessite rempublicam. Non agitur nunc de sociorum injuriis ; LIBERTAS & ANIMA nostra in dubio est. Dux hostium cum exercitu supra caput est. Vos cunctamini etiam nunc, & dubitatis quid faciatis ?. Scilicet, res ipsa aspera est, sed vos non timetis eam. Imo vero maxume ; sed inertia & mollitia animi, alius alium exspectantes, cunctamini ; videlicet, Diis immortalibus confisi, qui hanc rempublicam in maxumis periculis servavere. NON VOTIS, NEQUE SUPPLICIIS MULIEBRIBUS, AUXILIA DEORUM PARANTUR : vigilando, agendo, bene consulendo, prospere omnia cedunt. Ubi socordiæ tête atque ignaviæ tradideris, nequicquam Deos implores ; irati, infestique sunt. M. POR. CAT. *in* SALUST.

Printed in the YEAR MDCCXLVII.

Non Votis, &c.

often surpriz'd by it, unprovided of the proper Means of Security. When 'tis too late they are sensible of their Imprudence: After great Fires, they provide Buckets and Engines: After a Pestilence they think of keeping clean their Streets and common Shores: and when a Town has been sack'd by their Enemies, they provide for its Defence, &c. This Kind of AFTER-WISDOM is indeed so common with us, as to occasion the vulgar, tho' very significant Saying, *When the Steed is stolen, you shut the Stable Door.*

But the more insensible we generally are of publick Danger, and indifferent when warn'd of it, so much the more freely, openly, and earnestly, ought such as apprehend it, to speak their Sentiments; that if possible, those who seem to sleep, may be awaken'd, to think of some Means of Avoiding or Preventing the Mischief before it be too late.

Believing therefore that 'tis my DUTY, I shall honestly speak my Mind in the following Paper.

War, at this Time, rages over a great Part of the known World; our News-Papers are Weekly filled with fresh Accounts of the Destruction it every where occasions. Pennsylvania, indeed, situate in the Center of the Colonies, has hitherto enjoy'd profound Repose; and tho' our Nation is engag'd in a bloody War, with two great and powerful Kingdoms, yet, defended, in a great Degree, from the French on the one Hand by the Northern Provinces, and from the Spaniards on the other by the Southern, at no small Expence to each, our People have, till lately, slept securely in their Habitations.

There is no British Colony excepting this, but has made some Kind of Provision for its Defence; many of them have therefore never been attempted by an Enemy; and others that were attack'd, have generally defended themselves with Success. The Length and Difficulty of our Bay and River has been thought so effectual a Security to us, that hitherto no Means have been entered into that might discourage an Attempt upon us, or prevent its succeeding.

But whatever Security this might have been while both Country and City were poor, and the Advantage to be expected scarce worth the Hazard of an Attempt, it is now doubted whether we can any longer safely depend upon it. Our Wealth, of late Years much encreas'd, is one strong Temptation, our defenceless State another, to induce an Enemy to attack us; while the Acquaintance they have lately gained with our Bay and River, by Means of the Prisoners and Flags of Truce they have had among us; by Spies which they almost every where maintain, and perhaps from Traitors among ourselves; with the Facility of getting Pilots to conduct them; and the known Absence of Ships of War, during the greatest Part of the Year, from both Virginia and New-York, ever since the War began, render the Appearance of Success to the Enemy far more promising, and therefore highly encrease our DANGER.

That our Enemies may have Spies abroad, and some even in these Colonies, will not be made much doubt of, when 'tis considered, that such has been the Practice of all Nations in all Ages, whenever they were engaged, or intended to engage in War. Of this we have an early Example in the Book of Judges (too too [*sic*] pertinent to our Case, and therefore I must beg leave a little to enlarge upon it) where we are told, Chap. xviii, v. 2, That *the Children of Dan sent of their Family five Men from their Coasts to spie out the Land, and search it, saying, Go, search the* LAND. These Danites it seems were at this Time not very orthodox in their Religion, and their Spies met with a certain idolatrous Priest of their own Persuasion, v. 3, and they said to him, *Who brought thee hither! what makest thou in this Place? and what hast thou here?* [would to God no such Priests were to be found among us.]⁹ And they said unto him, verse 5, *Ask Counsel of God, that we may know whether our Way which we go shall be prosperous? And the Priest said unto them, Go in Peace; before the Lord is your Way wherein you go.* [Are there no Priests among us, think you, that might, in the like Case, give an Enemy as good Encouragement? 'Tis well known, that we have Numbers of the same Religion with those who of late encouraged the French to invade our Mother-Country.]¹ *And they came,* Verse 7, *to Laish, and saw the People that were therein, how they dwelt* CARELESS, *after the Manner of the Zidonians,* QUIET *and* SECURE. They *thought* themselves secure, no doubt; and as they *never had been* disturbed, vainly imagined they *never should.* 'Tis not unlikely that some might see

9. Brackets in this paragraph in the original.
1. Roman Catholics, who supported the Young Pretender's invasion of Britain.

the Danger they were exposed to by living in that *careless* Manner; but that if these publickly expressed their Apprehensions, the rest reproached them as timorous Persons, wanting Courage or Confidence in their Gods, who (they might say) had hitherto protected them. But the Spies, Verse 8, returned, and said to their Countrymen, Verse 9, *Arise that we may go up against them; for we have seen the Land, and behold it is very good! And are ye still? Be not slothful to go.* Verse 10, *When ye go, ye shall come unto a People* SECURE; [that is, a People that apprehend no Danger, and therefore have made no Provision against it; great Encouragement this!] *and to a large Land, and a Place where there is no Want of any Thing.* What could they desire more? Accordingly we find, in the following Verses, that *Six hundred Men* only, *appointed with Weapons of War,* undertook the Conquest of this *large Land;* knowing that 600 Men, armed and disciplined, would be an Over-match perhaps for 60,000, unarmed, undisciplined, and off their Guard. And when they went against it, the idolatrous Priest, Verse 17, *with his graven Image, and his Ephod, and his Teraphim, and his molten Image,* [Plenty of superstitious Trinkets] joined with them, and, no doubt, gave them all the Intelligence and Assistance in his Power; his Heart, as the Text assures us, *being glad,* perhaps for Reasons more than one. And now, what was the Fate of poor Laish! The 600 Men being arrived, found, as the Spies had reported, a People QUIET and SECURE, Verse 20, 21.[2] *And they smote them with the Edge of the Sword, and burnt the City with* FIRE; *and there was no* DELIVERER, *because it was far from Zidon.* Not so far from Zidon, however, as Pennsylvania is from Britain; and yet we are, if possible, more *careless* than the People of Laish! As the Scriptures are given for our Reproof, Instruction and Warning, may we make a due Use of this Example, before it be too late!

And is our *Country,* any more than our City, altogether free from Danger? Perhaps not. We have, 'tis true, had a long Peace with the Indians: But it is a long Peace indeed, as well as a long Lane, that has no Ending. The French know the Power and Importance of the Six Nations, and spare no Artifice, Pains or Expence, to gain them to their Interest. By their Priests they have

2. Should be: verses 27, 28.

converted many to their Religion, and these‡ have openly es-
poused their Cause. The rest appear irresolute which Part to take;
no Persuasions, tho' enforced with costly Presents, having yet
been able to engage them generally on our Side, tho' we had
numerous Forces on their Borders, ready to second and support
them. What then may be expected, now those Forces are, by
Orders from the Crown, to be disbanded; when our boasted Expedition is laid aside, thro' want (as it may appear to them) either
of Strength or Courage; when they see that the French, and their
Indians, boldly, and with Impunity, ravage the Frontiers of New-
York, and scalp the Inhabitants; when those few Indians that
engaged with us against the French, are left exposed to their Resentment: When they consider these Things, is there no Danger
that, thro' Disgust at our Usage, joined with Fear of the French
Power, and greater Confidence in their Promises and Protection
than in ours, they may be wholly gained over by our Enemies,
and join in the War against us? If such should be the Case, which
God forbid, how soon may the Mischief spread to our Frontier
Counties? And what may we expect to be the Consequence, but
deserting of Plantations, Ruin, Bloodshed and Confusion!

Perhaps some in the City, Towns and Plantations near the
River, may say to themselves, *An Indian War on the Frontiers will
not affect us; the Enemy will never come near our Habitations; let
those concern'd take Care of themselves.* And others who live in the
Country, when they are told of the Danger the City is in from
Attempts by Sea, may say, *What is that to us? The Enemy will be
satisfied with the Plunder of the Town, and never think it worth his
while to visit our Plantations: Let the Town take care of itself.* These
are not mere Suppositions, for I have heard some talk in this
strange Manner. But are these the Sentiments of true Pennsyl-

‡The Praying Indians.[3]

3. A branch of the Mohawks who, accepted as hostages by the French,
"were at length seduced by the Artifices of the Priests, to desert their Countrey, and take up their Residence altogether in Canada, and having been
converted to their Superstition, and reconciled to their foolish Customs, to
say their Prayers by Tale of Beeds. The English Mohawks, by way of Derision
call them the *Praying Indians*. . . ." Paul A. W. Wallace, *Conrad Weiser*
(Phila., 1945), p. 593. See also Cadwallader Colden's description in his
History of the Five Indian Nations (London, 1747), p. 52.

vanians, of Fellow-Countrymen, or even of Men that have common Sense or Goodness? Is not the whole Province one Body, united by living under the same Laws, and enjoying the same Priviledges? Are not the People of City and Country connected as Relations both by Blood and Marriage, and in Friendships equally dear? Are they not likewise united in Interest, and mutually useful and necessary to each other? When the Feet are wounded, shall the Head say, *It is not me; I will not trouble myself to contrive Relief!* Or if the Head is in Danger, shall the Hands say, *We are not affected, and therefore will lend no Assistance!* No. For so would the Body be easily destroyed: But when all Parts join their Endeavours for its Security, it is often preserved. And such should be the Union between the Country and the Town; and such their mutual Endeavours for the Safety of the Whole. When New-England, a distant Colony, involv'd itself in a grievous Debt to reduce Cape-Breton, we freely gave *Four Thousand Pounds* for *their* Relief.[4] And at another Time, remembring that Great Britain, still more distant, groan'd under heavy Taxes in Supporting the War, we threw in our Mite to their Assistance, by a free Gift of *Three Thousand Pounds:*[5] And shall Country and Town join in helping Strangers (as those comparatively are) and yet refuse to assist each other?

But whatever different Opinions we have of our Security in other Respects, our TRADE, all seem to agree, is in Danger of being ruin'd in another Year. The great Success of our Enemies, in two different Cruizes this last Summer in our Bay, must give them the greatest Encouragement to repeat more frequently their

4. In July 1745 the Assembly voted £4000 "to the King's Use . . . to be laid out . . . in the purchase of Bread, Beef, Port, Flour, Wheat or other Grain, or any of them, within this Province. . . ." 8 *Pa. Arch.*, IV, 3042. According to BF, some members of the Council advised Governor Thomas to reject the bill, since it did not specifically authorize the purchase of gunpowder; but Thomas, wiser, replied, "I shall take the Money, for I understand very well their Meaning; *Other Grain*, is Gunpowder." The Assembly made no objection. Par. Text edit., p. 290.

5. Out of consideration for the many taxes their fellow subjects in Great Britain paid, and "to demonstrate the Fidelity, Loyalty, and Affection, of the Inhabitants of this Province to our gracious King"—so they publicly declared—the Assembly in October 1741 unanimously voted £3000 "for the Use of the King . . . to be applied to such Uses as he . . . shall think fit to direct and appoint." 8 *Pa. Arch.*, IV, 2709.

Visits, the Profit being almost certain, and the Risque next to nothing. Will not the first Effect of this be, an Enhauncing of the Price of all foreign Goods to the Tradesman and Farmer, who use or consume them? For the Rate of Insurance will increase in Proportion to the Hazard of Importing them; and in the same Proportion will the Price of those Goods increase. If the Price of the Tradesman's Work and the Farmer's Produce would encrease equally with the Price of foreign Commodities, the Damage would not be so great: But the direct contrary must happen. For the same Hazard, or Rate of Insurance, that raises the Price of what is imported, must be deducted out of, and lower the Price of what is exported. Without this Addition and Deduction, as long as the Enemy cruize at our Capes, and take those Vessels that attempt to *go out*, as well as those that endeavour to *come in*, none can afford to trade, and Business must be soon at a Stand. And will not the Consequences be, A discouraging of many of the Vessels that us'd to come from other Places to purchase our Produce, and thereby a Turning of the Trade to Ports that can be entered with less Danger, and capable of furnishing them with the same Commodities, as New-York, &c? A Lessening of Business to every Shopkeeper, together with Multitudes of bad Debts; the high Rate of Goods discouraging the Buyers, and the low Rates of their Labour and Produce rendering them unable to pay for what they had bought: Loss of Employment to the Tradesman, and bad Pay for what little he does: And lastly, Loss of many Inhabitants, who will retire to other Provinces not subject to the like Inconveniencies; whence a Lowering of the Value of Lands, Lots, and Houses.

The Enemy, no doubt, have been told, That the People of Pennsylvania are Quakers, and against all Defence, from a Principle of Conscience; this, tho' true of a Part, and that a small Part only of the Inhabitants, is commonly said of the Whole; and what may make it look probable to Strangers, is, that in Fact, nothing is done by any Part of the People towards their Defence. But to refuse Defending one's self or one's Country, is so unusual a Thing among Mankind, that possibly they may not believe it, till by Experience they find, they can come higher and higher up our River, seize our Vessels, land and plunder our Plantations and Villages, and retire with their Booty unmolested. Will not this confirm the Report, and give them the greatest Encouragement to strike one bold Stroke for the City, and for the whole Plunder of the River?

It is said by some, that the Expence of a Vessel to guard our Trade, would be very heavy, greater than perhaps all the Enemy can be supposed to take from us at Sea would amount to; and that it would be cheaper for the Government to open an Insurance-Office, and pay all Losses. But is this right Reasoning? I think not: For what the Enemy takes is clear Loss to us, and Gain to him; encreasing his Riches and Strength as much as it diminishes ours, so making the Difference double; whereas the Money paid our own Tradesmen for Building and Fitting out a Vessel of Defence, remains in the Country, and circulates among us; what is paid to the Officers and Seamen that navigate her, is also spent ashore, and soon gets into other Hands; the Farmer receives the Money for her Provisions; and on the whole, nothing is clearly lost to the Country but her Wear and Tear, or so much as she sells for at the End of the War less than her first Cost. This Loss, and a trifling one it is, is all the Inconvenience; But how many and how great are the Conveniencies and Advantages! And should the Enemy, thro' our Supineness and Neglect to provide for the Defence both of our Trade and Country, be encouraged to attempt this City, and after plundering us of our Goods, either *burn it,* or put it to Ransom; how great would that Loss be! Besides the Confusion, Terror, and Distress, so many Hundreds of Families would be involv'd in!

The Thought of this latter Circumstance so much affects me, that I cannot forbear expatiating somewhat more upon it. You have, my dear Countrymen, and Fellow Citizens, Riches to tempt a considerable Force to unite and attack you, but are under no Ties or Engagements to unite for your Defence. Hence, on the first Alarm, *Terror* will spread over All; and as no Man can with Certainty depend that another will stand by him, beyond Doubt very many will seek Safety by a speedy Flight. Those that are reputed rich, will flee, thro' Fear of Torture, to make them produce more than they are able. The Man that has a Wife and Children, will find them hanging on his Neck, beseeching him with Tears to quit the City, and save his Life, to guide and protect them in that Time of general Desolation and Ruin. All will run into Confusion, amidst Cries and Lamentations, and the Hurry and Disorder of Departers, carrying away their Effects. The Few that remain will be unable to resist. *Sacking* the City will be the first, and *Burning* it, in all Probability, the last Act of the Enemy. This, I believe, will be the Case, if you have timely Notice. But what must be your Condition, if suddenly surprized, without previous Alarm, perhaps in the Night! Confined to your Houses, you will have nothing to trust to but the Enemy's Mercy. Your best Fortune will be, to fall under the Power of Commanders of King's Ships, able to controul the Mariners; and not into the Hands of *licentious Privateers.* Who can, without the utmost Horror, conceive the Miseries of the Latter! when your Persons, Fortunes, Wives and Daughters, shall be subject to the wanton and unbridled Rage, Rapine and Lust, of *Negroes, Molattoes,* and others, the vilest and most abandoned of Mankind.* A dreadful Scene! which some may represent as exaggerated. I think it my Duty to warn you: Judge for yourselves.

'Tis true, with very little Notice, the Rich may shift for themselves. The Means of speedy Flight are ready in their Hands; and with some previous Care to lodge Money and Effects in distant and secure Places, tho' they should lose much, yet enough may be left them, and to spare. But most unhappily circumstanced

*By Accounts, the ragged Crew of the Spanish Privateer that plundered Mr. Liston's, and another Plantation, a little below Newcastle, was composed of such as these.[6] The *Honour* and *Humanity* of their Officers may be judg'd of, by the Treatment they gave poor Capt. Brown, whom they took with Martin's Ship in Returning from their Cruize. Because he bravely defended himself and Vessel longer than they expected, for which every generous Enemy would have esteem'd him, did they, after he had struck and submitted, barbarously *stab* and *murder* him, tho' on his Knees begging Quarter![7]

6. See above, p. 180; also *Pa. Col. Recs.,* v, 117–8; 1 *Pa. Arch.,* I, 759–60; *Pa. Gaz.,* July 16, 1747.

7. The ship *Mary,* Captain Bernard Martin, on a voyage from Antigua to Philadelphia, was attacked and boarded near Cape Henlopen on July 14 by a party of some 30 armed men, mostly French and Spanish, from the privateer whose men attacked the plantations of Liston and Hart two days before. They drove the crew below deck, shot and wounded Martin, and seized the vessel. Martin and seven of his crew were put ashore next day. *Pa. Col. Recs.,* v, 115–7; *Pa. Gaz.,* July 23, 1747.

indeed are we, the middling People, the Tradesmen, Shopkeepers, and Farmers of this Province and City! We cannot all fly with our Families; and if we could, how shall we subsist? No; we and they, and what little we have gained by hard Labour and Industry, must bear the Brunt: The Weight of Contributions, extorted by the Enemy (as it is of Taxes among ourselves) must be surely borne by us. Nor can it be avoided as we stand at present; for tho' we are numerous, we are quite defenceless, having neither Forts, Arms, Union, nor Discipline. And tho' it were true, that our Trade might be protected at no great Expence, and our Country and our City easily defended, if proper Measures were but taken; yet who shall take these Measures? Who shall pay that Expence? On whom may we fix our Eyes with the least Expectation that they will do any one Thing for our Security? Should we address that wealthy and powerful Body of People, who have ever since the War governed our Elections, and filled almost every Seat in our Assembly; should we intreat them to consider, if not as Friends, at least as Legislators, that *Protection* is as truly due from the Government to the People, as *Obedience* from the People to the Government; and that if on account of their religious Scruples, they themselves could do no Act for our Defence, yet they might retire, relinquish their Power for a Season, quit the Helm to freer Hands during the present Tempest, to Hands chosen by their own Interest too, whose Prudence and Moderation, with regard to them, they might safely confide in; secure, from their own native Strength, of resuming again their present Stations, whenever it shall please them: Should we remind them, that the Publick Money, raised *from All,* belongs *to All;* that since they have, for their own Ease, and to secure themselves in the quiet Enjoyment of their Religious Principles (and may they long enjoy them) expended such large Sums to oppose Petitions, and engage favourable Representations of their Conduct, if they themselves could by no Means be free to appropriate any Part of the Publick Money for our Defence; yet it would be no more than Justice to spare us a reasonable Sum for that Purpose, which they might easily give to the King's Use as heretofore, leaving all the Appropriation to others, who would faithfully apply it as we desired: Should we tell them, that tho' the Treasury be at present empty, it may soon be filled by the outstanding Publick Debts collected; or at least Credit might be had for such a Sum, on a single Vote of the Assembly: That tho' *they* themselves may be resigned and easy under this naked, defenceless State of the Country, it is far otherwise with a very great Part of the People; with *us,* who can have no Confidence that God will protect those that neglect the Use of rational Means for their Security; nor have any Reason to hope, that our Losses, if we should suffer any, may be made up by Collections in our Favour at Home? Should we conjure them by all the Ties of Neighbourhood, Friendship, Justice and Humanity, to consider these Things; and what Distraction, Misery and Confusion, what Desolation and Distress, may possibly be the Effect of their *un-seasonable* Predominancy and Perseverance; yet all would be in vain: For they have already been by great Numbers of the People petitioned in vain. Our late Governor did for Years sollicit, request, and even threaten them in vain. The Council have since twice remonstrated to them in vain. Their religious Prepossessions are unchangeable, their Obstinacy invincible. Is there then the least Hope remaining, that from that Quarter any Thing should arise for our Security?

And is our Prospect better, if we turn our Eyes to the Strength of the *opposite Party,* those Great and rich Men, Merchants and others, who are ever railing at Quakers for doing what their Principles seem to require, and what in Charity we ought to believe they think their Duty, but take no one Step themselves for the Publick Safety? They have so much Wealth and Influence, if they would use it, that they might easily, by their Endeavours and Example, raise a military Spirit among us, make us fond, studious of, and expert in Martial Discipline, and effect every Thing that is necessary, under God, for our Protection. But Envy seems to have taken Possession of their Hearts, and to have eaten out and destroyed every generous, noble, Publick-spirited Sentiment. *Rage* at the Disappointment of their little Schemes for Power, gnaws their Souls, and fills them with such cordial Hatred to their Opponents, that every Proposal, by the Execution of which *those* may receive Benefit as well as themselves, is rejected with Indignation. *What,* say they, *shall we lay out our Money to protect the Trade of Quakers? Shall we fight to defend Quakers? No; Let the Trade perish, and the City burn; let what will happen, we shall never lift a Finger to prevent it.* Yet the Quakers have *Conscience* to plead for their Resolution not to fight, which these Gentlemen have not: *Conscience* with you, Gentlemen, is on the other Side of the Question: *Conscience* enjoins it as a DUTY on you (and indeed I think it such on every Man) to defend your Country, your Friends, your aged Parents, your Wives, and helpless Children: And yet you resolve not to perform this Duty, but act *contrary* to *your own* Consciences, because the Quakers act *according* to *theirs.* 'Till of late I could scarce believe the Story of him who refused to pump in a sinking Ship, because one on board, whom he hated, would be saved by it as well as himself. But such, it seems, is the Unhappiness of human Nature, that our Passions, when violent, often are too hard for the united Force of *Reason, Duty* and *Religion.*

Thus unfortunately are we circumstanc'd at this Time, my dear Countrymen and Fellow-Citizens; we, I mean, the middling People, the Farmers, Shopkeepers and Tradesmen of this City and Country. Thro' the Dissensions of our Leaders, thro' *mistaken Principles* of *Religion,* join'd with a Love of Worldly Power, on the one Hand; thro' *Pride, Envy* and *implacable Resentment* on the other; our Lives, our Families and little Fortunes, dear to us as any Great Man's can be to him, are to remain continually expos'd to Destruction, from an enterprizing, cruel, now well-inform'd, and by Success encourag'd Enemy. It seems as if Heaven, justly displeas'd at our growing Wickedness, and determin'd to punish* this once favour'd Land, had suffered our Chiefs to engage in these foolish and mischievous Contentions, for *little Posts* and *paltry Distinctions,* that our Hands might be bound up, our Understandings darkned and misled, and every Means of our Security

*When God determined to punish his chosen People, the Inhabitants of Jerusalem, who, tho' Breakers of his other Laws, were scrupulous Observers of that ONE which required keeping holy the Sabbath Day; he suffered even the strict Observation of that Command to be their Ruin: For Pompey observing that they *then* obstinately refused to fight, made a general Assault on that Day, took the Town, and butcher'd them with as little Mercy as he found Resistance. JOSEPHUS.[8]

8. For Pompey's siege and entry into Jerusalem, see Josephus, *Antiquities of the Jews,* XIV, iv, 1–4, and *Wars of the Jews,* I, vii, 3–4; on fanatic Sabbath observance, see *Antiquities,* XII, vi, 2. All are loosely paraphrased here.

neglected. It seems as if our greatest Men, our *Cives nobilissimi*‡ of both Parties, had *sworn the Ruin of the Country, and invited the French, our most inveterate Enemy, to destroy it.* Where then shall we seek for Succour and Protection? The Government we are immediately under denies it to us; and if the Enemy comes, we are *far from* ZIDON, *and there is no Deliverer near.* Our Case indeed is dangerously bad; but perhaps there is yet a Remedy, if we have but the Prudence and the Spirit to apply it.

If this now flourishing City, and greatly improving Colony, is destroy'd and ruin'd, it will not be for want of Numbers of Inhabitants able to bear Arms in its Defence. 'Tis computed that we have at least (exclusive of the Quakers) 60,000 Fighting Men, acquainted with Fire-Arms, many of them Hunters and Marksmen, hardy and bold. All we want is Order, Discipline, and a few Cannon. At present we are like the separate Filaments of Flax before the Thread is form'd, without Strength because without Connection; but UNION would make us strong and even formidable: Tho' the *Great* should neither help nor join us; tho' they should even oppose our Uniting, from some mean Views of their own, yet, if we resolve upon it, and it please GOD to inspire us with the necessary Prudence and Vigour, it *may* be effected. Great Numbers of our People are of BRITISH RACE, and tho' the fierce fighting Animals of those happy Islands, are said to abate their native Fire and Intrepidity, when removed to a Foreign Clime, yet with the People 'tis not so; Our Neighbours of New-England afford the World a convincing Proof, that BRITONS, tho' a Hundred Years transplanted, and to the remotest Part of the Earth, may yet retain, even to the third and fourth Descent, that *Zeal* for the *Publick Good,* that *military Prowess,* and that *undaunted Spirit,* which has in every Age distinguished their Nation. What Numbers have we likewise of *those brave People,* whose Fathers in the last Age made so glorious a Stand for our Religion and Liberties, when invaded by a powerful French Army, join'd by Irish Catholicks, under a bigotted Popish King! Let the memorable SIEGE of LON-

‡Conjuravere cives nobilissimi Patriam incendere; GALLORUM GENTEM, infestissimam nomini Romano, ad Bellum arcessunt.
CAT. in SALUST.[9]

9. Sallust, *De Conjuratione Catilinae,* 52: 24.

DONDERRY,[1] and the signal Actions of the INISKILLINGERS,[2] by which the Heart of that Prince's Schemes was broken, be perpetual Testimonies of the *Courage* and *Conduct* of those *noble Warriors!* Nor are there wanting amongst us, Thousands of *that Warlike Nation,* whose Sons have ever since the Time of Caesar maintained the Character he gave their Fathers, of joining the most *obstinate Courage* to all the other military Virtues. I mean the *brave* and *steady* GERMANS. Numbers of whom have actually borne Arms in the Service of their respective Princes; and if they fought well for their Tyrants and Oppressors, would they refuse to unite with us in Defence of their *newly acquired* and most precious *Liberty* and *Property?* Were this Union form'd, were we once united, thoroughly arm'd and disciplin'd, was every Thing in our Power done for our Security, as far as human Means and Foresight could provide, we might then, *with more Propriety,* humbly ask the Assistance of Heaven, and a Blessing on our lawful Endeavours. The very Fame of our Strength and Readiness would be a Means of Discouraging our Enemies; for 'tis a wise and true Saying, that *One Sword often keeps another in the Scabbard.* The Way to secure Peace is to be prepared for War. They that are on their Guard, and appear ready to receive their Adversaries, are in much less Danger of being attack'd, than the supine, secure and negligent. We have yet a Winter before us, which may afford a good and almost sufficient Opportunity for this, if we seize and improve it with a becoming Vigour. And if the Hints contained in this Paper are so happy as to meet with a suitable Disposition of Mind in his Countrymen and Fellow Citizens, the Writer of it will, in a few Days, lay before them a Form of an ASSOCIATION for the

1. Londonderry, the chief Protestant stronghold in Ireland, was besieged by the forces of James II, April 19–July 30, 1689, when ships broke through the harbor obstructions and brought relief. Through their leader and spokesman George Walker, rector of Donaghmere, the men of Derry had proudly rejected every proposal of the besiegers: "No surrender." *DNB*, under Walker.
2. During the siege of Londonderry, offensive operations by the Protestant forces were directed from Enniskillen (or Inniskilling), Co. Fermanaugh. Organized into a troop of horse and a regiment of foot, the citizens, under Col. William Wolseley, defeated a much superior force sent against the town by James II, at the battle of Newtown Butler, July 31, 1689. J. W. Fortescue, *A History of the British Army,* I (London, 1910), 344; *DNB*, under Wolseley.

Purposes herein mentioned, together with a practicable Scheme for raising the Money necessary for the Defence of our Trade, City, and Country, without laying a Burthen on any Man.

May the GOD *of* WISDOM, STRENGTH *and* POWER, *the Lord of the Armies of Israel, inspire us with Prudence in this Time of* DANGER; *take away from us all the Seeds of Contention and Division, and unite the Hearts and Counsels of all of us, of whatever* SECT *or* NATION, *in one Bond of Peace, Brotherly Love, and generous Publick Spirit; May he give us Strength and Resolution to amend our Lives, and remove from among us every Thing that is displeasing to him; afford us his most gracious Protection, confound the Designs of our Enemies, and give* PEACE *in all our Borders, is the sincere Prayer of*

A TRADESMAN *of* Philadelphia.³

3. The title page contained a quotation from Marcus Porcius Cato's speech in Sallust, *De Conjuratione Catilinae*, 52: 4–6, 24–5, 28–9. BF printed in *Pa. Gaʒ.*, Nov. 19, a translation submitted by a reader, and reprinted it in the second edition of the pamphlet at the end of the text: "Should the City be taken, all will be lost to the Conquered. Therefore if you desire to preserve your Buildings, Houses and Country Seats, your Statues, Paintings, and all your other Possessions, which you so highly esteem; if you wish to continue in the Enjoyment of them, or to have Leisure for any future Pleasures; I beseech you by the immortal Gods, *rouse* at last, *awake* from your Lethargy, and save the Common-Wealth. It is not the trifling Concern of Injuries from your Allies that demands your Attention; your *Liberties*, *Lives* and *Fortunes*, with every Thing that is interesting and dear to you, are in the most imminent *Danger*.

"Can you doubt of, or delay what you ought to do, *now*, when the Enemies Swords are unsheath'd, and descending on your Heads?—The Affair is shocking and horrid! Yet, perhaps, you are not afraid.—Yes—You are terrified to the highest Degree. But thro' *Indolence* and *Supineness* of Soul, gazing at each other, to see who shall first rise to your Succour; and a *presumptuous Dependance* on the immortal *Gods*, who have indeed preserv'd this Republick in many dangerous Seasons; you *delay* and *neglect* every Thing necessary for your Preservation. Be not deceived—*Divine Assistance and Protection are not to be obtain'd by timorous Prayers, and womanish Supplications*. To succeed, you must *join salutary Counsels, Vigilance*, and *couragious Actions*. If you sink into Effeminacy and Cowardice; if you *desert* the *Tender* and *Helpless*, by Providence committed to your Charge; *never presume* to implore the Gods:—It will provoke them, and raise their *Indignation* against you."

Form of Association

Broadside: Historical Society of Pennsylvania; also printed (with "Remarks") in *The Pennsylvania Gazette*, December 3, 1747.

Franklin had promised in *Plain Truth* to present a plan of voluntary association for defense. He did so within a week. "Having settled the Draft of it with a few Friends," he wrote in his memoirs, "I appointed a Meeting of the Citizens" at Walton's schoolhouse on November 21. The plan was agreed to, and on November 23 was submitted to "a great Meeting of the principal Gentlemen, Merchants and others," who also unanimously approved it. A third meeting was called for November 24 in the New Building to sign the instrument. "The House was pretty full," Franklin wrote, "I had prepared a Number of printed Copies, and provided Pens and Ink dispers'd all over the Room. I harangu'd them a little on the Subject, read the Paper and explain'd it, and then distributed the Copies, which were eagerly signed, not the least Objection being made." Upwards of 500 men signed that night; the signing continued briskly throughout the town in the following days, until over a thousand were soon enrolled from the city alone.[4]

Franklin printed 500 copies of the Form of Association;[5] and he reprinted it in the *Gazette*, December 3, with an explanation of each article. These explanations were probably essentially those made in the meeting of November 24. The text of the Association is reprinted here from the original broadside; the explanatory notes are from the *Gazette*.

[November 24, 1747]

WE whose Names are hereunto subscribed, Inhabitants of the Province of Pennsylvania in America, taking into serious Consideration, that Great Britain, to which we are subject, is now engag'd in a War with two powerful Nations: That it is become too well known to our Enemies, that this Colony is in a naked, defenceless State, without Fortifications or Militia of any Sort, and is therefore exposed daily to Destruction from the Attacks of a very small Force: That we are at a great Distance from our Mother Country, and cannot, on any Emergency, receive Assistance from thence: That thro' the Multiplicity of other Affairs

4. Par Text edit., p. 278. Compare this with *Pa. Gaz.*, Nov. 26, below, p. 238; and with Richard Peters' report to Thomas and Richard Penn, Nov. 29, below, p. 216. Walton's school was kept in Chancellor's sail loft, which Peters gave as the location of the meeting of November 21.
5. Eddy, *Ledger "D,"* p. 80.

of greater Importance (as we presume) no particular Care hath hitherto been taken by the Government at Home of our Protection, an humble Petition to the Crown for that purpose, sign'd by a great Number of Hands, having yet had no visible Effect. That the Assemblies of this Province, by reason of their religious Principles, have not done, nor are likely to do any Thing for our Defence, notwithstanding repeated Applications to them for that Purpose: That being thus unprotected by the Government under which we live, against our foreign Enemies that may come to invade us, As we think it absolutely necessary, WE DO hereby, for our mutual Defence and Security, and for the Security of our Wives, Children and Estates, and the Preservation of the Persons and Estates of others, our Neighbours and Fellow Subjects, form ourselves into an ASSOCIATION, and, imploring the Blessing of Heaven on our Undertaking, do agree *solemnly* with each other in Manner following; that is to say;

First, THAT we will each of us, before the first Day of January next, or as soon as possible, provide ourselves with a good Firelock, Cartouch Box, and at least twelve Charges of Powder and Ball, and as many of us as conveniently can, with a good Sword, Cutlass or Hanger, to be kept always in our respective Dwellings, in Readiness, and good Order.

Secondly, THAT we will before the said Day, form ourselves into Companies, from Fifty to One Hundred Men each, consisting of such as are situated most conveniently for meeting together.

Thirdly, THAT at the first Meetings of each Company, which shall be on the Day aforesaid, three Persons shall be chosen by Ballot out of, and by each Company, to be Captain, Lieutenant and Ensign of the same, whose Names shall be presented to the Governor for the Time being, or in his Absence to the President and Council of this Province, in order to obtain Commissions accordingly. Which Persons, so commissioned, shall be the Captains, Lieutenants and Ensigns, of each Company, respectively, for the ensuing Year.

Fourthly, THAT after the Election of the said Captains, Lieutenants and Ensigns, they who are chosen within each County shall immediately meet, and they, or the Majority of them, shall form the said Companies into a Regiment or Regiments, and shall elect Colonels, Lieutenant-Colonels, Majors, and other superior

Officers, whose Names shall be likewise presented to the Governor for the Time being, or, in his Absence, to the President and Council, to receive Commissions as above mentioned, for one Year. To all which Officers (who shall serve *gratis,* without Wages, Salary or Pay) we will, in our several Stations, respectively, pay due Obedience. And the superior Officers so chosen, shall, on the third Monday in March next, meet together at Philadelphia, and frame such general Regulations as shall be necessary for uniting our whole Force on any Occasion, or such Part of it as shall be requisite; which Regulations shall continue, and be observed, until the Meeting of our General Military Council hereafter mentioned.

Fifthly, THAT we will meet in our respective Companies, to improve ourselves in military Discipline, at the Times and Places appointed by our said superior Officers, and hereafter to be fixed by the General Military Council herein after mentioned, not exceeding four Times in one Year, unless called together on some Emergency by the Governor, or, in his Absence, the President and Council. And on the third Monday in August yearly, all the Regiments in each County shall meet at the County Town, for a general Exercise and Review.

Sixthly, THAT at the said annual Meetings, we will chuse, by Ballot, in the fairest Manner, four Deputies for each County, from among such of our Association as shall be of most Note for their Virtue, Prudence and Ability, who shall meet together at Philadelphia in fourteen Days after their Election, at their own Expence, and form a GENERAL MILITARY COUNCIL, to consult upon and frame such *Regulations* as shall be requisite for the better ordering our military Affairs, improving us in military Knowledge, and uniting and ordering our Strength, so as to make it of the most Service for our common Security. And whatever Orders and Regulations shall be so made by the said Council, or the Majority of them, shall have the Force of LAWS with us, and we promise to pay them all the Obedience in our Power, until they shall be altered or repealed by the same Authority.

Seventhly, PROVIDED always, that our said General Military Council shall not, by any Laws made as aforesaid, subject us to any Pecuniary Mulcts, Fines, or Corporal Penalties, on any Account whatever; We being determined, in this whole Affair, to act *only* on Principles of REASON, DUTY and HONOUR. Nor shall they lay any Tax upon us, nor shall we be obliged, by their Authority, to contribute towards any Batteries or Fortifications; but whatever of that kind is judg'd necessary to be done, and recommended by them, shall be left to voluntary Subscription.

Eighthly, THIS Association shall continue firm, and every Part of this Agreement be faithfully observed by us (unless the KING'S MAJESTY shall order otherwise) until some more effectual Provision be made to answer the same good Ends and Purposes, or until Peace shall be established between Great Britain, and France and Spain, and no longer.

REMARKS on the PREAMBLE.

This contains the Reasons and the Necessity of our associating. Where a Government takes proper Measures to protect the People under its Care, such a Proceeding might have been thought both unnecessary and unjustifiable: But here it is quite the Reverse. For in our State (and perhaps if you search the World through, you will find it in ours only) the Government, that Part of it at least that holds the Purse, has always, from religious Considerations, refused to use the common Means for the Defence of the Country against an Enemy.

REMARKS on ARTICLE I.

As *Use* is in our Case more to be regarded than *Uniformity*, and it would be difficult so suddenly to procure such a Number of Arms, exactly of the same Kind, the general Word *Firelock* is used (rather than *Musket*, which is the Name of a particular kind of Gun) most People having a Firelock of some kind or other already in their Hands. If the Cartouch Box should not contain the 12 Charges, the rest may be ready in the Pocket. It is said by some military Writers, that one fourth Part of the Weight of the Ball, is Powder sufficient for a Charge; an Over-quantity, that makes a Gun violently recoil, rendering the Shot less certain. They add, that the nicest Care ought to be taken in casting Bullets so much less than the Bore, that they may slip down with Ease, when rolled in Cartridges, even into a foul Gun, otherwise there is great Loss of Time and Fire in an Engagement, to the no small Advantage of the Enemy. Tho' Bayonets are not required, it would be well enough for some to provide them; for they may be as useful against a violent Onset from irregular Foot, as against Horse. Those who on Account of their Age or Infirmities ought to be excused from the common Exercises, yet will do well to keep Arms and Ammunition ready in their Houses, that when Occasion calls, they may either use them if they can, or lend them to those who happen to be unprovided. The Expence of providing these Arms is small, and may be saved in some other Article: and they will always fetch near the Money they cost.

Remarks on Article II.

This Article is intended to prevent People's sorting themselves into Companies, according to their Ranks in Life, their Quality or Station. 'Tis designed to mix the Great and Small together, for the sake of Union and Encouragement. Where Danger and Duty are equal to All, there should be no Distinction from Circumstances, but All be on the Level.

Remarks on Article III.

Where the Officers of a Militia are appointed by the Governor (as in some Colonies) it often happens, that Persons absolutely disagreeable to the People are impower'd to command them. This is attended with very ill Consequences, rendering the Meetings for military Exercise, instead of a Pleasure, a most grievous Burthen, and by Degrees discouraging them even to a total Disuse. But where those to be commanded chuse those that are to command, it is to be presumed the Choice will naturally fall on Men of the best Character for their military Skill; on such too, from whose Prudence and Good-nature there may be no Fear of Injustice or military Oppression: And as the Ballot prevents all Resentments, so the Choice for one Year only, will keep all Officers within the Bounds of Moderation and Decorum in the Exercise of their Power, and excite an Emulation in All to qualify themselves for being chosen in their Turn. The Rotation of military Offices may be objected to, as contrary to modern Practice; but the wonderful Success of the Old Romans proves it absolutely right. The Romans, without Doubt, affected Glory and Command as much as other People; but yet they disdained not to obey in their Armies the same Persons whom they had formerly commanded; and to serve as private Soldiers, where they had been formerly Generals. The Application to the Governor, &c. for Commissions, preserves the Prerogative, at the same time that these frequent Elections secure the Liberty of the People. And what can give more Spirit and martial Vigour to an Army of FREEMEN, than to be led by those of whom they have the best Opinion?

REMARKS on ARTICLE IV.

If it is reasonable for the People to chuse those Officers who are immediately over *them*, it is no less so for the Officers themselves to chuse their immediate Superiors. The whole Choice, indeed, may, in one Sense, be said to be in the People, as it takes its Rise from them. Without some general Regulations for uniting our Force, or such Part of it as may be requisite, our general arming would be to little Purpose. And as every Neighbourhood would be glad of Assistance if attacked, so it ought to be willing to give Assistance where it is needed. The great Number of Horses in this Province are in this Respect a vast Advantage; for tho' perhaps we may not form Regiments of Horse, yet those who are to fight on Foot, may, by *their* Means, be suddenly assembled in great Numbers where wanted, even from very distant Places. The Romans, in sudden Expeditions, sometimes put two Men to a Horse. One on Foot was greatly assisted in his March by holding on the Horse's Mane, while the other rid; and they alternately relieved each other. The modern Horsemen, on the like Occasions, sometimes take up each a Foot Soldier behind them.

REMARKS on ARTICLE V.

Those who from their Years or Infirmity of Body, are not able to undergo the military Exercises, would do well, notwithstanding, to attend the Meetings of the Companies, and observe what the others do, that they may not on Occasion be wholly at a Loss: Their Presence and Approbation may encourage younger Men; and the gravest and wisest among us need not be ashamed to countenance Exercises so manifestly tending to the publick Good. The Number of Meetings for Exercise is limited to four in one Year, that People may not be called too often from their Business. 4 Exercisings in a Year are sufficient to keep what we have learnt in Memory; but more frequent Meetings may be necessary at first, till we are become expert in the Discipline. On any Emergency, that is, on an actual Invasion by our Enemies, we agree to assemble on the Governor's Call; but when 'tis known that we are all prepared, well armed and disciplined, &c. there is Reason to hope such an Emergency may never happen. That there should be Meetings of Regiments, as well as of particular Companies, is necessary, there being Parts of the military Discipline best learnt when great Bodies are together: The 3d Monday in August is chosen for these Meetings, as a Time of most Leisure, being after Harvest, the Days of a middling Length, and the Heats chiefly over. To make these Meetings more entertaining and useful, Prizes may be set up for the best Marksmen, and others most expert in any of the martial Exercises.

REMARKS on ARTICLE VI.

There are a Number of Regulations necessary to be made, which could not well be particulariz'd in these Articles; and which, as Circumstances change, may often want Amendment or Alteration. To form these Regulations, this Article provides a *Military Council,* to be compos'd of prudent, good and able Men. The old and wise, unfit for personal Duty, may here be of Service; many being good at contriving, that are not so fit to put what is contriv'd, in Execution, as younger and more vigorous Spirits. This General Military Council is the Common-Band that unites all Parts of the whole Association in one Body. The Regulations they shall make, we promise to observe as Laws; and it will behove our Lawgivers to see that they are reasonable Ones, since, by the subsequent Article, they cannot annex any Penalty to the Breach of them. But however that be, it will certainly be reasonable to observe them till repealed or altered.

REMARKS on ARTICLE VII.

A Militia of FREEMEN, ought not to be subject to any corporal Penalties. In worthy Minds, the Principles of *Reason, Duty* and *Honour,* work more strongly than the Fears of Punishment. The Military Council therefore is not impowered to appoint any such, nor yet even pecuniary Mulcts or Fines; that it may clearly appear we act only on the most honourable Motives. If the Persons who compose the several Companies should think fit (as Juries sometimes do) to make a temporary Agreement, to pay little Fines when they do not appear in good Time, or the like, to be apply'd to the Purchasing of Drums, Colours, &c. or to be given in Prizes, or to refresh their weary Spirits after Exercise; they are not hereby restrain'd from doing so, but left to their Liberty.

REMARKS on ARTICLE VIII.

This Article, as well as several of the others, expresses a dutiful Regard to the Government we are under. As to the Continuance of the Association, 'tis certainly necessary no longer than the War continues; and 'tis heartily to be wish'd, that a safe and honourable Peace may the very next Year render it useless.

'Tis hoped this whole Affair will be conducted with *good Order* and *Sobriety*, and that no *ill-natured* Reflections, no *Injuries* or *Insults* will be offered our *peaceable Friends, Neighbours* and *Fellow-subjects*, who, from their *religious Scruples*, cannot allow themselves to join us. Such Proceedings tending rather to give them an *Aversion* to the proper Method of Defence, than to *engage* them to *unite* in it.

To Cadwallader Colden   ALS: New-York Historical Society

Sir   Philada. Nov. 27. 1747
The violent Party Spirit that appears in all the Votes &c. of your Assembly, seems to me extreamly unseasonable as well as unjust, and to threaten Mischief not only to your selves but to your Neighbours.[6] It begins to be plain, that the French may reap great Advantages from your Divisions: God grant they may be as blind to their own Interest, and as negligent of it, as the English are of theirs. It must be inconvenient to you to remove your Family, but more so to you and them, to live under continual Apprehensions and Alarms.[7] I shall be glad to hear you are all in a Place of Safety.

6. Throughout the summer and fall Governor Clinton and Colden had been engaged in a bitter partisan quarrel with the Assembly over defense measures, Indian trade, and plans to attack Crown Point. Alice M. Keys, *Cadwallader Colden* (N.Y., 1906), pp. 176–93.

7. Apprehensive of what the "mutinous new Levies had threatened they wou'd do in their marching through the Countrey," the Colden family sent

Tho' *Plain Truth* bore somewhat hard on both Parties here, it has had the Happiness not to give much Offence to either. It has wonderfully spirited us up to defend our selves and Country, to which End great Numbers are entring into an Association, of which I send you a Copy enclos'd. We are likewise setting on foot a Lottery to raise £3000 for erecting a Battery of Cannon below the City. We have petition'd the Proprietor to send us some from England, and have order'd our Correspondents to send us over a Parcel, if the Application to the Proprietor fails. But lest by any Accident they should miscarry, I am desired to write to you, and desire your Opinion, whether if our Government should apply to Governor Clinton, to borrow a few of your spare Cannon, till we could be supply'd, such Application might probably meet with Success. Pray excuse the Effects of Haste in this Letter. I am, Sir, with the greatest Respect, Your most obliged humble Servant   B FRANKLIN

Addressed: To   The honble Cadwallader Colden Esq   New York
Free B FRANKLIN

To William Strahan

ALS: American Philosophical Society

Sir   Philada. Nov. 28. 1747
I received your Favour of June 11. per Capt. Tiffin, with the Books, &c. all in good Order. Mr. Parks,[8] who drew the Bill on Guidart & Sons, is surpriz'd at their Protesting it, they having, as he says, large Effects of his in their Hands: He will speedily renew that Bill. Enclos'd I send you a Bill on Xr. Kilby Esqr,[9] for £19.7.1½ Sterling, which I hope will be readily paid: And you may soon expect other Bills from me for larger Sums. What Books

---

their valuables from Coldengham to the safety of New York and prepared to flee "if there was necessity for it." Mrs. Colden to Colden, Nov. 22, 1747, *Colden Paps.*, III, 429–30.

8. William Parks (d. 1750), maintained printing offices in Annapolis, 1726–36, and in Williamsburg, 1730–50. Lawrence C. Wroth, *William Parks: Printer and Journalist of England and Colonial America* (Richmond, 1926). "Guidart" was probably Richard Guildart or Gildart of Liverpool.

9. Christopher Kilby (1705–1771), Boston merchant, government contractor, and Massachusetts agent. *DAB*, Supplement I.

will be wanted for the Shop hereafter, Mr. Hall will write for: I shall send for no more, unless for myself or a Friend. I must desire you to send per first Opportunity the Maps formerly wrote for, viz. Popple's large One of North America pasted on Rollers; Ditto bound in a Book: and 8 or 10 other Maps of equal Size if to be had; they are for the long Gallery and the Assembly Room in the Statehouse.[1] If none so large are to be got, let Prospects of Cities, Buildings, &c. be pasted round them, to make them as large. I want also Folard's Polybius, in French; it is 6 Vols. 4to. printed at Paris, and costs about 3 Guineas.[2] My best Respects to good Mrs. Strahan; I know not but in another Year, I may have the Pleasure of seeing you both in London. Please to deliver the Enclos'd to Mr. Acworth:[3] I know not where to direct to him. I am, dear Sir, Your most obliged humble Servant   B FRANKLIN

Addressed: To   Mr Wm Strahan   Printer in Wine Office Court Fleetstreet   London   Per favr of Mr Wallace in the Widow

Richard Peters[4] to the Proprietaries

Letterbook copy: Historical Society of Pennsylvania

Honour'd Proprietaries,   29th Novr 1747

Abundance of Stories have been told by Sailors and others who have been taken by French Privateers and carried into Martinico and Guardalupe that the French know our Bay and River as well as we do, that they are sure the Quakers will not consent to the raising Fortifications, that there are no Men of War upon the Coast and that vast Wealth may be got from the Plunder of the City, and that some Merchants and Captains of Ships in the French Islands have actually concerted a Scheme to be executed by Six Privateers of Force against the City some time next Year. They tell further that the Captains of the English Men of War have orders to detain every French Sailor they take and to send

1. See above, p. 77.
2. *Histoire de Polybe, nouvellement traduite du Grec par Dom Vincent Thuillier . . . Avec un commentaire ou un corps de science militaire, enriché de notes . . . par M. de Folard* (Paris, 1727–30).
3. Possibly Edmund Acworth, whose account appears in Ledger D.
4. On Peters, see above, p. 187 n.

214

them to England and never to suffer any of them to be exchang'd or to go to any of the French Ports in the West Indies. I know not what Truth there is in this but they say the French have got this Notion, and therefore think that the French Privateers will quit their Cruizes in the West Indies and come by Shoals on this Coast next Summer, and if a number of them shou'd by chance meet together, they may, having some of our pilots on board, encourage one another to make an attempt on the City, especially if there shou'd be no Men of War at New York or Virginia: These Accounts are handed about amongst the Tradesmen and have made strong Impressions on Numbers. The Quakers too have exasperated several of their People by an unseasonable Inquisition into the Names of all such of their Persuasion as contributed to the manning out the *Warren* Privateer[5] for a Cruize on our Coast in order to drive away the French and Spanish Privateers that infested the Bay last Summer, with an Intent to excommunicate all who will not recant and not only moderate Friends are disoblig'd at these imperious Measures of the Meeting, but it has rais'd an Universal Odium in the Members of all the other Congregations. Ben: Franklyn, who has for some time past been really apprehensive of a Visit from the French, observing this Turn in the Peoples minds, thought he cou'd by some well wrote Papers improve this opportunity, take an advantage of their Fears and spirit them up to an Association for their Defence. He communicated this opinion to Mr. Francis, Mr. Coleman and Mr. Hopkinson[6] on which a Scheme was form'd to assume the Character of a Tradesman, to fall foul of the Quakers and their opposers equally, as People from whom no good cou'd be expected, and by this Artifice to

5. The *Warren*, Capt. Alexander Kattur, a privateer fitted out by a subscription of Philadelphia merchants, sailed in May 1747 for a month's cruise between the Virginia capes and Sandy Hook. Quakers who contributed to the expedition were dealt with by a committee of the Monthly Meeting. Robert Strettel justified his conduct, charging Friends with persecution; and William Coleman and Reese Meredith also refused to acknowledge any error. All were disowned. Albert C. Myers, ed., *Hannah Logan's Courtship* (Phila., 1904), pp. 125–6, 130–1; William W. Hinshaw, ed., *Encyclopedia of American Quaker Genealogy*, II (Ann Arbor, Mich., 1938), 491, 662.

6. Tench Francis, attorney general of the province; William Coleman, member of the Philadelphia Common Council and clerk of the City Court; Thomas Hopkinson, judge of admiralty and member of the Provincial Council.

animate all the middling Persons to undertake their own Defence in opposition to the Quakers and the Gentlemen. If this shou'd take effect, Mr. Allen[7] and his Friends might publish a vindication of their Conduct and modestly offer a Junction of their Interest to promote the Publick Good. Franklyn offer'd to print all Papers gratis in his Gazette and if they shou'd be too Voluminous to be inserted there he wou'd not only print them gratis Pamphletwise but send them with the Gazette to every one of his Customers. The first thing that was done in Consequence of this Overture was the Publication of some Verses in praise of Robert Barclay taken as I suppose out of one of the Magazines, then a Quotation out of his apology on the Subject of Defence with some sly but strong observations which any pious and well inclin'd Quaker might make.[8] This had its effect in dividing moderate Men from Bigotts, and begot open exclamations against the Inquisition set up by the Meeting from Men who but just before were observ'd to stifle their disgust. On the 17th: Instant there appear'd a strong and pathetick appeal to the People, mostly of Franklyn's own doing, and in the next weekly Paper some Quotations were inserted from Thomas Edmundson. On Saturday there was a Meeting of 150 Persons, mostly Tradesmen, in Chancellor's Sail Loft, and Franklyn after having address'd them as the first Movers in every useful undertaking that had been projected for the good of the City—Library Company, Fire Companys &c., he pull'd a Draught of an intended Association out of his Pocket and read it, all approv'd and offer'd to Sign. No says he let us not sign yet, let us offer it at least to the Gentlemen and if they come into it, well and good, we shall be the better able to carry it into Execution. On this all the better sort of the People met on monday at the Coffee House where Franklyn produc'd his Draught and it was unanimously agreed that several shou'd be printed and sign'd at the new Building the next night, which was accordingly done, and I am told by Mr. Franklyn there will be a thousand hands to it before Night.[9] I have given You a full Relation of every

7. William Allen (see below, p. 296 n), leader of the "Gentlemen's Party," which, though opposed to the Quakers, also opposed the cost of defensive measures.
8. The pieces alluded to appeared in *Pa. Gaz.*, Oct. 22, Nov. 5, 19, 1747.
9. For another account of these meetings, see below, p. 238.

thing that is come to my knowledge relating to this affair, having had no hand in it neither privately nor publickly myself, but in Justice to Mr. Allen I must tell You that when he first communicated the affair to me, which was before it was reduc'd to any settled form or Plan, he told me, Mr. Franklyn and the other Persons concern'd desir'd I shou'd be made acquainted with every step since they had nothing in view but the security of their Lives and Properties, and thought they were at the same time doing the Proprietaries true Service in defending the Country by a voluntary association which the Legislature had refus'd to do and therefore they expected the Countenance and Assistance of the Proprietaries and depended on me to make their regards to the Proprietors Family known to them in such a manner as to induce them to believe the Associators were heartily in their Interest, and as vast numbers wou'd accede to them it wou'd be mightily for their advantage to encourage them by a generous Supply of Cannon and small Arms. In short the Scheme took its rise from the just fears and apprehensions all sorts of People were under for their Lives and Properties and tho' there may be at the bottom of it a personal antipathy to Quakers who brought the Country into this dilemma, yet they really desire to recommend themselves to the Proprietaries. I have had no time to consider the Paper call'd the Association Paper, of that I will give you my opinion by the *Beulah*.

In support of this Association a Petition was presented to the Assembly, Sign'd by 250, Sixty of which are Quakers. In further support another Petition is preparing from the Merchants and Traders to the Lords of the Admiralty for a Man of War,[1] this is to be back'd by an application from the Agent Victuallers, and Mr. Kinsey writes to Partridge[2] to apply to Friends to enforce it as much as they can. The Merchants Petition to the Lords of the Admiralty will I suppose be sent to Mr. Simpson & Company[3] to be presented and it is expected he will be attended by a body of London Merchants. This day the Council appointed a Committee to prepare an address to You on the Subject of the Associ-

1. *Pa. Col. Recs.*, v, 158.
2. John Kinsey was Speaker of the Assembly; Richard Partridge, London merchant, was the Province's agent in England.
3. Not identified.

217

ation,[4] and the Corporation likewise resolv'd upon an address of the like nature,[5] both which will go by this Conveyance. The Associators propose to raise £3,000 by a Lottery of £20,000, sinking 15 per Cent and the Inspection of it is to be committed to Persons to be chosen by the Common Council.

The Assembly this Day return'd an answer to the Council's Message relating to His Majesties Request to them to advance the Sums due to the four Pennsylvania Companies,[6] and it is such an answer as amounts to a denial. Soon after its delivery two Members were sent from the House to inform the Council that they had adjourn'd to the first Monday in January; the Council gave for answer that there were several matters worthy of their Consideration before them, but if they wou'd adjourn it cou'd not be help'd. So that it is plain they will not yet come to any determination on any of the things recommended to them by the Council, tho' they were Summon'd to meet for that purpose, nor do I hear that they intend to take notice of the Petition for the Defence of the City. I suppose their design is to see how it will work, to draw off Friends from the Association, and to sow the Seeds of dissension amongst the Chief Encouragers of it if they can, or at least they may entertain hopes that as they are to sit again in January something may turn out from which they may take an handle to reject it. I have taken care to put up in the Box Copies of every publick Paper, and have inclos'd the List of them that You may see that I have omitted nothing material. . . .[7]

Endorsed: By Mr Wallis in the Ship Widow
　　　　　Duplicate by way of New York in the Brig Exchange Captn. Hilton
　　　　　Triplicate by the Beulah

4. The address is printed in *Pa. Col. Recs.*, V, 160–2.

5. The City Council's appeal for cannon is printed in *Minutes of the Common Council of Philadelphia. 1704 to 1776* (Phila., 1847), pp. 489–90.

6. These were the companies that were stationed at Albany, 1747–48. The Assembly's reply is in *Pa. Col. Recs.*, V, 159–60.

7. The final paragraph, relating to the purchase of the late Peter Evans' plantation for the Proprietors, has been omitted.

From James Logan   Reprinted from Sparks, *Works*, VII, 24–7.

My Friend B. Franklin,   3 December, 1747
 I have expected to see thee here[8] for several weeks, according to my son's information, with Euclid's title-page printed, and my Mattaire's Lives of the Stephenses;[9] but it is probable thy thoughts of thy new excellent project[1] have in some measure diverted thee, to which I most heartily wish all possible success; of which, notwithstanding, I have some doubts, partly for want of arms for some of the common people, who may be willing to enlist, and for want of will in many others, as well of the Dutch[2] as of our people, and both these for want of a militia act to compel them. Ever since I have had the power of thinking, I have clearly seen that government without arms is an inconsistency. Our Friends spare no pains to get and accumulate estates, and are yet against defending them, though these very estates are in a great measure the sole cause of their being invaded, as I showed to our Yearly Meeting, last September was six years, in a paper thou then printed.[3] But I request to be informed, as soon as thou hast any leisure, what measures are proposed to furnish small arms, powder, and ball to those in the country; and particularly what

8. Logan's house, Stenton.
9. Logan's copy of Euclid's *Elements* was the handsome edition printed at Paris in 1516 by the celebrated typographer Henri Estienne; but it lacked a title page. Logan asked BF to print a substitute, lending him for the purpose his copy of Michael Maittaire's *Stephanorum Historia* (London, 1709), which contained (pt. 2, p. 6) a transcription of the original title page of the Euclid. After some delay (see below, p. 276) BF did the job, and the volume (now in Lib. Co. Phila.) contains two printed title pages, at the foot of the first of which Logan has written, "This was printed from the original itself as it was given by the famous P. Mattaire in the Lives of the Estiennes." Lib. Co. Phila., *Annual Report*, 1957, pp. 9–10.
1. The Association.
2. The Germans, of course.
3. Logan sent a letter to the Philadelphia Yearly Meeting of Friends, Sept. 22, 1741, strongly stating the case for defensive military measures and proposing that those conscientiously unable to support such measures should refuse to run for, or serve in, the Assembly. When the Quakers would not lay the letter before the general meeting, Logan had BF print 30 copies, under the title *To Robert Jordan, and others the Friends of the Yearly Meeting for Business, now conven'd in Philadelphia*. This letter is reprinted in *PMHB*, VI (1882), 402–11.

measures are taken to defend our river, especially at the Red Bank, on the Jersey side, and on our own,[4] where there ought not to be less than forty guns, from six to twelve pounders. What gunners are to be depended on?

Thy project of a lottery to clear £3,000 is excellent, and I hope it will be speedily filled; nor shall I be wanting. But thou wilt answer all these questions and much more, if thou wilt visit me here, as on First day, to dine with me, and thou wilt exceedingly oblige thy very loving friend,   JAMES LOGAN

Scheme of the First Philadelphia Lottery

Printed in *The Pennsylvania Gazette*, December 12, 1747.

The most urgent problem for the Association was not armed men, but money. Volunteering for military service, especially when there was no likelihood of being called to duty unless one's own city was actually threatened, was one thing; it was another to make a free gift of money to buy supplies. Franklin's solution was a lottery. Managers were appointed; the Mayor and Corporation of the city gave their approval and appointed overseers;[5] Franklin ran off a thousand handbills of the scheme and printed 10,000 tickets for the drawings.[6] The *Gazette* announced on December 3 that the Scheme of the Lottery would be published "on Saturday next" (i.e., December 5) and that copies might be had gratis at the post office; and the next week the *Gazette* reprinted it. To give the public confidence Franklin prepared a precise explanation of its operation (see below, p. 229). James Logan put £250 into the lottery;[7] the city of Philadelphia bought 200 tickets;[8] the Hand-in-

4. The Association battery was constructed on the Pennsylvania side, at Wicaco, just outside Philadelphia. Red Bank, farther down, was opposite the mouth of the Schuylkill, at a bend in the Delaware, where Hog, Mud, and League Islands make the river narrow for large vessels. Its importance was recognized during the Revolution, when Fort Mercer was erected there to guard the approaches to Philadelphia.

5. *Minutes of the Common Council of the City of Philadelphia. 1704 to 1776* (Phila., 1847), p. 490.

6. Eddy, *Ledger "D,"* p. 80.

7. See below, p. 274 n. BF remembered that Logan "put into my Hands Sixty Pounds to be laid out in Lottery Tickets." Par. Text edit., p. 286.

8. Common Council, *Minutes*, pp. 492–3; *Pa. Gaz.*, Jan. 19, 1748.

Hand Fire Company took 100.⁹ The managers sent them for sale to Maryland, Virginia, New York, and New Jersey. The Philadelphians, Franklin boasted, came as near to selling out in seven weeks as New York and New England lotteries did in as many months.¹

The lottery was designed to raise £20,000, of which £3000 was to go to the Association. The drawings were held between February 8 and 17. William Allen, for example, won £312; the city of Philadelphia £262; both turned back their prizes, as did Franklin, who drew several small prizes totaling £12.²

Meanwhile the Mayor and Corporation of the city and the President and Council of the province had petitioned the Proprietors for cannon, arms, and ammunition. The Lottery Managers ordered cannon from London and made a census of what was available on the city wharves, locating nearly 70 of different sorts.³ On December 29 the Council appealed to Governor Shirley of Massachusetts and Governor Clinton of New York to borrow guns from those colonies; they made similar requests of the governor of Jamaica and the commander-in-chief at Cape Breton. Shirley replied that he had none to spare, but promised to send a guardship to watch Delaware Bay and River. Clinton at first made a similar reply.⁴ But the Pennsylvania Council renewed their plea in March 1748, sending two of their members, Abraham Taylor, colonel of the Associators, and Thomas Lawrence, with William Allen and Franklin, to New York to present it in person. Clinton again refused them, "but," Franklin remembered, "at a Dinner with his Council where there was great Drinking of Madeira Wine, as the Custom

9. Phila. Lottery Journal. MS, Yale Univ. Lib. BF's Union Fire Company also subscribed. He relates how the Quaker members, though a large majority, absented themselves so that the non-Quakers could act. From this BF calculated that only one of 21 Quakers was sincerely against defense. Before the meeting, when he expected the proposal to buy lottery tickets would be defeated, BF half seriously, half jokingly proposed to Philip Syng that a motion be made to buy a fire engine, to which he thought the Quakers could have no objection. "And then if you nominate me, and I you, as a Committee for that purpose, we will buy a great Gun, which is certainly a *Fire-Engine*." Par. Text edit., pp. 284–6, 290. Another fire company, however, voted 19 to 3 against subscribing, apparently because of conscientious scruples against lotteries. Albert C. Myers, ed., *Hannah Logan's Courtship* (Phila., 1904), pp. 135–6.

1. *Pa. Gaz.*, Jan. 19, 1748.
2. Common Council, *Minutes*, pp. 498–9; Phila. Lottery Journal.
3. *Pa. Gaz.*, April 28, 1748.
4. *Pa. Col. Recs.*, V, 172–4, 187, 189, 198–9, 204–5, 228.

at that Place then was, he soften'd by degrees, and said he would lend us Six. After a few more Bumpers he advanc'd to Ten. And at length he very good-naturedly conceded Eighteen."[5]

From the income from the lottery the managers, together with a committee appointed for the purpose, defrayed the mounting costs of defense. Though not a lottery manager, Franklin was a member of the committee. By virtue of their control of funds these men became the principal figures in the Association. They selected a site for a strong battery on William Allen's land below Gloria Dei Church at Wicaco, south of the city, and a smaller one of eleven guns on William Atwood's wharf under Society Hill, and considered constructing similar works on other wharves. Planking and other materials were ordered in January; by early spring the Wicaco battery, 400 feet long, was ready for cannon.[6] Those from New York arrived in April. John Stamper seems to have been in charge of construction. Much of the work mounting the guns was done by John Pass, and old Gustavus Hesselius earned £4 painting the gun carriages, possibly with stripes and coats of arms. A flagpole was erected at a cost of £2 11s. It was, the Council informed the Proprietors in July, "one of the compleatest Batteries, of its size, on the Continent."[7] At Wicaco, Franklin wrote, "the Associators kept a nightly Guard while the War lasted: And among the rest I regularly took my Turn of Duty there as a common Soldier."[8]

The Lottery Managers' journal and ledger, with some related papers, are in the Yale University Library. From these the Managers published in 1752 a full accounting of their expenditures in a small pamphlet entitled *Philadelphia Lottery Accounts*.

5. Par. Text edit., p. 280; *Pa. Col. Recs.*, V, 205–6, 215. The Philadelphians got not eighteen, as BF remembered, but twelve 12-pounders and two 18-pounders from New York. "They met with an ill-natur'd disposition in the generality of the People, who said Pennsylvania deserv'd nothing at their hands, as they had asked them to join with them in defending their Frontiers against the Indian and French Enemy, and they always refus'd." Chief Justice DeLancey was at first opposed to lending the guns. Peters to Penn, March 25, 1748, Penn MSS, Official Corres., IV, 93, Hist. Soc. Pa.

6. Same to same, May 11, 1748, *ibid.*, 123. "The Association Battery," which was kept in repair for some years, is represented on Scull and Heap's "East Prospect of the City of Philadelphia," 1754. *PMHB*, LXXIII (1949), 22. For a summary account of the erection of the battery, see 1 *Pa. Arch.*, XII, 437–42.

7. *Pa. Col. Recs.*, V, 322.

8. Par. Text edit., p. 280.

THE ASSOCIATION, 1747–48.
Above: A ticket in the First Philadelphia Lottery.
Below: The Association Battery.

[December 5, 1747]

SCHEME of the Philadelphia Lottery,
For Raising Three Thousand Pounds for the PUBLICK USE.

Number of Prizes.		Value of each.		Total Value.
		£		£
2	of	500	are	1000
3	of	300	are	900
5	of	200	are	1000
10	of	100	are	1000
20	of	50	are	1000
40	of	25	are	1000
80	of	15	are	1200
100	of	10	are	1000
502	of	5	are	2510
2080	of	3	are	6240
Prizes 2842			First drawn	50
Blanks 7158			Last drawn	100
10000				£17000

Tickets at Forty Shillings each, is } £20000 { From which deduct 15 per Cent. for the Publick Use, is } £ 3000

£20000

The fortunate are to receive their prizes intire, the 15 per Cent. being deducted not from the prizes after they are drawn, but from the whole sum produced by sale of the tickets before the drawing begins.

The lottery to be under the care, management and direction of William Allen, Joshua Maddox, William Masters, Samuel M'Call, senior, Edward Shippen, Thomas Leech, Charles Willing, John Kearsley, William Clymer, senior, Thomas Lawrence, junior, William Coleman, and Thomas Hopkinson; who are to dispose of the tickets, and to be on oath, and give bond for the faithful discharge of their trust.

The 15 per Cent. to be applied to such use as the said managers, together with William Wallace, John Stamper, Samuel Hazard, Philip Syng, John Mifflin, James Coultas, William Branson, Rees Meredith, Thomas Lloyd, and Benjamin Franklin, or the majority of them, shall judge most for the benefit and advantage of this city and province, our present circumstances considered.

The whole to be regulated, with respect to the tickets, the drawing, keeping the accounts, and other particulars, as near as can be according to the method practised in England. The Drawing to commence on Monday, the eighteenth day of January next, at the Court-House, in Philadelphia, under the inspection of at least three of the managers, and such other persons as shall be appointed for that purpose by the corporation of the said city, and in the presence of such adventurers as think fit to attend.

The numbers of the blanks, as well as of the prizes, will be published weekly in the *Pennsylvania Gazette.*

The money to be paid to the possessors of the benefit tickets, as soon as the drawing is finished, of which publick notice will be given in the *Gazette.*

All prizes not called for within three months after the drawing is finished, to be deemed as generously given for the same use as the 15 per Cent. and not to be demanded afterwards, but shall faithfully be applied accordingly.

The managers, and their assistants, to make up fair accounts of the disposition of the money, and publish the same within twelve months after the lottery is drawn.

Tickets are now disposing of by the said managers at their respective dwellings.

To James Logan MS not found; reprinted from Sparks, *Works,* VII, 28.

Sir, Monday Noon [December 7, 1747][9]

I am heartily glad you approve of our proceedings. We shall have arms for the poor in the spring, and a number of battering cannon. The place for the batteries is not yet fixed; but it is generally thought that near Red Bank will be most suitable, as the enemy must there have natural difficulties to struggle with, besides the channel being narrow. The Dutch are as hearty as the English. "Plain Truth" and the "Association" are in their language,[1] and their parsons encourage them. It is proposed to breed gunners by forming an artillery club, to go down weekly to the battery and exercise the great guns. The best engineers against Cape Breton

9. Incorrectly dated December 4 by Sparks; that was a Friday in 1747.
1. See above, p. 184, on the German translation of *Plain Truth.*

were of such a club, tradesmen and shopkeepers of Boston. I was with them at the Castle at their exercise in 1743.[2]

I have not time to write larger nor to wait on you till next week. In general all goes well, and there is a surprising unanimity in all ranks. Near eight hundred have signed the *Association,* and more are signing hourly. One company of Dutch is complete. I am with great respect, Sir, &c.   B. FRANKLIN

Address to the Associators

MS (fragment): American Philosophical Society

The Associators—almost 600 in number—assembled with their arms at the court house on December 7 for their first meeting. Secretary Richard Peters, at the order of the President and Council, informed them that their "Proceedings are not disapprov'd by the Government," and assured them that commissions would be "readily granted" to the officers chosen in accordance with the Association articles.[3] Franklin made proposals for dividing the city into districts and companies and for conducting the forthcoming election of officers, both of which the Associators approved. Among his manuscripts are two sheets—hitherto separated—fragments of his paper read on this occasion.

Gentlemen   [December 7, 1747]

The second Article of the Association we have entred into, is this, *That we will before the said Day,* that is, before the first Day of January next, *form ourselves into Companies consisting of such as are situated most conveniently for meeting together.* But as the Manner of forming ourselves into Companies is not particularly express'd, I am now to acquaint you what previous Steps have been taken to that purpose. As the Association was sign'd promiscuously by Persons dwelling in all Parts of the Town, and it was difficult as their Names stood, to sort them into their respective Neighbour-hoods, two Inhabitants of each Ward were called together, to con-

2. The Massachusetts Assembly had authorized Governor Shirley to raise two companies of 60 men each "to be exerciz'd and disciplin'd in the use of the Great Artillery" at Castle William. They were the first troops trained to use "the Great Guns" in case of enemy attack. Shirley to the Lords of Trade, Jan. 30, 1743, Charles H. Lincoln, ed., *Correspondence of William Shirley* (N.Y., 1912), I, 100.

3. *Pa. Col. Recs.*, V, 168; see below, p. 239.

sider of the properest Means of dividing the Associators into Companies according to the Article. After some Consideration they agreed to go round their respective Wards, and take down the Names of the Associators of each Ward in separate Lists, by which Lists they might see whether there were a Number of Members in each Ward sufficient to form a Company. When the Lists were brought in, it appear'd that some Wards contain'd Associators more than sufficient for a [*missing*]

The first Company to the southward, is Dock Ward Company, and contains, &c.

(read em all)

Mulberry Ward being very large is divided into two Companies, and as our German Brethren who are as hearty and as forward as [any of] us, have desired to be by themselves, [one] of those Companies is accordingly German, [and the] other English.

If you approve of these Divisions, Gentlemen, I will deliver Lists of each Company, to some among you who will undertake to call you to[gether wh]en the Time comes for chusing your Officers, w[hich] by the Articles is the first Day of January next. In the mean time, if each Company shall think fit to meet by itself one Evening in a Week or oftner, to improve in the Exercise of Arms, those who have the Lists will look out for and provide convenient Rooms in different Parts of the Town to accommodate the several Companies. By these private Meetings and Exercises, we shall not only improve in the Discipline, but become acquainted with each other, and so be better able to judge, when the Day of Election comes, who among us are fittest to be our Officers.

Tis hoped all will endeavour to have their Arms and Ammunition ready by that Day, according to the Articles, and as our Numbers are daily encreasing, I do not doubt but you will then be able to make a noble Appearance. [*Remainder missing.*]

Proclamation for a General Fast

Broadside:[4] Yale University Library

The minutes of the Governor's Council of December 8, 1747, record that that body, "taking into Consideration the State of the War in

4. At the bottom: "Philadelphia: Printed by B. Franklin, MDCCXLVII." Evans 6043.

general, the Sickness that lately rag'd over this City and the Province, the probability of our Enemies making a Descent on the City, and the Calamitous Situation of our Frontiers," in order to awaken the inhabitants to "a just Sense of their Condition," appointed Abraham Taylor and Thomas Hopkinson to draft a suitable proclamation for a general fast. Their draft was submitted the following day, it was read and approved, and the Council ordered that it be engrossed and published on December 10 "forenoon at the Court House with the usual Solemnity."[5]

In this bare recital Franklin's name is not mentioned and no suggestion made as to where Taylor and Hopkinson might have turned for a model. Franklin's autobiography supplies the deficiency. His activity in the Association, he relates, won him the confidence of the members of the Council, and they consulted him in matters of importance to the Association. "Calling in the Aid of Religion, I propos'd to them the Proclaiming a Fast, to promote Reformation, and implore the Blessing of Heaven on our Undertaking. They embrac'd the Motion, but as it was the first Fast ever thought of in the Province, the Secretary had no Precedent from which to draw the Proclamation. My Education in New England, where a Fast is proclaim'd every Year, was here of some Advantage. I drew it in the accustomed Stile, it was translated into German, printed in both Languages and divulg'd thro' the Province."[6]

5. *Pa. Col. Recs.*, v, 168–9. As BF remembered it, the secretary of the Council, Rev. Richard Peters, was designated to draft the proclamation, not Taylor and Hopkinson. A model might have been Governor Shirley's proclamation of Oct. 6, 1746. Evans 5808. BF's established a precedent in Pennsylvania: Governor Morris proclaimed a fast during a disastrous drought in 1756 (*Pa. Col. Recs.*, VI, 422); and thereafter such fast days were occasionally proclaimed.

6. Par. Text edit., pp. 280–2. The fast day was the occasion for several sermons supporting the Association. William Currie in *A Sermon, Preached in Radnor Church* (Evans 6119) warned his hearers of what they might expect from "a lawless Crew of French and Spanish Privateers; and which is a worse Enemy than even those, the barbarous, cruel, and inhuman Indians"; and, warmly endorsing *Plain Truth*, urged them to join the Association as "the only Means that seems to be in our Power at present." Gilbert Tennent in *A Sermon Preach'd at Philadelphia* (Evans 6248) hailed the Association as "an important, necessary, and noble Undertaking," and continued: "If any imagine that their *Faith* and *Piety* are sufficient to *protect* them from a *temporal Enemy*, without the Use of *temporal Means*, let them try for a while, if they please, the Vertue and Influence of them, (seperate from temporal or secular Means) to build *Houses*, furnish their *Tables*, and keep their *Money* and *Goods* from *Thieves*, and see what they can do; possibly this may convince them of their unhappy Mistake!"

[December 9, 1747]

By the Honourable the PRESIDENT and COUNCIL of the
Province of Pennsylvania,
A PROCLAMATION For a GENERAL FAST.

FORASMUCH as it is the Duty of Mankind, on all suitable Occasions, to acknowledge their Dependance on the DIVINE BEING, to give Thanks for the Mercies received, and no less to deprecate his Judgments, and humbly pray for his Protection: And as the Calamities of a bloody War, in which our Nation is now engaged, seem every Year more nearly to approach us, and the Expedition form'd for the Security of these Plantations, hath been laid aside: As the Inhabitants of this Province and City have been sorely visited with mortal Sickness in the Summer past,[7] and there is just Reason to fear, that unless we humble ourselves before the Lord, and amend our Ways, we may be chastised with yet heavier Judgments: WE HAVE THEREFORE thought fit, on due Consideration thereof, to appoint Thursday, the seventh Day of January next, to be observed throughout this Province as a Day of FASTING and PRAYER; exhorting all, both Ministers and People, to observe the same with becoming Seriousness and Attention, and to join with one Accord in the most humble and fervent Supplications, That Almighty GOD would mercifully interpose, and still the Rage of War among the Nations, and put a Stop to the Effusion of Christian Blood: That he would preserve and bless our Gracious KING, guide his Councils, and give him Victory over his Enemies, to the Establishing a speedy and lasting PEACE: That he would bless, prosper and preserve all the British Colonies, and particularly, that he would take this Province under his Protection, confound the Designs and defeat the Attempts of its Enemies, and unite our Hearts, and strengthen our Hands in every Undertaking that may be for the Publick Good, and for our Defence and Security in this Time of Danger: That he would graciously please to bless the succeeding Year with Health, Peace and Plenty, and enable us to make a right Use of his late afflicting Hand, in a sincere and thorough Reformation of our Lives and Manners, to which the Ministers of all religious Societies are desired earnestly to exhort their People. And it is

7. The disease was supposed to have come from mud and stagnant water in Dock Creek. *Pa. Col. Recs.*, v, 244.

228

recommended to all Persons to abstain from servile Labour on the said Day.

Given at Philadelphia, under the Great Seal of the said Province, the Ninth Day of December, in the Twenty-first Year of the Reign of our Sovereign Lord GEORGE II. by the Grace of GOD, of Great-Britain, France and Ireland, King, Defender of the Faith, &c. Annoq; Domini, 1747.　　　　ANTHONY PALMER, President

By Order of the Honourable the President and
　Council, RICHARD PETERS, Secretary.

GOD Save the KING.

The Manner of Drawing a Public Lottery

Printed in *The Pennsylvania Gazette*, December 22, 1747.

This explanation is an integral part of the proposals for a lottery (see above, p. 220). Franklin very likely composed it, though there is no proof that he did.

An Account of the Manner of Drawing
a Publick LOTTERY.

Suppose a Lottery to consist of Ten Thousand Tickets; as the present Philadelphia Lottery does. Before the Tickets are sold, they are numbered from 1 to 10,000, each Ticket having its Number. These Tickets remain in the Hands of the Purchasers, and 'tis by them a Claim is made to the Prizes that shall happen to come up in the Drawing against their respective Numbers.

To prevent any Fraud in altering of Numbers, the Tickets are indented, and other Measures taken.

For the Drawing, two round Boxes, or hollow Wheels, are prepar'd, being about three Foot Diameter, and 6 or 8 Inches deep, each having a little Door near one Side. These Wheels are put on Axeltrees, and hung in the Manner of a Grindstone, so as to be easily turn'd round by a Handle. In one of them are put 10,000 little pieces of Paper, all of a Size, number'd from 1 to 10000, as the sold Tickets were, each Piece having its Number; these are closely roll'd up and ty'd with Thread, each by itself, so that by turning the Wheel many Times round, they may be all mix'd together, and it becomes impossible to know where among them any particular Number lies. In the other Wheel are likewise put 10,000 little Pieces of Paper of equal Size, roll'd up and ty'd in the same Manner each by itself: These are not number'd; but in *Two* of them (in the Philadelphia Lottery) will be wrote FIVE HUNDRED POUNDS; in *Three* of them will be wrote THREE HUNDRED POUNDS; in *Five* of them will be wrote TWO HUNDRED POUNDS; in *Ten* of them will be wrote ONE HUNDRED POUNDS; in *Twenty* of them will be wrote FIFTY POUNDS; in *Forty* of them, TWENTY FIVE POUNDS; in *Eighty* of them, FIFTEEN POUNDS; in *One Hundred* of them, TEN POUNDS; in *Five Hundred and two* of them, FIVE POUNDS; and in *Two Thousand and Eighty* of them, THREE POUNDS; the rest have nothing wrote in them, but are called the Blanks.

The Cutting, Rolling up, and putting in the Papers into the Boxes or Wheels, is to be done in Publick; Notice being beforehand given of the Day, that any concern'd may be present, and be satisfied that all the Numbers are put into one Wheel, and all the Prizes with the Blanks into the other, as they ought to be. The Managers besides have taken an Oath for the faithful Performance of their Trust, and a Committee of the Corporation are to inspect the Whole. Then the Wheels are shut and seal'd, and lock'd in a strong Chest, having several different Locks, the Keys of which to be kept by different Managers 'till the Day of Drawing.

On that Day the Chest is opened, and the Wheels taken out in publick View, and the Seals taken off. Then the Wheels being whirl'd round, 'till the Company is satisfy'd that the Papers in both Wheels are sufficiently mix'd, a little Boy standing high by the Wheel in View of all, puts his Hand into that Wheel that contains the 10,000 numbered Papers, takes out one of them, and gives it to a Manager, or one of the Corporation Inspectors, who cuts the Thread, opens it, and reads the Number aloud, and hands it to the others, that they may see it has been rightly read. Then another little Boy, standing by the Wheel containing the Blanks and Prizes, puts his Hand into that, and takes out one of the Pieces of Paper, gives it to a Manager, or inspector, who opens it, &c. If it proves a Prize, whatever Prize it is, it belongs to the Number just before drawn; and whoever has the Ticket with that Number, claims the said Prize; if it is a Blank, the Ticket of that Number claims nothing. Sworn Clerks are present, who enter down the Lot of every Number before another is drawn, and the Numbers, with their Lots, are filed together, to prevent any Mistakes, or to rectify such if they should happen to be made. After Drawing a few Tickets, the Wheels are turned again, to keep the Papers continually mixing. And thus the Numbers being in one Wheel, the Lots in the other, all mixed; as 'tis impossible to know what Number one Boy will lay his Hand on and take out of the one, or what Lot the other will take out of the other Wheel, so 'tis impossible to know, 'till drawn, what Fortune any Ticket will have; and in this consists the Fairness of the Lottery.

The first drawn Number claims FIFTY POUNDS, and the last drawn Number ONE HUNDRED POUNDS, besides the Prize that may happen to be drawn against them.

As the Drawing cannot be finished in one Day, but will require several; every Evening the Wheels are to be secur'd in the Chest, as aforementioned.

Extracts from the Gazette, 1747

Printed in *The Pennsylvania Gazette*, January 6 to December 29, 1747.

Extracts from *The Pennsylvania Gazette* have been printed for each of the years that Franklin personally conducted his printing office (see above, I, 164). With the establishment of the partnership of Franklin and Hall on January 1, 1748, however, the latter took over the daily oversight of the office, though Franklin, of course, from time to time contributed both original essays and excerpts from private letters containing news of general interest. The extracts for 1747 are, therefore, the last group of unsigned miscellaneous items that will be printed at the end of the year in this work.

Philadelphia, Feb. 3. 1746–7.

To be LETT for Three Years, A Bakehouse, with two ovens, very well situate for carrying on said Trade, being some years standing, and has continual Employ, by loaf bread, bisket baking, and for dinner baking (fixed) fit for any person to go on with said business the first day's entrance. Likewise to be sold or hired, two bolting-mills and chests, with all necessaries whatever for carrying on the business of loaf bread and bisket baking, with two servant lads time, brought up to said business. Any person inclining to purchase, may enter into said business one month after the day of agreement. For further information, enquire of Benjamin Franklin.

[February 3]

[ADVERTISEMENT] A Refiner and Hammerman is wanted for a Forge in the Government of New-York. One who is a good Workman, and can be well recommended, will have good Encouragement. Enquire of the Printer hereof. [February 24]

A Gentleman who came from Georgia, informs us, that the Reverend Mr. George Whitefield is safe arrived there.[8]

[March 16]

[ADVERTISEMENT] Lately imported, and to be sold by B. Franklin, Bibles of various Sizes, from large Folio, down to the smallest Pocket Bibles; Ditto in 2 Vols. Testaments, Common Prayers, Confessions of Faith, large and small, Independent Whig, Willwood's Glimpse of Glory, Rutherford's Letters, Brown on Prayer, Ditto's Christ the Way, &c. Boston's Fourfold State of Man, Gray's Works, complete, Willison's Sacramental Catechism, Flavell's Husbandry Spiritualized, Shephard's Sound Believer, Bunyan's Holy War, Ditto's Sighs from Hell, Ditto's Grace Abounding, Practice of Piety, Dilworth's Spelling-Books, Brown's Ditto, Play-Book for Children, Vincent on Judgment, Dyer's Golden Chain, Life of Monsieur De Renty; Cocker's Arithmetick, &c. &c. Also most Sorts of School Books, Latin, French and Dutch. Likewise Navigation Books.

With Psalters, Primmers, Paper, Sealing Wax, Ink-powder, and all Sorts of Stationary Ware. [April 9]

Philadelphia, May 7. 1747.
Deserted from Captain John Diemer's company of foot, now lying at Albany, the following men, viz. [*Here follow 17 names.*]

Whoever takes up and secures any of the said deserters, and gives information to the Subscriber, at the Post-Office, Phila-

---

8. Whitefield reached Georgia in December, but in late January went to Charleston, S. C., on a preaching tour. Tyerman, *Whitefield*, II, 167-8.

delphia, or to the said Capt. Diemer, so that they may be brought to his company, shall have *Three Pounds* reward for each.

W. FRANKLIN[9]

[May 7]

Philadelphia, May 21. 1747.

Strayed from off the commons of Philadelphia, a white horse, low in flesh, long sided, long switch tail, pretty well set, of middling heighth, unshod, is a cart horse, and has a heavy, lubberly trott. Whoever finds him, and brings him to the printer hereof, shall have *Ten Shillings* reward, when, by his directions, deliver'd to the owner in Philadelphia. [May 21]

Friday last the Reverend Mr. Whitefield came to Town, and preached twice on Sunday, and once on Monday, at the New-Building.[1] [June 4]

Monday last, in the Afternoon, the Governor, with his Lady and Daughter, embarked for London, on board the Greyhound, Capt. Budden: They were respectfully attended to the Wharff by the Corporation, the Grand Jury, and the principal Gentlemen and Ladies of the City. [June 4]

Philadelphia, June 4. 1747.

Whoever will discover to the printer hereof any effects belong-

9. William Franklin was an ensign in Captain John Diemer's company, raised for an expedition against Canada. The troops were in winter quarters at Albany, N. Y., 1746–7 (see above, pp. 89 n, 142). Diemer and his captains explained to Governor Clinton, June 8, 1747, that the desertions and mutinous conduct of their men was owing to the local people spreading rumors among them that they were being cheated of their pay and that Clinton intended to keep them in service in New York without hope of discharge. E. B. O'Callaghan, ed., *Documents relative to the Colonial History of the State of New York* (Albany, 1855), VI, 375–6. Diemer's return of his company, September 1746, is in 2 *Pa. Arch.*, II, 420–2.

1. Whitefield left Charleston March 21 and reached Philadelphia May 29. Though exhausted from preaching and weakened by fever and convulsions, he preached again May 30. "To oblige my friends, and with great regret," he wrote June 4, "I have omitted preaching one night, and purpose to do so once more, that they may not charge me with murdering myself; but I hope yet to die in the pulpit, or soon after I come out of it." Tyerman, *Whitefield*, II, 171, 172.

ing, or debts due, to the estate of Captain John Spence, late a merchant in this city, deceased, shall receive *Twenty per Cent.* or a fifth part of such effects and debts, immediately on the recovery thereof.[2] [June 4]

Philadelphia, June 18. 1747.
Lost between Germantown and Philadelphia, the 8th instant, a silver watch, the maker's name Tomlinson, London; with two seals, one silver, with a coat of arms; the other bathmetal, with glass faces, a crown on one side, and King William's and Queen Mary's heads in one on the other. Whoever brings it to the printer hereof, shall have *Forty Shillings* reward. [June 18]

We hear that several People have died suddenly within these few Days, by drinking cold Water too greedily while they were hot. [July 9]

Philadelphia, July 8. 1747.
Lost last night, a large pair of plain Silver Buckles, mark'd GPY. Whoever brings them to the printer hereof, shall receive *Ten Shillings* reward, and no questions ask'd. Silversmiths and others are desired to take notice of this Advertisement, and stop them if offer'd to sale. [July 9]

Philadelphia, August 6. 1747.
Stolen or stray'd last Night, out of B. Franklin's pasture, near this city, a likely young sorrel Horse, about 14 hands high, with silver Mane and Tail, four white feet, a blaze in his face, no brand, a large belly, and is in good case, paces well, but trots sometimes, very small ears, and is shod all round. Also a small bay horse, without shoes, low in flesh, long dark tail and mane. Whoever brings them to the subscriber, shall have *Forty Shillings* reward for the first, and *Ten Shillings* for the other: If stolen, and the thief detected, so that he may be brought to justice, FIVE POUNDS, with reasonable charges, paid by   B. FRANKLIN
[August 6]

2. Spence's account with BF, which includes a bill for an advertisement (probably a handbill) for a sale of rigging, is in Ledger D, in APS. Nothing more has been learned about Spence.

[ADVERTISEMENT] Just imported, and sold by B. Franklin, The Circle of the Sciences, &c. In Three Volumes.

Vol. I. An easy Introduction to the English Language; or, a pretty Spelling-book for little Masters and Misses.

Vol. II. An easy Introduction to the English Language; or, a Compendious Grammar for the Use of Young Gentlemen, Ladies, and Foreigners.

Vol. III. An easy Spelling-Dictionary of the English Language, on a new Plan; for the Use of Young Gentlemen, Ladies, and Foreigners.

Also The Child's Guide to Polite Learning; or a natural, plain and easy Spelling-Book and Grammar of the English Tongue. By Way of Question and Answer; To which is prefixed, A short Historical Account of Language in general, for the Perusal of such as are more advanc'd in Years.

Likewise the following Books for Children. Tom Thumb's Play-Book. Tommy Thumb's Song-Book. A Christmass-Box for Masters and Misses. The Trifle or gilded Toy, To humour every Girl and Boy. The Child's New-Years-Gift, or a Collection of chaste and significant Riddles. Nancy Cock's Riddle Book: With Proverbial Precepts on Education. Nancy Cock's Song-Book, for all little Misses and Masters. The Child's Entertainer: Being a New Collection of Riddles, upon the most familiar Subjects. The Child's Delight; or little Master and Misses instructive and diverting Companion. The Child's New Play-Thing: Being a Spelling-Book intended to make the Learning to Read, a Diversion instead of a Task, &c. &c.   [September 3]

Philadelphia, Sept. 3. 1747.
John Murphy having declined riding post to Maryland, gives notice, that he is ready to serve gentlemen as a messenger or express to any part of this or the neighbouring provinces; for which purpose he keeps good horses in readiness, and will perform what he undertakes with the utmost diligence and dispatch, giving security for his honesty, where required.

N.B. Said Murphy has lost a light-colour'd great-coat with the cape patched; the person that has found it, is desired to bring it to him at the Seven Stars, in Elbow lane, and they shall have Five shillings reward.[3] [September 3]

The same Day [Monday, September 14] the Rev. Mr. White-field set out from this Place for Maryland, in his Way to Georgia: During his Stay here, he preached frequently at the New-Building to very large and attentive Auditories.[4] [September 17]

Monday next will be published, and sold by B. Franklin, POOR RICHARD IMPROVED; And Half as big again as heretofore: Being an Almanack and Ephemeris of the Motions of the Sun and Moon; the true Places and Aspects of the Planets; the Rising and Setting of the Sun; and the Rising, Setting and Southing, of the Moon, for the Bissextile Year 1748. Containing also, The Lunations, Conjunctions, Eclipses, Judgment of the Weather, rising and setting of the Planets, Length of Days and Nights, Fairs, Courts, Roads, &c. Together with useful Tables, Chronological Observations, and entertaining Remarks. Fitted to the Latitude of Forty Degrees, and a Meridian of near five Hours West from London; but may, without sensible Error, serve all the Northern Colonies.

Containing moreover, Verses on the Death of Jacob Taylor. Particular Account of the Winter in Hudson's Bay. Table of Interest. Luke's Dying Request. Great and small Robbers. The Systems compared. Faith and Reason. A good Rule for Preserving Health. Three great Destroyers, Plague, Famine and Hero. Heathens dying. Poetical Strokes on Sir Isaac Newton. Education. Life, wherein it consists. Oliver Cromwell, Richard, and Julius Cesar. Fight at Lahogue. Verses on Warren, Anson and Boscawen. Use of Reading. What is the Chief Female Charm. A Philosophic Thought. Remark on Addison's Death and Writings. A spinning Empress. The true Hero, who. Remarks of Strada, a Spanish Historian, and the Duke of Parma. The good Wife. Difficulty of driving black Hogs in the Dark. Battle of Hochstet. Muskitoes, useful Remarks on them. Art of succeeding in Conversation. The

3. Murphy's account with BF, 1742–45, is in Ledger D, in APS. Nothing more is known about him.

4. During the summer Whitefield preached in New York and New England, to audiences as large as ever; and Sir William and Lady Pepperell invited him to dinner. Tyerman, *Whitefield*, II, 175.

amiable Doctress. Vigo. Observations on the Birth-day of the Founder of this Province. The Man of Taste. On Sir Walter Raleigh. English explained by Greek. Locke, the famous John, Esq; Of Parties. Benefits of Winter. The good Husband. Account of Niagara Falls, the greatest Cataract in the World. Story of the Emperor's Daughter, &c. &c. &c. With many other Matters (useful and entertaining) too many to mention here.

Jacob Taylor's Testimony in Favour of Poor Richard's Almanack.
  They have a Right to write who understand
  The Skill profest, the Theme they have in Hand;
  All useful Arts in true Professors shine,
  And just Applause, Poor Richard, shall be thine;
  For equal Justice must return thy Due,
  Thy Words good Sense, thy Numbers pure and true.
          Vide Taylor's Almanack, 1745.

Where likewise may be had, just published, Moore's American Country Almanack, For the Year 1748.   [September 17]

[ADVERTISEMENT] If Timothy Wastle, barber, of Barnard castle, in the county of Durham, Old England, will come to the Post-office, Philadelphia, he will hear of something to his advantage.
          [September 24]

Just published, and to be sold by the Printer hereof, The Pocket Almanack, For the Year 1748. Of whom may be also had, The Votes of the last Sessions of the Assembly of the Province of Pennsylvania.   [November 5]

Philadelphia, November 5. 1747.
All Persons indebted to the Printer hereof for a Year's Gazette, or more, are desired to pay.   [November 5]

Philadelphia, November 5. 1747.
  Lent some time ago, but forgot to whom, by Thomas Godfrey, of this city, Gravesend, 2 vols. Newton's Opticks, and a pair of round pliers: And left some where a Quarto blue paper book, containing about two sheets, having in one end of it Doctor Hally's Numbers and Radixes of the Planets; at the other end, a collection of about

237

100 observations of the Moon from Flamsted. Whoever has any of the above, is desired to return them.[5]   [November 5]

Last night came to Town some Indians from Ohio, a Branch of the Missisippi, all Warriors, and among them one Captain, on a Visit to this Government, about some particular Affairs relating to the War betwixt the English and French in those Parts.

[November 12]

The Indians from Ohio, now here, who are Deputies from a mix'd Body of Indians, collected from all the neighbouring Nations, and consisting of about 500 fighting Men, settled near the Head of that River, and the South Side of Lake Erie, have acquainted the Government, that the French did last Spring send them a Hatchet with Presents, as an Invitation to join in the War against the English; that to prevent any of their People accepting of the same, they immediately declared War against the French, and had already commenced Hostilities: To keep them firm in their Friendship to the English, a considerable Sum is now given them in Goods, and a Quantity likewise sent by them to a small neighbouring Nation in Alliance with them.[6]   [November 19]

Last Saturday Evening a great Number of the Inhabitants of this City met at Mr. Walton's School-House in Arch-street, when a Form of an Association for our common Security and Defence against the Enemy was consider'd and agreed to. On Monday following, the same was laid before a great Meeting of the principal Gentlemen, Merchants and others, at Roberts's Coffee-House, where after due Deliberation, it was unanimously approv'd of,

5. On Godfrey, see above, I, 190 n.
6. The Ohio Indians had asked for a present of goods as a reward for their loyalty, as well as to carry on war against the French who, they had discovered, "have hard Heads, and . . . we have nothing strong enough to break them." On advice from Conrad Weiser, the province interpreter, the Council voted a present valued at £143 10s. 9d. consisting of cloth, paint, tools, trinkets, four barrels of gunpowder, 500 lb. of bar lead, 8 guns, and 18 tomahawks for cracking French skulls. A smaller present of guns, powder, lead, flints, and knives went to the neighboring Canayiahaga; and a personal gift of cloth, clothing, powder, lead, and knives was made to old Shikellamy (see below, p. 285 n). *Pa. Col. Recs.*, v, 146–52; Paul A. W. Wallace, *Conrad Weiser* (Phila., 1945), pp. 258–61.

and another Meeting appointed to be the next Day following at the New-Building, in Order to begin Signing. Accordingly on Tuesday Evening upwards of Five Hundred Men of all Ranks subscribed their Names; and as the Subscription is still going on briskly in all Parts of the Town, 'tis not doubted but that in a few Days the Number will exceed a Thousand, in this City only, exclusive of the neighbouring Towns and Country. 'Tis hop'd the same laudable Spirit will spread itself throughout the Province; it being certain that we have Numbers more than sufficient, to defeat (with the Blessing of God) any Enterprize our Enemies can be suppos'd to form against us: All we wanted was Union and Discipline. The Form of the Association will be printed in our next; as also the Scheme of a Lottery for raising a Sum of Money for the general Service.[7]   [November 26]

The Scheme of the Lottery for raising a Sum of money for the Publick Service, will be published on Saturday next, and may be had gratis on calling for [it] at the Post-Office.[8] [December 3]

Philadelphia, November 12. 1747.
This is to give Notice, That George Heap, in Third-street, be-tween Arch-street and Market-street, makes Cartouch-boxes, Sword Belts and Scabbards, after the best and neatest manner.

[December 3]
On Monday Afternoon a great Body of the Associators met with their Arms at the State-House, and from thence marched down to the Court-House, in Market-Street, where they agreed to the proposed Divisions of the City into Companies. His Honour the President, and several of the Gentlemen of the Council being present, the Secretary, by Order, acquainted the Associators, That their Proceedings were not disapproved by the Government; and that the Officers they should chuse, in Pursuance of their Articles, would readily obtain Commissions. 'Tis not doubted but on the first of January, the Day of Election, there will be a very full Appearance of the Associated in this City, all Hands being busy in providing Arms, putting them in Order, and improving themselves in military Discipline.

7. On the Association, see above, pp. 184–8.
8. See above, p. 220.

And Yesterday the Reverend Mr. Jenny[9] preach'd an excellent Sermon on the Lawfulness of Self-Defence, and of Associating for that Purpose, to a very considerable Auditory; in the Church of England.   [December 12]

Philadelphia, December 10. 1747.
[ADVERTISEMENT] Dropt from a watch, last Wednesday se'n-night, a red Cornelian seal, set in gold, with part of a steel chain, on which it hung, the impression [of] a Homer's head. Whoever brings it to the printer hereof, shall have 5 shillings reward.
[December 12]

*⁎*The Northern Post begins his Fortnight's Stage this After-noon at Three o'Clock, during which Time this Paper will be pub-lished on Tuesdays.   [December 15]

Philadelphia, December 22. 1747.
Tickets in the Philadelphia Lottery, are sold by William Allen, Joshua Maddox, William Masters, Samuel M'Call, senior, Edward Shippen, Thomas Leech, Charles Willing, John Kearsley, William Clymer, senior, Thomas Lawrence, junior, William Coleman, and Thomas Hopkinson, at their respective Dwellings; and by B. Franklin, at the Post-Office.   [December 22]

Thursday last the Reverend Mr. Gilbert Tennent preached an excellent Sermon in the New-Building, on the Lawfulness of War, and on the Usefulness of the Association, into which great Num-bers of the Inhabitants of this Province have lately enter'd, and are still entering.[1]   [December 29]

PHILADELPHIA: Printed by B. FRANKLIN, Post-Master, at the New-Printing-Office, near the Market.

9. Robert Jenney (1687–1762), rector of Christ Church from 1742 until his death. Amer. Antiq. Soc., *Proc.*, LXVI (1956), 246.
1. Gilbert Tennent's *The Late Association for Defence, encourag'd, or, The lawfulness of a Defensive War*, printed in two editions by Bradford in 1748. Evans 6244, 6245. So moved was John Smith by the "deceit and Quirks" in Tennent's sermon that he composed a reply to vindicate the Quakers. Approved by the overseers of the Monthly Meeting, it was printed in 1000 copies by Franklin and Hall, half for free distribution. On January 30, the day of publication, Smith recorded in his diary, so many people demanded

Note, This ALMANACK us'd to contain but 24 Pages, and now has 36; yet the Price is very little advanc'd.

Poor RICHARD improved:

BEING AN

ALMANACK

AND

EPHEMERIS

OF THE

MOTIONS of the SUN and MOON;

THE TRUE

PLACES and ASPECTS of the PLANETS;

THE

RISING and *SETTING* of the *SUN;*

AND THE

Rifing, Setting *and* Southing *of the* Moon,

FOR THE

BISSEXTILE YEAR, 1748.

Containing also;
The Lunations, Conjunctions, Eclipses, Judgment of the Weather, Rising and Setting of the Planets, Length of Days and Nights, Fairs, Courts, Roads, &c. Together with useful Tables, chronological Observations, and entertaining Remarks.

Fitted to the Latitude of Forty Degrees, and a Meridian of near five Hours West from *London* ; but may, without senfible Error, ferve all the NORTHERN COLONIES.

By *RICHARD SAUNDERS,* Philom.

PHILADELPHIA:
Printed and Sold by B. FRANKLIN.

Poor Richard Improved, 1748

Poor Richard improved: Being an Almanack and Ephemeris of the Motions of the Sun and Moon; the True Places and Aspects of the Planets; the Rising and Setting of the Sun; and the Rising, Setting and Southing of the Moon, for the Bissextile Year, 1748. . . . By Richard Saunders, Philom. Philadelphia: Printed and Sold by B. Franklin. (Yale University Library)

For fifteen years Franklin had published his almanac in essentially the same format:[2] twenty-four pages in all, six of introductory and general information at the front, six more of general information at the back, and twelve in the middle section, one for each month. The front and back sections varied a little in subject matter and arrangement from year to year,[3] but the form and character of the monthly pages did not.

With the almanac for 1748 Franklin introduced an important change which he continued in the years that followed: he expanded his pamphlet to thirty-six pages and gave two facing pages to each month. With some minor differences the left-hand one was like the single monthly page of the earlier issues.[4] Part of each right-hand page was given to additional tabular matter and the rest was filled with "literary" material.[5] By using very small type in this space when necessary and sometimes by borrowing parts of the front or back sections, Franklin added substantially to the reading matter in the almanac. The new material changed considerably in character during the eleven years he

---

copies that his house and the printing office were "like a fair," and Hall told him that not even in London had he seen a pamphlet in such demand on first coming out. Albert C. Myers, ed., *Hannah Logan's Courtship* (Phila., 1904), pp. 139, 141–2. The printers issued a second edition of Smith's *Doctrine of Christianity . . . Vindicated* soon afterwards (Evans 6239, 6240). Tennent published a rejoinder, *The Late Association for Defence Farther Encouraged: or, Defensive War Defended* (Evans 6247), which was considered so effective that the Lottery Managers bought some for distribution. Eddy, *Ledger "D,"* p. 81.

2. For this format see the photographic facsimiles of all 24 pages of the 1733 issue, above I, 287–310.

3. The 1747 almanac divided the front and back pages five and seven with a consequent rearrangement of the material.

4. Occasionally, BF used for the verse material at the top a poem so long that it was spread through the left-hand pages of several months.

5. Beginning with the almanac for 1749 BF also introduced on these pages a series of small woodcuts depicting activities appropriate to the various months.

personally prepared *Poor Richard improved*, as he called the new version. In the first few almanacs he dwelt mostly on historical events which had occurred during corresponding months of previous years, and the lessons to be derived from them; later he introduced literary or scientific essays, some of which may have been original with him; most were obviously taken, at least in part, from other writers. Some of these essays occupy only a single page; others run through several months or even a whole year.[6] Related verses often accompany the prose passages. *Poor Richard improved*, therefore, became more than an almanac and compendium of useful information; it was a sort of miniature general magazine, issued annually to delight and educate its readers.

The varied nature and length of the pieces and their mixed authorship present problems of selection for the present edition. While Franklin's function was more often that of editor than of author, his choices and combinations of borrowed materials reflect his own tastes and attitudes. To omit here everything that cannot be established as original would destroy much of the flavor of the publication as a whole and would do less than justice to Franklin's editorial ingenuity or his views. Selections from these almanacs will include nearly all the shorter items, regardless of authorship; though a few, standing alone and clearly identified as extracts from other writers, will be omitted. Long articles obviously written by others will be merely cited in the annotation.

Kind Reader,

The favourable Reception my annual Labours have met with from the Publick these 15 Years past, has engaged me in Gratitude to endeavour some Improvement of my Almanack. And since my Friend Taylor[7] is no more, whose *Ephemerides* so long and so agreeably serv'd and entertain'd these Provinces, I have taken the Liberty to imitate his well-known Method, and give two Pages for each Month; which affords me Room for several valuable Additions, as will best appear on Inspection and Comparison with former Almanacks. Yet I have not so far follow'd his Method, as not to continue my own where I thought it preferable; and thus my Book is increas'd to a Size beyond his, and contains much more Matter.

6. One long essay occupied all the available space in the issues of both 1753 and 1754.
7. On Jacob Taylor, see above, pp. 101 n, 237.

Hail Night serene! thro' Thee where'er we turn
Our wond'ring Eyes, Heav'n's Lamps profusely burn;
And Stars unnumber'd all the Sky adorn.
    But lo!—what's that I see appear?
    It seems far off a pointed flame;
From Earthwards too the shining Meteor came:
    How swift it climbs th' etherial Space!
    And now it traverses each Sphere,
And seems some knowing Mind, familiar to the Place.
Dame, hand my Glass, the longest, strait prepare;—
'Tis He—'tis Taylor's Soul, that travels there.
O stay! thou happy Spirit, stay,
And lead me on thro' all th' unbeaten Wilds of Day;
Where Planets in pure Streams of Ether driven,
    Swim thro' the blue Expanse of Heav'n.
There let me, thy Companion, stray
    From Orb to Orb, and now behold
    Unnumber'd Suns, all Seas of molten Gold,
And trace each Comet's wandring Way.——[8]

Souse down into Prose again, my Muse; for Poetry's no more thy Element, than Air is that of the Flying-Fish; whose Flights, like thine, are therefore always short and heavy.

We complain sometimes of hard Winters in this Country; but our Winters will appear as Summers, when compar'd with those that some of our Countrymen undergo in the most Northern British Colony on this Continent, which is that upon Churchill River, in Hudson's Bay, Lat. 58d. 56m. Long. from London 94d. 50m. West. Captain Middleton, a Member of the Royal Society, who had made many Voyages thither, and winter'd there 1741–2, when he was in Search of the North-West Passage to the South-Sea, gives an Account of it to that Society, from which I have extracted these Particulars, viz.[9]

8. As Alan D. McKillop has pointed out ("Some Newtonian Verses in *Poor Richard*," *New Eng. Quar.*, XXI, 1948, pp. 383–5), BF adapted these lines from parts of John Hughes's poem in honor of Sir Isaac Newton, *The Ecstasy* (London, 1720), reprinted in Hughes, *Poems on Several Occasions* (London, 1735), II, 304–7.

9. Christopher Middleton (d. 1770), a servant of the Hudson's Bay Company and commander in the Royal Navy, led an expedition in search of the

The Hares, Rabbits, Foxes, and Partridges, in September and the Beginning of October, change their Colour to a snowy White, and continue white till the following Spring.

The Lakes and standing Waters, which are not above 10 or 12 Feet deep, are frozen to the Ground in Winter, and the Fishes therein all perish. Yet in Rivers near the Sea, and Lakes of a greater Depth than 10 or 12 Feet, Fishes are caught all the Winter, by cutting Holes thro' the Ice, and therein putting Lines and Hooks. As soon as the Fish are brought into the open Air, they instantly freeze stiff.

Beef, Pork, Mutton, and Venison, kill'd in the Beginning of the Winter, are preserved by the Frost for 6 or 7 Months, entirely free from Putrefaction. Likewise Geese, Partridges, and other Fowls, kill'd at the same Time, and kept with their Feathers on and Guts in, are preserv'd by the Frost, and prove good Eating. All Kinds of Fish are preserv'd in the same Manner.

In large Lakes and Rivers, the Ice is sometimes broken by imprison'd Vapours; and the Rocks, Trees, Joists, and Rafters of our Buildings, are burst with a Noise not less terrible than the firing of many Guns together. The Rocks which are split by the Frost, are heaved up in great Heaps, leaving large Cavities behind. If Beer or Water be left even in Copper Pots by the Bed-side, the Pots will be split before Morning. Bottles of strong Beer, Brandy, strong Brine, Spirits of Wine, set out in the open Air for 3 or 4 Hours, freeze to solid Ice. The Frost is never out of the Ground, how deep is not certain; but on digging 10 or 12 Feet down in the two Summer Months, it has been found hard frozen.

All the Water they use for Cooking, Brewing, &c. is melted Snow and Ice; no Spring is yet found free from freezing, tho' dug ever so deep down. All Waters inland, are frozen fast by the Beginning of October, and continue so to the Middle of May.

Northwest Passage, starting from England in June 1741 with two vessels. The party arrived at Churchill River in August, rebuilt an old fort, and remained there in winter quarters until the following July, the men suffering terribly from scurvy. After some further exploration of the northwest coast of Hudson Bay, Middleton sailed for home, reaching the Orkney Islands in September. His report of negative results aroused the criticism of Arthur Dobbs, who had helped promote the expedition, and a bitter controversy ensued (see above, II, 410 n). The account which BF reproduced here with some omissions and verbal changes was printed in *Phil. Trans.*, XLII (1743), 469.

The Walls of the Houses are of Stone, two Feet thick; the Windows very small, with thick wooden Shutters, which are close shut 18 Hours every Day in Winter. In the Cellars they put their Wines, Brandies, &c. Four large Fires are made every Day, in great Stoves to warm the Rooms: As soon as the Wood is burnt down to a Coal, the Tops of the Chimnies are close stopped, with an Iron Cover; this keeps the Heat in, but almost stifles the People. And notwithstanding this, in 4 or 5 Hours after the Fire is out, the Inside of the Walls and Bed-places will be 2 or 3 Inches thick with Ice, which is every Morning cut away with a Hatchet. Three or four Times a Day, Iron Shot, of 24 Pounds Weight, are made red hot, and hung up in the Windows of their Apartments, to moderate the Air that comes in at Crevices; yet this, with a Fire kept burning the greatest Part of 24 Hours, will not prevent Beer, Wine, Ink, &c. from Freezing.

For their Winter Dress, a Man makes use of three Pair of Socks, of coarse Blanketting, or Duffeld, for the Feet, with a Pair of Deerskin Shoes over them; two Pair of thick English Stockings, and a Pair of Cloth Stockings upon them; Breeches lined with Flannel; two or three English Jackets, and a Fur, or Leather Gown over them; a large Beaver Cap, double, to come over the Face and Shoulders, and a Cloth of Blanketting under the Chin; with Yarn Gloves, and a large Pair of Beaver Mittins, hanging down from the Shoulders before, to put the Hands in, reaching up as high as the Elbows. Yet notwithstanding this warm Clothing, those that stir Abroad when any Wind blows from the Northward, are sometimes dreadfully frozen; some have their Hands, Arms, and Face blistered and froze in a terrible Manner, the Skin coming off soon after they enter a warm House, and some lose their Toes. And keeping House, or lying-in for the Cure of these Disorders, brings on the Scurvy, which many die of, and few are free from; nothing preventing it but Exercise and stirring Abroad.

The Fogs and Mists, brought by northerly Winds in Winter, appear visible to the naked Eye to be Icicles innumerable, as small as fine Hairs, and pointed as sharp as Needles. These Icicles lodge in their Clothes, and if their Faces and Hands are uncover'd, presently raise Blisters as white as a Linnen Cloth, and as hard as Horn. Yet if they immediately turn their Back to the Weather, and can bear a Hand out of the Mitten, and with it rub the blister'd Part for a small Time, they sometimes bring the Skin to its former State; if not, they make the best of their Way to a Fire, bathe the Part in hot Water, and thereby dissipate the Humours raised by the frozen Air; otherwise the Skin wou'd be off in a short Time, with much hot, serous, watry Matter, coming from under along with the Skin; and this happens to some almost every Time they go Abroad, for 5 or 6 Months in the Winter, so extreme cold is the Air, when the Wind blows any Thing strong.——Thus far Captain Middleton. And now, my tender Reader, thou that shudderest when the Wind blows a little at N-West, and criest, *'Tis extrrrrrream cohohold!* *'Tis terrrrrrible cohold!* what dost thou think of removing to that delightful Country? Or dost thou not rather chuse to stay in Pennsylvania, thanking God that *He has caused thy Lines to fall in pleasant Places.*[1] I am, Thy Friend to serve thee,   R. Saunders

January. *XI Month.*

    Luke, on his dying Bed, embrac'd his Wife,
And begg'd one Favour: Swear, my dearest Life,
Swear, if you love me, never more to wed,
Nor take a second Husband to your Bed.
Anne dropt a Tear. You know, my dear, says she,
Your least Desires have still been Laws to me;
But from this Oath, I beg you'd me excuse;
For I'm already promis'd to J——n H——s.

Robbers must exalted be,
Small ones on the Gallow-Tree,
While greater ones ascend to Thrones,
But what is that to thee or me?

Lost Time is never found again.

    On the 16th Day of this Month, *Anno* 1707, the Union Act pass'd in Scotland.

    On the 19th of this Month, *Anno* 1493, was born the famous Astronomer Copernicus, to whom we owe the Invention, or rather the Revival (it being taught by Pythagoras near 2000 Years before)

1. "The lines are fallen unto me in pleasant places; yea, I have a goodly heritage." Psalms 16:6.

of that now generally receiv'd System of the World which bears his Name, and supposes the Sun in the Center, this Earth a Planet revolving round it in 365 Days, 6 Hours, &c. and that Day and Night are caused by the Turning of the Earth on its own Axis once round in 24 h. &c. The Ptolomean System, which prevail'd before Copernicus, suppos'd the Earth to be fix'd, and that the Sun went round it daily. Mr. Whiston, a modern Astronomer, says, the Sun is 230,000 times bigger than the Earth, and 81 Millions of Miles distant from it:[2] That vast Body must then have mov'd more than 480 Millions of Miles in 24 h. A prodigious Journey round this little Spot! How much more natural is Copernicus's Scheme! Ptolomy is compar'd to a whimsical Cook, who, instead of Turning his Meat in Roasting, should fix That, and contrive to have his whole Fire, Kitchen and all, whirling continually round it.

FEBRUARY. *XII Month.*

> Don't after foreign Food and Cloathing roam,
> But learn to eat and wear what's rais'd at Home.
> Kind Nature suits each Clime with what it wants,
> Sufficient to subsist th' Inhabitants.
> Observing this, we less impair our Health,
> And by this Rule we more increase our Wealth:
> Our Minds a great Advantage also gain,
> And more sedate and uncorrupt remain.

To lead a virtuous Life, my Friends, and get to Heaven in Season, You've just so much more Need of *Faith*, as you have less of *Reason.*

To avoid Pleurisies, &c. in cool Weather; Fevers, Fluxes, &c. in hot; beware of *Over-Eating* and *Over-Heating.*

On the 4th day of this month, *Anno* 1710, was born Lewis the 15th, present king of France, called his *most christian* majesty. He bids fair to be as great a mischief-maker as his grandfather; or, in the language of poets and orators, a *Hero.* There are three great destroyers of mankind, *Plague, Famine,* and *Hero.* Plague and Fam-

2. William Whiston, *A New Theory of the Earth* (3d edit., London, 1722), pp. 34, 36. BF rounded out Whiston's 227,500 to 230,000.

ine destroy your persons only, and leave your goods to your Heirs; but Hero, when he comes, takes life and goods together; his business and glory it is, to destroy man and the works of man.

> In horrid grandeur haughty *Hero* reigns,
> And thrives on mankind's miseries and pains.
> What slaughter'd hosts! What cities in a blaze!
> What wasted countries! and what crimson seas!
> With orphans tears his impious bowl o'erflows;
> And cries of kingdoms lull him to repose.

Hero, therefore, is the worst of the three; and thence David, who understood well the effects of heroism, when he had his choice, wisely pitch'd on *Plague* as the milder mischief.[3]

MARCH. *I Month.*

> The Sun, whose unexhausted Light
>   Does Life and Heat to Earth convey;
> The Moon, who, Regent of the Night,
>   Shines with delegated Ray;
> The Stars, which constant seem to Sight,
>   And Stars that regularly stray:
> All these God's plastick Will from Nothing brought,
> Assign'd their Stations, and their Courses taught.

The Heathens when they dy'd, went to Bed without a Candle.

> Knaves and Nettles are akin;
> Stroak 'em kindly, yet they'll sting.

On the 20th of this month, 1727, died the prince of astronomers and philosophers, sir Isaac Newton, aged 85 years: Who, as Thomson expresses it, *Trac'd the boundless works of God, from laws sublimely simple.*[4]

3. II Sam. 24: 12–15. Although David rejected the punishment of war, he actually left it to the Lord to choose between famine and pestilence.

4. James Thomson, *The Seasons.* "*Summer*," 1559–62:
Let NEWTON, *pure Intelligence*, whom GOD
To mortals lent, to trace his boundless works
From laws sublimely simple, speak thy fame
In all philosophy . . . .

What were his raptures then! how pure! how strong!
And what the triumphs of old Greece and Rome,
By his diminish'd, but the pride of boys
In some small fray victorious! when instead
Of shatter'd parcels of this earth usurp'd
By violence unmanly, and sore deeds
Of cruelty and blood; Nature herself
Stood all-subdu'd by him, and open laid
Her every latent glory to his view.[5]

Mr. Pope's epitaph on sir Isaac Newton,[6] is justly admired for its conciseness, strength, boldness, and sublimity:

Nature and nature's laws lay hid in night;
God said, *Let* NEWTON *be,* and all was light.

APRIL. *II Month.*

On EDUCATION all our Lives depend;
And few to that, too few, with Care attend:
Soon as Mamma permits her darling Joy
To quit her Knee, and trusts at School her Boy,
O, touch him not, whate'er he does is right,
His Spirit's tender, tho' his Parts are bright.
Thus all the Bad he can, he learns at School,
Does what he will, and grows a lusty Fool.

Life with Fools consists in Drinking;
With the wise Man Living's Thinking.

Eilen thut selten gut.[7]

On the 25th of this month, *Anno* 1599, was OLIVER CROMWELL born, the son of a private gentleman, but became the conqueror and protector (some say the tyrant) of three great kingdoms. His son Richard succeeded him, but being of an easy peaceable disposition, he soon descended from that lofty station, and became a pri-

5. James Thomson, *A Poem Sacred to the Memory of Sir Isaac Newton* (London, 1727), 30–8.
6. Epitaph XII in the collected works of Alexander Pope.
7. Hurry seldom does well.

vate man, living, unmolested, to a good old age; for he died not till about the latter end of queen Anne's reign, at his lodgings in Lombard-street, where he had lived many years unknown, and seen great changes in government, and violent struggles for that, which, by experience, he knew could afford no solid happiness.

Oliver was once about to remove to New-England, his goods being on shipboard; but somewhat alter'd his mind. There he would doubtless have risen to be a *Select Man,* perhaps a *Governor;* and then might have had 100 bushels of Indian corn *per Annum,* the salary of a governor of that then small colony in those days.

> Great Julius on the mountains bred,
> A flock, perhaps, or herd had led;
> He that the world subdu'd had been
> But the best wrestler on the green.   Waller.[8]

MAY. *III Month.*

> Read much; the Mind, which never can be still,
> If not intent on Good, is prone to Ill.
> And where bright Thoughts, or Reas'nings just you find,
> Repose them careful in your inmost Mind.
> To deck his Chloe's Bosom thus the Swain
> With pleasing Toil surveys th' enamel'd Plain,
> With Care selects each fragrant flow'r he meets,
> And forms one Garland of their mingled sweets.

Sell-cheap kept Shop on Goodwin Sands, and yet had Store of Custom.

Liberality is not giving much but giving wisely.

> Finikin Dick, curs'd with nice Taste,
> Ne'er meets with good dinner, half starv'd at a feast.

On the 21st of this month, *Anno* 1692, the brave admiral Russel beat the French fleet near La Hogue, and burnt, sunk, and destroy'd, near 20 sail of their men of war, in sight of Lewis XIV and K. James II, who were encamped on the shore with a considerable

---

8. Edmund Waller, "To Zelinda," 19–23.

army that was to be transported under convoy of that fleet to Ireland, in order to replace the latter on the throne of the 3 kingdoms. That design was defeated, and this glorious victory obtained with very little loss on our side. But

> O when shall (long-lost) HONOUR guide the war,
> See Britain blushes for each dastard tar;
> Lost to all sense of shame, the fight who flies,
> And leaves the convoy to secure the prize.[9]
> Not so, when Britain to each distant shore,
> O'er subject seas her conquering thunders bore;
> Fame then upon the tow'ring top-mast show'd
> Her waving pinions whereso'er they flow'd;
> And Victory, thro' all the yielding deep,
> With eagle wings, hung o'er each valiant ship.
> Then honour struck the stroke, true love of fame
> In each brave breast glow'd with a gen'rous flame,
> Not yet extinct in All; the same we view
> Boscawen, Warren, Anson, still in you.

For (to mention a late instance only) on the 3d of this same month, in the year preceding, these gallant and successful seamen, defeated at once two grand designs of the enemy (the retaking of Louisburgh, and total destruction of our East-India settlements) by attacking their joint fleets, just after they came out of port, taking 6 men of war of the line, and 6 Indiamen, with some others of lesser note, and dispersing the rest.[1]

JUNE. *IV Month.*

> Of all the Charms the Female Sex desire,
> That Lovers doat on, and that Friends admire,
> Those most deserve your Wish that longest last,

9. The British Navy suffered a series of disappointing and humiliating experiences during 1739–46. Among other officers charged with misconduct, Captain Fitzroy Lee was accused in 1747 of neglecting convoys in the West Indies and sending ships to the Spanish Main to cruise for private profit. He was recalled and court-martialed. Herbert W. Richmond, *The Navy in the War of 1739–48* (Cambridge, 1920), III, 66–7.

1. The battle of Cape Finisterre, May 3, 1747.

Not like the Bloom of Beauty, quickly past;
VIRTUE the Chief: This Men and Angels prize,
Above the finest Shape and brightest Eyes.
By this alone, untainted Joys we find,
As large and as immortal as the Mind.

Alas! that Heroes ever were made!
The *Plague,* and the *Hero,* are both of a Trade!
Yet the Plague spares our Goods which the Heroe does not;
So a Plague take such Heroes and let their Fames rot. Q.P.D.

On the 20th of this month, 1743, commodore Anson took the
Spanish Acapulco ship, valued at a million Sterling.

On the 27th, *Anno* 1709, Charles XII. of Sweden, was defeated
in the battle of Pultawa, by the Muscovites. This man had a great
mind to be a *Hero,* too; and, besides doing much mischief to his
neighbours, he brought his own country to the brink of ruin.

A philosophic Thought.[2]

I pluck'd this morn these beauteous flow'rs,
Emblem of my fleeting hours;
'Tis thus, said I, my life-time flies,
So it blooms, and so it dies.
And, lo! how soon they steal away,
Wither'd e'er the noon of day.
Adieu! well-pleas'd my end I see,
Gently taught philosophy:
Fragrance and ornament alive,
Physic after death they give.
Let me, throughout my little stay,
Be as useful and as gay;
My close as early let me meet,
So my odour be as sweet.

The 19th of this month, 1719, died the celebrated Joseph Addison, Esq; aged 47, whose writings have contributed more to the
improvement of the minds of the British nation, and polishing their
manners, than those of any other English pen whatever.

2. Not identified.

254

JULY. *V Month.*

When great Augustus rul'd the World and Rome, ⎫
The Cloth he wore was spun and wove at Home, ⎬
His EMPRESS ply'd the Distaff and the Loom. ⎭
Old England's Laws the proudest beauty name, ⎫
When single, *Spinster,* and when married, *Dame,* ⎬
For *Housewifery* is Woman's noblest Fame. ⎭
The Wisest houshold Cares to Women yield,
A large, an useful, and a grateful Field.

To Friend, Lawyer, Doctor, tell plain your whole Case;
Nor think on bad Matters to put a good Face:
How can they advise, if they see but a Part?
'Tis very ill driving black Hogs in the dark.

On the 1st of this month *Anno* 1690, was fought the memorable battle of the Boyne, in Ireland; when God crown'd our great deliverer, King WILLIAM, with success and victory. He was one of the right sort of *Heroes.* Your *true* hero fights to *preserve,* and not to *destroy,* the lives, liberties, and estates, of his people. His neighbours also, and all that are oppress'd, share his cares and his protection. But this sort is thin sown, and comes up thinner. Hercules was one, among the ancients; and our glorious BILLY, of Cumberland,[3] another among the moderns; God bless him! I might have mention'd, in the month of April, his happy victory over the rebels; who, with the united assistance of the kings of France and Spain, the Pope and the Devil, threatened destruction to our religion and liberties; but had all their schemes defeated by this battle. The sacred names of *justice* and *religion* were made use of as the cloaks of that invasion, wicked as it was. A pretended prince was to be restor'd to his *rights,* forsooth; and we were all to be converted to the Catholick faith! Strada says, that when the duke of Parma heard of the defeat of the Spanish Armada, in 1588 (which by the way happen'd the 21st of this same month) he said very piously, *That it was an enterprize so well concerted, as nothing could have disappointed but the* sins *of the people of England.* It seems they were

3. William Augustus, Duke of Cumberland (1721–1765), third son of George II, defeated the Scottish rebels at the battle of Culloden, April 16, 1746. *DNB.*

unworthy so great a blessing. And he makes this further reflection on queen Elizabeth's proclaiming a thanksgiving: *Mistaken woman! Blind nation!* says he, *to return thanks for the greatest* misfortune *that could have befallen them! For had that enterprize succeeded, they would all have been converted to the true Catholick Faith.* The *most christian* king, and his *catholick* majesty, and his *Holiness,* and the sham *defender of the faith,* (Fine titles all!) have now an opportunity of making the same pious reflections.

AUGUST. *VI Month.*

> To make the cleanly Kitchen send up Food,
> Not costly vain, but plentifully Good.
> To bid the Cellar's Fountain never fail,
> Of sparkling Cyder, or of well-brew'd Ale;
> To buy, to pay, to blame, or to approve,
> Within, without, below-stairs, and above;
> To shine in every Corner, like the Sun,
> Still working every where, or looking on.

Suspicion may be no Fault, but shewing it may be a great one.

He that's secure is not safe.

The second Vice is Lying; the first is Running in Debt.

The Muses love the Morning.

On the 2d of this month, *Anno* 1704, was fought the famous battle of Hochstet,[4] in which the joint armies of the French and Bavarians were totally defeated, by the duke of Marlborough and prince Eugene, 20,000 killed, and 13,000 taken prisoners, with the French general, marshal Tallard. There was never any victory, the news of which gave greater joy in England; the nation being under the greatest apprehensions for their army, when it was known that the French and Bavarians were joined, and were much more numerous than the English and Dutch: For it was generally thought, that if the English were beaten, at so great a distance from home, very few would ever be able to reach their native country again; Hochstet being on the banks of the Danube, very far in Germany.

4. This one of the several battles fought at Höchstädt is commonly known as the battle of Blenheim.

Muschitoes, or *Musketoes,* a little venomous fly, so light, that perhaps 50 of them, before they've fill'd their bellies, scarce weigh a
grain, yet each has all the parts necessary to life, motion, digestion,
generation, &c. as veins, arteries, muscles, &c. each has in his
little body room for the five senses of seeing, hearing, feeling,
smelling, tasting: How inconceivably small must their organs be!
How inexpressibly fine the workmanship! And yet there are little
animals discovered by the microscope, to whom a *Musketo* is an
Elephant! In a scarce summer any citizen may provide Musketoes
sufficient for his own family, by leaving tubs of rain-water uncover'd in his yard; for in such water they lay their eggs, which
when hatch'd, become first little fish, afterwards put forth legs and
wings, leave the water, and fly into your windows. *Probatum est.*

SEPTEMBER. *VII Month.*

> One glorious Scene of Action still behind,
> The Fair that likes it is secure to find;
> Cordials and Med'cines *gratis* to dispense,
> A beauteous Instrument of Providence;
> Plaisters, and Salves, and Sores, to understand,
> The Surgeon's Art befits a tender Hand,
> To friendless Pain unhop'd-for Ease to give,
> And bid the Hungry eat, and Sickly live.

> Two Faults of one a Fool will make;
> He half repairs, that owns and does forsake.

> Harry Smatter,
> Has a Mouth for every Matter.

When you're good to others, you are best to yourself.

On the first of this month, *Anno,* 1733, Stanislaus, originally a
private gentleman of Poland, was chosen the *second time* king of
that nation. The power of Charles XII. of Sweden, caused his first
election, that of Louis XV. of France, his second. But neither of
them could keep him on the throne; for PROVIDENCE, often opposite to the wills of princes, reduc'd him to the condition of a private
gentleman again.

On the 2d of this month, *Anno* 1666, began the fire of London,

257

which reduc'd to ashes 13,200 houses and 89 churches: Near ten times as much building as Philadelphia!

The great ART of succeeding in CONVERSATION (saith Mons. St. Evremond)[5] is, To admire little, to hear much, *always* to distrust our own reason, and *sometimes* that of our friends; never to pretend to wit; but to make that of others appear as much as possibly we can; to hearken to what is said, and to answer to the purpose.

Ut jam nunc dicat jam nunc debentia dici.

Observe, the precept is *hear much,* not *speak much.* Herbert, the poet, says,

———a well bred guest,
Will no more *talk all* than *eat all* the feast.[6]

And, *When you do speak,* says another, *speak to the purpose; Or else to what purpose do you speak?*[7] Observe the present disposition of the company; and

Let what you say the converse suit,
Not say things merely 'cause they're good.
For if you thus intrude your sense,
It then becomes impertinence:
Your salt is good, we may agree,
But pray don't salt our Punch and Tea.

OCTOBER. *VIII Month.*

And thus, if we may credit Fame's Report,
The best and fairest in the Gallic Court,
An Hour sometimes in Hospitals employ,
To give the dying Wretch a Glimpse of Joy;
T' attend the Crouds that hopeless Pangs endure,
And soothe the Anguish which they cannot cure;

5. "Of Study and Conversation," *The Works of Monsieur de St. Evremond* (2d edit., London, 1728), III, 273, with minor variations, but including the complete quotation from Horace. BF had copied this passage into his Commonplace Book some years before. See above, I, 270.

6. George Herbert, *The Church-Porch*, 305–6:
. . . A civil guest
Will no more talk all, than eat all, the feast.

7. This quotation and the verses which follow have not been identified.

To clothe the Bare, and give the Empty Food;
As bright as Guardian Angels, and as good.

Half Wits talk much but say little.

If Jack's in love, he's no judge of Jill's Beauty.

Most Fools think they are only ignorant.

On the 12th of this month, *Anno* 1702, admiral Rooke and the duke of Ormond attack'd the French and Spanish fleet, and the town of Vigo. Nine galeons and 6 of their men of war were taken; 14 men of war and 4 galeons, were sunk and burnt.

On the 14th of this month, *Anno* 1644, was born WILLIAM PENN, the great founder of this Province; who prudently and benevolently sought success to himself by no other means, than securing the *liberty,* and endeavouring the *happiness* of his people. Let no envious mind grudge his posterity those advantages which arise to them from the wisdom and goodness of their ancestor; and to which their own merit, as well as the laws, give them an additional title.

On the 28th, *Anno* 1704, died the famous John Locke, Esq; the Newton of the *Microcosm:* For, as Thomson says,

He made the whole *internal world* his own.[8]

His book on the *Human Understanding,* shows it. *Microcosm,* honest reader, is a hard word, and, they say, signifies the *little world,* man being so called, as containing within himself the four elements of the *greater,* &c. &c. I here explain Greek to thee by English, which, I think, is rather a more intelligible way, than explaining English by Greek, as a certain writer does, who gravely tells us, *Man is rightly called* a little world, *because he is a* Microcosm.

On the 29th, *Anno* 1618, was the famous sir Walter Rawleigh beheaded; to the eternal shame of the attorney-general, who first prosecuted him, and of the king, who ratify'd the sentence.

How happy is he who can satisfy his hunger with any food, quench his thirst with any drink, please his ear with any musick, delight his eye with any painting, any sculpture, any architecture, and divert his mind with any book or any company! How many

8. James Thomson, *The Seasons.* "Summer," 1558.

mortifications must he suffer, that cannot bear any thing but beauty, order, elegance and perfection! *Your man of* taste, *is nothing but a man of* distaste.

NOVEMBER. *IX Month.*

    Nor be the Husband idle, tho' his Land
Yields plenteous Crops without his lab'ring Hand:
Tho' his collected Rent his Bags supply,
Or honest, careful Slaves scarce need his Eye.
Let him whom Choice allures, or Fortune yields,
To live amidst his own extended Fields,
Diffuse those Blessings which from Heav'n he found,
In copious Streams to bless the World around;

Pardoning the Bad, is injuring the Good.

He is not well-bred, that cannot bear Ill-Breeding in others.

    On the 2d of this month, *Anno* 1641, the Long Parliament met, who began the *great rebellion,* as some call it, or the *glorious opposition* to arbitrary power, as others term it; for to this day *party* divides us on this head, and we are not (perhaps never shall be) agreed about it. *Party,* says one, *is the madness of many, for the gain of a few:* To which may be added, *There are* honest *men in* all *parties,* wise men *in* none: Unless those may be call'd *wise,* for whose profit the rest are *mad.*

    To thy lov'd haunt return, my happy muse,
For now behold the joyous winter-days
Frosty, succeed; and thro' the blue serene
For sight too fine, th' etherial nitre flies,
Killing infectious damps, and the spent air
Storing afresh with elemental life.
Close crouds the shining atmosphere; and binds
Our strengthen'd bodies in its cold embrace,
Constringent; feeds and animates our blood;
Refines our spirits, thro' the new-strung nerves
In swifter sallies darting to the brain;
Where sits the soul, intense, collected, cool,

Bright as the skies, and as the season keen.
All nature feels the renovating force
Of WINTER, only to the thoughtless eye
Is Ruin seen ———.⁹

*Muse, Shoes; Days, Stays; Serene, between; Air, Fair; Life, Wife,
Strife,* &c. &c. Rhimes, you see, are plenty enow; he that does not
like blank verse, may add them at his leisure, as the poets do at
Manhatan.

DECEMBER. *X Month.*

Open to all his hospitable Door,
His Tennent's Patron, Parent to the Poor:
In Friendships dear, discording Neighbours bind,
Aid the distress'd, and humanise Mankind:
Wipe off the sorrowing Tear from Virtue's Eyes,
Bid Honesty oppress'd, again arise:
Protect the Widow, give the Aged Rest,
And blessing live, and die for ever blest.

In Christmas feasting pray take care;
Let not your table be a Snare;
But with the Poor God's Bounty share.

Adieu my Friends! till the next Year.

On the 13th of this month, 1545, the famous council of Trent
began.

On the 23d, 1688, K. James abdicated his kingdoms, and embarked for France.

The fall of Niagara, which Popple's map¹ lays down in the
N-West corner of this province, is, according to Henepin,² compounded of two great cross streams of water, and two falls, with

9. *Ibid.,* "Winter," 691–706.
1. Henry Popple, *A Map of the British Empire in America with the French
and Spanish Settlements adjacent thereto* (London, 1733). Sheet I shows Niagara
as in the northwest corner of Pennsylvania and has an engraving of "the
famous cataract of Niagara." See above, p. 77 n.
2. Father Lewis Hennepin, *A New Discovery of a Vast Country in America*
(London, 1698), pp. 215–22.

an isle sloping along between. The waters fall from a horrible precipice above 600 foot, and foam and boil in an hideous manner, making an outrageous noise, more terrible than thunder; for when the wind blows out of the South, their dismal roaring may be heard more than 15 Leagues off.

Conrad, the 3d emperor of Germany, besieged Guelph, duke of Bavaria, in the city of Wansburg. The women perceiving the town could not hold out, petitioned the emperor that they might depart only with so much as they could carry on their backs; which the emperor condescended to, expecting they would have laden themselves with silver and gold; but they all came forth with every one her husband on her back; whereat the emperor was so moved that he wept, received the duke into his favour, gave all the men their lives, and extolled the women with deserved praises. *Quere,* Is this story more to the honour of the wives or of the husbands? My dame BRIDGET *says* the first, I *think* the latter: But we submit our dispute to the decision of the candid reader.

> A wit's a *feather,* and a chief a *rod;*
> An *honest man's* the noblest work of God.   Pope.[3]

LEAP-YEAR, or Bissextile, is every fourth year:[4] It is so called, by reason it leaps a day more that year than in a common year; for in a common year any fix'd day of the month does change the day of the week to the day following; but in Bissextile, it skips or leaps over a day. This Leap-Year is occasioned by the odd 6 hours in a year, over and above 365 days, which odd hours make a day in 4 years; and because the month of February is the shortest month in the year, this day is added thereto; so that every 4th year February has 29 days, and makes the year to consist of 366 days; that is, two

---

3. *Essay on Man,* Epistle IV, lines 247–8.

4. In most surviving copies of this almanac the 34th page (third from the end) contains a chronological list of the governors and speakers of Pennsylvania and the mayors of Philadelphia. Some copies substitute calendars of the New England court sessions on this page. The copy in Lib. Co. Phila., however, substitutes a calendar of court sessions in Virginia, North Carolina, and South Carolina, and, because this is too short to occupy the entire page, adds this explanation of Leap Year. These variants suggest that by 1748 *Poor Richard* had attained such a wide circulation as to justify what amounted to different editions for distribution in New England, the Middle Colonies, and the South.

days above 52 weeks; and this is the sole reason why, in Leap-Year, any fix'd feast (as Christmas Day for example) is found two days in the week further on than it was the Year before. To know when it is Leap-Year, divide the year of our Lord by 4, and if nothing remains, it is Leap-Year; but if 1, 2, or 3 remains, then it is accordingly the 1st, 2d, or 3d year after Leap-Year.

Articles of Agreement with David Hall

DS: Haverford College Library; also copy: Department of Records, Recorder of Deeds, Philadelphia[5]

Strahan sent David Hall[6] to Franklin in 1744, where, as journeyman, he proved to be so skillful, so industrious, discreet, and honest, that Franklin arranged to set him up in the West Indies.[7] This project was abandoned, however, and Hall became Franklin's foreman instead. By the summer of 1747 Franklin had decided to withdraw from the business and make Hall a partner in the shop,[8] a successful and profitable venture for both men. Hall conducted the enterprise, Franklin wrote Strahan, Feb. 4, 1751, "perfectly to my Satisfaction"; his payments to Franklin during the first nine years of the partnership amounted to £6056 5s. 3¾d., or an average of £673 a year. Isaiah Thomas wrote: "Had he [Hall] not been connected with Franklin, he might have been a formidable rival to him in the business of printing and bookselling."[9]

[January 1, 1748, N.S.]

ARTICLES OF AGREEMENT, indented and made the First Day of January in the Year of our Lord, One Thousand Seven Hundred and Forty Seven between Benjamin Franklin, of the City of Philadelphia, in the Province of Pennsylvania, Printer, of the one Part, and David Hall, of the same Place, Printer, of the other Part: Whereas the said Benjamin Franklin and David Hall have determined to enter into a Copartnership for the carrying on the Business of Printing in the City aforesaid, It is therefore covenanted, granted and agreed, by and between the said Parties to these Presents; and the said Benjamin Franklin and David Hall do each

5. Some words made illegible by creases or tears in the original have been silently supplied from the recorded copy.
6. See above, II, 409 n.   8. See above, p. 165.
7. See above, p. 46.   9. *Printing*, I, 246.

of them covenant and mutually agree each with the other of them, and to and with the Heirs, Executors and Administrators, of the other of them, in Manner following; that is to say,

That they the said Benjamin Franklin and David Hall shall be Partners in carrying on the Trade and Business of Printing in Philadelphia aforesaid, for and during the Term of Eighteen Years, if they the said Benjamin and David shall so long live, to commence the Twenty first Day of January One Thousand Seven Hundred and Forty Seven, on or before which Day the Printing Presses, Types and Materials, now commonly used by the said Benjamin Franklin, shall be put into the Hands, and under the Care of the said David Hall.[1] That the Business, and working Part of Printing, and of disposing of the Work printed, and of receiving and collecting the Money thence becoming due, shall be under the Care, Management and Direction of, and performed by the said David Hall, or at his Expence. That all Charges for Paper, Ink, Balls, Tympans, Wool, Oil, and other Things necessary to Printing, together with the Charge of all common and necessary Repairs of the Press and its Appurtenances; and also the Charge of Rent for so much Room as is necessary to be used in the Management of the Business of Printing aforesaid, shall be divided into two equal Parts, one of which said Parts shall be defrayed by, and paid as due from the said David Hall, and the other Part shall be defrayed, and allowed to be paid as due from the said Benjamin Franklin, and deducted out of the Income next herein after mentioned. That all Money received, or to be received for Printing, or for any thing done, or to be done relating to the Business of Printing aforesaid, by the said David Hall, either as Gratuity, Premium, Reward, or Salary, from the Government, or from others, shall be divided into two equal Parts, one of which said Parts the said David Hall shall have for his Care, Management and Performance aforesaid, and the said Benjamin Franklin shall have the remaining Part thereof. That for the regular transacting the Affairs in Copartnership aforesaid, the said David Hall shall keep fair and exact Books of Accounts, of and concerning all Work done and delivered or sold by him, and of all his Receipts and Disbursements relating to the Business of Printing in Copartnership aforesaid, with the Day,

1. Hall's inventory of "Books &c. left in my Hands by Mr. Franklin," Jan. 23, valued the stock at £681 1s. See below, p. 271.

Month and Year, of each Entry, and submit the same to the View of the said Benjamin Franklin, his lawful Attorney, Executors and Administrators, as often as thereunto required. And that all the Accounts of the Copartners in Copartnership aforesaid, shall be drawn out fair, and communicated to each other, and settled once a Month, to wit, on the first Monday of each Month during the Copartnership aforesaid, or oftener, if either of them the said Co-partners shall require it. And that upon such Settlement, the said David Hall shall pay the Part by this Agreement belonging to the said Benjamin Franklin, unto him the said Benjamin, or, in case of his Absence, or Death, the Accounts shall be settled with, and the Money paid to his lawful Attorney, or to his Executors, Adminis-trators or Assigns. That the said David Hall shall not work with any other Printing Presses, Types or Materials, than those belong-ing to the said Benjamin Franklin, nor follow any other Business but Printing, during the Continuance of the Copartnership afore-said, occasional buying and selling in the Stationary and Book-selling Way excepted. Nor shall the said Benjamin Franklin, during the Continuance of the Copartnership aforesaid, work with, or be concerned in the working with any other Types and Materials in this Place, than those by this Agreement to be put into the Hands of the said David Hall, so as to perform, or cause to be performed, any Piece of Printing in another Printing-house, which the said David Hall could perform with the abovesaid Types and Materials, without acquainting the said David Hall with the Intention of doing such Piece of Printing-work, and admitting him to be an equal Sharer therein, if he shall be so disposed. That the Loss by bad Debts shall be divided and sustained by both Parties in the same Proportion as the Money ought to have been divided by this Agreement, if it had been received. That the said Benjamin Frank-lin, or his legal Representative, shall, during the Copartnership aforesaid, have free Ingress and Egress in the Printing-house by this Agreement to be managed by the said David Hall, that it may be seen how the Business is carried on, and what Care is taken of the Materials, Utensils, &c. And if any thing is observed that may be prejudicial to the Interest of the said Benjamin Franklin in par-ticular, or to the Interest of the Partnership in general, the same, on Notice thereof being given to the said David Hall, shall be amended, guarded against, removed or altered, to the Satisfaction

of the said Benjamin Franklin, or of his Representative, as aforesaid. And before any Piece of Work of great Importance, either
on account of its Cost or Consequence, be enterd upon and begun,
the Advice and Consent of the said Benjamin Franklin, or his Representative, shall be asked and obtained by the said David Hall.
That neither of the said Parties shall reap any Benefit or Advantage
by Survivorship, if the other of them shall depart this Life before
the Expiration of the said Term of Eighteen Years; but that if the
said David Hall shall depart this Life before the Expiration of
the said Term, his Executors or Administrators shall provide a skilful and suitable Person, to the Satisfaction of the said Benjamin
Franklin, to continue and carry on the Business aforesaid, and perform all the Parts of this Agreement undertaken by the said David
Hall, or deliver up the Presses, Types, and all other Materials of
Printing, which have been or shall be provided by the said Benjamin Franklin, or at his Charge, to the said Benjamin, his certain
Attorney, Executors or Administrators, upon Demand, in good
Order and Condition, allowing for the usual Wear and Decay of
such Things; as also the Share of Money, Effects and Debts, belonging to the said Benjamin by this Agreement. And if the said
Benjamin Franklin shall depart this Life before the Expiration of
the Term of Copartnership aforesaid, the said David Hall shall
continue the Business nevertheless, paying the Part by this Agreement belonging to the said Benjamin Franklin, unto the Executors, Administrators or Assigns, of the said Benjamin, they performing all Parts of this Agreement to the said David, which the said
Benjamin ought to have done if he had lived. And at the Expiration of the Term of Eighteen Years aforesaid, the said David Hall
shall have the Preference of purchasing the said Printing-Presses,
Types and Materials, (if he shall be so disposed, and shall have
given Notice of such his Intention in Writing under his Hand at
least Twelve Months before, to the said Benjamin Franklin, his
Executors or Administrators) at their present Value, allowing for
the Wear thereof what shall be judged a reasonable Abatement,
considering the Time they shall have been used: But if the said
David Hall shall not be inclined to purchase the same, or shall not
have given Notice as aforesaid, then he shall at the Expiration
of the Term aforesaid, deliver or cause to be delivered the said
Printing Presses, Types and Materials, to the said Benjamin Franklin, his Heirs, Executors or Administrators; together with all such

Books of Accounts, Papers, Memorandums, and Writings what-soever, or authentic Copies of the same, as shall be necessary or useful to the said Benjamin Franklin, his Executors or Adminis-trators, for the recovering or securing his or their Right or Interest in any Affair relating to this Partnership, or to continuing and carrying on the Business aforesaid. And if any unusual Damage, by bad Usage or Negligence, shall have happened to the Printing-Presses, Types or Materials aforesaid, the said David Hall shall make it good: But if the Damage be occasioned by some unavoid-able Accident, the Loss shall be divided and sustained by both Parties, in the same Manner as the Loss by bad Debts is by this Agreement to be divided and sustained. In Witness whereof, the Parties to these Presents have interchangeably set their Hands and Seals hereunto. Dated the Day and Year first above written.

Signed Sealed and Deliver'd in Presence of   DAVID HALL
  JOSEPH KENT
  THOMAS SMITH

MEMORANDUM the fourteenth Day of February Ao. Di. 1757 Before me Charles Brockden Esqr. One of the Justices of the Peace &c. the within named David Hall acknowledged this Writing, or Articles of Agreement indented, to be his Deed and desired that the same might be Recorded as his Deed. IN WITNESS whereof I have hereunto set my Hand and Seal the Day and Year abovesaid.
    C BROCKDEN

[Seal]   RECORDED in the Office for Recording of Deeds for the City and County of Philadelphia in Book H Vol. 7. page 421 &ca. the 17th Day of Feb-ruary Ao. Di. 1757. As WITNESSETH my Hand and Seal of my Office.   C BROCKDEN

Endorsed: Articles of Agreemt B F and D Hall
    Ackd. 14 Feb. 57 C B

Colors of the Associator Companies

Printed in *The Pennsylvania Gazette*, January 12 and April 16, 1748.

The companies of Associators, numbering about 800 men, with "Drums beating and Colours flying," appeared under arms at the State House on January 1 to elect company officers, according to the terms of the

Association.[2] After the election they presented their choices to the President and Council, who, having ordered commissions prepared in blank, directed them to be filled in and delivered. The company officers then withdrew to choose regimental officers. They wanted to make Franklin their colonel, "but conceiving myself unfit, I declin'd that Station."[3] Abraham Taylor, a member of the Council, was chosen colonel, Thomas Lawrence lieutenant colonel, and Samuel McCall major. On January 8 they took the oath of allegiance to the government.[4]

When the companies were formed, Franklin wrote, "the Women, by Subscriptions among themselves, provided Silk Colours, which they presented to the Companies, painted with different Devices and Mottos which I supplied."[5] The first ten company colors, certainly of Franklin's design, were described in the *Gazette* of January 12; the remaining ten, which were for other city and some country units, in that of April 16. None of the standards is known to have survived.[6]

[January 12, 1748]
DEVICES and MOTTOES painted on some of the Silk Colours of the Regiments of ASSOCIATORS, in and near Philadelphia.

I. A Lion erect, a naked Scymeter in one Paw, the other holding the Pennsylvania Scutcheon. Motto, PRO PATRIA.

II. Three Arms, wearing different Linnen, ruffled, plain and chequed; the Hands joined by grasping each the other's Wrist, denoting the Union of all Ranks. Motto, UNITA VIRTUS VALET.

III. An Eagle, the Emblem of Victory, descending from the Skies. Motto, A DEO VICTORIA.

IV. The Figure of LIBERTY, sitting on a Cube, holding a Spear with the Cap of Freedom on its Point. Motto, INESTIMABILIS.

V. An armed Arm, with a naked Faulchion in its Hand. Motto, DEUS ADJUVAT FORTES.

2. The election of company officers was reported in *Pa. Gaz.*, Jan. 5, 1748; see also *Pa. Col. Recs.*, V, 174–5. By the division of Mulberry Ward there were eleven companies.

3. Par. Text edit., p. 280.

4. Peters to Penn, Feb. 1, 1748, Penn MSS, Official Corres., IV, 89, Hist. Soc. Pa.

5. Par. Text edit., p. 280.

6. A conjectural sketch of the flag of the first company was made to illustrate Frances O. Allen, "The Provincial or Colonial Flag of Pennsylvania," *PMHB*, XVIII (1894), 249.

VI. An Elephant, being the Emblem of a Warrior always on his Guard, as that Creature is said never to lie down, and hath his Arms ever in Readiness. Motto, SEMPER PARATUS.

VII. A City walled around. Motto, SALUS PATRIAE, SUMMA LEX.

VIII. A Soldier, with his Piece recover'd, ready to present. Motto, SIC PACEM QUERIMUS.

IX. A Coronet and Plume of Feathers. Motto, IN GOD WE TRUST.

X. A Man with a Sword drawn. Motto, PRO ARIS ET FOCIS. &c. &c.

Most of the above Colours, together with the Officers Half-Pikes and Spontons, and even the Halberts, Drums, &c. have been given by the good Ladies of this City, who raised Money by Sub-scription among themselves for that Purpose.

[April 16, 1748]

Continuation of Devices and Mottoes painted on some of the Silk Colours of the Regiments of Associators in this City and Country adjacent.

XI. Three of the Associators marching with their Muskets shoulder'd, and dressed in different Clothes, intimating the Unanimity of the different Sorts of People in the Association; Motto, Vis Unita Fortior.

XII. A Musket and Sword crossing each other; Motto, Pro Rege & Grege.

XIII. Representation of a Glory, in the Middle of which is wrote *Jehovah Nissi*, in English, The Lord our Banner.

XIV. A Castle, at the Gate of which a Soldier stands Centinel; Motto, Cavendo Tutus.

XV. David, as he advanced against Goliath, and slung the Stone; Motto, In Nomine Domini.

XVI. A Lion rampant, one Paw holding up a Scymiter, another on a Sheaf of Wheat; Motto, Domine Protege Alimentum.

XVII. A sleeping Lion; Motto, Rouze me if you dare.

XVIII. Hope, represented by a Woman standing cloathed in blue, holding one Hand on an Anchor; Motto, Spero per Deum vincere.

XIX. The Duke of Cumberland as a General; Motto, Pro Deo & Georgio Rege.

XX. A Soldier on Horseback; Motto, Pro Libertate Patriae.

Franklin and Hall: Accounts, 1748–1766

MS Account Book: American Philosophical Society

This ledger, labeled "Franklin & Hall No. 1," contains four separate lists and accounts relating to David Hall's operation of the partnership of Franklin and Hall from 1748 to 1766. Three are lists of cash payments for printing work; the fourth is an invoice of books and stationery in Franklin's shop when the partnership began. The amounts recorded in the ledger are recapitulated in James Parker's report on the examination of the partnership accounts which he made as Franklin's agent, Feb. 1, 1766. His first examination was made in the latter days of February 1765. It was followed by other examinations on June 13, Aug. 22, 1765, Jan. 17, and Feb. 1, 1766. Parker signed the accounts on the date of each inspection. In the following analysis the information in the ledger, from which a number of pages are missing, has been supplemented by Parker's report, especially in the matter of dates and amounts.

1. *Record of Money received by Hall for advertisements in the Gazette,* [*Jan. 26, 1748–Jan. 17, 1766*]. Pages [1]–[21], with pages 1–4, 9–10, 15–16, and 21 missing. The payments were made in advance, and are totaled and entered by the number and date of the *Gazette,* thus: "No. 1178, July 11 [1751]. Ten Advertisements (Two 7s. 6d. each) £2 15s." By Feb. 21, 1765, when Parker made his first examination, Hall had received a total of £3312 17s. 8d. When his final check was made, Jan. 17, 1766, £326 14s. 6d. additional had been entered.

2. *Record of advertisements, blanks, &c., printed for ready cash* [*Jan. 26, 1748*]–*Jan. 28, 1766*. Pages [22]–60, with pages 22, 27–8, 31–4, 39–40, 45–6, 51–4, 57–8 missing. This is a list of cash customers, principally for handbills (5s. each), although a few payments are for *Gazette* advertisements (3s. for one of ordinary length, 5s. for a long one) and miscellaneous printing. Nicholas Scull, surveyor general, is charged £1 2s. 8d. for "200 Copies of Grants of Land," Nov. 18, 1748. John Mifflin paid 7s. 6d., Nov. 28, 1749, for the "Union Fire Company List." "500 Mason's Notices" cost £1. The Germantown Library "for printing their Instrument of Partnership &c." paid £3 11s. 6d. on May 6, 1754. The most interesting entries in 1754 are payments by Lewis Hallam and other members of his theatrical company for playbills and tickets for performances in the theater in Southwark. Otherwise, though it contains hundreds of names, the list is almost devoid of biographical or historical value. Parker examined this account, Feb. 16, 1765, when it came to £484 14s. 9d. When his final check was made, Feb. 1, 1766, £15 7s. additional had been received.

3. "Account of Money received by David Hall for printing Work done by Franklin and Hall and charged in the Leidgers commencing Janry. 21st. 1748." Pages 61–77 [a and b] and four unnumbered pages, with pages 63–4, 69–70, 75–6 missing. This is a list of cash receipts from customers whose accounts were kept in the firm's "Old Leidger No. 1" and "New Leidger No. 2"—neither of which has been found. The accounts are undated, the reference being to a page of the earlier ledger. Among more than 800 entries, besides private persons and business firms, are such institutions and official bodies as the Germantown Library Company, St. Andrew's Society, the City Wardens, Masonic Lodge, Street Commissioners, County Commissioners, trustees of the College of Philadelphia, managers of the Pennsylvania Hospital, Philadelphia Contributionship, Commissioners of Indian Affairs, Library Company of Philadelphia, Union Library Company, and the managers of lotteries for Chester, Lancaster, Middletown, the Presbyterian Church, St. Paul's Church, and the Academy of Philadelphia. Parker examined these accounts, Feb. 25, 1765, when they came to £2393 12s. 8¼d. His final examination, Jan. 17, 1766, showed an additional £630 9s 3d. had been received. Hall continued to record (on four unnumbered pages) payments of accounts in the "Old Leidgers." In the margin of the fourth the following note appears: "Taken from the Ledger up to the 16th of February, 1770. For Account of more Cash taken from Ledger, see Quire Book, No. 2. Folio 22." This quire book has not been found.

4. "Invoice of Books &c. left in my Hands by Mr. Franklin, taken January 23d. 1748." Pages 78–9 only, remainder missing. The invoice mentions Bibles (including two Welsh ones), Testaments, Psalters, grammars, vocabularies, dictionaries, Latin and Greek texts, spelling books, works of religion and divinity, five copies of Whitefield's Sermons, and 35 copies of *Pamela*. Parker's valuation of the Franklin and Hall accounts, Feb. 1, 1766, showed the stock Franklin turned over to the partnership to be worth £681 1s.

To Cadwallader Colden AL: New-York Historical Society

Dear Sir   Philada. Jany. 27. 1747[/48]

I received your Favour relating to the Cannon.[7] We have petitioned our Proprietors for some, and have besides wrote absolutely to London for a Quantity, in case the Application to the Proprietors

7. Letter not found.

should not succeed; so that, Accidents excepted, we are sure of being supply'd some time next Summer.[8] But as we are extreamly desirous of having some mounted early in the Spring, and perhaps [if][9] your Engineer should propose to use all you have, the Works [he] may intend will not very soon be ready to receive them, we should think ourselves exceedingly oblig'd to your Government, if you could lend us a few for one Year only:[1] When you return to New York, I hope a great Deal from your Interest and Influence.

Mr. Read, to whom Osborne consign'd your Books, did not open or offer them to Sale till within these two Weeks, being about to remove when he receiv'd them, and having till now no Conveniency of Shelves, &c.[2] In our two last Papers he has advertis'd generally that he has a parcel of Books to sell, Greek, Latin, French and English, but makes no particular Mention of the Indian History; it is therefore no Wonder that he has sold none of them, as he told me [a] few days since. I had but one of them from London, which [I] sent you before any of my Friends saw it: So, as no one here has read it but myself, I can only tell you my own Opinion that 'tis a well wrote, entertaining and instructive Piece, and [must] be exceedingly useful to all those Colonies who have anything to [do] with Indian Affairs.

You have reason to be pleas'd with the Mathematicians [envious] Expression about your Tract on Gravitation.[3] I long to see from Europe [some] of the deliberate and mature Thoughts of their Philosophers upon it.

To obtain some Leisure, I have taken a Partner into the Printing

8. Twelve cannon, costing £1316 2s., arrived from England in mid-summer. *Pa Gaz.*, Sept. 1, 1748. The Proprietors sent nothing, ostensibly because the Association was extra-legal. *Pa. Col. Recs.*, v, 240–1.

9. Except in the last two insertions, the textual matter in brackets in this letter has been supplied by the editors from Sparks, *Works*, VII, 29–30.

1. See above, p. 221.

2. Thomas Osborne printed Colden's *History of the Five Indian Nations* in London, and sent copies for sale in America to Deborah Franklin's relative James Read in Philadelphia. See above, p. 170 n.

3. Presumably Colden had forwarded to BF Peter Collinson's report on "a Certain great Mathamatician" in England, who, on reading Colden's tract on gravitation, wondered how it had reached America, for he believed it must have been written in Europe. "This poor Man is a Little touched in his pericranium," Collinson observed, "So *That*, I hope will Excuse him." *Colden Paps.*, III, 411.

House, but tho' I am thereby a good deal disengag'd from private Business, I [find] myself still fully occupy'd. The Association, Lottery, Batteries, [&c. take] up at present great Part of my Time. I thank you for com[municating the] Sheet on the first Principles of Morality, the Continuation [of which I shall be] glad to [see].⁴ If this reaches you at Coldengham, pray [send me the paper on Vis Inert]iae, which I much want.

[I since]rely wish, for the sake of all these [*several words missing*] the Governor in better Temper⁵ [*remainder missing*].

Addressed: To   The honble. Cadwalader Colden Esqr   Coldengham   Free   B FRANKLIN

Endorsed: Benj. Frankelin

To James Logan

MS not found; reprinted from Sparks, *Works*, VII, 31–3.

Sir,   Philadelphia, 27 January, 1748
    I have not yet found the book,⁶ but suppose I shall to-morrow. The post goes out to-day, which allows me no time to look for it. We have a particular account from Boston of the guns there. They are in all thirty-nine, Spanish make and new; fifteen of them are twenty-eight pounders, and twenty-four are fourteen pounders. We offer by this post £1500, this currency, for them all, and suppose we shall get them.⁷

    The insurers, in consideration of the premium of twenty per cent, engage thus; that, if the prizes arising against the tickets insured do

---

4. Colden also sent a copy of this essay to Rev. Samuel Johnson of Stratford, Conn., who "read it with attention three times" and pronounced it a "beautiful little Draught." Colden undertook to show the inter-relations of physics, metaphysics, and morality. For the Colden-Johnson correspondence on the subject of the treatise, see *Colden Paps.*, III, 372–5, 398–400, and E. Edwards Beardsley, *Life and Correspondence of Samuel Johnson, D.D.* (N.Y., 1874), pp. 140–3. The essay was not separately printed.

5. BF commented on the bad temper of the New York Assembly in letters to Colden, Nov. 27, 1747 (above, p. 212), and Logan, Jan. 30, 1748 (below, p. 275).

6. Probably Maittaire's *Stephanorum Historia*. See above, p. 219 n.

7. The Sum offered was subscribed by the merchants. See above, p. 184.

not, one with another, make in the whole a sum equal to the first cost of the tickets, they will make up the deficiency. They now think it a disadvantageous agreement, and have left off insuring; for though they would gain, as you observe, £1000, if they insured the whole at that rate, in one lot, yet it will not be so when they insure a number of separate lots, as ten, twenty, or one hundred tickets in a lot; because the prizes, falling in one lot, do not help to make up the deficiencies in another. The person, that insured your one hundred and twenty-five, did the next day give the whole premium to another with six and a quarter per cent more, to be reinsured two thirds of them. I have not insured for anybody; so I shall neither lose nor gain that way. I will send the policy, that you may see it, with the book.[8] I am, Sir, &c.   B. Franklin

8. Purchasers of lottery tickets sometimes insured their investments against loss. The premium on a single ticket or even a small number of tickets was prohibitively high. Sometimes, therefore, several subscribers, as the members of a fire company, forming a "club," would insure their tickets, thus reducing their losses, but also their prizes.

Philip G. Nordell, Ambler, Pa., in a letter to the editors, analyzed the lottery in relation to Logan's insurance of his tickets: the scheme consisted of 10,000 tickets at £2 each, or £20,000. From this sum £3000 was to be deducted for the use of the beneficiary, i.e., the Association and related defense needs, leaving £17,000 to be distributed in 2842 plus 2, or 2844 prizes.

1. Suppose that one adventurer bought all the tickets (£20,000) and paid a 20 per cent premium on them (£4000). He would then win all the £17,000. The insurer would have to pay the deficiency of £3000, leaving him a profit of £1000, as BF points out.

2. But suppose that each ticket was bought by a different person. Then, since there were 2844 prizes (two of which in two instances might be won by the same person), and since the lowest prize was greater than the cost of a ticket, the insurer would not have to pay anything to the holders of those tickets. But he would have to pay £2 to each of the adventurers who drew blanks, that is, 7156 persons, or £14,312. After deducting the 20 per cent premium paid him (£4000), the insurer would take a loss of £10,312.

3. Suppose that the 10,000 tickets were sold in 1000 lots of ten each and that all of the prizes fell to 700 of these 1000 lots. Even if the prize or prizes in each case reached the full cost of the lot, the insurer would have to pay the full cost of the 3000 tickets in the remaining 300 lots, or £6000. Since he received only £4000 in premiums, his loss would be £2000.

Logan's 125 tickets cost him £250, but if his insurance premium was 20 per cent, he could not lose more than £50. Thus he took 125 tickets off the hands of the managers and at the same time limited the cost to himself to £50.

To James Logan MS not found; reprinted from Sparks, *Works*, VII, 33.

Sir, Philadelphia, 30 January, 1748
   I send you herewith the book, and enclosed is the policy.[9] Here is no news but what is bad, namely, the taking of Mesnard, an account of which we have by way of Lisbon. He was carried into St. Malo.[1] And just now we have advice from New York, that an express was arrived there from New England to inform the government that two prisoners, who had escaped from different parts of Canada and arrived in New England, agreed in declaring, that three thousand men were getting ready to march against Albany, which they intended to besiege and take; and that they were to be joined by a great body of Indians. They write from New York, that the advice is credited there. I wish it may not prove too true, the wretched divisions and misunderstandings among the principal men in that government giving the enemy too much encouragement and advantage.
   I hope you and your good family continue well, being with sincere respect and affection, &c. B. FRANKLIN

To William Strahan ALS: Huntington Library

Dear Sir Philada. Feby. 4. 1747,8
   Enclos'd is a second Bill for £19 7s. 1½d. Sterling. The first I sent you some time since.[2] Mr. Hall will write, tho' neither of us have much Time, the Vessel hurrying away for fear of the Ice. I shall soon send you more Bills. With my best Respects to Mrs. Strahan, in which my Dame joins, and hearty Wishes for the Welfare of you and yours, I am, Dear Sir, Your obliged Friend and most humble Servant B FRANKLIN

9. See above, p. 273.
1. The news of the taking of Captain Mesnard's ship, en route from Philadelphia to London, and the report of a projected French invasion of New York were printed in *Pa. Gaz.*, Feb. 2, 1748.
2. See above, p. 213.

Account of Money Received from David Hall, 1748–1757

MS Account Book: American Philosophical Society

This little book contains in eight pages headed "Acct. of Money received'd at different Times from Mr. David Hall" Franklin's record of his income from the partnership with Hall from Feb. 7, 1748, to March 28, 1757. It shows that Hall paid Franklin £45 a year in semi-annual installments as his share of the £55 rent due from Franklin to Robert Grace by the terms of his lease for the property on Market Street in which Hall now lived and in which the partners' printing office was located (see above, p. 51). Hall's other payments were frequent but irregular; and Franklin sometimes took books instead of cash. The total amount Franklin received from Hall in this period was £6056 5s. 3¾d. Deducting the rent payments, his net income from the partnership averaged about £620 a year.

On three other pages of the book are partial accounts and memoranda, 1747–67, in which appear the names of only Theophilus Grew, Hugh Roberts, and William Parks of Williamsburg, Va.

From James Logan

Letterbook abstract: Historical Society of Pennsylvania

Feb. 19th [1748]

My Friend B.F. I wrote to him about the Title page of Euclid and the Lottery now fully drawn[3] and desired his direction concluding his Affectionate friend.

Report on the Swamp

MS Minutes of the Common Council: Free Library of Philadelphia

By 1740 the banks of Dock Creek and the low, swampy ground lying between it and Society Hill to the west had become a public nuisance. Six tanyards threw their refuse into the creek, fouling the water and filling the bed so that the tide water moved only sluggishly, exposing mud and filth and creating offensive pools of stagnant, mosquito-breeding water.[4] After members of several prominent families had been carried off in the yellow fever epidemic of 1747, public indigna-

3. See above, p. 219.   4. Watson, *Annals*, I, 336–41.

tion was aroused, and the Provincial Council directed its secretary Richard Peters to ask the Proprietor to have the Dock cleaned out.[5] The City Council, informed on October 19 "that the Swamp between Budd's Buildings and Society Hill,[6] in the Condition it now lies, is a very great nusance, and injurious to the Health of the Inhabitants of the City living near it," appointed Samuel Powel, John Stamper, Samuel Rhoads, Edward Warner, Franklin, and William Logan a committee "to view the said Swamp, and consider of the best Means of removing the Nusance complain'd of, and what will be the best Method of improving the said Swamp for the general Use and Benefit of the City." The Council's response to the committee's report was that the recommendations were too costly, and that they would consult with the City Assessors before taking action.[7] Not until after the Revolution was Dock Creek covered.

[February 24, 1748]

In pursuance of the above Order we have viewed the Swamp between Budd's Buildings and Society Hill, and are of Opinion, and find it also to be the Opinion of many of our Fellow Citizens with whom we have conferr'd,

That a convenient Dock of Sixty Feet wide as far as the said Swamp extends Westward, a Branch of thirty Feet wide on the South West, and forty Feet wide on the North West, be left open for the Reception of Flats, Boats and other small Craft which may be used on the said Dock. That the Remainder ought to be fill'd up above the Tide, and walled in with a good sufficient Stone Wall, and made Landing Places for Wood or other Things, which may hereafter be brought by Water for the Use of the Inhabitants of this City; That the said Dock be dug out and cleansed so deep that the Bottom may be always cover'd with Water; That the

5. 1 *Pa. Arch.*, I, 769. Thomas Penn replied that while he approved anything that would promote the health of Philadelphia's citizens, he thought it more likely the disease was brought in by vessels from the West Indies. *Pa. Col. Recs.*, V, 244.

6. Budd's Buildings, among the earliest constructed in Philadelphia, were a row of ten houses on the west side of Front Street extending north from the drawbridge over the Dock. Watson, *Annals*, I, 343; Nicholas B. Wainwright, "Plan of Philadelphia," *PMHB*, LXXX (1956), 183. The structure appears in Cooper's Prospect of Philadelphia, above, I, facing p. 140. Society Hill, which took its name from The Free Society of Traders, was in the area between Walnut and Spruce, Second and Fifth Streets.

7. Phila. Common Council, *Minutes* (Phila., 1847), pp. 487–8, 496.

Channel under the Bridge in Front Street be continued the Width of the said Bridge to the East Side of Water Street, there to widen gradually by sloap Lines on each Side, so as to be sixty or eighty Feet wide, and to continue that Width to the River Channel, and to be dug out and walled as aforesaid agreeable to a Plan now laid before the Board; That the Common Sewer on the South West Branch be continued to the Dock. But as this will be attended with a considerable Expence, and the dangerous Nusance complain'd of not effectually removed unless the whole Dock so far as to the Third Street be in like manner dug out, cleansed and walled up, We have, (least it should appear too great a Burden to be borne by the City) applied to several of the Inhabitants Owners of Ground adjoining the said Dock, who taking the Premises into serious Consideration, have (for Removal of so publick and dangerous a Nusance as far as in them lies, and also for procuring a sufficient Quantity of Water in Case of Fire in that part of the City) agreed each for himself, his Heirs, Executors and Administrators, to dig out, cleanse and wall, their several and respective Shares of the said Dock which are opposite to their respective Lots, and to keep them forever clean and in good Repair; ON CONDITION That the Profits arising from the landing of Wood and other Things on the Bank of the said Dock opposite to their Lots, may belong to them, their Heirs and Assigns respectively; And that the City shall make Flood-Gates at the several Bridges, and do all their Part in the Premises.

And this Method we hope will be approved of by the Board notwithstanding the Conditions proposed by the said Undertakers, when it is consider'd that the whole Dock from Budd's Buildings to Third Street, has generally been made at a Private Expence, and landing Places in those narrow Streets will not answer the Charge of making to any but to such whose Estates will in other Respects be benefitted thereby.

Upon the whole, as the Nusance is of such a Nature, and should it continue may be of fatal Consequence, in preventing the Growth and Increase of this City by discouraging Strangers (to whom every Mortality at a Distance is greatly magnified) from coming among us, or filling our own Inhabitants with Fears and perpetual Apprehensions, while it is suspected to propagate infectious Distempers, We humbly propose that a Tax be laid on the City and

Money raised for doing all those parts which appertain to the Publick, and the whole Nusance be removed. It is nevertheless submitted to the Judgment of the Board by,

SAMUEL POWELL B. FRANKLIN
JOHN STAMPER   WILLM. LOGAN
SAMUEL RHOADS

To James Logan

MS not found; abstracted in Worthington C. Ford, comp., *List of the Benjamin Franklin Papers in the Library of Congress* (Washington, 1905), p. 10.[8]

Philadelphia, March 7, 1747/8

ABSTRACT: Pass's[9] opinion as to cost of casting cannon; favors purchasing from New England.

Proposal to the Associators MS: American Philosophical Society

By March 1 fifty-three companies of Associators had been organized, not only in Philadelphia city and county, but also in Bucks, Chester, and Lancaster counties. By the terms of the Association the superior officers met on March 21 to adopt general regulations to unite the forces for action in case of need. On March 25 Richard Peters informed Thomas Penn there were eighty companies, "who behave very orderly. Signals and Words of Command are Settled all over the Country, and the Alarms are as far as I can judge well contriv'd."[1] Proposals Franklin made, probably at the meeting March 21, survive in this undated manuscript.

The spring and summer of 1748 were full of anxiety for Philadelphia, as depredations continued. With a French privateer prowling in Delaware Bay in late May, and a Spanish privateer reported a few days later lying off Elsingborough, ten miles below New Castle, the alarms and events of the preceding November were repeated. Again the Assembly was called into special session, and again it refused aid. The Council did what it could: posted a guard of ten men at the powder house; set two

8. The ALS is known to have been missing from Lib. Cong. since 1951. In Ford's *List* the addressee is given as "James Logan, Trenton"—obviously a misreading of "Stenton."

9. On John Pass, see below, p. 297 n.

1. Peters to Penn, March 25, 1748, Penn MSS, Official Corres., IV, 93, Hist. Soc. Pa.

pilot boats cruising in the bay; forbade all except daylight traffic past the battery; and gave Abraham Taylor command of the defense. An artillery company was organized; efforts were made to put a privateer to sea. Meanwhile the batteries at Wicaco and Atwood's Wharf were pressed to completion and then strengthened as cannon from New York, Boston, and London arrived. On May 22 a British man-of-war, the *Otter*, reached Philadelphia with orders to patrol the river and bay. She required refitting on arrival and her captain lacked energy; the crisis was almost over before she put to sea, June 22.[2]

Propos'd   [March 21, 1748]
That the Managers of the Lottery be apply'd to, to appoint suitable Persons to go down the River to the Capes, and there consult with the Persons in Authority and concert with them such Manners of conveying Intelligence to Philadelphia whether by Express or otherways when any Enemys appear of such Force as to make an Alarm necessary; or even such as may endanger our Trade. Who may likewise in returning land at such Places as they judge suitable to give Signals from, and endeavour to agree with the neighbouring Inhabitants, to keep Watch and give the Signals that may be agreed on, and engage to furnish them with Guns, Tarbarrels, or whatever else may be necessary for that Purpose.

That for the more certain alarming the Country on any Occasion, as soon as the Commander in chief at Philadelphia is well inform'd of the Approach on our Coasts of any considerable Force of the Enemy, Letters and Orders may be dispatch'd by Expresses to the Colonels of some or all of the Regiments, as the Occasion may require, who may immediately communicate the same to the other Officers of the Regiments, and they to the Men of the respective Companies, who are immediately to meet at their usual Place of Rendezvous, and from thence march to such Place as the Colonel shall appoint for assembling his Regiment; and when all the Companies are assembled, the Regiment to march to such Place as the Commander in chief shall have directed.

That in Case of any Attempt on the Inhabitants of the Frontiers by small Parties, as the Indian Custom is, the superior Officers of the Regiment being well inform'd of the Facts, may dispatch away on horseback suitable Bodies of active Men, well acquainted with the Woods, to such Places or Passes among the Mountains, or near

2. *Pa. Col. Recs.*, v, 233–67 *passim;* see also below, pp. 310–16.

the Conflux of such Rivers, &c. by which it is probable the Enemy must endeavour to make their Retreat, there to take Post and lie in wait till their Return, keeping proper Scouts or Centinels at a Distance from the Body to give Notice of their Approach, &c. by which Means they may be cut off and the Prisoners they take recover'd; a few Instances of which would probably much intimidate those Cowardly People, and make them afraid of attempting to attack us thereafter. And that such Places may be known to more People, it might be proper for the Officers beforehand to make a few Journeys to them, (guided by Indian Traders or Hunters) accompanied by such of their Men as would be suitable to act on occasion, and are disposed that way, there observing and pointing out all the proper Places for Ambushes, &c.; the Expence of which Journeys might be defray'd by the Managers of the Lottery.

That if there be certain Accounts of any large Body of the Enemy marching towards any Part of the Frontiers, the Colonels of the nearest Frontier Regiments may dispatch Expresses to the Commander in Chief at Philadelphia, with the Vouchers of the Intelligence, from whom Orders may issue to raise such Force as may be necessary to march to the Assistance of such threatned Frontier.

That the People on the Frontiers be advised to pitch on some suitable Places at proper Distances, and there enclose Pieces of Ground with Palisades or Stockadoes, so as to make them defensible against Indians, whereto on Occasion their Wives, Children, and ancient Persons may retire in Time of Danger. In Parts where there may not be had sufficient voluntary Labour to erect such Defences, and the Neighbours being poor cannot bear the Expence, some Assistance might be obtain'd from the Lottery Managers, if another Lottery should go on.

That those Managers be apply'd to, to offer Rewards by a Publick Declaration to such as should be maimed in Action, and Pensions to poor Widows whose Husbands should happen to fall in Defence of their Country.

That a Number of Spades, Pickaxes, Shovels, &c. be provided for the City Regiment, to be used by the Negro's and others as Pioneers for casting up sudden Retrenchments on Occasion.

Endorsed: Adjd. to Monday April 4 at 9 in the Morning

To James Logan   ALS: Riverdale Country School, New York City

Sir   Ap. 3. 48.
I have a Letter from Mr. Samuel Lawrence of New York,[3] (who undertook to ship the Guns for us) informing, that two small Vessels had been agreed with to bring them round; but a Sloop arriving there on Sunday last that had been chas'd in Lat. 35. by a Ship and Brigt. [brigantine] that were suppos'd to be Don Pedro[4] with a Consort coming on this Coast, the Governor and Council thought it more advisable to send them to Brunswick, which we since hear is done: Capt. Wallace, a discreet old Sea-Commander of this Place,[5] goes today or tomorrow to receive them there, and provide Carriages &c. to bring them to Philadelphia. The Postmaster at New York, and another Correspondent there, write me, that the Ship seen was certainly that of Dom Pedro; the Capt. of the Vessel chas'd knowing her well, having often seen her at the Havana where he has been several Voyages with a Flag of Truce. He was very near being taken, but escaped by Favour of the Night. We are glad to hear the Don is come out with one Consort only, as, by some Accounts, we apprehended he intended to bring a small Fleet with him. It now looks as if his Design was more against our Trade than our City.

With this I send you a Pacquet from London, and a Pamphlet from Sweden, both left with me for you by the new Swedish Missionary, Mr. Sandin.[6]

You must have heard that Mr. James Hamilton is appointed our

3. Merchant; an active and influential member of the New York City Common Council.

4. The *Gazette* and other papers reported several times on the movements and whereabouts of the Spanish warship *Don Pedro* this summer.

5. Possibly the Captain William Wallace mentioned in BF's Ledger D, but not otherwise identified.

6. Rev. John Sandin came to America in April 1748 to serve as rector of the Swedish congregation at Raccoon (now Swedesboro), N. J. He died within six months, and Peter Kalm married his widow. *PMHB*, XVI (1892), 351; Kalm, *Travels*, II, 639. The pamphlet Sandin brought for Logan was *Sponsalia plantarum* (Stockholm, 1746), the Uppsala dissertation of Johan Gustav Wahlboom (1724–1788), student of Linnaeus, physician, and professor of natural history. Also, see below, p. 323.

Governor;[7] an Event that gives us the more Pleasure, as we esteem him a benevolent and upright as well as a sensible Man. I hope he will arrive here early in the Summer, and bring with him some Cannon from the Proprietor. I am, Sir, Your most obliged humble Servant   B FRANKLIN

Addressed: To James Logan Esqr

Endorsed: Ben Franklin Apr 3d 1748

From Jonathan Belcher[8]

Letterbook copy: Massachusetts Historical Society

Sir,   Burlington (NJ) April 9: 1748
    I received yours of 2d Instant last night and am obliged for your care of my Letters as I shall for any others [that] may come to you. I desire you to Send me your weekly news Paper at the price others give you. Sir with my Compliments to Mrs. Franklin, Your Ready Friend and humble Servant.

From Peter Collinson   ALS: Library Company of Philadelphia

Respected Friend   Lond Aprill 12 1747/8
    I was very fortunate to receive both thy Curious Experiments on Electricity. I have Imparted them to the Royal Society to whome they are very acceptable and they are now in the hands of our Ingenious Friend Mr. Watson Who has promised as soone as his accounts are printed to send them to Thee with a Letter and hopes for thy further Favours.[9]

7. Governor James Hamilton reached Philadelphia Nov. 23, 1748, but brought no guns from the Proprietor, who considered the construction of a battery "a Wild project." Penn to Peters, March 30, 1748, Penn Letter Book, II, 226, Hist. Soc. Pa. On Hamilton, see below, p. 327 n.

8. On Belcher, see above, I, 176 n. He was appointed governor of New Jersey in July 1746, his commission was dated February 1747, and he arrived in his government in August 1747.

9. Watson's report on BF's papers was read to the Royal Society, Jan. 11, 1750. A copy was given to Collinson to send BF. It is reprinted below, p. 457.

My Letters and Books for the Lib: Com: by Mesnard Last fall was luckkyly saved[1] and are in the hands of E: Bland[2] to Come by this ship, which I Wish Safe to hand, and am thy Sincere friend
P COLLINSON

Great Numbers of Ingenious Men are very Earnestly Engaged in Electrical Experiment in applying them to various purposes. I have lately seen a Letter from a Doctor of Physick att Turin,[3] who gives 3 Instances of the Electrical power on Human Bodies By filling the Electrical Phyal with a purgative Portion [sic] and Transferring it into a Patient and it had all the Effects as if taken into the Stomach. The like account has been communicated from another Hand.[4]

I am much Obliged to thee for thine of Novr: 28: 1747 with the pamphlets Inclosed[5] of which in my Next.

Doctor Mitchell has been out of Order himself this Winter for His Wife was so very Ill he had near Lost Her.[6] He desires his Kind Respects and Intends to Write by this Ship.

I am much Concern'd for the State of the Colonies Northward of you and for our friend Colden. As Mesnard was taken I conclude thine to Doctor Mitchell and Fothergill never came to hand [line missing].

Aprill 25 Wee have a Strong Report of a Peace. I wish it may prove True. Our Stocks are advanced 3 per Cent on it.

1. Capt. Stephen Mesnard's vessel was captured by the French.
2. Elias Bland, London merchant. See above, p. 141 n.
3. Probably Giovanni Battista Bianchi (1681–1761), director of hospitals and professor of anatomy at Turin. See Abbé Nollet, "An Examination of certain Phaenomena in Electricity, published in Italy," *Phil. Trans.*, XLVI (1749–50), 375–83.
4. A letter in Latin on the subject from Johann Heinrich Winkler of Leipzig to Cromwell Mortimer, secretary of the Royal Society, was read in the Society, March 31, 1748, and printed in *Phil. Trans.*, XLV (1748), 262–70.
5. *Plain Truth.*
6. On Dr. John Mitchell, see above, p. 17, and II, 415 n.

From James Logan

Letterbook copy: Historical Society of Pennsylvania

My Friend BF   Apr. 16th [1748]
I was well pleased with thine of the 13th Inst. on both Accounts, that of the Guns and that also of the Militia[7] with which Conr. Weiser was So well Satisfied that he declared at his Return hither, that he would not for Some pounds out of his own Pocket, but that Shekallemy one of the 6 Nations and his Son had Seen it,[8] and these Indians declare they never Saw Such a Sight before.

My Son who was here last night will deliver thee Jared Elliots discourse of husbandry and inclosed is his Letter,[9] for the Sight of both which I thank thee and am Thy assured Loving friend   J L

To Charles Carter[1]

MS not found; reprinted from Anderson Galleries, Sales Catalogue No. 800 (January 18, 1910), item 90.

Philadelphia, April 18, 1748
To Charles Carter, Esq., Virginia.
Please to pay Mr. Robert Dade[2] or Order Thirty-one Penny-weight of Gold, and charge it to Account of, Sir Your humble Servant   B. FRANKLIN[3]

7. See below, p. 311.
8. Shikellamy (d. 1748), Oneida chief, statesman and diplomat, through whom Pennsylvania handled its Indian affairs; from his seat at Shamokin he protected the interests of the Six Nations in the Susquehanna Valley from 1728 until his death. Paul A. W. Wallace, *Conrad Weiser* (Phila., 1945), pp. 39–40, 262–3, 274; C. Hale Sipe, *The Indian Chiefs of Pennsylvania* (Butler, Pa., 1927), pp. 122–64. Shikellamy and Weiser attended a Council meeting in Philadelphia, April 11. *Pa. Col. Recs.*, V, 222.
9. Jared Eliot, *Essays upon Field-Husbandry in New England* (New London, Conn., 1748). See above, p. 147 n. The letter has not been found.
1. Col. Charles Carter (1707–1764), of Cleve, King George Co., Va.; son of Robert "King" Carter of Corotoman and uncle of Robert Carter of Nomini Hall, the Councillor. *Va. Mag. Hist. Biog.*, XXXI (1923), 39–69. He is charged with glass, lottery tickets, and a few other items, 1749–52, in BF's Ledger D.
2. Robert Dade, of King George Co., Va., where he married, 1743. 2 *Wm. and Mary Quar.*, X (1930), 45.

James Logan to Franklin and Hall

Letterbook copy: Historical Society of Pennsylvania

Friends B. Franklin and David Hall   May the 7th [1748]

As I intirely condemn your Publication in your last Gazette of J.F.'s Paper in relation to me,[4] without my approbation which I should never have granted and impute it more as the forward Act of D. Hall than of you both together, I desire that you would publish this in your next Gazette that you may make me all the Amends that now lies in your Power to your friend   J LOGAN

P.S. As you put the Latin one first So put this.

From James Logan

Letterbook copy (incomplete): Historical Society of Pennsylvania

My good Friend   May 9th [1748]

I have wrote a few lines to thee and D.H. as Authors of the Gazette of what you have inserted in your last in relation to me

3. Noted in the sales catalogue as "With the endorsement of Robert Dade on the reverse."

4. What so annoyed and angered Logan was an extravagantly worded tribute in Latin, addressed "Dignissime Domine," composed by "J.F.," and printed in the *Gazette* on May 5. It saluted Logan as a man whose reputation for learning was wide-ranging, unbounded, and unblemished by envy, and continued with fulsome glorification of his translation of *Cato Major* and of his work in mathematics and on the generation of plants. It hailed his perspicacity, character, and universal erudition, and ended with hexameters:

> Vive igitur felix, nec sit felicior alter,
> Qui *Deus* es patriae et florida fama tuae,
> Doctorum Doctor, doctrina splendida Fultor,
> Gentis delicium, Cultor et aonidum . . . .

> (Live then in joy, may none more joyous be,
> God in thy land, may thy fame nourish thee.
> Teacher of teachers, trustee of learning's pages,
> Dear to thy people's hearts, heir of all ages.)

Publication of the verses may have been (or Logan may have suspected it was) connected with Governor Belcher's effort to get him to become a

which thou may put into what Language thou pleases provided it answers my End. I impute it to D.H. and not to thy Self. But this comes to inquire particularly into the [*incomplete*].[5]

To B. Franklin Postmaster

To James Logan

MS not found; reprinted from extract in Stan V. Henkels, Catalogue No. 1082 (April 11–12, 1913), p. 38.

Philadelphia, May 10, 1748

As to the Battery,[6] it goes on very well, a great Number of Hands being employ'd upon it, who work with the utmost Diligence. I suppose that in a few Days the Platform will be ready to receive the cannon and the carriages are all made, a particular committee is employ'd in providing cartridges, &c., and Jno. Pass has already cast a great number of large shot.

From George Whitefield

MS not found; reprinted from *A Select Collection of Letters of the Late Reverend George Whitefield, M.A.* . . . . (London, 1772), II, 141–2.

My dear Mr. F[ranklin],   Bermudas, May 27, 1748

Inclosed you have a letter which you may print in your weekly paper.[7] It brings good news from this little pleasant spot. If you

trustee of the College of New Jersey. 1 *N.J. Arch.*, VII, 124–5. Logan declined because of poor health, reluctance to be identified with the Presbyterian clergymen who were in control, and (according to Frederick B. Tolles, *James Logan and the Culture of Provincial America*, Boston, 1957, p. 214) a suspicion that the invitation was designed to get him to give his library to the College.

5. BF's reply, May 10, suggests that the remainder of this letter had to do with the battery.

6. According to Henkels' Catalogue, this paragraph was preceded by one or more in which BF exonerated Hall of knowledge of the publication of the offending article and advised Logan not to publish a reply, but to pass over the matter in silence. Logan took the advice.

7. This was probably *A Letter from the Reverend Mr. Whitefield to A Reverend Divine in Boston: Giving a Short Account of his late Visit to Bermuda*, dated May 17, 1748, which Franklin & Hall printed, 1748, as a small pamphlet.

could print it on half a sheet of paper, to distribute among the Bermudas captains, it might perhaps be serviceable. The inhabitants here have received me so well, that I think publishing their kindness is a debt justly due to them. I am now waiting for a fair wind, and then we shall sail for England. The Governor's lady[8] goes with me. His Excellency is very civil to me, and I believe many souls have been benefited by this visit to Bermudas.[9] I desire to give the LORD JESUS all the glory. You will remember me to Mrs. F[ranklin], and all my dear Philadelphia friends. I do not forget them, and hope they will always remember, dear Sir, Their and your most affectionate, obliged friend and servant,   G.W.

Scheme of the Second Philadelphia Lottery

Printed in *The Pennsylvania Gazette*, June 2, 1748.

The drawing of the First Philadelphia Lottery was followed immediately with a proposal to open a second, in which the tickets should be of four classes and prices instead of one, and prizes would be pieces of eight. To meet the demand for coin the Lottery Managers bought dollars in New York, Rhode Island, and Boston. Franklin printed 500 copies of the scheme,[1] and published it in the *Gazette* on June 2 and several ensuing weeks. The first class was drawn on September 10, the fourth and last on March 27, 1749.[2] With the proceeds the Association battery at Wicaco was further equipped and strengthened.

8. Widow of Governor Alured Popple, who had died 1744. The Bermuda Assembly made a grant of £100 to assist Mrs. Popple and her children to return to England, where she died 1773. Henry C. Wilkinson, *Bermuda in the Old Empire* (London, 1950), p. 201; *Gent. Mag.*, XLIII (1773), 526.
9. Whitefield arrived in Bermuda from Charleston, S.C., March 15, 1748. He spent eleven weeks there, preaching at least once daily. The clergy, the governor (William Popple, brother of the deceased Alured), and many of the Council received him warmly, entertained him, and came to hear him. He sailed for England June 2. Tyerman, *Whitefield*, II, 180–2. For his journal of this stay in Bermuda, see John Gillies, *Memoirs of the Life of the Reverend George Whitefield* (London, 1772), pp. 154–72.
1. Eddy, *Ledger "D,"* pp. 80–1.
2. *Pa. Gaz.*, Sept. 15, 1748; April 5, 1749.

Scheme of the Philadelphia Lottery, to raise 9375 Pieces of
Eight for the Publick Use of the City of Philadelphia, and
Province of Pennsylvania.

This Lottery consists of 7500 Tickets, and is divided into four
Classes, to be drawn at four different times. Each Ticket is divided
into four Billets, one for each Class. The Price of each Billet is, for
the first Class one Piece of Eight, for the second two Pieces of
Eight, for the third three Pieces of Eight, and for the fourth four
Pieces of Eight.

The First Class, at One Piece of Eight, each Billet.

Prizes.	Value in Pieces of Eight.		Sum in Do.
1	of 500	is	500
2	of 250	are	500
3	of 100	are	300
3	of 80	are	240
4	of 40	are	160
10	of 20	are	200
10	of 10	are	100
125	of 4	are	500
750	of 2	are	1500
2 The first and last drawn each	10	are	20
2 The Tickets drawn next before and after the Prize of 500, each	10	are	20
912 Prizes			4040

Cash Dr. received on
7500 Tickets,   7500 Pieces,
Cr. paid in Prizes,   4040
                        Remains 3460
              To be carried to the Fourth Class.

The SECOND CLASS, at 2 Pieces of Eight each Billet.

Prizes.	Value in Pieces of Eight.		Sum in Do.
1	of	750	is	750
1	of	500	is	500
2	of	250	are	500
3	of	150	are	450
4	of	100	are	400
6	of	80	are	480
10	of	50	are	500
12	of	40	are	480
26	of	20	are	520
10	of	15	are	150
45	of	10	are	450
50	of	6	are	300
250	of	4	are	1000
750	of	3	are	2250
2 The first and last drawn each	}	15	are	30
2 The Tickets drawn next before and after the 750, each	}	15	are	30
2 The Tickets drawn next before and after the 500, each	}	10	are	20
1176 Prizes				8810

Cash Dr. received on

7500 Tickets,	15000 Pieces,
Cr. paid in Prizes	8810
Remains	6190

To be carried to the Fourth Class.

The THIRD CLASS, at 3 Pieces of Eight each Billet.

Prizes.	Value in Pieces of Eight.		Sum in Do.
1	of 1000	is	1000
1	of 750	is	750
1	of 500	is	500
2	of 400	are	800
3	of 250	are	750
5	of 150	are	750
8	of 100	are	800
10	of 60	are	600
15	of 40	are	600
20	of 30	are	600
30	of 20	are	600
50	of 15	are	750
100	of 10	are	1000
250	of 6	are	1500
750	of 4	are	3000
2 The first and last drawn each	20	are	40
2 The Tickets drawn next before and after the 1000, each	20	are	40
2 The Tickets drawn next before and after the 750, each	15	are	30
2 The Tickets drawn next before and after the 500, each	10	are	20
1254 Prizes			14130

Cash Dr. received on

7500 Tickets,	22500 Pieces,
Cr. paid in Prizes,	14130
Remains	8370

To be carried to the Fourth Class.

The FOURTH and LAST CLASS, at 4 Pieces of Eight each Billet.

Prizes.		Value in Pieces of Eight.		Sum in Do.
1	of	1500	is	1500
2	of	1000	are	2000
3	of	750	are	2250
4	of	500	are	2000
6	of	400	are	2400
10	of	250	are	2500
10	of	150	are	1500
15	of	100	are	1500
20	of	80	are	1600
30	of	60	are	1800
24	of	50	are	1200
60	of	40	are	2400
1248	of	20	are	24960
2	The first and last drawn each	50	are	100
2	The Tickets drawn next before and after the 1500, each	30	are	60
4	The Tickets drawn next before and after the two of 1000, each	20	are	80
6	The Tickets drawn next before and after the three of 750, each	15	are	90
8	The Tickets next drawn before and after the four of 500, each	10	are	80

1455	Prizes.			48020
	Cash Dr. received on 7500 Tickets			30000
	Paid more than received in this Class			18020

Being what was brought forward from the preceding Classes.

STATE of the Account of the FOUR CLASSES, viz.

Received.	Pieces of Eight.	Pieces.
For 7500 Billets in first Class, at 1 each,		7500
For Ditto, in second Class, at 2 each,		15000
For Ditto, in third Class, at 3 each,		22500
For Ditto, in fourth Class, at 4 each,		30000
		75000

Prizes paid.		Amounting to
In first Class,	912	4040
In second Class,	1176	8810
In third Class,	1254	14130
In fourth Class	1455	48020
		75000

Twelve and a Half per Cent. deducted from 75000 Pieces of Eight, is 9375 Pieces, to be applied to the Publick Use.

EXPLANATION.

A LOTTERY, in the common Form, is subject to these Inconveniencies. If the Price of each Ticket be high, many who would have been Purchasers are discouraged and excluded. If low, the Number of Tickets must be great, and that occasions the Drawing to take up more Time, which increases the Expence, and is an Injury to many, who neglect other Business to attend it. If the Capital of the Lottery is large, 'tis an Inconveniency that so much Money as is necessary to fill it, should be damm'd up, and restrained from being current in Trade, till the whole is compleated, and all the Lottery drawn.

The present Scheme is calculated to remedy these Inconveniencies. It divides the Lottery into four distinct Classes, to be drawn at four different Times, and is so contrived, as that all the four Drawings will take but little more Time than one Drawing would do in the common Way. The Price of a Ticket is also divided into four gradual Payments, to be made, if the Buyer pleases, at four different and distant Times. The first Entry is low and easy, and if the Adventurer is successful in the first Class, he is enabled as well as encouraged to go on. And a very great Part of the Money is to return several times into the Hands of the People before the Conclusion.

The four Billets into which each Ticket is divided, are all of the same Number, but of different Prices, according to the several Classes to which they belong.

293

Every Adventurer in the first Class receives a Billet for each Piece of Eight he pays, entitling the Bearer to such Prize in that Class as may be drawn against its Number, subject to no Deduction, unless the Prize be Twenty Pieces of Eight, or upwards. For a like Billet in the second Class he pays two Pieces of Eight. For a Billet in the third Class three Pieces of Eight; and four for a Billet in the fourth Class: So that the Price of a whole Ticket to go through the Lottery is Ten Pieces of Eight.

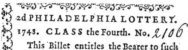

2d PHILADELPHIA LOTTERY. 1748. CLASS the Fourth. No. 2106 This Billet entitles the Bearer to such Prize as may be drawn againſt its Number in the fourth Claſs (if demanded within Six Months after the laſt Drawing is finiſhed) ſubject to no Deduction i under Twenty Pieces of Eight. f B — A Taylor

2d PHILADELPHIA LOTTERY. 1748. CLASS the Third No. 2114 This Billet entitles the Bearer to such Prize as may be drawn againſt its Number in the third Claſs (if demanded within Six Months after the laſt Drawing is finiſhed) ſubject to no Deduction if under Twenty Pieces of Eight. d B — A Taylor

Adventurers in the first Class have a Right to go thro' the subsequent Classes, but are not obliged to do it. If any neglect or decline taking out, or paying the Price of their Billets for a subsequent Class, till within three Days of the Drawing of such Class, the common Stock is to have the Benefit of it to the End; unless such Adventurers have left equivalent Prizes for that Purpose in the Hands of the Managers, which is the same Thing as paying: And the greatest Number of Prizes in the first, second, and third Classes, are made just the Price of a Billet in the Class next succeeding, that such Prizes may defray the Charge of new Billets, without the Trouble of paying Money.

A Sum equal to Twelve and a Half per Cent. on the whole, is to be deducted from the fortunate Tickets for the publick Use: But as it would occasion Trouble in making Change, and be otherwise inconvenient, if such Deduction were to be made from the smaller Prizes (which indeed cannot so well afford it) therefore nothing is deducted from any Prize that is under Twenty Pieces of Eight. And the Prizes are so calculated and order'd, that 15 per Cent. which is to be deducted from such as are Twenty Pieces of Eight and upwards, is equal to Twelve and a Half per Cent. on the Whole, and no more. Thus this Lottery is Two and a Half per Cent. more advantageous to Adventurers, than any that have hitherto been made on this Continent. And there are yet several other Advantages, for, in the first Place, the Adventurer's whole Ticket cannot be struck dead at a Blow, as in common Lotteries. If he has a Blank in the first Class, 'tis a Blank only of One Tenth of his Ticket, and he has still three good Chances left for the remaining nine Tenths, every Chance better than the preceding One, and the last best of all. Then he is under no Necessity of paying the whole Ten Pieces of Eight for each Ticket at once; and, if fortunate in the first Class, may have Occasion to advance no more than the first. In our former Lottery, the Price of a Ticket was *Forty Shillings,* the whole to be paid at once, and yet its best Chance was to be doubled but 250 times: In this Lottery one Piece of Eight may possibly gain several Thousands. And lastly, the Number of Prizes is more than Half the Number of Tickets.

Publick Notice is to be given before each Drawing, of the Time and Place when and where the Numbers and Prizes are to be put into the Wheels, that such Adventurers as think fit may be present if they please.

The Manner of Drawing is this: All the 7500 Numbers are to be put into one Wheel, and well mixed, the Wheel to be frequently turn'd during the Drawing. In the other Wheel are put the Prizes of the first Class, without any Blanks among them. Then a Number is drawn out of one Wheel, and a Prize against it out of the other, till the Prizes are all drawn; so ends the Drawing of the first Class, which may be finished in one Day.

The rest of the Numbers remain in their Wheel, seal'd up, till the Drawing of the second Class.

The Prizes drawn in each Class may be demanded within three Days after the Drawing of that Class is finished.

Six Weeks Time to be allowed between the Drawings, to take out Billets for the succeeding Class, prepare for drawing it, &c.

Before drawing the second Class, all the Numbers drawn out in the first Class are again to be roll'd up and tied, put into the Wheel to the rest, and well mixed among them.

Then the Prizes of the second Class being put into the other Wheel, without Blanks, the drawing proceeds as in the first Class.

In the same Manner is the third Class managed.

In drawing the fourth and last Class, Blanks are to be mixed with the Prizes, so many as to draw out all the Numbers in the Number Wheel, and complete the whole.

The drawing of the first Class is to begin on the first Monday in September next, without postponing or Delay, or sooner if sooner full; if any Tickets should then remain unsold, they are to be drawn on Account of the Stock.

The following Persons are appointed Managers of this Lottery, viz. Joseph Turner, Abraham Taylor, Tench Francis, John Inglis, Samuel Hazard, John Sober, William Plumsted, Patrick Baird, Philip Syng, Evan Morgan, jun., Jacob Duche, Austin Hicks, Samuel M'Call, jun., Joseph Sims, and Richard Nixon; who are to give Bond, and be on Oath for the faithful Performance of their Trust, and to lay out the Money arising, for such Uses, as to them, in Conjunction with William Allen, Joshua Maddox, William Masters, Samuel M'Call, senior, Edward Shippen, Thomas Leech, Charles Willing, John Kearsley, William Clymer, senior, Thomas Lawrence, junior, William Coleman, Thomas Hopkinson, William Wallace, John Stamper, John Mifflin, James Coultas, William Branson, Rees Meredith, Thomas Lloyd, and Benjamin Franklin, Managers and Assistants of the former Lottery, or to the Majority of the whole, shall seem most for the publick Benefit.

Prizes not demanded within six Months after the last Drawing, to be deem'd as generously given to the common Stock, for the same Use as the Twelve and a Half per Ct. and not to be demanded afterwards, but applied accordingly.

The Managers are to adjust their Accounts, and publish them within twelve Months after the Drawing is finished.

The Tickets will begin to be sold by the Managers at their respective Houses, on Thursday, the 16th Instant.

Miscellaneous Lottery Papers

DS: nos. 1, 2, 3, 4, 6, Yale University Library; no. 5, Edgar Fahs Smith Library, University of Pennsylvania

The Philadelphia Lottery Papers in the Yale University Library contain many orders by the Managers to their treasurer William Allen[3] to pay

3. William Allen (1704–1780), recorder of Philadelphia; member of the City Council; member of the Assembly, 1731–39; mayor of Philadelphia, 1735; chief justice of the Province, 1750–74; Provincial Grand Master of Masons, 1750; a principal representative of the proprietary interests.

for gun carriages and repairs or for personal services and expenses.[4] Franklin was not one of the managers of either lottery; he was, however, a member of a committee which joined them in spending the money (see above, p. 222). Documents illustrating this participation are grouped together here rather than in their respective chronological places.

[1]   March 21. 1748,9
Pay to John Pass[5] or Order the Sum of Seventy Pounds, out of the Lottery-Money in your Hands, on his Account for making the Field Carriages.   WM: CLYMER

To William Allen, Esqr   ⎫   SAMUEL M'CALL SENR
Treasurer of the Philadelphia Lottery. ⎭   B FRANKLIN

Recd. March 22d. 1748/9 of William Allen Seventy pounds being in full of the within Order   his
                                    per JOHN X PASS
                                         Mark

Memd. he gave three Receipts which were for parts of the seventy pound above mentioned to be cancelled now.

Endorsed: John Pass's Receipt £70.

Educated at the Middle Temple, London, sometime pensioner of Clare Hall, Cambridge, this wealthy, cultivated gentleman was distinguished for public service and philanthropy. He was the largest contributor of the first trustees of the Academy of Philadelphia, a trustee of the Loganian Library, a manager of the Pennsylvania Hospital; he advanced money to purchase the lot for the statehouse, and he underwrote the costs of European study and travel for several promising young Philadelphians, notably the artist Benjamin West, believing it wrong that "such a Genius should be cramped for want of a little Cash." By his will he freed his slaves. He remained a Loyalist during the Revolution. His wife was the daughter of Speaker Andrew Hamilton; Governor James Hamilton was his brother-in-law; one of his daughters married John Penn, and another James DeLancey of New York. Carl and Jessica Bridenbaugh, *Rebels and Gentlemen: Philadelphia in the Age of Franklin* (N.Y., 1942), pp. 184–91; *DAB*.
    4. Page 221. The accounts in these papers were published in a pamphlet, *Philadelphia Lottery Accounts* (Phila., 1752). The MS Ledger and Journal of the Second Philadelphia Lottery, as well as some other papers in the Yale collection, include accounts of receipts and expenditures in behalf of the Association of 1755–56.
    5. Payments to John Pass, ironmonger, are recorded in *Philadelphia Lottery Accounts*. One of £258 5s. 6d., Dec. 2, 1748, was "for Spikes, and

[2]   March 21. 1748/9
    Pay to Mr. Samuel M'call[6] or Order Nine Pounds, being for
Powder he furnish'd to try the Guns brought from N York.

To William Allen Esqr   ⎫   WM: CLYMER
Treasurer of the first Philadelphia Lottery ⎭   B FRANKLIN

Recd the 21st. March 1748/9 of Willm. Allen Esqr. payment of
the above Order.   per SAMUEL M'CALL SENR

Endorsed: Managers Order pd. S. M'call senr. £9.

[3]   June 6. 1749.
We whose Names are hereunto subscribed are of Opinion, that
Jno Pass should be paid the Ballance of his Account for making the
Field Carriages.   WM: CLYMER
                                       B FRANKLIN
Sir
    In Consequence of the within opinion of two of the Managers
for the Lottery, you will please to pay the Ballance of Mr. Pass's
Account.   SAMUEL M'CALL SENR.
To Wm. Allen Esqr

    Recd. Philadelphia June 7th. 1749 of William Allen Seventeen
pounds Seventeen Shillings and eleven pence being the full Ballance
of my Account of Field Pieces against the Lottery Managers.
                                              his
Test. Alexr. Stuart   per JOHN X PASS
                                              Mark
[4]
Sir   Nov. 23. 1749
    Mr. Kent serv'd at the last Lottery as one of the Clerks,[7] for
which he has not yet receiv'd any thing. He is just going to N.

---

other Iron-work, &c." and there are five more, totaling £87 17s. 11d., in
1748–49.
    6. Samuel McCall (1710–1761), major of the Associated Regiment, 1748;
member of the Library Company and one of the original members of the St.
Andrew's Society of Philadelphia, 1748; merchant, partner of John Inglis.
His business ledger (Hist. Soc. Pa.) shows that he sold BF "a Sett of small
moulds for Printing Ships, Sloops &c.," i.e., the devices used in *Pa. Gaz.* to
advertise ships' sailings. Usually designated "senior," his brother-in-law
was Samuel McCall, "junior" (1721–1762). *PMHB*, V (1881), 341–2.
    7. Not further identified.

England. It is scarce worth while to call the Managers together on this Occasion. We suppose they will not disapprove of his being allow'd the same Pay as he had for his Service in the first Lottery, especially as the latter requir'd more Days Attendance.

To Wm. Allen Esqr B FRANKLIN
  Treasurer of the Lottery PHIL SYNG

Recd. Philadelphia Novr. 23d. 1749 of William Allen the sum of Ten pounds in pursuance of the within Order being in full for my Service as Clerk to the second Philadelphia Lottery.

JOSEPH KENT

Endorsed: Lotty Order

[5]

To The menagers of The Lottery Dr.
  To painting four Field cariages £4. 0. 0
  GUSTAVUS HESSELIUS[8]

Sir Jan. 10. 1749,50
  The above has been long due, and I think it should be paid.
Your humble Servant B FRANKLIN
To Majr. M'Call

Recd. Jany 11th. 1749/50 of William Allen four pounds in full of the above Account JOHN HESSELIUS

[6]

Recd. Apl. 25th. 1750 of William Allen Three hundred and fourteen pounds ten Shillings being to pay for the Guns brought from Boston per me B FRANKLIN

Endorsed: Mr. Franklin's Receipt £314.10

8. Gustavus Hesselius (1682–1755), portrait painter and craftsman, builder of the first organ in America, advertised in 1740 that he would paint coats of arms on coaches and chaises. The amount of his bill indicates that something more than plain paint was spread on the gun carriages. His son John (1728–1778), also a painter, was itinerant in Maryland and Virginia from about 1748 until 1763, when, having married, he settled in Annapolis, Md. *PMHB*, XXIX (1905), 129–33; LXII (1938), 442.

From Peter Collinson

ALS: University of Pennsylvania Library

Friend Franklin   Londn June 14th 1748

The Bearer Mr. Kalm[9] Is an Ingenious Man and comes over on purpose to Improve himself in all Natural Inquiries. He is a Sweed per Nation and is as I am informed Imployed by the Academy of Upsal to make Observations on your Parts of the World. I recommend Him to thy Favour and Notice—by Him I send the first Vol. of the Voyage to Discover NorWest passage.[1] I hope the pacquett &c. sent under the Care of Hunt & Greenlease[2] is come safe to Hand. I am thy sincere friend P COLLINSON

Addressed: To   Ben: Franklin   Philadelphia

9. Pehr Kalm (1716–1779), a botanist especially interested in medicinal and dye-yielding plants, was a pupil of Linnaeus, whom he had accompanied to Russia and the Ukraine, 1744. He was elected to the Swedish Academy of Sciences, 1745, and appointed professor of natural history at the University of Åbo, 1747. The account of his tour of America, 1748–51, was published at Stockholm in three volumes, 1753–61; it was translated into German, 1754–64; into English by Johann Reinhold Forster, 1770–71; and into Dutch, 1772. BF wrote to David Colden, March 5, 1773, that it was "full of idle Stories, which he picked up amongst ignorant People, and . . . ascribed . . . to Persons of Reputation who never heard of them till they were found in his Book"; and was mortified to read some of the things attributed to him. Kalm also published in the transactions of the Swedish Academy of Sciences papers on such American products as maple sugar, Indian corn, grasshoppers, wild pigeons, spruce beer, and rattlesnakes. His description of Niagara Falls (printed in *Pa. Ga*7., Sept. 20, 1750) was one of the earliest in English. Kalm was ordained a Lutheran clergyman, 1757 (he had sometimes preached in Swedish churches in America, and married the widow of Johann Sandin, pastor at Raccoon, N.J.), and received an honorary degree in theology from the University of Lund, 1768. He was offered, but declined, a post at St. Petersburg as professor of botany. Kalm, *Travels*, I, vii-ix, II, 770–3; Esther V. Larsen, "Peter Kalm, Preceptor," *PMHB*, LXXIV (1950), 500–11.

1. Probably the first volume of [Charles Swaine], *An Account of a Voyage For the Discovery of a North-West Passage by Hudson's Streights*, which was published in May 1748. *Gent. Mag.*, XVIII (1748), 240. The second volume appeared 1749.

2. Not identified.

To [Nathaniel Sparhawk³]

ALS: Joseph W. P. Frost, Kittery Point, Maine (1954)

Philada. June 15. 1748

I receiv'd yours per Mr. Baynton with the Money as therein speci-
fied; and have since deliver'd it to Mr. Warren (who is now here)
with Mr. Pepperill's Letter; of which please advise Mr. Pepperill.⁴
I am Sir, Your most humble Servant   B FRANKLIN

To Jane Mecom

MS not found; reprinted from Jared Sparks, ed., *A Collection of the Familiar Letters and Miscellaneous Papers of Benjamin Franklin* (Boston, 1833), pp. 10–15.

Dear Sister,   Philadelphia, [June? 1748]⁵

I received your letter, with one for Benny,⁶ and one for Mr.
Parker, and also two of Benny's letters of complaint, which, as you
observe, do not amount to much. I should have had a very bad
opinion of him, if he had written to you those accusations of his
master, which you mention; because, from long acquaintance with
his master, who lived some years in my house, I know him to be a
sober, pious, and conscientious man; so that Newport,⁷ to whom
you seem to have given too much credit, must have wronged Mr.
Parker very much in his accounts, and have wronged Benny too, if
he says Benny told him such things, for I am confident he never did.

3. Nathaniel Sparhawk (1715–1776), merchant at Portsmouth and Boston;
married the daughter of Sir William Pepperrell, 1742. 6 Mass. Hist. Soc.
Colls., X, 118 n.
4. Probably Andrew Pepperrell (d. 1751), A.B., Harvard, 1743; business
partner of his father, Sir William, from 1744 until his death. Byron Fair-
child, *Messrs. William Pepperrell: Merchants at Piscataqua* (Ithaca, N.Y.,
1954). Baynton may be John Baynton (1726–1773), merchant of Philadelphia.
Warren has not been identified.
5. Undated by Sparks; written after June 6 (see below, p. 303 n). Van Doren
(*Franklin-Mecom*, p. 41) pointed out that it was written after March, 1748,
when BF visited New York.
6. Benjamin Mecom (C.17.3), BF's nephew, was apprenticed to the New
York printer James Parker (see above, II, 341 n). He was now in his sixteenth
year.
7. Not identified.

As to the bad attendance afforded him in the smallpox, I believe, if the negro woman did not do her duty, her master or mistress would, if they had known it, have had that matter mended. But Mrs. Parker was herself, if I am not mistaken, sick at that time, and her child also.[8] And though he gives the woman a bad character in general, all he charges her with in particular, is, that she never brought him what he called for directly, and sometimes not at all. He had the distemper favorably, and yet I suppose was bad enough to be, like other sick people, a little impatient, and perhaps might think a short time long, and sometimes call for things not proper for one in his condition.

As to clothes, I am frequently at New York, and I never saw him unprovided with what was good, decent, and sufficient. I was there no longer ago than March last, and he was then well clothed, and made no complaint to me of any kind. I heard both his master and mistress call upon him on Sunday morning to get ready to go to meeting, and tell him of his frequently delaying and shuffling till it was too late, and he made not the least objection about clothes. I did not think it any thing extraordinary, that he should be sometimes willing to evade going to meeting, for I believe it is the case with all boys, or almost all. I have brought up four or five myself, and have frequently observed, that if their shoes were bad, they would say nothing of a new pair till Sunday morning, just as the bell rung, when, if you asked them why they did not get ready, the answer was prepared, "I have no shoes," and so of other things, hats and the like; or if they knew of any thing that wanted mending, it was a secret till Sunday morning, and sometimes I believe they would rather tear a little, than be without the excuse.

As to going on petty errands, no boys love it, but all must do it. As soon as they become fit for better business, they naturally get rid of that, for the master's interest comes in to their relief. I make no doubt but Mr. Parker will take another apprentice, as soon as he can meet with a likely one. In the mean time I should be glad if Benny would exercise a little patience. There is a negro woman that does a great many of those errands.

I do not think his going on board the privateer arose from any difference between him and his master, or any ill usage he had re-

8. Mrs. Parker and her son were ill during an epidemic in the summer of 1747. See above, p. 173.

ceived. When boys see prizes brought in, and quantities of money shared among the men, and their gay living, it fills their heads with notions, that half distract them, and put them quite out of conceit with trades, and the dull ways of getting money by working. This I suppose was Ben's case, the *Catherine* being just before arrived with three rich prizes;[9] and that the glory of having taken a privateer of the enemy, for which both officers and men were highly extolled, treated, presented, &c. worked strongly upon his imagination, you will see, by his answer to my letter, is not unlikely. I send it to you enclosed.[1] I wrote him largely on the occasion; and though he might possibly, to excuse that slip to others, complain of his place, you may see he says not a syllable of any such thing to me. My only son, before I permitted him to go to Albany, left my house unknown to us all, and got on board a privateer, from whence I fetched him. No one imagined it was hard usage at home, that made him do this. Every one, that knows me, thinks I am too indulgent a parent, as well as master.

I shall tire you, perhaps, with the length of this letter; but I am the more particular, in order, if possible, to satisfy your mind about your son's situation. His master has, by a letter this post,[2] desired me to write to him about his staying out of nights, sometimes all night, and refusing to give an account where he spends his time, or in what company. This I had not heard of before, though I perceive you have. I do not wonder at his correcting him for that. If he was my own son, I should think his master did not do his duty by him, if he omitted it, for to be sure it is the high road to destruction. And I think the correction very light, and not likely to be very effectual, if the strokes left no marks.

His master says farther, as follows; "I think I can't charge my conscience with being much short of my duty to him. I shall now desire you, if you have not done it already, to invite him to lay his complaints before you, that I may know how to remedy them."

9. The privateer *Royal Catherine* returned triumphantly to New York, June 6, with two French prizes; her third conquest, in charge of a prize crew, arrived June 10. The Corporation voted Captain Burges the freedom of the city, and grateful merchants opened a subscription for two pieces of plate to be presented to him and his lieutenant. Howard M. Chapin, *Privateering in King George's War, 1739–1748* (Providence, R.I., 1928), pp. 170–1.

1. Not found.   2. Not found.

Thus far the words of his letter, which giving me a fair opening to inquire into the affair, I shall accordingly do it, and I hope settle every thing to all your satisfactions. In the mean time, I have laid by your letters both to Mr. Parker and Benny, and shall not send them till I hear again from you, because I think your appearing to give ear to such groundless stories may give offence, and create a greater misunderstanding, and because I think what you write to Benny, about getting him discharged, may tend to unsettle his mind, and therefore improper at this time.

I have a very good opinion of Benny in the main, and have great hopes of his becoming a worthy man, his faults being only such as are commonly incident to boys of his years, and he has many good qualities, for which I love him. I never knew an apprentice contented with the clothes allowed him by his master, let them be what they would. Jemmy Franklin, when with me, was always dissatisfied and grumbling.[3] When I was last in Boston, his aunt bid him go to a shop and please himself, which the gentleman did, and bought a suit of clothes on my account dearer by one half, than any I ever afforded myself, one suit excepted; which I don't mention by way of complaint of Jemmy, for he and I are good friends, but only to show you the nature of boys.

The letters to Mr. Vanhorne were sent by Mr. Whitfield, under my cover.[4]

I am, with love to brother and all yours, and duty to mother, to whom I have not time now to write, your affectionate brother,

B. FRANKLIN

Advice to a Young Tradesman

Printed in George Fisher, *The American Instructor: or Young Man's Best Companion.* . . . The Ninth Edition Revised and Corrected. Philadelphia: Printed by B. Franklin and D. Hall, at the New-Printing-Office, in Market-Street, 1748. Pp. 375–7. (Yale University Library)

George Fisher's *The Instructor: or Young Man's Best Companion* was a popular manual of English grammar, penmanship, composition, arithmetic, bookkeeping, and other useful matters for young men entering

3. For James Franklin's apprenticeship to his uncle BF, see above, II, 261–3.
4. Vanhorne has not been identified. Whitefield sailed from Charleston, S.C., to Bermuda in March, and from Bermuda to England, June 2. Tyerman, *Whitefield*, II, 180, 182.

business.[5] A competitor of William Mather's *The Young Man's Companion*,[6] on which it was based and from which it copied many particulars, it was first published in London in 1730 or earlier; a sixth edition appeared in 1742, and an eighth presumably before 1748. Franklin imported two dozen copies in 1745; in 1747 he began to get an American edition ready. This was the "Ninth Edition" and was announced in the *Gazette* of July 21, 1748, as "just published."

It was essentially but not entirely a reprinting of the English original. Franklin changed the name to *The American Instructor,* he omitted some parts of Fisher's book and added new material for American readers.[7] Instead of the English *Instructor's* brief medical prescriptions, for example, *The American Instructor* reprinted John Tennent's *Every Man his own Doctor*.[8] There were accounts of the history and government of the several colonies; of Pennsylvania, however, Franklin wrote simply: "One of the happiest Countries at this Time in the World. God grant it may long so continue." To promote the teaching of penmanship Franklin, like William Mather, included four plates of examples of good handwriting,[9] as well as a description of the Twelve

5. Little is known of the author. His name appears on an arithmetic of which there was a fifth edition in 1740, and the many editions of Cocker's Arithmetic between 1725 and 1767 were "carefully corrected and amended" by him. Fisher was not, as has been suggested, the pseudonym of Mrs. Thomas Slack (née Anne Fisher), author of several elementary educational works and wife of a Newcastle printer who was himself the author of several books of mathematical character. Ambrose Heal, *The English Writing-Masters and their Copy-Books, 1570–1800* (Cambridge, 1931), pp. 50–1; Louis C. Karpinski, "The Elusive George Fisher 'Accomptant'—Writer or Editor of Three Popular Arithmetics," *Scripta Mathematica*, III (1935), 337–9; William E. Lingelbach, "Franklin's *American Instructor:* Early Americanism in the Art of Writing," APS *Proc.*, XCVI (1952), 375–81; H. R. Plomer and others, *A Dictionary of the Printers and Booksellers . . . in England . . . 1726 to 1775* (Oxford, 1932), p. 230.

6. This work first appeared in 1681; a fifteenth edition appeared in 1737, with four plates illustrating the round and Italian hands.

7. With unimportant differences the English preface was reprinted in the Philadelphia edition, but a final paragraph was added: "In the British Edition of this Book, there were many Things of little or no Use in these Parts of the World: In this Edition those Things are omitted, and in their Room many other Matters inserted, more immediately useful to us Americans. And many Errors in the Arithmetical Part are here carefully corrected." The American preface ended: "Vale & Fruere."

8. See above, II, 155.

9. The round hand illustrated in one of these plates has been thought to be a creation of BF, but was not. Ray Nash, *American Writing Masters and Copybooks* (Boston, 1959), pp. 11, 23.

Ciphers which his late friend Joseph Breintnall had designed. And finally he offered this advice to young tradesmen.[1]

[July 21, 1748]

ADVICE TO A YOUNG TRADESMAN, WRITTEN BY AN OLD ONE.[2]

To my Friend A. B.

As you have desired it of me, I write the following Hints, which have been of Service to me, and may, if observed, be so to you.

Remember that TIME is Money. He that can earn Ten Shillings a Day by his Labour, and goes abroad, or sits idle one half of that Day, tho' he spends but Sixpence during his Diversion or Idleness, ought not to reckon That the only Expence; he has really spent or rather thrown away Five Shillings besides.

Remember that CREDIT is Money. If a Man lets his Money lie in my Hands after it is due, he gives me the Interest, or so much as I can make of it during that Time. This amounts to a considerable Sum where a Man has good and large Credit, and makes good Use of it.

Remember that Money is of a prolific generating Nature. Money can beget Money, and its Offspring can beget more, and so on. Five Shillings turn'd, is *Six:* Turn'd again, 'tis Seven and Three Pence; and so on 'til it becomes an Hundred Pound. The more there is of it, the more it produces every Turning, so that the Profits rise quicker and quicker. He that kills a breeding Sow, destroys all her Offspring to the thousandth Generation. He that murders a Crown, destroys all it might have produc'd, even Scores of Pounds.

Remember that Six Pounds a Year is but a Groat a Day. For this little Sum (which may be daily wasted either in Time or Expence

1. This is the earliest known printing. The Advice was reprinted by Benjamin Mecom in *New England Mag.*, No. 3 (1759), 27–8, with minor variations and the addition of one sentence. Mecom's version was followed in a broadside printed by Daniel Humphreys about 1785 (Evans 19011). Worthington C. Ford, "Franklin's Advice to a Young Tradesman. Two Unique Impressions," *The Bibliographer,* 1 (1902), 89–96. None of BF's principal editors—Duane, Temple Franklin, Sparks, Bigelow, or Smyth—included the paragraph beginning: "Good-natur'd Creditors."

2. In subsequent printings the title was generally omitted, and the Advice was given a signature, "An old Tradesman."

unperceiv'd) a Man of Credit may on his own Security have the constant Possession and Use of an Hundred Pounds. So much in Stock briskly turn'd by an industrious Man, produces great Advantage.

Remember this Saying, *That the good Paymaster is Lord of another Man's Purse.* He that is known to pay punctually and exactly to the Time he promises, may at any Time, and on any Occasion, raise all the Money his Friends can spare. This is sometimes of great Use: Therefore never keep borrow'd Money an Hour beyond the Time you promis'd, lest a Disappointment shuts up your Friends Purse forever.

The most trifling Actions that affect a Man's Credit, are to be regarded. The Sound of your Hammer at Five in the Morning or Nine at Night, heard by a Creditor, makes him easy Six Months longer. But if he sees you at a Billiard Table, or hears your Voice in a Tavern, when you should be at Work, he sends for his Money the next Day. Finer Cloaths than he or his Wife wears, or greater Expence in any particular than he affords himself, shocks his Pride, and he duns you to humble you. Creditors are a kind of People, that have the sharpest Eyes and Ears, as well as the best Memories of any in the World.

Good-natur'd Creditors (and such one would always chuse to[3] deal with if one could) feel Pain when they are oblig'd to ask for Money. Spare 'em that Pain, and they will love you. When you receive a Sum of Money, divide it among 'em in Proportion to your Debts. Don't be asham'd of paying a small Sum because you owe a greater. Money, more or less, is always welcome; and your Creditor had rather be at the Trouble of receiving Ten Pounds voluntarily brought him, tho' at ten different Times or Payments, than be oblig'd to go ten Times to demand it before he can receive it in a Lump. It shews, besides, that you are mindful of what you owe; it makes you appear a careful as well as an honest Man; and that still encreases your Credit.

Beware of thinking all your own that you possess, and of living accordingly. 'Tis a Mistake that many People who have Credit fall into. To prevent this, keep an exact Account for some Time of both your Expences and your Incomes. If you take the Pains at first to mention Particulars, it will have this good Effect; you will

3. Mecom, Humphreys, and later printings omit "chuse to."

discover how wonderfully small trifling Expences mount up to large Sums, and will discern what might have been, and may for the future be saved, without occasioning any great Inconvenience.

In short, the Way to Wealth, if you desire it, is as plain as the Way to Market. It depends chiefly on two Words, INDUSTRY and FRUGALITY; i.e. Waste neither Time nor Money, but make the best Use of both.[4] He that gets all he can honestly, and saves all he gets (necessary Expences excepted) will certainly become RICH; If that Being who governs the World, to whom all should look for a Blessing on their honest Endeavours, doth not in his wise Providence otherwise determine.

Notes on the Association

Printed in *The Pennsylvania Gazette*, January 5 to September 1, 1748.

Between November 1747 and September 1748 the *Pennsylvania Gazette* printed many items about enemy privateering in the Delaware Bay and River, about defense, and about the Association. These notes are helpful in understanding many of the documents printed above. Because of their importance, not only as reference materials but as illustrations of many of Franklin's activities during these hectic months, a generous selection is included here.

Friday last Nine Companies of the Associators of this City, and one of Moyamensing, having chosen their Officers for the ensuing Year, marched up, and met at the State-House; where the President and Council were sitting, who immediately granted the Commissions.[5] The Officers then withdrawing into a Room by themselves, elected Abraham Taylor, Esq; Colonel; Thomas Lawrence, Esq; Lieutenant Colonel; and Samuel M'Call, Esq; Major of the Regiment; which soon after began to March through the Town to the Court-House, in Market-Street, where it was drawn up in three Divisions, and after three general Discharges from each Division, separated, each Captain leading off his own Company. The whole was performed with the greatest Order and Regularity, and without occasioning the least Disturbance. Some of the Companies exceed 100 Men each, and most of them fall but little short of that

4. Mecom, Humphreys, and later printings add a sentence at this point: "Without Industry and Frugality nothing will do, and with them everything."
5. See above, p. 225.

Number. On the same Day the Kingsess Company met at Jenkins's Ferry, and chose their Officers. Several other Companies of Associators in the neighbouring Towns met also; but the Accounts of their Elections are not yet come to hand.

Order of the several Companies, determined by Lot, with the Names of the Officers, viz.

Number I.

Charles Willing, Captain; Atwood Shute, Lieutenant; James Claypole, Ensign.

Number II.

Thomas Bond, Captain; Richard Farmer, Lieutenant; Plunket Fleeson, Ensign.

Number III.

John Inglis, Captain; Lyn-Ford Lardner, Lieutenant; Thomas Lawrence, jun. Ensign.

Number IV.

James Polegreen, Captain; William Bradford, Lieutenant; William Bingham, Ensign.

Number V.

Peacock Bigger, Captain; Joseph Redman, Lieutenant; Joseph Ward, Ensign.

Number VI.

Thomas Bourne, Captain; Robert Owen, Lieutenant; Peter Etter, Ensign.

Number VII.

William Cuzzins, Captain; George Spafford, Lieutenant; Abraham Mason, Ensign.

Number VIII.

Septimus Robinson, Captain; William Clemm, Lieutenant; William Rush, Ensign.

Number IX.

James Coultas, Captain; George Gray, jun. Lieutenant; Abraham Jones, Ensign.

Number X.

John Ross, Captain; Richard Swan, Lieutenant; Philip Benezet, Ensign.

Number XI.

Richard Nixon, Captain; Richard Renshaw, Lieutenant; Francis Garrigues, Ensign. [January 5]

Yesterday the Mayor and Common-Council of this City met, and agreed, for the Encouragement of the Lottery, and promoting the PUBLICK BENEFIT design'd by it, to take 2000 of the remaining Tickets; so that there are now but a few left. 'Tis observable, that the late Lotteries in New-England and New-York, have taken more *Months* to fill than this has *Weeks;* it being but 7 Weeks since the first Tickets were ready to sell, tho' the Season has been so severe, as almost to cut off the Communication with the Country and neighbouring Provinces; and were it not that no Return is yet made of some Tickets sent for Sale to distant Places, the Drawing might immediately proceed.[6]　　　　　　　　　　[January 19]

Plank for the Platforms, and all other Materials, are preparing with all Diligence, for erecting strong BATTERIES on the River below this Town; and such is the *Zeal* and *Industry* of all concern'd, that 'tis not doubted they will be in good Condition very early in the Spring.[7]　　　　　　　　　　[January 19]

We learn from different Parts of the Country, that the ASSOCIA-TION goes on with great Success, notwithstanding the Season. If there are any Quantities of Small Arms to spare in the neighbouring Governments, they would meet here with a ready Market.
　　　　　　　　　　[January 19]

Preparations are making to begin the Drawing of the Lottery on Monday next. The Managers having no Tickets left, and the Demand still continuing, the Corporation continue to spare of the Number they bought, which may be had at the Post-Office till Saturday next.[8]　　　　　　　　　　[February 2]

The greatest Part of the Prize Money in the late Lottery being now paid, the Managers have agreed to give Attendance for Payment of the Remainder on Wednesdays and Saturdays only, from Ten to Twelve in the Morning, and from Three to Five in the Afternoon, at the House of William Allen, Esq; where also all concerned may see and inspect the Books.　　　　　[March 1]

It being proposed to erect at least two good Batteries on the River for the Defence of this City, the Managers of the Lottery,

6. See above, p. 220.　　　7. See above, p. 222.　　　8. See above, p. 221.

with their Assistants, intend to meet on Monday next, to determine the Places where to fix them, and to consider and conclude on several other Matters relating to the immediate beginning and carrying on the Work, &c. in all which they would be glad to receive the Advice of those that have Judgment or Experience in such Affairs, who are therefore desired to reduce their Sentiments to Writing, with their Reasons, and communicate them to the Managers for their Consideration at the said Meeting.

[March 1]

[ADVERTISEMENT] A Parcel of good Muskets, all well fitted with Bayonets, Belts and Cartouch-Boxes, and Buff Slings to cast over the Shoulder, very useful to such as have Occasion to ride with their Arms; To be sold by B. FRANKLIN.   [March 8]

The Field Officers of the Associated Regiment of this City, hereby give Notice, That said Regiment is to meet on Easter-Tuesday, the 12th of April next, at 10 o'Clock in the Forenoon: On Tuesday, the 24th of May: In August, on the Day agreed upon in the Articles of Association: And on Tuesday, the 4th of October next. And that if the Weather proves bad or rainy on any of these Days, then they are to meet on the very next fair Day following.

[March 29]

Tuesday last near 1000 Associators of this City were under Arms, and review'd by their Honours the President and Council in the Field; from whence they march'd into Town, drew up in Market-street, fired three general Vollies, and then separated, each Captain leading off his own Company to its respective Ward. The Appearance they made, the Regularity with which they perform'd their Exercise, and the good Order observ'd throughout the whole, gave great Satisfaction to the Spectators, who were very numerous, and to the City in general. While they were in the Field, Col. Taylor represented to them in a short Speech, that several of the Country Regiments had generously express'd their Readiness to come to the Defence of this City on Occasion; but as no Provision was made by the Publick for their Subsistence in such Cases, and it would not be reasonable to expect they should be among us at their own Expence, therefore it was propos'd that every Housholder of the City-Associators, would freely entertain three or four, or as many as his House would accommodate of his Country

Brethren, till the threaten'd Danger should be over, and that their Horses should be well provided for *gratis*. The Proposal was universally approv'd of and agreed to, and the general Assent of the whole declar'd by three hearty and unanimous Huzza's.[9]

[April 16]

The Cannon which have been so kindly lent us by the Government of N. York, are all deliver'd at Trenton on this River, and expected in Town in a few Days. [April 16]

On a Review made last Week of the Cannon lying on the several Wharves of this City, there were found to be near 70 of different Sizes, fit for Service on Occasion. And Committees being appointed by the Managers of the Lottery to erect Fascine Batteries on the Wharves that are best situated for that Purpose, a Number of the Guns were immediately removed and distributed in the most proper Places, and such Provision made for erecting those Batteries, that they may be compleated at an Hour's Warning.

The Grand Battery at Wicacoa below this Town is also near finished, and 'tis thought will be ready the Beginning of next Week to receive the heavy Cannon borrowed from N. York.[1]

Last Monday Morning was begun, and on Tuesday Evening compleatly finished, a Battery of 13 fine Guns, under Society Hill, on the Wharff of William Atwood, Esq; our present Mayor; the Breastwork is 8 or 10 Foot thick, compos'd of Timber and Plank fill'd in with Earth rammed down. The Building of the Breastwork and Merlons, laying the Platform, &c. was done by a Number of the House-Carpenters of this City, who voluntarily and generously offered their Labour *gratis*, and perform'd the Work with the greatest Alacrity and surprizing Dispatch. [April 28]

The Field Officers of the Associated Regiment of this City, hereby give Notice, that Tuesday next is the Day appointed for the general Review of said Regiment; that therefore the respective Companies are desired to meet at their Captain's Quarters precisely at 3 o'Clock in the Afternoon, so as to march from thence, and be in the Field (the same they were review'd in last general Muster) exactly at Four: And whereas last Review-day, several of

9. See above, p. 285.   1. See illustration, facing p. 222 above.

the Companies were a long Time in the Field before the others came, which was very fatiguing to them; 'tis therefore desir'd and expected, that all the Companies will be punctual, as to the Time of being on the Ground, so that they may not wait for one another.
[May 19]

Sunday last arrived here the *Otter* man of war, Capt. Ballet, in 7 weeks from Portsmouth, who is stationed here for the protection of our trade; so that we have reason to hope (particularly from the character of the Commander) that our coast will soon be clear'd of the privateers now infesting it. Captain Ballet came out with the Virginia fleet, under convoy of the *Hector* man of war, but parted with them about six hundred leagues off. In his passage, about 300 leagues off, he met, and had a smart engagement with, a very large ship for 4 hours, and would have carried her had not the Night come on. He had one of his hands killed, and seven or eight wounded.[2]
[May 26]

Tuesday last Col. Taylor's regiment of associators in this city, consisting of eleven companies, was under arms, and review'd by their honours the President and Council, in the field. Strangers who were present agree, that the progress this regiment has made in military discipline in so short a time, was truly extraordinary.
[May 26]

Last night there was a report in town that the enemy's privateers were as high up as Bomba-Hook, and had taken two shallops there.
[May 26]

Philadelphia, May 30. 1748.
Notice is hereby given, that it has been thought necessary, for His Majesty's Service, and the Safety of this City, that no Ship, Vessel or Boat, be permitted to pass the Lower Battery, from the Hour of Eight in the Evening, to Four in the Morning, until the Master of such Vessel have sent his Boat on Shore, or have otherwise made himself known to the Garrison; for which Purpose Orders have been issued to the commanding Officer of the Batteries.
By Order of the Honourable the President and Council,
RICHARD PETERS, Secretary.[3]
[June 2]

2. See *Pa. Col. Recs.*, V, 241–3.   3. *Ibid.*, 260.

On Thursday last an express arrived from Elsingborough, in Salem county, to acquaint this government, that one George Proctor had swam ashore there the night before, from a brigt. then lying off in the river, and deposed before the magistrates, that she was a Spanish privateer from the Havanna, mounting 14 carriage guns, 6 and 4 pounders, with 160 men.[4]   [June 2]

Soon after it was known that the enemies privateers were in our River, a subscription was proposed to raise a sum of money, either by way of gift, or of advance to the government, in expectation of being repay'd by the assembly when they should next meet, in order to fit out immediately one or more armed vessels, to clear the bay and coast, and protect our trade: But it seems to be at a stand at present; the little thanks and great censure those met with, who generously equipp'd the *Warren* for the same purpose last year, together with the consideration of the last message from the assembly, having very much discouraged it.[5] All foreign trade is now at a stand, and the port as much shut up, as if the river was frozen. 'Tis tho't the damage already done by the enemy is many times greater than the expence that might have been sufficient, with God's blessing, to prevent it. But that which would have been easy for ALL to bear, is really too hard for a FEW.   [June 2]

The Associators mount guard every night in their turns, at the Great Battery, near this city. In case of any alarm in the night, all well disposed persons are desired to place candles in their lower windows and doors, for the more convenient marching of the militia and other well-affected persons who may join them.
[June 2]

On Friday last five Companies of Col. Jones's Regiment of Associators were reviewed at Germantown. They made a very handsome Appearance, went thro' their Exercise and performed their Firings exceedingly well, and had great Applause from the most

4. *Ibid.*, 252–4.
5. See above, p. 215. The Assembly declared, a little testily, May 21, 1748, that it was impractical to send a vessel in pursuit of the enemy as the latter "very probably would be out of reach before any Vessel cou'd get thither," and that to keep a guard ship at the Capes would be too expensive. *Pa. Col. Recs.*, V, 237–8.

judicious Spectators. We hear that four other Companies of the same Regiment were review'd on Monday following at Norrinton, and performed likewise to general Satisfaction. A very commendable Sobriety and good Order has hitherto been observed at those Meetings of the Associators, which it is hoped will always continue. [June 9]

Philadelphia, June 9. 1748.
Now fitting out for a cruizing voyage against his majesty's enemies, and will sail in 14 days, The Privateer Brigt. TREMBLEUR, Abraham Matthews, Commander, To carry 16 carriage guns, 6 pounders, and 16 swivels, with 120 men.
All gentlemen sailors, and others, inclined to enter on board said privateer, may repair to the commander aforesaid, or to the sign of the Trembleur, in Water-street, where the articles are to be seen and signed by those who are willing to go the Cruize.[6] [June 9]

Yesterday His Majesty's Ship *Otter,* Captain Ballet, fell down on a Cruize. [June 23]

We hear that Captain Ballet, Commander of his Majesty's Ship *Otter,* has taken a French Flag of Truce at our Capes, bound in here; but had before been taken, and carried into Providence, where most of her Cargoe was condemned, and taken out of her: And also Capt. Hogg, belonging to this Place, supposed to have been trading with the Spaniards; and has carried them both into Virginia, in order to be tried. [July 14]

In Pursuance of his Majesty's Command, signified to the Honourable the President and Council of this Province, by his grace the Duke of Bedford, his Majesty's Proclamation for a Cessation of Arms was published here Wednesday last.[7] [August 18]

Notice is hereby given, that Monday the 29th of this Inst. August, is appointed for a General Review of the City Regiment, which is to be at the usual Place of Parade, at 9 o'Clock in the Forenoon; at which Time the Artillery Company are to be at their respective Posts, at the GRAND BATTERY. [August 18]

6. *Ibid.,* 249.   7. *Ibid.,* 330-2.

The new large Cannon that lately arrived from England, purchased by the Managers of the Lottery, being mounted on the Great Battery; on Monday last the Associators of this City met under Arms, and march'd thither; where they were saluted with One and Twenty Guns, and nam'd the Battery, THE ASSOCIATION.

[September 1]

From William Strahan: Power of Attorney

MS form with MS insertions in blanks: American Philosophical Society

James Read (see above, p. 39 n), Franklin's neighbor and rival bookseller, in May received from the London printer William Strahan, whom he knew, a consignment of books valued at £131 16s. 4d. When three years passed without payment, Strahan gave Franklin power of attorney to collect the debt. "I have hitherto waited with Patience," he explained to Read, "but you cannot expect that my Patience will hold out forever." Franklin got Read's bond acknowledging the debt, but did not press him hard. Strahan, still receiving no money, sent three more agents, including his former journeyman David Hall, to dun Read; they all failed. Finally in 1771, Thomas Wharton, an attorney appointed by Strahan, frightened Read into sending his creditor £60, but, apparently considering Strahan oppressive, Read appealed to Franklin, who gave him "the most friendly advice" he could, which was "to begin paying the Debt immediately." Wharton obtained a new bond from Read, but the American Revolution prevented further action. Strahan died in 1784 and Read in 1793—the balance of the debt still unpaid. The details of this affair are pleasantly related by J. Bennett Nolan, *Printer Strahan's Book Account: A Colonial Controversy* (Reading, Pa., 1939).

[September 2, 1748]

KNOW all men by these presents that I *William Strahan of London, Stationer* have made ordained constituted and appointed and by these presents do make ordain constitute and appoint *Benjamin Franklin of Philadelphia, Postmaster* my true and lawful Attorney for me and in my name and for *my* use to ask Demand and receive of *James Read Attorney at Law at Philadelphia all Sums, as well Principal as Interest due to me from him* and upon non payment thereof the said *Benjamin Franklin, his* Executors or Administrators for me and in my name to sue arrest imprison implead and prosecute for the same and upon such suit to proceed to Judgment and Execution. And thereupon the said *James Read*, *his* Executors and Administrators in prison to hold and keep until payment thereof be made with all costs and Damages sustained and to be sustained by occasion of the detaining of the same and upon payment thereof the said *Benjamin Franklin his* Executors and Administrators forth of prison to discharge. And Acquitances for the same or any part thereof for me and in my name to make seal and deliver. And also to do perform and execute all and every other lawfull and reasonable Acts and things whatsoever both for obtaining and discharging of the same as shall be needfull to be done. Giving and by these presents granting unto my said Attorney my full and absolute power in the premisses Ratifying and holding firm all and whatsoever my said Attorney shall lawfully do or cause to be done in or about the premisses by vertue of these presents.

IN WITNESS whereof I have hereunto set my hand and seal the *Second* day of *September* in the *twenty Second* Year of the reign of Our Sovereign Lord *George the Second* by the Grace of God of Great Britain France and Ireland King Defender of the faith and in the Year of our Lord One Thousand Seven Hundred and *forty eight.* WILL: STRAHAN [Seal]

SEALED and delivered (being first
    duly Stampt) in the presence of
    JAMES TROTTER
    JOHN WALLACE

Endorsed: Mr Strahan's Powr. Atty

To Cadwallader Colden   ALS: New-York Historical Society

Sir   Philada. Sept. 29. 1748
    I received your Favour of the 12th Inst.[8] which gave me the greater Pleasure, as 'twas so long since I had heard from you. I

8. Not found.

congratulate you on your Return to your beloved Retirement: I too am taking the proper Measures for obtaining Leisure to enjoy Life and my Friends more than heretofore, having put my Printing house under the Care of my Partner David Hall, absolutely left off Bookselling, and remov'd to a more quiet Part of the Town,[9] where I am settling my old Accounts and hope soon to be quite a Master of my own Time, and no longer (as the Song has it) *at every one's Call but my own.* If Health continues, I hope to be able in another Year to visit the most distant Friend I have, without Inconvenience. With the same Views I have refus'd engaging further in publick Affairs; The Share I had in the late Association, &c. having given me a little present Run of Popularity, there was a pretty general Intention of chusing me a Representative for the City at the next Election of Assemblymen; but I have desired all my Friends who spoke to me about it, to discourage it, declaring that I should not serve if chosen. Thus you see I am in a fair Way of having no other Tasks than such as I shall like to give my self, and of enjoying what I look upon as a great Happiness, Leisure to read, study, make Experiments, and converse at large with such ingenious and worthy Men as are pleas'd to honour me with their Friendship or Acquaintance, on such Points as may produce something for the common Benefit of Mankind, uninterrupted by the little Cares and Fatigues of Business. Among other Pleasures I promise my self, that of Corresponding more frequently and fully with Dr. Colden is none of the least; I shall only wish that what must be so agreable to me, may not prove troublesome to you.

I thank you for your kind recommending of me to Mr. Osborne.[1] Mr. Read would readily have put the Books into my Hands, but it being now out of my Way to dispose of them, I propos'd to Mr. Hall the Taking them into his Shop; but he having look'd over the Invoice, says they are charg'd so extravagantly high, that he cannot sell them for any Profit to himself, without

9. At the northwest corner of Second and Sassafras (or Race) Streets. *Pa. Gaʒ.,* May 31, 1750.

1. Thomas Osborne of London printed Colden's *History of the Five Indian Nations* and sent 50 copies to Deborah Franklin's relative James Read to sell in Philadelphia. See above, p. 170 n. The books that Hall would not sell are not identified. See also above, p. 175, and below, p. 322.

hurting the Character of his Shop: He will however, at my Request, take the Indian Histories and put them on Sale; but the rest of the Cargo must lie I believe for Mr. Osborne's further Orders: I shall write to him by our next Vessels.

I am glad you have had an Opportunity of gaining the Friendship of Govr. Shirley, with whom tho' I have not the honour of being particularly acquainted, I take him to be a wise, good and worthy Man.[2] He is now a Fellow-Sufferer with you, in being made the Subject of some public virulent and senseless Libels: I hope they give him as little Pain.[3]

Mr. Bartram continues well. Here is a Swedish Gentleman, a Professor of Botany, lately arriv'd,[4] and I suppose will soon be your Way, as he intends for Canada. Mr. Collinson and Dr. Mitchel recommend him to me as a very ingenious Man: Perhaps the enclos'd (left at the Post Office for you)[5] may be from him. I have not seen him since the first Day he came. I deliver'd yours

2. William Shirley (1694–1771), London barrister, emigrated to Boston in 1731. After holding various public offices in New England, he was governor of Massachusetts, 1741–57. Appointed major general in 1755, he acted as commander in chief of the British forces in North America from Braddock's death that summer until the arrival of James Abercromby the following June. He was governor of the Bahamas, 1759–67. Charles H. Lincoln, ed., *Correspondence of William Shirley* (N.Y., 1912), I, xxi–xxxi; *DAB;* Amer. Hist. Assoc. *Report* for 1911 (Washington, 1913), I, 404, 469.

3. Colden had accompanied Governor Clinton of New York and Governor Shirley of Massachusetts to an Indian conference at Albany in July. Mutual liking and respect had developed between Colden and Shirley, and the latter urged Clinton to call Colden back into public life: he had withdrawn under the bitter attacks of Chief Justice DeLancey's party. For his defense of his conduct, see *Colden Paps.*, III, 433, and Alice M. Keys, *Cadwallader Colden* (N.Y., 1906), pp. 199–215. Some of the "senseless Libels" against Shirley were that he had profited personally in handling public funds and disposing of commissions in the army. A refutation of the charges is in Lincoln, ed., *Shirley Correspondence*, I, 457–60.

4. Peter Kalm (see above, p. 300 n.) landed at Philadelphia Sept. 4, but went immediately into the country to botanize. In the next few weeks he visited John Bartram frequently, at least once with the painter Gustavus Hesselius; was a guest of Peter Cock (or Kock) at the latter's country place near Germantown; and traveled among the Swedish settlements in New Jersey. Kalm *Travels*, I, 17, 114–24.

5. Probably Kalm's letter to Colden, dated Philadelphia, Sept. 29, enclosing a letter from Linnaeus and some pamphlets. It is printed in *Colden Paps.*, IV, 77–8.

to Mr. Evans;[6] and when I next see Mr. Bartram, shall acquaint him with what you say. I am, with great Esteem and Respect, Dear Sir Your most obliged humble Servant   B FRANKLIN

Addressed: To The honble Cadwalader Colden Esqr Coldengham   Free B FRANKLIN

To Peter Collinson

ALS: Pierpont Morgan Library

Sir   Philada. Oct. 18. 1748
I have receiv'd your several Favours of April 1. June 2. June 14 and Augt. 20, and some others,[7] with all the Books and Pamphlets you have sent at sundry Times for the Library Company: We wish it were in our Power to do you or any Friend of yours some Service in Return for your long-continued Kindness to us.

I am pleas'd to hear that my Electrical Experiments were acceptable to the Society, and shall be glad to see the Ingenious Mr. Watson's new Piece on that Subject, when he thinks fit to publish it.[8] Of late we have done but little here in that Way; but possibly may resume those Enquiries this coming Winter, as the approaching Peace gives us a Prospect of being more at Ease in our Minds: If any thing new arises among us, I shall not fail to communicate it to you.

Our Friend Bartram show'd me some Queries you sent him relating to the Country back of us.[9] My Son is just return'd from a Journey to Ohio with Conrad Weiser;[1] from their Journals, &c. he may collect Answers to most of them; if John has not done it by this Vessel, I will by the next.

6. Colden may have been providing information to Lewis Evans for his map of 1749. Evans to Colden, March 13, 1749, *Colden Paps.*, IV, 107–8.

7. Collinson's letters of April 1, June 2, and Aug. 20, not found; for his letter of June 14, see above, p. 300.

8. William Watson, *An Account of some Experiments made by some Gentlemen of the Royal Society for Discovering the Force of Electricity at a Distance* was published at London in November 1748. *Gent. Mag.*, XVIII (1748), 528.

9. Not found.

1. William Franklin accompanied the province interpreter Conrad Weiser to a conference with the Ohio Indians at Logstown, July–October 1748. Paul A. W. Wallace, *Conrad Weiser* (Phila., 1945), pp. 263–9. Weiser's journal is printed in *Pa. Col. Recs.*, V, 348–58.

Mr. Kalm has been much out of Town since his Arrival, and is now gone to New York.[2] I hear he proposes to Winter here; no Service I can do him shall be wanting; but hitherto we have but little Acquaintance.

The L. Company will shortly send you a Bill. I am, with great Esteem and Respect, Sir, Your most obliged humble Servant

B FRANKLIN

Mr. Collinson

To William Strahan

ALS: Pierpont Morgan Library

Dear Sir   Philada. Oct. 19. 1748

I receiv'd your Favour of April 25,[3] with the Maps, &c. I am glad the Polybius did not come,[4] and hope you will not have sent it when this reaches your Hands; it was intended for my Son, who was then in the Army, and seemed bent on a military Life; but as Peace cuts off his Prospect of Advancement in that Way, he will apply himself to other Business.[5] Enclos'd I send you his Certificate from the Governor of New York, by which he is entitled to £98 16s. 4d. Sterling, being his Pay; with a Letter of Attorney impowering you to receive it; I know not what the Deductions will be at the Pay Office; but desire you will give my Account Credit for the net Proceeds. I am in daily Expectation of a Bill from Virginia of £50 which I shall remit you towards the Ballance, and Mr. Hall will account with you for those Things you have sent me, that are put in his Invoice. Our Accounts agree, except that I have charg'd you £1 9s. 7d. for the Ainsworth[6] d[elivere]d James Read, the 6s. 7d. being the Proportion of Charges on that Book, and the Bill

2. Kalm set out for New York Oct. 16 (o.s.) and returned Oct. 25. Kalm, *Travels*, I, 115, 143.
3. Not found.
4. BF had ordered the maps and Polybius, Nov. 28, 1747. See above, p. 214.
5. William was an ensign of Pennsylvania troops stationed at Albany, 1747–48. See above, p. 89 n. The men were to be paid by the British government; the Pennsylvania Assembly therefore refused even to advance the sums due them. Parliament finally authorized payment in 1750. See above, p. 218, and below, p. 479.
6. Robert Ainsworth's Latin-English and English-Latin dictionary, entitled *Thesaurus linguae Latinae compendiarius* (2d edit., 1746).

on Geo. Rigge[7] my Account calls £15 7s. 11d., yours £15 7s. 1d.; which is but a small Variation; and I know not but yours may be right.

I have lately sent a Printing-house to Antigua, by a very sober, honest and diligent young Man, who has already (as I am inform'd by divers Hands) gain'd the Friendship of the principal People, and is like to get into good Business. This will open another Market for your Books if you think fit to use it; for I am persuaded, that if you shall send him a Parcel with any Quantity of Stationary he may write to you for, he will make you good and punctual Returns. His Name is Thomas Smith; he is the only Printer on that Island: had work'd with me here, and at my Printing-house in N York, 3 or 4 Years, and always behav'd extreamly well.[8]

Mr. Thos Osborne, Bookseller of London, is endeavouring to open a Correspondence in the Plantations for the Sale of his Books: He has accordingly sent several Parcels, 1 to Mr. Parker of N York, 1 to Mr. Read here, and one to Mr. Parks in Virginia. I have seen the Invoices to Parker and Read; and observe the Books to be very high charg'd, so that I believe they will not sell. I recommended Parker to you for Books, but he tells me he has wrote you several Letters, and in two of them sent a Guinea to purchase some small Things, but never receiv'd any Answer. Perhaps the Guineas made the Letters miscarry. He is a very honest punctual Man, and will be in the Way of selling a great many Books; I think you might find your Account in Writing to him. Mr. Read having left off Bookselling Osborne has wrote to me and desired me to take those Books into my Hands, proposing a

7. Not identified.

8. Thomas Smith (d. 1752) went to Antigua about April 1748, at which time he is charged (in BF's Ledger D) for skins, ink, paper, binding parchment, a barrel of limes, and a "Pot Sweetmeats." He began printing the *Antigua Gazette* at St. John's that summer. BF frequently reprinted extracts from it, 1748–51; and he offered for sale a dispensatory which Smith printed, 1750, *Medulla Medicinae Universae.* BF wrote (to Jane Mecom, Sept. 14, 1752), that Smith died prematurely, but was healthy until he "grew careless and got to sitting up late in Taverns." He installed his nephew Benjamin Mecom (C.17.3) as Smith's successor. Wilberforce Eames, "The Antigua Press and Benjamin Mecom, 1748–1765," Amer. Antiq. Soc. *Proc.*, n.s., XXXVIII (1928), 303–48.

Correspondence, &c. but I have declin'd it in a Letter per this Ship.

My Spouse will write to Mrs. Strahan, to whom my best Respects. By this time twelvemonth, if nothing extraordinary happens to prevent it, I hope to have the Pleasure of seeing you both in London; being, with great Esteem and Affection, Dear Sir, Your obliged Friend and Servant   B FRANKLIN

P.S. You will find Mr. Geo. Smith,[9] one of the Witnesses to the Power of Attorney at the Pensilvania Coffee House. He goes over in this Ship.

Mr. Strahan

To James Logan

MS not found; reprinted from Sparks, *Works*, VII, 37–8.

Sir,   Philadelphia, October 30, 1748

I received your favor of the 28th,[1] with the piece on the Generation of Plants, for which I thank you. Mr. Sandin, the Swedish missionary,[2] who gave me Wahlboom's Oration to send you, (as he passed through this town from New York, where he just arrived, to Racoon Creek, where he was to be settled,) I have never seen since. Mr. Kalm came to see me the day he arrived, and brought me letters from Mr. Collinson and Dr. Mitchell, both recommending him. I invited him to lodge at my house, and offered him any service in my power; but I never saw him afterwards till yesterday, when he told me that he had been much in the country, and at New York, since his arrival, but was now come to settle in town for the winter.[3] Today he dined with me; and, as I had re-

9. George Smith settled the estate of Cornelia Bradford, widow of the printer Andrew Bradford. Thomas, *Printing*, I, 244.

1. Not found.

2. See above, p. 282 n.

3. Peter Kalm (see above, p. 300 n) returned to Philadelphia from New York Oct. 25 (o.s.). In his journal covering the days after this visit with BF are several of his host's anecdotes and observations: evidence that land around Philadelphia was once under water, the report of a Boston ship captain on the inhabitants of northern Greenland, an experiment to prove that ants communicate, and an experiment of Josiah Franklin on the migratory instinct of herring. BF also showed him some New England asbestos and described

ceived yours in the morning, I took occasion to ask him if he had not yet seen Mr. Logan. He said, no; that he had once been out with his countryman, Mr. Kock,[4] proposing to wait on you as they returned; but it proved later in the evening than they had expected, and he thought a visit then would be unseasonable, but proposed soon to pay his respects to you. Possibly he might at that time have[5] the packet for you at Naglee's.[6] I did not ask him about that. Inquiring of him what was become of Mr. Sandin, he told me that soon after he got to Racoon Creek, he was taken with the fever and ague, which was followed by several other disorders, that constantly harassed him, and at length carried him off, just as Kalm arrived here, who, hearing that he was dangerously ill, hurried down to see him, but found him dead.

Sandin had a family with him, and, when here, was in haste to get to his settlement, but might intend to wait on you when he should come again to Philadelphia. Kalm, I suppose, might be in haste to see as much of the country as he could, and make his journey to New York, before cold weather came on. I mention these things so particularly, that you may see you have not been purposely avoided by both these gentlemen, as you seem to imagine. I did not let Kalm know that you had mentioned him to me in your letter. I shall write to Mr. Hugh Jones,[7] as you desire. I am, Sir, &c.   B. FRANKLIN

---

the purse he had given Sir Hans Sloane (see above, I, 54); and described two moose he had seen in Boston as a boy. They were a present for Queen Anne, and a kindly merchant paid the admission charge of 2d. for BF and a number of his schoolmates. Kalm, *Travels*, I, 106, 143, 154–61. Kalm wrote (*ibid.*, I, 17) that BF "was the first who took notice of me and introduced me to many of his friends. He gave me all necessary instruction and showed me kindness on many occasions."

4. Peter Cock (d. 1749), Philadelphia merchant, native of Sweden. He received Kalm with "extraordinary kindness," and did him "unusual favors" in his country place near Germantown. *Ibid.*, II, 625.

5. So in Sparks, but probably a misreading for "leave."

6. Probably the house of John Naglee (d. 1751) on the Germantown road, close to Stenton. Harry M. and Margaret B. Tinkcom and Grant M. Simon, *Historic Germantown*, APS *Memoirs*, XXXIX (1955), p. 34.

7. Rev. Hugh Jones (*c.* 1692–1760), rector of St. Stephen's Church, North Sassafras Parish in Bohemia Manor, Md., 1731–60. A graduate of Jesus College, Oxford, he was professor of natural philosophy at the College of William and Mary, 1717–21. A competent mathematician, he was on Mary-

To James Logan

MS not found; reprinted from extract in Sparks, *Works*, VII, 39–40.

[November 7, 1748]
I send you herewith the late Voyage for the Discovery of the Northwest Passage,[8] which I hope may afford you some entertainment. If you have the Journal of the French Academicians to Lapland,[9] I should be glad to see it.

From James Logan

Letterbook copy: Historical Society of Pennsylvania

My friend B F.   9br [November] 9th [1748]
I here return thee Hen: Ellis's Tract of his Voyage to Hudson's Bay,[1] which I have perused and I thank thee for the Loan of it. But I'm Sorry for the Loss of Sandin the Swedish Minister for they generally use to be a good Sort of People, their Ministers I

---

land's commission to settle the boundary dispute with Pennsylvania, 1732–33 (when he met Logan). *DAB*. His writings on measurement, "Natural Arithmetic," and the "Universal Georgian Calendar," were published as *The Pancronometer* (London, 1753). His *Present State of Virginia* (London, 1724) has been edited, with a detailed biographical introduction, by Richard L. Morton (Chapel Hill, N.C., 1956). Jones appears as one of BF's customers in Ledger D.

8. Probably [Charles Swaine], *An Account of a Voyage For the Discovery of a North-West Passage by Hudson's Streight*, which Collinson had sent BF June 14 (see above, p. 300).

9. Pierre Louis Moreau de Maupertuis, *La Figure de la Terre, déterminée par les Observations de Messieurs de Maupertuis, Clairaut, Camus, Le Monnier ... et de M. l'abbé Outhier* (Paris, 1738). Logan owned a copy of the English translation, *The Figure of the Earth* (London, 1738). The commission was appointed by the King of France. The first four were members of the Royal Academy of Sciences; Outhier was a correspondent of that body. The expedition also included Anders Celsius, professor of astronomy at Uppsala. Peter Kalm was surprised to find on his visit to Canada, 1749, that his expenses were paid by the French government because Sweden had allowed Maupertuis and his companions to have "all thing the wanted gratis, or for nothing." Kalm to Bartram, Aug. 6, 1749, Darlington, *Memorials*, p. 369.

1. Henry Ellis, *A Voyage to Hudson's Bay, by the Dobbs Galley and California*, published in London, August 1748. *Gent. Mag.*, XVIII (1748), 384.

mean. I know not what to think of Kalm.[2] I had a Letter from Linnaeus 10 or 11 years Since when he was in Holland, and another recommendation from the Same Linnaeus, in Gustav Wahlbom's Inauguration [dissertation] which as I have Said before, is called Sponsalia Plantarum and in this he mentions my little piece[3] that I Sent thee in my last 4 times, and yet carries not the matter as far as I have done which I admire at, And thereto I would willingly Speak with Kalm tho' I'm very Sensible Age and the Palsey have weakned me much, and the hesitation in my Speech has greatly disabled me.[4] But he Surprizes me if he comes on no other design than he told to P. Collinson. I would gladly See thee when thou canst make it Suit thy own time and if thou keeps not a horse my Son will furnish thee with one. I am with Sincere respect Thy real friend   J L

To Benj. Franklin

To William Strahan   ALS: Buffalo Historical Society

Dear Sir   Philada. Nov. 23. 1748
    I have just Time to acquaint you that yours per Cowie is this moment come to hand, with Mr. Read's Account &c.[5] I shall use

2. Logan suspected Kalm's purpose in traveling to Canada, where, as it turned out, he was well received, his patron Count Tessin, president of the Swedish Academy of Sciences, being a leader of the pro-French party in Sweden. Kalm, *Travels*, II, 681. Furthermore, Kalm's travels among the Swedish inhabitants along the Delaware may have seemed to Logan to have political implications. In any event, Kalm was casual, to say the least, in paying his respects to the American philosophers. Darlington, *Memorials*, pp. 371, 372.
    3. Logan's *Experimenta et meletemata de plantarum generatione* (Leyden, 1739), which reported his experiments in plant fertilization, using Indian corn. An English translation was published in London, 1747. Frederick B. Tolles, *James Logan and the Culture of Provincial America* (Boston, 1957), pp. 199–202.
    4. A stroke in 1740 had left Logan's right side partially paralyzed; he made some recovery, but by 1750 additional strokes had deprived him of speech. Tolles, *Logan*, p. 195; Albert C. Myers, ed. *Hannah Logan's Courtship* (Phila., 1904), p. 281. Kalm did not call on Logan until Feb. 28, 1750. See below, p. 469.
    5. On James Read's account, see above, p. 316.

my best Endeavours to get your Money, and am not without Hopes of Succeeding. I wrote you the 19th past,[6] and sent a Power with the first of the enclos'd Certificates, which I hope will get safe to hand. You may depend on having the Ballance of my Account in a few Months. I am, Sir, Your obliged humble Servant

B FRANKLIN

I have desired Dr. Mitchel to pay you 3 Guineas, being the Price of a Fireplace sent him for the D. of Argyle.[7]

Mr. Strahan

Philadelphia Common Council to James Hamilton and Reply

Printed in *The Pennsylvania Gazette*, December 1, 1748; also copy: MS Minutes, Philadelphia Common Council, The Free Library of Philadelphia.

Franklin was chosen a member of the Philadelphia Common Council, Oct. 4, 1748. Mayor Charles Willing proposed, Nov. 24, a congratulatory address to James Hamilton, newly appointed governor, upon his arrival in Pennsylvania; the Council agreed, and named Willing, William Allen, Benjamin Shoemaker, Thomas Hopkinson, and Franklin to draft the address. The committee laid the draft before the Council the next day; after some amendments, it was ordered engrossed and was presented to Hamilton.[8]

[November 25, 1748]

To the Honourable JAMES HAMILTON, Esq;[9] Lieutenant-Governor of the Province of Pennsylvania, and Counties of New-castle, Kent and Sussex, on Delaware;

6. See above, p. 321.

7. Archibald Campbell, third Duke of Argyll (1682–1761). He began building Inveraray Castle, 1745, but did not live to complete it. The Franklin stove was probably for one of his other houses. *DNB;* William Rhind, ed., *The Scottish Tourist* (9th edit., Edinburgh, [1845]), p. 158. Dr. John Mitchell was a correspondent of the duke, for whom he collected plants and seeds, and was his traveling companion in 1748–49. Darlington, *Memorials*, p. 366; see above, I, 415 n.

8. *Minutes of the Common Council of . . . Philadelphia, 1704 to 1776* (Phila., 1847), pp. 506–8.

9. James Hamilton (*c.* 1710–1783), son of Andrew Hamilton (see above, I, 333); educated in Philadelphia and England; succeeded his father as pro-

NOVEMBER 25, 1748

The humble Address of the Mayor and Commonalty of the City of Philadelphia, in Common Council assembled.

May it please Your Honour,

WE, the Mayor and Commonalty, beg Leave to congratulate You, in the sincerest Manner,[1] on Your happy return to Your Country, and Accession to the Government; Events that fill the Hearts of the People of all Ranks and Denominations with unfeigned Joy.

WE cannot but esteem it a peculiar Happiness to have a Gentleman appointed our Governor, who is so perfectly acquainted with our publick Affairs, and whose real Regard for the Welfare of this Province, and Affection for its Inhabitants, are so well known to us.

FROM the long Acquaintance we have had with Your amiable private Character, and the Benevolence of Your Disposition; and from our Experience of Your Integrity and Ability in the Discharge of the several publick Offices You have heretofore sustained among us; we assure ourselves that this City and Province will be happy under Your Administration; and that we shall always have the highest reason to be thankful to our Proprietors for an Appointment so favourable to the People.

Signed by Order of the Board,   CHARLES WILLING, Mayor

To which the Governor was pleased to make the following Answer.

Gentlemen,

I am extremely obliged to you for this early Mark of Respect; but more particularly so, for the favourable Opinion you are

thonotary of the Supreme Court, 1733; member of the Assembly, 1734–39; mayor of Philadelphia, 1745–46; provincial councilor, 1746. During a visit to England he was appointed governor and returned to Philadelphia, Nov. 23, 1748. His appointment was generally approved, but he resigned, 1754, after several years of frustrating conflict with the Assembly over defense, paper money, taxation of proprietary lands, and related issues. He served again as governor, 1759–63. A man of wealth and public spirit, he was trustee of the College and Academy and a patron of young Benjamin West. When the Philosophical and American Societies merged in 1769, Hamilton was president of the older body and was the unsuccessful candidate for the presidency of the newly constituted APS in opposition to BF. His sister Margaret was the wife of Chief Justice William Allen. *DAB; Pa. Col. Recs.*, V, 362–3.

1. "In the sincerest Manner" omitted from the copy in the MS Minutes of the Council.

pleased to entertain of my private Character: And altho', on the one Hand, I am conscious to myself how far short I fall of what your Partiality in Favour of a Countryman may have induced you to ascribe to me; yet, on the other, I am proud to say, that with regard to the sincere Affection I have for the Inhabitants of this City and Province, you have done me no more than Justice.

As I have lately had the Honour to be admitted to some Share of Confidence with your Proprietors, I can, with the greater Certainty, declare to you their real Regard for the People, and the great Satisfaction they take in the Welfare and Prosperity of this Province; and I am persuaded I cannot so effectually recommend myself to their future Favour, as by making use of the Powers they have been pleased to intrust me with, for the Benefit and Advantage of all those under my Government; which I beg you to assure yourselves it is my hearty Inclination to do.

To James Logan   ALS: Historical Society of Pennsylvania

Sir   Philada. Nov. 29. 1748
I received your Favour of the 9th Inst.[2] with the Voyage in Search of the N.W. Passage; I have been several Times since at Kalm's Lodgings, but never happen'd to meet with him, he being almost always in the Country. I have got the 2d Vol. of Dialogues on Education,[3] which your Son Jemmey told me you once had a Desire to see. If you have not since seen it, I will send it to you. I am, with great Respect, Sir Your most obliged humble Servant
                                                          B FRANKLIN
Endorsed: Benj: Franklin 9br. 29th 1748. Has received the voyage to Hudsons Bay of Kalm.

To James Read[4]   Draft: New York Public Library

Sir   [December 5, 1748]
'Tis some Time since I receiv'd a considerable Account against

2. See above, p. 325.
3. David Fordyce, *Dialogues concerning Education,* II (London, 1748). *DNB.*
4. Probably the draft letter which BF enclosed to Strahan, April 29, 1749 (below, p. 378). For the background, see that letter and p. 316 above.

you from England. An Unwillingness to give you Concern has hitherto prevented my mentioning it to you. By comparing the Moderation and long Forbearance towards you of Mr. Strahan, to whom you owe so much, with your Treatment of an old Friend in Distress, bred up with you under the same Roof, and who owes you so little, you may perceive how much you have misunderstood yourself. 'Tis with Regret I now acquaint you, that (even while you were talking to me in that lofty Strain yesterday concerning Mr. Grace,)[5] I had in my Pocket a Power of Attorney to recover of you £131 16s. 4d. Sterling, a Ballance long due. It will be your own Fault if it comes to be known, for I have mention'd it to nobody. And I now ask you how you would in your own Case like those pretty Pieces of Practice you so highly contended for, of Summoning a Day only before the Court, lest the Cause should be made up and Fees thereby prevented; and of carrying on a Suit privately against a Man in another County than that in which he lives and may every Day be found, getting a judgment by Default, and taking him by Surprize with an Execution when he happens to come where you have su'd him, &c. &c. I should be glad to have the Account against my Friend Grace, with all the little Charges you have so cunningly accumulated on it, that I may communicate it to him; and doubt not but he will immediately order you Payment. It appears not unlikely to me, that he may soon get thro' all his Difficulties, and as I know him good-natur'd and benevolent to a high Degree, so I believe he will be above resenting the Ill-Treatment he has receiv'd from some that are now so fond of insulting him, and from whom he might have expected better Things: But I think you would do well not to treat others in the same Manner, for Fortune's Wheel is often turning, and all are not alike forgiving. I request, as soon as it suits your Convenience, that you will take the proper Measures with Regard to Mr. Strahan's Account and am Your humble Servant B F.

Endorsed: Letter to J Read Dec. 5. 1748

5. BF characterized his good friend Robert Grace (above, I, 209) as "generous, lively and witty, a Lover of Punning and of his Friends." Grace and William Coleman put up the money for BF to set up his own business when his partnership with Meredith ended. Par. Text edit., pp. 154, 166–8. He lived well, both in his Philadelphia house and at his iron furnace at Coventry, Chester Co.

Poor Richard Improved, 1749

Poor Richard improved: Being an Almanack and Ephemeris ... for the Year of our Lord 1749. . . . By Richard Saunders, Philom. Philadelphia: Printed and Sold by B. Franklin, and D. Hall. (Yale University Library)

Kind Reader,

By way of preface (for *custom* says there must be a preface to every almanack) I present thee with an *essay* wrote by a celebrated *naturalist* of our country, which, if duly attended to, may be of more service to the publick, than 375 prefaces of my own writing: Take it as follows, viz. *An Essay for the improvement of estates, by raising a durable timber for fencing, and other uses.*[6]

By a diligent observation in our province, and several adjacent, I apprehend that timber will soon be very much destroyed, occasioned in part by the necessity that our farmers have to clear the greatest part of their land for tillage and pasture, and partly for fuel and fencing. The greatest quantity of our timber for fencing is oak, which is long in growing to maturity, and at best is but of short duration; therefore I believe it would be to our advantage to endeavour to raise some other kind of timber, that will grow faster, or come sooner to maturity, and continue longer before it decays.

The red cedar (a species of juniper) I take to be the most profitable tree for fencing, and several other uses, that we can raise in our country, considering how easily it may be raised from seed; its readiness to grow on most kinds of soil; its quick growth; the profits it will afford while it is arriving to maturity; and the long duration of the wood when grown to a proper size for the materials we want for our several occasions in husbandry or building. The way I propose at first to raise a nursery of them, is to dig a piece of ground, suppose two square rod, clear away the weeds and grass-roots, as you would prepare a bed for parsnips or onions; then sow half a gallon of good berries evenly upon it, and rake them well in; this may be done in the latter end of October, as soon as the berries are ripe; they generally come up the Spring after sowing. Take care to pull up the grass or weeds the first or second year. If the ground be poor, very little attendance will

6. Peter Kalm (*Travels*, 1, 303) noted in his journal under date of May 5, that John Bartram wrote this essay. Internal evidence supports the attribution.

331

serve, and the cedars will grow well enough. The Seeds may be easily gathered in great quantities on the beaches by the seashore; but when you have got a few bearing trees, the birds will carry the berries all over your plantation, which will come up, and grow finely; so that you may dig up as many as you please to plant, or leave as many as you think proper to grow where they came up, which will soonest come to maturity, if the soil is suitable: But the most danger is their being broke or molested with horn cattle, nothing else is more hurtful to them. I know no other tree that will grow so well on such different soils as this will; for upon our sandy beaches, which are nothing but beds of sand, they grow as thick as possible; from whence many thousand posts for fencing are brought into Pennsylvania and York governments; and I have seen, in a great miry swamp, upon a branch of Sasquehannah, great trees growing, near 18 inches diameter, 70 foot high, and very streight. And the inhabitants near the mountains, up Hudson's river, make great use of them for making large hovels or barracks to put their corn in before it is threshed. They will grow well in high gravelly or clay soil, in rich or poor, or even upon a rock, if there be but half a foot of sand or earth upon it. It is much to be valued for its quick growth from seed, the little sap, and its much durable heart, which it acquireth sooner than any tree that we can raise on common land. Indeed the mulberry and locust are of quick growth in very rich land, but not upon poor. A cedar tree, from the berry, will in eight years be fit for hoops, in ten for bean-poles, in twelve for hop-poles, in sixteen or eighteen for ladders, and in twenty will be big enough to make three posts, besides a good stake at top; with this care, that they are not removed, bruised or broken, which very much retards their growth, makes them deformed, and spoils their streight pyramidal growth; which form this tree naturally inclines to grow in more than most trees, and in which we must enjoy the greatest profit from it. And we may in this assist nature by art, in carefully trimming them every three or four years, cutting the branches close and smooth off to the bole; so that these wounds may soon be closed, which will make the tree smooth on the surface, and the grain strait, which will be of great service, if we make boards or rails of them, which will be much the better for being clear of knots: But if we let this tree grow without trimming, as it naturally shoots out branches on

332

all sides in all the degrees of its growth, the lower ones die, but do not rot off near the bole, as in other trees; so that the sap can't close over them, but grows round, which makes the grain crooked, and instead of being streight and even, it appears as if drove full of spikes, as we may observe by the posts (especially the second cut) that are brought from the sea-coast, where they grow naturally, tho' not so large or tall as these beyond our northern mountains. It is now generally used for posts, which, as I am informed, will last fifty years, or longer: so that one sett of these posts about a plantation, would last a mature age, which would be of great advantage to farmers, and at the first cost, with white cedar or chestnut rails, would be no dearer than a quick-set hedge and ditch, which must be often repaired; this wood would be of extraordinary service in building, for sills for barns, stables and out-houses, and for door and window cases, and boards for floors, I suppose one of the best of woods, as not being subject to swell with moisture, or shrink with dryness; whether or not would it be very good to make large cisterns for the maltsters to steep their barley in, and for the brewers for coolers? I have seen sloops abuilding at Albany of this wood; indeed the bottom, as I remember, was made of oak; for as the river there is shallow, and the vessels often strike upon sand or gravel, which oak, as being a stronger wood, is better able to bear such a shock than cedar, which is more tender; yet notwithstanding the Bermudians build fine durable vessels thereof; and I have seen cedar-trees growing in Pennsylvania large enough to make wider planks than any I have seen in a Bermuda built vessel. I believe it would make curious lasting boats, which would swim light, row well, and want but little repair for many years. I don't doubt but my countrymen will think, if not say, What signifies telling us of such great advantages which we can't obtain? We don't know how to get either hoop or bean-poles of cedar, much less trees for house or ship-building: But I am of opinion, that with care, ingenuity and industry, we may make the very raising of them to a proper magnitude (exclusive of the value of them when cut down) to be easy, ornamental and profitable.

And first, I think it is easy to raise great numbers of them after this manner: Dig them out of the nursery when three or four years old, or about the plantation, as I mentioned before; and if you have an old worn-out field, which many of our country farmers either

333

already have, or I am apt to think soon will have, a field of ten acres, which contains 1600 square perches, will hold as many trees; for a square perch is sufficient room for each tree to stand in, while they are of a middle growth; these trees thus planted in rows, when grown eight or ten foot high, which they will in five years after planting, will put forth their fragrant male blossoms; and the females will begin to produce their aromatick berries, which to behold in upright and regular rows, will be very ornamental. And now some or other of them will yearly want trimming, as I mentioned before, to make a smooth strait-grained bole; the branches thus cut, will make withes, poles, stakes, and furnish brush for dry hedges, and at last fuel for the fire. And if they stand too close, you may cut every other one down for the several occasions mentioned before. When they have been thus order'd for twenty years, I believe one tree will make seven posts, and a rail or pole at top; and in forty or fifty years will make good boards for floors, or planks for naval uses. I have a tree in an old field, which hath stood about eighteen years, that would now make seven good posts.

Note, A field thus planted, will yield good pasture while the trees are growing; for either grass or corn will grow very well near the cedars (but oaks and hickories are very destructive to both, as the walnut is to most fruit-trees) and when cut down will be fresh land for tillage. But the horn-cattle must be kept out until the trees are as thick as one's wrist, else they will break them to pieces with their horns; but horses and sheep may go in when you please.

There is another method I would propose, which I believe may be altogether as profitable; that is, To plant them close to all the fences belonging to our plantations; whereby we may not only preserve all our fields for tillage, but while they grow, they may support our fences from blowing down. They must be planted close to the fence, if planted young, and trimmed near the top every year, until they are out of the reach of the cattle, else they will break them with their horns. They may be planted one to every pannel, or three to two rod. Then supposing a field of ten acres will take 160 rod of fence to inclose it, you may plant it round with 240 trees, at one to a pannel of fence. Supposing a farmer hath 150 acres within fence, divided into fields of ten acres; but very likely he may have some fields above ten, and some under, and allowing for several partition fences; I will suppose he may plant by all the fences about his plantation 2400 trees; so that if he plants every year 100 trees, he may after 24 years cut down every year 100 successively; which, allowing every tree to yield eight posts, every post to fetch one shilling, which they will now readily do (and hereafter may be more) which amounts to forty pounds; a fine yearly profit, considering we lose so little ground from tillage, and the trouble and expence of raising them is but little, and the profits so great, that I believe we can't generally fall into a method that will afford the farmer more profit with less expence, and more sure to hit. If we should fall into this method, it will be necessary, that two or three years before we cut a parcel down, we plant a young one between every one that we intend to fall; so that we may always have the same number of growing trees. One inconveniency attending planting them too close to the fence is, that the wind forcibly blowing the young tree to and fro, is apt to rub the bark off next the fence; but when they are grown pretty large, they stand too stiff to be moved by any common blast of wind, and will support the fence. *Vale et fruere.*

JANUARY. *XI Month.*

Advice to Youth.

First, Let the Fear of HIM who form'd thy Frame,
Whose Hand sustain'd thee e'er thou hadst a Name,
Who brought thee into Birth, with Pow'r of Thought
Receptive of immortal Good, be wrought
Deep in thy Soul. His, not thy own, thou art;
To him resign the Empire of thy Heart.
His Will, thy Law; His Service, thy Employ;
His Frown, thy Dread, his Smile be all thy Joy.

Wealth and Content are not always Bed-fellows.

Wise Men learn by others harms; Fools by their own.

On the 7th of this month 1692 died Robert Boyle, Esq; one of the greatest philosophers the last age produced. He first brought the machine called an *Airpump*, into use; by which many of the surprizing properties of that wonderful element were discovered and demonstrated. His knowledge of natural history, and skill in

335

chymistry, were very great and extensive; and his piety inferior to neither.

> ——BOYLE, whose pious search
> Amid the dark recesses of his works
> The great CREATOR sought:—— Thomson.[7]

is therefore an instance, that tho' *Ignorance* may in some be the *Mother of Devotion*, yet true learning and exalted piety are by no means inconsistent.

When we read in antient history of the speeches made by generals to very numerous armies, we sometimes wonder how they could be well heard; but supposing the men got together so close, that each took up no more ground than two foot in breadth, and one in depth, 45000 might stand in a space that was but 100 yards square, and 21780 on a single acre of ground. There are many voices that may be heard at 100 yards distance.[8]

FEBRUARY. *XII Month.*

> Wak'd by the Call of Morn, on early Knee,
> Ere the World thrust between thy God and thee,
> Let thy pure Oraisons, ascending, gain
> His Ear, and Succour of his Grace obtain,
> In Wants, in Toils, in Perils of the Day,
> And strong Temptations that beset thy Way.
> Thy best Resolves then in his Strength renew
> To walk in Virtue's Paths, and Vice eschew.

The end of Passion is the beginning of Repentance.

Words may shew a man's Wit, but *Actions* his Meaning.

On the 18th of this month, *anno* 1546 died that famous reformer, LUTHER: who struck the great blow to papal tyranny in Europe.

---

7. James Thomson, *The Seasons*. "Summer," 1555–7.
8. In his autobiography BF describes a similar calculation of the number of auditors George Whitefield might be able to reach at one time. After experimenting during a sermon preached from the Philadelphia Courthouse steps, he concluded "that he might well be heard by more than Thirty-Thousand." Par. Text edit., p. 272.

He was remarkably *temperate* in meat and drink, sometimes fasting four days together; and at other times, for many days eating only a little bread and a herring. Cicero says, *There was never any* great *man who was not an* industrious *man;*[9] to which may, perhaps, be added, *There was never any* industrious *man who was not a* temperate *man:* For intemperance in diet, abates the vigour and dulls the action both of mind and body.

Of Sound.

Mr. Flamstead, Dr. Halley and Mr. Derham, agree that sound moves 1142 feet in a second, which is one English mile in 4 seconds and 5 8ths; that it moves in the same time in every different state of the atmosphere; that winds hardly make any difference in its velocity; that a languid or loud sound moves with the same velocity; and that different kinds of sounds, as of bells, guns, &c. have the same velocity, and are equally swift in the beginning as end of their motion.[1]

March. *I Month.*

To Him intrust thy Slumbers, and prepare
The fragrant Incense of thy Ev'ning Prayer.
But first tread back the Day, with Search severe,
And Conscience, chiding or applauding, hear.
Review each Step; *Where, acting, did I err?*
Omitting, where? Guilt either Way infer.
Labour this Point, and while thy Frailties last,
Still let each following Day correct the last.

'Tis a well spent penny that saves a groat.

Many Foxes grow grey, but few grow good.

Presumption first blinds a Man, then sets him a running.

9. Not located. But see Busy-Body, No. 3 (above, I, 121): "If we were as industrious to become Good, as to make ourselves Great, we should become really Great by being Good, . . . and I pronounce it as certain, *that there was never yet a truly Great Man that was not at the same Time truly Virtuous.*"
1. John Flamsteed (1646–1719), Edmond Halley (1656–1742), and William Derham (1657–1735). *Phil. Trans.*, XXVI (1708), 2.

On the 13th of this month, 1741, the river Delaware became navigable again, having been fast froze up to that day, from the 19th of December in the preceding year. The longest and hardest winter remembred here.[2]

The earth according to Mr.Whiston, is 7970 miles in diameter,[3] which will make nigh 4000 miles[4] in circumference. It revolves about its axis in 23 hours and 56 minutes: It moves in the space of one hour 56,000 miles; and is 365 days 6 hours and 9 minutes revolving about the sun.

The nose of a lady here, is not delighted with perfumes that she understands are in Arabia. Fine musick in China gives no pleasure to the nicest ear in Pennsilvania. Nor does the most exquisite dish serv'd up in Japan, regale a luxurious palate in any other country. But the benevolent mind of a virtuous man, is pleas'd, when it is inform'd of good and generous actions, in what part of the world soever they are done.

APRIL. *II Month.*

LIFE is a shelvy Sea, the Passage fear,
And not without a skilful Pilot steer.
Distrust thy Youth, experienc'd Age implore,
And borrow all the Wisdom of Threescore.
But chief a Father's, Mother's Voice revere;
'Tis Love that chides, 'tis Love that counsels here.
Thrice happy is the Youth, whose pliant Mind
To all a Parent's Culture is resign'd.

A cold April,
The Barn will fill.

Content makes poor men rich; Discontent makes rich Men poor.

2. See above, II, 316, 320–1.
3. William Whiston, *A New Theory of the Earth* (3d edit., London, 1722), p. 36.
4. As first set in type the almanac gave the circumference of the earth erroneously as "nigh 4000 miles." The error was caught part way through the press run and the figure changed to "24000" in the rest of the edition. Copies of both states of the almanac survive. BF apologized for this and other misprints in the preface to *Poor Richard* for 1750. See below, p. 437.

338

Too much plenty makes Mouth dainty.

On the 7th of this month, 1626, died that *great little* man, Sir
FRANCIS BACON; *great* in his prodigious genius, parts and learning;
and *little,* in his servile compliances with a *little* court, and sub-
missive flattery of a *little* prince. Pope characterises him thus, in
one strong line;[5]

> If Parts allure thee, think how BACON shin'd,
> The wisest, brightest, meanest of mankind.

He is justly esteem'd the father of the modern experimental philosophy. And another poet treats him more favourably, ascribing his
blemishes to a wrong unfortunate choice of his way of Life;

> ————BACON, hapless in his choice,
> Unfit to stand the civil storm of state,
> And thro' the smooth barbarity of courts,
> With firm, but pliant virtue, forward still
> To urge his course. Him for the studious shade
> Kind nature form'd, deep, comprehensive, clear,
> Exact, and elegant; in one rich soul,
> PLATO, the STAGYRITE, and TULLY join'd.
> The great deliverer he! who from the gloom
> Of cloister'd monks, and jargon-teaching schools,
> Led forth the true Philosophy, there long
> Held in the magic chain of words and forms,
> And definitions void: He led her forth,
> Daughter of HEAV'N! that slow ascending still,
> Investigating sure the chain of things,
> With radiant finger points to HEAV'N again.[6]

MAY. *III Month.*

> O, well begun, Virtue's great Work pursue,
> Passions at first we may with Ease subdue;
> But if neglected, unrestrain'd too long,
> Prevailing in their Growth, by Habit strong,
> They've wrapp'd[7] the Mind, have fix'd the stubborn Bent,
> And Force of Custom to wild Nature lent;

5. *Essay on Man,* Epistle IV, 281–2.
6. Thomson, *The Seasons.* "Summer," 1534–49.

Who then would set the crooked Tree aright,
As soon may wash the tawny Indian white.

If *Passion* drives, let *Reason* hold the Reins.

Neither trust, nor contend, nor lay wagers, nor lend;
And you'll have peace to your Lives end.

Drink does not drown *Care,* but waters it, and makes it grow faster.

Who dainties love, shall Beggars prove.

On the 18th of this Month, 1684, the superbe city of GENOA, was barbarously bombarded by the French, and a great part of its beautiful buildings reduced to rubbish; in chastisement of a small affront taken by the Gallic King.[8] The English, tho' lately in open war with that republic, have generously and humanely abstain'd from so cruel a proceeding.

On the 27th, anno 1564, died at Geneva that famous reformer, Mr. John Calvin, A man of equal *temperance* and *sobriety* with Luther, and perhaps yet greater *industry*. His lectures were yearly 186, his sermons yearly 286; he published besides every year some great volume in folio; to which add his constant employments, in governing the church, answering letters from all parts of the reformed world, from pastors, concerning doubts, or asking counsel, &c. &c. He ate little meat, and slept but very little; and as his whole time was filled up with useful action, he may be said to have *lived* long, tho' he died at 55 years of age; since *sleep* and *sloth* can hardly be called *living*.

JUNE. *IV Month.*

Industry's bounteous Hand may *Plenty* bring,
But wanting *frugal Care,* 'twill soon take wing.

7. In the preface to *Poor Richard* for 1750 Richard Saunders called attention to the printer's error in rendering "warp'd" as "wrapp'd" here, "to the utter demolishing of all Sense in those Lines, leaving nothing standing but the Rhime." See below, pp. 437–8.
8. Louis XIV demanded the surrender, with apologies, of galleys being built and armed in Genoa for Spain; following a refusal, the French fleet bombarded the city.

Small thy Supplies, and scanty in their Source,
'Twixt *Av'rice* and *Profusion* steer thy Course.
Av'rice is deaf to *Want*'s Heart-bursting Groan,
Profusion makes the Beggar's Rags thy own:
Close Fraud and Wrong from griping *Av'rice* grow,
From rash *Profusion* desp'rate Acts and Woe.

A Man has no more *Goods* than he gets Good by.

Welcome, Mischief, if thou comest alone.

Different Sects like different clocks, may be all near the matter,
tho' they don't quite agree.

On the 15th of this month, anno 1215, was *Magna Charta* sign'd
by King John, for declaring and establishing *English Liberty*.

It was wise counsel given to a young man, *Pitch upon that course
of life which is most excellent, and* CUSTOM *will make it the most
delightful*. But many pitch on no course of life at all, nor form any
scheme of living, by which to attain any valuable end; but wander
perpetually from one thing to another.

Hast thou not yet propos'd some certain end,
To which thy life, thy every act may tend?
Hast thou no mark at which to bend thy bow?
Or like a boy pursu'st the carrion crow
With pellets and with stones, from tree to tree,
A fruitless toil, and liv'st *extempore?*
Watch the disease in time: For when, within
The dropsy rages, and extends the skin,
In vain for helebore the patient cries,
And sees the doctor, but too late is wise:
Too late for cure, he proffers half his wealth;
Ten thousand doctors cannot give him health.
  Learn, wretches, learn the motions of the mind,
Why you were mad,[9] for what you were design'd,
And the great *moral end* of human kind.

9. The printer "somewhat niggardly of his Vowels," according to Richard
Saunders' preface for 1750, unhappily converted "made" into "mad," with a
curious effect upon the sense of the line. See below, p. 437.

Study thy self; what rank or what degree,
The wise creator has ordain'd for thee:
And all the offices of that estate,
Perform, and with thy prudence guide thy fate.

JULY. *V Month.*

Honour the softer Sex; with courteous Style,
And Gentleness of Manners, win their Smile;
Nor shun their virtuous Converse; but when Age
And Circumstance consent, thy Faith engage
To some discreet, well-natur'd chearful Fair,
One not too stately for the Houshold Care,
One form'd in Person and in Mind to please,
To season Life, and all its Labours ease.

If your head is wax, don't walk in the Sun.

Pretty and Witty,
Will wound if they hit ye.

Having been poor is no shame, but being ashamed of it, is.

On the 12th of this month, *anno* 1712, died Richard the son of Oliver Cromwell, aged 90 years. And on the 13th, *anno* 1713, was the treaty of Utrecht signed, ending a glorious war by an inglorious peace. *The Preliminaries of the new Peace, are copied from those of the old one; 'tis to be hoped the Peace itself will be better.*[1]

'Tis raging NOON, and, vertical, the Sun
Darts on the Head direct his forceful rays.
All-conqu'ring HEAT, oh intermit thy wrath!
And on my throbbing temples potent thus
Beam not so fierce! Incessant still you flow,
And still another fervent flood succeeds,
Pour'd on the head profuse. In vain I sigh,
And restless turn, and look around for night;
Night is far off; and hotter hours approach.

1. The preliminaries of the Peace of Aix-la-Chapelle were signed April 30, 1748, between Great Britain, the United Provinces, and France, the other powers acceding later.

342

Thrice happy he! that on the sunless side
Of a romantick mountain, forest-crown'd,
Beneath the whole collected shade reclines:
Or in the gelid caverns, woodbine-wrought,
And fresh bedew'd with ever-spouting streams,
Sits coolly calm; while all the world without
Unsatisfy'd and sick, tosses in noon,
Emblem instructive of the virtuous man,
Who keeps his temper'd mind serene and pure,
And every Passion aptly harmoniz'd,
Amid a jarring world, with vice enflam'd.[2]

AUGUST. *VI Month.*

Gaming, the Vice of Knaves and Fools, detest,
Miner of Time, of Substance and of Rest;
Which, in the Winning or the Losing Part,
Undoing or undone, will wring the Heart:
Undone, self-curs'd, thy Madness thou wilt rue;
Undoing, Curse of others will pursue
Thy hated Head. A Parent's, Houshold's Tear,
A Neighbour's Groan, and *Heav'n's* Displeasure fear.

'Tis a laudable Ambition, that aims at being better than his Neighbours.

The wise Man draws more Advantage from his Enemies, than the Fool from his Friends.

On the 17th of this month, *anno* 1657, died the famous Admiral Blake, who was a soldier as well as seaman, and by several examples taught Great-Britain, that her *wooden castles,* properly managed, were an over-match for the stone-walls of her enemies.[3]

PRIDE is said to be the *last* vice the good man gets clear of. 'Tis a meer Proteus, and disguises itself under all manner of ap-

2. Thomson, *The Seasons.* "Summer," 432–3, 451–68.
3. Robert Blake (1599–1657) served with distinction in the Parliamentary army during the Civil Wars, and in 1649 became one of the commanders of the fleet. Upon him devolved the chief responsibility for defending the English coast in the First Dutch War. *DNB.*

pearances, putting on sometimes even the mask of *humility*.[4] If some are proud of neatness and propriety of dress; others are equally so of despising it, and acting the perpetual sloven.

Morose is sunk with shame, whene'er surpriz'd
In linnen clean, or peruke undisguis'd.
No sublunary chance his vestments fear,
Valu'd, like leopards, as their spots appear.
A fam'd surtout he wears, which once was blue,
And his foot swims in a capacious shoe.
One day his wife (for who can wives reclaim)
Level'd her barbarous needle at his fame;
But open force was vain; by night she went,
And while he slept, surpriz'd the darling rent;
Where yawn'd the frize, is now become a doubt,
And glory at one entrance quite shut out.[5]

Numbers that are equal to the sum of all their aliquot parts, are called *perfect numbers;* such are 6, 28, 120, &c.[6] Of these numbers Mr. Stone, in his *Mathematical Dictionary*, says, there are but ten, between 1 and 1,000000,000000.[7] I shall leave my curious reader to find the rest.

SEPTEMBER. *VII Month.*

Wouldst thou extract the purest Sweet of Life,
Be nor Ally nor Principal in Strife.
A Mediator there, thy Balsam bring,
And lenify the Wound, and draw the Sting;

4. Writing in 1784 BF discussed the same point in his autobiography: "In reality there is perhaps no one of our natural Passions so hard to subdue as *Pride*. Disguise it, struggle with it, beat it down, stifle it, mortify it as much as one pleases, it is still alive, and will every now and then peep out and show itself. You will see it perhaps often in this History. For even if I could conceive that I had compleatly overcome it, I should probably by [be] proud of my Humility." Par. Text edit., p. 236.
5. Edward Young, *Love of Fame, the Universal Passion*, Satire II, 239–50.
6. The preface to *Poor Richard* for 1750 confesses to a mistake here: 120 is not a perfect number, the next after 28 being 496. See below, p. 437.
7. Edmund Stone, *A New Mathematical Dictionary* (2d edit., London, 1743), under "Perfect Numbers."

344

On *Hate* let *Kindness* her warm Embers throw,
    And mould into a Friend the melting Foe.
The weakest Foe boasts some revenging Pow'r;
The weakest Friend some serviceable Hour.

All would live long, but none would be old.

Declaiming against Pride, is not always a Sign of Humility.

Neglect kills Injuries, Revenge increases them.

On the 12th of this month, *anno* 1604, the town of Ostend was surrender'd to the Spaniards, after a siege of three years, in which they lost 70,000 men. In the two last sieges, it was taken in fewer weeks.[8]

It is the opinion of all the modern philosophers and mathematicians, that the planets are habitable worlds. If so, what sort of constitutions must those people have who live in the planet Mercury? where, says Sir Isaac Newton, the heat of the sun is seven times as great as it is with us; and would make our Water boil away. For the same person found by experiments, that an heat seven times as great as the heat of the sun in summer, is sufficient to set water a boiling.

In the machine at Derby in England for winding Italian silk, there are 26,586 wheels, 97,746 movements; 73,728 yards of silk wound every time the water-wheel goes round, which is three times every minute; 318,504,960 yards of silk in one day and night; and consequently 99,373,547,550 yards of silk in a year. One water-wheel communicates motion to all the rest of the wheels and movements, of which any one may be stopped separately, and independent of the rest. One *fire-engine* conveys air to every individual part of the machine, and one *regulator* governs the whole work.[9]

8. By the British in 1706 and the French in 1745.
9. Sir Thomas Lombe (1685–1739) introduced silk-throwing machinery into England; securing a patent in 1718, he set up a mill in Derby the following year. When the patent expired in 1732 Parliament refused to renew it, but granted Lombe a reward of £14,000. *DNB.* BF copied this description of Lombe's machine almost *verbatim* from *Gent. Mag.*, II (1732), 719.

OCTOBER. *VIII Month.*

In Converse be reserv'd, yet not morose,
In Season grave, in Season, too, jocose.
Shun Party-Wranglings, mix not in Debate
With Bigots in Religion or the State.
No Arms to Scandal or Detraction lend,
Abhor to wound, be fervent to defend.
Aspiring still to know, a Babbler scorn,
But watch where Wisdom opes her golden Horn.

9 Men in 10 are suicides.

Doing an Injury puts you below your Enemy; *Revenging* one makes you but *even* with him; *Forgiving* it sets you *above* him.

On the 14th of this month, 1722, was the present King of France crowned.

That famous specific for the cure of intermitting fevers, agues, &c. called the JESUITS BARK,[1] after it had been introduced into Europe with great applause, fell into a general disrepute (from some accidents attending the injudicious use of it) and was a long time neglected. At length one Talbot,[2] an illiterate Englishman, grew remarkable for curing those disorders speedily and effectually, by a medicine which no one knew; and his fame reaching France, Lewis XIV. sent for him to the Dauphin, who had long labour'd under an obstinate ague, that resisted all the medicines then used by the best physicians. When he arriv'd at Paris, and had seen the Dauphin, he boldly undertook his cure; but being first, for form-sake, examined by the King's physicians, they asked among other things, *What he judg'd the Dauphin's distemper to be?*

1. The bark of the cinchona tree (also called Peruvian bark), from which quinine is derived.
2. Sir Robert Tabor, or Talbor (1642?–1681), apothecary's apprentice and physician. After extended experimentation he improved the method of administering quinine by giving smaller doses at more frequent intervals, thereby reducing the dangerous after-effects of the customary procedures. He published the results of his research as *Pyretologia, a Rational Account of the Cause and Cure of Feavers* (London, 1672). For curing Charles II of a serious ague he was knighted in 1678 and soon after was sent by the King to France to treat the dauphin. *DNB.*

'Tis an ague, says he. *What is an ague?* said they, *give us a definition of it. Pray,* says he, *what is a definition? A definition,* says one, *is a clear, short, and proper description of a thing in words. Why then, gentlemen,* says he, *I will give you a definition of an ague; 'Tis a distemper—that I can cure, and you can't.* They were affronted, told the King that Talbot was an ignorant quack, and not fit to be trusted with the Dauphin's health. The King however was resolv'd to try him and the Dauphin was cured. That munificent prince, besides rewarding Talbot, bought his secret at a great price for the publick good, and it prov'd no other thing than the Bark disguis'd, and some rules for giving it, now well known to physicians. Thenceforward the bark grew into repute again, and is now in high esteem, daily gaining ground, and overcoming by the success attending it the prejudices that were once so universal against the use of it. 'Tis not unlikely, that some other valuable old medicines have been disused, from like causes, and may in time be advantageously revived again, to the benefit of mankind.

NOVEMBER. *IX Month.*

> In quest of Gain be just: A Conscience clear
> Is Lucre, more than Thousands in a Year;
> Treasure no Moth can touch, no Rust consume;
> Safe from the Knave, the Robber, and the Tomb.
> Unrighteous Gain is the curs'd Seed of Woe,
> Predestin'd to be reap'd by them who sow;
> A dreadful Harvest! when th'avenging Day
> Shall like a Tempest, sweep the Unjust away.

Most of the Learning in use, is of no great Use.

Great Good-nature, without Prudence, is a great Misfortune.

> Keep Conscience clear,
> Then never fear.

The 5th of this month, NOVEMBER, seems to be a lucky day to the English church and British liberty; for on that day 1604, the popish gunpowder treason was detected; and on the same day in 1688, our glorious deliverer from popery and slavery, King

347

WILLIAM, landed at Torbay. *Eighty-eight* seems likewise a lucky year; for in 1588 was the Spanish *Armada* defeated.

Numbers that are mutually equal to the Sum of each others aliquot Parts, are called *Amicable Numbers;* of these the first pair is 220 and 284; the second pair is 17296 and 18416. I shall be obliged to any of my Readers that will tell me the third pair.

DECEMBER. *X Month.*

> But not from Wrong alone thy Hand restrain,
> The *Appetite* of Gold demands the Rein.
> What Nature asks, what Decency requires,
> Be this the Bound that limits thy Desires:
> This, and the gen'rous godlike Pow'r to feed
> The Hungry, and to warm the Loins of *Need:*
> To dry *Misfortune*'s Tear, and scatter wide
> Thy Blessings, like the Nile's o'erflowing Tide.

A Man in a Passion rides a mad Horse.

> Reader farewel, all Happiness attend thee;
> May each New-Year, better and richer find thee.

On the 25th of this month, *anno* 1642, was born the great Sir ISAAC NEWTON, prince of the modern astronomers and philosophers. But what is all our little boasted knowledge, compar'd with that of the angels? If they see our actions, and are acquainted with our affairs, our whole body of science must appear to them as little better than ignorance; and the common herd of our learned men, scarce worth their notice. Now and then one of our very great philosophers, an Aristotle, or a Newton, may, perhaps, by his most refined speculations, afford them a little entertainment, as it seems a mimicking of their own sublime amusements. Hence Pope says of the latter,

> Superior beings, when of late they saw
> A mortal man unfold all nature's law,
> Admir'd such wisdom in a human shape,
> And shew'd a Newton, as we shew an ape.[3]

3. *Essay on Man*, Epistle II, 31–4.

348

On WINTER.[4]

'Tis done! dread Winter spreads his latest glooms,
And reigns tremendous o'er the conquer'd year!
How dead the vegetable kingdon lies!
How dumb the tuneful! Horror wide extends
His melancholy empire. Here fond man!
Behold thy pictur'd life! pass some few years,
Thy flowering Spring, thy Summer's ardent strength,
Thy sober Autumn fading into age,
And pale concluding Winter comes at last,
And shuts the scene. Ah! whither now are fled
Those dreams of greatness? Those unsolid hopes
Of happiness? Those longings after fame?
Those restless cares? those busy bustling days?
Those gay-spent festive nights? those veering thoughts,
Lost between good and ill, that shar'd thy life?
All now are vanish'd! VIRTUE sole survives,
Immortal, never-failing friend of man,
His guide to happiness on high.   Thompson.

How to get RICHES.

The Art of getting Riches consists very much in THRIFT. All Men are not equally qualified for getting Money, but it is in the Power of every one alike to practise this Virtue.

He that would be beforehand in the World, must be beforehand with his Business: It is not only ill Management, but discovers a slothful Disposition, to do that in the Afternoon, which should have been done in the Morning.

Useful Attainments in your Minority will procure Riches in Maturity, of which Writing and Accounts are not the meanest.

Learning, whether Speculative or Practical, is, in Popular or Mixt Governments, the Natural Source of Wealth and Honour.

PRECEPT I.

In Things of moment, on thy self depend,
Nor trust too far thy Servant or thy Friend:

---

4. Thomson, *The Seasons*. "Winter," 1024–41.

With private Views, thy Friend may promise fair,
And Servants very seldom prove sincere.

PRECEPT II.

What can be done, with Care perform to Day,
Dangers unthought-of will attend Delay;
Your distant Prospects all precarious are,
And Fortune is as fickle as she's fair.

PRECEPT III.

Nor trivial Loss, nor trivial Gain despise;
Molehills, if often heap'd, to Mountains rise:
Weigh every small Expence, and nothing waste,
Farthings long sav'd, amount to Pounds at last.

To William Strahan   ALS: Yale University Library

Dear Sir   Philada. Jan. 9. 1748,9
   This just serves to cover a Bill of Exchange for £8 8s. 0d. Sterling, and to let you know we are all well. It goes via New York, our River being full of Ice. I shall write you largely per our next Vessel, particularly about Mr. Read's Affair.[5] I wrote to you per our two last Vessels. The Post just going, cannot add but that I am Dear Sir, Your obliged Friend and Servant   B FRANKLIN

Addressed: To   Mr Wm Strahan   Printer   London

From James Logan

Letterbook abstract: Historical Society of Pennsylvania

To B Franklin   Febry 13th [1749]
   I return'd him the Reliquiae Bodleianae[6] which he took out of

---

5. On James Read's indebtedness to Strahan, see above, p. 316.
6. *Reliquiae Bodleianae: or Some Genuine Remains of Sir Thomas Bodley* (London, 1703). Most of the volume is composed of Bodley's letters to Dr. Thomas James, first Keeper of the library; as Logan complained, they are not arranged in chronological order. Logan ordered a copy from John Whiston, London bookseller, Nov. 27, 1749. Letterbook, Hist. Soc. Pa.

the Library for me, blaming the Editor for not digesting the Letters according to their date, and kept Peter Kalm's Fauna Suecica by Linnaeus[7] taking notice of his being of Aboae in Finland which as being in that Province I wonder'd he should call their Academy Stockholmiae.[8]

To William Strahan

MS not found; extract reprinted from Stan V. Henkels, Catalogue No. 906, pt. 2, supplement (October 26, 1904), item 2910.

Philada. Feby. 28. 1748–9
Our Friend Hall goes on exceedingly well: Has lately got a Daughter.[9]

Directors of Library Company to Thomas Penn[1]

Copy: Historical Society of Pennsylvania

Sir   Philada: March 14th 1748/9
    This waits of You to acknowledge the Receipt of Your generous present to the Library Company by the Hands of Mr. Richard Hockley of a curious reflecting Telescope and five Volumes of Voyages.
    The Occasions of returning Thanks for Your several generous Donations have been so frequent that it is not easy to find new Expressions of Gratitude for this fresh Instance of Your Regard but the Directors in behalf of the Library Company beg leave to

7. Carolus Linnaeus, *Fauna Svecica, Sistens Animalia Sveciae Regni* (Stockholm, 1746).
8. Logan seems to be confusing the University of Åbo, where Kalm was professor, with the Royal Academy of Sciences at Stockholm, of which he was a member.
9. Mary, first child of David and Mary Hall, was born Feb. 7, 1749, and died before Sept. 27, 1750. *PMHB*, XVI (1892), 364; LX (1936), 458.
1. A minute in BF's hand, appearing at the bottom of Peter Collinson's bill for books sent the Library, June 16, 1742–Oct. 15, 1745, records that John Sober, William Coleman, and BF were appointed in Dec. 1748 "to write a Letter of Thanks to the Proprietary for the Telescope and Books they are now inform'd he has sent them." Sober reported, May 8, 1749, that the letter had been sent. MS Minutes (also in BF's hand), Yale Univ. Lib.

assure You they have the highest Sense of the Favours You have conferrd on them and particularly of this last the Instrument being far the best and most Valuable they have heard of in America and we hope may put some of our Members upon the Study of that Noble Science, the Attainment of which it so much facilitates.

With the most grateful Regard we are Your Honours most faithful obligd humble Servants.

Signd by Order and in behalf of the Directors of the Library Company   BN: FRANKLIN Secry

To Peter Collinson Copy: American Academy of Arts and Sciences[2]

Sir   Philada. Apl. 29. 1749[3]

I now send you some[4] Further Experiments and Observations in Electricity made in Philadelphia 1748. viz.

§1. There will be the same Explosion and Shock if the electrified Phial is held in one Hand by the Hook, and the Coating touched by the other; as when held by the Coating and touched at the Hook.[5]

§2. To take the charged Phial safely by the Hook, and not at the same Time diminish it's Force, it must first be set down on an Electric per se.[6]

2. In Bowdoin MS and in 1751, 1754, and 1760 editions of *Exper. and Obser.*: Letter III; in 1769 and 1774 editions: Letter IV. See above, pp. 115–18.

3. The date line, salutation, and opening sentence are reproduced here as they stand in the Bowdoin MS. In all printed editions of *Exper. and Obser.* three changes appear: 1. Part of the opening sentence is converted into a heading "Farther Experiments and Observations in Electricity," placed above the date line and salutation. 2. The date line is changed to "1748" (obviously taken from the opening sentence as given in the Bowdoin MS), and the date "April 29, 1749" (but without "Philada.") is placed at the very end of the letter. 3. The salutation "Sir" is followed directly by the first *numbered* paragraph of the text. The problem of dating is discussed in I. Bernard Cohen, "Some Problems in Relation to the Dates of Benjamin Franklin's First Letters on Electricity," APS *Proc.*, C (1956), 537–42, and Francis S. Philbrick's reply based on a consideration of the printed editions only (*ibid.*, pp. 542–4).

4. The first five words, written on a separate line, are in BF's hand.

5. Opposite this paragraph in the margin of his own copy of the 1751 edition BF has written the name of Ebenezer Kinnersley, apparently to indicate that Kinnersley first performed the experiment.

6. Opposite this paragraph in the margin of his own copy of the 1751 edition BF has written the name of Ebenezer Kinnersley.

§3. The Phial will be electrified as strongly, if held by the Hook, and the Coating apply'd to the Globe, or Tube, as when held by the Coating and the Hook apply'd.[7]

§4. But the Direction of the Electrical Fire being different in Charging, will also be different in the Explosion. The Bottle charged thro' the Hook will be discharged thro' the Hook. The Bottle charged thro' the Coating, will be discharged thro' the Coating and not otherwise: For the Fire must come out the same Way it went in.

§5. To prove this; Take two Bottles that were equally charg'd thro' the Hooks, one in each Hand; bring their Hooks near each other, and no Spark or Shock will follow; because each Hook is disposed to give Fire, and neither to receive it. Set one of the Bottles down on Glass, take it up by the Hook, and apply it's Coating to the Hook of the other; then there will be an Explosion and Shock, and both Bottles will be discharged.

§6. Vary the Experiment, by Charging two Vials equally, one thro' Hook,[8] the other thro' the Coating: Hold that by the Coating which was charged thro' the Hook; and that by the Hook which was charged thro' the Coating. Apply the Hook of the first to the Coating of the other and there will be no Shock or Spark. Set that down on Glass, which you held by the Hook, take it up by the Coating, and bring the two Hooks together; a Spark and Shock will follow, and both Phials be discharged.

In this Experiment the Bottles are totally discharged, or the Equilibrium within them restored. The *Abounding* of Fire in one of the Hooks (or rather in the internal Surface of one Bottle) being exactly equal to the *Wanting* of the other: and therefore, as each Bottle has in itself the *Abounding* as well as the *Wanting*, the Wanting and Abounding must be equal in each Bottle. See §§8, 9, 10, 11. But if a Man holds in his Hands two Bottles, one fully electrified, the other not at all; and brings their Hooks together; he has but half a Shock, and the Bottles will both remain half electrified; the one being half discharged and the other half charged.

7. Opposite this paragraph in the margin of his own copy of the 1751 edition BF has written the name of Ebenezer Kinnersley. Footnote in 1769 and 1774 editions: "This was a Discovery of the very ingenious Mr. Kinnersley's, and by him communicated to me."

8. In all printed editions: "the hook."

7. Farther,[9] Place two Vials equally charged on a Table at 5 or 6 Inches Distance; Let a Cork Ball, suspended by a Silk Thread, hang between them. If the Vials were both charg'd thro' their Hooks, the Cork, when it has been attracted and repell'd by the one, will not be attracted but equally repell'd by the other. But if the Vials were charged, the one thro the Hook and the other thro' the Coating,* the Ball when it is repell'd from one Hook will be as strongly attracted by the other, and play vigorously between them,[2] till both Vials are nearly discharg'd.

8. When we use the Terms of *Charging* and *Discharging* the Phial, 'tis in Compliance with Custom, and for want of others more suitable: since We are of Opinion, that there is really no more electrical Fire in the Phial, after what is called it's *Charging* than before; nor less after it's *Discharging;* (excepting only the small Spark that might be given to and taken from the Non-electric Matter, if separated from the Bottle, which Spark may not be equal to a 500th. Part of what is called the Explosion) For, if on the Explosion, the Electrical Fire came out of the Bottle by one Part, and did not enter in again by another; then, if a Man standing on Wax and holding the Bottle in one Hand, takes the Spark by touching the Wire Hook with the other, the Bottle being thereby *discharg'd,* the Man would be *charg'd;* or, whatever Fire was lost by one, would be found in the other; since there is[3] no Way for it's Escape. But the Contrary is true.

9. Besides, the Vial will not suffer what is called a *Charging,* unless as much Fire can go out of it one Way as is thrown in by another. A Phial can not be charged, standing on Wax, or Glass, or hanging on the prime Conductor, unless a Communication be form'd between it's Coating and the Floor.

*To charge a Bottle commodiously thro' the Coating, place it on a Glass Stand; form a Communication from the prime Conductor to the Coating, and another from the Hook to the Wall or Floor. When 'tis charg'd remove the latter Communication before you take hold of the Bottle; otherwise great Part of the Fire will escape by it.[1]

9. All printed editions omit "Farther."
1. The footnote appears in all printed editions.
2. Added in 1774 edition: "fetching the electric fluid from the one, and delivering it to the other."
3. In 1760, 1769, and 1774 editions: "was."

10. But suspend two or more Phials on the prime Conductor, one hanging to the Tail of the other, and a Wire from the last to the Floor: an equal Number of Turns of the Wheel shall charge them all equally; and every one as much as one alone would have been. What is driven out at the Tail of the first, serving to charge the second; what is driven out of the second charging the third, and so on. By this Means, a great Number of Bottles might be charged with the same Labour, and equally high with one alone, were it not that every Bottle receives new Fire and loses it's old with some Reluctance, or rather gives some small Resistance to the Charging, which in a Number of Bottles becomes more equal to the Charging Power, and so repels the Fire back again on the Globe, sooner⁴ than a single Bottle would do.

11. When a Bottle is charg'd in the common Way, it's inside and outside Surfaces stand ready, the one to give Fire by the Hook, the other to receive it by the Coating: The one is full and ready to throw out, the other empty and extreamly hungry: yet as the first will not *give out,* unless the other can at the same Instant *receive in;* so neither will the latter *receive in,* unless the first can at the same Instant *give out.* When both can be done at once, 'tis done with inconceivable Quickness and Violence.

12. So a strait Spring (tho' the Comparison does not agree in every Particular) when forcibly bent, must, to restore itself contract that Side, which in the bending was extended, and extend that which was contracted; if either of these two Operations be hindered, the other can not be done. But the Spring is not said to be *charged* with Elasticity when bent, and *discharg'd* when unbent; it's Quantity of Elasticity is always the same.

13. Glass, in like Manner, has, within it's Substance⁵ always the same Quantity of Electrical Fire; and that, a very great Quantity in Proportion to the Mass of Glass, as shall be shewn hereafter. §26.⁶

14. This Quantity, proportioned to the Glass, it strongly and obstinately retains, and will neither have more nor less; tho it will

4. Added in 1774 edition: "in proportion."
5. In his own copy of the 1754 edition BF has inserted a marginal note after "substance," beginning: "When in its so [ ]," the remainder being cropped in the binding.
6. All printed editions omit the cross-reference to §26.

suffer a Change to be made in it's Parts and Situation; that is, We may take away Part of it from one of the Sides, provided we throw an equal Quantity into the other.

15. Yet when the Situation of the Electrical Fire is thus altered in the Glass, when some has been taken from one Side, and some added to the other; it will not be at Rest or in its natural State, till 'tis restored to it's original Equality. And this Restitution can not be made thro the Substance of the Glass, but must be done by a Non-electric Communication formed without, from Surface to Surface.[7]

16. Thus the whole Force of the Bottle and Power of giving a Shock, is in the Glass itself; the Non-electrics in Contact with the two Surfaces serving only to give and receive to and from the several Parts of the Glass; that is, to give on one Side, and take away from the other.

17. This was discovered here in the following Manner. Purposing to analize the electrified Bottle, in Order to find where it's Strength lay; we placed it on Glass, and drew out the Cork and Wire, which, for that Purpose, had been loosly put in. Then taking the Bottle in one Hand, and bringing a Finger of the other near its Mouth, a strong Spark came from the Water, and the Shock was as violent as if the Wire had remained in it; which shew'd that the Force did not lie in the Wire. Then to find if it resided in the Water, being crowded into and condensed in it, as confined by the Glass; which had been our former Opinion; we electrified the Bottle again, and placing it on Glass, drew out the Wire and Cork as before, then taking up the Bottle, we decanted all its Water into an empty Bottle, which likewise stood on Glass; and taking up that other Bottle, we expected, if the Force resided in the Water, to find a Shock from it; but there was none. We judged then, that it must either be lost in Decanting, or remain in the first Bottle. The latter we found to be true: For that Bottle on Trial gave the Shock, tho' filled up as it stood with fresh unelectrify'd Water from a Tea Pot. To find then whether Glass had this Property merely as Glass, or whether the Form contributed any Thing to it; we took a Pane of Sash Glass, and laying it on the Hand, placed a Plate of thin[8] Lead on it's upper Surface; then electrified

7. BF's marginal MS note in his own copy of 1754 edition adds: "by removing [the a]ir between [the] Surfaces."
8. All printed editions omit "thin."

that Plate, and bringing a Finger to it, there was a Spark and Shock. We then took two Plates of Lead of equal Dimensions, but less than the Glass by two Inches every Way, and electrified the Glass between them, by electrifying the uppermost Lead; then separated the Glass from the Lead; in doing which, what little Fire might be in the Lead was taken out; and the Glass being touched in the electrified Part[9] with a Finger, afforded only very small pricking Sparks, but a great Number of them might be taken from different Places. Then dextrously placing it again between the Plates of Lead,[1] and completing the Circle between the two Surfaces, a violent Shock ensu'd. Which demonstrated the Power to reside in the Glass as *Glass;* and that the Non-electrics in Contact served only like the Armature of the[2] Loadstone, to unite the Forces[3] of the several Parts, and bring them at once to any Point desired. It being a Property of a Nonelectric, that the whole Body instantly receives or gives what Electrical Fire is given to or taken from any one of its Parts.

18. Upon this We made what we call'd an *Electrical Battery,* consisting of eleven Panes of large Sash Glass, arm'd with thin leaden Plates, pasted on each Side, placed vertically, and supported at two Inches Distance on Silk Cords; with Hooks of thick Leaden Wire[4] one from each Side standing upright, distant from each other; and convenient Communications of Wire and Chain from the giving Side of one Pane to the receiving Side of the other; that so the whole might be charg'd together, and with the same Labour as one single Pane; and another Contrivance to bring the giving Sides, after charging in Contact with one long Wire, and the Receivers with another; which two long Wires would give the Force of all the Plates of Glass at once thro' the Body of any Animal forming the Circle with them. The Plates may also be discharg'd separately, or any Number together that is required. But this Machine is not much used, as not perfectly answering our Intention with Regard to the Ease of Charging, for the Reasons given §10. We made also, of large Glass Panes, *Magical Pictures,* and self moving animated Wheels, presently to be described.

9. In all printed editions: "parts."
1. In all printed editions: "leaden plates" replaces "Plates of Lead."
2. In all printed editions: "a" replaces "the."
3. In all printed editions: "force."
4. In all printed editions: "with thick hooks of leaden wire."

19. I perceive by the ingenious Mr. Watson's last Book, lately received, that Dr. Bevis had used Panes of Glass to give a Shock before us;[5] tho' till that Book came to Hand, I thought to have communicated it to you as a Novelty. The Excuse for mentioning it here, is, that we try'd the Experiment differently, drew different Consequences from it (for Mr. Watson still seems to think the Fire accumulated on the Non-electric that is in Contact with the Glass pag. 72) and, as far as we hitherto know, have carry'd it further.

20. The Magical Picture is made thus.[6] Having a large Mezzotinto with a Frame and Glass (Suppose of the King, God preserve him) Take out the Print, and cut a Pannel out of it, near two Inches all round distant from the Frame;[7] if the Cut is thro' the Picture, tis not the Worse. With thin Paste or Gum Water, fix the Border, that is cut off, on the inside of the Glass, pressing it smoothe and close; then fill up the Vacancy by Gilding the Glass well with Leaf Gold or Brass; gild likewise the inner Edge of the Back of the Frame all round except the Top Part, and form a Communication between that Gilding and the Gilding behind the Glass: then put in the Board, and that side is finished. Turn up the Glass, and gild the foreside exactly over the Back Gilding; and when this is dry, cover it by pasting on the Pannel of the Picture that had been cut out, observing to bring the corresponding Parts of the Border and Picture together; by which the Picture will appear of a Piece as at first, only Part is behind the Glass and Part before. Hold the Picture horizontally by the Top, and place a little moveable gilt Crown on the Kings Head. If now the Picture be moderately electrified, and another Person take hold of the Frame with one Hand, so that his Fingers touch it's inside Gilding, and with the other Hand endeavour to take off the Crown, he will receive a terrible Blow and fail in the Attempt. If the Picture were highly charg'd, the

5. All printed editions read: "that Dr. Bevis had used, before we had, panes of glass to give a shock." BF's marginal MS note in his own copy of 1754 edition reads: "Smeaton first used Panes &c." Footnote in 1769 and 1774 editions: "I have since heard that Mr. Smeaton was the first who made use of panes of glass for that purpose."

6. Opposite this paragraph in the margin of his own copy of the 1751 edition BF has written the name of Ebenezer Kinnersley. Footnote in 1769 and 1774 editions: "Contrived by Mr. Kinnersley."

7. In all printed editions: "near two inches distant from the frame all round."

Consequence might perhaps be as fatal[8] as that of High Treason: For when the Spark is taken thro' a Quire of Paper laid on the Picture, by Means of a Wire Communication, it makes a fair Hole thro' every Sheet; that is thro' 48 Leaves (tho' a Quire of Paper is thought good Armour against the Push of a Sword, or even against a Pistol Bullet) and the Crack is exceeding loud. The Operator, who, to prevent its falling,[9] holds the Picture by the upper End, where the inside of the Frame is not gilt, feels Nothing of the Shock, and may touch the Crown[1] without Danger, which he pretends is a Test of his Loyalty. If a Ring of Persons take a Shock among them the Experiment is called the *Conspiracy*.[2]

21. On the Principle in §7. That the Hooks of Bottles, differently charged, will attract and repel differently, is made an electrical Wheel, that turns with considerable Strength. A small upright Shaft of Wood passes at right Angles thro' a thin round Board of about a Foot[3] Diameter, and turns on a sharp Point of Iron, fixt in the lower End, while a strong Wire in the upper End, passing thro' a small Hole in a thin Brass Plate, keeps the Shaft truly vertical. About 30 Radii of equal Length made of Sash Glass, cut in narrow Strips, issue Horizontally from the Circumference of the Board; the Ends most distant from the Center being about 4 Inches apart. On the End of every one, a Brass Thimble is fixt. If now the Wire of a Bottle, electrified in the Common Way, be brought near the Circumference of this Wheel, it will attract the nearest Thimble, and so put the Wheel in Motion: That Thimble, in passing by, receives a Spark, and thereby being electrified is repell'd and so driven forwards, while a second, being attracted, approaches the Wire, receives a Spark and is driven after the first; and so on till the Wheel has gone once round, when the Thimbles, before Electrified, approaching the Wire, instead of being attracted, as they

8. Printed emendation in 1751, 1754 and 1760 editions: "We have found it fatal to small animals, but 'tis not strong enough to kill large ones. The biggest we have killed is a hen." This emendation appears as a footnote in 1769 and 1774 editions, with slight variations and the addition of the date 1750.

9. In all printed editions: "to prevent its falling" is inserted later in the sentence, after "the frame is not gilt."

1. In all printed editions: "the Crown" is replaced by "the face of the picture."

2. All printed editions call the experiment "*The Conspirators*."

3. In all printed editions: "twelve inches" instead of "a foot."

were at first, are repell'd; and the Motion presently ceases. But if another Bottle, which had been charg'd thro' the Coating be placed near the same Wheel, it's Wire will attract the Thimbles[4] repell'd by the first, and thereby doubles the Force that carries the Wheel round; and not only, taking out the Fire that had been communicated to the Thimbles by the first Bottle, but even robbing them of their natural Quantity, instead of being repell'd when they come again towards the first Bottle, they are more strongly attracted: so that the Wheel mends its Pace till it goes with great Rapidity, 12 or 15 Rounds in a Minute; and with such Strength, as that the Weight of 100 Spanish Dollars, with which we once loaded it, did not seem in the least to retard it's Motion. This is called an *Electrical Jack;* and if a large Fowl were spitted on the upright Shaft, it would be carried round before a Fire with a Motion fit for Roasting.

22. But this Wheel, like those driven by Wind, Water or Weights, moves by a foreign Force, viz. that of the Bottles. The *Selfmoving Wheel,* tho constructed on the same Principles, appears more surprizing. 'Tis made of a thin round Plate of Window Glass, 17 Inches Diameter, well gilt on both Sides, all but two Inches next the Edge. Two small Hemispheres of Wood are then fixt with Cement to the Middle of the upper and under Sides, centrally opposite, and in each of them a thick strong Wire 8 or 10 Inches long, which together make the Axis of the Wheel. It turns horizontally on a Point at the lower End of it's Axis which rests on a Bit of Brass, cemented within a Glass Salt-Seller. The upper End of it's Axis passes thro' a Hole in a thin Brass Plate, cemented to a long strong Piece of Glass, which keeps it 6 or 8 Inches Distant from any Non-electric, and has a small Ball of Wax or Metal on its Top to keep in the Fire. In a Circle on the Table, which supports the Wheel, are fixt 12 small Pillars of Glass, at about 4 Inches Distance, with a Thimble on the Top of each. On the Edge of the Wheel is a small leaden Bullet, communicating by a Wire with the Gilding of the upper Surface of the Wheel: and about 6 Inches from it, is another Bullet, communicating in like Manner with the under Surface. When the Wheel is to be charg'd by the upper Surface, a Communication must be made from the under Surface to the Table. When it is well chargd it begins to move; the Bullet nearest to a Pillar, moving[5] towards the Thimble on that Pillar;

4. In all printed editions: "thimble."
5. In all printed editions: "moves."

and passing by, electrifies it, and then pushes itself from it: The succeeding Bullet, which communicates with the other Surface of the Glass, more strongly attracting[6] that Thimble, on Account of it's being before electrified by the other Bullet: and thus the Wheel increases it's Motion, till it comes to such a Height, as that the Resistance of the Air regulates it. It will go half an Hour, and make, one Minute with another, 20 Turns in a Minute; which is 600 Turns in the whole: The Bullet of the upper Surface giving in each Turn 12 Sparks to the Thimbles, which makes 7200 Sparks, and the Bullet of the under Surface receiving as many from the Thimbles: these Bullets moving in the Time, near 2500 Feet. The Thimbles are well fixt, and in so exact a Circle, that the Bullets may pass within a very small Distance of each of them. If instead of 2 Bullets, you put 8, 4 communicating with the upper Surface, and four with the under Surface, placed alternately; which 8, at about 6 Inches Distance completes the Circumference; the Force and Swiftness will be greatly increased; the Wheel making 50 Turns in a Minute;[7] but then it will not go so long. These Wheels may perhaps be apply'd to the Ringing of Chimes[8] and Moving Orreries.

23. A small Wire bent circularly, with a loop at each End; Let one End rest against the under Surface of the Wheel, and bring the other End near[9] the upper Surface, it will give a terrible Crack; The Force will be discharg'd, and the Wheel will stop.[1]

24. Every Spark drawn in that Manner from the Surface of the Wheel, makes a round Hole in the Gilding, tearing off a Part of it in coming out; which shews that the Fire is not accumulated on the Gilding, but is in the Glass itself.

25. The Gilding being varnished over with Turpentine Varnish; the Varnish, tho' dry and hard, is burnt by the Spark drawn thro' it, gives a strong Smell and visible Smoke. And when the Spark is drawn thro' Paper, all round the Hole made by it, the Paper will

6. In all printed editions: "attracts."

7. From this point to the end of the paragraph all printed editions read: "but then it will not continue moving so long. These wheels may be applied, perhaps, to the ringing of chimes, the moving of light-made orreries."

8. Printed emendation in 1751, 1754, and 1760 editions: "This is since done." Footnote in 1769 and 1774 editions: "This was afterwards done with success by Mr. Kinnersley."

9. In 1754 and 1760 editions: "nearer."

1. All printed editions omit: "and the Wheel will stop."

be blackt by the Smoke, which Sometimes penetrates several of the Leaves. Parts of the Gilding, torn off, are[2] also found forcibly driven into the Hole made in the paper by the Stroke.

26. 'Tis amazing to observe in how small a Portion of Glass a great Electrical Force may lie. A thin Glass Bubble about an Inch Diameter, weighing only six Grains, being half filled with Water, partly gilt on the outside, and furnished with a Wire Hook, gives when electrified, as great a Shock as a Man is willing[3] to bear. As the Glass is thickest near the Orifice, I suppose the lower half, which being gilt, was electrified, and gave the Shock, did not exceed two Grains; for it appeared, when broke, much thinner than the upper half. If one of these thin Bottles be electrified by the Coating, and the Spark taken out thro the Gilding, it will break the Glass inwards, at the same Time that it breaks the Gilding outwards.

27. And allowing, for the Reasons before given §§8, 9, 10, that there is no more Electrical Fire in a Bottle after Charging than before, how great must the Quantity be in this small Portion of Glass! It seems as if it were of its very Substance and Essence. Perhaps if that due Quantity of Electrical Fire, so obstinately retain'd by Glass, could be separated from it, it would no longer be Glass, it might loose it's Transparency, or its Fragility, or Elasticity.[4] Experiments may possibly be invented hereafter to discover this.[5]

28.[6] We are[7] surprized at the Account given in Mr. Watson's Book, of a Shock communicated thro' a great Space of dry Ground, and suspect[8] some metalline Quality in the Gravel of that Ground:

2. In all printed editions: "Part . . . is."

3. In all printed editions: "is willing to" is replaced by "can well."

4. In all printed editions: "or its brittleness, or its elasticity."

5. In his own copy of the 1751 edition BF has written the name of Ebenezer Kinnersley three times in the margin opposite the second, third, and fourth sentences, apparently to indicate that Kinnersley first performed these experiments.

6. In all printed editions this section, like the one before it, was numbered 27, so that while the final section in the MS is 29, that in the printed editions is 28.

7. In 1754 and all later editions: "were" replaces "are."

8. Added in all printed editions: "there must be."

having found, that simple dry Earth ramm'd in a Glass Tube open at both Ends, and a Wire Hook inserted in the Earth at each End; the Earth and Wires making Part of a Circle,[9] would not conduct the least perceptible Shock. And indeed when one Wire was electrified, the other hardly shew'd any Signs of it's being in Connexion with it.[1] Even a thoroughly wet Packthread sometimes fails of conducting a Shock, tho' it otherwise conducts Electricity very well. A dry Cake of Ice, or an Iceicle, held between two Persons[2] in a Circle, likewise prevents the Shock, which one would not expect, as Water conducts it so perfectly well. Gilding on a new Book, tho' at first it conducts the Shock extreamly well; yet fails after 10 or a Dozen Experiments;[3] tho' it appears otherwise in all Respects the same; which we can not account for.[4]

29. There is one Experiment more, which surprizes us, and is hitherto not satisfactorily accounted for. It is this. Place an Iron Shot on a Glass Stand, and let a damp Cork Ball,[5] suspended by a Silk Thread hang in Contact with the Shot. Take a Bottle in each Hand, one that is electrified thro' the Hook, the other thro' the Coating. Apply the *giving* Wire to the Shot, which will electrify it positively, and the Cork shall be repell'd. Then apply the *requiring* Wire, which will take out the Spark given by the other, when the Cork will return to the Shot. Apply the same again, and take out another Spark, so will the Shot be electrified negatively, and the

9. In 1774 edition: "circuit" replaces "circle."

1. Footnote to 1769 and 1774 editions: "Probably the ground is never so dry."

2. All printed editions omit "Persons."

3. Printed emendation in 1751, 1754, and 1760 editions: "This was by a small bottle. And since found to fail after [one], with a large glass." The bracketed word was added in MS in BF's copy of the 1751 edition.

4. Footnote in 1769 and 1774 editions: "We afterwards found that it failed after one stroke with a large bottle; and the continuity of the gold appearing broken, and many of its parts dissipated, the Electricity could not pass the remaining parts without leaping from part to part through the air, which always resists the motion of this fluid, and was probably the cause of the gold's not conducting so well as before." To this footnote the 1774 edition adds: "the number of interruptions in the line of gold, making, when added together, a space larger perhaps than the striking distance." For remarks on §28 by Prof. Thornbern Bergman of Uppsala, see *Phil. Trans.*, LI (1760), 907–9.

5. In all printed editions: "a ball of damp cork."

Cork in that Case shall be repell'd equally as before. Then apply the giving Wire, and give to the Shot[6] the Spark it wanted, so will the Cork return: Give it another, which will be an Addition to it's natural Quantity, so will the Cork be repell'd again; And so may the Experiment be repeated, as long as there is any Charge remaining[7] in the Bottles; Which shews that Bodies, having less than the common Quantity of Electricity, repel each other, as well as those that have more.

Chagrin'd a little that We have hitherto been able to discover Nothing[8] in this Way of Use to Mankind, and the hot Weather coming on, when Electrical Experiments are not so agreable; 'tis proposed to put an End to them for this Season somewhat humorously in a Party of Pleasure on the Banks of SchuylKill,[9] (where Spirits are at the same Time to be fired by a Spark sent from Side to Side thro' the River).†[1] A Turky is to be killed for our Dinners

†This was since done.

6. In all printed editions: "Then apply the giving wire to the shot, and give the spark it wanted."

7. All printed editions omit "remaining."

8. In 1769 and 1774 editions: "that we have been hitherto"; in all printed editions: "able to produce nothing."

9. Footnote in all printed editions: "The river that washes one side of Philadelphia, as the Delaware does the other; both are ornamented with the summer habitations, of the citizens, and the agreeable mansions of the principal people of this colony." BF's MS note in his own copy of 1751 edition: "Editor's Note."

1. All printed editions read: "Spirits, at the same time, are to be fired by a spark sent from side to side through the river, without any other conductor than the water; an experiment which we some time since performed, to the amazement of many." A footnote keyed to "many" in the 1769 and 1774 editions reads: "As the possibility of this experiment has not been easily conceived, I shall here describe it. Two iron rods, about three feet long, were planted just within the margin of the river, on the opposite sides. A thick piece of wire, with a small round knob at its end, was fixed to ["on" in 1774 edition] the top of one of the rods, bending downwards, so as to deliver commodiously the spark upon the surface of the spirit. A small wire fastened by one end to the handle of the spoon, containing the spirit, was carried a-cross the river, and supported in the air by the rope commonly used to hold by, in drawing the ferry-boats over. The other end of this wire was tied round the coating of the bottle; which being charged, the spark was delivered from the hook to the top of the rod standing in the water on that side. At the same instant the rod on the other side delivered a spark into the spoon, and fired the spirit. The electric fire returning to the coating of the bottle, through the handle of the spoon and the supported wire connected with them.

by the Electrical Shock; and roasted by the electrical Jack, before a Fire kindled by the Electrified Bottle; when the Healths of all the famous Electricians in England,[2] France and Germany, are to be drank in Electrified Bumpers,* under the Discharge of Guns from the Electrical Battery.[5]

To Peter Collinson Esqr. F.R.S. London

To John Mitchell[6] Copy: American Academy of Arts and Sciences[7]

Sir   Philada. Apl. 29. 1749[8]
Observations and Suppositions towards forming a new Hypothesis for explaining the several Phaenomena of Thunder Gusts.[9]

*An electrified Bumper is a small thin Glass Tumbler, near filled with Wine and electrified.[3] This when brought to the Lips, gives a Shock; if the Party be close shaved, and does not breathe on the Liquor.[4]

"That the electric fire thus actually passes through the water, has since been satisfactorily demonstrated to many by an experiment of Mr. Kinnersley's, performed in a trough of water about ten feet long. The hand being placed under water in the direction of the spark (which always takes the strait or shortest course [if sufficient, and other circumstances are equal]) is struck and penetrated by it as it passes." The words in brackets are in the 1774 edition only.

2. The electricians of Holland are mentioned at this point in all printed editions.

3. All printed editions add: "as the bottle."

4. This note appears as a footnote in all printed editions.

5. For comment on this letter by William Watson, see below, p. 457.

6. So stated in Bowdoin MS and confirmed by BF in a letter to Cadwallader Colden, June 28, 1750 (below, p. 482). No edition of *Exper. and Obser.* gives the addressee, but Dubourg (*Oeuvres*, I, 38), Sparks (*Works*, V, 211), Bigelow (*Works*, II, 137), and Smyth (*Writings*, II, 411) all erroneously indicate that this letter was written to Peter Collinson.

7. In Bowdoin MS and in 1751, 1754, and 1760 editions of *Exper. and Obser.*: Letter IV; in 1769 and 1774 editions: Letter V.

8. This letter is undated in the editions of *Exper. and Obser.* and in Dubourg, Sparks, Bigelow, and Smyth.

9. Footnote in all printed editions: "Thunder-gusts are sudden storms of thunder and lightning, which are frequently of short duration, but sometimes produce mischievous effects." For the publication of BF's theory in summarized form as a note on Lewis Evans' map, see below, p. 392 n.

§1. Non-Electrical[1] Bodies, that have Electric Fire thrown into [or on][2] them, will retain it, 'till other Non-electrics, that have less, approach; and then 'tis communicated by a Snap, and becomes equally divided.

§2. Electrical Fire loves Water, is strongly attracted by it, and they can subsist together.

3. Air is an Electric per Se, and when dry, will not [readily][3] conduct the Electrical Fire; it will neither receive it, nor give it to other Bodies; otherwise, no Body surrounded by Air could be electrified positively and negatively: For should it be attempted *positively*, the Air would immediately take away the Overplus; or *negatively*, the Air would supply what was wanting.

4. Water being electrified, the Vapours arising from it will be equally electrified; and floating in the Air, in the Form of Clouds, or otherwise, will retain that Quantity of Electrical Fire, 'till they meet with other Clouds or Bodies not so much electrified; and then will communicate as before mentioned.

5. Every Particle of Matter electrified is repell'd by every other Particle equally electrified. Thus the Stream of an artificial[4] Fountain, naturally dense and continual, when electrified will separate and spread in Form of a Brush; every Drop endeavouring to recede from every other Drop; but on taking out the Electrical Fire, they close again.

Profile of a Piece of Water, C&D are among the Particles of the Surface; A & B above the Surface Small Shot would represent it better than this Figure—

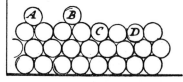

6. Water being strongly electrified, (as well as when heated by common Fire) rises in Vapours more copiously: the Attraction of Cohesion among it's Particles being greatly weakned by the opposite Power of Repulsion introduced with the Electrical Fire. And when any Particle

1. In all printed editions: "non-electric."
2. Added by BF in his copy of 1754 edition (Yale Univ. Lib.), but not included in printed editions.
3. Added by BF in his own copy of 1754 edition, but not included in printed editions.
4. All printed editions omit "artificial."

is by any Means disengaged, tis immediately repell'd and so flies into the Air.

7. Particles situated[5] as *A* and *B*[6] are more easily disengaged than *C*, and *D*, as each is held by Contact with three only; whereas *C* and *D* are each in Contact with nine. When the Surface is in Motion,[7] Particles are continually pusht in this Situation.[8]

8. Friction between a Non-Electric and an Electric per Se, will produce Electrical Fire; not by *creating* but collecting it: For it is equally diffused in our Walls, Floors, Earth, and the whole Mass of common Matter. Thus the whirling Glass Globe, during it's Friction against the Cushion draws Fire from the Cushion, the Cushion is supply'd from the Frame of the Machine, that from the Floor on which it stands. Cut off the Communication by thick Glass or Wax, placed under the Cushion, and no Fire can be *produced*, because it can not be collected.

9. The Ocean is a Compound of Water a Non-Electric, and Salt an Electric per Se.

10. When there is a Friction among the Parts near it's Surface, the Electrical Fire is collected from the Parts below. It is then plainly visible in the Night. It appears at the Stern and in the Wake of every sailing Vessel; every Dash of an Oar shews it, and every Surf and Spray: In Storms, the whole Sea seems on Fire. The detacht Particles of Water, then repelled from the Electrified Surface continually carry off the Fire as it is collected; they rise and form Clouds, and those Clouds are highly electrified, and retain the Fire, 'till they have an Opportunity of communicating it.

11. The Particles of Water rising in Vapour,[9] attatch themselves to Particles of Air.

12. The Particles of Air are said to be hard, round, separate and distant from each other; every Particle strongly repelling every other Particle; whereby they recede from each other, as far as common Gravity will permit.

5. In all printed editions: "Particles happening to be situated."
6. Added in 1769 and 1774 editions: "(Fig. VI. representing the profile of a vessel of water)."
7. In all printed editions: "the Surface is in Motion" is replaced by "the surface of water has the least motion."
8. In 1754 and subsequent editions: "into the situation represented by *A* and *B*, Fig. 6," except that "Fig. 6" is omitted in 1769 and 1774 editions.
9. In all printed editions: "vapours."

13. The Space between any three Particles equally repelling each other, will be an equilateral Triangle.

14. In Air comprest, these Triangles are smaller; in rarified Air they are larger.

15. Common Fire joyned with Air, increases the Repulsion, enlarges the Triangles, and thereby makes the Air specifically lighter. Such Air among denser Air will rise.

16. Common Fire, as well as Electrical Fire, gives Repulsion to the Particles of Water, and destroys their Attraction of Cohesion; Hence common Fire, as well as electrical Fire assists in raising Vapours.

17. Particles of Water having no Fire with them,[1] mutually attract each other. Three Particles of cold[2] Water then, being attatcht to the three Particles of a Triangle of Air; would by their mutual Attraction, operating against the Air's Repulsion, shorten the Sides and lessen the Triangle; whereby that Portion of the Air being made denser, would sink to the Earth with it's Water, and not rise to contribute[3] to the Formation of a Cloud.

18. But if every Particle of Water attatching itself to Air, brings with it a Particle of common Fire: the Repulsion of the Air being assisted and strengthned by the Fire, more than obstructed by the mutual Attraction of the Particles of Water, the Triangle dilates, and that Portion of Air becoming rarer and specifically lighter, rises.

19. If the Particles of Water bring Electrical Fire when they attach themselves to Air, the Repulsion between the Particles of Water electrified, joyns with the natural Repulsion of Air, to force it's Particles to a greater Distance, whereby the Triangles are dilated, and the Air rises, carrying up with it the Water.

20. If the Particles of Water bring with them Portions of both Sorts of Fire, the Repulsion of the Particles of Air is still more strengthned and encreased, and the Triangles further enlarged.

21. One Particle of Air may be surrounded by 12 Particles of Water of equal Size with itself, all in contact with it; and by more added to those.

22. Particles of Air thus loaded, would be drawn nearer to-

1. In all printed editions: "in them."
2. All printed editions omit "cold."
3. Omitted from 1774 edition: "to contribute."

gether by the mutual Attraction of the Particles of Water, did not Fire common or electrical assist their Repulsion.

23. If Air thus loaded be comprest by adverse Winds, or by being driven against Mountains &c. or condensed, by taking away the Fire that assisted it in Expanding, the Triangles, contract, the Air with it's Water will descend as a *Dew:* or, if the Water surrounding one Particle of Air, comes in Contact with the Water surrounding another, they coalesce, and form a Drop, and we have *Rain.*

24. The Sun supplies, (or seems to supply) common Fire to all[4] Vapours, whether raised from the Earth or Sea.

25. Those Vapours, which have both common and electrical Fire in them, are better supported in the Air; and may be longer supported[5] than those which have only common Fire in them. For when the Vapours rise into the coldest Regions above the Earth, the Cold will not diminish the Electrical Fire, if it doth the common.

26. Hence Clouds form'd by Vapours raised from fresh Waters within Land, from growing Vegetables, moist Earth &c. more speedily and easily deposite their Water, having but little Electrical Fire to repel and keep the Particles separate. So that the greatest Part of the Water rais'd from the Land, is let fall on the Land again; and the Winds blowing from the Land to the Sea are dry; there being but[6] little Use for Rain on the Sea; and to rob the Land of it's Moisture, in Order to rain on the Sea, would not appear reasonable.

27. But Clouds form'd by Vapours, raised from the Sea, having both Fires, and particularly a great Quantity of the Electrical, support their Water Strongly, raise it high; and, being moved by the Winds, may bring it over the Middle of the broadest Continent, from the Middle of the widest Ocean.

28. How these Ocean Clouds, so strongly supporting their Water, are made to deposite it on the Land, where 'tis wanted, is next to be considered.

29. If they are driven by Winds against Mountains, those Mountains being less electrified attract them; and on Contact, take away

4. Omitted in 1774 edition: "all."
5. All printed editions omit: "in the Air; and may be longer supported."
6. All printed editions omit "but."

their Electrical Fire (and being cold their[7] common Fire also). Hence the Particles close towards the Mountains and towards each other. If the Air was not much loaded, it only falls in Dews on the Mountain Tops and Sides, forms Springs, and descends to the Vales in Rivulets, which united make larger Streams and Rivers. If much loaded, the Electrical Fire is at once taken from the whole Cloud, and in leaving it, flashes brightly and cracks loudly; The Particles instantly coalescing for Want of that Fire, and falling in a heavy Shower.

30. When a Ridge of Mountains thus dams the Clouds, and draws the Electrical Fire from the Cloud first approaching it; That which next follows, when it comes near the first Cloud now deprived of it's Fire, flashes into it, and begins to deposite it's own Water: The first Cloud again flashing into the Mountains. The third approaching Cloud, and all the succeeding ones, acting in the same Manner as far back as they extend, which may be over many hundred Miles of Country.

31. Hence the continual Storms of Rain, Thunder and Lightning on the East Side of the Andes, which running North and South, and being vastly high, intercept all the Clouds brought against them from the Atlantic Ocean, by the Trade Winds, and oblige them to deposite their Water:[8] By which the vast Rivers Amazones, La Plata and Oroonoko are form'd, which return the Water again[9] into the same Sea, after it has[1] fertilized a Country of very great Extent.

32. If a Country be plain, having no Mountains to intercept the electrified Clouds, yet it is not without Means to make them deposite their Water. For if an electrified Cloud, coming from the Sea, meets in the Air a Cloud raised from the Land, and therefore not electrified; the first will flash it's Fire into the latter, and thereby both Clouds shall be made suddenly to deposite Water.

33. The electrified Particles of the first Cloud, close when they lose their Fire: the Particles of the other Cloud[2] close in receiving it: in both they have thereby an Opportunity of Coalescing into

7. In all printed editions: "their" is replaced by "the."
8. In all printed editions: "waters."
9. All printed editions omit "again."
1. In all printed editions: "it has" is replaced by "having."
2. In 1774 edition: "clouds."

Drops. The Concussion, or Jerk, given to the Air, contributes also to shake down the Water; not only from those two Clouds but from others near them. Hence the sudden Fall of Rain immediately after a Flash[3] of Lightning.

34. To shew this by an easy Experiment. Take two round Pieces of Pastboard, two Inches diameter: from the Center and Circumference of each of them, suspend by fine silk Threads, 18 Inches long, 7 small Balls of Wood (or 7 Peas) equal in Bigness:[4] so will the Balls appending to each Pastboard form equal equilateral Triangles, one Ball being in the Center, and six at equal Distances from that and from each other; and thus they represent Particles of Air. Dip both Sets in Water, and some cohering[5] to each Ball, they will represent Air loaded. Dextrously electrify one Sett, and it's Balls will repel each other to a greater Distance, enlarging the Triangles. Could the Water, supported by the seven Balls, come into Contact, 'twould form a Drop or Drops so heavy as to break the Cohesion it had with the Balls, and so fall. Let the two Sets of Balls[6] then represent two Clouds, the one a Sea Cloud electrified, the other a Land Cloud. Bring them within the Sphere of Attraction, and they will draw towards each other, and you will see the separated Balls close thus; The first electrified Ball that comes near an unelectrified Ball by Attraction, joyns it, and gives it Fire; instantly they separate, and each flies to another Ball of it's own Party, one to give and the other to receive Fire, and so it proceeds thro both Sets, but so quick as to be in a Manner instantaneous. In the Collision[7] they shake off and drop their Water which represents Rain.

35. Thus when Sea and Land Clouds would pass at too great a Distance for[8] the Flash, they are attracted towards each other 'till within that Distance: For the Sphere of electrical Attraction is far beyond the Distance of Flashing.

36. When a great Number of Clouds from the Sea, meet a Number of Clouds raised from the Land, the Electrical Flashes appear

3. In all printed editions: "flashes."
4. In 1774 edition: "Bigness" replaced by "goodness."
5. In 1769 and 1774 editions: "cohering" is replaced by "adhering."
6. All printed editions omit "of Balls."
7. In 1774 edition: "Collision" is replaced by "cohesion."
8. In 1760 and 1769 editions: "for" is replaced by "from."

to Strike in different Parts; and as the Clouds are jostled and mixed by the Winds, or brought near by the Electrical Attraction, they continue to give and receive Flash after Flash, till the Electrical Fire is equally diffused.

37. When the Gun Barrel, in Electrical Experiments, has but little Electrical Fire in it, you must approach it very near with your knuckle, before you can draw a Spark. Give it more Fire, and it will give a Spark at a greater Distance. Two Gun Barrels united, and as highly electrified, will give a Spark at a still greater Distance. But if two Gun Barrels electrified will strike at two Inches Distance, and make a loud Snap; to what a great Distance may 10,000 Acres of Electrified Cloud strike and give its Fire, and how loud must be that Crack!

38. It is a common Thing to see Clouds, at different Heights, passing different Ways, which shews different Currents of Air, one under the other. As the Air between the Tropics is rarified by the Sun, it rises, the denser Northern and Southern Air pressing into it's Place. The Air so rarified and forced up, passes Northward and Southward, and must descend in the Polar Regions, if it has no Opportunity before, that the Circulation may be carried on.

39. As Currents of Air, with the Clouds therein, pass different Ways, 'tis easy to conceive, how the Clouds passing over each other, may attract each other, and so come near enough for the electrical Stroke; and also how Electrical Clouds may be carried within Land very far from the Sea, before they have an Opportunity to strike.

40. When the Air, with it's Vapours raised from the Oceans between the Tropicks comes to descend in the Polar Regions, and to be in Contact with the Vapours arising there: the Electrical Fire they brought begins to be communicated, and is seen in clear Nights, being first visible where it is first in Motion, that is, where the Contact begins, or in the most Northern Part; from thence the Streams of Light seem to shoot Southerly, even up to the Zenith of Northern Countries. But tho' the Light seems to shoot from the North Southerly, the Progress of the Fire is really from the South Northerly; it's Motion begining in the North being the Reason that it is there first seen.

For the Electrical Fire is never visible but when in Motion, and leaping from Body to Body; or from Particle to Particle thro' the

Air. When it passes through dense Bodies 'tis unseen. When a Wire makes Part of the Circle, in the Explosion of the Electrical Phial, the Fire tho' in great Quantity, passes in the Wire invisibly. But in passing along a Chain, it becomes visible as it leaps from Link to Link. In passing along Leaf Gold[9] Gilding 'tis visible: For the Leaf Gold is full of Pores. Hold a Leaf to the Light, and it appears like a Net; and the Fire is seen in it's Leaping over the Vacancies.

And as when a long Canal fill'd with still Water, is opened at one End in Order to be discharg'd; the Motion of the Water begins first near the opened End, and proceeds towards the close End, tho' the Water itself moves from the close towards the opened End. So the Electrical Fire discharg'd into the Polar Regions, perhaps from a thousand Leagues Length of vapourized Air, appears first, where tis first in Motion, i.e. in the most Northern Part, and the Appearance proceeds Southward, tho' the Fire really moves Northward.[1]

Sometimes the Case may be, that electrified Vapours arising from the Polar Ocean (for Cold is no Hindrance to Electrical Operations) may meet with great Quantities of unelectrified Vapours brought by the Southern Currents of Air from the Continents in warmer Climes. Then the Fire on Contact, must proceed from North to South, thro' those unelectrified Vapours, and would appear so. But if any Part of the Northern electrified Vapours, from which they receive their Fire, are above the Horizon of the Place, from whence the Lights are seen, some Flashes from the Place of Meeting would appear to shoot Northerly, for the Reasons before mentioned.

Perhaps the Suppositions contained in this Section, may help to account for some of the Phaenomena of the Aurora Borealis.

41. When there is great Heat on the Land in a particular Region, the Sun having shone on it perhaps several Days, while the Surrounding Countries have been screened by Clouds, the lower Air is rarified and rises, the cooler denser Air above descends; the Clouds in that Air meet from all Sides, and joyn over the heated Place; and if some are electrified, others not, Lightning and Thun-

9. All printed editions omit "Gold."
1. All printed editions omit the remainder of this section, but insert at this point: "This is supposed to account for the Aurora Borealis."

der succeed, and Showers fall. Hence Gusts[2] after Heats, and cool Air after Gusts; the Water and the Clouds that bring it, coming from a higher and therefore a cooler Region.

42. An Electrical Spark drawn from an irregular Body at some Distance is scarce ever strait, but shews crooked and waving in the Air; So do the Flashes of Lightning; the Clouds being very irregular Bodies.

43. As electrified Clouds pass over a Country, high Hills and high Trees, lofty Towers, Spires, Masts of Ships, Chimneys &c. as so many Prominences and Points, draw the Electrical Fire, and the whole Cloud discharges there.

44. Dangerous therefore is it to take Shelter under a single[3] Tree during a Thunder Gust. It has been fatal to many, both Men and Beasts.

45. It is safer to be in the open Field for another Reason. When the Cloaths are wet, if a Flash, in it's Way to the Ground, should strike your Head, it will run[4] in the Water over the Surface of your Body; whereas if your Cloaths were dry, it would go thro' the Body.[5]

Hence a wet Rat can not be kill'd by the exploding Electrical Bottle, when a dry Rat may.[6]

46. Common Fire [i.e. Culinary][7] is in all Bodies more or less, as well as Electrical Fire. Perhaps they may be different Modifications of the same Element; Or they may be different Elements. The latter is by some suspected.

47. If they are different Things, yet they may and do subsist together in the same Body.

48. When Electrical Fire strikes through a combustible[8] Body, it acts upon the common Fire contain'd in it, and puts that Fire in

2. In all printed editions: "thunder-gusts."
3. All printed editions omit "single."
4. In 1769 and 1774 editions: "may run."
5. Added in 1774 edition: "because the blood and other humours, containing so much water, are more readily conductors."
6. Footnote in 1769 and 1774 editions: "This was tried with a bottle, containing about a quart. It is since thought that one of the large glass jars, mentioned in these papers, might have killed him, though wet."
7. Added by BF in his own copy of 1754 edition.
8. All printed editions omit "combustible."

Motion; and if there be a sufficient Quantity of each Kind of Fire, the Body will be enflamed.

49. When the Quantity of common Fire in the Body is small, the Quantity of electrical Fire, or the Electrical Stroke, should be greater: If the Quantity of common Fire be great, less Electrical Fire suffices, to produce the Effect.

50. Thus Spirits must be heated before we can fire them by the Electrical Spark. If they are much heated, a small Spark will do; if not the Spark must be greater.[9]

51. 'Till lately we could only fire warm Vapours, but now we can burn hard dry Resin. And when we can procure greater Electrical Sparks, we may be able to fire, not only unwarmed Spirits as Lightning does, but even Wood, by Giving a sufficient Agitation to the common Fire contained in it, as Friction we know will do.

52. Sulphureous and inflammable Vapours arising from the Earth are easily kindled by Lightning. Besides what arise from the Earth, such Vapours are sent out by Stacks of moist Hay, Corn or other Vegetables, which heat and reek. Wood rotting in old Trees or Buildings does the same: such therefore are easily and often fired.

53. Metals are often melted by Lightning; tho' perhaps, not from Heat in the Lightning nor altogether from agitated Fire in the Metals.

For as whatever Body can insinuate itself between the Particles of Metal, and overcome the Attraction by which they cohere (as sundry Menstrua can) will make the *solid* become a *Fluid*, as well as Fire, yet without heating it: So the Electrical Fire, or Lightning, creating a violent Repulsion between the Particles of the Metal it passes thro', the Metal is fused.

54. If you would by a violent Fire melt off the End of a Nail which is half driven into a Door; the Heat given the whole Nail before a Part would melt, must burn the Board it sticks in; and the melted Part would burn the Floor it dropt on. But if a Sword

9. Printed emendation in 1751, 1754, and 1760 editions: "We have since fired spirits without heating, when the weather is warm." In 1769 and 1774 editions this sentence appears as a footnote, with two additional sentences: "A little poured into the palm of the hand, will be warmed sufficiently by the hand, if the spirit be well rectified. Aether takes fire most readily."

375

can be melted in the Scabbard, and Money in a Mans Pocket, by Lightning, without burning either; it must be a cold Fusion.[1]

55. Lightning rends some Bodies. The Electrical Spark will strike a Hole thro' a Quire of strong Paper.[2]

56. If the foregoing Hypothesis be a true one there ought to be but little Thunder and Lightning far at Sea, or in the Islands remote from the Continent. On Enquiry, the Writer has been informed by an old Sea Captain, that they seldom meet with it on the great Ocean, till they come into Soundings. And an intelligent Person, who lived 13 Years at Bermudas, and many Years at South Carolina, says, That he has observed more Thunder and Lightning in one Month at the latter Place, than happened during the whole Term of his living at the Former.[3]

To Dr. John Mitchel, F. R. S. London

1. Footnote in 1769 and 1774 editions: "These facts, though related in several accounts, are now doubted; since it has been observed that the parts of a bell-wire which fell on the floor being broken and partly melted by lightning, did actually burn into the boards. (See *Philos. Trans.* Vol. LI. Part 1. and Mr. Kinnersley has found that a fine iron wire, melted by Electricity, has had the same effect.)"

2. Opposite this paragraph in the margin of his own copy of 1751 edition BF wrote "EK & BF," apparently meaning that Ebenezer Kinnersley and he first performed the experiment.

3. In all printed editions this paragraph reads: "If the source of lightning, assigned in this paper, be the true one, there should be little thunder heard at sea far from land. And accordingly some old sea-captains, of whom enquiry has been made, do affirm, that the fact agrees perfectly with the hypothesis; for that in crossing the great ocean, they seldom meet with thunder till they come into soundings; and that the islands far from the continent have very little of it. And a curious observer, who lived 13 years at Bermudas, says, there was less thunder there in that whole time than he has sometimes heard in a month at Carolina."

BF's paper was read to the Royal Society, November 9 and 16, 1749. Though it was not published, William Stukeley cited it approvingly in his diary (*Family Memoirs*, II, Surtees Soc. *Pubs.*, LXXVI, 1883, 378–9) and in his paper "On the Causes of Earthquakes," *Phil. Trans.* XLVI (1749–50), 643. For Collinson's report, Feb. 5, 1750, on the cordial reception accorded to it, see below, p. 460. These facts are at variance with BF's recollection, that the paper was read in the Society, but "laught at by the Connoisseurs." Par. Text edit., p. 382. Ezra Stiles apparently had a copy of this letter to Mitchell, the substance of which he communicated to his uncle Abel Stiles, Feb. 20, 1750. Stiles MSS, Yale Univ. Lib.

To William Strahan

ALS: Pierpont Morgan Library

Sir Philada. April 29. 1749

I suppose Mr. Hall will acquaint you that I have settled with him for those Things you sent me that were charg'd in his Invoice. Enclos'd are the following Bills, viz.

Richard Graham's	£22. 0.0
James M'Nab's	3.10.0
Hammond & Co's	2.13.7
Do	8. 8.0
Do	9. 0.0
	£45.11.7

which with my Son's Wages, and a Remittance I order'd you from the W. Indies, and suppose may be in your Hands before this Time, will I imagine near ballance our Accounts.

In a former Letter I promis'd to write you largely about your Affair with Mr. Read,[4] and the Measures taken to recover your Money. Before I received your Power of Attorney and Account, there was a Misunderstanding between us, occasion'd by his endeavouring to get a small Office from me (Clerk to the Assembly) which I took the more amiss, as we had always been good Friends and the Office could not have been of much Service to him, the Salary being small; but valuable to me; as a Means of securing the Publick Business to our Printing House. So as we were not on Speaking Terms when your Account came to hand and the Influence I had over him as a Friend was become little or nothing, it was some Time before I mention'd it to him. But at length the Ice was broke in the following Manner. I have a Friend in the Country that assisted me when I first set up, whose Affairs have lately been in some Disorder (occasion'd chiefly by his too great Good Nature) his Creditors coming at the same time in a Croud upon him.[5] I had made up with several of them for him, but Mr. Read being employ'd in one small Case (a Debt of £12 only) early on, (by some Contrivance in the Law which I dont understand) a private Action against him, by summoning him in this County when he lives in another, and obtain'd a Judgment against

4. See above, pp. 316, 350.

5. Robert Grace. See above, pp. 50, 330.

him without his or my knowing anything of the matter; and then came to me, knowing I had a great Affection for Mr. Grace, and in a very insulting Manner ask'd, *"What shall I do with your Friend Grace? I have got Judgment against him, and must take out Execution if the Debt is not immediately satisfy'd. &c."* Upon enquiring into the Matter, and understanding how it had been carry'd on, I grew a little warm, blam'd his Practice as irregular and unfair, and his Conduct towards Mr. Grace, to whom his Father and Family had been much oblig'd, as ungrateful; and said, that since he look'd on me as Mr. Grace's Friend, he should have told me of the Action before he commenc'd it, that I might have prevented it, and sav'd the Charges arising on it; and his not doing so could be only from a View to the small Fees it produc'd him, in carrying it thro' all the Courts, &c. He justify'd his Practice, and said it was legal and frequent; deny'd that his Father or Family were under any Obligation to Mr. Grace; alledg'd that Grace had us'd him ill in employing another Lawyer in some of his own Actions, when at the same Time he owed him near Five Pounds; and added haughtily that he was determin'd to sue Grace on his own Account, if not speedily paid; and so saying left me very abruptly. I thought this a good Opportunity of introducing your Affair, imagining that a Consciousness of his ill Behaviour to me and my Friend would pique him to make immediate Payment. Accordingly I wrote him a Letter the next Day, of which I send you the rough Draft enclos'd, together with his Answer;[6] since which several other Letters pass'd on the same Subject, of which [I] have no Copies. All I insisted on, since he declar'd his Inability to pay at present, was, that he should give you his Bond, so that in Case of his Death you might come in for Payment prior to common Creditors, and that he should allow you Interest from the Time the Money became due in the common Course of Payments. He agreed to give his Bond, but it has been delay'd from time to time till this Day, when on my Writing to him again, to know what Account I should send you, I receiv'd from him the enclos'd Billet,[7] in which he refuses to allow Interest for the Time past. As he cannot be compell'd to pay Interest on a Book Ac-

6. The "rough Draft" is printed above, p. 329, but Read's reply and the other letters have not been found.
7. Not found.

count I desired him then to fill up and execute a Bond to you for the Principal, and he might settle the Affair of the Interest with you hereafter. Accordingly he has just now done it, so that Interest will arise for the Time to come: But as he threatens to pay very speedily, and I am persuaded may easily do it by the Help of his Relations, who are wealthy, I hope you will not have much Interest to receive. He has a great [many good] Qualities for which I love him; but I believe he is, as you say, sometimes a little crazy. If the Debt were to me, I could not sue him; so I believe you will not desire me to do it for you; but he shall not want Pressing (tho' I scarcely ever dun for myself) because I think his Relations may [and] will help him if properly apply'd to; and Mr. Hall thinks with me, that urging him frequently may make him more considerate, and induce him to abridge some of his unnecessary Expences. The Bond is made payable in a Month from this Day; and, for your Encouragement I may add that notwithstanding what he affects to say of the Badness of his Circumstances, I look on the Debt to be far from desperate.

Please to send me Chambers's Dictionary,[8] the best Edition, and charge it in Mr. Hall's Invoice. My Compliments to good Mrs. Strahan: My Dame writes to her. I am, with great Esteem and Affection, Dear Sir, Your most obliged Friend and humble Servant   B FRANKLIN

Addressed: To Mr William Strahan Printer in Wine Office Court Fleetstreet London

From James Logan

Letterbook abstract: Historical Society of Pennsylvania

To B Franklin   3 mo. [May] 19th [1749]
Sent him Capt. Smiths voyages or Travels to Virginia. Greg. Leti's Sisto 5to. 2 Voll and Marchetti's Lucrezzio in Italian[9] and

8. Ephraim Chambers, *Cyclopaedia: or, An Universal Dictionary of Arts and Sciences,* of which a fourth edition appeared in London in 1741, and a fifth in 1743.

9. "Capt. Smiths voyages" was probably *The True Travels, Adventures, and Observations of Captaine John Smith, In Europe, Asia, Affrica, and*

379

desired him to Send me what Classics he has published by M. Mattaire.[1]

To James Logan

MS not found; reprinted from extract in Sparks, *Works*, VII, 40.

[May 19, 1749]

I send you the third and fourth volumes of the Harleian Miscellany,[2] and also what I have of Mattaire's Classics. I think I promised to send you something else, but have forgotten what it was. You complain of the decay of your memory, but mine is a miserable one, and never was good. I thank you for your favor in lending me Marchetti's *Lucrezio* and Smith's Travels, which I shall take care duly to return.

From James Logan

Letterbook abstract: Historical Society of Pennsylvania

4 [mo. June] 11 [1749]

Wrote to B. Franklin to come up and See my Books.

America, from Anno Domini 1593 to 1629 (London, 1630), which Logan owned. The other books are Gregorio Leti, *Vita di Sisto V.*, *Pontefice Romano* (Amsterdam, 1686), and Alessandro Marchetti's translation, *Di T. Lucrezio Caro della Natura della cose* (London, 1717). All are in Loganian Lib. Cat.

1. Michael Maittaire (1668–1747), scholar and typographer, edited a series of Latin classics, printed by Tonson and Watts of London, 1713–19. His many other writings include *Stephanorum Historia* (London, 1709), and *Annales Typographici* (5 vols., The Hague, Amsterdam, London, 1719–41). For BF's use of the first book to print a title page for Logan's Euclid of 1516, see above, p. 219 n. Maittaire's large library, rich in classical authors and early printed editions, was sold at auction in London, 1748. *DNB*.

2. *The Harleian Miscellany:* . . . (8 vols., London, 1744–56). The third and fourth volumes, published in 1745, contain respectively an account of Cardinal Mazarin's library and Sir Thomas Bodley's autobiography.

To William Strahan

MS not found; reprinted from Bigelow, *Works*, X, 252–3.

Dear Sir,   Philadelphia, July 3, 1749
I wrote to you very fully per Arthur concerning your affair
with Mr. Read,³ and shall have nothing to add on that subject
till I hear further from you. I acquainted you that he had given
his bond for the balance due to you, and that I do not look on
the debt as desperate.

Enclosed I send you several second bills, having sent the firsts
per Arthur. I hope to hear per next ship that you have received
my son's pay, since I understand there was a [Bill of]⁴ Parliament
in March last, for a sum to defray all the charges of the Canada
expedition.⁵ If it should prove otherwise, I will send the balance
from hence in the fall, and make you satisfaction for the delay
and disappointment.

The Library Company send to Mr. Collinson by this ship for a
parcel of books. I have recommended you to him on the occasion,
and hope you will have the selling of them. If you should, and
the Company judge your charges reasonable, I doubt not but
you will keep their custom.

I fear I shall not have the pleasure of seeing you this year, perhaps the next I may.

Please to send me a book lately advertised; I think it is called
A Collection of Sentences, Wise Sayings, etc., by some officer
about the Parliament House; his name I have forgot.⁶

3. See above, p. 377.
4. Missing words supplied from extract in Rosenbach Company, *1776
Americana* . . . (Phila., 1926), p. 28, no. 53.
5. The Secretary at War, March 10, 1749, laid before Parliament bills for
expenses incurred during the war in America, including Clinton's accounts.
This is probably what BF referred to. Additional accounts, including the
charges for supporting the troops from Pennsylvania, were presented to
Parliament, March 12, 1750; a committee recommended payment; and the
bill passed. Leo F. Stock, ed., *Proceedings and Debates of the British Parlia-
ments respecting North America*, V (Washington, 1941), 299–300, 416, 425;
below, p. 479.
6. *A Collection of select Aphorisms and Maxims* (London, 1748), by Charles
Palmer, deputy-serjeant of the House of Commons. BF drew many aphorisms
for *Poor Richard* from it. See above, I, 282.

With all our best respects to you and yours, I am, dear sir, your most obliged friend and servant, B. FRANKLIN

What is the price of printing paper in London?

To James Logan
ALS: American Philosophical Society

Sir July 4. 49

I sent word today to N. Holland,[7] that you desired to see him, and offer'd him my Horse. He sent me word, he could get a Horse in the Neighbourhood, and would wait on you.

I return you Smith's Travels with Thanks.[8] I send you also Wr. Pope's Life of Ward Bishop of Salisbury.[9] I am, Sir, with great Respect Your most humble Servant B FRANKLIN

Endorsed: Benj: Franklin July 4 1749

To George Whitefield

Reprinted from *The Evangelical Magazine*, XI (1803), 27–8; also AL (fragment): American Philosophical Society.[1]

Dear Sir, Philadelphia, July 6, 1749

Since your being in England, I have received two of your favours, and a box of books to be disposed of.[2] It gives me great pleasure to hear of your welfare, and that you purpose soon to return to America.

7. Possibly "Holland the bookbinder" who is mentioned by John Smith as doing work for the Quaker Monthly Meeting, 1749. Albert C. Myers, ed., *Hannah Logan's Courtship* (Phila., 1904), p. 267.

8. See above, p. 379.

9. Walter Pope, *The Life of the Right Reverend Father in God Seth, Lord Bishop of Salisbury* (London, 1697), listed in Loganian Lib. Cat. Ward was Savilian professor of astronomy at Oxford, 1649–60, and the author of *Astronomica Geometrica* (London, 1656), also in Loganian Lib. Cat.

1. Because the surviving MS fragment consists only of a narrow vertical strip of pages 1 and 2, the editors have followed the printed version, with two exceptions: following the MS, they have capitalized the "A" in *Ad Exemplum Regis* and eliminated an exclamation point after "fashion."

2. Whitefield returned to England, July 1748. Neither the letters nor any reference to the books have been found. A letter "To Mr. F——," July 7, 1748, announcing his safe arrival, printed in his *Select Collection of Letters* (London, 1772), II, 147, may have been addressed to BF.

We have no kind of news here worth writing to you. The affair of the building remains in *statu quo,* there having been no new application to the Assembly about it, nor any thing done in consequence of the former.[3]

I have received no money on your account from Mr. Thanklin,[4] or from Boston. Mrs. Read, and your other friends here in general are well, and will rejoice to see you again.

I am glad to hear that you have frequent opportunities of preaching among the great. If you can gain them to a good and exemplary life, wonderful changes will follow in the manners of the lower ranks; for, *Ad Exemplum Regis, &c.* On this principle Confucius, the famous eastern reformer, proceeded. When he saw his country sunk in vice, and wickedness of all kinds triumphant, he applied himself first to the grandees; and having by his doctrine won them to the cause of virtue, the commons followed in multitudes. The mode has a wonderful influence on mankind; and there are numbers that perhaps fear less the being in Hell, than out of the fashion. Our more western reformations began with the ignorant mob; and when numbers of them were gained, interest and party-views drew in the wise and great. Where both methods can be used, reformations are like to be more speedy. O that some method could be found to make them lasting! He that shall discover that, will, in my opinion, deserve more, ten thousand times, than the inventor of the longtitude.

My wife and family join in the most cordial salutations to you and good Mrs. Whitefield. I am, dear Sir, your very affectionate friend, and most obliged humble servant,   B. FRANKLIN

From Peter Kalm

MS not found; reprinted from extract in *The Pennsylvania Gazette,* October 12, 1749.[5]

[Quebec, August 6, 1749]
I have found more learned Men in Canada, than I imagined had been in all America. The Jesuits in general excel in several Parts

3. On the New Building, see below, p. 435.
4. Not identified. Possibly the original editor's error for "Franklin."
5. This letter was also printed in *N.-Y. Gaz.,* Oct. 16, 1749, and in *Md. Gaz.,* Nov. 29, 1749. Kalm wrote of it in New York: "From the gazettes which were printed here in town I discovered also that Mr. Franklin, the

of Learning; and the King's Officers also are skilful in the Arts and Sciences. The new General Governor, Monsieur Jonquiere,[6] who was taken Prisoner by the English in the last War, arrived here on Friday last from France. He was received with all imaginable Marks of Honour. All the Great Men met him at his Landing (when all the Cannon of the City were discharged) and attended him to the Cathedral Church, the Streets being lined on both Sides with Soldiers. When he came to the Door of the Church, he was met by the Bishop and all the Priests in their finest Habits. The Bishop made him a long congratulatory Oration; and after he had kissed a silver Crucifix, he went into the Church, the Bishop and Priests going and singing before him, carrying Candles and Crucifixes. There he assisted at the High Mass, which was perform'd by the Bishop himself. From the Church he went to the Castle, where all the Citizens and others came to pay their Reverence to him, with many Speeches and Orations. I had the honour to be invited to assist at all this Ceremony, and to dine in the Castle. In the Afternoon there was a great Procession through all the Streets, in honour of the Virgin Mary. Monsieur Gallissoniere,[7] who was Vice Governor General, returns to France in

---

postmaster at Philadelphia, my very special friend, had had printed in the Philadelphia gazette an extract from the letter which I had written to him from Quebec, Canada. . . . All of the French were especially pleased at this, as they had [in this article] been given considerable honor for their learning." Kalm, *Travels*, II, 625; Benson's brackets. Kalm set out for Canada from New York with a pass from Gov. Clinton on May 30. *Colden Paps.*, IX, 10. For a fuller account of the governor's arrival, see Kalm, *Travels*, II, 464–5, under date of Aug. 15 (N.S.).

6. Pierre-Jacques de Taffanel, Marquis de la Jonquière (1685–1752), was the French admiral defeated by Anson, Boscawen, and Warren off Cape Finisterre, May 3, 1747. See above, p. 253.

7. Rolland Michel Barrin, Marquis de la Gallissonière (1693–1756), acting governor general, 1747–49, while La Jonquière was a prisoner of war. A man of scientific interests, he instructed soldiers, officers, and travelers in Canada to observe and collect minerals, plants, and animals. Kalm regarded him highly, imagining that in him "I saw our great Linné under a new form." On his return to France La Gallissonière became director of the bureau of maps and plans of the French Navy, and in 1750–54 was one of the French commissioners to determine the New England-Canadian boundary.

In his English translation of Kalm's *Travels* (Warrington, 1770–71), John R. Forster inserted a protest against Kalm's prejudice in favor of the French

about two Weeks. 'Tis said here that he will be made Secretaire d'Etat de France. He is the most learned Man in all Sciences, but especially in Natural History, that I have yet seen: It is hard to conceive where he could have acquir'd so much Knowledge. The new General Governor is a tall Man, between 60 and 70 Years of Age, of a benevolent Disposition, very agreeable in Conversation, &c.[8]

On the Need for an Academy

Printed in *The Pennsylvania Gazette*, August 24, 1749.

By 1740 Franklin was well satisfied with his condition and prospects in Pennsylvania, but he regretted that no provision was made "for a compleat Education of Youth." He "therefore in 1743, drew up a Proposal for establishing an Academy,"[9] which he discussed with Rev. Richard Peters, whom he considered suitable to head such an institution. Peters declined, "having more profitable Views in the Service of the Proprietors";[1] and Franklin "let the Scheme lie a while dormant." He revived it in 1749 with the support of "a Number of active Friends, of whom the Junto furnished a good Part,"[2] and gave notice of their project by reprinting Pliny's letter on education.

To the Printers of the GAZETTE.

In the settling of new countries, the first care of the planters must be to provide and secure the necessaries of life; This en-

---

scientists in Canada. Benson points out that BF and his friends were private persons, whereas the French and Swedish scientists had government support. Kalm might have altered his opinions had he met Logan or visited the philosophers and colleges in New England and the South. Kalm, *Travels*, I, 374–6; II, 504–6.

8. La Gallissonière was short and hunchbacked; the Indians were impressed by the contrast between his great spirit and mean body. *Ibid.*, II, 504; E.B. O'Callaghan, ed., *Documents relative to the Colonial History of . . . New York*, VI (Albany, 1855), 533 n.

9. Nothing is known of its contents.

1. He had some hopes of being appointed chief justice succeeding Jeremiah Langhorne, who died Oct. 11, 1742. John Kinsey's appointment to the office was announced to the Council, April 5, 1743. Hubertis Cummings, *Richard Peters* (Phila., 1944), pp. 81, 84; *Pa. Col. Recs.*, IV, 640.

2. Par. Text edit., pp. 276–8, 296.

grosses their attention, and affords them little time to think of any thing farther. We may therefore excuse our ancestors, that they established no ACADEMY or college in this province, wherein their youth might receive a polite and learned education. *Agriculture* and *mechanic arts*, were of the most immediate importance; the *culture* of *minds* by the *finer arts* and *sciences*, was necessarily postpon'd to times of more wealth and leisure.

Since those times are come, and numbers of our inhabitants are both able and willing to give their sons a good education, if it might be had at home, free from the extraordinary expence and hazard in sending them abroad for that purpose; and since a proportion of men of learning is useful in every country, and those who of late years come to settle among us, are chiefly foreigners, unacquainted with our language, laws and customs; it is thought, a proposal for establishing an ACADEMY in this province, will not now be deem'd unseasonable. Such a proposal the publick may therefore shortly expect. In the mean time, please to give the following letter of the younger Pliny to Cornelius Tacitus, a place in your paper, as it seems *apropos* to the design above mentioned.

PLINY junior to CORNELIUS TACITUS.[3]

I rejoice that you are safely arrived in Rome; for tho' I am always desirous to see you, I am more particularly so now. I purpose to continue a few days longer at my house at Tusculum, in order to finish a work which I have upon my hands: For I am afraid, should I put a stop to this design, now that it is so nearly compleated, I shall find it difficult to resume it. In the mean while, that I may lose no time, I send this letter before me, to request a favour of you, which I hope shortly to ask in person: But before I inform you what my request is, I must let you into the occasion of it. Being lately at Comum, the place of my nativity, a young lad, son to one of my neighbours, made me a visit. I asked him whether he studied, and where? He told me he did, and at Mediolanum.* And why not here? Because (said his father, who

*Milan.

3. Pliny, *Letters*, IV, xiii. The extract, with unimportant changes, is from William Melmoth's translation, of which the fourth edition appeared in London, 1747.

came with him) we have no masters. "No! said I, surely it nearly concerns you, who are fathers (and very opportunely several of the company were so) that your sons should receive their education here, rather than any where else: For where can they be placed more agreeably, than in their own country, or instructed with more safety, and less expence, than at home, and under the eye of their parents? Upon what very easy terms might you, by a general contribution, procure proper masters, if you would only apply towards the raising a salary for them, the extraordinary expence it costs you for your sons journies, lodgings, and what-soever else you pay for upon account of their being abroad; as pay indeed you must in such a case for every thing? Tho' I have no children myself, yet I shall willingly contribute to a design so beneficial to (what I look upon as a child, or a parent) my country; and therefore I will advance a third part of any sum you shall think proper to raise for this purpose. I would take upon myself the whole expence, were I not apprehensive that my benefaction might hereafter be abused, and perverted to private ends; as I have observed to be the case in several places where publick foundations of this nature have been established. The single means to prevent this mischief is, to have the choice of the masters entirely in the breast of the parents, who will be so much the more careful to determine properly, as they shall be obliged to share the expence of maintaining them: For tho' they may be careless in disposing of another's bounty, they will certainly be cautious how they apply their own; and will see that none but those who deserve it shall receive my money, when they must at the same time receive theirs too. Let my example then en-courage you to unite heartily in this useful design, and be as-sured, the greater the sum my share shall amount to, the more agreeable it will be to me. You can undertake nothing that will be more advantageous to your children, nor more acceptable to your country. They will, by this means, receive their education where they receive their birth, and be accustomed, from their infancy, to inhabit and affect their native soil. May you be able to procure professors of such distinguished abilities, that the neighbouring towns shall be glad to draw their learning from hence; and as you now send your children to foreigners for edu-cation, may foreigners in their turn flock hither for their instruction." I thought proper thus to lay open to you the rise of this affair, that you might be the more sensible how agreeable it will be to me, if you undertake the office I request. I intreat you, therefore, with all the earnestness a matter of so much importance deserves, to look out, amongst the great numbers of men of letters, which the reputation of your genius brings to you, proper persons to whom we may apply for this purpose; but without entering into any agreement with them on my part: For I would leave it entirely free to the parents to judge and choose as they shall see proper: All the share I pretend to claim is, that of contributing my care and my money: If therefore any one shall be found, who thinks himself qualified for the undertaking, he may repair thither; but without relying upon any thing but his merit. Farewell.

To Abiah Franklin

MS not found; reprinted from *London Magazine: and Monthly Chronologer*, XII (1825), 606.

Honoured Mother,   Philadelphia, Sep. [7]. 1749[4]

We received your kind Letter[5] by this Post, and are glad to hear you still continue to enjoy such a share of Health. Cousin Josiah and his Spouse[6] arrived here hearty and well last Saturday noon; I met them the Evening before at Trenton, 30 miles off and accompany'd them to Town. They went into their own House on Monday and I believe will do very well for he seems bent on Industry and she appears a discreet notable young Woman. My Wife has been to see them every Day, calling in as she passes by, and I suspect has fallen in Love with our new Cousin, for she entertains me a deal when she comes home with what Cousin Sally does and what Cousin Sally says and what a good contriver she is and the like.

4. The *London Magazine* dates this letter Sept. 17; Sparks (*Familiar Letters*, pp. 15–16; *Works*, VII, 39–41) and some later editors date it Sept. 7. Sparks is followed here because Sept. 7, which fell on Thursday in 1749, better fits BF's account of the movements of Josiah Davenport and his wife than does Sept. 17, a Sunday.

5. Not found.

6. Josiah Franklin Davenport (C.12.4), BF's nephew, had married Sarah Billings in Boston, June 29. He set up as a baker in Philadelphia.

I believe it might be of service to me in the matter of getting in my debts, if I were to make a voyage to London; but I have not yet determined on it in my own mind, and think I am grown almost too lazy to undertake it.

The Indians are gone homewards, loaded with presents; in a week or two the Treaty with them will be printed and I will send you one.[7]

My Love to Brother and sister Mecom and to all enquiring Friends. I am your dutiful Son   B. FRANKLIN

To James Logan   ALS (fragment): Historical Society of Pennsylvania

Philada. Sept. 12. 49

[*First part missing*] [Ad]vertisement, by which you will see the Language of the Picts is now under Consideration at home.[8] If I had a Copy of what you have wrote on that Subject, I would take Care it should not be lost.[9]

Please to favour me with the short Account of your Library, contain'd in the Paper I read the other Day at your House, that I may insert it in a Note to the Proposals for an Academy. I am, with great Respect, Sir, Your most obliged humble Servant

B FRANKLIN

7. The minutes of the conference with the Indians, Aug. 16–21, were reported to the Council and Assembly (*Pa. Col. Recs.*, V, 398–410), but were not separately printed, as BF expected. Their presents included 10 half barrels of gunpowder, 10 hundredweight of bar lead, 3 hundredweight of small shot, 140 plain and 50 ruffled shirts, guns, knives, hatchets, mirrors, ribbons, rings, beads, tobacco, pipes, and "1 Groce & a half of small Brass Jews Harps."

8. The advertisement was of Dr. John Free (1711–1791), *An Essay towards an History of the English Tongue* (London, 1749), the third section or "dissertation" of which was "Of the Pyhtas, corruptly called Picts." The *Essay* had greater ethnological than philological interest, and if BF thought it would help him in preparing the curriculum for the academy at Philadelphia (see below, p. 397), he was disappointed. A graduate of Oxford in 1730, Free held various livings and became master of St. Saviour Grammar School, Southwark, 1747. He wrote countless sermons, pamphlets, poems, and lectures; attacked Popery and Methodism; and published an astonishing plan for a free university to be founded in England by the Empress of Russia for all peoples and religions. John Nichols, *Literary Anecdotes of the Eighteenth Century* (9 vols., London, 1812–15), V, 687–95; IX, 631.

9. Nothing more seems to be known about Logan's writing on the Picts' language.

From James Logan

Letterbook copy: Historical Society of Pennsylvania

My Friend B F   7br. [September] 13. 49

I received thine of Yesterdays date this day about 11 but do not believe that discourse of Doctor Frees explains the Discourse of the Picts or as he calls them the Pyhtas as I have done for he mentions the duration of their Language.[1] I shall cause my younger Son[2] next Month when he is out of his time [to] copy out that discourse: Thou may mention my Library as thou pleases but it [truly?] contains the Polyglot Bible and Castels Lexicon on it in 3 large Voll. Aldus's Septuagint and divers other Editions of the Bible with most of the Fathers, almost all the Greek Authors from Homer himself of whom there are Several Editions and one of them with Eustathius's Comm[entaries] of the Roman Edit. in 4 Voll. with Politi's Translation of him in Greek and Latin attempted in 3 large Voll. to near the end of the 4th Cent[ury] in more than 100 Voll. in folio comprising all the old Mathem[aticia]ns as Archimedes, Apollonius, Euclid, Ptolemy's Geography and his Syntaxis or Almagest and divers of the valuable Photius, Suidas, Several of the Byzantine much later with all the Roman Classicks without exception and many of them in Several Editions as all Cicero's Works in 4 [several Editions] all Graevius, Gronovius, Salengre, and Poleni's Collections of the Roman and Greek Antiq. in some 33 Tomes bound in 31 Voll. with some hundreds of other Writers as Vossius, Lipsius, Grotius &c. a large Collection of later, as well as the before mentioned Ancient Mathema[tician]s in divers languages Some oriental French and Italian and a great many more English &c.[3]

This is a Summary of my Library, the whole of which I can not well expect thou wilt insert in that discourse but leaving thee perfectly at thy Liberty thou shuld not displease me provided thou mentions it at all to which I shall add no more but that I am with Sincere respect Thy Affectionate friend   J L

1. See below, p. 393 n.
2. James Logan, Jr. (1728–1803), Logan's fifth and youngest child, was apprenticed to the merchant John Reynell.
3. BF used this information with little change in a footnote to his *Proposals relating to the Education of Youth* (see below, p. 401–2).

James Logan

From Peter Collinson ALS: Historical Society of Pennsylvania

Respected friend   Lond Septr 14t 1749
I was unwilling to loose the Opertunity per Cap. Rice—So in 5 or 6 Days time I ordred all the Books to your Order that Could be gott together. I was so much engaged I could not go to see them before they was packed—but Hope the Bookseller has been carefull to send such as will Meet with your aprobation.

What can be gott to the remainder of your Order may be sent in the Spring with the things for the Air pump.

Your Bill is in its way to Scotland for Acceptance.

I am concern'd Capt. Clark was oblig'd to putt into Rhoad Island.

I have lately receivd a Book on Electricity from Paris,[4] which I send for thy perusal. Return it by any private hand. I am perswaded it will afford thee some Entertainment.

I am with much Esteem thy sincere friend   P COLLINSON

Pray Remember Mee to J: Bartram. If I have leisure I will answer his Entertaining Letter of 28th July on the Locasts and Dragon flies &c. I Desire he would make Mee a Collection of them. I Long for the arrival of Budden to see what He has sent Mee.

I wonder he takes no Notice of what of my Orders are come to hand—for I have sent by several Ships for 13 boxes and now I have an order for another. I wish the year may prove plentyfull in Seeds for John Sake besides on order From Powell the Seedsman in Holbourn[5] sent per J Pemberton[6] for a Tenn or Twenty Guinea Cargo.

I hope J. Pemberton is safe arrived by whome have sent 1 Vol. Lives of Popes &c.[7] Pray give my Love to him.

4. Not identified.

5. Possibly Anthony Powell, gardener to George II and author of *The Royal Gardener* (London, 1769). George W. Johnson, *A History of English Gardening* (London, 1829), p. 230.

6. James Pemberton, who sailed home from England in July or August, 1749. Pemberton Papers, v, Hist. Soc. Pa.

7. Archibald Bower, *The History of the Popes* (7 vols., London, 1748–66). In 1752 BF presented to Yale College a copy of Vol. 1 (2d edit., 1749), possibly the copy Collinson refers to here, and followed this gift in 1754 with Vol. 11 (3d edit., 1750).

I Desire my friend John will send Mee in the next Ships $\frac{1}{2}$ doz. young plants of the small Magnolia for my own Garden and of the flowering Ivy or next year which he thinks best.

	By Mesnard	£1: 1:3
Pamphlets	By the Macclesfield	2:6
sent	By the beula	12:8
per	By Legross	2:–
	By J. Pemberton	1:17:–

I just now receivd a Present of a New Mapp of your Province and who I am to thank I [dont] know except Lewis Evans.[8]

[*Addressed:*] For   Mr Benn Franklin   In   Philadelphia   per Capt Rice

8. On Lewis Evans, see above, p. 48 n. His *Map of Pensilvania, New-Jersey, New-York, And the Three Delaware Counties* was engraved by Lawrence Hebert of Philadelphia, and a few trial copies were printed (possibly by Franklin and Hall) in the late winter of 1749, when subscriptions were opened. It was advertised as "just published" in *Pa. Gaz.*, Aug. 3, 1749. The map is reproduced in facsimile in Henry N. Stevens, *Lewis Evans: His Map of the Middle British Colonies in America* (2d edit., London, 1920). See also Lawrence C. Wroth, *An American Bookshelf, 1755* (Phila., 1934), pp. 150–4; Lawrence H. Gipson, *Lewis Evans* (Phila., 1939), pp. 17–24. The map has a special Franklin interest because Evans printed in one of the empty spaces some data on northeast storms and thundergusts which BF evidently provided. Although he had developed his theory about the course of northeast storms in 1743, this is the first published statement of it. See above, p. 149, also above, p. 365, on thundergusts, and below, p. 463, on storms. William E. Lingelbach, "Franklin and the Lewis Evans Map of 1749," APS *Year Book 1945*, pp. 63–73. Evans' paragraphs are as follows:

"All our great Storms begin to Leeward: thus a NE Storm shall be a Day sooner in Virginia than Boston. There are generally remarkable Changes in the Degrees of Heat and Cold at Philadelphia every 3 or 4 Days, but not so often to the Northward. The Navigation of Philadelphia is almost every Winter stopt by Ice for 2 or 3 Months; and tho' North River is longer froze than Delaware, yet N. York, being on Salt Water affords better Winter Navigation. Both Delaware and N. York Bays are quite free from the Ship Worms. Land Wind in dry Weather raises the thickest Fogs, attracting the Moisture on the Rivers and Coasts, it comes in Contact with, in such large Quantities, that, untill it is dissipated by the Sun and other Causes, it obstructs the Vibrations of Light in direct Lines. After this Dissipation of Fogs, we have the most intense Heats; and very often Thunder Gusts towards Evening.

"Thunder never happens, but with the Meeting of Sea and Land Clouds. The Sea Clouds coming freighted with Electricity, and meeting others less

To James Logan

MS not found; reprinted from extract in Sparks, *Works*, VII, 40.

[September 18, 1749]

For the reason you mention, I am of the same opinion, that Dr. Free has not considered the Picts' language as you have done, but imagines with other writers that the Pict nation was totally destroyed and its language with it.[9]

From James Logan

Letterbook copy: Historical Society of Pennsylvania

My friend B Fr   8br [October] 6th [1749]

I absolutely forgot to mention what I principally intended yesterday. Thy telling me what were the most likely paper Mills to Supply me with 6 or 7 sheets or more of Pastboard of about 19 or 20 inches in length and 15 in breadth and what rolling presses were [in] town to smooth them, an exact account of which to be prepared to day and Sent in the Morning with thy proposal for the Academy will very much [oblige] thine Affectionately J L

---

so, the Equilibrium is restored by Snaps of Lightning: and the more opposite the Winds, and the larger and compacter the Clouds, the more dreadful are the Shocks: The Sea Clouds, thus suddenly bereft of that universal Element of Repellency, contract, and their Water gushes down in Torrents.

"Land Winds passing over a large shaded (and very often frozen) Continent (on both Sides of the Mountains) are always dry and cold, and the Sea Winds wet and warm. NE is a settled high Wind, and most often wet, and SW, squawly and unsettled. The hottest Weather is with a S Wind and Calms, and the coldest with NW. Snow comes from N to NE; Rainy Storms from NE to E; and high dry Wind from the W. The Land Winds blow above $\frac{3}{4}$ of the Year."

9. See above, p. 390. John Free wrote of the Pictish language that, with "the Saxon to the South, and the Gaelick to the North of the Friths gaining daily such Ground upon it, at the last it was quite extinguished." *An Essay towards an History of the English Tongue* (London, 1749), p. 56. Free used other writers, notably Thomas Innes, *A Critical Essay on the Ancient Inhabitants of the Northern Parts of Britain, or Scotland* (2 vols., London, 1729), accepting his views on the extinction of the Picts, although disagreeing with him on their origin.

Be pleas'd also to inform me what the Translators name of the fr[ench] Polybius is. Tis M. Folard in 6 Voll. 4to with many Cuts.[1]

To William Strahan

MS not found; reprinted from Bigelow, *Works*, X, 253–4.

Dear Sir,   Philadelphia, October 23, 1749

I hope before this can reach you your Parliament will have met and ordered payment of what has been so long due on account of the Canada expedition.[2] In the settling our account I will make you a reasonable allowance for the disappointment occasioned by the delay of my son's bill.

J. Read has removed into a house of less rent, which I was well pleased with. I have had no talk with him lately about your affairs, but still hope the best; and it shall not be long before I take an opportunity of urging him to discharge some part of the bond.[3]

I am now engaged in a new public affair, as you will see by the enclosed,[4] which I hope, with God's blessing, will very soon be in good train. I have not laid aside my intention of seeing England, and believe shall execute it next year, if nothing extraordinary occurs, in which your conversation is not one of the least pleasures I propose to myself.

I hope this will find you and good Mrs. Strahan safe returned from your northern journey. I am just setting out on one, and have only time to add that I am, with great esteem and sincere affection, dear sir, your most obliged humble servant,

B. FRANKLIN

P.S. Please to give my account credit for what you receive by the enclosed power of attorney,[5] and let me know the sum, that I may pay the person here.

1. *Histoire de Polybe*, translated from the Greek by Dom Vincent Thuillier, with a commentary by M. de Folard (6 vols., Paris, 1727–30); in Loganian Lib. Cat.

2. BF had sent Strahan his son William's certificate from the governor of New York for payment for his military service at Albany, 1747–48. Parliament finally authorized payment in 1750. See above, p. 321, and below, p. 479.

3. On BF's efforts to collect James Read's debt to Strahan, see above, pp. 316, 329, 377.

4. BF's *Proposals Relating to the Education of Youth*.

5. Not found.

PROPOSALS N. 2

RELATING TO THE

EDUCATION

OF

YOUTH

IN

PENSILVANIA.

PHILADELPHIA:
Printed in the Year, M.DCC.XLIX

Proposals Relating to the Education
of Youth in Pennsylvania

Proposals Relating to the Education of Youth in Pensilvania. Philadelphia: Printed in the Year, M,DCC,XLIX. (Yale University Library)

This pamphlet was printed after September 13, 1749, when Logan wrote the account of his library which Franklin printed in a footnote. It was printed before October 23, if, as seems likely, he enclosed it to Strahan, to whom he wrote on that day, "I am now engaged in a new public affair." A mid-October date seems reasonable since a subscription had to be opened, the subscribers had to choose trustees, and the trustees had to adopt a constitution—all of which was done by November 13.

ADVERTISEMENT TO THE READER.

It has long been regretted as a Misfortune to the Youth of this Province, that we have no ACADEMY, in which they might receive the Accomplishments of a regular Education.

The following Paper of *Hints* towards forming a Plan for that Purpose, is so far approv'd by some publick-spirited Gentlemen, to whom it has been privately communicated, that they have directed a Number of Copies to be made by the Press, and properly distributed, in order to obtain the Sentiments and Advice of Men of Learning, Understanding, and Experience in these Matters; and have determin'd to use their Interest and best Endeavours, to have the Scheme, when compleated, carried gradually into Execution; in which they have Reason to believe they shall have the hearty Concurrence and Assistance of many who are Wellwishers to their Country.

Those who incline to favour the Design with their Advice, either as to the Parts of Learning to be taught, the Order of Study, the Method of Teaching, the Oeconomy of the School, or any other Matter of Importance to the Success of the Undertaking, are desired to communicate their Sentiments as soon as may be, by Letter directed to B. Franklin, Printer, in Philadelphia.

AUTHORS quoted in this PAPER.[6]

1. The famous Milton, whose Learning and Abilities are well

6. BF's quotations are from the following: John Milton, *Paradise Regain'd ... To which is added. Samson Agonistes. And Poems upon several Occasions.*

397

known and who had practised some Time the Education of Youth, so could speak from Experience.

2. The great Mr. Locke, who wrote a Treatise on Education, well known, and much esteemed, being translated into most of the modern Languages of Europe.

3. *Dialogues on Education*, 2 Vols. Octavo, that are much esteem'd, having had two Editions in 3 Years. Suppos'd to be wrote by the ingenious Mr. Hutcheson (Author of *A Treatise on the Passions*, and another on the *Ideas of Beauty and Virtue*) who has had much Experience in Educating of Youth, being a Professor in the College at Glasgow, &c.

4. The learned Mr. Obadiah Walker, who had been many Years a Tutor to young Noblemen, and wrote a Treatise *on the Education of a young Gentleman;* of which the Fifth Edition was printed 1687.

5. The much admired Mons. Rollin, whose whole Life was spent in a College; and wrote 4 Vols. on Education, under the Title of, *The Method of Teaching and Studying the Belles Lettres;* which are translated into English, Italian, and most of the modern Languages.

6. The learned and ingenious Dr. George Turnbull, Chaplain to the present Prince of Wales; who has had much Experience in the Educating of Youth, and publish'd a Book, Octavo, intituled, *Observations on Liberal Education, in all its Branches,* 1742.

With some others.

With a Tractate of Education (5th edit., London, 1721); John Locke, *Some Thoughts concerning Education* (11th edit., London, 1745); [David Fordyce], *Dialogues concerning Education* (2 vols., London, 1745–48), which BF erred in attributing to Francis Hutcheson, as he recognized in a letter to James Logan, Dec. 17, 1749; Obadiah Walker, *Of Education. Especially of Young Gentlemen* (5th impression, Oxford, 1687); Charles Rollin, *The Method of Studying and Teaching the Belles Lettres* (4th edit., 4 vols., London, 1749); George Turnbull, *Observations upon Liberal Education, In all its Branches* (London, 1742).

BF characteristically quoted his authorities with casual accuracy, altering and telescoping sentences and paragraphs, italicizing and capitalizing to suit his mood and promote his purpose, rather than to make a display of pedantic literalness. No attempt has been made to collate his versions with the originals, but in a few instances the editors have clarified his citations by inserting missing volume numbers, and they have regularly italicized the titles of books mentioned in his text and notes, and have inserted opening and closing quotation marks that BF occasionally overlooked.

PROPOSALS, &C.

The good Education of Youth has been esteemed by wise Men in all Ages, as the surest Foundation of the Happiness both of private Families and of Common-wealths.* Almost all Governments have therefore made it a principal Object of their Attention, to establish and endow with proper Revenues, such Seminaries of Learning, as might supply the succeeding Age with Men qualified to serve the Publick with Honour to themselves, and to their Country.

Many of the first Settlers of these Provinces, were Men who had received a good Education in Europe, and to their Wisdom and good Management we owe much of our present Prosperity. But their Hands were full, and they could not do all Things. The present Race are not thought to be generally of equal Ability: For though the American Youth are allow'd not to want Capacity; yet the best Capacities require Cultivation, it being truly with them, as with the best Ground, which unless well tilled and sowed with profitable Seed, produces only ranker Weeds.

*As some Things here propos'd may be found to differ a little from the Forms of Education in common Use, the following Quotations are to shew the Opinions of several learned Men, who have carefully considered and wrote expresly on the Subject; such as Milton, Locke, Rollin, Turnbull, and others. They generally complain, that the *old Method* is in many Respects wrong; but long settled Forms are not easily changed. For us, who are now to make a Beginning, 'tis, at least, as easy to set out right as wrong; and therefore their Sentiments are on this Occasion well worth our Consideration.

Mr. Rollin says (*Belles Lett.* [IV] p. 249. speaking of the Manner of Educating Youth) "Though it be generally a very wise and judicious Rule to avoid all Singularity, and to follow the received Customs, yet I question whether, in the Point we now treat of, this Principle does not admit of some Exception, and whether we ought not to apprehend the Dangers and Inconveniencies of blindly following the Footsteps of those who have gone before us, so as to consult *Custom* more than *Reason*, and the governing our Actions rather by what others *do*, than by what they *should do;* from whence it often happens, that an Error once established is handed down from Age to Age, and becomes almost a certain Law, from a Notion, that we ought to act like the rest of Mankind, and follow the Example of the greatest Number. But human Nature is not so happy as to have the greatest Number always make the best Choice, and we too frequently observe the contrary."

399

That we may obtain the Advantages arising from an Increase of Knowledge, and prevent as much as may be the mischievous Consequences that would attend a general Ignorance among us, the following *Hints* are offered towards forming a Plan for the Education of the Youth of Pennsylvania, viz.

It is propos'd,

THAT some Persons of Leisure and publick Spirit, apply for a CHARTER, by which they may be incorporated, with Power to erect an ACADEMY for the Education of Youth, to govern the same, provide Masters, make Rules, receive Donations, purchase Lands, &c. and to add to their Number, from Time to Time such other Persons as they shall judge suitable.

That the Members of the Corporation make it their Pleasure, and in some Degree their Business, to visit the Academy often, encourage and countenance† the Youth, countenance and assist the Masters, and by all Means in their Power advance the Usefulness and Reputation of the Design; that they look on the Students as in some Sort their Children, treat them with Familiarity and Affection, and when they have behav'd well, and gone through their Studies, and are to enter the World, zealously unite, and make all the Interest that can be made to establish them,‡ whether in Business, Offices, Marriages, or any other Thing for their Advantage, preferably to all other Persons whatsoever even of equal Merit.

And if Men may, and frequently do, catch such a Taste for cultivating Flowers, for Planting, Grafting, Inoculating, and the

†Rollin, Vol. 2. p. 371. mentions a French Gentleman, Mons. Hersan, who, "at his own Expence, built a School for the Use of poor Children, one of the finest in the Kingdom; and left a Stipend for the Master. That he himself taught them very often, and generally had some of them at his Table. He clothed several of them; and distributed Rewards among them from Time to Time, in order to encourage them to study."

‡Something seems wanting in America to incite and stimulate Youth to Study. In Europe the Encouragements to Learning are of themselves much greater than can be given here. Whoever distinguishes himself there, in either of the three learned Professions, gains Fame, and often Wealth and Power: A poor Man's Son has a Chance, if he studies hard, to rise, either in the Law or the Church, to gainful Offices or Benefices; to an extraordinary Pitch of Grandeur; to have a Voice in Parliament, a Seat among the Peers; as a Statesman or first Minister to govern Nations, and even to mix his Blood with Princes.

like, as to despise all other Amusements for their Sake, why may not we expect they should acquire a Relish for that *more useful* Culture of young Minds. Thompson says,[7]

> 'Tis Joy to see the human Blossoms blow,
> When infant Reason grows apace, and calls
> For the kind Hand of an assiduous Care;
> Delightful Task! to rear the tender Thought,
> To teach the young Idea how to shoot,
> To pour the fresh Instruction o'er the Mind,
> To breathe th' enliv'ning Spirit, and to fix
> The generous Purpose in the glowing Breast.

That a House be provided for the ACADEMY, if not in the Town, not many Miles from it; the Situation high and dry, and if it may be, not far from a River, having a Garden, Orchard, Meadow, and a Field or two.

That the House be furnished with a Library (if in the Country, if in the Town, the Town Libraries* may serve) with Maps of all

*Besides the English Library begun and carried on by Subscription in Philadelphia, we may expect the Benefit of another much more valuable in the Learned Languages, which has been many Years collecting with the greatest Care, by a Gentleman distinguish'd for his universal Knowledge, no less than for his Judgment in Books.[8] It contains many hundred Volumes of the best Authors in the best Editions, among which are the Polyglot Bible, and Castel's Lexicon on it, in 8 large Vols. Aldus's Septuagint, Apocrypha and New Testament, in Greek, and some other Editions of the same; most of the Fathers; almost all the Greek Authors from Homer himself, in divers Editions (and one of them in that of Rome, with Eustathius's Commentaries, in 4 Vols.) to near the End of the 4th Century, with divers later, as Photius, Suidas, divers of the Byzantine Historians; all the old Mathematicians, as Archimedes, Apollonius, Euclid, Ptolomy's Geography and Almagest, with Theon's Commentaries and Diophantus, in the whole above 100 Vols.

7. James Thomson, *The Seasons*. "Spring," 1143–4, 1147–53. The first line reads:
  . . . By degrees,
  The human blossom blows . . .
and "When infant Reason" is "Then infant Reason" in the poet's words.

8. This collector was James Logan, who in response to BF's request provided the material for this note, Sept. 13, 1749. The works referred to are listed in *Catalogue of the Books belonging to the Loganian Library* (Phila., 1837).

Countries, Globes, some mathematical Instruments, an Apparatus for Experiments in Natural Philosophy, and for Mechanics; Prints, of all Kinds, Prospects, Buildings, Machines, &c.†

That the RECTOR be a Man of good Understanding, good Morals, diligent and patient, learn'd in the Languages and Sciences, and a correct pure Speaker and Writer of the English Tongue; to have such Tutors under him as shall be necessary.

That the boarding Scholars diet‡ together, plainly, temperately, and frugally.

That to keep them in Health, and to strengthen and render active their Bodies, they be frequently exercis'd* in Running, Leaping, Wrestling, and Swimming,** &c.

---

in Greek Folio's. All the old Roman Classics without Exception, and some of them in several Editions (as all Tully's Works in four Editions). All Graevius, Gronovius, Salengre's and Poleni's Collections of Roman and Greek Antiquities, containing above Five Hundred distinct Discourses in 33 Tomes, with some Hundreds of late Authors in Latin, as Vossius, Lipsius, Grotius, &c. A good Collection of Mathematical Pieces, as Newton in all the three Editions, Wallis, Huygens, Tacquet, Dechales, &c. in near 100 Vols. in all Sizes, with some Orientals, French and Italian Authors, and many more English, &c. A handsome Building above 60 Feet in front, is now erected in this City, at the private Expence of that Gentleman, for the Reception of this Library, where it is soon to be deposited, and remain for the publick Use, with a valuable yearly Income duly to enlarge it; and I have his Permission to mention it as an Encouragement to the propos'd Academy; to which this noble Benefaction will doubtless be of the greatest Advantage, as not only the Students, but even the Masters themselves, may very much improve by it.

†See in Turnbull, p. 415. the Description of the Furniture of the School called the Instituto at Bologna, procur'd by the Care and Direction of Count Marsigli, and originally at his private Expence.

‡Perhaps it would be best if none of the Scholars were to diet abroad. Milton is of that Opinion (*Tractate of Education*) for that much Time would else be lost, and many ill Habits got.

*Milton proposes, that an Hour and Half before Dinner should be allow'd for Exercise, and recommends among other Exercises, the handling of Arms, but perhaps this may not be thought necessary here. Turnbull, p. 318. says, "Corporal Exercise invigorates the Soul as well as the Body; let one be kept closely to Reading, without allowing him any Respite from Thinking, or any Exercise to his Body, and were it

That they have peculiar Habits to distinguish them from other Youth, if the Academy be in or near the Town; for this, among other Reasons, that their Behaviour may be the better observed.

---

possible to preserve long, by such a Method, his Liking to Study and Knowledge, yet we should soon find such an one become no less soft in his Mind than in his outward Man. Both Mind and Body would thus become gradually too relaxed, too much unbraced for the Fatigues and Duties of active Life. Such is the Union between Soul and Body, that the same Exercises which are conducive, when rightly managed, to consolidate or strengthen the former, are likewise equally necessary and fit to produce Courage, Firmness, and manly Vigour, in the latter. For this, and other Reasons, certain hardy Exercises were reckoned by the Antients an essential Part in the Formation of a liberal Character; and ought to have their Place in Schools where Youth are taught the Languages and Sciences." See p. 318 to 323.

**'Tis suppos'd that every Parent would be glad to have their Children skill'd in *Swimming*, if it might be learnt in a Place chosen for its Safety, and under the Eye of a careful Person. Mr. Locke says, p. 9. in his *Treatise of Education;* "'Tis that saves many a Man's Life; and the Romans thought it so necessary, that they rank'd it with Letters; and it was the common Phrase to mark one ill educated, and good for nothing, that he had neither learnt to read nor to swim; *Nec Literas didicit nec Natare.* But besides the gaining a Skill which may serve him at Need, the Advantages to Health by often Bathing in cold Water during the Heat of the Summer, are so many, that I think nothing need be said to encourage it."

'Tis some Advantage besides, to be free from the slavish Terrors many of those feel who cannot swim, when they are oblig'd to be on the Water even in crossing a Ferry.

Mr. Hutchinson [i.e., Fordyce], in his *Dialogues concerning Education*, 2 Vols. Octavo, lately publish'd, says, Vol. 2. p. 297. "I would have the Youth accustomed to such Exercises as will harden their Constitution, as Riding, Running, Swimming, Shooting, and the like."

Charlemagne, Founder of the German Empire, brought up his Sons hardily, and even his Daughters were inur'd to Industry. Henry the Great of France, saith Mons. Rhodez,[9] "was not permitted by his Grandfather to be brought up with Delicacy, who well knew that *seldom lodgeth other than a mean and feeble Spirit in an effeminate and tender Body.* He commanded that the Boy should be accustomed to run, to leap, to climb the Rocks and Mountains; that by such Means he might be inured to Labour, &c. His ordinary Food also was of coarse Bread,

9. The whole paragraph is from Walker, not Rhodez.

As to their STUDIES, it would be well if they could be taught *every Thing* that is useful, and *every Thing* that is ornamental: But Art is long, and their Time is short. It is therefore propos'd that they learn those Things that are likely to be *most useful* and *most ornamental*, Regard being had to the several Professions for which they are intended.

All should be taught to write a *fair Hand*, and swift, as that is useful to All. And with it may be learnt something of *Drawing*,‡ by

---

Beef, Cheese and Garlick; his Cloathing plain and coarse, and often he went barefoot and bareheaded." Walker *of Education*, p. 17, 18.

‡*Drawing* is a kind of Universal Language, understood by all Nations. A Man may often express his Ideas, even to his own Countrymen, more clearly with a Lead Pencil, or Bit of Chalk, than with his Tongue. And many can understand a Figure, that do not comprehend a Description in Words, tho' ever so properly chosen. All Boys have an early Inclination to this Improvement, and begin to make Figures of Animals, Ships, Machines, &c. as soon as they can use a Pen: But for want of a little Instruction at that Time, generally are discouraged, and quit the Pursuit.

Mr. Locke says, p. 234. "When your Son can write well and quick, I think it may be convenient not only to continue the Exercise of his Hand in Writing, but also to improve the Use of it further in *Drawing;* a Thing very useful to a Gentleman on several Occasions; but especially if he travel; as that which helps a Man often to express in a *few Lines* well put together, what a *whole Sheet of Paper in Writing* would not be able to represent and make intelligible. How many Buildings may a Man see, how many *Machines* and Habits meet with, the Ideas whereof would be easily retain'd, and communicated by a little Skill in Drawing; which being committed to Words, are in Danger to be lost, or at best but ill retained in the most exact Descriptions? I do not mean that I would have him a perfect Painter; to be that to any tolerable Degree, will require more Time than he can spare from his other Improvements of greater Moment. But so much Insight into Perspective and Skill in Drawing, as will enable him to represent tolerably on Paper any Thing he sees, except Faces, may, I think, be got in a little Time."

Drawing is no less useful to a *Mechanic* than to a Gentleman. Several Handicrafts seem to require it; as the Carpenter's, Shipwright's, Engraver's, Painter's, Carver's, Cabinet-maker's, Gardiner's, and other Businesses. By a little Skill of this kind, the Workman may perfect his own Idea of the Thing to be done, before he begins to work; and show a Draft for the Encouragement and Satisfaction of his Employer.

Imitation of Prints, and some of the first Principles of Perspective. *Arithmetick,** *Accounts,* and some of the first Principles of *Geometry* and *Astronomy.*

The English Language† might be taught by Grammar; in which some of our best Writers, as Tillotson, Addison, Pope,

---

*Mr. Locke is of Opinion, p. 269. that a Child should be early enter'd in Arithmetick, Geography, Chronology, History and Geometry. "Merchants Accounts, he says, if it is not necessary to help a Gentleman to *get* an Estate, yet there is nothing of more Use and Efficacy to make him *preserve* the Estate he has. 'Tis seldom observ'd that he who keeps an Account of his Income and Expences, and thereby has constantly under View the Course of his Domestic Affairs, lets them run to Ruin: And I doubt not but many a Man gets behind-hand before he is aware, or runs farther on when he is once in, for want of this Care, or the Skill to do it. I would therefore advise all Gentlemen to learn perfectly *Merchants Accounts;* and not to think 'tis a Skill that belongs not to them, because it has received its Name, and has been chiefly practis'd by Men of Traffick." p. 316.

Not only the *Skill,* but the *Habit* of keeping Accounts, should be acquir'd by all, as being necessary to all.

†Mr. Locke, speaking of *Grammar,* p. 252. says, "That to those the greatest Part of whose Business in this World is to be done with their Tongues, and with their Pens, it is convenient, if not necessary, that they should speak properly and correctly, whereby they may let their Thoughts into other Mens Minds the more easily, and with the greater Impression. Upon this Account it is, that any sort of Speaking, so as will make him be understood, is not thought enough for a Gentleman. He ought to study *Grammar,* among the other Helps of Speaking well, but it *must be* THE GRAMMAR OF HIS OWN TONGUE, of the Language he uses, that he may understand his own Country Speech nicely, and speak it properly, without shocking the Ears of those it is addressed to with Solecisms and offensive Irregularities. And to this Purpose *Grammar is necessary;* but it is the Grammar *only* of *their own proper Tongues,* and to those who would take Pains in cultivating their Language, and perfecting their Stiles. Whether all Gentlemen should not do this, I leave to be considered, since the Want of Propriety and Grammatical Exactness is thought very misbecoming one of that Rank, and usually draws on one guilty of such Faults, the Imputation of having had a lower Breeding and worse Company than suits with his Quality. If this be so (as I suppose it is) it will be Matter of Wonder, why young Gentlemen are forc'd to learn the Grammars of foreign and dead Languages, and are never once told of the Grammar of their own Tongues.

Algernon Sidney, Cato's Letters, &c. should be Classicks: The *Stiles* principally to be cultivated, being the *clear* and the *concise*.

They do not so much as know there is any such Thing, much less is it made their Business to be instructed in it. Nor is their own Language ever propos'd to them as worthy their Care and Cultivating, tho' they have *daily Use* of it, and are not seldom, in the future Course of their Lives, judg'd of by their handsome or awkward Way of expressing themselves in it. Whereas the Languages whose Grammars they have been so much employed in, are such as probably they shall scarce ever speak or write; or if upon Occasion this should happen, they should be excused for the Mistakes and Faults they make in it. Would not a Chinese, who took Notice of this Way of Breeding, be apt to imagine, that all our young Gentlemen were designed to be Teachers and Professors of the dead Languages of foreign Countries, and not to be Men of Business in their own." Page 255. the same Author adds, "That if Grammar ought to be taught at any Time, it must be to one that can speak the Language already; how else can he be taught the Grammar of it? This at least is evident from the Practice of the wise and learned Nations among the Antients. They made it a *Part of Education* to cultivate *their own*, not foreign Tongues. The Greeks counted all other Nations barbarous, and had a Contempt for their Languages. And though the Greek Learning grew in Credit amongst the Romans towards the End of their Commonwealth, yet it was the Roman Tongue that was made the Study of their Youth: *Their own* Language they were to make Use of, and therefore it was *their own* Language they were *instructed* and *exercised* in." And p. 281. "There can scarce be a greater Defect (says he) in a Gentleman, than not to express himself well either in Writing or Speaking. But yet I think I may ask the Reader, whether he doth not know a great many, who live upon their Estates, and so, with the Name, should have the Qualities of Gentlemen, who cannot so much as tell a Story as they should, much less speak clearly and persuasively in any Business. This I think not to be so much their Fault as the *Fault of their Education*." Thus far Locke.

Mons. Rollin, reckons the Neglect of Teaching their own Tongue a great Fault in the French Universities. He spends great Part of his first Vol. of *Belles Lettres*, on that Subject; and lays down some excellent Rules or Methods of Teaching French to Frenchmen grammatically, and making them Masters therein, which are very applicable to our Language, but too long to be inserted here. He practis'd them on the Youth under his Care with great Success.

Mr. Hutchinson, *Dial.* [II] p. 297. says, "To perfect them in the Knowledge of their Mother Tongue, they should learn it in the Grammatical Way, that they may not only speak it purely, but be able both

Reading should also be taught, and pronouncing, properly, distinctly, emphatically; not with an even Tone, which *under-does*,
nor a theatrical, which *over-does* Nature.

to correct their own Idiom, and afterwards enrich the Language on
the same Foundation."

Dr. Turnbull, in his *Observations on a liberal Education*, says, p. 262.
"The Greeks, perhaps, made more early Advances in the most useful
Sciences than any Youth have done since, chiefly on this Account, that
they studied no other Language but their own. This no Doubt saved
them very much Time; but they *applied themselves carefully* to the
Study of *their own* Language, and were *early* able to speak and write it
in *the greatest Perfection*. The Roman Youth, though they learned the
Greek, did not neglect their own Tongue, but studied it more carefully
than we now do Greek and Latin, without giving ourselves any Trouble
about our own Tongue."

Mons. Simon, in an elegant Discourse of his among the Memoirs
of the Academy of Belles Lettres at Paris,[1] speaking of the Stress the
Romans laid on Purity of Language and graceful Pronunciation, adds,
"May I here make a Reflection on the Education we commonly give
our Children? It is very remote from the Precepts I have mentioned.
Hath the Child arrived to six or seven Years of Age, he mixes with a
Herd of ill-bred Boys at School, where under the Pretext of Teaching
him *Latin*, no Regard is had to his *Mother Tongue*. And what happens?
What we see every Day. A young Gentleman of eighteen, who has had
this Education, CANNOT READ. For to articulate the Words, and join
them together, I do not call *Reading*, unless one can pronounce well,
observe all the proper Stops, vary the Voice, express the Sentiments,
and read with a delicate Intelligence. Nor can he speak a Jot better. A
Proof of this is, that he cannot write ten Lines without committing
gross Faults; and because he did not learn his own Language well in
his early Years, he will never know it well. I except a few, who being
afterwards engaged by their Profession, or their natural Taste, cultivate
their Minds by Study. And yet even they, if they attempt to write, will
find by the *Labour* Composition costs them, what a *Loss it is*, not to
have learned their Language in the proper Season. Education among
the Romans was upon a quite different Footing. Masters of Rhetoric
taught them early the Principles, the Difficulties, the Beauties, the
Subtleties, the Depths, the Riches of their own Language. When they
went from these Schools, they were perfect Masters of it, they were
never at a Loss for proper Expressions; and I am much deceived if it

1. Jean-François Simon in *Mémoires de l'Académie des Inscriptions et Belles-
Lettres*, v, quoted from Turnbull, pp. 333–5.

To form their Stile, they should be put on Writing Letters‡ to each other, making Abstracts of what they read; or writing the same Things in their own Words; telling or writing Stories lately

was not owing to this, that they produced such excellent Works with so *marvellous Facility.*"

Pliny, in his Letter to a Lady on chusing a Tutor for her Son,[2] speaks of it as the most material Thing in his Education, that he should have a good Latin Master of Rhetoric, and recommends Julius Genitor for his *eloquent, open and plain Faculty of Speaking.* He does not advise her to a Greek Master of Rhetoric, tho' the Greeks were famous for that Science; but to a Latin Master, because Latin was the Boy's Mother Tongue. In the above Quotation from Mons. Simon, we see what was the Office and Duty of the Master of Rhetoric.

‡This Mr. Locke recommends, *Educ.* p. 284. and says, "The Writing of Letters has so much to do in all the Occurrences of human Life, that no Gentleman can avoid shewing himself in this Kind of Writing. Occasions will daily force him to make this Use of his Pen, which, besides the Consequences that, in his Affairs, the well or ill managing it often draws after it, always lays him open to a severer Examination of his Breeding, Sense and Abilities, than oral Discourses, whose transient Faults dying for the most Part with the Sound that gives them Life, and so not subject to a strict Review, more easily escape Observation and Censure." He adds,

"Had the Methods of Education been directed to their right End, one would have thought this so necessary a Part could not have been neglected, whilst Themes and Verses in Latin, of no Use at all, were so constantly every where pressed, to the Racking of Childrens Inventions beyond their Strength, and hindring their chearful Progress by unnatural Difficulties. But Custom has so ordained it, and who dares disobey? And would it not be very unreasonable to require of a learned Country Schoolmaster (who has all the Tropes and Figures in Farnaby's Rhetorick[3] at his Finger's Ends) to teach his Scholar to express himself handsomely in English, when it appears to be so little his Business or Thought, that the Boy's Mother (despised, 'tis like, as illiterate for not having read a System of Logic or Rhetoric) outdoes him in it?

"To speak and write correctly, gives a Grace, and gains a favourable Attention to what one has to say: And since 'tis English that an Englishman will have constant Use of, that is the Language he should chiefly cultivate, and wherein most Care should be taken to polish and

2. Pliny, *Letters*, III, iii, quoted from Turnbull, p. 236.
3. Thomas Farnaby, *Index Rhetoricus scholis et institutioni tenerioris aetatis accomodatus* (London, 1633 and later edits.).

read, in their own Expressions. All to be revis'd and corrected by the Tutor, who should give his Reasons, explain the Force and Import of Words, &c.

———

perfect his Stile. To speak or write better Latin than English, may make a Man be talk'd of, but he will find it more to his Purpose to express himself well in his own Tongue, that he uses every Moment, than to have the vain Commendation of others for a very insignificant Quality. This I find universally neglected, nor no Care taken any where to improve young Men in their own Language, that they may thoroughly understand and be Masters of it. If any one among us have a Facility or Purity more than ordinary in his Mother Tongue, it is owing to Chance, or his Genius, or any Thing, rather than to his Education, or any Care of his Teacher. To mind what English his Pupil speaks or writes, is below the Dignity of one bred up among Greek and Latin, tho' he have but little of them himself. These are the Learned Languages, fit only for Learned Men to meddle with and teach: English is the Language of the illiterate Vulgar. Though the Great Men among the Romans were daily exercising themselves in their own Language; and we find yet upon Record the Names of Orators who taught some of their Emperors Latin, tho' it were their Mother Tongue. 'Tis plain the Greeks were yet more nice in theirs. All other Speech was barbarous to them but their own, and no foreign Language appears to have been studied or valued amongst that learned and acute People; tho' it be past Doubt, that they borrowed their Learning and Philosophy from abroad.

"I am not here speaking against Greek and Latin. I think Latin at least ought to be well understood by every Gentleman. But whatever foreign Languages a young Man meddles with, that which he should critically study, and labour to get a Facility, Clearness and Elegancy to express himself in, should be *his own;* and to this purpose *he should daily be* EXERCISED in it."

To the same Purpose writes a Person of eminent Learning in a Letter to Dr. Turnbull: "Nothing certainly (says he) can be of more Service to Mankind than a right Method of Educating the Youth, and I should be glad to hear ——————— ——————— to give an Example of the great Advantage it would be to the *rising Age,* and to our Nation. When our publick Schools were first establish'd, the Knowledge of Latin was thought Learning; and he that had a tolerable Skill in two or three Languages, tho' his Mind was not enlightened by any *real Knowledge,* was a profound Scholar. But it is not so at present; and People confess, that Men may have obtained a Perfection in these, and yet continue *deeply ignorant.* The Greek Education was of another Kind

To form their Pronunciation,* they may be put on making Declamations, repeating Speeches, delivering Orations, &c. The Tutor assisting at the Rehearsals, teaching, advising, correcting their Accent, &c.

But if HISTORY† be made a constant Part of their Reading, such as the Translations of the Greek and Roman Historians, and the modern Histories of antient Greece and Rome, &c. may not

---

[which he describes in several Particulars, and adds]⁴ They studied to write their *own Tongue* more accurately than we do Latin and Greek. But where is English taught at present? Who thinks it of Use to study correctly *that Language* which he is to use *every Day* in his Life, be his Station ever so high, or ever so insignificant. It is in *this* the Nobility and Gentry defend their Country, and serve their Prince in Parliament; in *this* the Lawyers plead, the Divines instruct, and all Ranks of People write their Letters, and transact all their Affairs; and yet who thinks it worth his learning to write *this* even accurately, not to say politely? Every one is suffer'd to form his Stile by Chance; to imitate the first wretched Model which falls in his Way, before he knows what is faulty, or can relish the Beauties of a just Simplicity. Few think their Children qualified for a Trade till they have been whipt at a Latin School for five or six Years, to learn a little of that which they are oblig'd to forget; when in those Years right Education would have improv'd their Minds, and taught them to acquire Habits of Writing *their own Language* easily under right Direction; and this would have been useful to them as long as they lived." *Introd.* p. 3, 4, 5.

Since Mr. Locke's Time, several good Grammars have been wrote and publish'd for the Use of Schools; as Brightland's, Greenwood's, &c.⁵

*By Pronunciation is here meant, the proper Modulation of the Voice, to suit the Subject with due Emphasis, Action, &c. In delivering a Discourse in Publick, design'd to persuade, the *Manner*, perhaps, contributes more to Success, than either the *Matter* or *Method*. Yet the two latter seem to engross the Attention of most Preachers and other Publick Speakers, and the former to be almost totally neglected.

†As nothing *teaches* (saith Mr. Locke) so nothing *delights* more than HISTORY. The first of these recommends it to the Study of grown

4. BF's brackets.
5. John Brightland, *A Grammar of the English Tongue* (London, 1711 and later edits.), and James Greenwood, *An Essay towards a practical English Grammar* (London, 1711 and later edits.).

almost all Kinds of useful Knowledge be that Way introduc'd to Advantage, and with Pleasure to the Student? As

GEOGRAPHY, by reading with Maps, and being required to point out the Places *where* the greatest Actions were done, to give their old and new Names, with the Bounds, Situation, Extent of the Countries concern'd, &c.

CHRONOLOGY, by the Help of Helvicus[6] or some other Writer of the Kind, who will enable them to tell *when* those Events happened; what Princes were Cotemporaries, what States or famous Men flourish'd about that Time, &c. The several principal Epochas to be first well fix'd in their Memories.

ANTIENT CUSTOMS, religious and civil, being frequently mentioned in History, will give Occasion for explaining them; in which the Prints‡ of Medals, Basso Relievo's, and antient Monuments will greatly assist.

———

Men, the latter makes me think it the *fittest* for a young Lad, who as soon as he is instructed in Chronology, and acquainted with the several Epochas in Use in this Part of the World, and can reduce them to the Julian Period, should then have some History put into his Hand. *Educ.* p. 276.

Mons. Rollin complains, that the College Education in France is defective in Teaching *History;* which he thinks may be made of great Advantage to Youth. This he demonstrates largely in his *Belles Lettres,* to the Satisfaction of all that read the Book. He lays down the following Rules for Studying History, viz. 1. To reduce the Study to Order and Method. 2. To observe what relates to Usages and Customs. 3. To enquire particularly, and above all Things, after the Truth. 4. To endeavour to find out the Causes of the Rise and Fall of States, of the Gaining or Losing of Battles, and other Events of Importance. 5. To study the Character of the Nations and great Men mentioned in History. 6. To be attentive to such Instructions as concern MORAL EXCELLENCY and the CONDUCT OF LIFE. 7. Carefully to note every Thing that relates to RELIGION. Vol. 3. p. 146.

‡Plenty of these are to be met with in Montfaucon;[7] and other Books of Antiquities.

6. Christophorus Helvicus, *The Historical and Chronological Theatre* (London, 1687).

7. Bernard de Montfaucon, *L'Antiquité expliquée et representée en figures* (5 vols., Paris, 1719), and other works.

MORALITY,* by descanting and making continual Observations on the Causes of the Rise or Fall of any Man's Character, Fortune, Power, &c. mention'd in History; the Advantages of Temperance, Order, Frugality, Industry, Perseverance, &c. &c.† Indeed the general natural Tendency of Reading good History, must be, to fix in the Minds of Youth deep Impressions of the Beauty and Usefulness of Virtue of all Kinds, Publick Spirit, Fortitude, &c.

History will show the wonderful Effects of ORATORY, in governing, turning and leading great Bodies of Mankind, Armies, Cities, Nations. When the Minds of Youth are struck with Admiration at this,‡ then is the Time to give them the Principles

*For the Importance and Necessity of moral Instructions to Youth, see the latter Notes.

†Dr. Turnbull, *Liberal Education,* p. 371, says, "That the useful Lessons which ought to be inculcated upon Youth, are much better taught and enforced from *Characters, Actions,* and *Events,* developing the inward Springs of human Conduct, and the different Consequences of Actions, whether with Respect to private or publick Good, than by abstract Philosophical Lectures. History points out in Examples, as in a Glass, all the Passions of the human Heart, and all their various Workings in different Circumstances, all the Virtues and all the Vices human Nature is capable of; all the Snares, all the Temptations, all the Vicissitudes and Incidents of human Life; and gives Occasion for Explaining all the Rules of Prudence, Decency, Justice and Integrity, in private Oeconomy, and in short all the Laws of natural Reason."

‡"Rules are best understood, when Examples that confirm them, and point out their Fitness or Necessity, naturally lead one, as it were by the Hand, to take Notice of them. One who is persuaded and moved by a Speech, and heartily admires its Force and Beauty, will with Pleasure enter into a critical Examination of its Excellencies; and willingly lay up in his Mind the Rules of Rhetoric such an Example of Eloquence plainly suggests. But to teach Rules abstractly, or without Examples, and before the agreeable Effects the Observance of them tends to produce (which are in Reality their Reason or Foundation)⁸ have been felt, *is exceedingly preposterous.*" Turnbull, p. 410.

"I have seldom or never observed any one to get the Skill of Speaking handsomely, by Studying the Rules which pretend to teach Rhetoric." Locke, p. 279.

8. BF's parenthetical remarks.

of that Art, which they will study with Taste and Application. Then they may be made acquainted with the best Models among the Antients, their Beauties being particularly pointed out to them. Modern Political Oratory being chiefly performed by the Pen and Press, its Advantages over the Antient in some Respects are to be shown; as that its Effects are more extensive, more lasting, &c.

History will also afford frequent Opportunities of showing the Necessity of a *Publick Religion,* from its Usefulness to the Publick; the Advantage of a Religious Character among private Persons; the Mischiefs of Superstition, &c. and the Excellency of the CHRISTIAN RELIGION above all others antient or modern.*

History will also give Occasion to expatiate on the Advantage of Civil Orders and Constitutions, how Men and their Properties are protected by joining in Societies and establishing Government; their Industry encouraged and rewarded, Arts invented, and Life made more comfortable: The Advantages of *Liberty,* Mischiefs of *Licentiousness,* Benefits arising from good Laws and a due Execution of Justice, &c. Thus may the first Principles of sound *Politicks*† be fix'd in the Minds of Youth.

On *Historical* Occasions, Questions of Right and Wrong, Justice and Injustice, will naturally arise, and may be put to Youth, which they may debate in Conversation and in Writing.‡ When they

*See Turnbull on this Head, from p. 386 to 390. very much to the Purpose, but too long to be transcribed here.

†Thus, as Milton says, *Educ.* p. 381. should they be instructed in the Beginning, End and Reasons of political Societies; that they may not, in a dangerous Fit of the Commonwealth, be such poor, shaken, uncertain Reeds, of such a tottering Conscience, as many of our great Councellors have lately shewn themselves, but stedfast Pillars of the State.

‡"After this, they are to dive into the Grounds of Law and legal Justice; deliver'd first and with best Warrant by Moses; and as far as human Prudence can be trusted, in those celebrated Remains of the antient Grecian and Roman Lawgivers, &c." [Milton,] p. 382.

"When he has pretty well digested Tully's Offices, says Mr. Locke, p. 277. and added to it Puffendorff *de Officio Hominis & Civis,* it may be seasonable to set him upon Grotius, *de Jure Belli & Pacis,* or which perhaps is the better of the two, Puffendorff *de Jure naturali* [*naturae*] & *Gentium;* wherein he will be instructed in the natural Rights of Men,

ardently desire Victory, for the Sake of the Praise attending it, they will begin to feel the Want, and be sensible of the Use of *Logic*, or the Art of Reasoning to *discover* Truth, and of Arguing to *defend* it, and *convince* Adversaries. This would be the Time to acquaint them with the Principles of that Art. Grotius, Puffendorff, and some other Writers of the same Kind, may be used on these Occasions to decide their Disputes. Publick Disputes* warm

---

and the Original and Foundations of Society, and the Duties resulting from thence. This *general Part of Civil Law* and History are Studies which a Gentleman should not barely touch at, but constantly dwell upon, and never have done with. A virtuous and well-behaved young Man, that is well versed in the *general Part of the Civil Law* (which concerns not the Chicane of private Cases, but the Affairs and Intercourse of civilized Nations in general, grounded upon Principles of Reason) understands Latin well, and can write a good Hand, one may turn loose into the World, with great Assurance that he will find Employment and Esteem every where."

*Mr. Walker, in his excellent Treatise of the Education of young Gentlemen, speaking of *Publick and open Argumentation pro and con*, says p. 124, 125. "*This is it* which brings a Question to a Point, and discovers the very Center and Knot of the Difficulty. *This* warms and *activates* the Spirit in the Search of Truth, excites Notions, and by replying and frequent Beating upon it, *cleanseth* it from the Ashes, and makes it shine and flame out the clearer. Besides, it puts them upon a continual *Stretch* of their Wits to defend their Cause, it makes them quick in Replies, intentive upon their Subject; where the *Opponent* useth all Means to drive his Adversary from his Hold; and the *Answerer* defends himself *sometimes* with the Force of Truth, *sometimes* with the Subtilty of his Wit; and *sometimes* also he escapes in a Mist of Words, and the Doubles of a Distinction, whilst he seeks all Holes and Recesses to shelter his persecuted Opinion and Reputation. This properly belongeth to the Disputations which are Exercises of young Students, who are by these Velitations and in this Palaestra brought up to a more serious Search of Truth. And in them I think it not a Fault *to dispute for Victory*, and to endeavour to save their Reputation; nor that their Questions and Subjects are concerning Things of small Moment and little Reality; yea, I have known some Governors that have absolutely forbidden such Questions, where the Truth was of Concernment, on purpose that the Youth might have the Liberty of exerting their Parts to the uttermost, and that there might be no Stint to their Emulation."

the Imagination, whet the Industry, and strengthen the natural Abilities.

When Youth are told, that the Great Men whose Lives and Actions they read in History, spoke two of the best Languages that ever were, the most expressive, copious, beautiful; and that the finest Writings, the most correct Compositions, the most perfect Productions of human Wit and Wisdom, are in those Languages, which have endured Ages, and will endure while there are Men; that no Translation can do them Justice, or give the Pleasure found in Reading the Originals; that those Languages contain all Science; that one of them is become almost universal, being the Language of Learned Men in all Countries; that to understand them is a distinguishing Ornament, &c. they may be thereby made desirous of learning those Languages, and their Industry sharpen'd in the Acquisition of them. All intended for Divinity should be taught the Latin and Greek; for Physick, the Latin, Greek and French; for Law, the Latin and French; Merchants, the French, German, and Spanish: And though all should not be compell'd to learn Latin, Greek, or the modern foreign Languages; yet none that have an ardent Desire to learn them should be refused; their English, Arithmetick, and other Studies absolutely necessary, being at the same Time not neglected.

If the new *Universal History*[9] were also read, it would give a *connected* Idea of human Affairs, so far as it goes, which should be follow'd by the best modern Histories, particularly of our Mother Country; then of these Colonies; which should be accompanied with Observations on their Rise, Encrease, Use to Great-Britain, Encouragements, Discouragements, &c. the Means to make them flourish, secure their Liberties, &c.

With the History of Men, Times and Nations, should be read at proper Hours or Days, some of the best *Histories of Nature*,†

†Rollin, Vol. 4. p. 211. speaking of *Natural Philosophy*, says, "That much of it falls within the Capacity of all Sorts of Persons, even of Children. It consists in attending to the Objects with which Nature presents us, in considering them with Care, and admiring their different Beauties, &c. Searching out their secret Causes indeed more properly belongs to the Learned.

"I say that even Children are capable of Studying Nature, for they

9. See above, p. 146 n.

which would not only be delightful to Youth, and furnish them with Matter for their Letters, &c. as well as other History; but afterwards of great Use to them, whether they are Merchants, Handicrafts, or Divines; enabling the first the better to understand many Commodities, Drugs, &c. the second to improve his Trade or Handicraft by new Mixtures, Materials, &c. and the last to adorn his Discourses by beautiful Comparisons, and strengthen them by new Proofs of Divine Providence. The Con-

---

have Eyes, and don't want Curiosity; they ask Questions, and love to be informed; and here we need only awaken and keep up in them the Desire of Learning and Knowing, which is natural to all Mankind. Besides this Study, if it is to be called a Study, instead of being painful and tedious, is pleasant and agreeable; it may be used as a Recreation, and should usually be made a Diversion. It is inconceivable, how many Things Children are capable of, if all the Opportunities of Instructing them were laid hold of, with which they themselves supply us.

"A Garden, a Country, a Plantation, are all so many Books which lie open to them; but they must have been taught and accustomed to read in them. Nothing is more common amongst us than the Use of Bread and Linnen. How seldom do Children know how either of them are prepared, through how many Operations and Hands the Corn and Flax must pass, before they are turned into Bread and Linnen? The same may be said of Cloth, which bears no Resemblance to the Wool whereof it is formed, any more than Paper to the Rags which are picked up in the Streets: And why should not Children be instructed in these wonderful Works of Nature and Art which they every Day make Use of without reflecting upon them?"

He adds, that "a careful Master may in this Way enrich the Mind of his Disciple with a great Number of useful and agreeable Ideas, and by a proper Mixture of short Reflections, will at the same Time take Care to form his Heart, and lead him by Nature to Religion."

Milton also recommends the Study of *Natural Philosophy* to Youth, *Educ.* p. 380. "In this," says he, "they may proceed leisurely from the History of Meteors, Minerals, Plants and living Creatures, as far as Anatomy; Then also in Course might be read to them out of some not tedious Writer, the Institution of Physick; that they may know the Tempers, the Humours, the Seasons, and how to manage a Crudity; which he who can wisely and timely do, is not only a great Physician to himself, and to his Friends, but also may at some Time or other save an Army by this frugal and expenseless Means only; and not let the healthy and stout Bodies of young Men rot away under him for want

versation of all will be improved by it, as Occasions frequently occur of making Natural Observations, which are instructive, agreeable, and entertaining in almost all Companies. *Natural History* will also afford Opportunities of introducing many Observations, relating to the Preservation of Health, which may be afterwards of great Use. Arbuthnot on Air and Aliment, Sanctorius on Perspiration, Lemery on Foods,[2] and some others, may now be read, and a very little Explanation will make them sufficiently intelligible to Youth.

While they are reading Natural History, might not a little *Gardening, Planting, Grafting, Inoculating,* &c. be taught and practised; and now and then Excursions made to the neighbouring Plantations of the best Farmers, their Methods observ'd and reason'd upon for the Information of Youth. The Improvement of Agriculture being useful to all,‡ and Skill in it no Disparagement to any.

The History of *Commerce,* of the Invention of Arts, Rise of Manufactures, Progress of Trade, Change of its Seats, with the

---

of this Discipline, which is a great Pity, and no less a Shame to the Commander."

Proper Books may be, Ray's *Wisdom of God in the Creation,* Derham's *Physico-Theology, Spectacle de la Nature,* &c.[1]

‡Milton would have the Latin Authors on Agriculture taught at School, as Cato, Varro and Columella; "for the Matter," says he, "is most easy, and if the Language be difficult, yet it may be master'd. And here will be an Occasion of *inciting* and *enabling* them hereafter to improve the Tillage of their Country, to recover the bad Soil, and to remedy the Waste that is made of Good; for this was one of Hercules' Praises." *Educ.* p. 379.

Hutcheson [i.e., Fordyce] *(Dialogues on Educ.* 303, 2d Vol.) says, "Nor should I think it below the Dignity or Regard of an University,

1. John Ray, *The Wisdom of God manifested in the Works of the Creation* (London, 1691 and later edits.); William Derham, *Physico-Theology: or a Demonstration of the Being and Attributes of God from his works of creation* (London, 1713 and later edits.); and [N. A. Pluche], *Le Spectacle de la Nature* (8 vols., Paris, 1732–51), English trans., London, 1733 and later edits. BF's gift to Mary Stevenson of the 8th edit. is in APS.

2. John Arbuthnot, *An Essay concerning the Effects of Air on Human Bodies* (London, 1733), and *An Essay concerning the Nature of Aliments* (2 vols., London, 1731–32); *Medicina Statica: being the Aphorisms of Sanctorius* (London, 1712); and Louis Lémery, *Traité des Aliments* (Paris, 1702).

Reasons, Causes, &c. may also be made entertaining to Youth, and will be useful to all. And this, with the Accounts in other History of the prodigious Force and Effect of Engines and Machines used in War, will naturally introduce a Desire to be instructed in *Mechanicks,** and to be inform'd of the Principles of that Art by which weak Men perform such Wonders, Labour is sav'd, Manufactures expedited, &c. &c. This will be the Time to show them Prints of antient and modern Machines, to explain them, to let them be copied,† and to give Lectures in Mechanical Philosophy.

With the whole should be constantly inculcated and cultivated, that *Benignity of Mind,*‡ which shows itself in *searching for* and

---

to descend even to the general Precepts of *Agriculture* and *Gardening*. Virgil, Varro, and others eminent in Learning, tho't it not below their Pen——and why should we think meanly of that Art, which was the Mother of Heroes, and of the Masters of the World."

Locke also recommends the Study of Husbandry and Gardening, as well as gaining an Insight in several of the manual Arts; *Educ.* p. 309, 314, 315. It would be a Pleasure and Diversion to Boys to be led now and then to the Shops of Artificers, and suffer'd to spend some Time there in observing their Manner of Working. For the Usefulness of Mechanic Skill, even to Gentlemen, see the Pages above cited, to which much might be added.

*How many Mills are built and Machines constructed, at great and fruitless Expence, which a little Knowledge in the Principles of Mechanics would have prevented?

†We are often told in the Journals of Travellers, that such and such Things are done in foreign Countries, by which Labour is sav'd, and Manufactures expedited, &c. but their Description of the Machines or Instruments used, are quite unintelligible for want of good Drafts. Copying Prints of Machines is of Use to fix the Attention on the several Parts, their Proportions, Reasons, Effects, &c. A Man that has been us'd to this Practice, is not only better able to make a Draft when the Machine is before him, but takes so much better Notice of its Appearance, that he can carry it off by Memory when he has not the Opportunity of Drawing it on the Spot. Thus may a Traveller bring home Things of great Use to his Country.

‡"Upon this excellent Disposition (says Turnbull, p. 326.) it will be *easy to build* that amiable Quality commonly called GOOD BREEDING, and upon *no other Foundation* can it be raised. For whence else can it

EDUCATION OF YOUTH, 1749

seizing every Opportunity *to serve* and *to oblige;* and is the Foundation of what is called GOOD BREEDING; highly useful to the Possessor, and most agreeable to all.*

The Idea of what is *true Merit,* should also be often presented to Youth, explain'd and impress'd on their Minds, as consisting in an *Inclination* join'd with an *Ability* to serve Mankind, one's Country, Friends and Family; which *Ability* is (with the Blessing of God) to be acquir'd or greatly encreas'd by *true Learning;* and should indeed be the great *Aim* and *End*† of all Learning.

---

spring, but from a general Good-will and Regard for all People, deeply rooted in the Heart, which makes any one that has it, careful not to shew in his Carriage, any Contempt, Disrespect, or Neglect of them, but to express a Value and Respect for them according to their Rank and Condition, suitable to the Fashion and Way of their Country? 'Tis a Disposition to make all we converse with easy and well pleased."

*"It is this lovely Quality which gives true Beauty to all other Accomplishments, or renders them useful to their Possessor, in procuring him the Esteem and Good-will of all that he comes near. Without it, his other Qualities, however good in themselves, make him but pass for proud, conceited, vain or foolish. Courage, says an excellent Writer, in an ill-bred Man has the Air, and escapes not the Opinion of Brutality; Learning becomes Pedantry; Wit, Buffoonery; Plainness, Rusticity; and there cannot be a good Quality in him which Ill-breeding will not warp and disfigure to his Disadvantage." Turnbull, p. 327.

†To have in View the *Glory* and *Service of God,* as some express themselves, is only the same Thing in other Words. For *Doing Good to Men* is the *only Service of God* in our Power; and to *imitate his Beneficence* is to *glorify him.* Hence Milton says, "The *End* of Learning is to repair the Ruins of our first Parents, by regaining to *know God aright,* and out of that Knowledge to *love him,* to *imitate him,* to be *like him,* as we may the nearest by possessing our Souls of true Virtue." *Educ.* p. 373. Mr. Hutcheson [i.e., Fordyce] says, *Dial.* v. 2. p. 97. "The *principal End* of Education is, to *form us wise and good Creatures, useful to others and happy ourselves.* The whole Art of Education lies within a narrow Compass, and is reducible to a very simple Practice; namely, *To assist in unfolding those Natural and Moral Powers with which Man is endowed, by presenting proper Objects and Occasions; to watch their Growth that they be not diverted from their End, or disturbed in their Operation by any foreign Violence; and gently to conduct and apply them to all the Purposes of private and of public Life."* And Mr. Locke (p. 84. *Educ.*) says, "'Tis VIRTUE, then, direct VIRTUE, which is to be *aim'd at* in Education. All

419

other Considerations and Accomplishments are nothing in Comparison to this. This is the *solid* and *substantial* Good, which Tutors should not only read Lectures and talk of, but the *Labour* and *Art of Education* should furnish the Mind with, and *fasten* there, and never cease till the young Man had a true Relish of it, and plac'd his *Strength*, his *Glory*, and his *Pleasure*, in it." And Mons. Rollin, *Belles Lettres*, Vol. 4. p. 249. to the same Purpose, "If we consult our Reason ever so little, it is easy to discern that the END which Masters should have in View, is not barely to teach their Scholars Greek and Latin, to learn them to make Exercises and Verses, to charge their Memory with Facts and historical Dates, to draw up Syllogisms in Form, or to trace Lines and Figures upon Paper. These Branches of Learning I own are useful and valuable, but as *Means*, and not as the *End;* when they conduct us to other Things, and not when we stop at them; when they serve us as Preparatives and Instruments for better Knowledge, without which the rest would be useless. Youth would have Cause to complain, if they were condemned to spend eight or ten of the best Years of their Life in learning, at a great Expence, and with incredible Pains, one or two Languages, and some other Matters of a like Nature, which perhaps they would seldom have Occasion to use. The end of Masters, in the long Course of their Studies, is to habituate their Scholars to serious Application of Mind, to make them love and value the Sciences, and to cultivate in them such a Taste, as shall make them thirst after them when they are gone from School; to point out the Method of attaining them; and make them thoroughly sensible of their Use and Value; and by that Means dispose them for the different Employments to which it shall please God to call them. Besides this, the *End* of Masters should be, *to improve their Hearts* and Understandings, to protect their Innocence, to *inspire* them with Principles of *Honour* and *Probity*, to train them up to good Habits; to correct and subdue in them by gentle Means, the ill Inclinations they shall be observed to have, such as Pride, Insolence, and high Opinion of themselves, and a saucy Vanity continually employed in lessening others; a blind Self-love solely attentive to its own Advantage; a Spirit of Raillery which is pleased with offending and insulting others; and Indolence[3] and Sloth, which renders all the good Qualities of the Mind useless."

Dr. Turnbull has the same Sentiments, with which we shall conclude this Note. "If," says he, "there be any such Thing as DUTY, or any such Thing as HAPPINESS; if there be any Difference between right and wrong Conduct; any Distinction between Virtue and Vice, or Wisdom and Folly; in fine, if there be any such Thing as Perfection or Imperfection belonging to the rational Powers which constitute moral Agents;

3. "Insolence" in Rollin, from whom BF quotes.

or if Enjoyments and Pursuits admit of Comparison; *Good Education* must of Necessity be acknowledged to mean, *proper Care* to instruct early in the Science of Happiness and Duty, or in the Art of Judging and *Acting aright* in Life. Whatever else one may have learned, if he comes into the World from his Schooling and Masters, quite unacquainted with the Nature, Rank and Condition, of Mankind, and the *Duties of human Life* (in its more ordinary Circumstances at least) he hath lost his Time; *he is not educated;* he is not prepared for the World; he is not qualified for Society; he is not fitted for discharging the *proper Business of Man.* The Way therefore to judge whether Education be on a right Footing or not, is to compare it with the END; or to consider what it does in order to accomplish Youth for choosing and *behaving well* in the various Conditions, *Relations* and Incidents, of Life. If Education be calculated and adapted to furnish young Minds betimes with proper Knowledge for their Guidance and Direction in the chief Affairs of the World, and in the principal Vicissitudes to which human Concerns are subject, then it is indeed *proper or right Education.* But if *such Instruction* be not the *principal Scope* to which all other Lessons are rendered subservient in what is called the *Institution of Youth,* either the *Art of Living and Acting well* is not Man's *most important* Business, or what ought to be the CHIEF END of Education is neglected, and sacrificed to something of *far inferior* Moment. *Observations on Liberal Education,* p. 175, 176.

Constitutions of the Academy of Philadelphia

MS Minutes: Trustees of the University of Pennsylvania; another MS version: University of Pennsylvania Archives

This document was drawn up by Franklin and Tench Francis.[4] The final and official version, spread on the Trustees' Minutes and printed here, contains corrections and additions by Franklin and his insertion of James Logan's name at the head of the list of trustees. It is of further interest because marginal marks indicate it was the copy Franklin used in 1789 when he was preparing his Observations relative to the Intentions of the Original Founders of the Academy in Philadelphia.[5] The printed version, a four-page pamphlet (Evans 6405), ends with the following note: "The above Constitutions were signed on the 13th of November, 1749; and are to be carried into Execution as early as may be in the ensuing Year, a considerable Sum being already subscribed for this Purpose by a few Hands; who hope, from the known

4. Par. Text edit., p. 296.
5. Printed in Smyth, *Writings,* x, 9–31.

Publick Spirit of the People of Pennsylvania, that such further Sums as are necessary to be subscribed for perfecting this useful Design, will not be wanting."

The same scrivener copied the Trustees' Minutes and the Archives versions. The latter, however, lacks the names of the trustees and their signatures, though it is followed by the subscription pledge made and signed November 14, printed here next below.

[November 13, 1749]

Constitutions Of the Publick Academy In the City of Philadelphia.

As Nothing can more effectually contribute to the Cultivation and Improvement of a Country, the Wisdom, Riches, and Strength, Virtue and Piety, the Welfare and Happiness of a People, than a proper Education of Youth, by forming their Manners, imbuing their tender Minds with Principles of Rectitude and Morality, instructing them in the dead and living Languages, particularly their Mother-Tongue, and all useful Branches of liberal Arts and Science,

For attaining these great and important Advantages, so far as the present State of our infant Country will admit, and laying a Foundation for Posterity to erect a Seminary of Learning more extensive, and suitable to their future Circumstances, An Acad-emy for teaching the Latin and Greek Languages, the English Tongue, gramatically and as a Language, the most useful living foreign Languages, French, German and Spanish: As Matters of Erudition naturally flowing from the Languages, History, Geography, Chronology, Logick and Rhetorick, Writing, Arithmetick, Algebra, the several Branches of the Mathematicks, Natural and Mechanick Philosophy, Drawing in Perspective, and every other useful Part of Learning and Knowledge, SHALL be set up, main-tained, and have Continuance, in the City of Philadelphia in Manner following: Twenty-four Persons, towit, James Logan, Thomas Lawrence, William Allen, John Inglis, Tench Francis, William Masters, Lloyd Zachery, Samuel M'Call Junr., Joseph Turner, Benjamin Franklin, Thomas Leech, William Shippen, Robert Strettell, Philip Syng, Charles Willing, Phineas Bond, Richard Peters, Abraham Taylor, Thomas Bond, Thomas Hop-kinson, William Plumsted, Joshua Maddox, Thomas White, and

William Coleman, all of the City of Philadelphia, shall be Trustees, to begin, and carry into Execution, this good and pious Undertaking; who shall not for any Services, by them as Trustees performed, claim or receive any Reward or Compensation. Which Number shall always be continued, but never exceeded upon any Motive whatever.

WHEN any Trustee shall remove his Habitation far from the City of Philadelphia, reside beyond Sea, or dye, the remaining Trustees shall, with all convenient Speed, proceed to elect another, residing in or near the City, to fill the Place of the absenting or deceased Person.

THE Trustees shall have general Conventions once in every Month, and may, on special Occasions, meet at other Times on Notice, at some convenient Place within the City of Philadelphia, to transact the Business incumbent on them, and shall, in the Gazette, advertise the Time and Place of their general Conventions.

NOTHING shall be transacted by the Trustees, or under their Authority, alone, unless the same be voted by a Majority of their whole Number, if at a general Convention; and if at a special Meeting, by the like Majority, upon personal Notice given to each Trustee, at least one Day before, to attend.

THE Trustees shall, at their first Meeting, elect a President for one Year, whose particular Duty it shall be, when present, to regulate their Debates, and state the proper Questions arising from them, and to order Notices to be given, of the Times, and Places of their special Conventions. And the like Election shall be annually made, at their first Meeting, after the Expiration of each Year.

THE Trustees shall annually choose one of their own Members for a Treasurer, who shall receive all Donations and Money due to them, and disburse and lay out the same, according to their Orders, and at the End of each Year, pay the Sum remaining in his Hands to his Successor.

ALL Contracts and Assurances, for Payment of Money to them, shall be made in the Name of the Treasurer for the Time being, and declared to be in Trust for the Use of the Trustees.

THE Trustees may appoint a Clerk, whose Duty in particular it shall be, to attend them in their general and special Conventions; to give Notice in Writing to the Members of the Time, and Place, and Design, of any special Meetings; to register all their Proceedings; and extract a State of their Accounts annually, to be published in the Gazette; for which they may pay him such Salary as they shall think reasonable.

THE Trustees shall, with all convenient Speed, after signing these Constitutions, contract with any Person that offers, who they shall judge most capable of teaching the Latin and Greek Languages, History, Geography, Chronology, and Rhetorick; having great Regard at the same Time, to his polite Speaking, Writing, and Understanding the English Tongue. Which Person shall in Fact be, and shall be stiled, the Rector of the Academy.

THE Trustees may contract with the Rector, for the Term of Five Years, or less at their Discretion, for the Sum of Two Hundred Pounds a Year.

THE Rector shall be obliged, without the Assistance of any Usher, to teach Twenty[6] Scholars the Latin and Greek Languages; and at the same Time, according to the best of his Capacity, to instruct them in History, Geography, Chronology, Logick, Rhetorick, and the English Tongue and Twenty five Scholars more, for every Usher provided for him, who shall be intirely subject to his Direction.

THE Rector shall, upon all Occasions, consistent with his Duty in the Latin School, assist the English Master, in improving the Youth under his Care; and superintend the Instruction of all the Scholars, in the other Branches of Learning taught within the Academy; and see that the Masters in each Art and Science, perform their Dutys.

THE Trustees shall, with all convenient Speed, contract with any Person that offers, who they shall judge most capable, of teaching the English Tongue gramatically and as a Language, History, Geography, Chronology, Logick and Oratory. Which Person shall be stiled the English Master.

THE Trustees may contract with the English Master, for the Term of Five Years, or less at their Discretion, for the Sum of One Hundred Pounds a Year.[7]

6. This amount has been written over an earlier figure, erased. The Archives MS gives "Ten Scholars."

7. This figure was inserted after the Constitutions were drawn up; the Archives version has only a blank here.

424

The English Master shall be obliged, without the Assistance of any Usher, to teach Forty[8] Scholars, the English Tongue gramatically and as a Language; and at the same Time, according to the best of his Capacity, to instruct them in History, Geography, Chronology, Logick and Oratory; and Sixty Scholars more, for every Usher provided for him.

The Ushers for the Latin and Greek School, shall be admitted, and at Pleasure removed, by the Trustees and the Rector, or a Majority of them.

The Ushers for the English School shall be admitted, and at Pleasure removed, by the Trustees and the English Master, or a Majority of them.

The Trustees shall contract with each Usher, to pay him what they shall judge proportionable to his Capacity and Merit.

Neither the Rector, nor English Master shall be removed, unless disabled by Sickness, or other natural Infirmity, or for gross voluntary Neglect of Duty continued after two Admonitions from the Trustees; or for committing infamous Crimes, and such Removal be voted by three Fourths of the Trustees; after which their Salarys respectively shall cease.

The Trustees shall, with all convenient Speed, endeavour to engage Persons, capable of teaching the French, Spanish and German Languages, Writing, Arithmetick, Algebra, the several Branches of the Mathematicks, Natural and Mechanick Philosophy, and Drawing; who shall give their Attendance, as soon as a sufficient Number of Scholars shall offer to be instructed in those Parts of Learning; and be paid such Salarys and Rewards, as the Trustees shall from Time to Time be able to allow.

---

8. The difference in the salaries and duties of the rector and English master show how the intentions of some of the founders were frustrated. "When the Constitutions were first drawn," BF wrote in the "Observations" of 1789, "Blanks were left for the Salaries, and for the Number of Boys the Latin Master was to teach. The first Instance of Partiality in favor of the Latin Part of the Institution was in giving the Title of Rector to the Latin Master; and no Title to the English One. But the most striking Instance was when we met to sign, and the Blanks were first to be fill'd up, the Votes of a Majority carry'd it, to give twice as much Salary to the Latin Master as to the English, and yet require twice as much Duty from the English Master as from the Latin, viz. £200 to the Latin Master to teach 20 Boys, £100 to the English Master to teach 40!"

EACH Scholar shall pay such Sum or Sums quarterly, according to the particular Branches of Learning they shall desire to be taught, as the Trustees shall from Time to Time settle and appoint.

No Scholar shall be admitted, or taught within the Academy, without the Consent of the major Part of the Trustees in Writing, signed with their Names.

IN Case of the Disability of the Rector or any Master, established on the Foundation, by receiving a certain Salary, through Sickness or any other natural Infirmity, whereby he may be reduced to Poverty, the Trustees shall have Power to contribute to his Support, in Proportion to his Distress and Merit, and the Stock in their Hands.

FOR the Security of the Trustees, in contracting with the Rector, Masters and Ushers; to enable them to provide and fit up convenient Schools, furnish them with Books of general Use, that may be too expensive for each Scholar; Maps, Draughts, and other Things generally necessary for the Improvement of the Youth; and to bear the incumbent Charges that will unavoidably attend this Undertaking, especially in the Beginning; the Donations of all Persons inclined to encourage it, are to be cheerfully and thankfully accepted.

THE Academy shall be opened with all convenient Speed, by accepting the first good Master that offers, either for teaching the Latin and Greek, or English, under the Terms above proposed.

ALL Rules for the Attendance and Duty of the Masters, the Conduct of the Youth, and facilitating their Progress in Virtue and Learning, shall be framed by the Masters in Conjunction with the Trustees.

IF the Scholars shall hereafter grow very numerous, and the Funds be sufficient, the Trustees may at their Discretion, augment the Salarys of the Rector or Masters.

THE Trustees to increase their Stock, may let their Money out at Interest.

IN general, the Trustees shall have Power to dispose of all Money received by them, as they shall think best for the Advantage, Promotion and even Enlargement of this Design.

THE Trustees may hereafter, add to or change any of these Constitutions, except that hereby declared to be invariable.

ALL Trustees, Rectors, Masters, Ushers, Clerks and other Ministers, hereafter to be elected or appointed, for carrying this Undertaking into Execution, shall, before they be admitted to the Exercise of their respective Trusts or Duties, sign these Constitutions, or some others to be hereafter framed by the Trustees in their Stead, in Testimony of their then approving of, and resolving to observe them.

UPON the Death or Absence as aforesaid of any Trustee, the remaining Trustees shall not have Authority, to exercise any of the Powers reposed in them, until they have chosen a new Trustee in his Place, and such new Trustee shall have signed the established Constitutions; which if he shall refuse to do, they shall proceed to elect another, and so toties quoties, until the Person elected shall sign the Constitutions.

WHEN the Fund is sufficient to bear the Charge, which it is hoped, thro' the Bounty and Charity of well-disposed Persons, will soon come to pass, poor Children shall be admitted and taught gratis, what shall be thought suitable to their Capacities and Circumstances.

IT is hoped and expected, that the Trustees will make it their Pleasure and in some Degree their Business, to visit the Academy often; to encourage and countenance the Youth, countenance and assist the Masters, and by all Means in their Power, advance the Usefulness, and Reputation of the Design; that they will look on the Students as, in some Measure, their own Children, treat them with Familiarity and Affection; and when they have behaved well, gone thro' their Studies, and are to enter the World, they shall zealously unite, and make all the Interest that can be made, to promote and establish them, whether in Business, Offices, Marriages, or any other Thing for their Advantage, preferable to all other Persons whatsoever, even of equal Merit.

THE Trustees shall in a Body, visit the Academy, once a Year extraordinary, to view and hear the Performances and Lectures of the Scholars, in such Modes, as their respective Masters shall think proper; and shall have Power, out of their Stock, to make

427

Presents to the most meritorious Scholars, according to their several Deserts.

WM. SHIPPEN[9]	JOSH. MADDOX	B FRANKLIN
ROBT. STRETTELL	THO LAWRENCE	THOS LEECH
PHILIP SYNG	WILL: ALLEN	THOS: CADWALADER
CHAS. WILLING	JOHN INGLIS	ISAAC NORRIS
PHINEAS BOND	TENCH FRANCIS	THOS. WHITE
RICHARD PETERS	WM: MASTERS	WM: COLEMAN
ABRAM. TAYLOR	LLOYD ZACHARY	D. MARTIN
THOS. BOND	SAM: M'CALL	Rector
THOS. HOPKINSON	JUNR	THEOS: GREW
WM PLUMSTED	JO TURNER	Mathl. Professor

Subscriptions to the Academy

DS: University of Pennsylvania Archives

The 14th: Day of November in the Year of our Lord One Thousand seven Hundred and forty-nine.

9. Biographical and identifying notes on most of these men appear elsewhere in this and the preceding volumes (see indexes). The following persons have not hitherto been identified: John Inglis (1708–1775), merchant; common councilor; captain of the Association, 1748; president of the St. Andrew's Society. Tench Francis (d. 1758), attorney general, 1741–55; recorder of Philadelphia, 1750–55. William Masters (d. 1760), member of the Assembly. Samuel McCall, Jr. (1721–1762), merchant; common councilor; a founder of the St. Andrew's Society and also of St. Peter's Church. Thomas Leech (c. 1686–1762), clerk of the Assembly, 1723–27; member of the Assembly for Philadelphia County; Speaker pro tem., 1758; vestryman and warden of Christ Church. William Shippen (1712–1801), physician; one of the first physicians of the Pennsylvania Hospital; a founder of the Second Presbyterian Church; trustee of the College of New Jersey (Princeton), 1765–96; member of the Continental Congress, 1778. Robert Strettell (1693–1761), a Quaker who supported defensive war; provincial councilor; mayor of Philadelphia, 1751. Abraham Taylor (c.1703–1772), merchant; provincial councilor; colonel of the Associators, 1748; deputy collector of customs; removed to England, 1762. Joshua Maddox (1685–1759), merchant; judge of the Orphans Court; vestryman and warden of Christ Church. Thomas White (1704–1775), lawyer; practiced some years in Maryland, where he owned plantations for raising tobacco and producing iron; colonel of Maryland militia; moved to Philadelphia; justice of the peace in Philadelphia, 1752. Montgomery, *Hist. Univ. Pa.*, pp. 53–108.

For the Encouragement of this useful good and charitable Undertaking, to enable the Trustees and their Successors to begin, promote, continue and enlarge the same, humbly hoping, through the Favour of Almighty God, and the Bounty and Patronage of pious and well-disposed Persons that it may prove of great and lasting Benefit to the present and future rising Generations, WE, THE SUBSCRIBERS, do promise to pay to the Treasurer elected according to the above Constitutions, or to his Successor, or Successors for the Time being, the several Sums of Money by us respectively subscribed to be paid, at the Times in our Subscriptions respectively mentioned. WITNESS our Hands

Per Annum for five Years

ROBT. STRETTELL Ten pounds per Ann

PHILIP SYNG Six Pounds per Year

THOS LEECH Six pounds per [Year]

THOS. WHITE Six Pounds

THOS. HOPKINSON Ten Pounds

THOS: CADWALADER for 3 years from 14th. of Nov: 1751 eight pounds

JAMES HAMILTON Fifty pounds £50

THO LAWRENCE Fifteen pds. £15

JO TURNER Twenty pounds £20

WILL: ALLEN seventy five pounds £75

WM MASTERS Twenty pounds £20

LLOYD ZACHARY Twenty pounds £20

Per Annum for five Years

WM PLUMSTED fifteen pounds £15

ABRAM. TAYLOR Fifteen pounds £15

SAM: M'CALL JUNR Fifteen Pounds £15

JOHN INGLIS Ten pounds £10

CHAS. WILLING Fifteen pounds per Ann. 15

TH BOND Fifteen Pounds per An. 15

TENCH FRANCIS ten pound per Ann. 10

WM. SHIPPEN ten pound £10

B FRANKLIN Ten Pounds per ann 10

PHINEAS BOND per Annum £10

WM: COLEMAN per Annum Ten pounds 10

RICHARD PETERS Ten Pounds 10

JOSH: MADDOX Ten Pounds £10

From Cadwallader Colden Draft: New-York Historical Society

[November, 1749]

I receiv'd by the last opportunity from New York the Proposals relating to the Education of Youth in Pensylvania. I have read it with much pleasure and heartily wish the Gentlemen success that are endeavouring to promote so usefull a Design. I have no objection to any thing in the proposals. I am pleased with every part of them. Tho I do not pretend to have my thoughts in any manner so well digested as yours are who have applied your self particularly to the subject (for from your generous attempts on several other occasions for the good of your Country I take you to be principally the Author of that performance) yet I believe you will not be displeased with any hints which may come from others tho' in themselves but trivial when compared with the great[ness] of the subject you have in view. While you keep the Great [end] of Education in view viz. to enable men and to incline them to be more usefull to mankind in General and to their own Country in particular and at the same time to render their own life more happy you cannot be in great danger of taking wrong steps while all of them tend to that end. But I think one of the Principal things for this purpose will be in the choice of the Trustees and Rector who is to oversee the Masters and schollars to direct both their lessons and studies in such manner as they may most effectually promote this grand purpose for which they are intended and in this choice as great a regard must be had to the heart as to the head of the Rector that he be a man that will have this great purpose allwise at heart. Such a person will find so much employment for every hour in life that he will have no time to take care of his own private affairs and therefor it will be necessary that he have so much incouragement by a proper Sallary as to make him easy in his private affairs and it may not be amiss that he have likewise a small annual gratuity from [every] schollar that as his care may increase the number of Schollars and the number will increase his trouble so he may find some benefite to himself in it. I do not think it proper that his whole subsistence should depend upon [such] gratuity because that might make him too much dependent upon the humours of the Schollars or there parents. It seems to me better that the least part of his incouragements should come that way. But as to the Masters or Teachers the greatest [part of] their incouragement may come from the rewards they are to receive from the Schollars as this is likely to make them the more assiduous and while they are under the direction of the Rector and Trustees I can see no inconveniency likely to happen by it. I am pleased with your mentioning Agriculture as one of the Sciences to be taught because I am of opinion it may be made as much a Science as any of those that are not purely Mathematicall and none of them deserve so much to be taught as this at least none more since it is truely the foundation of the Wealth and wellfare of the Country and it may be personally usefull to a greater number than any of the other Sciences. For this reason I think there should be a Professor on purpose who should likewise have contingent allowances given him for making experiments and to correspond with the noted farmers for [his] information. For this purpose and for several other reasons I am of Opinion the College would do best in the Country at a distance from the City. By this the Schollars will be freed from many temptations to idleness and some worse vices that they must meet with in the [City] and it may be an advantage to many children to be at a distance from their parents. The chief objection to the College's being in the Country I think is that the schollars cannot acquire that advantage of behaviour and address which they would acquire by a more general conversation with Gentlemen. But this I think may be remedied by obliging them to use the same good manners towards one another with a proper regard to their several ranks as is used among well bred Gentlemen [and] by having them taught Dancing and other accomplishments an easy carriage and address in Company and other Exercises usually taught Gentlemen. Their being obliged to declame or dispute or Act plays may take off that Bashfullness which frequently [gives] Schollars an aukwardness on their first appearance in publick. And as no doubt they must be allow'd to go to the City [sometimes] I am of opinion the advantages from the Country are [no?] less than what may arise [from] the College's being in or near the town.

It is a common argument that the Power and strenth of a Nation consists in its riches and Money. No doubt money can do great things but I think the Power of a Nation consists in the knowledge and Virtue of its inhabitants and in proof of this history every where allmost shews us that the Richest Nations abounding most in Silver and Gold have been generally conquer'd by poor but in some sense Virtuous nations. If Riches be not accompanied with virtue they on that very account expose a nation to ruin by their being a temptation for others to invade them while luxury the usual consequence of Riches makes them an easy prey.

I would not oblige all the schollars to learn latin and Greek. I would be so far from making the knowledge of those languages or of any foreign language a condition of the Schollars being admitted into the Colledge that I would have all the Sciences taught in English. I am of opinion it would be of greater service to the Generality of the Schollars to have the most eminent English Authors both in prose and verse explain'd to them by shewing the beauties and energy of our own language than to have the learned languages taught to them who afterwards in their course of life perhaps may never make use of them. Never the less they who are design'd for the Learned Professions [viz.] Divinity, Law and Physic [ought?] to understand the learned languages and Merchants and others who may have business with other Nations ought to understand the French at least but in all cases our own language ought to be our principal care.

From James Logan

Letterbook abstract: Historical Society of Pennsylvania

My Friend   10br [December] 13 [1749]
I wrote to him[1] that Lewis Evans has been here yesterday to advise of T. Godfrey's Decease[2] which I supposed had prevented his coming today the last he had appointed but that to morrow was a new one and that he might apply to my Son for his Charges.[3]

1. That is, BF. Logan usually recorded only the substance of very short letters, referring to the addressee in the third person.
2. *Pa. Gaz.*, Dec. 19, 1749, reporting that Godfrey (see above, I, 190 n) had died "last week," declared he "had an uncommon Genius for all kinds of *Mathematical Learning*, with which he was extreamly well acquainted."
3. The charges may have been for Evans' drafting Logan's deed of trust for his library. See Logan to John Kinsey, Nov. 24, Dec. 13, 1749, Letterbook, Hist. Soc. Pa.; Edwin Wolf, 2nd, "The Romance of James Logan's Books," 3 *Wm. and Mary Quar.*, XIII (1956), 348.

Some here would be pleased to see his Experiments[4] [*two words illegible*].

To B. Franklin

To James Logan

MS not found; reprinted from extract in Sparks, *Works*, VII, 40.

[December 16, 1749]

I send you herewith a new French piece on electricity,[5] in which you will find a journal of experiments on a paralytic person. I also send Neal on Electricity,[6] and the last Philosophical Transactions,[7] in which you will find some other pieces on the same subject. If you should desire to see any of the experiments mentioned in those pieces repeated, or if any new ones should occur to you to propose, which you cannot well try yourself, when I come to fetch the apparatus they may be tried. I shall be glad to hear that the shocks had some good effect on your disordered side.[8]

4. The references may be to experiments by BF or by Evans, who made experiments in electricity, and in 1751 lectured on natural philosophy, including electricity, at New York, Newark, N.J., and Philadelphia. Lawrence H. Gipson, *Lewis Evans* (Phila., 1939), pp. 9–10.

5. Probably Jean Jallabert, *Expériences sur l'Electricité* (Geneva, 1748), which contains a "Journal de quelques Expériences faites sur un Paralytique," pp. 127–44, *129–*36.

6. John Neale, *Directions for Gentlemen, who have Electrical Machines, How to proceed in making their Experiments* (London, 1747). At the close of the pamphlet the author appealed to the public for accounts of the application of electricity to paralytics.

7. Probably No. 486, which was reported in *Gent. Mag.* of Sept. 1749 (XIX, 415) as just published. It contained two articles, by Johann Heinrich Winkler and Henry Baker, on the medical use of electricity. *Phil. Trans.*, XLV (1748), 262–75.

8. A stroke in 1740 partially paralyzed Logan's right side; by the end of 1749 recurrent attacks of palsy left him weak and often helpless. Frederick B. Tolles, *James Logan and the Culture of Provincial America* (Boston, 1957), p. 195.

From James Logan

Letterbook abstract: Historical Society of Pennsylvania

My Friend   10br [December] 17 [1749]
I Send him his borrowed Praeceptor. I thought to have bought that and Turnbull for my Son who is at home with me and to deliver him Those others that I had wrote for. Desire him to Send me Milton and Hutcheson dis[sertation] of Senses with the last &c. Hutcheson says there are more than 5 Senses and reckons Pain and hunger which goes the last.[9]

To B. Franklin

To James Logan

MS not found; reprinted from extract in Sparks, *Works*, VII, 40.

[December 17, 1749]
I send the Dialogues on Education, which I ascribed to Hutcheson, but am since informed they were wrote by Mr. Forbes, Professor of Philosophy in the University of Aberdeen;[1] the same who wrote the Inquiry into the Life and Writings of Homer. I also send Milton.[2]

9. The references are to Robert Dodsley, *The Preceptor: Containing A General Course of Education* (2 vols., London, 1748); George Turnbull, *Observations upon Liberal Education, In all its Branches* (London, 1742); Milton, *Tractate on Education;* and possibly Francis Hutcheson, *An Essay on the Nature and Conduct of the Passions and Affections* (London, 1728). See above, pp. 397–98.

1. BF and his informant were both mistaken in ascribing the "Dialogues on Education" to Francis Hutcheson in the preface of his *Proposals* (see above, p. 398): the author was David Fordyce, professor of moral philosophy in Marischal College, Aberdeen; his *Dialogues concerning Education* was published anonymously at London in two volumes, 1745–48. Nor was Fordyce the author of the famous *Enquiry into the Life and Writings of Homer* (London, 1735); that was written by his uncle, Thomas Blackwell the younger, professor of Greek and, after 1748, principal of Marischal College. *DNB.* See also BF to William Smith, May 3, 1753.

2. See above, p. 397 n.

Proposals for Preparing the Academy Building

AD (fragment): American Philosophical Society

With by-laws signed and funds promised for the Academy, the trustees had next to decide on its location.[3] Some (including Franklin at first) favored a country town as less corrupting to students' morals; others preferred Philadelphia, where James Logan offered a lot in Sixth Street. In either case a suitable building would cost a good deal of money. It may have been Franklin who proposed renting the meeting-hall part of the New Building, 100 by 70 feet, built for George Whitefield ten years before[4] and now little used, except by Gilbert Tennent's congregation. The Academy trustees accordingly named a committee, Nov. 13, 1749, to confer with the Whitefield trustees and to get an estimate of the cost of remodeling it. It was at this point that Franklin outlined the proposals, of which only this undated fragment, in his hand, survives. The Whitefield trustees offered the entire building to the Academy, and on December 26 the Academy trustees accepted.

Franklin's memoirs describe what happened: he had been elected one of the four trustees of the New Building, principally, he wrote, because when the Moravian member died, in order to avoid having another from the same religion, the choice after some discussion fell on Franklin, who was "merely an honest Man, and of no Sect at all." He discovered that the Whitefield trustees owed several years' ground rent as well as other debts and that, with the decline of evangelical fervor, there was scant prospect of their being discharged, to say nothing of keeping the building in repair. They had not even fulfilled their obligation to build a free school. "Being now a Member of both Sets of Trustees, that for the Building and that for the Academy, I had good Opportunity of negociating with both, and brought them finally to an Agreement." The trustees of the New Building ceded it to the Academy in exchange for discharging the debts—£775 16s. 1¾d. The Academy also accepted the New Building's other obligations, agreeing to keep a large hall for preaching and to establish the free school for poor children. The transfer took place Feb. 1, 1750.

Franklin took on the job of getting the building ready for students, hired the workmen, purchased the materials, and superintended the work of "dividing the great and lofty Hall in Stories, and different

3. Par. Text edit., pp. 296–300; Montgomery, *Hist. Univ. Pa.*, pp. 109–11, 116–8. A contemporary account of these events is in Richard Peters, *A Sermon on Education* (Phila., 1751), preached at the opening of the Academy, Jan. 7, 1751.
4. See above, II, 290 n.

Rooms above and below for the several Schools." The suggestion he had made in this fragment—to partition the south end (or third) of the building into four rooms—appears to have been adopted.[5] Pending completion of the remodeling, instruction began, Jan. 7, 1751, and continued for several weeks in a warehouse belonging to William Allen at Second and Arch Streets.[6]

Proposed   [December ? 1749]
    That the South End of the New B[uilding be set] off by a substantial Partition, and divided [into four] Rooms, two on a Floor, each about 33 Feet square and the Lot fenc'd off to the Street.
    That three of those Rooms be for the Use of the Academy, to be taken for a Term of Years at a certain Rent.
    That the Trustees of the Academy do at present defray the Expence of the Partitions, &c. and undertake to [dis]charge the Debts that arose from the Roofing [remainder missing].

[To Jared Eliot, c. 1749]   MS: Yale University Library

This document, consisting of the first four pages of a letter, undated and unsigned, describes the operation of the writer's farm near Burlington, N.J. It was long thought to be by Franklin and has been the basis for several discussions of his knowledge of practical agriculture. Sparks printed it (*Works*, VI, 83–6), thinking it might have been written "as early as 1747;" Bigelow included it in his edition (*Works*, II, 80–3); as did Smyth (*Writings*, II, 383–6), who dated it more correctly 1749. The letter is not by Franklin, however, as George DeCou demonstrated in 1940; it was written to Eliot by Charles Read of New Jersey. For a documented account of this identification, see Carl R. Woodward, *Ploughs and Politicks: Charles Read of New Jersey* (New Brunswick, N.J., 1941), pp. xi-xxiv.

    5. The trustees "are now altering the south half of the great building into four rooms for four masters." Peters to Thomas Penn, Feb. 17, 1750, Sparks, *Works*, I, 570 n. An earlier proposal had been to divide the first floor into four large schoolrooms. William L. Turner, "The Charity School, the Academy, and the College," APS *Trans.*, n.s., XLIII, pt. 1 (1953), 180 n.
    6. Edward P. Cheyney, *History of the University of Pennsylvania, 1740–1940* (Phila., 1940), p. 38.

Poor Richard Improved, 1750

Poor Richard improved: Being an Almanack and Ephemeris . . . for the Year of our Lord 1750. . . . By Richard Saunders, Philom. Philadelphia: Printed and Sold by B. Franklin, and D. Hall. (Yale University Library)

To the READER.

The Hope of acquiring lasting FAME, is, with many Authors, a most powerful Motive to Writing. Some, tho' few, have succeeded; and others, tho' perhaps fewer, may succeed hereafter, and be as well known to Posterity by their Works, as the Antients are to us. We Philomaths, as ambitious of Fame as any other Writers whatever, after all our painful Watchings and laborious Calculations, have the constant Mortification to see our Works thrown by at the End of the Year, and treated as mere waste Paper. Our only Consolation is, that short-lived as they are, they out-live those of most of our Cotemporaries.

Yet, condemned to renew the Sisyphean Toil, we every Year heave another heavy Mass up the Muses Hill, which never can the Summit reach, and soon comes tumbling down again.

This, kind Reader, is my seventeenth Labour of the Kind. Thro' thy continued Good-will, they have procur'd me, if no *Bays*, at least *Pence;* and the latter is perhaps the better of the two; since 'tis not improbable that a Man may receive more solid Satisfaction from *Pudding*, while he is *living*, than from *Praise*, after he is *dead*.

In my last, a few Faults escap'd; some belong to the Author, but most to the Printer: Let each take his Share of the Blame, confess, and amend for the future. In the second Page of *August*,[7] I mention'd 120 as the next perfect Number to 28; it was wrong, 120 being no perfect Number; the next to 28 I find to be 496. The first is 6; let the curious Reader, fond of mathematical Questions, find the fourth. In the 2d Page of *March*,[8] in some Copies, the Earth's Circumference was said to be nigh 4000, instead of 24000 Miles, the Figure 2 being omitted at the Beginning. This was Mr. Printer's Fault; who being also somewhat niggardly of his Vowels, as well as profuse of his Consonants, put in one Place, among the Poetry, *mad*, instead of *made*, and in another *wrapp'd*,

---

7. See above, p. 344.   8. See above, p. 338.

instead of *warp'd;* to the utter demolishing of all Sense in those Lines, leaving nothing standing but the Rhime.[9] These, and some others, of the like kind, let the Readers forgive, or rebuke him for, as to their Wisdom and Goodness shall seem meet: For in such Cases the Loss and Damage is chiefly to the Reader, who, if he does not take my Sense at first Reading, 'tis odds he never gets it; for ten to one he does not read my Works a second Time.

Printers indeed should be very careful how they omit a Figure or a Letter: For by such Means sometimes a terrible Alteration is made in the Sense. I have heard, that once, in a new Edition of the *Common Prayer,* the following Sentence, *We shall all be changed in a Moment, in the Twinkling of an Eye;* by the Omission of a single Letter, became, *We shall all be hanged in a Moment,* &c. to the no small Surprize of the first Congregation it was read to.[1]

May this Year prove a happy One to Thee and Thine, is the hearty Wish of, Kind Reader, Thy obliged Friend,   R. SAUNDERS

The Number of People in New-Jersey, taken by Order of Government in 1737–8.

Counties.	Males above 16.	Females above 16.	Males under 16.	Females under 16.	Slaves. Males,	Females	Total of Whites,	Total of Slaves,
Middlesex,	1134	1085	1086	956	272	231	4261	503
Essex,	1118	1720	1619	1494	198	177	6644	375
Bergen,	939	822	820	708	443	363	3289	806
Somerset,	967	940	999	867	425	307	3773	732
Monmouth,	1508	1339	1289	1295	362	293	5431	655
Burlington,	1487	1222	1190	996	192	151	4895	343
Gloucester,	930	757	782	676	74	48	3145	122
Salem,	1669	1391	1313	1327	97	87	5700	184
Cape-May,	261	219	271	211	21	21	962	42
Hunterdon,	1618	1230	1270	1170	124	95	5288	219
Totals,	11631	10725	10639	9700	2208	1773	43388	3981

9. See above, pp. 341, 339.

1. BF had cited this same mistake in his essay on Printer's Errors in 1730. See above, I, 169.

Number of Ditto, taken in 1745, by order of Gov. MORRIS.

Morris,	1109	957	1190	1087	57	36	4343	93
Hunterdon,	2302	2117	2182	2090	244	216	8691	460
Burlington,	1786	1605	1528	1454	233	197	6373	430
Gloucester,	913	797	786	808	121	81	3304	202
Salem,	1716	1603	1746	1595	90	97	6660	187
Cape-May,	306	272	284	274	30	22	1136	52
Bergen,	721	590	494	585	379	237	2390	616
Essex,	1694	1649	1652	1548	244	201	6543	445
Middlesex,	1728	1659	1651	1695	483	396	6733	879
Monmouth,	2071	1783	1975	1899	513	386	7728	899
Somerset,	740	672	765	719	194	149	2896	343
Totals,	15086	13704	14253	13754	2588	2018	56797	4606

Note, That Morris and Hunterdon Counties, were both in one, under the Name of Hunterdon, in 1737–8. In 1745, the Number of the People called Quakers in New-Jersey, was found to be 6079; no distinct Account was taken of them in 1737–8. Total of Souls in 1737, 47369; Ditto in 1745, 61403; Increase 14034. Query, At this Rate of Increase, in what Number of Years will that Province double its Inhabitants?[2]

Buried in the several Burying Grounds of PHILADELPHIA, belonging to the

In the Years	Church of England,	Swedish Church	Presby-terians,	Baptist Meeting,	Quaker Meeting,	Strangers,	Negroes,
1738	113	24	29	15	46	269	54
1739	109	16	18	7	56	97	47
1740	105	8	22	12	29	80	34
1741	165	30	41	20	120	300	69
1742	126	35	21	9	70	98	50
1743	117		19	21	68	150	50
1744	123	16	29	14	81	100	47
	858	129	179	98	470	1094	351

Note; No Account of Burials in the Swedish Ground, was taken in the Year 1743, and those Germans buried in the new Dutch Burying Ground, are numbered among the Strangers, who were chiefly Palatines: The Mortality among them is not owing to any Unhealthiness of this Climate, but to Diseases they contract on Shipboard, the Voyage sometimes happening to be long, and too great a Number crowded together. Exclusive of those, the Total of Deaths in seven Years is about 2100, which is 300 *per Annum:* By which we should have had nearly 10,500 Inhabitants during those seven Years, at a Medium; for in a healthy Country (as this is) political Arithmeticians compute, there dies yearly One in Thirty-five. But in these last five Years, from 1744, the Town is greatly increased.

2. The tables reprinted above reproduce, slightly condensed, the data on two manuscripts, one a rough draft and the other a fair copy, among the

In the Province of Massachusetts Bay, in New-England, *Anno* 1735, there were 35,427 Polls of white Men of 16 Years and up- wards, 2600 Negroes, 27,420 Horse-kind of three Years old and upwards, 52,000 Neat Cattle of three to four Years old and upwards, 130,001 sheep of one year old and upwards. In 1742 there was 41,000 Polls of white Men, from 16 Years upwards. Increase of Men in seven Years 5573, which is near one Sixth. New-Jersey increased in the same Time near one Third.

By the New-Jersey Accounts it appears, that the Number of Males, aged above 16, is nearly one fourth Part of the whole Number of Souls. If the same Proportion holds in the Massachusetts, they should have had in that Province, in 1742, about 164000 Souls. There are three other Provinces in New-England, viz. Connecticut, Rhode-Island, and New-Hampshire.

In 1742, a Year of middling Health in Boston, were buried about 515, which multiplied by 35, makes nearly 18,000 Inhabitants. In the same Year were found in that Town, Dwelling-houses 1719, Warehouses 166, Widows 1200, of which 1000 poor; in the Alms- house 111 Persons; in the Work-house 36; Negroes 1514; Horses 418; Cows 141.

In 1748–9, the Dwelling-houses in Philadelphia were 2076. The following Summer arrived 24 or 25 Sail of Ships with German Families, supposed to bring near 12,000 Souls.

It has been computed in England, that the Colonies on the Continent, taken one with another, double the Number of their Inhabitants every Thirty Years. This quick Increase is owing not so much to natural Generation, as the Accession of Strangers. What the natural Increase of Mankind is, is a curious Question. In Breslaw, the Capital of Silesia, a healthy inland City, to which many Strangers do not come, the Number of Inhabitants was found to be generally about 34,000. An exact Register is kept

---

Franklin Papers in APS. The collection of these statistics and those which follow and the accompanying discussion of population growth show that as early as the autumn of 1749, when BF was preparing this almanac, he had become interested in the subject at large and especially in the much more rapid increase of population in the colonies than in "old settled Countries." The final paragraph clearly foreshadows the "Observations concerning the Increase of Mankind, Peopling of Countries, &c.," which he wrote in 1751.

there of the Births and Burials, which taken for 30 Years together, amount, as follows,

Births *per Annum*,	1238
Deaths *per Annum*,	1174
Yearly Increase but	64

Let the expert Calculator say, how long it will be, before by an Increase of 64 *per Annum*, 34,000 People will double themselves? Yet I believe People increase faster by Generation in these Colonies, where all can have full Employ, and there is Room and Business for Millions yet unborn. For in old settled Countries, as England for Instance, as soon as the Number of People is as great as can be supported by all the Tillage, Manufactures, Trade and Offices of the Country, the Overplus must quit the Country, or they will perish by Poverty, Diseases, and want of Necessaries. Marriage too, is discouraged, many declining it, till they can see how they shall be able to maintain a Family.

JANUARY. *XI Month.*

> So weak are human Kind by Nature made,
> Or to such Weakness by their Vice betray'd,
> Almighty *Vanity!* to thee they owe
> Their Zest of Pleasure, and their Balm of Woe.
> Thou, like the Sun, all Colours dost contain,
> Varying like Rays of Light on Drops of Rain;
> For every Soul finds Reason to be proud,
> Tho' hiss'd and hooted by the pointing Croud.

There are three Things extreamly hard, Steel, a Diamond and to know one's self.

Hunger is the best Pickle.

He is a Governor that governs his Passions, and he a Servant that serves them.

On the 9th of this Month, 1744-5, died CHARLES ALBERT, Elector of Bavaria, and Emperor of Germany. 'Tis thought his Death was hastened by Grief and Vexation at the Success of the

441

Queen of Hungary, and the Disappointments of his own Ambition. O *Content!* What art thou! And where to be found! Art thou not an inseparable Companion of Honour, Wealth and Power? No. This Man was rich, great, a Sovereign Prince: But he wanted to be *richer, greater,* and *more a Sovereign.* At first his Arms had vast Success; but a Campaign or two left him not a Foot of Land he could call his own, and reduc'd him to live with his Empress in a *hired House* at Frankfort!

> The bold Bavarian, in a luckless Hour,
> Tries the dread summits of Cesarean Power,
> With unexpected Legions bursts away,
> And sees defenceless Realms receive his Sway;
> Short Sway! Fair Austria spreads her mournful Charms,
> The Queen, the Beauty, sets the World in Arms;
> From Hill to Hill the Beacon's rousing Blaze
> Spreads wide the Hope of Plunder and of Praise;
> The fierce Croatian, and the wild Hussar,
> And all the Sons of Ravage, crowd the War;
> The baffled Prince, in Honour's flatt'ring Bloom,
> Of hasty Greatness, finds the fatal Doom;
> His Foes Derision, and his Subjects Blame,
> And steals to Death from Anguish, and from Shame.[3]

FEBRUARY. *XII Month.*

> We smile at Florists, we despise their Joy,
> And think their Hearts enamour'd of a Toy;
> But are those wiser, whom we most admire,
> Survey with Envy, and pursue with Fire?
> What's he, who fights for Wealth, or Fame, or Power?
> Another Florio, doating on a Flower,
> A short-liv'd Flower, and which has often sprung,
> From sordid Arts, as Florio's out of Dung.

A Cypher and Humility make the other Figures and Virtues of ten fold Value.

If it were not for the Belly, the Back might wear Gold.

3. Samuel Johnson, *The Vanity of Human Wishes; in Imitation of the Tenth Satire of Juvenal,* 239–52.

442

On the 19th of this Month, 1653, was a great Sea-Fight between the English and Dutch. The Fleet of the former commanded by Blake and Dean, Admirals: That of the latter by Van Trump. The Dutch were beaten, lost 11 Men of War, and 30 Merchant Ships, and 1500 Men killed. The English lost but one Ship, the *Sampson,* which was sunk; but the Number of their Slain supposed to be nearly equal.[4]

For LIBERALITY.

Tho' safe thou think'st thy Treasure lies,
Hidden in Chests from Human Eyes,
Thieves, Fire, may come, and it may be
Convey'd, my Friend, as far from thee.
Thy Vessel that yon Ocean sails,
Tho' favour'd now with prosp'rous Gales,
Her Cargo which has Thousands cost,
All in a Tempest may be lost.
Cheats, Whores and Quacks, a thankless Crew,
Priests, Pickpockets, and Lawyers too,
All help by several Ways to drain,
Thanking themselves for what they gain;
The *Liberal* are secure alone,
For what they frankly give, for ever is their own.

MARCH. *I Month.*

What's the bent Brow, or Neck in Thought reclin'd?
The Body's Wisdom, to conceal the Mind.
A Man of Sense can Artifice disdain,
As Men of Wealth may venture to go plain;
And be this Truth eternal ne'er forgot,
Solemnity's a Cover for a Sot;
I find the Fool, when I behold the Screen:
For 'tis the Wise Man's Interest to be seen.

Wouldst thou confound thine Enemy, be good thy self.

4. In the three-day engagement off Portland and in the Channel, which began Feb. 18, 1653, Robert Blake and Richard Deane, aided by George Monck and William Penn (father of the founder of Pennsylvania), defeated the Dutch commander Cornelius Tromp.

Pride is as loud a Beggar as *Want,* and a great deal more saucy.

Pay what you owe, and what you're worth you'll know.

The Reason, says Swift, why so few Marriages are happy, is, because young Ladies spend their Time in making *Nets,* not in making *Cages.*[5]

> Why, Celia, is your spreading Waist
> So loose, so negligently lac'd?
> How ill that Dress adorns your Head;
> Distain'd and rumpled from the Bed?
> Those Clouds that shade your blooming Face,
> A little Water might displace,
> As Nature ev'ry Morn bestows
> The chrystal Dew to cleanse the Rose.
> Those Tresses as the Raven black,
> That wav'd in Ringlets down your Back,
> Uncomb'd, and injur'd by Neglect,
> Destroy the Face that once they deck'd,
> Whence this Forgetfulness of Dress?
> Pray, Madam, are you marry'd? *Yes.*
> Nay then indeed the Wonder ceases,
> No matter now how loose your Dress is;
> The End is won, your Fortune's made,
> Your Sister now may take the Trade.
> Alas, what Pity 'tis to find
> This Fault in Half the Female kind!
> From hence proceed Aversion, Strife,
> And all that sours the wedded Life.
> *Beauty* can only point the Dart,
> 'Tis *Neatness* guides it to the Heart;
> Let Neatness then, and Beauty strive
> To keep a wav'ring Flame alive.

APRIL. *II Month.*

> When e'er by seeming Chance, Fop throws his Eye
> On Mirrors flushing with his Finery,

5. Jonathan Swift, "Thoughts on Various Subjects, Moral and Diverting, October, 1706," *Works* (London, 1883), IX, 217.

With how sublime a Transport leaps his Heart;
Pity such Friends sincere should ever part.
  So have I seen on some bright Summer's Day,
A spotted *Calf,* sleek, frolicksome and gay;
Gaze from the Bank, and much delighted seem,
Fond of the pretty Fellow in the Stream.

Sorrow is good for nothing but Sin.

Many a Man thinks he is buying Pleasure, when he is really selling himself a Slave to it.

> Graft good Fruit all,
> Or graft not at all.

On the 17th of this Month, 1722, the Princesses Amelia and Carolina, were inoculated for the Small Pox, after the Experiment had been tried for the first Time in England on some condemned Malefactors. The Example of the Court was soon followed by many of the Nobility and Gentry, and Success attending the Practice, 'tis now grown more common in many Parts of Europe; and tho' at first it was reckoned by many to be a *rash* and almost *impious* Action, to give a Distemper to a Person in Health; so changeable are the Opinions of Men, that it now begins to be thought *rash* to hazard taking it in the common Way, by which one in seven is generally lost; and *impious* to reject a Method discovered to Mankind by God's good Providence, whereby 99 in 100 are saved.

The Indians of America generally suffer extreamly by this Distemper when it gets among them, perhaps from the Closeness and Hardness of their Skins. Monsieur Condamine,[6] a French Academician, who, in 1744, made a Voyage from Peru, down the River Amazones, thro' the Middle of South America, reports, that a few Years before, the Small-Pox getting among the Indians, full Half of those taken sick were carried off by it: Which a Portuguese Missionary observing, and having met by Chance with an Account of Inoculation in a News Paper, he try'd it on great Numbers of his Indian Disciples, and preserved them all; which gave a high Opinion both of the Man and his Religion.

6. Charles-Marie de La Condamine (1701–1774), soldier, explorer, chemist, whose writings helped to bring about general acceptance of inoculation.

MAY. *III Month.*

> Content let all your Virtues lie unknown,
> If there's no Tongue to praise them, but your own,
> Of Boasting more than of a Bomb afraid,
> Merit should be as modest as a Maid.
> *Fame* is a Bubble the Reserv'd enjoy,
> Who strive to grasp it, as they touch, destroy;
> 'Tis the World's Debt to Deeds of high Degree;
> But if you pay yourself, the World is free.

Tis hard (but glorious) to be poor and honest: An empty Sack can hardly stand upright; but if it does, 'tis a stout one!

He that can bear a Reproof, and mend by it, if he is not wise, is in a fair way of being so.

Beatus esse sine Virtute, nemo potest.

On the 22d of this Month, 1453, was the famous City of Constantinople, the Capital of the Greek Empire, taken from the Christians by the Turks, who have ever since held it in Possession. When it was besieg'd, the Emperor made most earnest Application to his People, that they would contribute Money to enable him to pay his Troops, and defray the Expence of defending it; but they thro' Covetousness refused, pretending Poverty, &c. Yet the Turks in pillaging it, found so much Wealth among them, that even their common Soldiers were enriched: And it became a Saying, which continues to this Day, when they observe a Man grown suddenly rich, *He has been at the Sack of Constantinople.*

O *Avarice!* How blind are thy Votaries! How often by grasping at too much, do they lose all, and themselves with it! The Thirst of *More*, encreases with the *Heap;* and to the *restless* Desire of Getting, is added the *cruel Fear* of Losing, a Torment from which the Poor are free. And Death often scatters all we have with so much Care and Toil been gathering;

> High built *Abundance*, Heap on Heap for what?
> To breed new Wants, and beggar us the more;
> Then make a richer Scramble for the Throng?
> Soon as this feeble Pulse, which leaps so long

Almost by Miracle, is tir'd with Play,
Like Rubbish from disploding Engines thrown,
Our Magazines of hoarded Trifles fly;
Fly diverse; fly to Foreigners, to Foes:
New Masters court, and call the former Fool,
(How justly!) for Dependance on their Stay,
Wide scatter, first, our Playthings, then our Dust.[7]

JUNE. *IV Month.*

"Daphnis, says Clio, has a charming Eye;
What Pity 'tis her Shoulder is awry?
Aspasia's Shape indeed—*but* then her Air,
'Twould ask a Conj'rer to find Beauty there."
Without a *But,* Hortensia she commends,
The first of Women, and the best of Friends;
Owns her in Person, Wit, Fame, Virtue, bright;
But how comes this to pass?—She dy'd last Night.

Sound, and sound Doctrine, may pass through a Ram's Horn, and a Preacher, without straitening the one, or amending the other.

Clean your Finger, before you point at my Spots.

On the 7th of this Month, 1692, the Town of Port Royal, in Jamaica, was sunk by a fearful Earthquake.

The Day was very clear, and afforded no Suspicion of the least Evil; but in the Space of three Minutes, about half an Hour after 11 in the Morning, that fine Town was shaken to Pieces, sunk into, and cover'd, for the greater Part, by the Sea: By the falling of the Houses, Opening of the Earth, and Inundation of the Waters, near 2000 Persons were lost, many of Note.

For some Days afterwards, 'twas dismal to see the Harbour cover'd with the dead Bodies of People of all Conditions, floating up and down without Burial: For the great Burial Place, was destroy'd by the Earthquake; which dashing to Pieces the Tombs, whereof there were Hundreds in that Place, the Sea washed the Carcasses of those who had been buried out of their Graves.

7. Edward Young, *Night Thoughts,* VI, 483–93.

447

A Sickness followed, which carried off some Thousands more. During the Earthquake, Thieves robbed and plundered the Sufferers, even among the Ruins, while the Earth trembled under their Feet. Some were killed in the very Act by falling Walls, &c.

JULY. *V Month.*

On TIME.

See TIME launch'd forth, in solemn Form proceed,
And Man on Man advance, and Deed on Deed!
No Pause, no Rest in all the World appears,
Ev'n live long Patriarchs waste their 1000 Years.
Some Periods void of Science and of Fame,
Scarce e'er exist, or leave behind a Name;
Meer sluggish Rounds, to let Succession climb,
Obscure, and idle Expletives of Time.

He that spills the Rum, loses that only; He that drinks it, often loses both that and himself.

That Ignorance makes devout, if right the Notion,
Troth, Rufus, thou'rt a Man of great Devotion.

A plain, clean, and decent Habit, proportioned to one's Circumstances, is one Mark of Wisdom. Gay Cloathing so generally betokens a light and empty Mind, that we are surpriz'd if we chance to find good Sense under that disguise.

Vain are the Studies of the Fop and Beau,
Who all their Care expend on outward Show.
Of late abroad was young Florello seen;
How blank his Look! How discompos'd his Mien!
So hard it proves in Grief sincere to feign,
Sunk were his Spirits,—for his Coat was plain?
Next Day his Breast regain'd its wonted Peace,
His Health was mended—with a Silver Lace.[8]

What an admirable Invention is Writing, by which a Man may

8. Edward Young, *Love of Fame, The Universal Passion*, Satire II, 211–17. In most editions the first two lines of the quoted passage read:
These all their care expend on outward show
For wealth and Fame; for Fame alone, the beau.

communicate his Mind without opening his Mouth, and at 1000 Leagues Distance, and even to future Ages, only by the Help of 22 Letters, which may be joined 5852616738497664000 Ways, and will express all Things in a very narrow Compass. 'Tis a Pity this excellent Art has not preserved the Name and Memory of its Inventor.

Bed-Bugs, by some called *Chinces,* because first brought from China in East-India Goods, are easily destroy'd, Root and Branch, by boiling Water, poured from a Teakettle into the Joints, &c. of the Bedstead, or squirted by a Syringe, where it cannot well be poured. The old Ones are scalded to Death, and the Nits spoilt, for a boil'd Egg never hatches. This done once a Fortnight, during the Summer, clears the House. *Probatum est.*

AUGUST. *VI Month.*

> Others behold each nobler Genius thrive,
> And in their generous Labours long survive;
> By Learning grac'd, extend a distant Light;
> Thus circling Science has her Day and Night.
> Rise, rise, ye dear Cotemporaries, rise;
> On whom devolve these Seasons and these Skies!
> Assert the Portion destin'd to your Share,
> And make the Honour of the Times your Care.

Those that have much Business must have much Pardon.

Discontented Minds, and Fevers of the Body are not to be cured by changing Beds or Businesses.

> Little Strokes,
> Fell great Oaks.

The 22d of this Month, 1711, the English Fleet, sent against Canada, was shipwrecked in the Bay of St. Lawrence.

From MARTIAL.[9]

Vitam quae faciunt beatiorem, &c.
I fancy, O my Friend, that this
In Life bids fair for Happiness;

9. *Epigrams,* X, 47.

449

Timely an Estate to gain,
Left, or purchased by your Pain:
Grounds that pay the Tiller's Hire,
Woods to furnish lasting Fire;
Safe from Law t'enjoy your own,
Seldom view the busy Town;
Health with moderate Vigour join'd;
True well-grounded Peace of Mind;
Friends, your Equals in Degree,
Prudent, plain Simplicity;
Easy Converse Mirth afford,
Artless Plenty fill the Board;
Temp'rate Joy your Ev'nings bless,
Free from Care as from Excess:
Short the Night by Sleep be made,
Chaste, not chearless, be the Bed:
Chuse to be but what you are;
And Dying neither wish nor fear.

SEPTEMBER. *VII Month.*

Still be your darling Study Nature's Laws;
And to its Fountain trace up every Cause.
Explore, for such it is, this high Abode,
And tread the Paths which Boyle and Newton trod.
Lo, Earth smiles wide, and radiant Heav'n looks down,
All fair, all gay, and urgent to be known!
Attend, and here are sown Delights immense,
For every Intellect, and every Sense.

You may be too cunning for One, but not for All.

Genius without Education is like Silver in the Mine.

Many would live by their Wits, but break for want of Stock.

Poor *Plain dealing!* dead without Issue!

The 3d of this Month, 1658, died OLIVER CROMWELL, aged
60 Years. A great Storm happen'd the Night he died, from whence
his Enemies took Occasion to say, The D---l fetch'd him away

in a Whirlwind: But his Poet Waller, in some Verses on his Death, gave that Circumstance quite a different Turn. He begins with these lofty Lines; viz.[1]

> We must resign, Heav'n his great Soul does claim,
> In Storms as loud as his immortal Fame;
> His dying Groans, his last Breath shakes our Isle,
> And Trees uncut fall for his Fun'ral Pile, &c.

When the King came in, Waller made his Peace by a congratulatory Poem to his Majesty: And one Day 'tis said the King asked him jocularly, *What is the Reason, Mr. Waller, that your Verses on Oliver are so much better than those you made on me?* We Poets, my Liege, reply'd he, *always succeed better in Fiction than in Truth.*

> Much Learning shows how little Mortals *know;*
> Much Wealth, how little Worldlings can *enjoy.*
> At best it baby's us with endless Toys,
> And keeps us Children 'till we drop to Dust.
> As Monkies at a Mirror stand amaz'd,
> They fail to find what they so plainly see;
> Thus Men, in shining Riches, see the Face
> Of Happiness, nor know it is a Shade;
> But gaze, and touch, and peep, and peep again,
> And wish, and wonder it is absent still.[2]

OCTOBER. *VIII Month.*

> With Adoration think, with Rapture gaze,
> And hear all Nature chant her Maker's Praise;
> With Reason stor'd, by Love of Knowledge fir'd,
> By Dread awaken'd, and by Love inspir'd,
> Can We, the Product of another's Hand,
> Nor whence, nor how, nor why we are, demand?
> And, not at all, or not aright employ'd,
> Behold a Length of Years, and all a Void?

1. Edmund Waller, "Upon the Late Storme, and of the Death of His Highness Ensuing the Same."
2. Young, *Night Thoughts,* VI, 519–28.

You can bear your own Faults, and why not a Fault in your Wife.

Tho' Modesty is a Virtue, Bashfulness is a Vice.

>Hide not your Talents, they for Use were made.
>What's a Sun-Dial in the Shade!

On the first of this Month, 1680, the great Comet appeared in England, and continued blazing near 3 Months. Of these surprizing Bodies, Astronomers hitherto know very little; Time and Observation, may make us better acquainted with them, and if their Motions are really regular, as they are supposed to be, enable us hereafter to calculate with some Certainty the Periods of their Return. They have heretofore been thought Forerunners of National Calamities, and Threateners of Divine Vengeance on a guilty World. Dr. Young, intimates this Opinion, in his Paraphrase on that Chapter of *Job,* where the Deity challenges the Patriarch, and convinces him of the Weakness of Man;[3]

>Who drew the Comet out to such a Size,
>And pour'd his flaming Train o'er Half the Skies!
>Did thy Resentment bang him out? Does he
>Glare on the Nations, and denounce from Thee?

>The Summer Fruits now gathered in,
>Let thankful Hearts in chearful Looks be seen;
>Ope the hospitable Gate,
>Ope for Friendship, not for State;
>Neighbours and Strangers enter there
>Equal to all of honest Air;
>To Rich or Poor of Soul sincere.
>Cheap bought Plenty, artless Store,
>Feed the Rich, and fill the Poor;
>Converse chear the sprightly Guest,
>Cordial Welcome crown the Feast;
>Easy Wit with Candour fraught,
>Laughter genuine and unsought;
>Jest from double Meaning free,
>Blameless, harmless Jollity;
>Mirth, that no repenting Gloom
>Treasures for our Years to come.

3. Edward Young, *A Paraphrase on Part of the Book of Job,* 133–6.

NOVEMBER. *IX Month.*

> Happy, thrice happy he! whose conscious Heart,
> Enquires his Purpose, and discerns his Part;
> Who runs with Heed, th' involuntary Race,
> Nor lets his Hours reproach him as they pass;
> Weighs how they steal away, how sure, how fast,
> And as he weighs them, apprehends the last.
> Or vacant, or engag'd, our Minutes fly;
> We may be negligent, but we must die.

What signifies knowing the Names, if you know not the Natures of Things.

Tim was so learned, that he could name a Horse in nine Languages; So ignorant, that he bought a Cow to ride on.

The Golden Age never was the present Age.

On the 30th of this Month, 1718, Charles XII. of Sweden, the modern Alexander, was kill'd before Fredericstadt. He had all the Virtues of a *Soldier*, but, as is said of the Virtues of Cesar, *They undid his Country:* Nor did they upon the whole afford himself any real Advantage. For after all his Victories and Conquests, he found his Power less than at first, his Money spent, his Funds exhausted, and his Subjects thinn'd extreamly. Yet he still warr'd on, in spite of Reason and Prudence, till a small Bit of Lead, more powerful than they, *persuaded* him to be quiet.

> On what Foundation stands the Warrior's Pride?
> How just his Hopes, let Swedish Charles decide;
> A Frame of Adamant, a Soul of Fire,
> No Dangers fright him, and no Labours tire;
> O'er Love, o'er Force, extends his wide Domain,
> Unconquer'd Lord of Pleasure and of Pain;
> No Joys to him pacific Scepters yield,
> War sounds the Trump, he rushes to the Field;
> Behold surrounding Kings their Pow'r combine,
> And one capitulate, and one resign;
> Peace courts his Hand, but spreads her Charms in vain,
> "Think nothing gain'd, he cries, 'till nought remain;
> On Moscow's Walls till Gothic Standards fly,

453

And all is mine beneath the Polar Sky."
    The March begins in military State,
And Nations on his Eye suspended wait;
Stern Famine guards the solitary Coast,
And Winter barricades the Realms of Frost;
He comes, nor Want nor Cold his Course delay;
Hide, blushing Glory, hide Pultowa's Day:
The vanquish'd Hero leaves his broken Bands,
And shews his Miseries in distant Lands;
Condemn'd a needy Supplicant to wait,
While Ladies interpose, and Slaves debate.
    But did not Chance at length her Error mend?
Did no subverted Empire mark his End?
Did rival Monarchs give the fatal Wound?
Or hostile Millions press him to the Ground?
His Fall was destin'd to a barren Strand,
A petty Fortress, and a dubious Hand;
He left the Name at which the World grew pale,
To point a Moral, or adorn a Tale.[4]

DECEMBER. *X Month.*

And thou *supreme of Beings* and of Things!
Who breath'st all Life, and giv'st Duration Wings;
Intense, O let me for thy Glory burn,
Nor fruitless view my Days and Nights return;
Give me with Wonder at thy Works to glow;
To grasp thy Vision, and thy Truths to know;
To reach at length thy everlasting Shore,
And live and sing 'till Time shall be no more.

'Tis a Shame that your Family is an Honour to you! You ought to be an Honour to your Family.

Glass, China, and Reputation, are easily crack'd, and never well mended.

Adieu, my Task's ended.

4. Johnson, *The Vanity of Human Wishes*, 189–220.

On the 7th of this Month, 1683, was the honourable Algernon Sidney, Esq; beheaded, charg'd with a pretended Plot, but whose chief Crime was the Writing an excellent Book, intituled, *Discourses on Government*. A Man of admirable Parts and great Integrity. Thompson calls him the British Cassius. The good Lord Russel and he were intimate Friends; and as they were Fellow Sufferers in their Death, the Poet joins them in his Verses,[5]

> Bring every sweetest Flower, and let me strow
> The Grave where Russel lies; whose temper'd Blood
> With calmest Chearfulness for Thee* resign'd,
> Stain'd the sad Annals of a giddy Reign,
> Aiming at lawless Power, tho' meanly sunk,
> In loose inglorious Luxury. With him
> His Friend, the British Cassius, fearless bled;
> Of high, determin'd Spirit, roughly brave,
> By ancient Learning to th' enlighten'd Love
> Of ancient Freedom warm'd.

Of Courts.

> If any Rogue vexatious Suits advance
> Against you for your known Inheritance:
> Enter by Violence your fruitful Grounds,
> Or take the sacred Land-mark from your Bounds;
> Or if your Debtors do not keep their Day,
> Deny their Hands, and then refuse to pay;
> You must with Patience all the Terms attend,
> Among the common Causes that depend,
> Till yours is call'd:—And that long-look'd-for Day,
> Is still encumber'd with some new Delay:
> Your Proofs and Deeds all on the Table spread,
> Some of the B------ch perhaps are sick a-bed;
> That J---ge steps out to light his Pipe, while this
> O'er night was boozy, and goes out to p---ss.

*Britannia

5. Thomson, *The Seasons*. "Summer," 1521–30. Algernon Sidney (1622–1683) and William Russell, Lord Russell (1639–1683), were executed for alleged complicity in the Rye House Plot.

Some Witness miss'd; some Lawyer not in Town,⎤
So many Rubs appear, the Time is gone,   ⎬
For Hearing, and the tedious Suit goes on.   ⎦
    Then rather let two Neighbours end your Cause,
And split the Difference; tho' you lose one Half;
    Than spend the Whole, entangled in the Laws,
While merry Lawyers sly, at both Sides laugh.

From James Logan

Letterbook copy: Historical Society of Pennsylvania

My Friend B.F.   Jan. 8th [1750]
If there be any convenient room left, Since my eldest Son[6] has rejected the Offer, I am willing my name Should be inserted amongst the Collegues of your Society,[7] tho' very uncapable of being in any manner useful to it, yet I am very desirous to have it by all means promoted, tho' I expect to be excused from contributing any thing to it more than that £35 Sterl. per an. Settled on my Library for ever.[8] I am Thy Affectionate friend
                                    J L

6. William Logan (1718–1776), educated at Bristol, England, by his uncle Dr. William Logan; a successful merchant in Philadelphia; common councilor and provincial councilor; inherited the Stenton estate. He was a more consistent Friend than his father. Albert C. Myers, ed., *Hannah Logan's Courtship* (Phila., 1904), p. 156 n.

7. Though at first declining it, Logan accepted this appointment after the Constitutions (see above, p. 421) were copied fair, and BF inserted his name at the head of the list of trustees of the Academy.

8. Logan drew up a deed of trust for his library, 1745, and erected a building to house it between Chestnut, Walnut, Sixth, and Seventh Streets. He canceled this deed, intending to make additional provision, but death intervened. His heirs, however, faithfully carried out his intentions, executing deeds of trust, Aug. 28, 1754, and March 25, 1760. The library was annexed to the Library Company by legislative act, 1792. Frederick B. Tolles, *James Logan and the Culture of Provincial America* (Boston, 1957), pp. 193–4; *Loganian Lib. Cat., First Supplement* (Phila., 1867), pp. x-xxvii; Edwin Wolf, 2nd, "The Romance of James Logan's Books," 3 *Wm. and Mary Quar.*, XIII (1956), 348 n. Logan offered the trustees a lot on Sixth Street for the academy building, but they declined with thanks, Dec. 26, 1749, as the New Building was reckoned "in all respects better suited to their present circumstances and future views." Montgomery, *Hist. Univ. Pa.*, pp. 57–8.

William Watson:[9] Notice of Franklin's Experiments

MS: The Royal Society; also copy: American Academy of Arts and Sciences

[January 11, 1750]

At the reading of this paper[1] Mr. Watson took notice, that several of Mr. Franklin's experiments were new and very curious; but, besides that Mr. Watson is not quite master of part of this gentleman's reasoning, there are two things therein more particularly to be attended to: and these are, first, that when this gentleman in this paper mentions, that the Electricity is in the glass, he always means the accumulated electricity; as he in his former papers, which Mr. Watson has seen, is of opinion constantly that the Electrical power is originally furnished by, what have been hitherto called, the non electric substances applied to the glasses in rubbing them, and not from the glasses themselves. Secondly, he imagines, contrary to what Mr. Watson has laid before the Society and in which opinion he finds by what has been published Mr. Watson does persist, that in all the improvements of the experiment of Leyden the violence of the Shock is not owing to any accumulation of electric matter in the water or other non electrics made use of in that experiment, but that the shock is owing to the glass that contains this water or such like. To this Mr. Watson observed, that as yet he has seen no reason to alter or

9. William Watson (1715–1787), physician, naturalist, pioneer in electrical studies, began his career as an apothecary in London. Elected to the Royal Society, 1741, he contributed to *Phil. Trans.* some 58 original papers and reports on others' work; received the Society's Copley Medal for his electrical discoveries, 1745. Several of his papers were reprinted as *Experiments and Observations Tending to illustrate the Nature and Properties of Electricity* and as *A Sequel to Experiments and Observations*, both in 1746. He took his M.D. at Halle, 1757, was made licentiate of the Royal College of Physicians, 1759, and fellow, 1784. He was knighted, 1786. *DNB.* Priestley characterized him as being in 1751 "the most interested and active person in the kingdom in every thing relating to electricity." *History and Present State of Electricity* (London, 1767), p. 153. He was one of those who recommended BF for election to the Royal Society. Raymond P. Stearns, "Colonial Fellows of the Royal Society of London, 1661–1788," 3 *Wm. and Mary Quar.*, III (1946), 245.

Collinson sent BF a copy of Watson's remarks, April 25, which BF inserted in the Bowdoin MS (see above, pp. 116–17). The two versions differ in spelling, capitalization, punctuation, and paragraphing, but not in substance.

1. BF's report of April 29, 1749 (above, p. 352), read in the Royal Society, December 21.

retract his former sentiments; and that he has frequently made an experiment, which in his opinion is very conclusive in determining this point. This experiment is, that if one person causes to be fully electrised a vial two thirds full of water, or other proper non electric matter, by means of a peice of wire connected with the prime conductor so as easily to be drawn out; if this person, he says, pours the water contained in this vial into a bason held in one hand of a second person supported by wax, who the instant of the pouring the water presents the finger of his other hand near some warm spirit of wine in the hand of a third person, there will ensue a snap, and the spirit will frequently be set on fire. This testifies the accumulation of electricity in the second person, which here he can receive by no other means than by the pouring of the water from the vial into the bason held in his hand. Now as the water only, and not the vial, touched the bason, the electricity, it must be presumed, came from the water.

Mr. Watson would further recommend to our worthy brother Mr. Collinson, in writing to his correspondent Mr. Franklin, to desire to know his success in attempting to kill a Turkey by the electrical strokes.[2]

Endorsed: Read at R. S. Janry 11. 1749[/50]. given a copy to Mr. Peter Collinson.

From James Logan

Letterbook abstract: Historical Society of Pennsylvania

My Esteemed Friend   11 [January] 12th [1750]
    I wrote to him to come up hither next first day if the weather was good Seeing while the Assembly Sits I can appoint no other day and if my Son has delivered him the Magic Squares I pray him to bring them with him.[3] His affectionate friend   J L
To B. Franklin

2. BF obliged Watson with an account of the electrocution of hens and of a ten-pound turkey, which tasted, he believed, better than fowl killed in the ordinary way. BF to Collinson, Feb. 4, 1751. He commented to Collinson on Watson's other remarks, July 27, 1750.

3. "Our Benj. Franklin is certainly an Extraordinary Man in most respects," Logan wrote Peter Collinson, Feb. 14, 1750, "—one of a singular good

To James Logan

MS not found; reprinted from extract in Sparks, *Works*, VI, 100.

[January 20, 1750]
The magical squares, how wonderful soever they may seem, are what I cannot value myself upon, but am rather ashamed to have it known I have spent any part of my time in an employment that cannot possibly be of any use to myself or others.

To James Logan   Transcript: Harvard College Library (Sparks)

Sir   Monday J any 29. 1750
    Enclosed I send you a Copy of the Constitution of the Academy. Your agreeing to be one of the Trustees gave great pleasure to all concerned. I shall wait on you with Mr. Kalm on Wednesday next, if the Weather be tolerable, and nothing extraordinary prevents.[4]
    I am with great respect Sir Your Affectionate humble Servant
                                                  B. FRANKLIN
To the Hon. James Logan Esqr. Stenton.

From Peter Collinson   ALS: American Philosophical Society

Londn. february 5: 1749/50
I have so many Obligations to my kind Friend, that I dedicated a time to Visit all the Booksellers in London to search for foreign

---

Judgment, but of Equal Modesty. He is Clerk of our Assembly, and there for want of other Employment, while he sate idle, he took it in his head to think of Magical Squares, in which he outdid Frenicle himself who published above 80 pages in folio on that subject alone." Transcript: Harvard Coll. Lib. (Sparks). Bernard Frénicle de Bessy's 84-page work appeared in *Divers Ouvrages de Mathématique et de Physique par Messieurs de l'Académie Royale des Sciences*, of which a copy was in Logan's library. Edwin Wolf, 2nd, "The Romance of James Logan's Books," 3 *Wm. and Mary Quar.*, XIII (1956), 349 n. For a full description of BF's magic squares and circles, see his letters to Collinson, 1752.
    4. See below, p. 469.

459

Electrical Books and could only find Two in French. One I take to be the same I sent for thy perusal but could not be certain which Elce [I] had not bought both for I sent it away just as I received it from France.

I have many Things to say but am att present so Engaged I cannot Collect my Thought together, but shall do it I hope by Next, for this is our busiest time a year shiping Goods to the plantations.

I have sent a Parcell of books to Elias Blands[5] and thine with them.

The Guinea came safe. I wish I could have laid it all out to thy satisfaction. Pray what must I do with the remainder?

Your very Curious peices relateing to Electricity and Thundergusts have been read before the Society[6] and have been Deservedly Admired not only for the Clear Intelligent Stile but also for the Novelty of the Subjects. I am collecting all these Tracts together: your first Account with the Drawings and your Two Letters in 1747 and your Two last Accounts with Intention to putt them into some printers Hand to be communicated to the publick.[7]

The Almanack had many Things very Acceptable.

On the Books and Scheme of Education[8] more in my Next, It is much Approved. If some prizes was given annually to the greatest proficients, on a publick Day in presence of the Magistrates, Governors, &c. it stimulats greatly and begets a Laudable ambition to Excel which produces surprising Effects. In short my Dear friend I scrawl any thing. Thy Candor will excuse and thy Ingenuity will find out my Meaning.

Your American Electrical Operator seems to putt ours out of Countenance by his Novelty and Variety. Certainly something very usefull to Mankind will be found out by an by.

5. Elias Bland, London merchant. See above, 141 n.

6. BF to John Mitchell, April 29, 1749, was read in the Royal Society Nov. 9 and 16, 1749; his letter written the same day to Collinson was read Dec. 21, 1749. See above, pp. 365, 362. William Stukeley, *Family Memoirs*, II (Surtees Soc. *Pubs.*, LXXVI, 1883), 378–9.

7. Precisely what pieces Collinson had in mind is not clear. For a list of those actually printed, see BF's *Experiments and Observations on Electricity*, 1751, below.

8. See above, p. 397.

Douglasses and Elliots Essays⁹ are productive of many pretty Entertaining Articles which I read with pleasure and the Elephant by [*blank*] has its Admirers.¹

I shall be glad to hear the Books came safe and print of London &c. I am now out of Town to shake off the Citty Dust so have not my Memorandums with Mee so my Dear friend fare well. Its Late and I am Tired. Thine P COLLINSON

But I must add—that on Thursday the Fifth Day of the Week on the 8 Instant at about 20 Minutes past 12 at Noone, Wee felt a very Surpriseing Shock of an Earthquake. It was more sensible and Violent in some places than others. To Mee and many others it seem'd as if a Bale of Heavy Goods had fell down by Accident at my Next Neighbours and shook my House which sometimes Happens. But a Friend of Mine whose House is near the Thames, hear'd, (as did others) a Loud rumbling sound like cannon at a distance and then so Terrible a shock ensued that he instantly ran out of Doors, thinking his new House was tumbled about his Ears. There is an Endless Variety of Relations about its Effects but its certain Extent and Direction is not yet known but accounts came that Day that it was felt from Twickenham on the Thames to Greenwich. I dont find any people that was rideing or Walking was sensible of It. At my House in the Country 10 Miles North of London near Barnet it was not felt nor in our Neighbourhood.²

To Cadwallader Colden ALS: Historical Society of Pennsylvania

Sir Philada. Feb. 13. 1749, 50

I receiv'd your very kind Letter relating to my Proposals for the Education of our Youth, and return you the Thanks of the

9. William Douglass, *A Summary, Historical and Political, of the first Planting, Progressive Improvements, and Present State of the British Settlements in North-America,* first published at Boston in separate numbers, 1747–48. The first bound volume appeared 1749, the second 1751. The first two parts of Jared Eliot, *Essays upon Field-Husbandry* appeared in 1748 and 1749 respectively.

1. The piece has not been located; probably it was about the American mastodon, whose remains were first uncovered in 1739.

2. Reports of this earthquake fill the whole of No. 497 of *Phil. Trans.,* XLVI (1749–50), 601–750.

461

Gentlemen concern'd, for the useful Hints you have favour'd us with.[3] It was long doubtful whether the Academy would be fix'd in the Town or Country; but a Majority of those from whose generous Subscriptions we expected to be able to carry the Scheme into Execution, being strongly for the Town, it was at last fix'd to be there. And we have for the purpose made an advantageous Purchase of the Building which was erected for itinerant Preaching; a House 100 foot long and 70 wide, with a large Lot of Ground, capable of additional Buildings; situate in an airy Part of the Town. It cost I suppose not less than £2000 Building; but we have it for less than half the Money. It is strongly built of Brick; and we are now about dividing it into Rooms for the Academy. The Subscription goes on with great Success; and will not I believe be much short of £5000, besides what we expect from the Proprietors. From our Government we expect nothing. Enclos'd I send you a Copy of our present Constitutions; but we are to have a Charter, and then such of the Constitutions as are found good on Experience will I suppose be enacted into Laws, and others amended, &c.

In this Affair, as well as in other publick Affairs I have been engag'd in, the Labouring Oar has lain and does lay very much upon me, which is one Cause of my not having of late kept up so regular a Correspondence with distant Friends as I should otherways have done; and have thereby been depriv'd of much Pleasure. I assure you with great Sincerity, that I always look'd on the Friendship you honour me with, as one of the Happinesses of my Life; and that I was never acquainted with any part of your Conduct in Publick or private Life, that did not encrease the Esteem and Respect I had for you. This is in Answer to a part of your Letter,[4] in which you are conjecturing at the Cause of the late Interruption of our Correspondence, which I beg you would attribute to any thing, rather than what you mention.

I have no Observations of Jupiter's Satellites to send you, as I expected I should have. Being my self otherwise engag'd, and not very skilful in those Matters, I depended on our Astronomer Mr. Godfrey, and put the Telescope into his Hands for that purpose: He had a fine Summer for it, but I am inform'd was so continually

3. See above, p. 430.
4. Not included in the surviving draft.

462

muddled with Drink, that our Surveyor General, Mr. Scull, who was his Neighbour, could never get him to assist in making the Meridian Line. He is now dead, and your Letter of Directions for making such a Line, which I put into his Hands, is lost.[5] Mr. Scull desires me to write to you for a Repetition of those Directions, and when you have a little Leisure, I shall be oblig'd to you for them: But it will now be Midsummer before we shall have an Opportunity of observing Jupiter again.[6]

I have wrote some additional Papers on Electricity, which I will get copied, and send to you per next Post. They go on much slower in those Discoveries at home, than might be expected.

I am glad you are about enlarging and explaining your Principles of Natural Philosophy: I believe the Work will be well receiv'd by the Learned World.[7] I am, Sir, with great Respect, Your affectionate humble Servant   B FRANKLIN

To Jared Eliot

ALS: Mrs. Richard D. Wood, Jr., Wawa, Pa. (1957); printed in *American Journal of Science, and Arts*, V (1822), 364–6.

Dear Sir   Philada. Feb. 13. 1749,50

You desire to know my Thoughts about the N.E. Storms beginning to Leeward.[8] Some Years since there was an Eclipse of the Moon at 9 in the Evening,[9] which I intended to observe, but be-

5. Thomas Godfrey (see above, I, 190 n) died in December 1749. His observations on Jupiter's occultations and eclipses in 1740 and 1745 were used by Lewis Evans and Nicholas Scull (see above, I, 177) to fix the meridian in Evans' map of the Middle Colonies, 1749. Lawrence H. Gipson, *Lewis Evans* (Phila., 1939), pp. 18–19 n, and the facsimiles in Henry N. Stevens, *Lewis Evans: His Map of the Middle British Colonies* (3d edit., London, 1924).

6. Colden criticized Evans' methods; for his advice on the use of Jupiter and its satellites, see his undated unaddressed letter in *Colden Paps.*, IX, 36–8.

7. The revised edition of Colden's *Principles of Action in Matter* was published in London with the imprint date of 1751, but apparently did not appear until sometime in 1752. *Colden Paps.*, IX, 111, 118.

8. On the first publication of BF's theory see above, p. 392 n.

9. The date was Oct. 21, 1743. Alexander D. Bache, "Attempt to Fix the Date of the Observations of Doctor Franklin, in relation to the North-East Storms of the Atlantic Coast of the United States," *Jour. Franklin Institute*, XVI (1833), 300, and above, p. 149.

fore 8 a Storm blew up at N E. and continued violent all Night and all next Day, the Sky thick clouded, dark and rainy, so that neither Moon nor Stars could be seen. The Storm did a great deal of Damage all along the Coast, for we had Accounts of it in the News Papers from Boston, Newport, New York, Maryland and Virginia. But what surpriz'd me, was to find in the Boston News-papers an Account of an Observation of that Eclipse made there: For I thought, as the Storm came from the N E. it must have be-gun sooner at Boston than with us, and consequently have pre-vented such Observation. I wrote to my Brother about it, and he inform'd me, that the Eclipse was over there, an hour before the Storm began. Since which I have made Enquiries from time to time of Travellers, and of my Correspondents N Eastward and S. Westward, and observ'd the Accounts in the Newspapers from N England, N York, Maryland, Virginia and South Carolina, and I find it to be a constant Fact, that N East Storms begin to Leeward; and are often more violent there than farther to Windward. Thus the last October Storm, which with you was on the 8th. began on the 7th in Virginia and N Carolina, and was most violent there. As to the Reason of this, I can only give you my Conjectures. Suppose a great Tract of Country, Land and Sea, to wit Florida and the Bay of Mexico, to have clear Weather for several Days, and to be heated by the Sun and its Air thereby exceedingly rari-fied; Suppose the Country North Eastward, as Pensilvania, New England, Nova Scotia, Newfoundland, &c. to be at the same time cover'd with Clouds, and its Air chill'd and condens'd. The rarified Air being lighter must rise, and the Dense Air next to it will press into its Place; that will be follow'd by the next denser Air, that by the next, and so on. Thus when I have a Fire in my Chimney, there is a Current of Air constantly flowing from the Door to the Chimney: but the beginning of the Motion was at the Chimney, where the Air being rarified by the Fire, rising, its Place was supply'd by the cooler Air that was next to it, and the Place of that by the next, and so on to the Door. So the Water in a long Sluice or Mill Race, being stop'd by a Gate, is at Rest like the Air in a Calm; but as soon as you open the Gate at one End to let it out, the Water next the Gate begins first to move, that which is next to it follows; and so tho' the Water proceeds forward to the Gate, the Motion which began there runs backwards, if one may so speak, to the upper End of the Race, where the Water is last in Motion. We have on this Continent a long Ridge of Mountains running from N East to S. West; and the Coast runs the same Course. These may, perhaps, contribute towards the Direction [of the winds or at least influence] them in some Degree, [missing]. If these Conjectures do not [satisfy you, I wish] to have yours on the Subject.[1]

I doubt not but those Mou[ntains which you mention contain valuable mines] which Time will discover. [I know of] but one valuable Mine in this [country] which is that of Schuyler's in the Jerseys. [This yields good] Copper, and has turn'd out vast Wealth to the Owners. I was at it last Fall; but they were not then at Work; the Water is grown too hard for them; and they waited for a Fire Engine from England to drain their Pits; I suppose they will have that at Work next Summer; it costs them £1000 Sterling.

Col. John Schuyler,[2] one of the Owners, has a Deer Park 5 Miles round, fenc'd with Cedar Logs, 5 Logs high, with chocks of Wood between; it contains variety of Land high and Low, woodland and clear. There are a great many Deer in it; and he expects in a few Years to be able to kill 200 head a Year, which will be a profitable Thing. He has likewise 600 Acres of Meadow, all within Bank.[3] The Mine is not far from Passaic Falls, which I went also to see. They are very curious: the Water falls 70 foot perpendicular, as we were told; but we had nothing to measure

1. A corner of the MS has been torn away. Bracketed words are supplied from the printed version.

2. Col. John Schuyler (d. 1773), of Pompton, N.J., member of the Governor's Council, 1745–46. He operated a copper mine on the Passaic river, which his father had opened. Kalm visited the mine in 1749. Kalm, *Travels*, II, 621. Andrew Burnaby noted in 1760 that the mine was kept free from water by "a fire-engine erected upon common principles." *Travels through the Middle Settlements in North-America* (London, 1775), p. 57. William Nelson, "Josiah Hornblower and the First Steam-Engine in America, with some notices of the Schuyler Copper Mines at Second River, N.J.," 2 N.J. Hist. Soc. *Proc.*, VII (1882), 175–247. A description of the house and manner of life there, recorded by a visitor in 1776, is quoted in Thomas A. Glenn, *Some Colonial Mansions* (2d ser., Phila., 1900), pp. 418–23; see also George W. Schuyler, *Colonial New York* (N.Y., 1885), II, 192–4, 206–7.

3. The mention of the banked meadows so interested Eliot that BF promised, after his visit to Connecticut later in the year, to get him an account of it from Colonel Schuyler.

with.[4] It [gives me great][5] Pleasure that your Sentiments [are in accord] with mine. I like your No[tion] [*missing*] ming; and tho' perhaps it [*missing*] n prudent, as we are circum[stanced] [*missing*] them in the Proposals; I doubt [not that they will] in time become Part of the [*missing*]. It will be agreable to you to hear, and therefore I inform you, that our Subscription goes on with great Success, and we suppose will exceed £5000 of our Currency: We have bought for the Academy, the House that was built for Itinerant Preaching, which stands on a large Lot of Ground capable of receiving more Buildings to lodge the Scholars, if it should come to be a regular Colledge. The House is 100 foot long and 70 wide, built of Brick; very strong; and sufficiently high for three lofty Stories: I suppose it did not cost less than £2000 building; but we bought it for £775 18s. 11¾d: tho' it will cost us 3 or perhaps 400 more to make the Partitions and Floors, and fit up the Rooms. I send you enclos'd a Copy of our present Constitutions;[6] but we expect a Charter from our Proprietaries this Summer, when they may prob'ly receive considerable Alterations.[7] The Paper admonishes me that 'tis Time to conclude. I am, Sir, Your obliged humble Servant   B FRANKLIN

To James Logan

MS not found; reprinted from extract in Sparks, *Works*, VII, 40.

[February 17, 1750]
I send Whiston's Life.[8] He seems to me to have been a man of great industry and little prudence. I have been lame these two

4. The falls are described by many eighteenth-century travelers, including Burnaby (*Travels*, pp. 56–7), who mentioned a legend that two Indians, venturing too close in a canoe, were carried over the precipice.
5. The mutilated passage is completely omitted in the printed version. The bracketed words are supplied conjecturally by the editors.
6. See above, p. 421.
7. The Proprietors did not grant a charter until July 13, 1753.
8. *Memoirs of the Life and Writings of Mr. William Whiston* (London, 1749). Whiston (1667–1752), mathematician and theologian, had an acute mind but little judgment. A graduate of Cambridge, he succeeded Newton as Lucasian professor, 1703; he was removed in 1710 for Arianism. A tireless writer and lecturer, he confirmed the narrative of Genesis by Newtonian

weeks past, but am now so much better, that I think I shall be able to wait on you next week with Mr. Kalm.[9] We had a very bright appearance of the Aurora Borealis last night. When I have the pleasure of seeing you, I shall give you a full account of the affairs of the Academy, which go on with all the success that could be expected.

From George Whitefield

MS not found; reprinted from *A Select Collection of Letters of the Late Reverend George Whitefield, M.A.* . . . (London, 1772), II, 335–7.

My dear Mr. F[ranklin],   Plymouth, Feb. 26, 1750

Ever since I received your last kind letter, I have been endeavouring to redeem some time to answer it, but till now have not had opportunity. Indeed even now a multiplicity of business obliges me to be much more brief than otherwise I should. However, I cannot help informing you, that I am glad that the gentlemen of Philadelphia are exerting their efforts to erect an academy. I have often thought such an institution was wanted exceedingly; and if well-conducted, am persuaded it will be of public service. Your plan I have read over, and do not wonder at its meeting with general approbation.[1] It is certainly well calculated to promote polite literature; but I think there wants *aliquid Christi* in it, to make it so useful as I would desire it might be. It is true, you say, "The youth are to be taught some public religion, and the excellency of the christian religion in particular:" but methinks this is mentioned too late, and too soon passed over. As we are all creatures of a day; as our whole life is but one small point between two eternities, it is reasonable to suppose, that the grand end of

principles and explained the Flood by a collision of the earth and a comet (*New Theory of the Earth*, London, 1696); he believed that the Tartars were the Lost Tribes, formed a society for promoting primitive Christianity, translated Josephus, and, becoming scrupulous about the Athanasian Creed, left the Church of England in 1747 to become a Baptist. *DNB*. Whiston's son John was one of the London booksellers with whom Logan dealt.

9. BF took Kalm to Stenton February 28. Logan was unfavorably impressed. See below, p. 469.

1. BF's *Proposals Relating to the Education of Youth in Pennsylvania*. See above, p. 397.

every christian institution for forming tender minds, should be to convince them of their natural depravity, of the means of recovering out of it, and of the necessity of preparing for the enjoyment of the supreme Being in a future state. These are the grand points in which christianity centers. Arts and sciences may be built on this, and serve to embellish and set off this superstructure, but without this, I think there cannot be any good foundation. Whether the little Dutch book I have sent over, will be of any service in directing to such a foundation, or how to build upon it, I cannot tell. Upon mentioning your desire to the King's German chaplain,[2] a worthy man of GOD, he sent it to me, and thought, if translated, it might be of service. Glad should I be of contributing, though it was but the least mite, in promoting so laudable an undertaking; but the gentlemen concerned are every way so superior to me, both in respect to knowledge of books and men, that any thing I could offer, I fear, would be of very little service. I think the main thing will be, to get proper masters that are acquainted with the world, with themselves, and with GOD, and who will consequently naturally care for the welfare of the youth that shall be committed to their care. I think also in such an institution, there should be a well-approved christian Orator, who should not be content with giving a public lecture in general upon oratory, but who should visit and take pains with every class, and teach them early how to speak, and read, and pronounce well. An hour or two in a day, I think, ought to be set apart for this. It would serve as an agreeable amusement, and would be of great service, whether the youth be intended for the pulpit, the bar, or any other profession whatsoever. I wish also, that the youth were to board in the academy, and by that means be always under the master's

2. Friedrich Michael Ziegenhagen (1694–1776), royal Lutheran chaplain at St. James's, 1722–76, was deeply interested in foreign missions, aiding the Salzburger emigrants to Georgia, 1737, and acting as sort of unofficial bishop to the Pennsylvania congregations, who asked him to get them a minister. Through Gotthilf August Francke of Halle he secured the services of Heinrich Melchior Muhlenberg, who visited him in London before departing for America in 1741. Theodore E. Schmauk, *A History of the Lutheran Church in Pennsylvania (1638–1820)* (Phila., 1903), I, 193; Theodore G. Tappert and John W. Doberstein, trans., *The Journals of Henry Melchior Muhlenberg* I (Phila., 1942), 18–22. The little German book he gave Whitefield for BF has not been identified.

eye. And if a fund could be raised, for the free education of the poorer sort, who should appear to have promising abilities, I think it would greatly answer the design proposed. It hath been often found, that some of our brightest men in church and state, have arisen from such an obscure condition. When I heard of the academy, I told Mr. B_____,[3] that the new building,[4] I thought, would admirably suit such a proposal; and I then determined in my next to mention some terms that might be offered to the consideration of the Trustees. But I find since, that you have done this already, and that matters are adjusted agreeable to the minds of the majority. I hope your agreement meets with the approbation of the inhabitants, and that it will be serviceable to the cause of vital piety and good education. If these ends are answered, a free-school erected, the debts paid, and a place preserved for public preaching, I do not see what reason there is for any one to complain. But all this depends on the integrity, disinterestedness, and piety of the gentlemen concerned. An institution, founded on such a basis, GOD will bless and succeed; but without these, the most promising schemes will prove abortive, and the most flourishing structures, in the end, turn out mere Babels. I wish you and the gentlemen concerned much prosperity; and pray the LORD of all lords to direct you to the best means to promote the best end; I mean, the glory of GOD, and the welfare of your fellow-creatures. Be pleased to remember me to them and all friends as they come in your way, and believe me, dear Sir, Yours, &c.

G.W.

James Logan to Peter Collinson

Letterbook copy: Historical Society of Pennsylvania

Dear Peter   Stenton 12 mo [February] 28 1749/50
I have Spent most of this day for the first time with thy friend Kalm accompanied with B. Franklin, and I know not what to make of him, nor of his Journey to Canada, where, after the whole last winter Spent at a Swedish Woman's House near Newcastle, he Spent near five Months, and dined many times at the Governors

3. Not identified.
4. On the New Building, see above, II, 290 n, and this volume, above, p. 435.

at Quebec, without Seeing during the 8 Months or more that he had been here, any one person that I could hear of, but B.Franklin and Jno. Bartram, and he talks of returning to Canada again, but on what business I cannot learn. The Swedes had a Colony Sent in this River under Christina their Queen, but because they were neglected by their own People at home, they were obliged to Surrender to the Low Dutch, who being attack'd by an English Fleet and army Surrendred to them about 1664, and the Same Lowlanders in 1672 recovering the Countrey again were obliged the Succeeding year to resign all their pretensions to it to the English. But the principal of these Actions were at the North River and New Amstel now called Hudsons River and New York. This Delaware was called the South River, and the Dutch in it built the town of Newcastle. The Swedes are not much encreased and in my time here (now above 50 years) are much Anglified as our Term is, nor if we had a War now with France Should we have any reason to apprehend the French in conjunction with the Swedes were they to joyn them, for B. Franklin found a way in 1747 to put the Countrey on raising above 120 Companies of Militia of which Philadelphia raised ten, of about a hundred men each with Some few Germans amongst them, and the women were So Zealous that they furnished ten pair of Silk Colours wrought with various Mottoes. The Serjeants had also Halberds &c. &c., but in all the rest Scarce one for they all vote for the Quakers purely to Save their own Money. Benjamin also was the Sole Author of two Lotteries that raised above Six thousand pounds of our Money to pay for the Charge of Batteries on the River. And tho' we had now a war with France we Should be Secure against any common Attempt, as lying So far up the River. In Short he is an excellent yet a humble man, and carried himself a Musket among the Common Soldiers. He is now also putting forward an Academy for the improvement of Youth, for which he is [has] already got Subscriptions for above five hundred pounds per annum for five years and has a full dependance of finding wayes to continue it for futurity. But I must here add that thou hast Seen my Tully of old Age of which he printed a thousand and of these I Sent over a dozen but they were taken in the first of the French War in 1744. He also Sent over to Wm. Strahan a Printer in or near Fleet Street 2 or 3 years after 300 of them (to whom he only directs to Wm.

Strahan Printer in London) of which he has no further account but that they were received and would not Sell, by reason that there was another version lately published which I Suspect, and therefore I beg thee to find that Strahan and expostulate with him, but on a further thought I shall write to Jno. Whiston William's Son at Boyles Head in Fleet Street and for the present bid thee [farewell.] Thy Affectionate   J.L.

P.S. I have read all the first Vol. of Wm. Whiston's life[5] and look'd over the 2d and I pity him.[6] Pray call on his Son telling him where I have wrote to thee of Wm. Strahan, and if thou canst learn, please to inform me what profession of Religion Jno. Makes.[7] His father now professes himself a Baptist.

2d P.S. Pray do not imagine that I overdoe it in my Character of BF for I am rather short in it and I hope to convince thee when an opportunity offers free of Postage that what I wrote in my last by Capt. James of his Magical Squares is truly Astonishing. And if thou art free in thy communication with our Proprietor he can shew thee his (B.F.'s) Proposals relating to the Education of Youth in Pensilvania, a tract 8vo, also a large Sheet called Constitutions of the Publick Academy in the City of Philadelphia in which he first put me at the Head of the Trustees unknown to me and I refused it, yet being left open in a few Weeks I accepted of it, for it was at first proposed to me that [the Library?][8] I was about to Settle on the Publick would be [remainder missing]. But what I principally esteem him for, is not those Squares tho' they are commendable but his real Service to the Countrey in being Instrumental in Saving it by his contriving the plan [of] his 2

5. Whiston's Life. See above, p. 466 n.
6. Above this point in the MS are the following words: "Speak to Strahan himself and not to John Whiston"; but where Logan meant this to appear is uncertain. The injunction seems to be canceled by his "further thought" at the end of the body of the letter.
7. John Whiston (d. 1780), one of the printers of the votes of the House of Commons, was one of the first booksellers to issue priced catalogues regularly. With Thomas Osborne, Strahan, and other bookseller-publishers, he actively promoted the *New and General Biographical Dictionary* (12 vols., London, 1761–62). *DNB*.
8. This insertion, required for sense, is made from Sparks's transcript in Harvard Coll. Lib. The remainder of the sentence is missing, as it was in Sparks's day.

Lotteries for the Charges of Batteries his borrowing Great Guns from N York but with W. Allen's Assistance but he is the prime actor in all this as he is in the Academy. Certain conceited people when Whitefield came first over and having had leave to preach in the publick Church two or three times and afterwards on its being denied to him, contributed to build a House large enough for him to preach in and therefore by the favour of a good woman who obliged them by Some means in the Ground for it built a House one hundred feet lo[ng] 70 ft. br[oad] and about 35 ft. high which the Trustees of the Academy have purchased. I have now wrote to John Whiston who I hope will take care of the business of Strahan and thou needs not to Speak to him about it otherwise than as thou pleases and thou may in like manner Speak to Strahan or forbear.   J L

To Peter Collinson[9]

MS not found; reprinted from *The Gentleman's Magazine*, XX (1750), 208.

[March 2, 1750][1]

I was very much pleased with some ingenious papers in the late *Transactions* on the subject of electricity.[2]

There is something however in the experiments of points, sending off, or drawing on, the electrical fire, which has not been fully explained, and which I intend to supply in my next. For the doctrine of *points* is very curious, and the effects of them truly wonderfull; and, from what I have observed on experiments, I

9. Entitled in *Gent. Mag.*: "A curious Remark on Electricity; from a Gentleman in America; whose ingenious Letters on this Subject will soon be published in a separate Pamphlet, illustrated with Cuts. Extract of a Letter to Mr. P. C. F.R.S."

1. This is believed to be the letter Collinson referred to in a letter to BF in June (see below, p. 484): "Per Next I may more particularly consider thine of March the 2d. There is Something very Marvelous in the Doctrine of Points." Furthermore, since the May issue of *Gent. Mag.* appeared early in June, the letter could not have left Philadelphia after early April; but March is more likely.

2. *Phil. Trans.*, No. 486 (XLV, 1748, 131–276), which was published Oct. 1749. *Gent. Mag.*, XIX (1749), 480. This number contained articles on electricity from Abbé Nollet, John Ellicott, and Henry Baker. Ellicott's experiments with electrical points, pp. 209–221, particularly interested BF.

472

am of opinion, that houses, ships, and even towns and churches may be effectually secured from the stroke of lightening by their means; for if, instead of the round balls of wood or metal, which are commonly placed on the tops of the weathercocks, vanes or spindles of churches, spires or masts, there should be put a rod of iron 8 or 10 feet in length, sharpen'd gradually to a point like a needle, and gilt to prevent rusting, or divided into a number of points, which would be better—the electrical fire would, I think, be drawn out of a cloud silently, before it could come near enough to strike; only a light would be seen at the point, like the sailors corpusante.*[3] This may seem whimsical, but let it pass for the present, until I send the experiments at large.[5]

I shall further remark on *the Transactions,* &c. that the leaf gold suspended is not always nearest the non-electric, and that its situation depends on the number, acuteness, or situation of its points.[6] By cutting a leaf into the shape underneath, it may be made to rest in the air, at any required distance from the electrified plate, from a quarter of an inch to a foot, while the nearest non-electric (the floor) may be at 3 or 4 feet distance. If it draws too near the electrified plate, make the top more sharp; if it keeps at too great a distance, make it more dull, or obtuse, by cutting off its points; then, by tryals and a little practice, it may be made to rest where desired.

[*It is usually taken for a meteor on the yards or shrouds, but is indeed no more than the spray of the sea saturated with luminous insects, frequent during the summer season in the Mediteranean.][4]

3. Note the similarity in thought and language of this paragraph and sect. 20 of BF's Opinions and Conjectures, July 29, 1750. Corposant (corpo santo): St. Elmo's fire.

4. Brackets in the printed version.

5. At this point a footnote was inserted stating that the experiments would appear in the forthcoming publication of BF's experiments. See his *Experiments and Observations on Electricity,* 1751, below.

6. See Ellicott's experiments with leaf-silver in *Phil. Trans.,* XLV (1748), 221–3.

To Abiah Franklin
ALS: Boston Athenaeum

Honoured Mother   Philada. April 12. 1750

We received your kind Letter of the 2d Instant,[7] and are glad to hear you still enjoy such a Measure of Health, notwithstanding your great Age. We read your Writing very easily; I never met with a Word in your Letters but what I could readily understand; for tho' the Hand is not always the best, the Sense makes every thing plain.

My Leg, which you enquire after, is now quite well.[8] I still keep those Servants, but the Man not in my own House: I have hired him out to the Man that takes Care of my Dutch Printing Office,[9] who agrees to keep him in Victuals and Clothes, and to pay me a Dollar a Week for his Work. His Wife since that Affair behaves exceeding well: But we conclude to sell them both the first good Opportunity; for we do not like Negro Servants. We got again about half what we lost.

As to your Grandchildren, Will. is now 19 Years of Age, a tall proper Youth, and much of a Beau.[1] He acquir'd a Habit of Idleness on the Expedition, but begins of late to apply himself to Business,

7. Not found.

8. BF told James Logan on Feb. 17 (see above, p. 466) he had been lame two weeks.

9. Johann Boehm was BF's partner for printing German almanacs and the *Philadelphier Teutsche Fama*, 1749–51. Oswald Seidensticker, *The First Century of German Printing in America, 1728–1830* (Phila., 1893), pp. 35–8. Nothing more is known about the servants' misconduct.

1. The general belief that William Franklin (D.1) was born in 1731, or very close to it, is based primarily on this statement of his father's in April 1750. It is possible, however, that BF deliberately understated the youth's age by one, two, or even three, years in order to leave with his mother an impression (perhaps first conveyed by earlier letters now missing) that William was BF's child by Deborah, whom he took to wife, Sept. 1, 1730, just as Francis Folger and Sarah undoubtedly were. If indeed William was the son of an earlier liaison with an unknown woman, BF may well have wished to conceal the matter from his mother in far-off Boston. This suggestion that William was actually born some time before 1731 is supported by the fact that he received an ensign's commission in the Pennsylvania troops raised for the Canada expedition in 1746, when, according to BF's present statement, he could have been only 15, unusually young for an officer, even in eighteenth-century America. Whether or not he himself ever knew the actual date of his birth, William was responsible for the belief that he was 82 when he died in 1813. *Gent. Mag.* LXXXIII (1813), 510.

and I hope will become an industrious Man. He imagin'd his Father had got enough for him: But I have assur'd him that I intend to spend what little I have, my self; if it please God that I live long enough: And as he by no means wants Sense, he can see by my going on, that I am like to be as good as my Word.

Sally grows a fine Girl, and is extreamly industrious with her Needle, and delights in her Book.[2] She is of a most affectionate Temper, and perfectly Dutiful and obliging, to her Parents and to all. Perhaps I flatter my self too much; but I have Hopes that she will prove an ingenious sensible notable and worthy Woman, like her Aunt Jenney.[3] She goes now to the Dancing School.

For my own Part, at present I pass my time agreably enough. I enjoy (thro' Mercy) a tolerable Share of Health; I read a great deal, ride a little, do a little Business for my self, more for others; retire when I can, and go [into] Company when I please; so the Years roll round, and the last will come; when I would rather have it said, *He lived usefully,* than, *He died rich.*

Cousins Josiah and Sally[4] are well, and I believe will do well, for they are an industrious saving young Couple: But they want a little more Stock to go on smoothly with their Business.

My Love to Brother and Sister Mecom and their Children, and to all my Relations in general. I am Your dutiful Son B FRANKLIN

Two further observations can be made: If, on the one hand, William's mother was not Deborah and he was born about 1731, the liaison was timed with extraordinary awkwardness, occurring as it must have done at just about the same time that Deborah became BF's wife. If, on the other hand, Deborah was William's mother, as Charles Henry Hart has argued, and the boy was indeed born about 1731, it is curious that even in his own lifetime he was often described as illegitimate, though "Franky" and Sarah never were. Their status as children of the same common-law wife would have been identical with his. Both these puzzles would be explained if William were significantly older than 19 in April 1750, whoever his mother may have been. For extended and contradictory discussions of William Franklin's parentage, see Paul L. Ford, *Who was the Mother of Franklin's Son? An Historical Conundrum hitherto Given Up—Now Partly Answered* (Brooklyn, 1889); reprinted with an afterword by John C. Oswald (New Rochelle, N.Y., 1932); and Charles H. Hart, "Who was the Mother of Franklin's Son. An Inquiry demonstrating that she was Deborah Read, wife of Benjamin Franklin," *PMHB,* xxxv (1911), 309–14.

2. Sarah Franklin (D.3) was seven years old.

3. Jane Franklin Mecom (C.17).

4. Josiah Davenport (C.12.4), a baker, and his wife Sarah settled in Philadelphia, 1749. See above, p. 388.

From Peter Collinson

ALS: American Philosophical Society

Lond. Aprill 25 1750

I wish I have before this advised my Worthy Friend that his pacquet per Cap. Clark came at last to my Hands, with the Electrical Papers, which are now on the Press under the Inspection and Correction of our Learned and Ingenious Friend Doctor Fothergill for Wee thought it a great Pitty that the Publick should be deprived the benefit of so many Curious Experiments.

Great Doctors will differ as may be seen by the Inclosed Paper from Mr. Watson[5] Which was read some Time after thy papers had been communicated to the Society, who was greatly pleased with them and Desired their Thanks for so kind a Communication.

Abbe Nolet has been at the pains to Travel on purpose to Turin to Venice and Bologna to see those Experiments Verified of Giveing Purges, Transfusion of Odours and Cureing the Gout &c. but to his great Surprise found very Little or no Satisfaction.[6] The Ingenious Men in those Citties had been too premature in publishing for Facts, Experiments [which,] if they did once succeed, could not be depended on for Certainty to do again, to the no small Disappointment of Abbe Nolet—Who Indeed could never make them do, but thought they might have a Knack in performing those Opperations that He was Ignorant Off.

I am Obliged to thee for the Constitutions.[7] They are very Rational and well Calculated for the Purposes Intended. I am glad to find so Laudable an Institution Meets with such Encouragement.

Wee have had Heithertoo the Warmest and Mildest Winter and Spring that Ever was known. Our Apricots and Peaches are sett Like ropes of Onions and the Face of plenty smiles Every Where—but our Neighbours complain Spain, Portugal and South of France by this Long Warm Dry Season are like to Loose their Crops of Corn unless suddenly retrieved by Rain. Our

5. See above, p. 457.
6. Nollet, "An Examination of certain Phaenomena in Electricity, published in Italy," *Phil. Trans.*, XLVI (1749–50), 370–97, was read in the Royal Society, March 29, 1750. Watson had read a letter, March 1, "declaring that he as well as many others have not been able to make Odours pass thro' Glass by means of Electricity." *Ibid.*, 348–56.
7. Constitutions of the Academy of Philadelphia. See above, p. 421.

476

Wheat is risen on this News. I have seen no Snow and Scarsly any Ice and Winter has been Insensibly Lost in a very Early Spring, but yett as the Season has been so agreeable on one Hand yett on the other it may have furnishd Materials or putt them in Action to the Great Surprise of all that Felt four Earthquakes —the 8th feby and March at London and then at Portsmouth and the Isle of Wight and Since at Chester and Liverpool. Divers Hypotheses's are advanced to Solve these Phenomena, Hales I send.[8] Others have been read before the Society wholy Accounting for it on the principle of Electricity. Others presume as Wee have had a very Long Dry Time for 6 months past, the Caverns are Exhausted of the Water, Air has Supplyed its Roome. This had putt the Beds of pyri[tes] in a Ferment. Such unusuall Warmth has Rarified it, an Explosion Ensued. Thus in short Hints my good friend take it as I can give, and be assured I am thine

P COLLINSON

From Samuel Johnson[9]

Letterbook copy (fragment): Columbia University Library

[May 10, 1750][1]
[*First part missing*] Seat of London. I drew it[2] up at first only for the use of my Son, and had no further tho'ts, but when I tho't

8. Stephen Hales, *Some Considerations on the Causes of Earthquakes* (London, 1750), read in the Royal Society, April 5, 1750, and printed in *Phil. Trans.*, XLVI (1749–50), 669–81.

9. Samuel Johnson (1696–1772), B.A., Yale, 1714; tutor in the college, 1716–19; minister at West Haven, 1720–22; one of those in and around Yale College, including its rector Timothy Cutler, who came to doubt or oppose the validity of presbyterian ordination, 1722 (see above, I, 43); was ordained in England in the Anglican communion, 1723. He settled at Stratford, Conn., 1723, as a missionary of the Society for the Propagation of the Gospel, the first clergyman of his faith settled in the colony. He became a warm friend of Dean (later Bishop) George Berkeley during the latter's residence at Newport, R.I., 1729–31, and enlisted his benefactions for Yale. He wrote several pieces defending and explaining Berkeleyan idealism. He often engaged in controversy over the rights of the Anglican church in New England's hostile climate. Oxford conferred on him the degree of doctor of divinity, 1743. BF and others urged him to head the new Academy of Philadelphia, 1750–51; he declined on the grounds of age and ill health (see his letter to BF, Jan. 1752, below), but accepted the presidency of King's (Columbia) College, 1754. On

it necessary to take the pains to transcribe it in order for your perusal, I could not forbear having the vanity to wish it might be useful to others, for I was always very desirous if I could, to contribute something towards promoting the Interest of Learning in the Country, and could therefore wish, (tho' I dare not expect,) that it might possibly obtain so favourable an Opinion with Gentlemen as to be thot not altogether undeserving the Press, but as to this I am intirely resigned to the Judgment of my Friends, and particularly do submit it to your Candid Judgment and that of any Friend to whom you may think it worth the while to give the perusal of it. Only if it were to be printed I should be glad you would suggest any defects you observe in it or any thing that might make it more intelligible and useful. I will only add that if it were tho't in some measure fit to be printed, and practicable to get it done, I had some thots of printing with it a new Edition of my Ethics with some Enlargements and Emendations, and that I beleive I could dispose of over 100 Copies of it here, and perhaps another 100 might be disposed of at Boston and some at N.Y. and the Jersies. However I intirely submit what I have thus had the assurance to write, to your free and candid animadversion, and remain Sir your most humble &c.   S.J.

To William Strahan

MS not found; facsimiles of ALS: Historical Society of Pennsylvania and Boston Public Library

Dear Sir   Philada. June 2. 1750
The Person from whom you had the Power of Attorney to receive a Legacy, was born in Holland, and at first call'd *Aletta Crell*; but not being Christen'd when the Family came to live among the English in America, she was baptiz'd by the Name

---

his retirement in 1763 he returned to Stratford as rector. *DAB;* E. Edwards Beardsley, *Life and Correspondence of Samuel Johnson, D.D.* (N.Y., 1874); Herbert W. and Carol Schneider, eds., *Samuel Johnson, President of King's College: His Career and Writings* (4 vols., N.Y., 1929).

1. The date is fixed by BF's letter to Johnson, April 15, 1754.
2. Johnson's *Noetica* which, with the second edition of his *Ethica* and *An Introduction to the Study of Philosophy,* Franklin and Hall published, 1752, under the title *Elementa Philosophica.*

of *Mary*.[3] This Change of Name probably might be unknown to the Testator, as it happen'd in Carolina, and so the Legacy might be left her by her first Name *Aletta*. She has wrote it on a Piece of Paper which I enclose, and desires you would take the Trouble of acquainting the Gentleman with these Particulars, which she thinks may induce him to pay the Money.

I am glad to understand by the Papers, that the Parliament has provided for paying off the Debts due on the Canada Expedition. I suppose my Son's Pay is now in your Hands.[4] I am willing to allow 6 per Cent (the Rate of Interest here) for the Delay; or more, if the Disappointment has been a greater Loss to you. I hope the £50 Bill I lately sent you, is come to hand, and paid.

The Description you give of the Company and Manner of Living in Scotland, would almost tempt one to remove thither. Your Sentiments of the general Foible of Mankind, in the Pursuit of Wealth to no End, are express'd in a Manner that gave me great Pleasure in reading: They are extreamly just, at least they are perfectly agreable to mine. But London Citizens, they say, are ambitious of what they call *dying worth* a great Sum: The very Notion seems to me absurd; and just the same as if a Man should run in debt for 1000 Superfluities, to the End that when he should be stript of all, and imprison'd by his Creditors, it might be said, he *broke worth* a great Sum. I imagine that what we have above what we can use, is not properly *ours*, tho' we possess it; and that the rich Man who *must die*, was no more *worth* what he leaves, than the Debtor who *must pay*.

I am glad to hear so good a Character of my Son-in Law.[5] Please to acquaint him that his Spouse grows finely, and will

3. Mary (Aletta) Crell, daughter of Joseph Crell (or Crellius), who translated BF's *Plain Truth* into German (see above, 184 n), came from Germany with her father and uncle, and settled at Saxe Gotha in the Congaree Valley in South Carolina, 1736, where she married Dr. Peter Neigh (or Nye). After his death she married a Scotsman who kept a tavern in Amsterdam, where she was living "very well" in 1761, when BF visited her and her father. Van Doren, *Autobiographical Writings*, p. 129; BF to Deborah F., Sept. 14, 1761.

4. See above, pp. 321, 381, 394.

5. A playful expression of the hope, entertained by both men for some years, that young William Strahan, now ten, would some day marry Sarah Franklin, now seven.

479

probably have an agreable Person. That with the best Natural Disposition in the World, she discovers daily the Seeds and Tokens of Industry, Oeconomy, and in short, of every Female Virtue, which her Parents will endeavour to cultivate for him; and if the Success answers their fond Wishes and Expectations, she will, in the true Sense of the Word, be *worth* a great deal of Money, and consequently a great Fortune.

I suppose my Wife writes to Mrs. Strahan. Our Friend Mr. Hall is well, and manages perfectly to my Satisfaction. I cannot tell how to accept your repeated Thanks for Services you think I have done to him, when I continually feel my self oblig'd to him, and to you for sending him. I sincerely wish all Happiness to you and yours, and am, Dear Sir, Your most obliged humble Servant   B FRANKLIN

Addressed: To   Mr Wm Strahan   Printer   London

Last Will and Testament

ADS (mutilated):[6] American Philosophical Society

[June 22, 1750]

I Benjamin Franklin of the City of Philadelphia Printer, being in perfect Health of Body and Mind, (blessed be God) do this twenty second Day of June, in the Year 1750, make, publish, sign and seal this my last Will and Testament, viz.

First, I give to my honoured Mother Abiah Franklin, Twenty Pounds per Annum during her Life, to be paid Quarterly out of the Incomes and Profits of my Printing Houses before the Division of that Part [*remainder of page missing*]
Street, with the Improvements thereon; and also my Share in the Library of Philadelphia; all of them to him and his Heirs or Assigns forever.

6. The MS lacks about two-thirds of the first two pages, on which specific bequests were recorded. There are interesting similarities and differences between this will and that of April 28, 1757, which superseded it. For example, the Library Company share which BF willed to William Franklin in 1750, was willed to Sarah in 1757; but the moving conclusion of 1750 was retained unchanged in 1757. Both early wills, however, differ substantially from that of July 17, 1788, when BF's financial and personal conditions were, of course, quite different.

Also I give to my Wife Deborah Franklin, during her natural Life, my Right to a House and Lot in High-street, now in Possession of her Mother Sarah Read; and after my Wife's Decease, I give the same to my Daughter Sarah Franklin, her Heirs or Assigns forever.

And the rest of my Estate, Goods and Chattels (except [*remainder of page missing*]
Wife die before the Expiration of the said Partnerships or any of them, then the Share of those Profits hereby allotted to her, is to go to my Children, and be equally divided between them.

And as the said Partnerships expire, I will that the said Printing Houses be sold one after the other, and the Money arising from such Sale divided between my Wife and Children, in the same Manner as the yearly Profits are before directed to be divided: Earnestly recommending to my little Family, that the Peace, Love, and affectionate Performance of mutual Duties [*two or three words missing*] among them, may continue to their Lives [End?[7] *two or three words missing*]. And I make my Wife Deborah Franklin [and my son?] William Franklin Executors of this my last Will [and Test]ament; and I desire my good Friends William Coleman and Philip Syng to give them from time to time their Advice where it may be needful in the Settlement of any of my Affairs.

And now humbly returning sincere Thanks to GOD for producing me into Being, and conducting me hitherto thro' Life so happily, so free from Sickness, Pain and Trouble, and with such a Competency of this World's Goods as might make a reasonable Mind easy: That he was pleased to give me such a Mind, with moderate Passions, or so much of his gracious Assistance in governing them; and to free it early from Ambition, Avarice and Superstition, common Causes of much Uneasiness to Men. That he gave me to live so long in a Land of Liberty, with a People that I love, and rais'd me, tho' a Stranger, so many Friends among them; bestowing on me moreover a loving and prudent Wife, and dutiful Children. For these and all his other innumerable Mercies and Favours, I bless that BEING OF BEINGS who does not disdain to care for the meanest of his Creatures. And I reflect on those Benefits received with the greater Satisfaction, as they give me such a Confidence in his Goodness, as will, I hope,

7. Word supplied from 1757 will.

enable me always in all things to submit freely to his Will, and to resign my Spirit chearfully into his Hands whenever he shall please to call for it; reposing myself securely in the Lap of God and Nature as a Child in the Arms of an affectionate Parent.

B FRANKLIN[8]

Signed, sealed and delivered by the said
Benjamin Franklin, as and for his last Will and
Testament, in the Presence of us
SAMUEL RHOADS
PHILIP SYNG
WM: COLEMAN

To Cadwallader Colden

ALS: New-York Historical Society

Sir   Philada. June 28. 1750

I wrote a Line to you last Post, and sent you some Electrical Observations and Experiments. You formerly had those Papers of mine out of which something has been taken by Mr. Watson, and inserted in the Transactions:[9] If you have forgot the Contents of those Papers, I am afraid some Things in that I last sent you will be hardly understood, as they depend on what went before. I send you herewith my Essay towards a new Hypothesis of the Cause and Effects of Lightning, &c. of which you may remember some Hints in my first Electrical Minutes.[1] I sent this Essay above a 12 month since to Dr. Mitchel in London, and have since heard nothing of it, which makes me doubt of its getting to hand. In some late Experiments, I have not only frequently fired unwarm'd Spirits, by the Electrical Stroke, but have even melted small Quantities of Copper, Silver and Gold, and not only melted but vitrified them, so as to incorporate them with common Glass; and this without any sensible Heat; which strengthens my Supposition that the Melting of Metals by Lightning may be a cold Fusion.[2] Of these Experiments I shall shortly write a particular

8. The signature has been firmly crossed out, probably by BF when he signed the new will of 1757.
9. See above, p. 126.
1. See above, p. 365.
2. BF to Collinson, July 29, 1750.

Account. I wrote to Mr. Collinson, on Reading in the Transactions the Accounts from Italy and Germany, of giving Purges, transferring Odours, &c. with the Electrical Effluvia, that I was persuaded they were not true. He since informs me,[3] that Abbé Nolet of Paris, who had try'd the Experiments without Success, was lately at the Pains to make a Journey to Turin, Bologna and Venice, to enquire into the Facts, and see the Experiments repeated, imagining they had there some Knacks of Operating that he was unacquainted with; but to his great Disappointment found little or no Satisfaction; the Gentlemen there having been too premature in Publishing their Imaginations and Expectations for real Experiments. Please to return me the Papers when you have perus'd them.

My good old Friend Mr. Logan, being about three Months since struck with a Palsey, continues Speechless, tho' he knows People, and seems in some Degree to retain his Memory and Understanding. I fear he will not recover.[4] Mr. Kalm is gone towards Canada again, and Mr. Evans is about to take a Journey to Lake Erie, which he intends next Week.[5] Mr. Bertram continues well and hearty. I thank you for what you write concerning celestial Observations. We are going on with our Building for the Academy, and propose to have an Observatory on the Top; and as we shall have a mathematical Professor, I doubt not but we shall soon be able to send you some Observations accurately made. I am, with great Esteem and Respect, Sir, Your most obliged Humble Servant   B FRANKLIN

3. April 25, 1750, above, p. 476.
4. James Logan died Oct. 31, 1751.
5. Peter Kalm traveled through the Iroquois country to Lake Ontario in the summer of 1750, visiting Forts Oswego and Niagara, and viewing Niagara Falls, which he described in a famous letter to BF, Sept. 2, printed in *Pa. Gaz.*, Sept. 20. Kalm, *Travels*, II, 694–6. Kalm's letter was also printed as an appendix to John Bartram's *Observations . . . In his Travels from Pensilvania To Onondago, Oswego and the Lake Ontario, In Canada* (London, 1751).

Lewis Evans changed his plans and did not leave Philadelphia. On the Proprietors' proposal to have Evans and John Bartram make a journey to the western parts ostensibly for scientific purposes but in reality to check the boundaries of the province, see Lawrence H. Gipson, *Lewis Evans* (Phila., 1939), pp. 33–8.

P.S. If you think it would be agreable to Mr. Alexander,[6] or any other Friend in N York, to peruse these Electrical Papers, you may return them to me thro' his Hands.

Cr. Colden Esqr

From Peter Collinson

AL (fragment): Library Company of Philadelphia

[June, 1750][7]

[*First part missing*] Pray give my respects to Lewis Evans.[8] I have not Time to write to Him but I putt his Mapps to Bowles one of the most noted Print and Mapp sellers near the Exchange[9] —and He Tells Mee he has disposed of few of them the Price is so High.

Thou will see by Byrd's[1] Letter the reason no Thermometers was done. So farewell.

The Books &c. for Lib: Com. I shall send to the Care of Friend Griffith.[2]

Per next I may more particularly consider thine of March the 2d. There is something very Marvelous in the Doctrine of Points.

Addressed: To Benjam Franklin Esqr Philadelphia

6. James Alexander, member of the New York Council, a man of mathematical interests. See above, p. 32 n, and II, 407.

7. Date assigned with reference to BF to Collinson, March 2, above, p. 472. The fragment seems to precede BF to Collinson, July 3, 1750.

8. See above, p. 392 n.

9. John Bowles (1701–1779), book-, map-, and print-seller in Cornhill, near the Royal Exchange. H. R. Plomer and others, *A Dictionary of the Printers and Booksellers ... in England ... from 1726 to 1775* (Oxford, 1932), pp. 31–2. About 1760 he pirated Evans' map of 1755, and reissued it several times. Henry N. Stevens, *Lewis Evans: His Map* (3d edit., London, 1924), pp. 19–20, 23–7, 46–50, 54–6.

1. John Bird (1709–1776), mathematical instrument maker in the Strand, London. In 1749–50 he built for the Royal Observatory a very accurate brass quadrant of eight feet radius, which brought in orders for duplicates from observatories at St. Petersburg, Cadiz, and Paris. *DNB*.

2. Collinson's invoice, amounting to £23 2s. 3d., for books and instruments "lately received," was presented to the Library Company directors, Sept. 10, 1750. MS Minutes, Lib. Co. Phila.

Index

Compiled by David Horne